SO-ABZ-870

THE ABERDEEN COALITION
1852–1855

THE EARL OF ABERDEEN, 1846

THE ABERDEEN
COALITION
1852-1855

A STUDY IN
MID-NINETEENTH-CENTURY
PARTY POLITICS

BY

J.B.CONACHER

Professor of History
University of Toronto

CAMBRIDGE
AT THE UNIVERSITY PRESS
1968

Published by the Syndics of the Cambridge University Press
Bentley House, P.O. Box 92, 200 Euston Road, London, N.W.1
American Branch: 32 East 57th Street, New York, N.Y.10022

Library of Congress Catalogue Card Number: 68–10148
Standard Book Number: 521 04711 0

Printed in Great Britain
at the University Printing House, Cambridge
(Brooke Crutchley, University Printer)

IN MEMORY OF
W.M.C.

CONTENTS

CONTENTS

ILLUSTRATIONS

PLATES

ILLUSTRATIONS

'PUNCH' CARTOONS

MAPS

PREFACE

Most political history, other than general surveys, is written in the form either of biography or of monographs dealing with particular themes or problems. I believe, however, that a case may be made for the study of an administration that is concerned with all its aspects and all its leading members. The purpose of this book is to examine the Aberdeen administration of 1852–55 in detail as an approach to mid-nineteenth-century British history.

I hope that the results will throw some light on the way the British parliamentary system worked in the high-Victorian period and also on the complicated subject of contemporary party relationships. To achieve this end I have deliberately explored all the major and many of the minor issues that faced the Aberdeen coalition during its relatively brief existence. The result is a long book, but I should like to think that the intrinsic interest of the story that emerges will succeed in carrying the reader with me.

Originally I had intended to write a history of the Peelites from 1846 to 1859 with much the same general purpose in mind, but in order to cope with the detail that seemed to be necessary to build up the picture, in the end I decided to limit the volume to its present scope. Thus the book begins abruptly with the fall of the Derby ministry in December 1852. I have sketched the developments leading up to the formation of the coalition in the barest detail, since I propose to deal with them in a separate study of the Peelites from 1846. Nevertheless, my interest still centres on the role of the Peelites in the coalition, because it points to the contribution that Peelism was to make in the development of a new Liberalism that was already challenging the Whiggism of an earlier day. Yet in the person of Lord John Russell Whiggism fought hard to maintain its old ascendancy and much of my attention is taken up with this struggle. Previous accounts of the coalition have been presented mainly through the medium of biography, which inevitably distorts the perspective of the whole picture. I have endeavoured to go beyond these individual biographies and in a sense to write a biography of the ministry as a whole.

Since my concern is primarily with political history in the broad sense, I have relied mainly on collections of private papers, supplemented by *Hansard* and some *Parliamentary Papers*, but I have not attempted to use the unpublished departmental papers of the various ministries. Thus, although the Eastern Question plays a big part in the history of the coalition and consequently in this book, I have approached it through the private correspondence of the ministers concerned, rather than the unpublished records of the Foreign Office. I am not concerned with the Eastern Question as a whole, but rather with the reaction of the British cabinet ministers to it. There is inevitably some overlapping with Temperley's *England and the Near East: the Crimea*; but that book is centred on Constantinople, mine on London. The story I tell is a complicated one, but the detail reveals much, not only about the individuals concerned, but also about the working of the British cabinet system of government in the mid nineteenth century, and more incidentally about British diplomacy.

My study ends as abruptly as it begins, with the sudden collapse of the coalition early in 1855. Some day I should like to deal with the sequel— the rise and fall of the first Palmerston administration, 1855-58, and its eventual re-organisation in 1859, which finally completed the work begun by Lord Aberdeen in 1852.

I have not attempted to develop the social, economic and intellectual background of the period, partly for lack of space, but mainly because this has been done so well in recent years by such historians as Asa Briggs, W. L. Burn, Kitson Clark and Norman Gash. Donald Southgate's *The Passing of the Whigs, 1832-1886* (London, 1962), which appeared when my earlier chapters on domestic politics were completed, covers some of the same ground, especially on the formation of the coalition, but necessarily more briefly.[1]

I wish to acknowledge the gracious permission of Her Majesty the Queen to use the royal archives at Windsor. I wish also to thank the duke of Newcastle, Lord Aberdeen, Lord Clarendon, Lord Herbert, Lord Russell, Sir Fergus Graham and Mr C. Gladstone for allowing me to use the papers of their ancestors who were in the ministry. Thanks are also due to the British Museum, the Public Record Office, the Bodleian Library, the Cambridge University Library, the University of Nottingham Library, and the Newberry Library, Chicago, for giving me access to their collections (or, in the case of the Graham Papers, to the microfilm of them). I should also like to acknowledge with thanks the kind

[1] Olive Anderson's *A Liberal State at War* (London, 1967) appeared while the present work was in the press.

permission of Macmillan and Co. Ltd to quote from Strachey and Fulford (editors), *The Greville Memoirs*, vols. VI and VII, and of John Murray (Publishers) Ltd to quote from John Martineau's *Life of Henry Pelham, fifth duke of Newcastle*. I am grateful to the Council of the Navy Records Society, London, for permission to base the maps on originals published in volume 83 of the Society's publications.

I must also express my appreciation to the Nuffield Foundation, the Canada Council, and the Humanities Research fund of the University of Toronto for generous assistance in the form of grants and fellowships without which this work could never have been done. It would be rash to try to name all those friends whose advice and encouragement have helped me to complete the task, but I must thank in particular several colleagues, Professors J. C. Cairns, R. Helmstadter, D. J. McDougall and C. P. Stacey, who have read substantial parts of the manuscript, and my wife who has assisted me at all stages.

J.B.CONACHER

Garden Island, Ontario
1 September 1966

ABBREVIATIONS

Ab. Cor.	*Aberdeen Correspondence*
Add. MSS. 43039–43358	Aberdeen Papers .
Add. MSS. 44086–44835	Gladstone Papers
A.H.R.	*American Historical Review*
Camb. Hist. J.	*Cambridge Historical Journal*
E.H.R.	*English Historical Review*
E.P.	*Eastern Papers* (in *P.P.*)
Hansard	*Hansard's Parliamentary Debates*, 3rd series
Hist. J.	*Historical Journal*
J.M.H.	*Journal of Modern History*
MS. Clar.	Clarendon Papers
P.P.	*Parliamentary Papers*
PRO 30/22/10, 11, 12	Public Record Office (Russell Papers)
R.A.	Royal Archives, Windsor Castle
T.R.H.S.	*Transactions of the Royal Historical Society*

Full details of all manuscript sources will be found
in the Bibliography, p. 568

I

THE FORMATION OF THE COALITION AND ITS EARLY PARLIAMENTARY SUCCESSES

1

THE FORMATION OF THE ABERDEEN COALITION, DECEMBER 1852

Preliminaries

For the half-dozen years following the repeal of the Corn Laws and the break-up of Sir Robert Peel's ministry in June 1846 British party politics were in a state of flux.[1] Lord John Russell's Liberal administration survived until February 1852,[2] largely owing to Peelite support, but the very words 'Liberal' and 'Peelite' are question-begging. The term Liberal party had only recently come into use[3] to describe all those who had given general support to the 'Reform' Administrations of Grey and Melbourne. The word Whig was still used to describe the point of view and social background of the aristocratic leaders of the party, while at the other extreme the word Radical covered a variety of ultra-Liberals, the Philosophical Radicals such as Hume and Roebuck, the Manchester Radicals such as Cobden and Bright, and more vaguely some social Radicals such as Fielden, all of varying independence and perhaps numbering about a third of the party in the House of Commons at the most.[4] Increasingly rank and file members of the party simply called themselves Liberal to judge from Dod's *Parliamentary Companion* in the 'forties and 'fifties.[5] Russell could consider himself as a Whig, but call himself the leader of the Liberal party. Finally there was the Irish Brigade, as they became known in the early 'fifties, Catholic or Catholic-supported Irish Liberals who broke with Russell over his

[1] See C. H. Stuart, 'The formation of the coalition cabinet of 1852', *T.R.H.S.*, 5th series, IV (1954), 45–68, my 'Peel and the Peelites, 1846–50', *E.H.R.* LXXIII (1958), 431–52, and Donald Southgate, *The passing of the Whigs 1832–86*, chs. V–IX.

[2] Dr F. Dreyer's doctoral thesis, 'The Russell administration, 1846–52', is an illuminating study of the Whig-Liberal party during these years.

[3] See E. Halévy, *A history of the English people in the nineteenth century*, III, *The triumph of reform 1830–41*, 180, n. 1, who says that the term became official in 1847.

[4] See S. Maccoby, *English radicalism, 1832–52*, Appendix A, 449–51, which lists the names of one hundred Liberals or Radicals who voted against Russell on Locke King's Reform motion.

[5] See my 'Party politics in the age of Palmerston', in P. Appleman, W. A. Madden and M. Wolff (eds.), *1859: Entering an age of crisis* (Bloomington, Indiana, 1959), p. 167.

Ecclesiastical Titles Bill of 1851 and who vaguely adhered to a tenants' rights programme for Ireland.[1]

Peelite is an even more elusive category to define. It was estimated that there were 117 free-trade or Liberal Conservatives elected in the general election of 1847,[2] but probably only forty-odd of these could properly be considered as Peelites, i.e. free trade Conservatives personally loyal to Peel and after his death to his memory and ready, if necessary, to remain indefinitely independent of the main body of the Conservatives, now known as Protectionists. The number of this group was indeterminate, but its hard core were those men who had held office under Peel. By and large they were men of liberal views, but distrust of the Radicals, distaste for Whig cliquishness, suspicion of Liberal ecclesiastical policy and the politician's natural disinclination to cross old party lines made it difficult for them to contemplate fusion with the Liberal party. Over the years, it is true, some had merged with the Liberals, but after the death of Peel, who refused to sanction any overt organisation of his followers after 1846, Gladstone and Sidney Herbert had kept together a band of about forty who sat as a group below the gangway on the opposition side of the House.[3]

Peelite support for the Russell ministry was less certain after Peel's death in June 1850. Russell's foolish and illiberal Ecclesiastical Titles Bill of 1851 was strongly opposed by the Peelite leaders in both Houses, as well as by some Radical and most Irish members of the Commons. Differences over this measure were a major factor in preventing the formation of a Liberal Peelite coalition after Russell's defeat on Locke King's motion for parliamentary reform in February 1851. The Peelites welcomed Palmerston's dismissal from the Russell ministry in December of that year, but they failed to come to Russell's support when Palmerston joined with the Protectionist opposition to defeat the government's Militia Bill.[4]

Lord Derby, who succeeded Russell as Prime Minister, managed to keep his minority Protectionist government in office until the end of the abortive 1852 session, thanks to divisions among the Liberals and a

[1] See J. H. Whyte, *The Independent Irish Party, 1850–9.*
[2] *The Times,* 3 September 1847.
[3] British Museum Add. MS. 44778, fols. 76–83, Gladstone memorandum no. 95, dated 29 November 1876, partly quoted in John Morley, *Life of William Ewart Gladstone,* I, 428.
[4] See W. D. Jones, *Lord Derby and Victorian Conservatism,* p. 159; H. F. C. Bell, *Lord Palmerston,* II, 58.

conscious decision of the Peelites to withhold judgment until the
Derbyites had shown where they stood with respect to free trade, the
income tax and other issues of the day. As soon as the essential business
of the session was completed parliament was dissolved, but the results of
the general election held in July were indecisive. *The Times*[1] gave the
ministry 284 safe seats, and the Liberal opposition, including the Radicals
and the Irish Brigade, 309 seats, while it listed separately the names
of fifty-eight 'Liberal Conservatives', but not all of these could be
called Peelite. Bonham, Peel's former party manager, counted fifty
'Peelites',[2] but Sir John Young, the former Conservative chief
whip, only found thirty-four and his names were not all the same as
Bonham's.[3]

Russell in opposition was less stand-offish than in office. Indeed he
was no longer in full control of his own party and it was clear that many
of his former colleagues and followers were reluctant to serve again
under his leadership. This was an irritating situation for a man of Lord
John's thin-skinned sensitivity, but he soon realised that a Liberal-
Peelite coalition was the only solution to the parliamentary situation
and the prospect of a closer relationship with the Peelite leaders was
more congenial now that the loyalty of some of his former colleagues
was in doubt. When the election results showed him that he would
have no majority of his own in the new House he entered into a long
and friendly correspondence with Lord Aberdeen, the titular head of the
Peelite group, to explore the possibilities of joint action in the coming
session.[4] Although a Tory of forty years standing, Aberdeen, always a
member of the upper House, had never been deeply involved in party
politics. His main interests were in the field of foreign affairs, but he was
a staunch supporter of Peel's free trade policy, and now showed himself
to be remarkably open-minded, indeed liberal in his general political
views. He and his close friend and colleague, Sir James Graham, a
former Whig, were ready enough to work with Russell, but the

---

[1] 28 July 1852; three seats were unaccounted for.

[2] Add. MS. 44110, fols. 228–31, to Gladstone, 29 July 1852.

[3] Add. MS. 44273, fols. 209–10, to Gladstone, 4 August 1852. Young gave the government a possible maximum of 315, but of these he only considered 272 as safe. He and
Bonham carried on a fascinating three-way correspondence with Gladstone as to the
number of Peelites elected that indicates how uncertain membership in the group was.

[4] The correspondence is in the Aberdeen Papers, Add. MS. 43066, fols. 87–120, 21 July–
18 September 1852, and the Russell Papers, PRO 30/22/10/C, /D and /E, 23 July–
16 September, and much of it is reproduced in Spencer Walpole, *The life of Lord John
Russell*, pp. 155–8.

younger Peelites such as Gladstone, Sidney Herbert and the duke of Newcastle had more reservations.[1]

All the Peelites were ready to join the Liberals in the House of Commons in forcing Disraeli to accept a free trade resolution when the new parliament met in November, although with Palmerston they were prepared to work out a modified wording to avoid the downfall of the government. They were anxious to see what sort of budget proposals Disraeli would produce before finally making up their minds where they stood. Disraeli's budget resolutions introduced in December, however, were decisive, for they simply did not come up to Peelite fiscal standards and they proposed to introduce the principle of differentiation in the income tax in a way that Gladstone found quite unacceptable. Disraeli's treatment of personalities in the debate was the last straw and late on the final night Gladstone wound up with an impassioned attack that was conclusive. Forty-two Conservatives, of whom thirty-nine may be classified as Peelites, joined the Liberals to defeat the Resolutions in the early morning hours of 17 December.[2]

At long last the hour of decision for the Peelites had come. For more than six years they had sat on the fence, hostile to any party or any government led by Peel's traducers, but suspicious of Whigs and Radicals as lifelong political rivals and opponents. By and large the Peelite reforming tradition was a better match for the main body of the Liberals than for the main body of the Conservatives, but human reluctance to change old associations remained strong to the end. Even while the debate was still in progress so staunch a Peelite as Sir John Young wrote to Gladstone warning him that 'politically' he was 'on

[1] The interesting correspondence between the ex-Peelite ministers and Aberdeen, who relayed it to Russell, is to be found in *Aberdeen Correspondence* (hereafter *Ab. Cor.*) *1850–60* (privately printed by Lord Stanmore and deposited in the British Museum), pp. 301–70.

[2] *Hansard's Parliamentary Debates*, 3rd series, CXXIII, 1693 (hereafter *Hansard* with a volume number). The thirty-nine Peelites who subsequently supported the Aberdeen coalition were afterwards joined by one other, the third Sir Robert Peel, who missed the division, and by four others who were defeated in the general election of 1852, but who later returned through by-elections, namely, E. Cardwell, T. Green, Roundell Palmer and R. J. Phillimore. The three Conservatives who opposed the Disraeli budget, but who did not give consistent support to the coalition, were James Johnstone, Colonel Jonathan Peel (brother of the Prime Minister) and G. Tomline. Thus the hard core of Peelites who supported the coalition proved to be forty-four (see Appendix A), although another thirty-six independent Conservatives, including James Johnstone, gave it not infrequent support (see Appendix B), but none of this was clear when the coalition was formed. Only twenty-four of the forty-four were survivors of the band of Peel's supporters in 1846.

the brink of a grave danger'. The inclination of such men was to win over as many as possible of the supporters of Lord Derby to a reconstituted Peelite Conservative party, not to achieve a union of the present small band of Peelites with the Liberals. Young made this point clear in a letter to Gladstone explaining the nature of the danger facing him. If Aberdeen were to head a coalition government with Russell leading the Commons and Graham in a prominent position, then in Young's view the whole Conservative party would follow Derby and Disraeli into opposition, 'nearly divide the House & render the succeeding Ministry weak and powerless—dependent on the Radicals and the Irish Brass Band for their existence from day to day'. He was also convinced that a dissolution for such a ministry would be disastrous since he believed the Conservatives were stronger in the country and would beat them. In conclusion he hinted at the dangerous influence that Sir James Graham might exercise, for all his great talents, because of his 'love of intrigue' and his extreme unpopularity with the Conservative party.[1]

Of this letter Gladstone noted: 'Yes—I agree quite in this view. As to political questions those affecting religion should be open.'[2] Yet subconsciously he may have felt that events were taking the course of a Greek drama in which he had to play his fore-ordained role. At any rate his apparent agreement did not stop him taking the risks against which Young warned him.[3]

Gladstone's friend and former secretary, Sir Stafford Northcote, wrote in a vein similar to Young's. He suggested that with free trade settled the Peelites were the natural leaders of the Conservative party, although the self-constituted chiefs of that party remained anxious to keep them out, and he asked:

Is it not then the policy of the Peelites to assert themselves as a purely Conservative Administration, claiming the support of the whole Conservative body, and that alone? And resting this claim to supersede Lord Derby on the simple ground of their superior capacity for administering the financial and other affairs of the country?

It would not be inconsistent with this position [he went on] that they should

[1] Add. MS. 44237, fols. 222–4, 13 December 1852.
[2] *Ibid.* fol. 226, 18 December 1852. The note is unsigned, but presumably Gladstone's.
[3] The action of some rowdy young Tory bloods who threatened to throw him out of the Carlton Club a few nights before the defeat of the government may have helped Gladstone to make up his mind that he no longer belonged in that atmosphere. See L. Strachey and R. Fulford, *The Greville Memoirs* (London, 1938), VI, 383; Morley, *Gladstone*, I, 440–1.

7

accept the services of a few of the Conservative Whigs, but it *is* inconsistent that they should join Ld. J. Russell the acknowledged leader of the Liberals, unless he abjures his old party, which is not the case.

In short he recommended the formation of a Liberal Conservative ministry which he believed could expect the support of most Conservatives and could rally the electorate at a general election.[1]

On the government's resignation Gladstone himself prepared a 'most Private memorandum' regarding the possibility of forming a 'mixed Government' to defend the income tax, which went a good deal further than either of his correspondents had suggested. In the existing situation, he reasoned, neither the Conservative nor the Liberal party was capable of forming a single government. The Liberals might like to form one with reinforcements from the Peelites, but the latter were not prepared to take office as members of the Liberal party 'and if they were they would be encountered by an Opposition numerically too strong for them in the present Parliament and one which they could not weaken by a Dissolution'. The only alternative, he concluded, was the formation of what he called a 'mixed Government'.

The formation of a mixed Government [he wrote] can only be warrantable or auspicious when its members have the most thorough confidence in the honour, integrity, and fidelity of each other; when they are agreed in principle upon all the great questions of public policy immediately emergent; and lastly when a great and palpable emergency of State calls for such a formation.

Gladstone considered that such an exigency existed at that moment, not only in the foreign situation, but more particularly in the field of finance. He analysed the history of the income tax at length and considered the dangerous innovations now proposed to differentiate between sources of income. Here he found the basis of a coalition between the temperate portions of the Conservative and Liberal parties to oppose such innovations. Thus he believed that the three conditions to justify a mixed government existed. 'By a mixed government', he wrote, 'I mean something different from a fusion of parties. A mixed government may honourably be formed, but a fusion of parties could not, with a reserve upon political questions more remotely impending, such as Parliamentary Reform; a reserve to this extent that upon all the particulars and details of such a measure...every man will retain an entire freedom.' The question of a differentiated income tax,

[1] Add. MS. 44778, fols. 72–5, December 1852.

he insisted, must be the subject of great deliberation, perhaps by a cabinet committee which might work out a reasonable plan. If not the cabinet must then take a united stand on another course.[1]

Gladstone's distinction between a mixed government (i.e. a coalition) and a fusion of parties is of particular interest, because, although he here appears as the protagonist of the former concept, in the long run the fusion was achieved under his leadership. Gladstone presumably made his views clear to Aberdeen, for the latter appears to have kept in close touch with him as well as with Herbert and Graham about the steps which he was now taking towards the formation of a government.[2]

Certainly Graham was in close communication with Aberdeen throughout the whole process of cabinet making, and indeed his Diary of events, although highly partial, is the most detailed source of information in print.[3] As the senior Peelite in the House of Commons and as a born politician he was anxious to ensure that his less worldly-wise friend and colleague in the House of Lords made no unnecessary mistakes. He strongly advised Aberdeen 'to send for each individual *without exception*' to whom a place was to be offered. 'You must make it felt *at once*', he wrote, 'that you are the head of the Government, and that the power of the Crown flows from you *alone*.'[4]

On the eve of the Derby government's fall the duke of Bedford, who had been in correspondence with Baron Stockmar, intervened to act as a secret and unofficial link between the Court and the opposition camp. He invited several Whig and Peelite leaders—Russell, Lansdowne, Clarendon, Aberdeen and Newcastle—to be his guests at Woburn from 15 to 17 December.[5] There they were joined on the 17th by Colonel Phipps, Prince Albert's private secretary. Both Bedford and Phipps sent much the same advice to Windsor, namely that in the event of Derby's resignation the queen should send for both Lansdowne and

[1] Add. MS. 44778, fols. 66–71, memo. 93, 18 December 1852.
[2] See Add. MS. 44778, fols. 60–5 and Add. MS. 44740, fols. 171–83 for a variety of lists of names in Gladstone's hand of Peelites and Liberals evidently being considered for office, and a letter from Gladstone to Aberdeen, dated 'Christmas, 1852', making suggestions for non-cabinet appointments.
[3] Graham Papers, Diary 17–30 December 1852, entitled 'Changes of Government' (printed in C. S. Parker, *Life and Letters of Sir James Graham*, II, 190–203, with some omissions).
[4] Add. MS. 43190, fols. 377–8, 23 December 1852.
[5] R.A. C42, fol. 48, Bedford to Stockmar, 15 December 1852; cf. L. Strachey and R. Fulford, *The Greville Memoirs*, VI, 377–82; Spencer Walpole, *Lord John Russell*, II, 161. Lansdowne, detained by gout, arrived on the 17th after Russell's departure.

Aberdeen 'to consult them'.[1] Neither attached much importance to the Manchester party, but they both expressed concern regarding the attitude of Palmerston, with whom Bedford had had some conversations at an earlier date. Bedford reported that Palmerston would not serve under Russell as Prime Minister again, but that both of them would be willing to serve under Lansdowne. The latter, however, had expressed strong objections to the idea of resuming public office. Regarding the results of the Woburn colloquium Bedford wrote to Stockmar: 'I think our little meeting of politicians here, including my brother for one day, has been of infinite use, by putting the parties in good humour with each other & by smoothing jealousies and asperities, for a common object—but it is impolitic to conceal from oneself that there must still be great difficulties in the formation of a new Government.' He said that Aberdeen was 'very friendly both personally & politically' with his brother and that Newcastle, also, was 'friendly, & quite prepared to do his best to facilitate the formation of a good government by a [juncture?] of Whigs and Peelites'. Bedford sounded out his brother's own views, without telling him that he was doing so at the queen's request. 'He will do everything that loyalty, & patriotism can require, without a particle of self', Bedford reported to Stockmar. 'In confidence, I add', he continued, 'that he does not wish to be sent for—but will readily confer with, & probably do whatever Lords Lansdowne & Aberdeen think best—but Ld Palmerston must still remain a difficulty.' In a postscript Bedford added: 'You are aware that great objections exist to my brother as head of a Govt, especially among Irish members, & the followers of Sir Robert Peel.'[2]

Colonel Phipps gave his master an account very similar to the duke's. He reported a conversation with Clarendon, whom he described as gloomy, to the effect that a combination with the Peelites was desirable, but that there would be difficulties; 'almost all the Peelites and many of the Whigs', he wrote, 'would refuse to serve under Lord John, whilst the liberals would possibly object to Lord Aberdeen alone'. Clarendon told him that the only thing for the queen to do was to send for Lansdowne and Aberdeen 'to *consult* them', but he was concerned about Palmerston, whom he feared might yet form an alliance with Disraeli. Phipps found Newcastle strong for a coalition, saying that 'there was no sacrifice of feelings or opinion that he was not prepared to make'.

[1] R.A. C42, fol. 49, Bedford to Stockmar, 16 December 1852; R.A. C28, fol. 12, Phipps to Prince Albert, 18 December.   [2] R.A. C28, fol. 7, 17 December 1852.

But he said it 'must be a real coalition, & not an attempt to join the Peelites to the Whigs and Liberals'. He thought the Peelites would rally to a Lansdowne–Aberdeen ministry, with Russell leading the Commons, but not to a ministry headed by either Russell or Lansdowne alone.[1]

On the same day, the 18th, Bedford wrote yet another letter to Stockmar saying that after much thought he believed that an Aberdeen administration with Russell leading the Commons would have the best chance of success, even though such an arrangement might not be quite satisfactory to the Whig party. 'No one knows that I am writing to you or that I have arrived at the opinion I have given you', he added.[2] Nevertheless, the secret soon got out; the Russells were very indignant with the duke for acting behind his brother's back, as they saw it, and Lady John in a letter to her father, Lord Minto, indulged in all sorts of foolish might-have-beens. She gave a highly coloured account of the affair, dwelling upon her brother-in-law's duplicity in not revealing the contents of the queen's letters to Lord John, who, she said, was convinced that the queen only wrote to the duke 'as a channel to himself wch wd make her communication to him less public'.

Now was there ever more extraordinary or weaker conduct than this [she continued] & is it not sad and strange that a man so afraid of & unfit for responsibility shd from the love of mystery have taken upon himself such an immense share of it—for to what he has done is I believe to be attributed the present state of things—At all events J. might have been sent for.[3]

On 17 December, immediately after his government's defeat in the House of Commons, Lord Derby proceeded to Osborne, where the queen was staying. He managed to cross over to the Isle of Wight on the same day and presented his resignation to the queen that evening. He advised the queen to send for Lord Lansdowne, 'who', he said, 'knew better than anybody the state of parties'. Rather oddly he explained his failure to recommend Lord Aberdeen by saying he feared that, in view of his own declared resolve to retire from public life, many of his followers 'would think it necessary to join Lord Aberdeen', if that nobleman were called to form a government on his recommendation. Prince Albert quite properly commented that constitutionally

---

[1] *Ibid.* fol. 12, 18 December 1852.   [2] *Ibid.* fol. 19, 18 December 1852.
[3] Minto Papers, Acc 2794, Box 136 (National Library of Scotland), dated 'Xmas day, 1852'; from a transcription kindly supplied to me by Dr F. Dreyer.

speaking no responsibility lay with the outgoing minister with regard to recommending the name of his successor. Lord Derby appeared to relish the difficulties that faced his rivals, saying that there would need to be a cabinet of thirty-two to meet the claims of all the ex-ministers.[1]

Cabinet bargainings, 18–25 December

The queen, guided by Bedford's information, proceeded to summon Lords Aberdeen and Lansdowne together, but the latter had to decline on account of an attack of gout that fortuitously laid him low. Aberdeen hesitated to proceed alone and informed the queen that he awaited her further instruction. This was telegraphed the same day and he succeeded in reaching Osborne at 3 p.m. on Sunday, 19 December.[2] While awaiting the queen's reply on 18 December Aberdeen had called on Lansdowne and Graham. The former had been very forthcoming, had intimated his own disinclination to assume 'the heavy duties of Prime Minister' and had encouraged Aberdeen to proceed alone, promising 'in general terms his co-operation and assistance, in arriving at a settlement with the Whigs'. Lansdowne had actually suggested to the queen that she should request Aberdeen and Russell jointly to work out a satisfactory arrangement of men and places, and he hinted at this in the course of their conversation. Graham strongly warned his friend of 'the impolicy of accepting any such joint commission', and Aberdeen agreed that he would only accept undivided authority.[3]

On the same day the duke of Bedford addressed letters to his brother and to Aberdeen, advocating an Aberdeen ministry with Russell leading the Commons. 'Do not', he wrote to his brother, 'for God's sake allow any personal feelings to prevent this arrangement.' By chance Aberdeen met Lord John as he walked back from Graham's house in

[1] A. C. Benson and Viscount Esher (eds.), *The letters of Queen Victoria*, 1st series, II, 500–2, Memorandum by Prince Albert, 18 December 1852.

[2] Add. MS. 43046, fols. 166–7, Queen Victoria, 17 December 1852, with a promise that a steamer would await the train at Southampton; *Ab. Cor. 1850–60*, to Queen Victoria, 18 December; Graham Diary, 18 December (Parker, *Graham*, II, 190); *Letters of Queen Victoria*, II, 502–4, memorandum by Prince Albert, 19 December.

[3] Graham Diary, 18 December 1852 (Parker, *Graham*, II, 190–1); Walpole, *Russell*, II, 161. According to Graham, Lansdowne admitted that he had been pressed by Palmerston and others to accept the lead; 'that he was opposed to further measures of parliamentary reform; that he was aware of the probable unwillingness of some of Peel's friends to serve under him; and that on the whole he considered Lord Aberdeen best fitted for the task at this juncture'.

Grosvenor Place on the 18th and the two took a stroll together in Hyde Park. According to Aberdeen's account of the conversation, Russell (perhaps with his brother's admonitions in mind) agreed to enter an Aberdeen ministry as Foreign Secretary and leader in the Commons.[1] Lord John's account as passed on by his wife to Lord Minto was vaguer. 'Well, he met Ld Ab'n by chance the day after the division', Lady John wrote, '& told him that his mind was not made up, he thought he shd not refuse office under him—the conditions of course, one of wch was the adoption of reform by the ministry.'[2] As so often is the case in human affairs both men, quite honestly no doubt, remembered the conversation in the way they wanted to. At any rate the misunderstanding pointed to the shoals that lay ahead, to use Sir James Graham's phrase.

While Lord Aberdeen was preparing to set out for the Isle of Wight, Sidney Herbert assembled his former Peelite colleagues, Graham, Goulburn, Gladstone, Newcastle, and Cardwell, at a Saturday evening dinner meeting. In the course of discussion there was general agreement, according to Graham, on the income tax, on which all were opposed to discrimination, and parliamentary reform, on which they agreed to a limited amount of disfranchisement. This meeting may be said to mark the reconciliation of Graham with his former Peelite colleagues,[3] although the *rapprochement* had clearly begun with the discussions on the free trade resolutions in November. In the ensuing negotiation there was no stronger advocate of Peelite claims than the veteran Sir James. In the course of the next few days he continued to discuss the situation with both Newcastle and Herbert and noted in his Diary: 'It is clear that the Peelites under Lord Aberdeen are ready to go as far in the Liberal sense as Lord John desires; but under Lord John they will not act, though they are willing to act with him.' He was also visited by Russell, but characteristically refused to allow Lord John to state his intended relationship to Aberdeen until the latter had communicated to Russell the queen's pleasure. They found themselves in general agreement on policy with respect to Reform, and the income tax and the

---

[1] Lord Stanmore, *The Earl of Aberdeen*, p. 213; Graham Diary, quoting Herbert (Parker, *Graham*, II, 192–3).

[2] Lady John Russell, *loc. cit.*; cf. Walpole, *Russell*, II, 161.

[3] In April the Peelites, instigated by Gladstone, had repudiated their connection with Graham following a speech he had made at Carlisle that appeared to announce his return to the Liberal party. Graham had just accepted the nomination for Carlisle in company with a Radical. See Morley, *Gladstone*, I, 420–1.

necessity of including Palmerston in any combination, but Russell complained of 'Gladstone's appeal to the "Conservative" country gentlemen' during the budget debate. Graham defended Gladstone by pointing out that it was of vital importance to sever some of the Conservative country members from Derby and Disraeli 'and that this was the time and Gladstone the person, for effecting so great a good'.[1]

At Osborne, on the afternoon of Sunday 19 December, Lord Aberdeen had an hour's frank conversation with the queen and the prince consort. In view of Lansdowne's health and disinclination to act he accepted the task of forming an administration, although protesting his unworthiness to do so. He made it clear that while he would invite Lord John Russell to lead the House of Commons and to take the Foreign Office, and while he would consult Lord John upon appointments, he considered that he must take the sole responsibility. He emphasised that 'the new Government must not be a revival of the old Whig Cabinet with an addition of some Peelites, but should be a liberal Conservative Government in the sense of that of Sir Robert Peel'. To this end he insisted that 'two Secretaries of State at least must be Peelites'. Indeed it was his hope that many Conservatives who supported Derby would now support such a government. All this helps to explain the otherwise surprisingly firm, not to say tough, line that Aberdeen took in his ensuing negotiations with the Whigs.

Lord Aberdeen talked frankly to the royal couple about Russell's lack of popularity, which he personally considered undeserved. He looked forward to the Peelites getting to know and respect him in office; happily he did not see what the future had in store. He recognised the necessity of trying to get Palmerston to accept office and spoke of the possibility of the queen conferring a peerage on either Graham or Herbert to strengthen the government in the House of Lords. In the course of the audience the prince presented Lord Aberdeen with a 'list of the possible distribution of Offices', which he himself had drawn up. If the Prime Minister designate was taken aback he showed no signs of it, for Prince Albert recorded with equanimity that he took the list with him 'as containing "valuable suggestions"'.[2]

Aberdeen returned to London the same afternoon and saw both Russell and Lansdowne that evening, finding them, as he said, 'in the

[1] Graham Diary, 19 December 1852 (Parker, *Graham*, II, 191–2).
[2] *Letters of Queen Victoria*, II, memorandum by Prince Albert, 19 December 1852, pp. 502–4.

same disposition with respect to the formation of the new Administration'. On Monday morning (20 December), however, he received a rude jolt with his breakfast in the form of a note from Russell, who wrote:

A night's reflection has convinced me that I am not equal to the work of the Foreign Office with the lead of the House of Commons.

Then comes the Home Office. I doubt whether this is an office I could take, but I will go to you directly after my breakfast & in the meantime beg you to do nothing.[1]

When Russell arrived shortly afterwards he indicated that he was no longer ready to form part of the administration, although willing to give it his support. His change of mind, he explained, was caused not only by his 'apprehension of the fatigue of the Foreign Office', but also by his consideration of the 'effect likely to be produced on his political friends by his acceptance of office'.[2] Sudden and unpredictable changes of mind were not uncommon with Lord John. According to Greville, quoting Clarendon, Romilly, David Dundas and possibly other friends had pressed him to reverse his decision.[3] Graham's suspicions lay closer to home. 'Wives sometimes have great influence on occasions, when pride and patronage are concerned', he commented in his Diary.[4] His diagnosis is partially confirmed in Lady John's excited account of the whole affair in the letter to her father in which she wrote:

I own that for the first few days before & after his [Russell's] decision to join the Ministry I did not behave with heroism—not, God knows, from any notion of dignity forbidd'g a man who has been first ever to be second—dignity be'g in such a case little better than selfish ambition to my mind—but from the terrible & inexpressible fear that ambition might not be the only thing sacrificed—that altho' a most rare & noble & disinterested patriotism was his only motive in tak'g the first step, other & almost imperceptible steps wd one by one be taken to the loss of the only things worth caring about, character & reputation, both of wch he must lose if he ceases to be the Leader of the great Liberal party in consequence of this union.[5]

For the moment it looked as if the long awaited coalition would be still-born, but other pressures began to build up to push Russell back

[1] Add. MS. 43066, fos. 129–30, 20 December 1852.
[2] *Letters of Queen Victoria*, II, 505, from Aberdeen, undated (copy in Add. MS. 43046, fo. 168, dated 20 December 1852).   [3] *Greville Memoirs*, VII, 18.
[4] Graham Papers, Diary, 20 December 1852 (deleted by Parker).
[5] Lady John Russell, *loc. cit.*

into the boat. On the same morning he received a letter from the queen dwelling on the necessity of 'patriotic sacrifice of personal interests and feelings to the public' and urging him to cooperate with Lord Aberdeen.[1] Lord Lansdowne, upon whom Russell called again for advice, added his weighty counsel, and while they were discussing the matter they were joined by Macaulay, who entered the debate with his accustomed energy and used all his great persuasive powers to urge Russell not to stand aside.[2] Shortly afterwards Clarendon made a final appeal[3] and the upshot was that Russell proposed he should lead the House and sit in the cabinet without office, a course which Graham immediately pronounced 'inadmissible'. Aberdeen 'objected to so great an innovation' and did not consider the duke of Wellington's case in 1841 a satisfactory precedent, since the duke was a peer and 'himself an exception to all rule'. Graham was especially emphatic on the necessity of Russell holding some office and in the end Lord John reluctantly agreed to accept some nominal office such as the Duchy of Lancaster 'if the arrangement should be found untenable in a parliamentary view'.[4]

Lord Aberdeen then resumed his task of assembling the other pieces of the puzzle. Lansdowne had warned Russell if he did not take the Foreign Office himself to make sure that it was put in the hands of someone in whom he could confide.[5] A mutually acceptable candidate was found in the person of Lord Clarendon. Graham was given his choice of the Home Office or the Exchequer, but consented 'to neither the one nor the other'. Another setback was sustained when Palmerston refused office on the grounds that he and Aberdeen had been too long in opposition to each other and that he did not favour the proposals for parliamentary reform under consideration. Aberdeen refused to be depressed by this development and wrote to the queen: 'In some respects Lord Aberdeen is by no means certain that Lord Palmerstons (sic) absence may not be attended with advantage.'[6] The only progress made at this stage was in the decision, on pressure from Russell, to offer the Great Seal to Lord Cranworth, a Whig legal luminary of long standing, although Aberdeen would have preferred to have kept the Conservative

[1] Walpole, *Russell*, II, 162.   [2] *Ibid.* pp. 162–3.
[3] *Greville Memoirs*, VI, 379–80.
[4] *Letters of Queen Victoria*, II, 506–7, from Lord Aberdeen, 20 December 1852; Graham Papers, Diary, 20–21 December (Parker, *Graham*, II, 194–5).
[5] PRO 30/22/10/F, fols. 1533–6, 21 December 1852.
[6] Add. MS. 43046, fol. 175, to the queen (copy), 21 December 1852; Graham Papers, Diary, 21 December (Parker, *Graham*, II, 195).

Chancellor, Lord St Leonards, who was probably the better man, and
who was one of the few Peelites whom Derby had enlisted.[1]

Lord John Russell's intentions remained obscure throughout the 21st.
Commenting on the situation in his Diary Graham wrote:

The Reform Club has got an inkling of his vacillation. Their indignation is
unmeasured and loudly expressed. If the arrangements fail from Ld. John's
indecision, he will be lost in public opinion and stamped as unfit for great
affairs. The Queen's absence from London is injudicious and unfortunate. It
throws some doubt on her real feelings with respect to the change in
ministry.[2]

In fact the queen returned to Windsor on the morning of Wednesday the 22nd and there Lord Aberdeen wearily proceeded to meet her
and report fresh troubles. He had just heard from Lord John who
wrote:

I am most anxious to see you succeed in the change which the Queen has
entrusted to you, & I should have been willing to accept the seals of the
Foreign Office under you had my health admitted of my doing so.

But I feel a laborious office with the conduct of the business of the House of
Commons on the part of the Government is more than I ought to undertake.

Unfortunately there is no office of dignity with light duties which can be
held with a seat in the House of Commons.

I propose therefore to decline office, but to accept if you wish it a seat in
the Cabinet, with a general charge of the Government business in the House
of Commons.

He again cited the precedent of the duke of Wellington and dismissed the objection that he would be evading the necessity of a by-
election by proposing to accept the Chiltern Hundreds and thus vacate
his seat in order to seek re-election. If Aberdeen was prepared to accept
these terms Russell undertook to join his administration. 'Wishing to be
a conservative Minister I feel you are persuaded that there is nothing so
conservative as judicious and enlightened progress', he wrote. 'I look
forward therefore with trust and hope to the maintenance of free trade,
the promotion of education, the advancement of liberty, civil and
religious, under your administration.'[3]

[1] Graham Papers, Diary, 21 December 1852. 'Ellice tells me also', Graham wrote, 'that
the supposed intention of retaining if possible, the services of Sugden [St Leonards] as
Ld Ch. is gall and wormwood to the Whigs.'
[2] *Ibid.* Parker omits the passage about the queen.
[3] Add. MS. 43066, fols. 131–4, 22 December 1852.

Lord John's avowed intention of applying for the Chiltern Hundreds scotched a suspicion that Graham had put in Aberdeen's mind on the previous day to the effect that Russell's reluctance to take office arose from his fear of vacating his seat for the City of London, where Rothschild was reported to be hostile in view of Lord Aberdeen's supposed opposition to a Jewish Emancipation Bill. Actually this fear was unfounded since Aberdeen was quite prepared to announce his support for such a bill. Nevertheless, Graham refused to be impressed by Russell's new proposal and confided to his Diary all the constitutional objections to a cabinet minister holding no office. Indeed he brought the argument to rather absurd lengths in contrasting the position of a minister without office and without pay with that of other ministers as follows:

He alone will be regarded as independent, they will be considered as Mercenaries; he will derive his authority exclusively from the H of Commons: they will be the humble Servants of the Crown; he will have no share in the Emoluments of office, and his motives will be considered pure and disinterested; they in comparison with him, will be exposed to the suspicion of time serving senility. In a word he will soon become the H of Commons Master, to whom all other Ministers must bend; and the Prime Minister himself in the H of Lords will be less the Servant of the Crown than of the Independent leader in the Lower House.

It will be difficult to accuse him of high Crimes and Misdemeanours; for he holds no office and presents no assailable Front; yet he may sway the Councils of the State in the most fatal direction and exercise an overweening influence over the deliberations of Parliament. The Servants of the Crown are the paid Servants of the Public; and (an) unpaid Leader of the H of Commons, if he court popularity and if there be reluctance, as there always is, to make up a Government, may become almost a Dictator.[1]

Graham did admit that 'in the person of Lord John Russell these Evils and these dangers are not to be anticipated', but he stressed the danger of precedent and objected to making exceptions.

There is no strain on Constitutional Principles [he continued] so severe as that of Special Cases said to be exceptional. The Duke of Wellington's lead of the House of Lords from 1841 to 1846 is cited as a case in point. The Duke of Wellington stood alone, and cannot be compared with any living Man, with reference either to public duties or personal responsibilities...and it must

[1] Graham Papers, Diary, 21 December 1852. The passage is deleted by Parker.

be remembered that the House of Lords is far different from the House of Commons both in practice and in power.[1]

These curious extracts reflect perhaps more on the writer than on the object of his criticisms. For some time Graham had been helping to bring Aberdeen and Russell together. He had been telling Russell how glad he was once more to be working closely with him. Yet now that the great moment had arrived his mind became obsessed with these pedantic objections that a later generation knows to be groundless.

Gladstone argued against Russell taking the leadership in the Commons without office in a dispassionate and closely reasoned memorandum which was in contrast to the rather peevish tone of Graham's opposition. He suggested that a leader without an office might lose weight, thus disposing of Graham's ridiculous arguments that such a leader might become a dictator; 'the leaning of my mind', Gladstone concluded, 'is towards the opinion that in a constitutional point of view the ground is not only untried but dangerous...and that Lord John Russell should accept at least to assume an office like the Presidency of the Council with easy duties attached to it but unquestioned dignity and considerable weight'.[2] Graham had dismissed the possibility of this office on the grounds that the Lord President could not sit in the Commons without special legislation, which he considered to be undesirable. The Chancellorship of the Duchy of Lancaster Russell considered beneath his dignity.[3]

Aberdeen agreed with Graham and Gladstone as to the impropriety of Russell leading the Commons without office and found the royal couple to be of the same opinion, as indeed were several of the Whigs. Palmerston, who had reconsidered his own position, entered the discussion by addressing a letter to Russell in which he argued against Lord John either combining the Foreign Office with the lead of the House, or the lead of the House with no office. He urged him to take the

---

[1] Graham Papers, Diary, 22 December 1852. All but one sentence is omitted by Parker, *Graham*, II, 196.

[2] Add. MS. 44777, memo. 82, 341–4, misdated 22 December 1851. In addition to the obvious objections Gladstone noted that 'the departmental function of the leader in the House of Commons is the basis of his attributes, and the real regulator of his relations to the first minister and to his colleagues. By that departmental function he is invested with well defined responsibilities strictly analogous to theirs, and the dividing line of their several responsibilities kept clear from his.'

[3] *Letters of Queen Victoria*, II, 512. Actually Baldwin was appointed Lord President in 1931 while still in the Commons, as were Chamberlain and Anderson in 1940.

Presidency of the Council, the Privy Seal or the Duchy of Lancaster as offices available for such occasions.[1] Russell apparently replied with reference to his dignity, for Palmerston rejoined with great tact telling him 'that the office which you may happen at any time to hold never can be the Measure of your Political Importance, but that on the Contrary you will always give Importance to any office which you may choose to hold'.[2] Lord Clarendon likewise joined in the effort to persuade Lord John to take office, magnanimously urging him to take the Foreign Office with the promise that he would be ready to take it over whenever Lord John found it too much.[3] On this basis, on the evening of 22 December, Russell finally accepted the Foreign Office, but with the intention of surrendering it at an early date.[4]

In the letter already quoted[5] Lady John gave her father a breathless account of the settlement which went far to confirm Graham's fears and which foreshadowed much of the trouble that was to afflict the coalition endlessly after it came into existence. In part she wrote:

Now as to the very important question of J's own part in the Ministry—I feel sure you will approve as I do what is agreed upon—that he shd take the F.O. merely to set it agoing, & sweep out Ld Malmesbury's cobwebs, & on the meeting of Parlt give it up to Ld Clarendon, & keep a seat in the cab't & the leadership without office—This is both *grander* & more useful, for he will have time to care for the general concern, to work at Reform, Education, &c, & in this way alone cn safely to himself or his cause undertake a responsibility greater than if he was really Prime Minister—Those, & they are not few alas even among his old friends who dread his hav'ng too much weight, urge him incessantly to take a permanent office—Ld Lans'ne among the rest, who I am afraid takes a part in the Ministry partly with a view of beat'g him down on reform, & Ld Clar'n who with all his ability is a dangerous ally, and will require much watch'g at the F.O.

[1] PRO 30/22/10/F, fols. 1559–60, 24 December 1852. On the previous day Palmerston had written a friendly letter to Russell saying 'we shall meet again as far as I am concerned just as good friends as if we had never separated'. *Ibid.* fols. 1557–8, 23 December. A few days later Palmerston wrote to Lord Broughton saying that his reconciliation with Russell was 'cordial & complete'. Add. MS. 43757, fol. 84, Broughton Diary, 28 December 1852.

[2] PRO 30/22/10/F, fol. 1579, 26 December 1852.

[3] H. Maxwell, *The life and letters of George William Frederick Fourth Earl of Clarendon*, I, 352; *Letters of Queen Victoria*, II, 511.

[4] Walpole, *Russell*, II, p. 164. According to Greville (*Memoirs*, VI, 380), it was the duke of Newcastle who first suggested that Russell should take the Foreign Office for a short period.

[5] See above, p. 11.

She urged her father to write to John ('& anybody else it will do any good to write to'), among other things to confirm his intention of recalling Lord Westmorland from Vienna. In view of Lord Aberdeen's 'old despotic tendencies', John, she said, must do what he could 'in one little month to set foreign affairs on a proper footing'. She went on to blame the Peelites for their selfishness with regard to other appointments once they had secured her husband. 'While he on his part has only been too confiding & scrupulous,' she wrote, 'several persons, some even members of the H. of C. whom he is to lead, have been written to without his consent with the offer of places—& in no single instance has Ld Ab'n proposed any but a Peelite *or a Tory* for anyth'g.'

Lord Aberdeen's difficulties seemed to be evaporating, for the same day, through the intercession of Lord Lansdowne, Palmerston was prevailed upon to join the ministry, taking the Home Office of his own choice. Aberdeen told the royal couple that even when Palmerston had first declined he had been exceedingly cordial, reminding Aberdeen that 'in fact they were great friends (! ! !) of sixty years standing, having been at school together'. Prince Albert, who recorded the story in a memorandum of the conversation with Lord Aberdeen, added in lighter vein: 'We could not help laughing heartily at the *Harrow Boys* and their friendship.'[1]

When he called on the queen at Windsor late on the afternoon of 22 December, Aberdeen discussed other cabinet appointments as well as the two key ones involving Russell and Palmerston. At this stage he was uncertain whether to appoint Graham to the Exchequer, as Russell wished, and Gladstone to the Colonies, or vice versa. Victoria and Albert greatly favoured Gladstone at the Exchequer and there he went. At this stage it was also proposed to make Newcastle Lord President and to place Herbert in the Admiralty, Wood at the Board of Control, Granville at the Board of Trade, Sir F. Baring at the Board of Works, Lord Canning at the Post Office and Cardwell as Secretary at War, these to comprise the cabinet, but, in fact, only three of them in the end took the offices here suggested, and Canning, Cardwell and Baring never got into the cabinet. At this point the only other decisions that were held to were to appoint Lord Cranworth Chancellor and the duke of Argyll Lord Privy Seal.[2]

This last appointment requires some explanation in view of the age

[1] *Letters of Queen Victoria*, II, 511. See also H. C. F. Bell, *Lord Palmerston*, II, 72.
[2] *Letters of Queen Victoria*, II, 510–12, memorandum by Prince Albert, 2 December 1852.

and inexperience of the young Scottish peer and the exclusion of so many better-known candidates from the cabinet. Indeed, when Argyll realised that he was in and his more experienced friend Canning outside the cabinet he wrote to Aberdeen to say that he would gladly withdraw in favour of the other. Aberdeen waived this generous offer, saying that it had been agreed upon from the first that Argyll should be offered the post.[1] It is difficult to give an entirely satisfactory explanation for the appointment, but there are three factors that help to shed some light upon it. Argyll was a great territorial magnate in Scotland and this still counted for something, although not necessarily in concrete terms of electoral influence. Perhaps more important was the fact that he was more acceptable to the Whigs than most Peelites since he had married into a great Whig family (his father-in-law was the duke of Sutherland) and had never played any official role against the Whigs. Indeed Russell had offered him office in 1851.[2] Finally, and this probably weighed with Aberdeen, without administrative duties his debating ability would be useful to the Prime Minister in the House of Lords.

On the following morning, Thursday 23 December, Aberdeen informed the queen of Russell's final acceptance and submitted 'a proposed list of Your Majesty's confidential servants almost complete as well as a list of other officers not in the Cabinet', in the hopes that the writs might be moved in the House of Commons on the next day.[3] He now proposed to put Graham at his old place in the Admiralty and to appoint Sir William Molesworth First Commissioner of the Board of Works, assuring the queen that she would find this erstwhile Radical baronet 'animated with the best of dispositions'.[4] The queen made no objection to Molesworth, but thought that Graham's appointment would be unpopular since 'his achievements at the Admiralty in former times were all *retrenchments*', which she considered had often proved injurious to the service. She also questioned the proposed appointment

---

[1] Dowager duchess of Argyll (ed.), *George Douglas, eighth Duke of Argyll (1823–1900), autobiography and memoirs*, I, 371–2, 374.

[2] *Ibid.* p. 341.

[3] Add. MS. 43046, fol. 181, 23 December 1852. It is not clear whether this was before or after he received from Russell a long list of Whig claims for lesser offices and household appointments (Add. MS. 43066, fols. 138–9).

[4] Add. MS. 43046, fol. 181. According to J. K. Laughton (*Memoirs of the life and correspondence of Henry Reeve*, I, 269) Molesworth was admitted to the cabinet at the urging of Reeve and Delane. According to the latter the Radical baronet would take nothing less than a cabinet seat and was anxious to get the Colonial Office (A. I. Dasent, *Life of J. T. Delane*, I, 151).

of Granville to the Duchy of Lancaster since he was the chief lessee and
urged that Clarendon should be made President of the Council.[1]

By now Sir James was at last becoming more optimistic as to the
prospects of the government, saying that he had 'great faith in the
strong cohesion of office'. Indeed under date of 23 December he wrote
in his Diary: 'The Government may be considered as formed. 7 Peelites, 5 Whigs, 1 Radical compose the Cabinet...We shall all look
somewhat strangely at each other when we first meet in cabinet.'[2] But
they were not yet out of the wood.

When word got out that the Peelites were to have 'the lion's share' of
the places,[3] some of Russell's Whig friends began to protest, with the
result that later on the 23rd he wrote to Aberdeen:

I am told that the whole complexion of the Government with the addition of
Harrowby will look too Peelite.

G. Grey suggests and I concur that Clarendon should be President of the
Council immediately, and when he leaves it, someone else may be named,
Harrowby or Granville.

I am seriously afraid that the whole thing will break down from the weakness of the old Liberal party (I must not say Whig) in the Cabinet.

To this must be added
President of B. of Trade
Postmaster
Chief Secy for Ireland
    all in Peelite hands...
Forgive all this trouble.[4]

He enclosed a memorandum from Lord Bessborough indicating that
fifty-seven Irish members meant to act as a body, that they were hostile
to the appointment of Blackburne or Redington, former Liberal Irish
officeholders, and expected to see the Irish member, Keogh, as Attorney
General and several other Brigadiers holding minor places in the government. This information is puzzling since Keogh was later criticised for
taking office, but the Irish independents were more friendly to an
Aberdeen government than to a Derby or a Russell one.[5]

---

[1] *Letters of Queen Victoria*, II, 513–14.
[2] Graham Diary, 23 December 1852 (Parker, *Graham*, II, 197). He also wrote in a sentence deleted by Parker: 'In the meantime it is necessary to keep out Ld Derby and the
common Enemy, and not to press points of difference prematurely and too eagerly.'
[3] See Broughton Diary for 'Sat. Xmas day': 'The Peelites have the Lion's share—& Russell goes into the Cabinet with scarcely a personal or even a party friend in it.' Add.
MS. 43757, fol. 83.
[4] Add. MS. 43066, fols. 136–7.   [5] See Whyte, *Independent Irish Party 1850–9.*

Aberdeen did not admit the justice of Russell's criticisms, but in a not unfriendly note proposed that they have a further talk on his return from Windsor. He did not object to Lord Clarendon but questioned whether he could do the business of the office proposed in the House of Lords: 'and we are so weak', he added (presumably referring to the Upper House), 'that I entertain very great apprehensions'.[1] Evidently he was referring to Clarendon's weakness as a debater since the Lord President normally sat in the Lords.

The battle raged on into Christmas eve to the queen's annoyance. She had waived her objections and she hoped 'that political parties would not fall short in patriotic spirit of the example she has thus herself set'.[2] But she was not beset by the same hungry pack of followers who made Lord John's life difficult. Now on the 24th not only did he demand three more Whig seats in the cabinet (Granville, F. Baring and G. Grey), but he also wanted Lord Carlisle to be Lord Lieutenant of Ireland instead of the Peelite Lord St Germans. Aberdeen agreed to bring in Granville as President of the Council and secured the service of Lord Lansdowne in the cabinet without office. Cardwell at the Board of Trade and Canning at the Post Office were excluded from the cabinet, but Molesworth at the Board of Works, as we have seen, was brought in as a gesture to the Radicals. It had already been settled that Newcastle would take the Colonial Office and Herbert be Secretary at War, both with seats in the cabinet. On pressure from Lansdowne, Russell finally accepted these arrangements and the composition of the cabinet was complete. 'It is indeed a tesselated pavement,' commented Graham. Lord Aberdeen reported the final arrangements to the queen on Christmas day.[3]

The battle over the lesser offices, 25–29 December

Herbert, stranded in London for the holiday, described it as the 'dreariest' Christmas in his memory. Writing to Gladstone, who had managed to get to Hawarden in the teeth of a hurricane, he reported fresh troubles, this time over Irish appointments, requiring an emergency meeting of Aberdeen, Russell and Graham at Argyll House that

[1] Add. MS. 43066, fol. 142, 23 December 1852 (copy).
[2] *Letters of Queen Victoria*, II, 515, the queen to Aberdeen, 24 December 1852.
[3] Graham Diary, 24 December 1852 (Parker, *Graham*, II, 198); *Letters of Queen Victoria*, II, 515–16, memorandum by the queen, 25 December; Add. MS. 43046, fols. 192 and 194, Aberdeen to the queen and the queen to Aberdeen, 24 December 1852.

night. 'The sooner you are back the better,' Herbert concluded, 'for one cannot tell at any moment what the next hour may bring. I envy you your Xmas at Hawarden.'[1] From his retreat Gladstone wrote to the Prime Minister to warn him that Strutt, the Liberal nominee for the Duchy of Lancaster, with all its church patronage, was or used to be a Unitarian, but suggesting some concession be made to the Whigs in the person of Redington, their former Irish Secretary.[2]

The situation was made more tense with the publication in *The Times* on Christmas day of a full and correct list of the cabinet appointments before they had been officially confirmed or announced. Worse still a leading article in the same edition applauded the Peelite and disparaged the Whig appointments, especially that of Russell to the Foreign Office which was deemed inappropriate. 'Lord John Russell has so little of the accomplishments specially required for his new office', it commented with obvious inside information, 'that we can only suppose he is keeping it for a successor, most probably Lord Clarendon, who otherwise will not have a seat in the Cabinet.' Russell was naturally much annoyed at this leak and at the hostile tone of the article towards himself.[3]

Clarendon complained strongly to Reeve of *The Times* of the unkind and unjust slur on Russell who had so sacrificed and exposed himself to blame from disappointed Liberals. Since Aberdeen's friendship with

---

[1] Add. MS. 44210, fol. 68, 'Xmas day (1852)'.

[2] Add. MS. 43070, fols. 275–8, 'Christmas D 52'. Of Redington Gladstone wrote: 'if he was undoubtedly efficient & you refuse to replace him from considerations other than those of merit, this would be a departure from the special ground on which you have stood throughout the proceedings'. This suggests that in the eyes of the Peelites their claim to so many places lay primarily on grounds of merit. On the other hand Gladstone did put in a word for Lord R. Clinton 'though Newcastle's proud purity would not hear of an appointment...because of relationship'. Gladstone concluded by expressing his admiration of the way in which Aberdeen had performed 'the extraordinary task of the past week', and told him that he was 'the only man in the country who could have surmounted such difficulties'.

[3] *The Times*, 25 December 1852; Graham Diary, 25 December; Add. MS. 43190, fols. 383–4, Graham to Aberdeen, 25 December.
    The Times had a series of well-informed leaders throughout the crisis. On 20 December it had proclaimed Aberdeen's fitness to form a government. It recognised that the co-operation of Russell and his friends was necessary, 'but the Liberal party do not rest solely with them', it added, emphasising that this was a time of party transformation. On 22 December it defended the formation of a coalition if that term was to be used, for 'there are many Conservatives more Radical than professed Reformers, many Whigs more Tory than professed Conservatives, many Reformers more so than either'. On 24 December, publishing the first of its accurate forecasts, it dwelt on the difficulties facing Lord Aberdeen, but expressed the belief that Whigs and Peelites were ready to co-operate.

Delane, the editor, was well known, the editorial would be thought to have the Prime Minister's approval. 'The Peelites should have been more self denying', Clarendon wrote; 'the general feeling was that the Peelites already wanted to kick down the Whig ladder by which *alone* they have climbed to power.' He hoped there might yet be a real fusion in the cabinet, but *The Times* leader made this difficult.[1]

On 26 December Russell addressed the following letter to Aberdeen in which he plainly expressed his pent-up feelings:

While I admit that you have every wish to act fairly I must submit to you the following results of your proposals:
Of 330 members of the House of Commons
   270 are Whigs and Radicals
   30 Irish Brigade
   30 Peelites
   To this party of 30 you propose to give 7 seats in the Cabinet
   To the Whigs & Radicals 5
   To Lord Palmerston   1   —13
   Of four important offices not in the Cabinet you propose to give 3 to the 30 Peelites, 1 to the 270.
   I am afraid the Liberal party will never stand this, and that the storm will overwhelm me.

He went on to suggest that Granville should be made Lord President, a proposal to which Aberdeen had already assented, that Francis Baring should take the Board of Trade with a seat in the cabinet, that Lord Stanley of Alderley should be Vice-President without a seat in the cabinet, and that Clarendon should enter the cabinet immediately as Chancellor of the Duchy of Lancaster. He said that he had already sent for Baring and that if he would not join George Grey would. 'Let me add to what I have said', he continued, like a terrier returning to his bone, 'that ten Whigs, members of former Cabinets, are omitted in this while only two Peelites are omitted, & one entirely new admitted. Let me propose further that the minor posts be recast with less disproportion. Cardwell ought not to have public office while Labouchere, Vernon Smith and others are excluded.'[2]

These difficulties were not imaginary, for a few days later Ellice, who was himself well disposed towards the Peelites, was writing to Brough-

---

[1] Maxwell, *Clarendon*, I, 355–6. According to Dasent, Delane was in close touch with Aberdeen during the period of cabinet making (*Delane*, I, 149–52).
[2] Add. MS. 43066, fols. 144–6, 26 December 1852.

ton saying that 'great discontent prevails at Brooks's and the Reform Club—and the Irish Brigade keep their seats on the opposition benches'.[1] Lady John, of course, was ever ready to relate her husband's troubles to her father, telling him what a 'weary & in many respects vexatious, disappoint'g & mortify'g business' it had been. 'You know how such a time brings out a man in his true colours,' she commented, alluding to the division between those who thought only of themselves and those who acted 'in total disregard of self'.

I am happy to say that many of our old gov't in and out of the cab't, are among these (she continued)—It was very desirable that even the liberals in the new Ministry shd not be all taken from that old set, & the public will be rather surprised not to see one Grey in the list—Ld Grey declared fortunately before be'g asked that nothing wd induce him to come in—Sir George was very unwilling but is com'g into Parlt as a warm supporter—Sir C. Wood not quite so amiable but very anxious that everybody else shd make sacrifices. Ld Carlisle & Mr. Labouchere have never reminded J. of their existence—Ld Clanricarde is thought to be out of humour—[2]

Russell's papers bear testimony to the various pressures to which he was subjected. Both Lansdowne and Palmerston pressed the claims of Lord Clanricarde.[3] Sir Francis Baring came up to London in the belief that he was to be offered a place only to be disappointed, but he praised Russell's public spirit in waiving his own claims and joining an Aberdeen government and promised himself to support it.[4] Lord Carlisle, writing on the same day that Lady John was noting his silence, accepted the news that he was left out with an attempt to be philosophical. 'I had certainly allowed myself to think', he wrote to Russell, 'that if there were any offices, for which my antecedents might have most fitted me, they would [have] been either Ireland or the Presidency of the Council. Probably in the long run these things are salutary for one.'[5] Lord Rutherford rejoiced at Russell's own return to office but admitted that things had not gone as he liked. He warned Russell that there was anxiety in Scotland about the law appointments and gave his opinion that 'nothing could be more grievous to the Liberal party here than any

[1] Add. MS. 43747, fols. 84–5, 29 December 1852.
[2] Lady John Russell, Minto Papers, Acc 2794, Box 136, 25 December 1852.
[3] PRO 30/22/10/F, fol. 1549, 23 December 1852 from Palmerston and fol. 1587, 26 December from Lansdowne. Palmerston passed on a message from Lady Clanricarde that the Irish members would be pleased to see her husband given office! Cf. Greville Memoirs, VI, 184.
[4] Ibid. fols. 1575–6, 25 December 1852.   [5] Ibid. fol. 1577, 26 December 1852.

hesitation in recurring to your own law officers'.[1] Moncrief in accepting office made the same point, saying that there were only two parties in Scotland, those for and those against Lord Derby, that all Peel's law officers had been among the former, and that there would be great resentment at the law appointment of any of them.[2] Lord Truro accepted Russell's explanation telling him why it was impossible to offer him the Irish Great Seal with dignity, saying that he had no regrets.[3] Labouchere was likewise accommodating, saying that he had no strong wish for office and no claims to be included under the circumstances.[4] Lord Panmure told Russell that he was glad for private reasons that he had not been offered anything, and promised his support, but he wondered what the Greys thought of their omission and urged Dalhousie as preferable to Newcastle.[5] Actually both Greys were offered office but declined, Lord Grey mainly because of his opposition to a further Reform Bill.[6]

Lord Normanby, who had told Russell earlier that he would like to be Irish Viceroy,[7] probably sounded a more typical note when he wrote:

I was quite prepared that the time was come when the Peelites must be admitted and [illegible] into the Liberal ranks—but one who is at a distance and therefore knows nothing of detail and who has been a Whig and nothing more for the last thirty years cannot but regret when he sees that great party absorbed in the smallest and as it appears by the last election the least popular section of the Tories.

Your own personal sacrifice was noble and patriotic...but I think undue advantage was taken of the difficulties of your position. You were at the head of a party containing about two hundred of the House of Commons and comprising [sic] about 18 who had been Cabinet Ministers.

The Peelites were at most thirty in the Commons and had only 7 who had ever been in the Cabinet even for a few months yet all these with one exception (old Goulburn) are included whilst you have at most only four who look up to you of which only three are your former colleagues and of these three one without office. I could make other remarks as to some

[1] PRO 30/22/10/F, fols. 1589–92, 26 December 1852.
[2] Ibid. fols. 1546–52, 30 December 1852.
[3] Ibid. fols. 1604–5, 27 December 1852.
[4] Ibid. fol. 1596, 27 December 1852.
[5] Ibid. fols. 1614–15, 28 December 1852. He also urged Russell not to drop reform.
[6] Ibid. 30/22/10/F, fols. 1553–6, 23 December 1852, partly in G. P. Gooch, Later correspondence of Lord John Russell 1840–1878, II, 118.
[7] Ibid. fols. 1472–6, 24 November 1852.

individual appointments but it is certainly now best for the country to forget one's feelings as soon as possible.[1]

This was bound to have been unsettling for Lord John, as were the comments later received from his father-in-law, Lord Minto, who wrote from Italy:

Nothing to be sure can be more unnatural than the footing on which it has been attempted to underbuild a slender & baseless Peelite fabric with a sound & substantial Whig foundation. The spirit in which such pretensions were conceived certainly does not promise much...I however endeavour to persuade myself that as many of them are keenly alive to the charm of office, and as they are wholly dependent for Parliamentary strength upon Whig support, they may become conscious of the necessity of accommodating themselves to our policy and gradually become absorbed in our ranks. But this is rather a hope than an expectation on my part.

While protesting his sincere wish for the 'success of the great experiment', he feared that Russell would lack support in the cabinet and expressed apprehensions about the new government's educational policy as likely to entail 'too much churchyness', especially in Scotland.[2]

On the evening of 26 December Russell and Hayter, the Whig whip, conferred with Aberdeen and the Peelite triumvirate of Graham, Newcastle and Herbert. Graham gloomily wrote of the meeting: 'the same wrangle continues for places, and the same unabated jealousy of Whigs against Peelites'. Nevertheless, Aberdeen did not go beyond the concession regarding Lord Granville and the cabinet remained six Peelites, six Whigs and one Radical.[3] The list of most of the subordinate ministers and Household appointments was supposedly settled the same evening, but the next day there was further trouble as Wood and Hayter visited Graham, looking for fresh concessions. Sir James delivered an ultimatum to the effect that he would withdraw his address to the

---

[1] PRO/30/22/10/G, fols. 1775–82, 7 January 1853.
[2] *Ibid.* fols. 1741–2, 4 January 1853.
[3] The Peelites: Aberdeen (Prime Minister), Gladstone (Exchequer), Newcastle (Colonies), Graham (Admiralty), Argyll (Privy Seal), Herbert (Secretary at War); the Whigs: Russell (Foreign Office and House leader), Palmerston (Home Office), Cranworth (Lord Chancellor), Wood (Board of Control), Granville (Lord President), Lansdowne (without office); the Radical Molesworth (Commissioner of Works) made a seventh Liberal, while Clarendon would make an eighth when he succeeded Russell at the Foreign Office.

electors of Carlisle and reveal all to the House unless the Whigs would abide by their bargain. They did not want any more Graham revelations and gave up the struggle on this point, but in the matter of some lesser offices still to be settled Aberdeen was prepared to be more flexible.[1]

The majority of the other ministerial appointments outside the cabinet in the end went to the Liberals, but Cardwell, as we have seen, was given the Board of Trade and Canning, to his chagrin,[2] the Post Office. Lord Hardinge, a onetime Peelite, was retained as Commander-in-Chief, while Lord Raglan, a Conservative soldier, was made Master-General of the Ordnance. The Liberals took seven other ministerial appointments and also the major Household offices, with the exception of the Mastership of the Horse, which was given to the new Duke of Wellington.[3]

Strutt's religious beliefs were canvassed before he was offered the Duchy of Lancaster. At the same time that Gladstone was questioning his fitness for this particular office, Russell was writing a note to Aberdeen reassuring him. 'Strutt is not as I supposed a Unitarian', he wrote, 'but goes regularly to Church.'[4] The correspondence on this interesting point went on for some days, for Aberdeen protested that he did not want it said that the first act of a Presbyterian Prime Minister was to put a Socinian in charge of Church of England patronage.[5] Russell told him to recollect that Socinianism was 'a nickname like Puseyism and other nicknames which it will be well not to bandy

---

[1] Graham Diary, 26 and 27 December 1852 (Parker, *Graham*, II, 199–200).

[2] *Letters of Queen Victoria*, II, 519–20, memorandum by Prince Albert, 28 December 1852, who wrote: 'Lord Canning seemed very much hurt at not being taken into the Cabinet, and felt inclined to refuse the Post Office. We agreed upon the impolicy of such a step, and encouraged Lord Aberdeen to press him. Lord Clanricarde, and particularly Lord Carlisle, were very much grieved at being left out altogether.'

[3] See *Annual Register, 1852* and *1853*. Actually Aberdeen first pressed the Mastership of the Horse on his Peelite friend the Duke of Buccleuch, saying that it was of vital importance to the government and greatly desired by the queen. Nevertheless, Buccleuch declined, expressing the opinion that he could be of greater value out of office. Add. MS. 43201, fol. 58, 30 December 1852, fols. 59–62, 31 December. Aberdeen also recommended Graham's nephew, Lord Dufferin, for a Court appointment, but the queen said 'he was too young and *looked* too young'. When the Prime Minister tried again some time later she again demurred, saying that 'he was an excellent young man'; but that 'he was too great a favourite with the ladies'. Graham Papers, 2 January and 22 September 1853. Two Peelites, Lord Drumlanrig and Lord E. Bruce, received minor Household appointments.

[4] Add. MS. 43066, fol. 152, 25 December 1852.

[5] PRO 30/22/10/F, fols. 1581–3, 26 December 1852 (two letters).

among us'.[1] In the end Aberdeen was satisfied that Strutt was a member of the Church of England and so assured the queen.[2]

It would be fruitless to try to follow the detailed discussion about lesser places that filled the week between Christmas and New Year's Day. Irish appointments were particularly thorny because of the unpopularity of Russell's candidates, such as Redington, who had been Irish Under-Secretary at the time of the Ecclesiastical Titles Bill. The Whigs begrudged the allocation of the two chief Irish posts to Peelites, Lord St Germans, who became Lord Lieutenant, and Sir John Young, who was made Secretary. They fought hard to have Redington made Under-Secretary, but finally accepted a compromise by which he was given the Secretaryship of the Board of Control, and another Whig, Brady, was made Irish Lord Chancellor. This switch displaced another Whig nominee, Layard, from the Board of Control, and left without office he proved of some embarrassment throughout the government's life, as a self-professed authority on Eastern affairs. Other Irish law appointments went to Brewster, a Peelite nominee, who became Attorney General, and William Keogh, a former Peelite and now an Irish Liberal associated with the Brigade, who condemned him for accepting office, along with Sadleir, another Brigadier, who was made a Lord of the Treasury. A third Irish Catholic to take office was Monsell, who became Clerk of the Ordnance, but he was less open to criticism than the other two, since he had not taken the Tenant League pledge of independence. Although the Irish Brigade were more inclined to support an Aberdeen government than any other, because of the Peelites' opposition to the Ecclesiastical Titles Bill, they preferred to remain independent of all English parties and strongly condemned Sadleir and Keogh for taking office. Their defection may well have weakened the Independent opposition, as it became known in 1853, but did not seem to have done much harm to their spirits.[3]

With Ireland finally settled there was still trouble with Scottish appointments, where Aberdeen's personal opinions carried more weight. 'Your Scotch Whigs are really too bad', he wrote to Russell. 'I am unwilling to recognize the necessity of delivering Scotland into the hands of these violent & exclusive partisans; and I think they might

[1] Add. MS. 43066, fols. 157–60, 26 December 1852.
[2] Add. MS. 43046, fol. 202, 27 December 1852 (copy).
[3] See Aberdeen–Russell correspondence in Add. MS. 43066 and PRO 30/22/10/G; Graham Diary, 28 December 1852; Whyte, *Independent Irish Party*, ch. VIII.

be improved by seeing a gentleman of more liberal feelings introduced among them. If this Scotch spirit were to prevail no government could exist, as I trust we may hope to do.'[1] In the end both Scottish law officers appointed were Liberals.[2] Russell in his turn preached moderation to the Scottish Liberals. 'The two parties must be fused & must endeavour to act in harmony in this country', he wrote to Lord Murray. 'In Scotland I am told there are no Peelites; the fewer there are the more easy it will be to satisfy them.'[3]

The Liberals received the bulk of the non-ministerial appointments at Westminster, but five more Peelites received places,[4] thus bringing the total number of Peelite appointments (not including Hardinge or Raglan) to seventeen. Charles Villiers became Judge-Advocate General, but Bright complained to Russell that he should have had the Board of Trade with a seat in the cabinet. 'The man whom Sir R. Peel followed', he commented, 'is somewhat better, I think, than a man who merely followed Sir R. Peel.'[5] Russell complimented Bright on his epigram but suggested that he would have been equally opposed to two brothers having seats in the cabinet.[6] This may have mystified Bright since Clarendon's appointment was still in the future.

By the middle of the week almost all the details were settled and, on Wednesday 29 December, Aberdeen and Russell, both weary of the struggle, addressed notes to each other in almost identical terms. 'I trust we have now nearly come to the end of our patronage difficulties', the Prime Minister wrote; 'but they might have been worse', he added philosophically. The other expressed similar relief when he wrote: 'I hope we are now coming to a conclusion upon these vexatious questions of patronage & we may hope to rest at nights. I am sure they plague you as much as me.'[7] The day before, the old ministers had

---

[1] Add. MS. 43066, fol. 186, 3 January 1853 (copy).

[2] *Annual Register, 1853.*

[3] PRO 30/22/10/G, 9 February 1853 (Gooch, *Later correspondence*, II, 121–2). Throughout the administration the Scottish Whigs remained a thorn in Lord Aberdeen's side and the young duke of Argyll was always ready to remind him of their excesses. See Aberdeen correspondence with both Russell and Argyll.

[4] Robert Lowe became the other Secretary to the Board of Control, Frederick Peel Under-Secretary at the Colonial Office, Henry Fitzroy Under-Secretary at the Home Office, and Lord A. Hervey and F. Charteris Lords of the Treasury. For a complete list of appointments see Appendix C.

[5] Gooch, *Later correspondence*, II, 120.   [6] *Ibid.* p. 121.

[7] Add. MS. 43066, fols. 169, 171–2. There are some nine letters from Russell to Aberdeen in the five days 25–29 December, fols. 150–70, and another five from Aberdeen to Russell in PRO 30/22/10/F, fols. 1581, 1583, 1618, 1612, 1620. On 31 December

travelled down to Windsor on the Great Western Railway to give up their seals and the new ministers had made the journey by the South Western to kiss hands and officially accept their offices.[1]

With the cabinet and other major offices settled, Aberdeen had announced the formation of the government on Monday the 27th, the same day that Graham had had the 'show-down' with Wood and Hayter. He began by denying Derby's charges of conspiracy, commenting that at the time the preceding government fell he had been arranging to engage a winter residence at Nice. He then described the circumstances under which he had undertaken the queen's commission. He had come to the conclusion, he said, 'that the time had arrived when it was possible for men whose political differences the course of events and recent legislation had almost, if not altogether, effaced or removed, and whose personal respect and friendship had never been interrupted ... to act together in the public service'. Consequently he had accepted the task, which he had succeeded in fulfilling, perhaps not without difficulty, but with good will on all sides.

He outlined the policy his government intended to follow, beginning with the field of foreign affairs. To the surprise of some of his listeners he asserted that there had been a continuity in British policy over the preceding thirty years and this he proposed to continue.

It has been marked by a respect due to all independent States [he said], a desire to abstain as much as possible from the internal affairs of other countries, an assertion of our honour and interests, and above all a desire to secure the general peace of Europe by all such means as were practicable and at our disposal.

At the same time there would be no relaxation in the defensive preparations recently initiated. The statement could have been made word for word a hundred years later, with a little elaboration as to means.

In the field of commercial policy he naturally promised 'the maintenance and the prudent extension of free trade, and the commercial and financial system established by Sir Robert Peel'. The most immediate concern of the government would be the settlement of the income tax. All this was to be expected, but perhaps more significant as an indication of the liberal and reforming complexion of the new administration was the promise of educational, law and parliamentary reform.

Aberdeen sent the queen a list of fifteen legal and non-ministerial appointments and ten household appointments that had been settled earlier in the week. R.A. C 28, fol. 71.
[1] *The Times*, 29 December 1852.

As to Lord Derby's query about the Conservativeness of the government, he simply said:

My Lords, I declare to the noble Earl that in my opinion no Government in this country is now possible except a Conservative Government; and to that I add another declaration which I take to be indubitably as true; that no Government in this country is now possible except a Liberal Government. The truth is that these terms have no definite meaning. I never should have thought of approaching my noble Friend the Member for the City of London (Lord John Russell), unless I had thought he was Conservative; and I am sure he never would have associated himself with me unless he had thought I was Liberal. My Lords, these names it may be convenient to keep up for the sake of party elections; but the country is sick of these distinctions, which have no real meaning, and which prevent men from acting together who are able to perform good service to the Crown and to the country. I trust, therefore, that in just acceptation of the word, whatever the measures proposed by the present Government may be, they will be Conservative measures as well as Liberal, for I consider both qualities to be essentially necessary.

He refused to be frightened by the supposed 'encroachments of democracy' that Lord Derby had warned against, because he could see no such dangers. 'I have great confidence in the people of this country,' he concluded; 'and I do believe the imputation, and even the existence of alarm at this moment, is almost a libel on the people.'[1]

Derby made a fighting rejoinder, defending at some length his charges that there had been a concert among the different parties opposed to his government to get rid of it, directing his shafts particularly in the direction of the duke of Newcastle and Sir James Graham. As to the new Prime Minister's statement of policy, he waxed sarcastic over the alleged continuity of foreign policy, welcomed the proposals for educational and administrative reforms, but expressed doubts about parliamentary reform, repeating his warning against increasing the democratic element in the constitution. He jeered at Aberdeen's use of the terms 'Liberal' and 'Conservative', which he switched around as the need arose to suit his convenience.[2]

Following this sharp exchange, both Houses were adjourned to 10 February 1853.

Greville commented on Aberdeen's statement that 'it was fair enough and not ill received but it was ill delivered, and he omitted to say all he

---

[1] *Hansard*, CXXIII, 1721–7.　　　　[2] *Ibid.* 1727–41.

might and ought to have said about Lord Lansdowne, nor did he say enough about John Russell'. When this was pointed out to him by Newcastle, Aberdeen accepted the criticism, pleading inexperience, and expressed regret that he could not make the speech over again.[1] This was unfortunate, for despite all the difficulties in forming the cabinet and making the other appointments, it must be emphasised that it never would have been done without the basic good will of the Whigs, with some exceptions, to Lord Aberdeen. In particular the strong support from the beginning of Bedford and Lansdowne is reflected in their friendly correspondence with the new Prime Minister.[2]

The most common observation to be made about the Aberdeen coalition both then and ever since has been that the Peelites were far out of proportion to their strength in the House of Commons, and this not unnaturally was a sore point with the Liberal rank and file and more particularly with some of those Whig ministers who were left without office or excluded from the cabinet. Of the seven Whig-Liberals one was a Radical who had never been in a Whig cabinet, one was an independent Whig who had been dismissed from the last Whig cabinet, one was a professional lawyer rather than a regular party politician, and one had already retired from official political life. This left a hard core of three active Whig party politicians, Russell, Wood and Granville! Such Whig notables as Lord Grey, Sir George Grey, Lord Carlisle, the Marquis of Clanricarde, Sir Francis Baring, Lord Broughton, Henry Labouchere and, for the time being, Lord Clarendon were all left out. Poor Russell, whom the Peelites had found so difficult throughout the negotiations, was blamed for this by many of the Whigs; indeed some of them had tried to persuade him to abandon the whole idea of a coalition.[3] The Peelite leaders perhaps failed sufficiently to realise the full difficulty of his position, partly because his sudden changes seemed to be so irrational and emotional. Indeed Russell's real fault lay in the primadonna-like way in which he treated the question of his own personal position, and here it was evident that he allowed himself to be unduly influenced by his wife.[4]

[1] *Greville Memoirs*, VI, 385–7.
[2] *Ab. Cor. 1850–60*, pp. 414, 415, 418, 420, 424–5, 428.
[3] *Greville Memoirs*, VI, 386.
[4] See R.A. C28, fol. 105, Col. Grey memorandum of conversation with Sir George Grey, 1 February 1853. Grey had urged Russell to take the Home Office but Lady John had vetoed it, determined that her husband should not strain himself by taking on any executive office.

There was reason, however, in Lord Aberdeen's insistence on having such a large number of his own friends in the cabinet, despite their lack of numbers in the Commons, quite apart from their alleged ability. Within the past year both Russell and Derby had been defeated by the votes of independent Liberals and independent Conservatives. The evidence suggested that party lines needed redrawing and this is what Aberdeen was doing (as he explained rather clumsily in his speech in the House of Lords). He was constructing a government that he anticipated would obtain support not only from the Liberal Conservatives who voted against the Disraeli budget, but from quite a few more followers of Lord Derby who would be ready, after Derby's failure, to give fair trial to an administration headed by a former Conservative Foreign Secretary and with a cabinet containing six former Conservative ministers.[1] To have included a predominant number of Liberal ministers in the cabinet would have been to close the ranks of the Conservatives behind Lord Derby. Such considerations, however, could not be expected to make the Liberals happy and so it was inevitable that the formation of the ministry should have been a protracted and painful business. On the whole, indeed, it was a surprise to all concerned that the new team settled down as easily and as quickly as it did to the task at hand.

[1] Greville anticipated rabid opposition from the Derbyites, but quoted Lord Drumlanrig, who said he knew 'several adherents of Derby who were resolved to give the new Government fair play' (*Memoirs*, VI, 381). Further evidence of such a shift is to be found in the following short news item in *The Times*, 3 January:

'The Government of Lord Aberdeen will have a good majority in the House of Lords, including the whole bench of bishops without we believe a single exception.

'In the House of Commons also, the adhesions are coming in day by day, from "the other side". Between 40 and 50 of the dispersed Derbyites, representing town constituencies, and some from the counties, too, have already fallen away from an allegiance that brought no benefit...'

2

THE COALITION CABINET

The new team — two generations

The first meeting of the new cabinet was held on 29 December in Argyll House, where Lord Aberdeen was host to his colleagues at a cabinet dinner. They have been well described on their initial appearance together by their youngest member, the duke of Argyll, who was attending the first cabinet meeting of his long life, and for him the interest of the occasion was heightened by the fact that it took place in his ancestral home, purchased years earlier by Lord Aberdeen but never renamed.[1]

The ministers fell into two main age groups, those who were born in the eighteenth century and those who were born after 1800. Eight, if we include Clarendon, who joined the cabinet in February, fell in the former group, but Wood (1800–85) and Clarendon (1800–70) only just slipped under the line. Three entered public life and held important offices during the Napoleonic Wars, Lansdowne (1781–1863), who was Chancellor of the Exchequer in 1806, Palmerston (1785–1865), who became Secretary at War in 1809, and Aberdeen (1784–1860), who went as special envoy to Austria in 1813. A particular lustre was attached to the two older members of this trio, to Lansdowne as the colleague of Fox in the first Ministry of All Talents, and to Aberdeen as the ward of the younger Pitt. Lord Lansdowne, as Argyll remarked, both began and ended his political life in a coalition cabinet; and Argyll himself (1823–1900) would live long enough to know the names of Lloyd George and Winston Churchill, leaders of the wartime coalitions of the twentieth century. Lansdowne, the son of Lord Shelburne, onetime Prime Minister and patron of Jeremy Bentham, was the most respected and beloved Whig nobleman of his day. Although now infirm with age, he was a good speaker when he undertook to enter debate. According to Argyll, 'he was as temperate and philosophical in his opinions as he was weighty and grave in the expression of them'.[2]

[1] *Argyll Memoirs*, I, 374–87. What follows is in part based on Argyll's reminiscence, written forty-five years later when he was the sole survivor.
[2] *Ibid.* p. 376.

37

Lord Aberdeen,[1] too, commanded great respect owing to his long experience and wide contacts, but especially because of his obvious integrity and disinterestedness. He was rather more remote from party politics than most of his colleagues, having spent all his public life in the House of Lords, where he had been a Scottish representative peer from 1806 to 1814, when he was created a peer of the United Kingdom. His official experience had begun with his mission to Vienna in 1813, where he had been sent to secure the cooperation of Austria in the war against Napoleon, and in 1814 he had participated in the peace settlement at Paris as a subordinate of Castlereagh. His mind was indelibly impressed by the ravages of war which he had witnessed on the field of Leipzig and in the following pursuit. Of a retiring disposition, he avoided political office until 1828, when he became Foreign Secretary under Wellington, an office he resumed under Peel between 1841 and 1846. He was not a great Foreign Secretary, but his peaceful policy, contrasting with Palmerston's more aggressive attitude, produced an *entente* with France, friendly relations with Russia, and boundary settlements with the United States. His relationship with Peel, who fully supported his policy, was warm and close, but he did not pretend to any real interest in or knowledge of those great fiscal questions that so concerned Peel and his disciples. Out of office he strongly opposed Palmerston's bellicose foreign policy, especially in the affair of Don Pacifico, but he had no thought of deserting Peel for the Protectionists.

Aberdeen did not have the great all-round abilities of Peel, the public appeal of the later Gladstone, or the parliamentary skill of Russell or Derby—indeed he was a poor public speaker; but he was a man of cultivated tastes, a trustee of the British Museum and a Fellow of the Royal Society. Moreover, he had a combination of common sense and broadmindedness that made him attractive to all who knew him well, although there were some outside his circle who thought him cold and dour. His natural reserve was probably accentuated by the tragedy of his private life, for he was twice widowed and three daughters died prematurely. Gladstone felt a greater affection for him than for any

[1] Sir Arthur Gordon's *The Earl of Aberdeen* is the best biography of Aberdeen. Gordon, later Lord Stanmore, was Aberdeen's youngest son. He was very close to his father and in possession of all the earl's private papers, but this life, one of a series, is unfortunately very brief. Lady Frances Balfour's *The life of George, 4th Earl of Aberdeen*, although longer, is less satisfactory.

other man he had known in his public life.[1] Indeed, as a man he was highly esteemed by all his colleagues and he was probably the only one who could have brought them all together.

The contrast between Aberdeen and Palmerston is striking: the one plain of feature, diffident and withdrawing in manner, but a firm believer in the essential unity of the European community and in the importance of keeping close and friendly relations with all its members; the other once handsome, still striking in appearance, self-confident and jovial, contemptuous of foreigners unless they were admirers of English ways and English ideas. Palmerston was not as sensitive or cultured as Aberdeen, nor as liberal in his views as Russell, but he showed great magnanimity in entering a cabinet headed by one of the strongest critics of his foreign policy and with the rival who had recently turned him out of the Foreign Office now holding those very seals.

Palmerston's entry into the coalition was almost casually made, but it was to mark a turning-point in his long career.[2] The 'thirties had been a decade of transition for him as 'Cupid' gave way to 'Lord Pumice-stone' and as he gradually sank his roots into the Whig-Liberal party. In middle age he married the widowed Lady Cooper, who was devoted to him and set about to promote his political career by her prowess as a London hostess. In the later 'forties Palmerston was emerging as a national hero, who seemed to symbolise the faults and virtues of John Bull, tough and outspoken, but straightforward and magnanimous, champion of all things English and, especially abroad, of her liberal institutions. He was not a great orator, but could express himself with force and clarity. These qualities were notably present in his letters and memoranda, both in their style and in their calligraphy. The bold, firm handwriting and the fluent, pungent style reveal the man for what he was. Sometimes his analyses of problems were absurdly optimistic, ignoring the difficulties arising from a particular policy, but the argument was always couched in clear and vigorous language.

While some of his Whig colleagues still viewed him with suspicion, he was often popular with the Roebuck type of Radical, who applauded

[1] 'He is the man in public life of all others whom I have *loved*', Gladstone told his grand-daughter-in-law many years later. 'I say emphatically *loved*. I have *loved* others but never like him.' See Lady Aberdeen's account of 'A Visit to the Gladstones in 1894' in *Victorian studies*, II (1958), 155–60.

[2] H. C. F. Bell's *Lord Palmerston* (two volumes) is the best of many biographies, but E. Ashley, *The life and correspondence of Henry John Temple Viscount Palmerston*, is still useful because of the long quotations from his correspondence.

his manner of dealing with the autocratic governments of Europe, and increasingly in the 'fifties by many backbench Tories, who liked his nationalism as well as his growing opposition to further parliamentary reform. His political strength had increased since the 'thirties, partly owing to his cultivation of the press, partly because he overshadowed Russell, who lacked the power of Grey and Melbourne to curb such a strong-willed Foreign Secretary. Russell's dismissal of Palmerston in 1851 hurt the former more than the latter. For the time being it left Palmerston in an independent position, courted by Tories and Radicals and by anti-Russell Whigs. It was too soon for him yet to supplant Russell as leader of the Liberal party, but if Lord John was given a little more rope he might effect the transformation himself. It was characteristic of Palmerston that whatever he undertook he did with relish, and his work at the Home Office, where he was open to the influence of his son-in-law, Lord Shaftesbury, although a brief episode in his career, was far from negligible. The Aberdeen coalition, ironically, was to be the prelude to the age of Palmerston.

Lord John Russell (1792–1878) was undoubtedly the most difficult and unmanageable member of the new team.[1] He was the very essence of Whiggism, incarnating its best and worst features, for he was high-minded and patriotic, in some respects genuinely liberal, but he was also notoriously exclusive and clannish. Moreover, he was extremely thin-skinned and absurdly concerned about what he called his honour and the respect that he considered due to him. For these reasons he was not a popular statesman and has fared badly with historians, but it should not be forgotten that he played a leading role in the achievement of a whole series of great reforms, including the repeal of the Test and Corporation Acts and Catholic Emancipation in the 'twenties, the reform of parliament, of the municipal corporations and of the Poor Law in the 'thirties, and the victory of free trade in the 'forties. Moreover, for all his prickly qualities, there was an attractive side to his personality that may be seen in his relations with his family and his more intimate friends. Indeed, Aberdeen and Graham, who had cause enough for exasperation with him and often showed it in their correspondence, nevertheless, always retained a certain affection for the 'Little Man', as they called him.

Sir James Graham (1792–1861), whom Argyll wittily said 'was a coalition in himself', came from a north of England land-owning

[1] Spencer Walpole's *Russell*, although partial and outdated, remains the best biography.

family of great antiquity. He was born in the same year as Russell and entered parliament also as a Whig, in 1818, five years after him.[1] They received their first ministerial appointments together in 1830 and both served on the famous committee that drafted the Great Reform Bill, but Graham preceded Russell in Grey's cabinet, which he entered on its formation as First Lord of the Admiralty. They parted, of course, with his resignation in 1834, and only now came together again after a separation of eighteen years. Graham, we are told, was a tall, handsome man, although growing a little bald. Argyll's description may be quoted further:

He was, indeed, one of the pillars of the Government. Although a man of large and powerful frame, he had rather a weak voice. He had no animation in his delivery, no action with his arms. He stood like a column, generally resting his weight on one leg, with the other foot against the table. But he spoke with a weight and gravity which made his speaking highly effective. I have heard Lord Aberdeen refer to it as 'Graham's sledge-hammer'.[2]

He had a high reputation as an efficient administrator, able debater and wise counsellor, but for all his acknowledged ability and masculine appearance there was a curious timidity that prevented him from ever being considered a party leader or a Prime Minister. As he himself readily acknowledged, there was an underlying strain of pessimism in his make-up, which deprived him of the self-confidence necessary for successful political leadership. Although of bluer blood, he had much in common with Sir Robert Peel, with whom he was most intimately associated from 1841, when he became Peel's Home Secretary, until Peel's death in 1850. Lacking Peel's personal stature and political nerve, Graham was less the statesman and more the politician. He did not inspire the same confidence and respect in his political associates, but in these years he was more intimate with Peel than with any other man. After 1834 their views were generally identical and they both had that seriousness of outlook which so characterised the Victorian England that they helped to make in contrast to the Regency England of their youth.

Of Sir Charles Wood, an uninspiring man of limited talents, Argyll charitably says that he showed greater ability at the Board of Control,

[1] Parker's *Graham*, despite its two volumes, is scrappy and incomplete, but it contains many useful quotations from his correspondence. A. B. Erickson's *The public career of Sir James Graham* is better in dealing with Graham as an administrator at the Admiralty and the Home Office.   [2] *Argyll Memoirs*, I, 379–80.

for which he was better suited, than at the Exchequer, where he had tried to model himself on Peel, but unsuccessfully. Yet he took himself seriously as a financial authority and on this ground bullied Russell, who was not. He was a strong party man and generally loyal to Russell, but he ended his official life as the Lord Halifax of Gladstone's first cabinet.

Clarendon[1] is a more attractive figure than Wood, generally liked, although not by Queen Victoria, who rightly suspected him of laughing at her. His reputation as a diplomat survived the Crimean War; indeed Bismarck is supposed to have suggested that he was the one man, had he lived, who might have averted the Franco-Prussian War. He too was to end his career in Gladstone's first ministry. He was outspoken and disinterested and had a good sense of humour. During the months preceding the outbreak of the Crimean War it was necessary for the cabinet to listen to many endless and often repetitive despatches. We are told that 'the liveliness and humour' which characterised the reading of the Foreign Secretary were a 'source of relief' to his weary colleagues. 'His running comments were inimitable,' Argyll wrote. 'His readings of the character of each diplomatist were often as good as a play, and were a real help in enabling us to judge how far we could trust each separate estimate of the situation at the separate Courts.'[2] Clarendon never sat in the House of Commons and he did not succeed his uncle in the peerage until 1838, but he entered the diplomatic service as early as 1820 and the Whig cabinet in 1839.

Little need be said of Lord Cranworth (R. B. Rolfe, 1790–1868), who had been called to the bar in 1816 and who had climbed the Whig legal ladder to the point where he was the obvious candidate of that party, although, as we have seen, Aberdeen, and the Court, would have preferred to have kept Lord St Leonards, a more distinguished lawyer. In his cabinet memoranda Gladstone generally observed that the Lord Chancellor said little, but agreed with the majority of his colleagues.

The remaining members of the cabinet were all of a younger generation that entered parliament after the passing of the great Reform Bill, Gladstone, Newcastle, Herbert and Molesworth in 1833, and Granville in 1836. Argyll,[3] as we have seen, never sat in the Commons, since he succeeded to his title in 1847, only three years after he had come of age. Consequently he had as yet made relatively little impression on the

[1] Sir Herbert Maxwell's two-volume biography is of limited value, but contains useful quotations from Clarendon's correspondence and Lady Clarendon's Journal.
[2] *Argyll Memoirs*, I, 451.
[3] See above, pp. 21–2.

political world, although those who knew him were clearly impressed with his potentiality. He sat in all Liberal cabinets from 1855 until he broke with Gladstone in the 1880s and ended his political life as a Liberal Unionist. Although he was in many respects a liberal-minded aristocrat his basic conservatism predominated in the end in his opposition to Irish land legislation and Home Rule. His *Memoirs* show him to have been a shrewd and intelligent observer of the contemporary political scene, but he never put himself in the centre of the stage. He had a remarkably wide range of interests, religious, scientific, and literary, and the full bibliography of his published works runs to several hundred items.

Sir William Molesworth (1810–55) stood out the most from the rest of his colleagues.[1] He was an avowed Benthamite, a reputed unbeliever, a proponent of the ballot, and an ardent colonial reformer. His appointment was a sop to the Radicals, but as heir to an old baronetcy his social background was quite acceptable. He proved more agreeable and less aggressive than some of his new colleagues anticipated, but was later suspected as a source of cabinet leaks to the press.

Lord Granville (1815–91), although a few years younger, had longer official experience and highly orthodox qualifications.[2] Since his father had been an ambassador, he had spent more time abroad as a boy than most members of his class, and consequently his outlook was less insular. As a schoolboy at Eton he had championed Catholic Emancipation, where it was an unpopular cause. Moreover, he had married into the distinguished German Catholic family of Dalberg. (His wife was the mother of the future Lord Acton by an earlier marriage.) He entered the House of Commons on coming of age in 1836 and became Under-Secretary for Foreign Affairs in 1839, but he was out of parliament from 1841 until he succeeded to his peerage in 1846. To his disappointment he was only offered the court appointment of Master of the Buckhounds when Russell formed his government in that year. To the indignation of John Bright, however, he received the unlikely appointment of Vice-President of the Board of Trade in 1848, but he won the respect even of Bright by his able and energetic promotion of the Great Exhibition of 1851. His appointment to cabinet office to replace Palmerston at the end of that year came as a general surprise, but in Aberdeen's opinion he was

---

[1] See Mrs Fawcett's *Rt. Hon. Sir William Molesworth, Bt, M.P.*

[2] Lord Edmund Fitzmaurice, *The life of Granville George Leveson Gower second Earl of Granville 1851–91*, the official biography, only has fifteen pages on the years of the coalition.

the best man the Whigs had for the post.[1] It did not last long, but it heralded Lord Granville's arrival on the bridge of the Whig ship. He was the sort of man who got along with everybody well—with the Court, where he was very popular; with all his colleagues, among whom he was often an intermediary between rival factions; with the diplomatic corps, where his tact was in contrast to Palmerston's blustering; and with the public at large, to the extent that they knew him. 'He was popular in society, not merely on account of his very agreeable powers of conversation', wrote Argyll, 'but for his great good temper, tact, and sagacity of character, and for other qualities, in short, which it was more easy to feel than to describe. The general impression of ability he produced among all who knew him had begun to spread among his opponents in politics, as well as among his friends.'[2] His biographer suggests that the fact he had a nickname in every circle in which he moved, 'Alcibiades' at school, 'Crichton' at Oxford, 'Gink' at home, was indication of his popularity,[3] but the sobriquet 'Pussy' by which he was known in the political world is not the most flattering, and perhaps reveals the weaker side of his character. On the whole Englishmen prefer the bulldog image.

Among the younger Peelites who served under Peel in 1846, seven were contemporaries or close contemporaries at Oxford, Sir John Young (born in 1807), Sidney Herbert (1808), W. E. Gladstone (1809), the duke of Newcastle, then Lord Lincoln (1811), Lord Canning (1812), Lord Dalhousie (1812) and Edward Cardwell (1813). Dalhousie was Governor General of India, appointed by Russell in 1847, when the coalition was formed, and the other six all held office in it, three in the cabinet. Indeed, the friendship of the distinguished trio of Gladstone, Newcastle and Herbert dates from their Oxford days.

The fifth duke of Newcastle (1811–64), who succeeded his father in 1851, was a zealous high churchman and a stout champion of Peel's fiscal programme. He was an aristocrat with a strong sense of public service, a capacity for hard work, and remarkably liberal political views. These qualities, combined with the great family connections associated with his name, clearly marked him as a young man with a future, but his private life was marked by tragedy that perhaps limited his public usefulness. His liberal views alienated him from his reactionary old

---

[1] *Argyll Memoirs*, I, 347; Fitzmaurice, *Granville*, I, 46.
[2] *Argyll Memoirs*, I, 347.
[3] Fitzmaurice, *Granville*, I, 22–3.

father, who only consented to reconciliation when on his deathbed. While still estranged from his father, he was deserted by his wife.[1]

He was elected to the House of Commons in 1833 and accepted office under Peel in 1834 and 1841, entering the cabinet in 1845. In 1846 he became Irish Secretary, representing the new liberal-conservative approach to Irish affairs that Peel adopted in his later years, and he acquired some popularity in Ireland during his short tenure of office. Prior to the formation of the coalition, Newcastle was known to be a sharp critic of Lord John and consequently it remained to be seen how he would settle down at the same council table with Russell and his friends. Yet he was after all a great landed aristocrat with liberal views, especially on parliamentary reform, and his family was Whig in origin, so there was no basic reason why he could not coalesce with onetime foes. Argyll probably made a fair assessment of him when he wrote: 'Newcastle was an industrious and conscientious worker, but he had no brilliancy and little initiative.'[2]

The most attractive of the younger Peelites was Sidney Herbert (1810–61), the handsome and gracious son of the eleventh earl of Pembroke, a man whose even temper, courteous manners and transparent good will made him generally liked and respected, but these were not necessarily the characteristics of an effective politician. Of him Argyll wrote:

He was handsome, refined, and graceful, all in a high degree; he had a winning smile, a most courteous manner, and great quickness of intellect and perception. He was a good speaker, and possibly his early death may have cut off from play much higher qualities; but my own conviction is that he never would have been a leader of men.[3]

He was a most devout Anglican, sharing his friends' high church views, and left as testimony of his zeal an imposing new parish church at Wilton built in the Lombardic style in striking contrast to the English village around it. His political views were similar to those of his two friends with whom he had entered parliament in 1833 and taken office in 1834 and 1841; indeed with Graham and Aberdeen he was one of the original trio to support Peel's initial proposal in the cabinet to repeal the Corn Laws (Gladstone was temporarily out of the cabinet at the time). Like Gladstone he was very happily married and in the years after 1846

[1] John Martineau's *The life of Henry Pelham fifth duke of Newcastle, 1811–64*, has little to say of Newcastle's domestic afflictions, but there are references to them in the correspondence of his friends.　　[2] *Argyll Memoirs*, I, 380.　　[3] *Ibid*.

devoted much time and energy to works of philanthropy, in particular the promotion of privately aided emigration of exploited female needle-workers.[1]

Of the younger Peelites, Gladstone (1809–98) was undoubtedly the outstanding.[2] He had a certain spark missing in his two friends, despite their native ability and aristocratic connections, as well as tremendous vitality and stamina that would keep him in active politics for more than thirty years after they had died. Although the son of a wealthy Liverpool merchant who had brought him up as a Tory in politics and an evangelical in religion, Gladstone had never entered his father's business. Receiving the traditional education of the aristocracy at Eton and Oxford, he had entered parliament in 1833 at the age of 23, married into an old Whig family and settled down on a country estate. Like his friends he had received junior office from Peel in 1834 and 1841, but he entered the cabinet two years ahead of them in 1843. Yet he was still something of an enigma to his chief and to most of his contemporaries. Few could follow the intricacies of a conscience that forced him to endanger his career by resigning office over the famous increase in the Maynooth grant, which, in fact, he was prepared to support with his vote. Fortunately Stanley's resignation later in 1845 had enabled him to return to the cabinet as Colonial Secretary, but his high standards of political morality made it difficult for him to find a new seat, once the influence of the duke of Newcastle had been withdrawn from Newark.[3] Eventually in the general election of 1847 he succeeded in obtaining the second seat for Oxford University, but only after a severe contest. His high-church views in religion and his increasingly

[1] Lord Stanmore's *Sidney Herbert* is a perceptive official biography; see vol. I, ch. IV.

[2] Of the many biographies of Gladstone, Morley's official three-volume *Life* is still by far the best, especially for these earlier years where the author is writing of a Gladstone whom he did not know personally. Considering that it was published only five years after Gladstone's death, Morley managed to make amazingly good use of the formidable mass of private papers that were then uncatalogued. Time after time the modern researcher in this great collection finds that Morley has been there before him, although by modern standards of scholarship he is sometimes a little cavalier in his use of sources. His basic work, however, is sound, but his artistry surpasses his scholarship. The modern scholar may be envious of the skill with which he effortlessly draws together a wide range of information to be found in the manuscript sources or the deft touch with which he vividly recreates the atmosphere of some forgotten debate. After sixty years this great biography stands up remarkably well, despite the inevitable partiality of its author, and on some topics still leaves little to be said.

[3] See my 'Mr Gladstone seeks a seat', *Canadian Historical Association Report* (1962), pp. 55–67, and W. R. Ward, *Victorian Oxford*, pp. 141–5.

liberal views in politics ensured him a strong opposition in that constituency for the eighteen years that he represented it. Gladstone had already travelled some way along the road from high Toryism to advanced Liberalism, which was the story of his political career. As Peel's lieutenant at the Board of Trade he had played an important role in promoting the new programme of fiscal reform and his formidable powers as a parliamentary debater already marked him as one of the ablest men of his generation. Within a year of Peel's death he had taken another long step away from the Toryism of his youth with the publication of his *Letter to Lord Aberdeen*, which appealed for justice to Italian liberals languishing in Neapolitan prisons. Nevertheless, none found it more difficult than Gladstone to repudiate all the ties of his youth and he criticised Peel sharply for a too slavish support of the Whig government. Often he walked into the opposition lobby with Disraeli, and sometimes on colonial matters with the Radicals, against the better judgment of Peel and Graham.[1]

Although he was one day to be their leader, to the Whigs in 1852 Gladstone was the most foreign of the Peelites. To many he may well have appeared as a cleric in civilian clothes; his election committee at Oxford was made up almost entirely of clergymen. Yet no one would ever call him 'Pussy'. There was a decidedly masculine side to his personality that made his pastime of chopping down giant trees quite in character. While some facets of Gladstone's make-up must have remained a closed book to most of his new colleagues, there were few areas of public business in which he did not take a lively and intelligent interest, and from the first they became aware that they had joined forces with a man of great ability and one whom they could always respect even when they did not understand him.

Since Gladstone's acceptance of office in the coalition of 1852 was clearly a turning-point in his career, and a decision that was to affect the future of both major political parties, the reasons for it deserve some further consideration. Of the leading Peelites he had probably been the most loath to make any final break with the Conservative party in which he had been nurtured and where he still counted many personal friends. One of these, Sir William Heathcote, who had acted as his election chairman at Oxford, now expressed doubts as to his ability to remain in that capacity. In response to this warning Gladstone hastened to explain his situation, saying: 'to tell you the truth all I have done...

[1] See my 'Peel and Peelites', *E.H.R.* LXXIII, 448.

has in my view flowed so simply and distinctly from the absolute dictates of duty that in the main I have not felt that I had an option to exercise.'[1] He was indignant at Derby's charges of combination against the late government, but reserved his strongest criticism for Derby's leader in the Commons.

My opinion indeed of Mr Disraeli's political character [he wrote], indifferent before has become worse since he made his speech on Mr Villiers' motion, nor do I feel sure that I would have accepted the responsibility, had all obstacles been removed, of becoming his colleague: while nothing would have induced me to lift a finger for the purpose of moving him from the leadership he has gained.

Gladstone made it clear that his difference with Derby's government was not over free trade, which he considered settled, but over the budget. Although he might have valued 'the existence of Ld Derby's Govt for the sake of religion', he could not on that account have refused to resist what he considered 'a dishonest & profligate scheme of finance'. 'To *you* I must frankly state', he wrote, 'that in...parts of that Budget, and in the prompt refusal of its framer to take time to consider the manner of his proceedings, I read on his part (not, mark, on Ld Derby's) a determined intention that there shd be no union with the Peelites; whose financial principles he knew very well.'

Having contributed to the fall of the government, Gladstone said he felt it his duty to help in providing an alternative as long as it was not incompatible with either 'principle or honour'. He did not propose to retire from the Oxford seat as long as such an act would affect 'the honour and credit' of Lord Aberdeen's government.[2] Heathcote was not convinced by this explanation, but readily supported Gladstone against the 'disgraceful tricks' that his opponents proceeded to mount in the ensuing by-election.[3]

As Graham said, it was 'a strong team', but it would require 'some driving', and it remained to be seen whether its gentle leader was capable of doing this. The first dinner meeting, which Argyll described as 'a most lively and agreeable party',[4] proved an auspicious beginning. 'But what interested me most', Argyll added, 'was to observe and feel

---

[1] Add. MS. 44208, fols. 33–6 (copy), 28 December 1852.
[2] *Ibid.* fols. 37 and 39, 30 December 1852 and 5 January 1853. See below, pp. 50–1.
[3] *Argyll Memoirs*, I, 383; Graham more cautiously recorded that 'the dinner passed off pleasantly' (Parker, *Graham*, II, 203). [4] *Argyll Memoirs*, I, 383.

THE COALITION CABINET, 1854

Left to right standing: WOOD, GRAHAM, MOLESWORTH, ARGYLL, CLARENDON, GRANVILLE, NEWCASTLE
Left to right seated: GLADSTONE, LANSDOWNE, RUSSELL, ABERDEEN, CRANWORTH, PALMERSTON, GREY, HERBERT

SIR JAMES GRAHAM

LORD JOHN RUSSELL, 1854

the sense of comradeship which was manifestly present in at least its incipient stage.'[1] By and large the comradeship observed at this first cabinet meeting was maintained and developed over the next two years despite the great stresses and strains to which the coalition was exposed, and when it finally broke up it was not due to any incompatible cleavage between the two sectors that comprised it.

Lord Aberdeen summed up his own opinions as to the strength and the prospects of the new administration which he headed in a private letter to an old American friend who had himself recently accepted cabinet office in his own country:

My own prospects are uncertain. I have formed a Government, undoubtedly composed of able and distinguished men, differing from each other in some respects, but united, as I trust, in a sincere desire to promote the welfare and prosperity of their own country, as well as the interests of humanity. As I have said it is a great experiment, hitherto unattempted, and of which the success must be considered doubtful. In the meantime, the Public have regarded the new administration with singular favour.

The Session of Parliament will be full of difficulty; for we shall have an opposition formidable in numbers, and animated with the most hostile feelings. At the same time, I confess, that I am sanguine in my belief, that our good measures will procure for us sufficient majorities in Parliament, as well as the support of the country.[2]

In a similar letter to the king of the Belgians he commented on the cordiality of the press in both London and the provinces,[2] while to Guizot he wrote:

Hitherto, I have every reason to be satisfied with the disposition of my colleagues, and trust it may continue. My position amongst them will be pretty much the same as that which I desire to see England occupy amongst the nations of Europe; viz., by acting the part of a moderator, and by reconciling differences, and removing misunderstandings,—to preserve harmony and peace.[3]

First steps—by-elections

Both Peelite and Liberal ministers sustained the test of re-election, with the exception only of the ex-Brigadier, John Sadleir, who went down to defeat by a small majority of 46 composed of a curious combination of Derbyites and Irish extremists who regarded him as a traitor

---

[1] *Ab. Cor. 1852–5*, pp. 11–12, to Edward Everett, 13 January 1853.
[2] *Ibid*. p. 26, 23 January 1853.   [3] *Ibid*. p. 31, 26 January 1853.

to the Brigade.[1] Graham was opposed by a Chartist at Carlisle, whom he easily defeated, rising to the occasion with his usual platform buoyancy.[2] Cardwell got back into parliament in a by-election for Oxford City, necessitated by the appointment of Sir W. P. Wood to the office of Vice-Chancellor. Gladstone faced the most serious opposition, owing to the bitterness of the low-church party, who fought hard to unseat him. They went to the unusual length of keeping the polls open for fifteen days to the great inconvenience of the dons who were Gladstone's party workers and of the Oxford electors who were forced to travel from all over the country, so close was the contest, reported daily in the national papers with all the excitement of a horse race. The venom of the opposition, however, rallied Gladstone's moderate Conservative supporters, men such as Heathcote, Stafford Northcote and S. T. Coleridge, all of whom devoted much time and effort to the campaign. In the end the reactionaries were defeated by a vote of 1022 to 898, giving Gladstone a majority of 124.[3] To Aberdeen Gladstone wrote: 'I will never willingly allow such people as these to make an inch of ground: but they will succeed in making the seat for the University not worth a dog's holding.'[4] To his committees in London and Oxford he addressed letters for publication in the press, assuring them that the church was as safe in the hands of Lord Aberdeen as of Lord Derby.[5] As Graham sagely observed to Aberdeen, Oxford was a thraldom for Gladstone as it had been for Peel, but it was not to be broken in Graham's own lifetime.[6]

Indeed, in view of the ferocity of the opposition, Sir Stafford Northcote, one of Gladstone's most active supporters, discussed with him the

[1] The Times, 21 January 1853; Whyte, Independent Irish Party, pp. 105–6. Some time later revelations of Sadleir's conduct in the 1852 election led to his resignation and in 1856 he took his own life. See Whyte, p. 161.

[2] The Times, 4 January 1853. Graham attacked the Tories with relish and dismissed Derby's taunts that he had become a Radical by saying that he was glad to reckon Bright, Cobden and Villiers as his friends. In reporting the speeches The Times commented: 'Sir James was, as usual, by far the most entertaining and also the most instructive.'

[3] Daily items on this election appeared in the news, editorial, correspondence and advertisement columns of The Times, 5–21 January 1853. For the attitude of Gladstone's Conservative supporters see Add. MS. 44138, fol. 384, Coleridge, 17 January 1853; Add. MS. 44208, fol. 39, Heathcote, 5 January 1853; Add. MS. 44216, fols. 194–203, Northcote, 5 and 13 January 1853. See also Ward, Victorian Oxford, pp. 177–9.

[4] Add. MS. 43070, fols. 284–5, 5 January 1853.

[5] The Times, 7 and 8 January 1853.

[6] Ab. Cor. 1852–5, pp. 6–7, 4 January 1853.

advisability of his continuing to represent the University. He noted that continued contests were wreaking havoc among his academic supporters, but the general conclusion appeared to be that the advantage of being represented by Gladstone 'was quite worth all the evils which appear to be inseparable from it'. Reporting the attitude of his chief supporters to Gladstone's continued representation of Oxford, Northcote wrote: 'It is they say the main thing which keeps the best men of the University together...they feel that you are after all a thorough Oxford man...that if an Oxford man were challenged to show what his system could produce you would be the man of all others to whom he would point.'[1] One detects a fierce loyalty among Gladstone's Oxford supporters which was nicely demonstrated in a testimonial luncheon given in his honour at Balliol after the election, at which he bravely discussed the contentious subject of university reform to a general murmur of applause.[2]

With by-elections out of the way the new ministers settled down to the task of preparing to meet parliament on 10 February. At least seven cabinet meetings were held in the month preceding that date.[3] The legislative programme was discussed in some detail and it was agreed that Russell should open with a statement as to 'various measures now ready or in preparation', but that he would do so 'without entering into any matter connected with general policy, or the formation of the Government'.[4] The ministers seemed to start off well together and Lord Aberdeen was able to tell the queen that 'he was much struck by the spirit of conciliation, and good will which prevailed'.[5]

The one rough spot in these early days was occasioned by Russell's insistence on going through with the transfer of the seals of the Foreign Office to Clarendon shortly after the opening of parliament. Aberdeen and the queen had been unhappy about the arrangement and were

---

[1] Add. MS. 44216, fols. 199–203, 13 January 1853. On 18 December Northcote had written: 'I am rather a stiff Conservative, and I do not feel at all sure that the next Administration will be one that I can work under; though if you form a leading element in it I can scarcely imagine my having any doubts. I am satisfied that the rejection of the Budget was right, and I am not at the bottom of my heart sorry that Disraeli should be beaten, but I am very grieved that things have taken the turn that they have, and that the Peelites and the country gentlemen do not seem likely to draw together.' It can be understood why Northcote never made a good leader of the opposition against a Gladstone government! (*ibid.* fols. 185–7).   [2] *The Times*, 1 February 1853.
[3] *The Times*, 10, 14, 18 and 21 January; 4, 7 and 9 February 1853.
[4] Add. MS. 43046, fols. 268–9 (copy), Aberdeen to Queen Victoria, 8 February 1853.
[5] Add. MS. 43046, fols. 266–7 (copy), 6 February 1853.

annoyed by a premature and inaccurate news item in the *Globe* of 15 January which announced that Russell would give up the Foreign Office at the beginning of the session, 'on public, and not on private or personal grounds'. They were most anxious to persuade Russell to remain until Easter and, when he went, to take the Duchy of Lancaster. To this purpose they enlisted the assistance of the duke of Bedford but without avail.[1] Walpole has published extracts from the somewhat lengthy exchange of letters between Russell and Aberdeen on the subject, an exchange that supplemented more informal conversations. Russell opened with a brusque letter calling upon Aberdeen to honour the pact that had been made. He said he chose to make the change on the commencement of the session because he would find the two jobs too exacting.[2] Aberdeen protested that he had not expected Russell to demand a change so soon and urged him to wait until Easter, emphasising the very bad public impression that would be created if he were to lead for the government in the House of Commons without holding office. To a hint from Lord John that the Home Office was compatible with the lead of the House, Aberdeen rejoined a little tartly that he might have had this or any other office for the asking when the government was formed (obviously it was too late to go after that particular office now).[3]

In a further letter Lord John responded:

To suppose that I should have taken the Foreign Office to descend at Easter to the Duchy of Lancaster to vacate my seat again in new circumstances, seems to me strange. I think your recollection must have failed you.

He proceeded to quote a note from Lady John's diary of 23 December to the effect that 'Lords Aberdeen and Clarendon gave me their words of honour as gentlemen that, on the meeting of Parliament I should leave the Foreign Office, & not be asked to take any other office'. Russell admitted that 'if objections fatal to such a plan on constitutional grounds could be started', he would 'be bound to take an office or leave the Government', but on weighing such objections he found them 'frivolous and superficial'.[4]

---

[1] Add. MS. 43046, fols. 248–9 (copy), Aberdeen to Queen Victoria, 18 January 1853; fols. 250–1, 19 January, Queen Victoria to Aberdeen; fol. 252, 19 January, Prince Albert to Aberdeen.

[2] Add. MS. 43066, fols. 226–8, 19 January 1843 (Walpole, *Russell*, II, 167).

[3] PRO 30/22/10/G, fols. 1888–90, 19 January 1853; only two of five paragraphs are printed in Walpole, *Russell*, II, 168.

[4] Add. MS. 43066, fols. 233–7, 21 January 1854; Walpole, *Russell*, II, 168–9.

Aberdeen accepted the evidence of Lady John's diary and admitted he might have been mistaken, but made it clear that he had been under the impression that Russell would take the Duchy on vacating the Foreign Office, and had so reported the conversation to the queen. 'I confess', he continued in language similar to Palmerston's, 'I am surprised to find you speak of *descending* to the Duchy of Lancaster. Surely you take a wrong estimate of your own position and character.' Aberdeen, however, expressed himself ready to abide by Russell's judgment as to what would be acceptable to the House of Commons and was ready to leave the matter there, saying he 'was quite sure the sooner this kind of conversation was brought to an end the better'.[1] It was not until 15 February that Russell actually informed Clarendon that the date of change would be the 21st of that month.[2]

Russell's last letter in the correspondence was much more friendly. He fully agreed that there had been a misapprehension between the two of them. 'The whole arrangement', he commented, 'is one which it requires infinite forbearance & good understanding among us to carry into effect successfully.' He promised on his side to do his best to make it work and to give full opportunity to the House to raise any question they might choose.[3] As it turned out, the changeover occasioned practically no comment in parliament, although Disraeli made a passing jibe on 18 February in a speech on foreign policy in which he alluded to the rumours of change. Protesting 'against this system of shutting up great men in small rooms', he said: 'I think I have a right to ask the noble lord frankly, "Are you Secretary of State or are you not?"'[4] On 24 February a Mr Cayley asked whether it was true that Lord John had resigned from the Foreign Office and was leading the House of Commons

[1] Walpole, *Russell*, II, 169–70; Add. MS. 43066, fol. 239, 21 January 1853.
[2] Maxwell, *Clarendon*, I, 362–3.
[3] Add. MS. 43066, fols. 245–6, 22 January 1853.
[4] Monypenny and Buckle, *Disraeli*, I, 1303. On 12 February Russell told the queen that Walpole had spoken to him privately 'as to his future position in leading the Government in the House of Commons without office' and had pronounced the opinion that 'it was neither illegal nor unconstitutional, but might prove inconvenient as a precedent'. The Speaker told him there were no constitutional objections and gave it as his opinion that the duties of Leader were so laborious that 'an office without other duties ought to be assigned to it' (*Letters of Queen Victoria*, II, 532). The queen must have commented adversely, for next day Lord John drafted a tart letter to her saying that he had personally made great sacrifices to launch the coalition and that he had never been granted an audience to explain his situation, but that the Speaker and Walpole had both assured him there was no constitutional objection. PRO 30/22/10/H, fol. 2098, 13 February 1853; *Letters of Queen Victoria*, II, 532–4.

without holding any other office. Lord John allowed that it was; whereupon Mr Cayley, instead of criticising this innovation, gave notice of a motion to bring in a bill attaching a salary to the onerous post of House leader.[1] Presumably he was persuaded of the undesirability of this proposal, for no more was heard from the gentleman on the subject.

The incident is not without interest in constitutional history, but occasioned surprisingly little public comment or concern at the time. Indeed, when the changeover was quietly effected, the business of both Houses was already well under way, and both ministers and members were becoming fully engaged with new problems, both domestic and foreign, that kept them fully occupied for the remainder of the session. It will be most convenient for us first to consider the success of the legislative programme of the new administration before turning to their foreign policy, which brought the country into a war scarcely expected when they took office. The success of the one has unhappily been long overshadowed by the failure of the other.

Parliamentary début

When parliament resumed its sittings on 10 February, the outlook in the House of Commons was promising, to judge from a note which Graham sent to the Prime Minister describing the first day's proceedings.

I liked the appearance of the House of Commons yesterday evening [he wrote]. Our Benches were well filled by many gentlemen not heretofore accustomed to sit together; and Lord John's quiet announcement of moderate measures, in well-arranged succession, was favourably received. He performed his part with great discretion, and a tact which seldom fails him in the House of Commons.[2]

Russell's statement outlined the measures which the government proposed to implement, the general principles laid down by Aberdeen in his December statement. A few days earlier *The Times* had said that there was nothing large on the horizon except the budget and that the time was appropriate for certain minor reforms. Russell's programme bore out this forecast. A government with such a precarious majority must tread gently. There would be some increase in the defence estimates, a pilotage bill, another attempt to settle the issue of Jewish

[1] *Hansard*, CXXIV, 548–9, 24 February 1853.
[2] *Ab. Cor. 1852–5*, p. 39, 11 February 1853.

disabilities, and proposals on the important subject of education; it was also hoped that some action might be taken respecting the reports on Oxford and Cambridge; the policy of the previous government with respect to the abandonment of transportation to Australia would be followed and a bill would be brought in to allow the Canadian legislature full control over its Clergy Reserves; all he could promise for Ireland was consideration of two bills relating to tenant–landlord relations, presently before a Select Committee of the House. Of the budget, which was to contain the government's most important proposals, he could only say that it would come after Easter. As for his own pet project of parliamentary reform, he had to announce that it had been decided to postpone it a year in order to allow time to deal with the income tax and the Lord Chancellor's proposed legal reforms, and also to obtain the necessary information.[1]

In the other House the start was less propitious, for, characteristically, the new Prime Minister had no pronouncement to make, since he felt that he had said all that was necessary in his statement of 28 December. This annoyed the leader of the opposition, who, on the first opportunity, rose to enquire whether Lord Aberdeen was not going to make some announcement with regard to the legislative programme of the government. He suggested this was only proper in the absence of a queen's speech and that it would be unbecoming the dignity of the House of Lords if its members should have to wait for their newspapers the next morning for an account of the ministerial statement in the House of Commons. While he promised support for any measures that might be 'useful and beneficial to the country', the general tone of his remarks and especially his allusion to Aberdeen's original statement was a hectoring one.[2]

Lord Aberdeen refused to be drawn. He reminded the House that he had already indicated the subjects on which the government hoped to introduce legislation. He said that the Lord Chancellor would make a statement with regard to proposed law reforms but that he did not believe it was normal practice to announce in the Lords measures which would be introduced in the Commons. Nevertheless, Derby repeated his appeal for information as a matter of respect for the House. Lord Aberdeen merely bowed his head and made no reply. Again Derby asked his question. 'Does silence mean none?' he snapped. 'Does the noble Earl, on the part of the Government, mean that no measures are

---

[1] *Hansard*, CXXIV, 17–23.   [2] *Ibid.* 10–16.

to be introduced into your Lordships' House this session?' According to *Hansard*, 'the Earl of Aberdeen again bowed'. 'May I be permitted to ask, again, what measures will be introduced into the House this Session?' Derby persisted. 'Still no answer?' With which the noble House adjourned until the next day.[1]

Greville, a detached friend of the government, called Aberdeen's behaviour awkward and foolish and described the whole scene as 'rather ridiculous'. 'He is unfortunately a very bad speaker at all times,' Greville observed, 'and, what is worse in a Prime Minister, has no readiness whatever.'[2] *The Times* praised the government's programme, especially the decision to postpone reform, but commented on the quiet start of the parliamentary year—Aberdeen's silence, Russell's restraint, the lack of debate or enthusiasm in the first few days, which resulted in the House rising as early as six o'clock. 'Not a dish has been kept cold,' the leader-writer observed. 'Not a place at table has been vacant for the public good.'[3]

The serious work of the session began the following week and on the preceding Saturday, 14 February, the cabinet met again to settle some of the details. The Prime Minister reported laconically to the queen that 'there was a good deal of desultory conversation connected with parliamentary business and prospects'. Among other matters consideration was given to motions tabled by Lord Clanricarde in the one House and Disraeli in the other regarding recent by-election speeches made by Wood and Graham in which they had made slighting remarks about the autocratic system of government in France under Louis Napoleon. 'The expressions were imprudent,' Aberdeen admitted to the Queen, 'but he hoped they would admit of explanation and apology'.[4]

On 18 February Disraeli seized upon the anti-French speeches of Wood and Graham to launch his first major attack on the new government. In a speech that was overly long, but in part lively and clever, he rehearsed the importance of a policy of good relations with France, which had been pursued by previous governments but which was imperilled by these injudicious ministerial pronouncements.[5] To the enjoyment of some, but by no means all, of his followers, he employed to the full his great powers of irony and sarcasm at the expense of the

[1] *Hansard*, CXXIV, 16–17.   [2] *Greville Memoirs*, VI, 400.
[3] *The Times*, 11 and 12 February 1853.
[4] Add. MS. 43046, fols. 277–8. For Wood's explanation to Russell see PRO 30/22/10/H, fols. 2110–11, 14 February 1853.   [5] *Hansard*, CXXIV, 246–81.

Ministry of All Talents, which, he maintained, here showed itself so lacking in discretion. 'That is the great quality on which I had thought this Cabinet was established,' he mocked. 'Vast experience, administrative adroitness—safe men, who never would blunder—men who might not only take the Government without a principle and without a party, but to whom the country ought to be grateful for taking it under such circumstances.'[1] In his peroration he managed to combine a general indictment of the government with a condemnation of its foreign policy. He touched some tender points when he said:

For we have now got a Ministry of 'progress', and every one stands still. We never hear the word 'reform' now; it is no longer a Ministry of reform; it is a Ministry of progress, every member of which agrees to do nothing. All difficult questions are suspended. All questions which cannot be agreed upon are open questions...Let Parliamentary reform, let the ballot, be open questions if you please; let every institution in Church and State be open questions; but, at least, let your answer to me to-night prove that, among your open questions, you are not going to make an open question of the peace of Europe.[2]

Although, as Greville allowed, the final part was 'clever and brilliant', it was an unscrupulous political speech; and Russell rightly rebuked him for stirring up trouble in the very area where he professed to seek friendly relations.[3] Aberdeen in the Lords and Russell and Graham in the Commons all protested that the government was most anxious to maintain a policy of good relations with France and that these passing allusions taken out of their context from speeches made on the hustings in no way indicated any policy to the contrary.[4] While Disraeli may have put heart in some of his more extreme supporters, on the whole he probably overplayed his hand and alienated the moderates. Indeed, Tom Baring, whom Greville called 'the most sensible and respectable of the Derbyites', told the diarist that 'he was so much disgusted [with Disraeli] that he was on the point of getting up to disavow him'.[5] The immediate political outlook for the coalition was not inauspicious.

[1] *Ibid.* 266.
[2] *Ibid.* 280–1; see also Monypenny and Buckle, *Disraeli*, I, 1301–14; *Greville Memoirs*, VI, 403.
[3] *Hansard*, CXXIV, 281–8.   [4] *Ibid.* 81–3, 84–5, 296–300.
[5] *Greville Memoirs*, VI, 404.

3

PEELITE FINANCE: GLADSTONE'S FIRST BUDGET

The preparation of the budget, December 1852–March 1853

The main achievement of the session of 1853 lay in the government's fiscal proposals, and for that reason we may consider these first, although, while they were being prepared, parliament dealt with more routine matters. In his masterly account of Gladstone's first budget, John Morley has alluded to the problem of presenting such a subject to a later generation with the remark that 'there is something repulsive to human nature in the simple reproduction of defunct budgets'.[1]

It is difficult today to imagine the intense interest taken in the middle of the last century in what must strike us as comparatively simple budgetary problems. This interest reached a climax in the year 1853 when a great Chancellor of the Exchequer appeared on the scene ready to dispose of the supposedly complex question of the income tax, but in the light of more recent experience the fiscal problems of that era and the amounts involved seem trivial. It is fascinating, if unprofitable, to conjecture how a Chancellor of Gladstone's genius would have dealt with a budget of five hundred million pounds and the complex problems connected with the balance of payments and the maintenance of the sterling bloc, which plague his modern successors. In history, however, comparisons should be made with earlier experience and not with developments still hidden by the veil of the future. To understand Gladstone's achievement in 1853 and the public response to it we must relate it to the history of public finance in the preceding half-century

[1] Morley, *Gladstone*, I, 461. I have endeavoured to avoid duplicating Morley's biographical account of Gladstone's role by considering the broader aspects of the budget as a government measure and the reaction of Gladstone's colleagues as described by him in memoranda written at the time and later. There are a great number of memoranda on various aspects of this budget running to hundreds of folios to be found in the Gladstone papers, ranging from a forty-page 'Memorandum on the Income Tax for Cabinet Committee' to an extract from Gibbon's *Decline and Fall of the Roman Empire*, I, 211, dealing with opposition to a legacy duty which Gladstone has entitled 'Augustus Caesar, His Budget' (Add MSS. 44741, fols. 123–42, and 44742, fols. 145–6).

and recognise the large role that such matters traditionally played in the public affairs of those times.

The Englishman's aversion to taxation has a long history; indeed it was an important factor in the development of parliamentary government. Early in the nineteenth century this national characteristic was further stimulated by the widespread acceptance of the views of the classical economists, who insisted that men were best able to look after their own affairs with the minimum of state interference, and of the utilitarians—often the same people—who demanded the application of the measuring-rod of utility in all matters connected with government and public finance. As a result, despite the great burden of national debt accrued during the Napoleonic Wars, there was a marked reduction in the cost of government in the years after 1815 and especially after 1826. In the latter year total national expenditures amounted to some £61,000,000, but by 1834 they had been reduced to a figure slightly less than £46,000,000 and only twice in the years 1834–52 did they go above £51,000,000.[1]

During the eighteenth century the landed classes who ran the country had managed to shift the burden of taxation from their own shoulders to that of the population at large by steady increases in customs and excise duties, which came greatly to overshadow the land tax and the assessed taxes directed at the wealthy. The reform and modernisation of the eighteenth-century fiscal system was begun by the younger Pitt in the decade prior to the outbreak of war in 1793, but the demands of war developed the need for new sources of taxation, which Pitt met with his legacy duty in 1796 and the income tax in 1799. Because of opposition in the House of Commons, however, he considerably reduced the scope of the legacy duty by excluding landed property. The income tax was accepted as a necessity of war and quickly demonstrated its great potentiality as an efficient instrument of taxation, but it was withdrawn immediately after the war because of political opposition objecting to its inquisitorial nature.[2]

The work begun by Pitt in the revision of the customs duties was greatly extended by Huskisson and Robinson, who in the 1820s took the first long steps on the road to free trade, and their work in turn was continued and much expanded by Peel in his great budgets of 1842,

[1] J. F. Rees, *Short fiscal and financial history of England 1815–1918*, pp. 54 and 82.
[2] For the view that the opposition to the tax was worked up for political reasons see F. Shehab, *Progressive taxation, a study in the development of the progressive principle in the British income tax*, pp. 64–9.

1845 and 1846. Peel's chief lieutenant in the preparation of the 1842 and 1845 budgets was Gladstone, who did the major work in preparing the extensive revisions of the customs schedules. To pay the immediate costs of the customs remissions and to repair the deficiencies of Whig finance in the preceding decade, Peel took the daring step of reinstituting the income tax as a temporary measure for three years. By 1845, thanks to the beneficent effect of these reforms, the lost revenue from customs and excise had virtually been restored, since increased trade ensured that lower duties provided a larger revenue. The early elimination of the income tax might have been contemplated, but Peel chose to renew it for another three years to effect still further reductions of duties, arguing that such taxes were more inimical than the income tax itself.[1] In 1848 the Whigs, who had opposed the introduction of the income tax in 1842, were quite content to renew it for another three years and indeed to do so again in 1851 since there was no other way of avoiding a serious deficit. On the latter occasion, however, Lord Stanley objected to the fact that the original temporary nature of the income tax was being forgotten, and the Radical Joseph Hume forced the government to accept an amendment limiting the renewal to one year in order that a Select Committee of the House might inquire into the mode of assessing and collecting it. Hume's committee heard much conflicting evidence, but was unable to come to any conclusions. It was apparent that there was a respectable weight of informed opinion in favour of the tax in principle, but a serious difference of opinion as to whether there should be some attempt to differentiate as to the source of income. When the one-year renewal lapsed in 1852, the Protectionists had just come into office and were in no position to make any radical changes in the system of taxation; consequently Disraeli's provisional budget renewed the tax for yet another single year. In his December budget, Disraeli found he had to retain the income tax, but as a sop to the Radicals to compensate for his proposed reduction of the malt tax he adopted the policy of differentiation, which was one of the features of his budget attacked most severely by Gladstone. Obviously the question of the income tax had to be settled one way or the other and it was the first business of the new Peelite Chancellor of the Exchequer to settle it.[2]

[1] See Sir Stafford H. Northcote, *Twenty years of financial policy*, pp. 68–71.
[2] For the background of this question see Northcote, *Twenty years of financial policy*, chs. I–III; Sydney Buxton, *Finance and politics, an historical study 1783–1885*, vol. I, chs. I–V; Shehab, *Progressive taxation*, chs. III–VI; Rees, *Fiscal and financial history*, chs. I–IV; J. H. Clapham, *An economic history of modern Britain: free trade and steel 1850–86*, ch. X.

Gladstone had never been a keen supporter of the income tax and indeed had been the only one of Peel's colleagues in 1842 to raise objections to it. He considered that it would be open to evasion, that it would be highly inquisitorial, and that it would be expensive and hard to collect. Nevertheless, he had accepted it as a temporary necessity and likewise its renewal in 1845. In 1851 he said that while he did not object to the renewal of this tax to effect major revisions of the customs duties as in 1842 and 1845, he did object to renewing it only to make minor revisions.[1] He opposed the appointment of Hume's committee and refused to sit on it,[2] presumably because of Hume's advocacy of the principle of differentiation between incomes.

The opportunity that this budget presented to settle the vexed problem of the income tax and to continue the fiscal programme of Peel was undoubtedly a major consideration with Gladstone when he accepted office in the coalition. From the moment that he did so the whole force of his powerful mind was concentrated on the problem. At the first cabinet dinner he asked for the appointment of a cabinet committee to advise him, but it appears that its members did no more than submit papers for his consideration. He also received a fair number of notes from Wood, Graham and Cardwell on various matters connected with the budget, and indeed in the final stages he discussed it in great detail with Cardwell, who sketched an alternative scheme that Gladstone considered using if his own was unacceptable. It is quite clear, however, that virtually the whole edifice was completed by Gladstone himself, and it is significant that by far the greater part of the papers alluded to above are in his own hand.

Early in January he drafted a lengthy memorandum of 'strictly preliminary observations',[3] nominally for the cabinet committee, in which he recorded his shock at finding that 'his Predecessor' had taken no steps whatsoever 'towards obtaining that clear and detailed knowledge of the working of the tax, and of its incidence on various classes affected by it, without which no practical progress can be made'. (It was this sort of thing that contributed to Gladstone's low opinion of Disraeli.[4]) Such information would now be obtained as quickly as

[1] Northcote, *Twenty years of financial policy*, p. 160.
[2] *Ibid.* p. 163.   [3] Add. MS. 44741, fols. 1–32.
[4] This opinion was, of course, mutual and was reflected in the unhappy quarrel between the two men over the disposition of the furniture at no. 11 Downing Street. The incident is described at length by Buckle, who reproduces the correspondence (*Disraeli*, I, 1292–6), but dismissed by Morley as a triviality (*Gladstone*, I, 457–8).

possible, but even at this stage Gladstone felt that there was no way of meeting the popular cry for a differentiated tax, although he was prepared to accept arguments for gradation.

Closely connected with the budget was an ambitious and elaborate plan of National Debt conversion and consolidation, which Gladstone presented to the House in a long and able speech on 8 April. Since enterprising Chancellors of the Exchequer had reduced the general level of interest on the National Debt to about three per cent by a number of great conversion measures carried out over the preceding thirty years, Gladstone's opportunities in this field did not look promising. Indeed there was no precedent for a lower rate and the only stock available for such an operation was three per cent Consols, which by their nature were protected against forced conversion. Nevertheless, he proceeded to offer several options to holders of Consols in an endeavour to obtain an arrangement in the long run more economical for the government. Provision was also made for the liquidation of the century-old South Sea Company stock and some Bank annuities of the same period. Despite some sharp objections from the opposition the necessary resolutions were passed without a division, and subsequently two consolidated fund bills were enacted without debate. As it turned out, the whole scheme proved abortive, for the sudden turn for the worse in the foreign situation made the Consol-holders unwilling to convert and the South Sea Company stockholders insisted on cash, which with the sudden change in the market that summer cost the government money.[1]

A few days later (15 April) and only four days before Gladstone actually introduced his budget, the government suffered a reverse, when, for once, the Radicals, the Irish and the Derbyites voted together in support of a resolution introduced by Milner Gibson for the abolition of the duties on advertisements which was carried by 200 to 169.[2] It was in vain that Gladstone admitted the unsatisfactory state of the law with respect to taxes on newspapers and announced the government's intention to bring in a bill. Indeed this very tax was one which Gladstone then intended to reduce. He could not directly say so, but by the tone of his speech, and 'by moving the previous question instead of a

---

[1] *Hansard*, CXXV, 810–78; CXXVII, 862, 964, 1207; CXXIX, 1535, 1598, 1705, 1823; Northcote, *Twenty years of financial policy*, pp. 220–31; Buxton, *Finance and politics*, pp. 126–9.

[2] *Hansard*, CXXV, 1117–87; the division list is not printed; *Ab. Cor. 1852–5*, p. 85, Graham, 14 April 1853.

direct negative he sufficiently indicated this intention', as Aberdeen told
Prince Albert; 'but the opportunity was too favourable', he added,
'for the combined opposition to resist'. 'Disraeli led the way', Graham
told Aberdeen, 'and the hostility of the House was strongly marked,
while the support which we received was luke warm.' He conferred
with the other senior ministers in the House, who all agreed that the
matter was one for concern and that a cabinet should be held the next
day.[1]

'It is impossible to deny that this is serious,' Aberdeen wrote to
Prince Albert about the night's events; 'for, although it has always been
evident that the union of two parties of entirely opposite principles
could ensure a majority, it was supposed that it would be difficult to
produce such co-operation. We have seen, however, that this is not the
case, and we may look for a repetition of the tactics of last night whenever the occasion seems favourable.'[2] In the end the cabinet decided to
submit, since it was agreed that the tax in question was objectionable
and since it had been intended to deal with it anyway. The incident was
a jolt that emphasised the danger of defeat on the budget itself, but here,
as Aberdeen observed, they would be on firmer ground for defence.
Moreover, the sign of danger, he felt, had 'produced a greater spirit of
conciliation and agreement' among the members. As it happened, the
incident had occurred in the middle of a series of momentous cabinet
meetings on the budget itself.

The budget proposals which Gladstone outlined to Prince Albert in
summary form in the space of one hour, to the cabinet in more detail in
a statement of three hours, and to the House of Commons in a speech of
five hours[3]—all listened to with rapt attention by their various audi-
ences—must here be summarised more briefly.

Its main objective was to continue Peel's great work of repealing or
reducing taxes that hampered trade or bore heavily on the consumer,
but at the same time Gladstone devised a plan for the gradual extinction
of the income tax. Because of some increases in the Army and Navy
estimates he anticipated expenditures of some £52,000,000, but he
thought that total expenditure could be reduced over the next few years
by reductions in debt charges that he planned. He anticipated that with

[1] *Ab. Cor. 1852–5*, p. 85, Graham, 14 April 1853.
[2] *Ibid.* p. 86, 15 April 1853.
[3] *Hansard*, CXXV, 1350–1425, reprinted in A. Tilney Bassett, *Gladstone's speeches*,
pp. 182–252. See Appendix D below for a summary of the budget taken from Northcote, *Financial policy*, p. 387.

the expansion of trade the revenue lost from the reduction of duties would be restored. Further revenue was to be obtained from an increase in the spirit duties in Ireland and Scotland (which were substantially less than the English duty) and by an extension of the legacy duty to inherited real property. All this made it possible for the Chancellor to plan ahead, not for one but for eight years, and it was the audacity of this long-range planning in contrast with the hand-to-mouth arrangements of his immediate predecessors that struck the public imagination when the budget plans were announced. Because of the need of more immediate revenue before his long-run calculations began to apply, the income tax was to be extended to Ireland and to incomes of £100, where the previous floor had been £150, but it was to be gradually reduced from 7d. in 1853 and 1854 to 6d. in 1855 and 1856, 5d. in 1857, 1858 and 1859, and to be abolished in 1860. The 5d. rate was to be charged immediately on the new taxpayers in the £100 to £150 category. Gladstone resolutely refused to differentiate between sources of income on the grounds that there was no way to do this that was both practicable and just. He did recognise, however, that the tax bore more heavily on persons whose incomes were earned and not permanent, and to provide some compensation for such people he made the one concession of exempting life insurance premiums up to one-seventh of the income in question.

Gladstone recognised the great advantages of the income tax, but considered that, in time of peace, in the long run the disadvantages outweighed them. Later in his budget speech he summed up his views succinctly when he said:

The general views of Her Majesty's Government, with respect to the Income Tax, are that it is an engine of gigantic power for great national purpose; but, at the same time, that there are circumstances attending its operation which make it difficult, perhaps impossible, at any rate in our opinion, not desirable, to maintain it as a portion of the permanent and ordinary finances of the country. The public feeling of its inequality is a fact more important of itself. The inquisition it entails is a most serious disadvantage; and the frauds to which it leads are an evil which it is not possible to characterize in terms too strong.

One thing I hope this House will never do; and that is, nibble at this great public question....: for, if as my noble friend (Lord John Russell) once said with universal applause, this country cannot bear a revolution once a year, I will venture to say that it cannot bear a reconstruction of the Income Tax once a year.

THE DUKE OF NEWCASTLE, 1856

W. E. GLADSTONE, 1858

SIDNEY HERBERT

THE DUKE OF ARGYLL, 1860

THE EARL OF CLARENDON   THE MARQUIS OF LANSDOWNE, 1838

VISCOUNT PALMERSTON, 1846

Whatever you do in regard to the Income Tax, you must be bold, you must be intelligible, you must be decisive.[1]

Boldness and incisiveness were the keynotes of Gladstone's budget, much more so than in those of the more cautious Peel.

These plans for extending and maintaining the revenue made possible a wide range of tax concessions in the Peelite tradition. The tax revisions were expected to net an additional £1,344,000 of revenue, to which there was added an anticipated surplus of £807,000, producing a total of £2,151,000 available for tax remissions. The import duties on all semi-manufactures other than timber were abolished, although reduced protective duties were retained 'on the last stage of the finished article', and all differential duties as between foreign and colonial manufactures were eliminated. The nine customs duties on glass, with the exception of some fancy glass, were to be gradually abolished. For the consumers there were to be tariff reductions on thirteen items of food including tea, fruits and dairy products. The reduction of the revenue duty on tea was most substantial—and costly. Immediately it was to be lowered from 2s. 2¼d. to 1s. 10d. and by 1856 to 1s., a reduction of £366,000 in the first year alone and eventually of over £3,000,000, although it was expected that more than a third of this would be regained by increased consumption. In all, customs duties were to be abolished on 123 and reduced on 146 articles. Perhaps the most important remission to the general consumer, and especially to the poor, was the abolition of the excise duty on soap, which would amount to a loss of over £1,000,000 in revenue a year, although the full amount would not be lost in the first year.[2]

In addition the budget provided for the reduction of the tax on life insurance, the simplification and reduction of the stamp duties, the reduction of advertisement duties, the newspaper stamp duty, the attorneys' and solicitors' duty, and the hackney carriage duty, as well as the reform of the whole system of assessed taxes.[3]

Despite the length of his presentation the cabinet gave Gladstone a good hearing. 'Nothing could have been more kind', he recorded, 'than the reception of the statement or more harmonious than the tone of half an hour's conversation which followed it. Not a single positive objection was taken to any of the propositions which made up the plan.

[1] Quoted in Northcote, *Financial policy*, pp. 188–9.
[2] Buxton, *Finance and politics*, p. 123. The customs duty on soap was also reduced and was to disappear by 1860.   [3] Northcote, *Financial policy*, p. 197.

Only Lord Palmerston stated some scruple about the extension of the Legacy Duty to land.'[1] 'If Gladstone can make it as intelligible to the House of Commons as he did to us,' Aberdeen wrote to the prince consort, 'I shall feel sanguine with respect to the result; but the subject is complicated and difficult, and it would be, indeed, the triumph of reason against prejudice.'[2] The lack of initial opposition from his colleagues may only have indicated that they were overcome by the *tour de force* of his presentation and that the full implications of the proposals had not yet sunk in. At any rate over the weekend doubts began to arise, especially with respect to Ireland and to the succession duty.

The cabinet met again on the 11th and in the course of a long discussion Lansdowne, Graham, Wood, Palmerston and Granville favoured some modification, but Russell, Newcastle, Clarendon, Molesworth, Argyll and Aberdeen all supported Gladstone, although the last two had some misgivings about the extension of the income tax downwards.[3] The Lord Chancellor was absent and Herbert silent. Gladstone's strongest supporter in the cabinet turned out to be Molesworth, who stressed the necessity of taking the plan as a whole.[4]

In a further cabinet on the following day the opposition increased. Palmerston even allowed that he thought Disraeli's budget 'a very good plan', while admitting the impracticability of it. He was prepared to go along with the cabinet, however, provided they would not go as far as resigning or dissolving over the income tax, but Russell claimed they would have no option but dissolution if they were defeated on differentiation. Gladstone's account of the meeting continues:

Graham portended certain failure...Molesworth Newcastle and I at one time appeared nearly alone: but Lord Aberdeen came in to help and said it was better to take the whole: the more you cut off from it, the less the remainder hung together.

Lord John echoed this. Newcastle pressed for a decision as time was hastening on. Duke of Argyll fell in with assent for the whole plan. Sidney Herbert on the other hand went with Wood, Graham and Lord Lansdowne.

[1] Add. MS. 44741, fol. 80.
[2] *Ab. Cor. 1852–5*, pp. 80–1, 9 April 1853.
[3] Gladstone's argument in defence of this was that free trade had reduced the cost of living of these people by more than the amount that they were to be taxed. See *Hansard*, CXXV, 1389–92.
[4] Add. MS. 44778, memo. 96, fols. 84–97, summarised by Morley, *Gladstone*, I, 465–6.

The Chancellor when called upon to give an opinion said 'that without professing to understand the matter well he was favourable to the Budget as it stood'. Clarendon was also favourable, while Granville spoke of making concessions, if necessary, to parliament.[1] In reporting the meeting to Prince Albert, Aberdeen indicated that while some details remained to be settled, Gladstone's plan, in all its more important features, was adopted. He admitted, nevertheless, that the difference of opinion on the part of two or three ministers was 'still very serious'. It was decided to postpone another meeting until Saturday (16 April) to avoid 'injurious speculation, both political and financial'.[2] In the meantime, however, the crisis over the advertisement duty forced the calling of an emergency meeting on the 15th.

On the evening after the third meeting Gladstone discussed the whole matter with Cardwell, his confidant outside the cabinet. The latter proposed an alternative plan, which Gladstone preferred to 'the more narrow modifications' that had already been raised.[3]

At this stage Gladstone had good cause to be apprehensive as various senior ministers began to convey their fears individually to the Prime Minister. 'The more I think of the budget, (admirable though it is as a whole),' Clarendon wrote to Aberdeen, 'the more I am convinced that the Irish part of it will be ruinous to the entire scheme.' He proposed the postponement of the Irish income tax until the first drop in the schedule occurred.[4] But the most serious opposition came from Sir Charles Wood, who was put in a very awkward position in that during the debate on the Disraeli budget he had given assurances to the Irish members on the matter of the income tax. He told Russell: 'I strongly disapprove of the extension of the Income Tax to Ireland and of lowering the limit to £100, under the circumstances of condemning the tax to early extinction; and I think the proposed Budget unfair to Ireland.' He recognised that on such matters a minister must accept the decision of the majority, but beyond that there was the question 'whether after what has passed between me and some of the Irish

---

[1] Add. MS. 44778, fols. 98–105, memo. 97, partially summarised by Morley, *Gladstone*, I, 466. Morley's next paragraph is misleading since it summarises an earlier conversation between Russell and Graham in which the latter was reassuring the former. Graham told Aberdeen of this conversation on 26 March (*Ab. Cor. 1852–5*, pp. 73–4). In the cabinet discussions they seemed to reverse positions.

[2] *Ab. Cor. 1852–5*, p. 81, 12 April 1853.

[3] Add. MS. 44118, fols. 52–5, 13 April 1853. See also Add. MS. 44778, fols. 106–7, memo. 98, 13 April, in which Gladstone discussed Cardwell's proposal.

[4] *Ab. Cor. 1852–5*, p. 83, 14 April 1853.

5-2

members, I can honourably be a party this year to extend the Income Tax to Ireland'.[1]

Russell forwarded Wood's letter to Aberdeen, asking him to talk seriously to Gladstone and urge on him a reduction of the Irish spirit duty.[2] Two days later Wood wrote to Aberdeen in the same vein. He promised to give the best opinion he could of the budget, but was uncertain whether he could honourably remain one of the cabinet proposing it in view of what he had said to the Irish members.[3]

There were various reactions to Cardwell's proposals. Graham preferred them, but professed his willingness to abide by the cabinet's previous decision. Newcastle and Argyll stood firmly for the whole budget. Aberdeen shrewdly pointed out that the government was formed to extend Peel's system, whereas Cardwell's plan forwent extension indefinitely.[4] When the cabinet met on 15 April Gladstone made it clear that he preferred Cardwell's plan to half measures; indeed he considered 'the entire budget was safer than a reduced one'. They discussed the possibility of dissolution, to which the older members were generally opposed. Clarendon, Herbert and Palmerston joined Wood in protesting that the proposals were too hard on Ireland. At last a compromise was found in the proposal to remit entirely the consolidated annuities owed by Ireland, which it was felt would justify levying the full income tax on Ireland. Wood still hung back, but the rest now seemed ready to swing into line.[5]

This decision was confirmed at a final cabinet meeting on the 16th. 'There is still some difference of opinion in the cabinet,' Aberdeen had to admit to Prince Albert; 'and, although a great spirit of conciliation prevails, I cannot say that absolute unanimity may be found to exist when it is most needed.' He considered that cabinet opinion anticipated defeat, but he himself was not entirely pessimistic. '*Differentiation* is a popular delusion, which it is very difficult to resist,' he wrote, 'but, in other respects, I think the Budget will be popular in the House, and, especially, in the country.'[6]

[1] *Ab. Cor. 1852-5*, pp. 84-5, Wood to Russell, 13 April 1853.
[2] *Ibid.* pp. 83-4, 13 April 1853.
[3] *Ibid.* p. 86, 16 April 1853. He had consulted Monsell, one of the Irish members who had joined the government. The latter was himself in favour of extending the income tax to Ireland, 'but', wrote Wood, 'he has no doubt my declaration in the House of Commons was used as an argument to induce Irish members to vote with us against [the] D'Israeli Budget'.   [4] Add. MS. 4478, fols. 108-11, memo. 99, 14 April 1853.
[5] *Ibid.* fols. 112-17, memo. 100 (summarised by Morley, *Gladstone*, 1, 467-8).
[6] *Ab. Cor. 1852-5*, pp. 87-8, 16 April 1853.

Judging from a letter of Palmerston's, the cabinet agreed to make defeat on any main point a matter for resignation or dissolution. Palmerston made his own opposition to the latter alternative quite clear to Aberdeen, because of his dislike of the succession duty. 'But, as to myself,' he wrote, 'holding strong objections to that measure, I have submitted to the opinion of my colleagues, in regard to proposing it to Parliament, as a part of our general plan; I am, however, bound, in fairness, to say, that I am not to be reckoned upon, as a party to a dissolution of Parliament on that question.'[1]

Finally on 18 April, the very day on which Gladstone was to present the budget to the House of Commons, Wood addressed a letter to the Prime Minister giving his grudging consent. He still objected to the extension of the income tax to Ireland and to taxpayers in the £100–150 bracket; he regarded the cabinet's decisions as 'unwise and impolitic' and saw 'little, or no prospect of their being carried', but he was unwilling to put the government in even greater danger by his own action. He continued:

I think that, taking into account the alteration of circumstances made by the remission of the whole of the Annuities, I can make a case for myself which will justify me in the eyes of all *reasonable* men.

I do not, myself, attach much importance to my singly leaving the Government, on the ground of my own peculiar position, but if you think that my resignation for that reason would materially embarrass the Government, I am willing to bear, and to meet, as I best can, the imputations which I may expect.[2]

Needless to say, Aberdeen warmly welcomed Wood's decision and insisted on the importance of his staying.[3]

The budget in parliament, April–July 1853

Thus only at the very last moment had the cabinet closed its ranks. The chances of similar success in the House of Commons did not seem as good. Gladstone, himself, was far from hopeful. Analysing the components of the House of Commons on the eve of his budget presentation, he could only count 310 government supporters, and of these the Radicals were undependable. The Derby opposition he counted at 250, to which he thought it not unlikely that 40 Irish Brigade might be

[1] *Ibid.* pp. 88–9, 17 April 1853. [2] *Ibid.* pp. 89–90, 18 April 1853.
[3] *Ibid.* p. 91, 19 April 1853.

added. Fifty or so Conservatives he regarded as doubtful. Clearly they held the balance and if the government got the necessary support from them, then the tactics of the Peelites ever since the election would have been justified. But the situation was a dangerous one, especially, as Gladstone wrote, 'with an ex-Finance Minister who is also leader of the Opposition, and who unlike all other leaders of Opposition stimulates and spurs faction instead of endeavouring to keep it within bounds'. He doubted whether the government could be carried on 'without a larger stress of party connection'. Yet it was imperative to get the matter settled before the income tax expired.[1]

Gladstone made his budget proposals to the Commons on 18 April in a speech described by the *Annual Register* as one of 'extraordinary power and ability'. Although it lasted for five hours, it made a great impression on its hearers and was greeted 'with a burst of enthusiastic and protracted cheering'.[2] Lord John Russell told the queen that it 'was one of the most powerful financial speeches ever made in the House of Commons', and expressed himself as 'very sanguine as to the success of the plan'. 'Mr Pitt', he added, 'in the days of his glory might have been more imposing, but he could not have been more persuasive.'[3] Lord Aberdeen gave it as his opinion that 'as a Finance Minister, he [Gladstone] has placed himself fully on the level of Sir Robert Peel'.[4] Congratulations, of course, poured in on the Chancellor from all sides. Clarendon, originally critical of the scheme, told him that it was 'the most perfect financial statement ever heard within the walls of Parlt for such it is allowed to be by friend & foe'.[5]

In acknowledging Aberdeen's congratulations, Gladstone wrote a most characteristic note, saying:

I had the deepest anxiety with regard to you, as our Chief, lest, by faults of my own, I should aggravate the cares and difficulties into which I had at least

[1] Add. MS. 44778, fols. 118–21, memo. 101, 15 April 1853; partly summarised by Morley, *Gladstone*, I, 448–9.

[2] *Annual Register*, 1853, pp. 50–61.

[3] *Letters of Queen Victoria*, II, 542. Prince Albert could not resist showing this report to Gladstone, 'trusting', he wrote, 'that your Christian humility will not allow you to become dangerously elated'.

[4] *Ab. Cor. 1852–5*, pp. 98–9, to the king of the Belgians, 4 May 1853.

[5] Add. MS. 44133, fol. 5, 19 April 1853. Cf. J. H. Clapham writing in 1932: 'Gladstone's Budget speech of 1853, which "changed the convictions of a large part of the nation on the income tax", diverted liberal opinion from the policy of differentiation, and determined the form of the tax for half a century, seems less convincing to-day than it did to contemporaries' (*Economic history*, p. 402).

helped to bring you; and the novelty of our political relations with many of our colleagues, together with the fact that I had been myself slow, and even reluctant, to the formation of a new connection, filled me with an almost feverish desire to do no injustice to that connection now that it is formed.[1]

After a few brief comments and questions the debate on Gladstone's motion on the income tax was adjourned one week. It went on intermittently for four nights, 25, 28 and 29 April and 2 May.[2] Bulwer Lytton led off for the opposition with an amendment holding that the income tax proposals, 'without any mitigation of the inequalities of its assessment, are alike unjust and impolitic'.[3] In all twenty-seven members spoke against the budget, eight of them Irish, concentrating their opposition on the Irish clauses. Twenty-three spoke in support of the Chancellor of the Exchequer, including seven Irish members, four Radicals, five Peelites and three Conservatives.[4]

While the Irish opposition was formidable, there were almost as many Irish members ready to defend the plan. H. Herbert, an Irish Peelite, speaking as the representative of an agricultural district, expressed the opinion that the Chancellor's proposals would be 'just, equitable, and statesmanlike, with respect to the tenant-farmers of Ireland'. He found it extraordinary that he should be asked to vote against the present proposals and 'against the Government, at the head of which was a statesman who possessed stronger claims than any living man on all those who valued the religious liberty for which they had so long struggled in Ireland'.[5]

The major opposition speech came at the end of the debate from Disraeli.[6] He professed to agree with the general principles on which the budget was grounded, saying that they were identical with those on which he based his own budget, but he found two main objections, namely 'the renewal of the income tax for seven years without any mitigation of the inequalities of assessment, and the injustice shown to

---

[1] *Ab. Cor. 1852–5*, p. 93, 19 April 1853. For further comment see Morley, *Gladstone*, I, 469–71.

[2] *Hansard*, CXXVI, 453–515, 682–750, 804–71, 912–1008.   [3] *Ibid.* 454.

[4] The Radicals were: Cobden, Hume, J. L. Ricardo and W. Williams; the Peelites: Cardwell, Denison, Lowe, Milnes and H. Herbert (also included in the Irish list); the Conservatives: G. Sandars, Col. Harcourt and H. Drummond, all of whom had supported Disraeli's budget. Drummond saw the succession duty as a tax on elder brothers rather than on land, while Harcourt strongly supported the income tax proposals, warning his party that it would be madness to force a dissolution on them. *Hansard*, CXXVI, 722–5 and 824–6.   [5] *Ibid.* 826–9.

[6] *Ibid.* 963–93. Cf. Monypenny and Buckle, *Disraeli*, I, 1323.

land. He expressed doubts as to the possibility of terminating the income tax in seven years, but mockingly professed to believe that if the Chancellor of the Exchequer should find himself in that same position in 1860 'he would resign his office sooner than propose the continuance of the tax for a further period'.[1] He took particular delight in pointing out the contradictions in the speeches of various members who supported the present budget and denounced his. In particular in his peroration he delivered a sarcastic and taunting attack on Russell who 'had thrown aside the Whig party' and had 'accepted a subordinate office under a subordinate officer of Sir Robert Peel'.

Russell closed for the government in a fairly short speech in which he pointed out the contradiction between Lytton's motion, which would have had landed income taxed at a higher rate, and Disraeli's, which claimed that the present budget was unfair to the landed interest. He concluded his speech with a warm tribute to his colleague the Chancellor of the Exchequer, who in his presentation of this budget had earned a name 'to be envied amongst Finance Ministers of this country'.[2] The only other cabinet minister to speak during the debate, significantly, was Sir Charles Wood, but strong support also came from Cardwell and from a future Chancellor, Robert Lowe. Another ex-Whig Chancellor, Sir F. Baring, spoke quite critically, but voted for the budget.[3]

When the vote was finally taken on 2 May the motion stood against the amendment 323 to 252.[4] The majority included 82 Conservatives or Liberal Conservatives. Of these probably 43 may now be classified as fairly dependable Peelites,[5] but some 39 had been won over from Derby,[6] including such a stout Tory as Sir R. Inglis. Almost half of these had at one time or another appeared on Peelite lists, but on the other hand a few names once included on such lists opposed the budget and were now clearly in the Derbyite camp.[7] Many of the Derbyites supporting the government probably felt that it was really an acceptable budget and that there was no valid party reason for opposing it and turning the

---

[1] *Hansard*, CXXVI, 976. One may wonder whether Gladstone remembered this sally when he brought in his 1860 budget with 10*d.* income tax.

[2] *Ibid.* 1003.

[3] For a summary of the Debate see *Annual Register 1853*, pp. 63–75.

[4] *Hansard*, CXXVI, 1004–8.

[5] See Appendix A.   [6] See Appendix B.

[7] J. Baird, R. Clive, H. Corry, Lord Jocelyn, R. M. Laffen, G. Tomline, H. C. Whitmore, Gen. Wyndham.

government out. Their own prospects were no better and would probably be worse than in 1852.

Thirty-three Irish Liberals or Independents opposed the budget, but some 26 Irish Liberals remained loyal to the government. On this occasion, of course, the Radicals were safe.[1]

Reverting to Gladstone's pre-budget analysis of the House it will be seen that he overestimated the adverse Irish vote by 7 and that most of his 50 uncertain Conservatives supported the government to give a much larger majority than he anticipated. Indeed, subtracting the 33 Irish Brigade votes from the opposition, it will be seen that Disraeli only marshalled 229 Conservatives in the opposition lobby, 31 fewer than Gladstone had allowed him. Of the 78 members who did not vote, some 32 were Conservatives.

The victory of 2 May, however, was only the first round in a long fight, where the forces ebbed and flowed, but the main citadel was never in mortal danger. With the official opposition amendment disposed of, other private amendments had to be met in the Committee of Ways and Means, especially several from the Irish Brigade. On 5 May an Irish member, who had supported the government on the previous vote, submitted an amendment that would have excluded Ireland from the income tax. This led to an Irish night, indeed two nights, for the proceedings were interrupted by a long procedural wrangle occasioned by the remark of a new Irish member, Gavan Duffy, that he did not 'think in the worst days of Walpole and the Pelhams more scandalous corruption existed' than he had seen with his own eyes 'practised upon Irish Members'.[2] Eventually the amendment was put to the vote and defeated 286 to 61.[3]

On 12 May the question of Whig assurances to the Irish members with regard to the income tax came up once again, and Sir Charles Wood made a reasonably straightforward statement, explaining that he thought the situation was greatly changed by the remission of the

[1] The main core of the Irish Independents as listed in Whyte's *Independent Irish Party*, pp. 180–1 voted against the budget, with the exception of one man, Bellew, whom he lists as uncertain. The two Irish Peelites, H. Herbert and Sir John Young, supported the budget.

[2] *Hansard*, CXXVI, 1192–3. This put the fat in the fire with a vengeance and the rest of that evening was spent in discussing what action should be taken with respect to such unpardonable remarks. In the end the gentleman was required to appear at the next sitting (it was now after midnight) when his words would be taken into consideration. As a result of his explanation on that occasion, in which he withdrew nothing, the matter was let pass.   [3] *Ibid.* 1193–1218, 1234–40.

consolidated annuities and consequently he was satisfied and the present proposals were advantageous to Ireland.[1] Several more unsuccessful amendments were moved by both Conservative and Irish Independent members, including a Tory motion on 9 May designed to provide some exemption for landowners that led to an argument between Gladstone and Disraeli as to which of their budgets offered the more to land-owners. This amendment was defeated by 276 to 201,[2] but it may be noted that six of the Derbyites who had opposed Lytton's amendment now returned to the opposition lobby.[3] On the other hand only ten of the Irish Brigadiers who had supported Lytton persisted in the opposi-tion lobby. Clearly the main concern of the majority was to protest the Irish income tax, not to turn the government out; eventually the main motion on the income tax was passed without a division.[4]

The second reading of the income tax bill was passed unopposed on 20 May[5] and it went into committee on 23 May. Once more the Irish returned to the fray with a motion asking for a Select Committee to consider the fiscal relations of Ireland and Great Britain. The Chan-cellor, advancing facts and figures to controvert the proposal, aroused the ire of at least one Irish spokesman, who expressed the opinion 'that there was no salvation for the true interests of that country [Ireland] but her entire freedom from all Chancellors of the Exchequer'.[6] Despite a sympathetic speech from Sir John Pakington, the motion was defeated by 194 to 61.[7]

In all, the bill survived some thirteen further amendments and seven divisions in the course of four nights in committee.[8] The third reading was finally passed on 6 June by a majority of 189 to 55[9] and the bill went to the House of Lords, where the second reading was moved by Lord Aberdeen on 21 June. It came in for some abuse from Lord Derby and several others, but Lord Wicklow, an Irish peer, gave it his blessing with the very sensible observation that he did not see why the general impoverishment of Ireland should be an excuse for those with money not paying their share of taxes. The second reading was not contested.[10] There was some further criticism, mainly on the Irish part of the bill, in committee,[11] and on the third reading, when two amendments were

---

[1] *Hansard*, CXXVII, 219–25. [2] *Ibid.* CXXVI, 1331–77.
[3] Colville, East, Gordon, Hudson, Stuart and Wood (*ibid.* 1376–7).
[4] *Ibid.* CXXVII, 258. [5] *Ibid.* 438–9.
[6] *Ibid.* 535. [7] *Ibid.* 504–36.
[8] *Ibid.* [9] *Ibid.* 1212–14.
[10] *Ibid.* CXXVIII, 476–501. [11] *Ibid.* 588–600.

offered and defeated, the second, according to *Hansard*, 'after a short discussion which was inaudible'.[1] The bill was then passed and received the royal assent on 28 June,[2] just in time to become effective.

The Resolution to bring in the succession duties was introduced by Gladstone in a speech of great length on 13 May and passed without a division,[3] but the Succession Duty Bill did not come up for consideration until June. Difficult and important details were not settled by the cabinet until late in May and the Prime Minister told the queen he expected it to 'be the most formidable part of the budget, especially in the House of Lords, although popular in the country'.[4] In 1805 Pitt had managed to extend his legacy duty to all bequests charged on real estate, but it was only now that inherited real property was to be made to pay such a tax. In view of the fact, however, that, unlike personal property, real property was subject to local rates, the payment of the new succession duty was to be spread over four years and the assessment was to be made, not on the capitalised value of the property, but on the heir's life interest.[5]

In the Commons the main debate took place in the committee stage, which lasted for six nights. On the motion to go into committee on 13 June Sir John Pakington precipitated a general debate by an amendment for a six-month postponement, which was defeated by a vote of 268–185.[6] The 40 firm Peelites in the House[7] supported the main motion. Of the 39 Derbyites who had broken with their party on the income tax, 20 still supported the government, 15 did not vote, and 4 now voted with the opposition.[8] Another 6 Derbyites who had opposed the income tax[9] and 2 others who had not voted in that division[10] now supported the succession duties to make a total of 28 Derbyites going into the government lobby on this occasion. The Irish Brigade, with one or two exceptions that cancelled out, abstained from voting.

---

[1] *Hansard*, 793–813.   [2] *Ibid.* 905.

[3] *Ibid.* CXXVII, 1331–77.

[4] *Ab. Cor. 1852–5*, p. 108, 21 May 1853.

[5] See Buxton, *Finance and politics*, I, 118. This provision was essential to protect holders of entailed property from injustice.

[6] *Hansard*, CXXVIII, 62–124.   [7] See Appendix A.

[8] See Appendix B. The four were Col. Harcourt, W. Stirling, Lord Wellesley and B. T. Woodd.

[9] Sir C. H. Coote, Lord Emlyn, C. S. Hardinge, Sir E. Lacon, R. M. Laffan, and C. Turner.

[10] W. R. S. Fitzgerald and A. Smollett.

The bill was fought throughout the committee stage and the third reading and numerous amendments were moved. In all the government survived twelve divisions,[1] but on one occasion the majority fell to six in a small house, and on another it was only sixteen in a large one. As with the income tax bill, the Chancellor was continually called upon to defend his proposals, clause by clause, which he did with skill, firmness and patience; indeed on several occasions he proposed amendments himself to meet difficulties raised. The third reading was finally passed on 18 July by 176 to 104.[2]

Opposition to the very idea of a succession duty on property bristled in the House of Lords from the first mention of it. Indeed Lord Malmesbury sought to have a Select Committee appointed to consider the effects of the proposed tax before the bill had even reached the Upper House. Aberdeen told the queen that this was 'a dexterous party measure', which he was uncertain whether to oppose.[3] In the end he did so with some support from Granville and very briefly from Argyll. The motion was only defeated by 139 to 126, a majority of thirteen that was secured by the thirteen episcopal votes, which all went to the government.[4]

The bill did not come to the Lords until late July, but it was debated on both second and third readings and through the committee stage. The main spokesmen for the government were Aberdeen, Granville, Argyll and, more briefly, Lansdowne. Two amendments were rejected, one by a majority of 102 to 68, and the bill was finally passed on 28 July.[5]

The Spirits Excise Bill passed with little debate, although there was some opposition from Irish members, who late on the night of the third reading were defeated on four successive motions of adjournment.[6]

The Customs Duties Bill, the various Stamp Duties Bills, and the bill to repeal the excise duty on soap also passed with little debate. On the

[1] *Hansard*, CXXVIII, 1174 (124–116); 1176 (108–92); 1383 (78–72); 1389 (97–86); 1391 (101–94); 1397 (195–125); 1407 (195–179); CXXIX, 222 (114–72); 398 (138–100); 416 (134–93); 409 (112–77); 417 (146–110).

[2] *Ibid.* CXXIX, 418.

[3] *Ab. Cor. 1852–5*, p. 108, 21 May 1853.

[4] *Hansard*, CXXVII, 659–706, 27 May; the votes included 69 proxies for and 66 against the motion. In the course of the debate Lord Malmesbury quoted an earlier opponent of the tax who had said that if they got it, 'this country, which was the best to live in, would be the worst to die in' (622).

[5] *Ibid.* CXXIX, 586–635, 697–743, 851–66.   [6] *Ibid.* 412–26, 674–8.

question of the tax on newspaper advertisements, however, the Chancellor suffered a reverse. In bringing in motions with respect to various stamp duties, he proposed to reduce the tax on newspaper advertisements to 6*d*. Milner Gibson, referring to the previous motion of the House to abolish this duty, moved an amendment for the repeal of all such duties. He was defeated by a majority of 109 to 99,[1] but a little later in the proceedings another Radical proposed to substitute a 'o' for the '6' in Gladstone's motion and this was passed by 70 to 61.[2] Too many of the government's supporters had left the House on the assumption that the matter was settled. It was an annoying, but minor, reversal. Gladstone's feat in piloting all these bills safely through such an independent House was an extraordinary achievement. 'The truth is', Lord Aberdeen told Madame Lieven, 'that Gladstone has raised himself to the highest pitch of financial reputation, and has given a strength and lustre to the Government, which it could not have derived from anything else.' As a result the government was 'infinitely better, and stronger' than he ever expected to see it.[3]

There was no question among contemporaries, and since then among economic historians, that the budget of 1853 was one of the great budgets of the century. Gladstone dealt with the outstanding fiscal problems of his time with a sureness of touch that eluded the Whig Chancellors. This is not to say that he was entirely successful, for, as we have seen, his debt conversion scheme raised more problems than it solved. Moreover, owing to a miscalculation, the new succession duty failed to bring in as much new revenue as had been anticipated. Nevertheless, when the financial year was completed there turned out to be a surplus of £3,500,000.[4] It was not Gladstone's fault that the outbreak of the Crimean War shattered all his long-range plans. It may be suggested that it was unrealistic for him to project a fairly static rate of expenditure for a period of eight years into the future, but the level of expenditures had scarcely changed to any appreciable amount over the

[1] *Hansard*, CXXVIII, 1111.
[2] *Ibid.* 1128. On the matter of parliamentary tactics following the defeat, Gladstone expressed himself as ready to follow Russell's advice: PRO 30/22/11/A fols. 132–3, 9 July 1853.
[3] *Ab. Cor. 1852–5*, pp. 109–10, 23 May 1853.
[4] Despite all the remissions there was a slight and unexpected increase in both customs and excise revenue. The reduced stamp duties also produced a larger revenue, and the extension of the income tax and of the Irish spirits duty likewise brought in rather more than had been anticipated (Northcote, *Financial policy*, pp. 239–40).

preceding fifteen years.[1] Unfortunately, by 1860, it was to rise to £70,000,000 and this was not simply a result of the Crimean War. We may, however, postpone consideration of the immediate political significance of the budget until we have examined the rest of the coalition's legislative programme of 1853, which was considerable, if less spectacular.

[1] Rees, *Short fiscal and financial history*, pp. 54 and 82. Expenditures in 1838 were £49,117,000, in 1852 £49,507,000.

4

THE INDIA ACT OF 1853

The evolution of the bill

In a leader on 28 March 1853 *The Times* asserted that there were three great questions awaiting a settlement, national education, the income tax and the government of India. The government sidestepped the first, and, as we have seen, settled the second to public satisfaction. The third could not be ignored, because the India Act of 1833 was about to expire. Since the days of Lord North successive India Acts had renewed the charter of the East India Company and provided for the government of its dominions for a period latterly limited to twenty years. During this period the role of the company had greatly changed and now even its participation in the government of the Indian sub-continent was being openly questioned. Since the beginning of March *The Times* had been harping almost daily on the necessity of grappling fearlessly with this thorny problem, insisting that parliament was completely free with the expiry of the old Act to bring about any changes it deemed expedient. It was pointed out that the Indians had been excessively taxed to support a warlike policy and that all too many of them had failed to get the justice that they deserved as subjects of the Crown. *The Times* did not insist that the dual system necessarily had to be discarded, but it did suggest that the quality of membership of the company's court of directors might be greatly improved.

Lord Broughton, President of the Board of Control in Russell's cabinet, had hoped that any changes required in the government of India when the charter lapsed might be left to the government of the day rather than be made the subject of public debate, but in 1852, when Derby came into office, both Houses of Parliament appointed committees to consider the operation of the expiring Act. Although these committees heard a good deal of evidence, their work was interrupted by the early dissolution of parliament, the need to reconstitute them when the new parliament met, and then the further change in administration.[1]

One of the expert witnesses with the most fully worked-out views on

[1] Sir William Lee-Warner, *The life of the marquis of Dalhousie*, II, 219–22.

the future of Indian government was the inevitable Sir Charles Trevelyan, who had first made his name as an Indian administrator and would
finally end his career in that country. In the utilitarian tradition he had
recommended 'a Supreme Government for the whole of India, entirely
separated from any local administrative responsibility; an expanded
Legislative Council; and presidencies under Governors appointed by
the Governor-General and dispensing with executive councils'. He also
urged further reforms in the judicial system and the completing of the
long-mooted codification of Indian law.[1] Many of the same points were
made in a comprehensive essay on the government of India, dated
13 October 1852, written by the Peelite governor general, Lord
Dalhousie. Both recognised that, in contrast with Madras and Bombay,
which had long been administered as separate presidencies, Bengal had
suffered from being the direct responsibility of the governor general
and his deputy, who did not have time to give the necessary close
supervision of local administration.[2] As we shall see, the bill eventually
introduced by Wood went a long way to meet these recommendations,
even though it did not fully satisfy the governor general or the
demands of the advanced critics.

From time to time during the earlier part of the session the Indian
question was brought up in both Houses of Parliament. Lord Ellenborough and other peers presented petitions received from India under-
lining the grievances of the Indian population and the serious attention
that had to be given to any recasting of the Indian system of government. In the Commons, Bright made himself the leading critic on
Indian affairs, taking an hour on one occasion to ask Russell what were
the government's intentions. As everybody knew, the existing India Act
terminated in April of 1854. Therefore, either a new Act had to be
passed this session, or the old one extended for a short period. Many of
the critics preferred the latter course in order to allow more time for a
thorough investigation, but the government, especially Aberdeen in the
Lords, refused to believe that delay was necessary. It was pointed out
that Select Committees had been appointed by both Houses early in
1852 and that these committees were continuing their sittings in the
present session. The critics said that the work of the committees was far
from finished. The government answered that enough had been done
and that many of the topics being examined had nothing to do with the

[1] Eric Stokes, *The English Utilitarians and India*, p. 253.
[2] Lee-Warner, *Dalhousie*, II, 219, 227–32.

actual form of government and that the recommendations of the committees when completed would be of value to whatever government should then exist.[1]

It was quite clear from these early skirmishes that the Indian question was a formidable one, given the government's uncertain strength. It soon became apparent that one of their most searching critics would be Lord Ellenborough, a former colleague of the Peelite leaders, who had remained aloof from them since 1846, but who had not joined Derby in 1852.[2] In the Commons debate of 11 March, precipitated by Bright's lengthy question, it was significant that most of the critics came from the Liberal ranks and that one of the few supporters of Russell was the Liberal Conservative Lord Jocelyn.

The differences and doubts that emerged in these occasional exchanges in parliament were reflected in cabinet discussions on the subject. It is clear that Aberdeen was very anxious to get the matter settled and was ready for a fairly radical measure. He was exasperated by Russell's changing attitude, which no doubt sprang from the uneasiness in Liberal ranks in the Commons. As early as 20 March he told the queen that in a cabinet meeting of the previous day the most important subject of discussion 'was the state of public feeling, and Parliamentary prospects, with respect to the India Bill'. He said that there was a strong desire for an interim bill for fear of opposition to any large reform, but he himself urged the latter with respect to freeing the Indian civil service of patronage and opening it to merit. The matter was referred to a select committee of the cabinet.[3]

Despite his endless labours in getting the various fiscal measures through parliament, Gladstone found the time to keep the most detailed account of what happened in the cabinet.[4] On the authority of Herbert he described the genesis of the bill as follows:

The history of the decision to bring forward the E.I. question this year is curious enough.

A committee of no less than eight members of the Cabinet was appointed to consider of a plan.

It consisted of Lord Aberdeen & Lord John Russell, Duke of Argyll, Sir J. Graham, Ld Granville, Sir C. Wood, S. Herbert, Molesworth.

---

[1] *Hansard*, CXXIV, 631–8, 1061–9; CXXV, 1–33, 37–70; 689–713; CXXVI, 1292–5.
[2] For Ellenborough's political position in these years see A. N. Imlah, *Lord Ellenborough*, pp. 240–2.
[3] *Ab. Cor. 1852–5*, pp. 66–7, to the queen, 19 March 1853.
[4] Add. MS. 44778, fols. 137–42, memo. 104, 10 June 1853.

81

When it brought its labours to a close Granville Herbert & Molesworth were decidedly favourable to single Government: Graham & Wood opposed to it: Ld Aberdeen inclining towards the former, Ld. J.R. and (I think) D. of Argyll towards the latter. The Committee however though apparently without a majority reported in favour of the plan produced by Wood [see below]: into which Ld Abn had suggested its by far best feature, namely the opening [of] Hayleybury and Addiscombe.

At a meeting of the cabinet on Saturday, 21 May, general approval was given to the proposals of the India committee, which decided to keep the court of directors but to improve its composition; opposition was anticipated to its retention.[1] Shortly afterwards, however, 'a fit of uncertainty of purpose' came suddenly upon Lord John, influenced, it was thought, by the press, by the Radicals, and by the Eliots.[2] He announced his change of opinion on 22 May to Graham, who immediately informed Wood. The latter was naturally 'very much annoyed' and threatened to resign.[3] 'He says, with truth, that there is no consideration for the feelings, or positions, of others', Graham wrote to Aberdeen.[4] Graham and Wood discussed how best to deal with Lord John and 'determined that it was more prudent not to write'. 'If he adhere to his resolution', Graham observed to Aberdeen, 'the proposal which we settled yesterday, cannot be made.'[5] Russell now wanted to limit the duration of the bill to a period of five or six years, but Aberdeen said that he did not think this would be acceptable to Wood. On the 25th he opened the matter up privately with Russell at Herbert's, where there was a cabinet dinner.[6] He found Russell 'very conciliatory' and yet at the meeting after dinner the latter started to discuss alternatives, saying, according to Gladstone, 'that he felt great difficulty about the indefiniteness of time for which we were about to legislate'.[7] 'This opened up the conversation afresh', Gladstone's account continues, 'and it appeared that the great majority of the Cabinet were either lukewarm or adverse: though Lord Aberdeen was much disinclined to alter what he had announced as already decided to the Queen viz. to go on at once.'[8]

[1] *Ab. Cor. 1852–5*, p. 108, Aberdeen to the queen, 21 May 1853.
[2] R.A. C47, fol. 38, memo. by Prince Albert of conversation between Graham and Stockmar, dated 28 May 1853. Sir H. Eliot was Russell's brother-in-law.
[3] *Ibid.*   [4] *Ab. Cor. 1852–5*, p. 109, 22 May 1853.
[5] *Ibid.*   [6] *Ibid.* pp. 112–14, Aberdeen to the queen, 26 May 1853.
[7] Add. MS. 44778, fols. 137–42, memo. 104, 10 June 1853.
[8] *Ibid.* Aberdeen's and Gladstone's accounts do not conflict, but Gladstone makes no mention of Russell's earlier objections, and Aberdeen ignores the general lukewarmness of the cabinet, since he was much keener on the measure than was Gladstone.

Queen Victoria expressed her surprise at Lord Aberdeen's report of the meeting of the 25th, for she said that Lord John had told her that after his conversation with Graham and Wood it had been agreed that he would propose postponement to the next session. She agreed, however, with her Prime Minister that 'it would have a *very bad* effect if the measure were withdrawn at the eleventh hour'.[1] Aberdeen was not unnaturally annoyed by this information of Russell's communication with the queen and a break-up of the cabinet seemed possible. To forestall this, at the next meeting on Saturday 28 May, Graham proposed postponement on public grounds, namely the length of time required for the passage of the budget.[2] On these grounds it was generally agreed that it would be impossible to pass an India Bill that session. 'On the whole', Aberdeen wrote to the queen, 'the discussion was perfectly friendly, and the decision unanimous.'[3] The ministers may not have known, but prior to the meeting Russell had written to the queen to say that he would abide by the cabinet's decision.[4] At any rate the matter was not yet settled.

The cabinet met again on 31 May and dramatically reversed its previous decision under circumstances that are vividly described in Gladstone's memorandum, which is most instructive in the way in which it lifts the veil of secrecy normally hiding cabinet discussion and reveals how cabinet business was at least sometimes conducted. Having given some account of the earlier discussions, Gladstone continued:

But all was not yet over. Our next Cabinet was held before the moment when Lord John was pledged to answer as to the in[tention] of the Government. No fact was recited as leading to this reversal, except a somewhat menacing communication from the Chairs [the court of directors], and a private letter of Dalhousie's to Argyll, which spoke generally but strongly in favour of delay.

The subject was discussed at [?such] length and with so much difference of opinion that at length it was necessary to take the voices separately.

There were thirteen members of the Cabinet present—the Lord Chancellor alone being away.

Of these there were for delay simply Granville, Molesworth, S. Herbert, W.E.G...   4

For delay with a late autumn session to legislate, and thus without any continuance bill, Sir J. Graham, Lord Lansdowne...   2

[1] *Ab. Cor. 1852–5*, p. 114, 27 May 1853.
[2] R.A. C47, fol. 39, memo. by Prince Albert, 28 May 1853.
[3] *Ab. Cor. 1852–5*, p. 115, 28 May 1853.   [4] R.A. C47, fol. 39, 28 May 1853.

Total for delay... 6

For going on *simpliciter* and positively Aberdeen, Lord J. Russell, Sir C. Wood... 3

Palmerston what is your opinion, said Lord John.

Which of my opinions, replied he, for I have had ten within the past ten minutes. But if you want my last opinion it is in favour of going on.

To this ten within ten minutes Clarendon answered that his case was the same. Thus were added votes... 2

Newcastle gave an opinion the last I should have expected from him viz. that we should go on but leave the question open whether in case of defeat on the question we should resort to one of the last alternatives or simply *take it*. For we had most of us been of the opinion that unless we made a Cabinet question of any motion for delay we should be beaten upon it. However this opinion of his was adopted by Argyll and so came out a further addition of votes... 2

Making in all for going on... 7

But I suppose a decision on a great question has rarely been settled, unsettled and resettled, in a Cabinet, after a fashion more queer.[1]

It was at this point that Russell precipitated a government crisis with its Irish members by an injudicious speech on ecclesiastical revenues, but, as we shall see, this storm was also weathered, and on Friday 3 June Wood asked leave to introduce his India Bill in a five-hour speech,[2] which Greville described as one of 'unexampled prolixity and dulness'.[3]

Wood began by explaining that, although extension for a year was possible, it was desirable to settle the matter that session, since in the next session parliament would be preoccupied with Reform, and the last India Act had been criticised (by Disraeli) because it was passed under the shadow of the Reform Bill. Moreover, the proposed bill was confined to the form of government at home and in India, and the Select Committees on India appointed in the previous session had practically completed their examination of this subject.

Defending the British achievement in India, Wood virtually ignored the swelling volume of criticism against it and emphasised what had been done in contrast to its critics who were always talking about what

[1] Add. MS. 44778, fols. 137–42, memo. 104, 10 June 1853. One is reminded of the 'Ten Minute Bill' of the Derby–Disraeli cabinet in 1867.

[2] *Hansard*, CXXVII, 1092–1169. For the ministerial crisis see below, pp. 107–10.

[3] *Greville Memoirs*, VI, p. 428. According to Lee-Warner (*Dalhousie*, II, 223) large portions of Wood's speech were taken directly from Dalhousie's essay. The speech did contain much information and some interesting observations about British government in India.

had not been done or what was being done badly. He recognised the anomalous nature of the British government in India, where a native population of many millions was 'ruled by a mere handful of foreigners, professing a different religion, speaking a different language, and accustomed to different habits', and he did not deny the innate absurdity of the way in which it was supervised. 'No man, if he were to sit down to the task of constructing a Government for India, would dream of constructing a Government upon such a system for so mighty an Empire,' he said. 'But it must be remembered that this form of government has grown up along with the growth of our Indian Empire.'[1] The fact remained, he argued, that the system worked and that changes had been adopted from time to time over the years to meet the needs of the country.

Wood then proceeded to defend the system of dual government against those who demanded a unitary system. He quoted such imposing experts as John Stuart Mill and Sir Charles Trevelyan in its defence and, while acknowledging that no less a person than Lord Ellenborough, who had been both Governor General and President of the Board of Control, was critical of the present system, he pointed out that Ellenborough wanted to improve the membership of the council which would advise the President of the Board of Control. He argued with some force that the system of double government made it possible to keep party considerations out of Indian affairs and pointed out the drawbacks of having these affairs under the constant scrutiny of parliament.

On the other hand he did admit that a defect existed in the manner in which the court of directors was chosen. Consequently he proposed to keep the present system, but to improve the method of choosing the directors, to curtail their patronage, and to impose 'some check on the higher appointments made by them in India'.[2] The court of directors was to be reduced from an effective twenty-four elected members to twelve elected and six appointed members. The latter were to be appointed by the government from persons who had served for at least ten years in India. Six of the twelve elected members must also have served in India for a similar period. Thus, in contrast to the existing court, the majority of the new membership would be men of experience in Indian affairs. The changeover was to be effected in two stages over a six-year period. No set term was to be attached to the Act, which would

---

[1] *Hansard*, CXXVII, 1134–5.   [2] *Ibid.* 1153.

remain in force until parliament saw fit to change it. Since the number of directors and their patronage was being reduced, their salaries were to be raised from £300 to £500 a year, with £1,000 each for the chairman and his deputy. Undoubtedly the most significant change proposed, however, was the abolition of patronage, which was hitherto one of the prize perquisites of members of the court of directors, a proposal first made by Lord Grenville in 1813. Macaulay had actually carried such a provision in the India Act of 1833, but subsequently backstairs intrigue had resulted in its repeal.[1] Entrance to Haileybury, the training college for Indian civil servants, and Addiscombe, where officers for the scientific branches of the Indian Army were trained, was to be governed by examination, but direct appointments to the army he did not consider as 'fit subjects for competition'.[2] The appointment of the members of council of all the presidencies by the court of directors was to be made subject to the approval of the Crown.[3] Little change was proposed for the executive government in India except that, following the advice of Dalhousie and Trevelyan, the office of Governor of Bengal was to be separated from that of the Governor General, and power was granted to make a new presidency in the Punjab. Contrary to the opinion of Dalhousie it was deemed inexpedient to place natives on the council.[4]

A temporary commission was to be appointed to draft acts for the consideration of the Indian council to meet the existing defects in Indian law. A legislative council was to be constituted consisting of the existing executive council, plus two legal members and one representative nominated by the Governor or Lieutenant-Governor of each district. It was also proposed to make some improvements in the constitution of the Superior Court of India.[5]

[1] R. J. Moore, 'Abolition of patronage in the Indian civil service and the closing of Haileybury college', *Hist. J.* VII (1964), 246–67.
[2] *Hansard*, CXXVII, 1156–8.
[3] *Ibid.* 1158–9.
[4] *Ibid.* 1159–61; Lee-Warner, *Dalhousie*, II, 230–3; Stokes, *English Utilitarians and India*, p. 255; A. B. Keith, *A constitutional history of India 1600–1935*, p. 137.
[5] *Hansard*, CXXVII, 1162–5. See further Keith, *Constitutional history of India*, pp. 137–8. Wood might also have added that it was proposed to increase the importance of the office of President of the Board of Control by raising the salary to that of a Secretary of State.

The debate in parliament

It was approaching midnight when the minister sat down, but despite the lateness of the hour John Bright immediately launched into a general attack on the government's proposals of another hour's duration.[1] Referring to Wood's speech he said:

There were some good things in it, no doubt. He did not suppose that any man could stand up, and go on speaking for five hours, without saying something that was useful. But as to the main question on which this matter rested, he did not believe that the plan which the government proposed to substitute would be one particle better than that which existed at the present moment.[2]

He grudgingly admitted some merit in the proposals regarding patronage, but the service into which the new recruits entered remained unreformed. He made great fun of the proposals to reconstitute the court of directors. To the amusement of his listeners he pictured the touching scene when the present twenty-four directors met to discuss the reduction of their number to fifteen.[3] 'The present constituency was so bad', he continued, 'that nothing the President of the Board of Control could do could make it worse.' To appoint six qualified members, he argued, 'was an admission that the remaining twelve members of the Board were not fit for their office. They had two ingredients—the one wholesome, the other poisonous; but there were two drops of poison to one of wholesome nutriment.' He had no doubt that the honourable Lord, the member for London, supported these proposals for sustaining the dual system of government. 'He only wished', the *Hansard* account continues, 'that some of the younger blood in the Cabinet might have had their way upon this question. Nothing could induce him to believe, after the evidence which was before the public, that this measure had the approbation of an united Cabinet. It was not possible that thirteen sensible gentlemen, who had any pretensions to form a Cabinet, could agree to a measure of this nature.' Indeed, the series of conflicting rumours during the preceding week, he suggested, indicated 'that there was a good deal of vacillation on the part of the Government'.[4]

Bright came closer to the truth than he may have realised and some

---

[1] *Hansard*, CXXVII, 1169–94.   [2] *Ibid.* 1171.

[3] *Ibid.* 1191. 'As the East India Company kept a writer to record their history, he hoped they also kept an artist to give us an historical painting of this great event.'

[4] *Ibid.* 1191–3.

members of the cabinet must have been uneasy as they listened to him. *The Times* renewed his criticisms, saying that Bright had left Wood with no ground to stand on even before the House rose. The minister's rosy picture of Indian affairs it labelled 'a laboured apology for British rule', and charged that the interests of the natives had been overlooked. While applauding the abolition of patronage it emphasised the pointlessness of retaining the patrons; there was no longer any reason for a dual system of government, since there was no longer any obligation to the East India Company. Moreover, the failure to set any fixed duration to the proposed Act would put the twelve elected directors in the power of the six appointed directors, who would always be able to advise the government to change the Act.[1] The Directors at India House were reported to have received the news with sullen resignation. The only thing to be said for the bill in their eyes was that it might have been worse.[2]

The debate continued for two more nights before leave was given to bring in the bill. Most of the speakers were critical of it and of the dual system of government, and those who defended it, as for instance Sir James Hogg, were more concerned to refute the arguments of Bright, which Hogg said 'consisted of shreds and patches, of bits and scraps, from old pamphlets and magazines', of fragments of old reports but, in no part, of the evidence before the present committee.[3]

When the bill came up for its second reading on 23 June Lord Stanley moved an amendment designed to postpone legislation until further information had been obtained. In his opening speech in the debate on this amendment, which lasted for four nights, Stanley complained about the limited amount of time allowed for so important a bill brought in late in the session and compared it to the amount of time allowed to debate such measures as the Reform Bill and the Ecclesiastical Titles Bill. Robert Lowe, answering Stanley on behalf of the government, pointed out that this bill had been brought in a little earlier in the session than either the two preceding India Bills (1813 and 1833)—nor could they ignore the fact that more time had to be allotted to the other bills mentioned because they excited more interest among members. 'If the noble Lord wanted to have any proof of the amount of interest felt in this measure, compared with the long discussions on the Reform Bill, or the Ecclesiastical Titles Bill, he could not have done

[1] *The Times,* 4 and 6 June 1853.
[2] *The Times,* 7 June 1853.   [3] *Hansard,* CXXVII, 1242.

better than have looked around him when he was speaking...had he been moving an Amendment with regard to the Reform Bill or the Ecclesiastical Titles Bill, he would not have been listened to in the solemn silence that he was to-night, but he would have been met with cheers and counter-cheers and other demonstrations of enthusiasm to his credit.'[1]

The main opposition to the bill had come and continued to come from what Sir Robert Inglis called the 'Young India' group, which another member identified with the Manchester School. Consequently in the debate, which lasted for four nights, despite Lowe's allegation of lack of interest, the division of speakers for and against the amendment did not follow party lines. Indeed only three Conservative speakers were found to support Lord Stanley, J. Napier, C. B. Adderley, a Conservative colonial reformer, and Disraeli, always ready to capitalise on a situation such as this. No less than nine Liberals, most of a Radical tinge, such as Cobden, Bright, and Hume, were opposed to the bill and in favour of the amendment. On the other hand, eight of the Derbyites, including Herries and Inglis, opposed the amendment, and of the government supporters who spoke in favour of the bill and against the amendment four were Peelites, Graham, Lowe (Secretary of the Board of Control), Sir James Hogg (an East India Company director) and Monckton Milnes. The only Liberals to speak for the bill were two ministers, Russell and Wood, an ex-minister, Macaulay, another East India Company director, R. D. Mangles, and John MacGregor (Chairman of the Eastern Archipelago Company).[2]

Probably no speech was looked forward to with as much anticipation as that of Macaulay, who only a week before had single-handedly killed the Judges' Exclusion Bill, a private measure, in a speech of 'extra-ordinary power and eloquence'.[3] Macaulay's appearances in the House were now infrequent because of growing ill health. He was, however, anxious to see the bill pass, since in his opinion its positive advantages outweighed all its shortcomings, and so he responded to Wood's plea for his intervention in the debate on 24 June, in what proved to be his last speech in the House of Commons. It was planned that he should speak in the afternoon to avoid the fatigue of a later hour, but unfortunately Hume secured the chosen time by moving the adjournment on the

[1] *Ibid.* cxxviii, 633–4.   [2] See *ibid.* cxxviii, 606–74, 735–78, 814–903, 978–1074.
[3] *Greville Memoirs*, vi, 426. This was his first appearance in the House since his re-election.

previous evening and refused to make way for the man everyone wanted to hear, saying that he too had a weak chest and that he knew just as much about India as Macaulay did. The House heard him through a long speech with great impatience and it was close to eight before Macaulay could rise. Although it was the 'deadest time of the evening' the House remained well filled. The speech he made is not one of Macaulay's best remembered, since he excluded it from his Collected Edition on the grounds that he had been unable to complete it. Nevertheless, even today it jumps to life from the dull pages of *Hansard*, in contrast to the dead speeches that preceded and followed it.[1]

Macaulay's major point was that the constitution of boards and courts in England was of minor importance compared to the choice of Englishmen who were actually to go to India and govern its hundred and fifty million inhabitants.[2] He vigorously repudiated the contention of Lord Ellenborough that academic worth was of no significance, indeed that it might be a drawback in 'the contest of active life', by pointing out the evidence of history to the contrary. 'Look at the Church, the Parliament, or the Bar [he said]. Look to the Parliament from the time when Parliamentary Government began in this country—from the days of Montagu and St John, to those of Canning and Peel. You need not stop there, but come down to the time of Lord Derby and my right hon. Friend the Chancellor of the Exchequer.'[3]

Turning to the question of native participation in the government of India, he strongly objected to the idea of appointing a man merely because he was a native, but he maintained that, should such a person win a place in competition with Europeans, then he was indeed to be welcomed. Macaulay strongly defended giving the natives the opportunity of Western education condemned by Lord Ellenborough and others and concluded his speech with these words:

I can only say, for myself, with regard to this question, that, in my opinion, we shall not secure or prolong our dominion in India by attempting to exclude the Natives of that country from a share in its government, or by attempting to discourage their study of western arts or learning; and I will only say, further, that, however that may be, I will never consent to keep them ignorant in order to keep them manageable, or to govern them in ignorance in order that we may govern them long.[4]

[1] G. O. Trevelyan, *The life and letters of Lord Macaulay*, II, 338–41; *Hansard*, CXXVIII, 739–59.
[2] *Ibid.* 745.
[3] *Ibid.* 751.   [4] *Ibid.* 758–9.

One of the longest and strongest speeches in favour of the bill came from Sir James Graham,[1] who had participated in the preparation of the India Act of 1833, who had taken a life-long interest in Indian affairs, and who had known intimately five Indian governors general. In particular he dwelt on the dangers of delay and defended the modified form of double government. In the latter connection he dwelt on the evidence of Mill, whose great scholarly reputation belied any charges of his dependence on the Company, which was in fact 'much more dependent upon him for the assistance which he [had] given them'. In the course of his speech Graham made two references to party considerations. He alluded to the fact that the government had brought in the bill at this time of the session and with the knowledge that it was likely to create a division among their friends as evidence of their good faith and sense of public duty; on the other hand he was happy to observe 'that, though much difference of opinion exists, there had not, up to the present moment, been mingled with the debate the slightest tincture of party or factious feeling'.

Disraeli took up this point when he spoke on the fourth and last night (30 June), saying:

We have been told frequently in this debate that this subject is not a party question—as if a party question were necessarily an improper question. We have been told frequently in this debate that the subject is not considered in a party spirit, as if a subject considered in a party spirit were necessarily considered in a partial and unjust spirit. Now, Sir, as we are all of us Members of that which is a House of party, and which, if it were not a House of party, you may depend upon it would not long exist in this country, I think this is a point on which there should be a clearer conception than at present prevails in this assembly. I look upon a purely party question as a question which concerns the distinctive principles of the two great parties into which a popular assembly is naturally divided...I cannot understand how a great party in this House can take refuge in neutrality on a subject like that which is before us... I say, we owe it to our constituents...fairly to place before Parliament and the country the reasons why we differ from the course recommended by the Government, and to give Parliament and the country an opportunity of expressing their opinions between the two policies that are placed before their consideration. I know I may be told that party government tends to great excesses. It is my opinion that the excesses of party government are not greater—perhaps they are not so great—as the excesses which are experienced under despotic government...I make these observations because I have the

[1] *Ibid.* 833–57.

misfortune to differ on this question from many Gentlemen for whom I entertain great respect, with whom I act in political connexion, and for whom I feel great personal regard. For my own part, I cannot incur the responsibility of giving my approbation to the measure.[1]

His listeners must have been puzzled as to why he insisted on emphasising the importance of making such measures party questions, when by his own confession the Conservative party was split down the middle on it, with Herries, who had been President to the Board of Control in the Derby administration, giving it his support. Perhaps the explanation is to be found in the suggestion that Disraeli delighted to put obstacles in his own path for the pleasure of then overcoming them.[2] At any rate he made a very clever and witty speech, reminding Macaulay, who had asserted that the real power in Indian government lay in India, that it was the court of directors that had forced the recall of the great proconsul of a great government, Lord Ellenborough, who had been sent out by his own colleagues in Peel's cabinet to take over India in time of crisis.[3] He had great fun with the proposals to reduce the number of elected directors, describing those who survived the decimation process as 'the fifteen Thugs', whose victims would be among their former friends, and he vigorously refuted the arguments for early action, jeering at the suggestion that an India Bill and a Reform Bill could not be introduced in the same session. He ended with another reference to the question of party:

We have had our party struggles, the subjects of which have often been confined to oblivion, but we are struggling now for something that will not be soon forgotten; and however I may go into the lobby, however my noble Friend may be attended, I shall be supported by the consciousness that upon a great occasion I at least attempted to do my duty by those who have deemed me worthy of their political confidence, and I shall at least do my utmost to connect their names with a course of policy which I think will be honourable to themselves, and which I believe will be beneficial to the country.[4]

Lord John Russell, following Disraeli at a very late hour, wound up the debate with a brief speech dwelling on the negative nature of the amendment. He took up Disraeli's remarks upon party, saying that he was in entire agreement with what the other said on the subject, but he

[1] *Hansard*, CXXVIII, 1033–5.
[2] See A. J. P. Taylor, *Englishmen and others*, p. 67.
[3] Here of course we may see the reason for Ellenborough's fierce opposition to the retention of the court of directors.　　　　[4] *Hansard*, CXXVIII, 1064.

found an inconsistency in his failure to point to any decided policy which his party should follow.

When the House divided shortly before 3 a.m. 322 supported the government, and only 140 were found to oppose the bill.[1] The 37 Peelites in the House at the time all entered the government lobby[2] and they were joined by 87 Conservatives.[3] On the other hand at least 24 Liberals voted against the government.[4] Indeed it will be seen that only 207 Liberals supported it. Of the Irish repealers voting, 5 supported the government,[5] and 6 opposed it.[6]

During nine nights in committee the bill was subject to many amendments and some sixteen divisions, but on only one occasion did the government suffer defeat, when it was forced to accept an additional clause proposed by Sir John Pakington, providing for the abolition of the East India Company's salt monopoly.[7] The third reading was finally passed in the Commons after three more divisions on additional clauses, one of which, curtailing the proposed salary increase of directors, was carried against the government. Ironically this clause was deleted by the House of Lords at the instigation of Lord Ellenborough, the bill's chief critic in the Upper House. In view of his earlier criticisms Ellenborough's remarks on the second reading were milder than might have been expected,[8] but he did propose numerous amendments in the committee stage, all but three of which were rejected.[9] The bill passed the Lords in fairly short order, for Lord Malmesbury, the official opposition spokesman, contented himself with a protest at the late date at which it was introduced.[10]

The India Act of 1853 received final assent on 20 August, the last day of the session. Although it represented a political victory for the government, it has received little attention from historians, since it was

---

[1] *Ibid.* CXXVIII, 1074–7.
[2] See Appendix A.   [3] See Appendix B.
[4] Barnes, T., Bell, J., Biggs, W., Blackett, J. F. B., Bright, J., Brockman, E. D., Chambers, M., Cheetham, J., Cobden, R., Crook, J., Gibson, T. M., Greville, Col., Hadfield, G., Hume, J., Kennedy, T., Laslett, W., Miall, E., Phillimore, J. G., Phinn, T., Pollard-Urquhart, W., Seymour, W. P., Sullivan, M., Talbot, C., Thompson, G.
[5] Bowyer, G., Corbally, M. E., M'Cann, J., O'Brien, P., Shee, W.
[6] Dunn, Col., Greene, J., Greville, Col., Kennedy, T., Moore, G., Sullivan, M.
[7] *Hansard*, CXXIX, 913–59. At least ten Derbyites who had supported the second reading voted for this clause, which was introduced at the instigation of English salt interests. It was passed by a vote of 117–107.
[8] *Ibid.* 1349–59.   [9] *Ibid.* 1426–51.
[10] *Ibid.* 1450–1. The Commons accepted the Lords' amendments (*ibid.* 1723–6).

soon replaced owing to the great convulsions that seized India a few years later. Indeed the Act has been criticised for clinging too closely to ideas which had once been liberal and progressive, but which now needed a radical revision that was not forthcoming.[1] Undoubtedly it was not an adventurous measure, nor a particularly popular one at the time, since it was a compromise, reluctantly accepted by the friends of the Company, but not going far enough for the Indian reformers.

Despite the fact that Wood had written to him saying that the bill had incorporated almost all his suggestions, Dalhousie in a letter to a friend called it 'a wretched thing'. The 'home part of it' had done either 'far too much or not half enough', while, 'for the India part', he wrote, 'they are to pay twice as much for doing half the quantity of good which I showed them the way to'.[2] This language may simply reflect the annoyance of an imperious man chagrined that his full advice was not followed, but at the time of writing he was greatly upset by the very recent news of the death of his wife on her way back to England. In any event Dalhousie proceeded without delay to implement the Indian parts of the new Act. Indeed, in constituting the new legislative council he went beyond the intentions of the President of the Board of Control, who had no wish to see the council grow into an independent parliamentary body. Dalhousie, on the other hand, sharply objected to Wood's suggestion that no legislation should be introduced in the council without the prior assent of the authorities at home.[3]

The India Act of 1853 left it an open question whether Bengal was to be made a separate presidency or placed under a lieutenant-governor. In April 1854 Dalhousie, glad to be rid of responsibility for its administration, took it upon himself to appoint a lieutenant-governor. On receiving this news Wood immediately rushed a new Act through parliament before the close of the 1854 session, regularising the situation and terming Bengal a presidency. This Act also increased the power of the central government to alter the boundaries of the various provinces with home approval.[4]

One unopposed and little noticed amendment to the India Act of

---

[1] H. H. Dodwell in *The Cambridge history of India*, VI, *The Indian empire 1858–1918*, 19.

[2] *Private letters of the marquis of Dalhousie*, p. 260, to J. G. A. Baird, 23 July 1853. Wood's letter dated 8 June may not yet have arrived (Lee-Warner, *Dalhousie*, II, 232–3). Dalhousie's biographer makes no allusion to his vexation and regards the Act as emanating from the Governor General.

[3] Lee-Warner, *Dalhousie*, II, 233–45.

[4] *Ibid.* pp. 247–51; Keith, *Constitutional history of India*, pp. 139–40.

1853, introduced by the government in the Lords, had broadened the qualifications for entrance into the Indian civil service in a way that was to have significant bearing on its implementation. The man responsible for this change was Benjamin Jowett of Balliol, who on hearing from his friend Trevelyan that it was proposed to limit admittance to Haileybury (and hence the Indian service) to candidates of not more than nineteen years of age, strongly objected that this would exclude university graduates. He immediately set about to lobby for an amendment to open the service to the universities; and, thanks to the intervention of no less a trio than Gladstone, Aberdeen and Granville, this was obtained at the very last moment with Wood's agreement. Subsequently Wood set up a small committee under the chairmanship of Macaulay, with Jowett now ensconced as a member, to recommend procedures for the implementation of the clauses dealing with entry into the Indian service. The report was written by Macaulay under the influence of Jowett, who at that time was working closely with Trevelyan in the matter of civil service reform, and submitted to the government in November 1854. It had the effect of undermining the position of Haileybury, and shortly afterwards Wood decided to close that institution, which by this time had served its purpose. The Indian civil service was henceforward to be a preserve for the students of Jowett and his colleagues at Oxford and Cambridge.[1]

Two other important sequels to the India Act of 1853 may be noted. A law commission was reconstituted in England, to Dalhousie's annoyance, to resume the task, left long in abeyance since Macaulay's departure from India, of codifying Indian law; the work was largely completed by the end of the decade thanks to Wood's initiative at this time.[2] Finally, it may be noted that in July 1854 Wood issued a celebrated educational despatch, enunciating a policy of higher education in English designed to create an educated middle class in India. Such a policy had long been advocated by Macaulay and Dalhousie and was zealously taken up by the Governor General, despite his pique that the despatch had ignored what he had already done.[3]

The coalition's Indian policy, although cautious as a result of the different forces operating on it, was on the whole an enlightened and

---

[1] R. J. Moore, 'Abolition of patronage in the Indian civil service', *Hist. J.* VII, 246–67, who gives the first full account of this intriguing story.

[2] Stokes, *English Utilitarians in India*, pp. 257–63; Lee-Warner, *Dalhousie*, II, 235–6.

[3] Stokes, *English Utilitarians in India*, pp. 251–2; Lee-Warner, *Dalhousie*, II, 206–9.

successful one. Important progress was made in the spheres of local administration, education and law reform, and approval was given to the important principle of appointment by merit,[1] which characterised the Peelite approach to public service and which Gladstone wished to apply to appointments in the home service. Moreover, the passage of the India Act of 1853 indicated that the days of indirect rule were numbered, even if the consequences of the Mutiny had not swept it away. It was a useful stepping-stone in the British tradition of evolutionary change and it was fortunate that there was a great reforming Governor General in India at the time to assist in its implementation.[2]

[1] Unfortunately, as it was pointed out, this reform had the drawback that it made Indian appointments to the service unlikely, if not impossible. See *Cambridge History of India*, VI, 19.

[2] R. J. Moore, *Sir Charles Wood's Indian policy 1853–66* (Manchester, 1967) has appeared while the present work was in the press.

5

RELIGIOUS ISSUES AND REFORM MEASURES IN THE SESSION OF 1853

Legal reforms

The budget and the India Bill comprised the major legislation of 1853, but there were a number of other useful, if less controversial, measures which we may consider more briefly. Most of these passed with relatively little debate, but as usual religious issues, whenever they arose, dissipated an inordinate amount of parliamentary time. Law reforms provided a fairly stable legislative diet for mid-Victorian parliaments and the session of 1853 was no exception. By and large such reforms were not made a party issue and one Lord Chancellor took up where another left off. Indeed, several of the measures passed under the supervision of Lord Cranworth had been initiated by his predecessor, Lord St Leonards.

Early in the session, on 14 February, the Lord Chancellor discussed the whole subject of law reform in a 'long and elaborate' speech full of appropriate references to the names of Bentham and Romilly and to the efforts of former Chancellors still in the House. He spoke of what had been done and what remained to be done, among other things alluding to the desirability of drawing up a great Code Victoria of English law to clear away the clutter of antiquated and outdated laws of former centuries.[1] His initial bill was a modest measure to register Assurances (in connection with transfers of property), which ran into trouble in the House of Commons, where it was referred to a Select Committee and never heard of again.[2] This was a poor start, but in actual fact a good deal of useful law reform was passed in the course of the session, including a Charitable Trusts Act,[3] an Evidence Amendment Act,[4] three Chancery Reform Acts,[5] several Acts dealing with Scottish law,[6] and a lengthy Common Law Court Act for Ireland, which ran to 243 clauses.[7]

---

[1] *Hansard*, CXXIV, 41–78.
[2] *Ibid.* CXXVII, 714–15.
[3] *A collection of public general statutes passed in the sixteenth and seventeenth years of the reign of Her Majesty Queen Victoria 1852–3*, ch. 137.
[4] *Statutes, 1852–3*, ch. 83.
[5] *Ibid.* chs. 22, 78 and 98.
[6] *Ibid.* chs. 53 and 94.
[7] *Ibid.* ch. 113.

There were also three substantial measures dealing with lunacy, introduced by Lord St Leonards with the support of the Chancellor, which were passed with very little debate.[1]

The Charitable Trusts Act was no routine measure, for its antecedents went as far back as 1818 to the appointment of a Charity Commission, at the instigation of Brougham, which laboured until 1830 and in a revived form till 1834, surveying the state of some 26,751 English charities (and even then the figure was not complete).[2] This great survey, the results of which were published in a huge 'Doomsday Book', pointed to many anomalies and worse crying out for supervision. Yet, despite all the time and money that had gone into the survey and despite the recommendations of a powerful Select Committee appointed to consider the findings of the commission, no legislation resulted. Numerous bills were introduced throughout the 1840s, but all foundered through apathy, lack of time, the resistance of vested interests, and, in 1846, the exigencies of the political situation that led the Whig peers to join the Protectionists to defeat a bill of the tottering Peel government. A new royal commission, appointed by the Russell government in 1850-1, renewed the pressure, and so it was not inappropriate that a coalition of Whigs and Peelites should finally secure the passage of a substantial measure, which aimed to remove the anomalies in the administration of old bequests, and generally to effect the better management of charitable trusts.[3]

Despite initial enthusiastic praise from *The Times* and the appointment of a well-qualified commission with able and energetic inspectors, the results were disappointing. Amendments to Cranworth's bill in the House of Lords had greatly reduced the commission's power to take effective action to right the wrongs that it uncovered, but nevertheless it was an important beginning and paved the way for more effective legislation some years later.[4]

---

[1] *Statutes, 1853*, chs. 70, 96 and 97. These were a Lunacy Regulation Act of 153 clauses, a Lunatics Care and Treatment Act of 39 clauses, and a Lunatic Asylum Act of 136 clauses. In general these measures aimed to protect the rights and interests of lunatics, of their families, and of the public, and to supervise more strictly the care of such people.

[2] For a full and lucid account of the whole subject see David Owen, *English philanthropy, 1660–1960*, ch. VII, 182–208, on which this paragraph is largely based.

[3] *Statutes, 1853*, ch. 137; *Hansard*, CXXV, 539–42 and CXXIX, 1153. The religious issue was raised in the House of Commons when Russell, in face of opposition, introduced an amendment to exclude Roman Catholic charities because of their very dubious legal status (Owen, *English philanthropy*, p. 201).

[4] Owen, *English philanthropy*, pp. 202–8.

Another important legal reform introduced in this session was the virtual abandonment of the practice of penal transportation, which, of course, was a measure of significance in the field of colonial policy. Lord Grey, the former Whig Colonial Secretary, reacted strongly to the government's announced intention of dealing with this matter by introducing a motion (on 10 May) to the effect that no alteration should be made to the present practice until the matter had been considered by parliament. This was defeated by a vote of 54 to 37 after an interesting debate in which Aberdeen attacked Grey's motion as an attempt to interfere with the royal prerogative; and in which Newcastle dwelt on the opposition of responsible colonists to the practice and pointed out that transportation was in fact a life sentence, since no provision was made for the return of the prisoner after the sentence was completed.[1]

In July the Lord Chancellor introduced a bill greatly curtailing the number of cases in which transportation remained a punishment, since Western Australia was now the only colony willing to accept convicts and its limit of absorption was less than 1000 a year. The bill passed through both Houses with very little debate, since even those who favoured transportation in theory, and the Lord Chancellor included himself among them, realised that convicts could no longer be sent to colonies unwilling to receive them.[2] The system had become quite anomalous with the granting of responsible government.

The colonial church: The Canadian Clergy Reserves Bill

The first noteworthy government measure brought into the House of Commons was the Canadian Clergy Reserves Bill. It was of more significance in Canada than in England, but because of its religious connotations it was a potentially controversial measure that could have proved dangerous to a government without a firm majority. In introducing the bill on 15 February Frederick Peel reminded his listeners that the principle of allotting one-seventh of all public land grants to the support of the Protestant clergy in Canada was embodied in Pitt's Constitutional Act of 1791.[3] Since this was regarded as an Anglican monopoly, it had long been considered as a grievance by the popular

---

[1] *Hansard*, cxxvii, 1–79. This motion was also criticised by the Lord Chancellor and by the duke of Argyll, who questioned the wisdom of making convicts the majority of the population of Van Diemen's Land; it was supported by Lords Derby and Campbell.

[2] *Hansard*, cxxviii, 7–11, 348–53, 1535–60, 1600–2, 1682–99; *Statutes, 1853*, ch. 99.

[3] *Hansard*, cxxiv, 133–46.

7-2

Assembly in Upper Canada. When the matter was referred to the judges they held that it was beyond the competence of the Canadian legislature to set aside the settlement of 1791. Lord John Russell had consequently secured the passage of a Clergy Reserves Bill in 1840 that met some, but not all, of the Canadian demands by extending the Clergy Reserves to other Protestants and to the Roman Catholics. In the meantime great changes had taken place in the colony, but the colonial legislature still remained powerless to deal with this matter that so clearly concerned it. 'All that we propose to do', Peel said, 'is to vest in the Legislature of Canada the power, if they think fit to exercise it, of securing the existing arrangement.' 'I think it precipitate', he added, 'to anticipate that these clergy reserves will, in consequence of this concession, be of necessity alienated from religious purposes and secularized by the Legislature of Canada.'[1]

The Tories, of course, did just that and raised the familiar cry that the church was in danger. The Act of 1840, which had once been an encroachment on the preserves of the Church of England, now became a bastion of defence. Not all good churchmen, however, were so reactionary in their views as the redoubtable Mr Spooner, a leading Tory critic of the bill. Gladstone defended the measure on the sound ground that clergy reserves were a local matter to be left to a local legislature. In language that was reminiscent of Burke he said: 'I think that it having pleased the Almighty to interpose 3,000 miles of ocean between you and them—having drawn that broad line of distinction which showed His will—it is fitting that they, and not you, should take the management of their concerns, with which they are better acquainted than you can possibly be.' Indeed he went so far as to say that he thought the surrender of parliament's control of the Canadian legislature afforded the best chance of keeping these church endowments in Canada.[2]

Nevertheless, despite this act of faith in the Canadian legislature, the cabinet decided on 12 March to delete a clause of the bill that would have abrogated the guarantee by the imperial parliament of an annual payment to the Protestant clergy of Canada, which had been made in 1840 to secure the support of the archbishop of Canterbury to the Act of that year. 'This alteration of the Bill will probably excite a good deal of

[1] *Hansard*, CXXIV, 138.
[2] *Ibid.* 1142–53. Gladstone also pointed out that the act of 1840, now upheld so strongly by the ultra-Protestant interest, actually provided for the endowment of the Roman Catholic Church in Canada.

fresh opposition,' Lord Aberdeen told the queen, 'but a well founded accusation of breach of good faith would have been much more formidable.'[1] The opposition to the proposed amendment, which was introduced by Russell on 4 April, came, of course, from the Radicals. Despite a taunting speech from Disraeli, he and other Conservatives supported the government to defeat a motion by Miall and Bright for the retention of the clause by a vote of 176 to 108.[2]

The second reading of the bill was passed in the Commons on 4 March by a vote of 275 to 192[3] and the third on 11 April by 288 to 208.[4] The 40 Peelites[5] in the House and 22 other Conservatives[6] voted in the majority on the latter occasion. The bill was introduced into the House of Lords by the duke of Newcastle, who went at length into its historical background. He was supported by his Peelite colleague, the duke of Argyll, by the independent Lord Grey, and by the bishops of Oxford and St Davids, but vigorously opposed by Lord Derby, who moved an amendment, Lord St Leonards, the bishop of Exeter and others.[7] The debate was enlivened by a 'scene' between Derby and Clarendon, which ended amicably with their 'drinking each other's health in water across the table'.[8] The amendment was defeated by 117 to 78 and the bill passed its third reading on 28 April without division and received the royal assent on 9 May.[9]

Lord Aberdeen, in reporting the debate and the division to the queen, observed that 'the Bishops were nearly divided, there being ten for, and nine against the amendment'. Lord Derby's 'ingenious and dexterous speech', he said, was well answered by the duke of Newcastle.[10] While not a measure of the greatest importance in the imperial parliament, this was a concrete achievement for the government, touching as it did on the vulnerable matter of religion.

Measures of this sort presented peculiar difficulties to men such as Gladstone and his high-church friends, who had to determine what course to take that was compatible with the true interests of the church on the one hand and the demands of equity and political reality on the

---

[1] R.A. A23, fol. 17, 13 March 1853.   [2] *Hansard*, CXXV, 481–506.
[3] *Ibid.* CXXIV, 1155–8.   [4] *Ibid.* CXXV, 995–8.
[5] See Appendix A. One of the absent Peelites, Sir Robert Peel, had supported the second reading.
[6] See Appendix B. Three other Conservatives not present had supported the bill on the second reading.
[7] *Hansard*, CXXVI, 381–450.   [8] *Greville Memoirs*, VI, 421.
[9] *Hansard*, CXXVI, 663, 1286.   [10] *Ab. Cor. 1852–5*, p. 95, 26 April 1853.

other. The crisis in conscience involved is nicely illustrated in a curious letter[1] addressed to Gladstone, while the bill was still being debated, by a group of able and distinguished men, most of whom probably stood to the right of him politically, but all of whom looked up to him as their ideal representative in parliament for Oxford University, with which they all appeared to have close ties. The prime mover was Sir J. Awdry, who was not personally known to Gladstone, but among the ten who signed the letter there were friends such as Justice J. T. Coleridge, John Keble, of Tractarian fame, Sir Stafford Northcote, the future Conservative leader, Roundell Palmer, one day to be Gladstone's Lord Chancellor, George Moberley, whom he would nominate to the see of Salisbury, and the faithful Sir William Heathcote, who explained that they might have collected more names, but preferred to keep the matter confidential.[2]

These gentlemen told Gladstone that they addressed him because of their confidence in the principles that led him 'to aim at the highest & best objects for the Church'. 'In considering the abandonment of the Clergy Reserves to the Canadian Parliament', they wrote, 'it occurs to us that the occasion urgently requires its accompaniment by that measure of Colonial Church liberty which the public have learned to associate with your name & principles.' Urging the 'necessity for some more perfect internal organization for the Colonial Church', they continued:

But it is notorious that a large proportion of sincere Churchmen look with apprehension upon some elements of the present Administration; and it is obvious that these men would be far better inclined to accept that Administration as a whole if they saw fair grounds for believing that their views would receive a reasonable amount of favour at the hands of the Government. It is therefore, as we venture to suggest, of no small importance to Her Majesty's Ministers, whose continuance in office is at present necessarily dependent on the union of parties recently opposed, that some measures should be carried which may obviously justify the adhesion [of] such persons as we have indicated.[3]

[1] Add. MS. 44208, fols. 45–6, 3 March 1853.
[2] *Ibid.* fols. 47–8, 15 March 1853, a covering letter from Heathcote. The other signers were T. D. Acland, William James and Montague Bermond.
[3] *Ibid.* fols. 45–6. Their concluding paragraph bears quotation: 'Wishing rather to cheer you by the expression of moral sympathy from some who hope that they appreciate your motives in entering upon a new course of action, than to urge you against your own better judgement, we have taken the liberty of addressing you, though collectively, in a somewhat private and confidential form, and trust that you will forgive the introduction of some names not honoured by your personal acquaintance.'

One measure calculated to meet the needs felt by these gentlemen was a Colonial Church Regulation Bill designed to provide a legal basis for the regulation of the Church of England in the colonies, 'without endeavouring to introduce the principle of a Church Establishment'.[1] Late in the session it was passed by the Lords, where it was sponsored by the archbishop of Canterbury, and supported by the Lord Chancellor and the Peelite dukes of Newcastle and Argyll. It only reached the Commons on 29 July, and on 3 August it was shelved by a vote postponing its second reading for three months. In the course of a brief debate Gladstone defended the principle of the bill, pointing out that he himself had been responsible for bringing the problem before the House in a former session, when he had introduced a bill that had been criticised as going too far in the direction of independence for the colonial churches. The episcopacy had now agreed on the proposals contained in the present bill and while he realised that the House was not prepared to act so late in the session he trusted they would give fair consideration to the proposals in the following session.[2]

The Jewish Disabilities Bill

Another measure bound to arouse religious prejudices was Lord John Russell's bill for the removal of Jewish disabilities, the fourth such bill that he had introduced since 1847. The Jews were still excluded, even after the Catholic Emancipation Act of 1829, by the words in the Abjuration Oath 'on the true faith of a Christian'. Various bills were unsuccessfully introduced in the 'thirties to remove the remaining Jewish disabilities and in 1845 Peel's government passed a Jewish Disabilities Removal Act enabling Jews to hold municipal office. The election of Baron Lionel de Rothschild to parliament as Russell's colleague for the City of London in 1847 revived the issue of parliamentary emancipation since his inability to subscribe to the oaths prevented his taking his seat. Accordingly Russell, as Prime Minister, brought in a Jewish Disabilities Bill in the session of 1847–8, which after great debate passed through the House of Commons with the support of Peel, Gladstone, Bentinck and Disraeli, but was defeated in the

---

[1] *Hansard*, CXXIX, 512–33.

[2] *Ibid.*, CXXIX, 1207–14. No such bill was passed in 1854. Sir George Grey, an Erastian Whig, who succeeded Newcastle at the Colonial Office, had no sympathy for such legislation and refused to give it his support.

Lords.[1] Further measures introduced in 1849 and 1851 suffered a similar fate, but now, back in office and with the full support of a Peelite Prime Minister, Russell returned to the fray.

The bill was opposed vigorously at all stages by the same old gang of reactionaries (Inglis, Newdegate, Sibthorp and Co.), with the same old arguments, and pressed three times to divisions in large houses. On all three occasions in the Commons, however, the government was successful, with votes of 234 to 205, 263 to 213, and 288 to 230. One of the strongest speeches in support of the measure came from Sidney Herbert, while another Peelite, Lord Drumlanrig, distinguished himself in a short speech in which he explained how he had come to the conclusion that his former opposition to this reform was unsound and why he was now prepared to support it. Two other Peelites entered the debate, the third Sir Robert Peel, to defend his opposition to the bill, and Henry Fitzroy, to rebuke Peel for the slur he cast on the character of Baron Rothschild, while trying to prove that his opposition to the measure was not bigoted.[2]

On the other hand one junior Peelite office-holder, Lord A. Hervey, felt forced to vote against the government on the first reading, although he abstained from later divisions. Gladstone wrote to Aberdeen on his behalf saying that Hervey was the only member of the government who had '*suffered* on account of that question'.[3] Aberdeen in turn sought to placate Russell with a note in which he wrote:

With respect to Lord Alfred Hervey's vote last night, he mentioned to me three or four days ago how he was situated, and perhaps might have offered to resign; but it really did not occur to me as necessary to exact it. I was so late a convert, myself, that I felt it would be unreasonable to do so. Indeed, to say the truth, I had not the least notion of the Government being so united on the subject; for I think it was half formed before you were aware of the change that had taken place in my own case.[4]

To show his own good will Aberdeen offered to take charge himself of the bill in the Upper House, where the opposition was bound to be formidable. Four other Peelites opposed either the second or the third

[1] For the historical background see Ursula Henriques, *Religious toleration in England 1787–1833*, ch. VI, 'Jewish emancipation', pp. 175–205, and Cecil Roth, *A history of the Jews in England*, ch. XI, 'Emancipation, 1815–58', pp. 241–66.

[2] *Hansard*, CXXIV, 590–625; CXXV, 71–118, 166–72, 1225–91.

[3] Add. MS. 43070, fol. 298–9, 27 February 1853.

[4] PRO 30/22/10/H, fols. 2144–5, 25 February 1853.

reading of the bill, but none of them had any official connection with the government. Given the speeches of Fitzroy, Drumlanrig and Herbert, the opposition of these five scarcely reflects a serious rift between Peelites and Liberals. The third reading was passed in a large house on 15 April by a vote of 288 to 230.[1] The Irish Independents voted with the government, as did 32 Peelites[2] and some 10 Conservatives, including Disraeli and young Lord Stanley.[3]

The bill was again defeated in the House of Lords by the large vote of 164 to 115 despite strong arguments made in its defence by Aberdeen, Argyll, Brougham, the archbishop of Dublin and the bishop of St Davids. Lord Aberdeen explained that, although he had opposed such a bill five years ago, he had determined, before the advent of Derby's government, not to do so again, and had so informed his friends Gladstone and Newcastle. He said this to make it clear that the change had nothing to do with 'recent political combinations'. He suggested that the opposition to the bill, which he once shared, was surely the relic of an old prejudice with understandable historical roots, but he reminded his hearers that 'vengeance was not ours'.[4] Aberdeen told the queen that the government lost seven or eight votes by an early division after a languid and spiritless debate.[5]

Although the measure was yet another failure, it was still a step towards the final goal that would eventually be won, as were so many parliamentary battles, by the erosive tactic of unremitting attack over the years. Lord John would try again in 1854 and some day the opposition would cave in, as in the end it did in 1858 when a Tory government arranged the compromise that solved the problem.

Maynooth

Another religious issue that inevitably arose was the perennial one of Maynooth, on which the opposition forced not less than four divisions in the course of the session. At an early date the irrepressible

---

[1] *Hansard*, CXXV, 1287–91.

[2] See Appendix A. Six Peelites were absent from the vote. Of these G. F. Heneage and Lewis supported the second reading, but A'Court opposed it (*Hansard*, CXXIV, 622–5; CXXV, 118–22). Goulburn, Legh, Lockhart and Sir R. Peel voted against the third reading.

[3] The majority of independent Conservatives, once reckoned as potential Peelites, opposed the bill. See Appendix B.

[4] *Hansard*, CXXVI, 754–95. The vote included 46 proxies for and 68 proxies against the bill.

[5] R.A. A23, fol. 22, 29 April 1853.

Spooner precipitated a lengthy and fruitless debate by moving for a committee to consider the Maynooth Act. For two nights (22 and 23 February) all the old arguments were rehashed and the motion was finally defeated by 192 to 162. There were 26 Peelites and at least 13 Conservatives in the majority, but two Peelites, Wortley and Wickham, voted for the motion.[1] After a third night of debate a radical amendment to replace the proposed committee by one to consider ecclesiastical expenditure from public revenues was also defeated by a vote of 262 to 68, but in this case the administration was at odds with its Radical tail and supported by Tory votes.[2]

The whole debate was mainly an affair of backbenchers, with Sir John Young, the only minister to speak, repeating the well-known arguments in justification of the grant. The most interesting intervention came from Lord Stanley, who indicated his liberal tendencies by explaining why he felt he must oppose the motion. It may be noted that no member of the previous cabinet took part in the original division.

Spooner later raised the matter again by moving an amendment to a supply estimate for public buildings in Ireland to delete a small sum for the repair of Maynooth College. He had made similar amendments, he said, in 1848, 1849, 1850 and 1851, and since the majority against him had declined over these years from 71 to 2, 'encouraged by this evident progress of opinion in the House of Commons', he now tried again. Despite some support from Radicals, who opposed all religious endowments, he was defeated by a vote of 80 to 43.[3]

Later in April Lord Winchilsea proposed a motion in the House of Lords for a committee on Maynooth. The Prime Minister defeated this by moving an amendment for the appointment of a royal commission to look into the operation of Maynooth College. This may have seemed a concession to the anti-Maynooth sentiment, but in fact it was a device to clear the air by getting an investigation out of the political atmosphere of a parliamentary committee, whose sponsors really sought the abolition of the institution to be investigated. A royal commission would approach the work of investigation with no animus and indeed its findings might be welcome to the authorities of the College.[4] Lord Aberdeen wrote to Prince Albert with evident satisfaction to announce the success of his amendment over Lord Winchilsea's motion by a vote

[1] *Hansard*, CXXIV, 413–65, 487–523.   [2] *Ibid.* 889–938.
[3] *Ibid.* CXXVII, 398–404. The item was then passed with another division of 74 to 54 (*ibid.* 405–6).   [4] *Ibid.* CXXV, 1291–1348.

of 110 to 53 in which he noted that all the bishops had supported the government.[1]

Another display of religious animosity was seen on 10 May in the introduction of a private bill purporting to facilitate the recovery of personal liberty on the part of girls locked up in 'conventual establishments'. The debate saw the usual fight between Irish Catholics and Protestant extremists and indeed the first round was won by the latter, who secured permission to introduce the bill by a vote of 138 to 115. Lord John Russell, however, expressed his opposition in the debate on the second reading but refused to support a compromise amendment, which in effect, prevented further consideration of the bill.[2]

A similar impasse was reached in the case of a private member's bill that sought to reach a compromise settlement of the vexed problem of church rates. Although receiving ministerial support and the silent vote of Disraeli, it was defeated by a combination of Tories who opposed any change and Radicals who felt the proposals did not go far enough.[3]

An Irish crisis, June 1853

Further debate calculated to arouse religious emotions was precipitated on 31 May, this time by an Irish Catholic motion for a Select Committee to enquire into the ecclesiastical revenues of Ireland. This was opposed by Young and by Russell, who both saw it as a direct attack on the

[1] *Ab. Cor. 1852–5*, pp. 90–1, 18 April 1853. The five Commissioners were Lord Harrowby, who, Aberdeen told the queen, although a liberal-minded man, held 'very strong opinions in all Church matters', Dr Twiss, whom he described as 'the author of the best work published against Papal Aggression in 1850', Mr Langfield, a distinguished Irish Protestant lawyer, and two Roman Catholics, Chief Baron Pigot, 'an upright man, and although a conscientious Catholic by no means unfriendly to the introduction of improvement', and a Mr James O'Farrell, who although unknown to the Prime Minister, was well recommended (R.A. A23, fol. 48, 27 August 1853).

The commission submitted a painstakingly detailed report on 1 March 1855 but by that time the coalition government that appointed it had come to an end. See *P.P. 1854–5*, Readex microprint edition, XXII, 1–68.

[2] *Hansard*, CXXVII, 79–134; CXXVIII, 534–88, 678–80; CXXIX, 484–512. The better part of another evening was wasted over the consideration of the amendment, which proposed the appointment of a Select Committee to enquire into the necessity of any such regulation. Both Russell and Inglis, a sponsor of the original bill, objected to the amendment, which actually was not put to the vote before the session ended, although on 22 June the House had voted against keeping the original wording.

[3] *Hansard*, CXXVII, 567–646. Sir George Grey opposed the bill on the grounds that satisfactory compromises were being worked out locally and that the provisions of the proposed measure were too severe on non-Dissenters.

Established Church of Ireland. Russell alluded to the fact that some years ago he had failed to satisfy either party by proposing to allocate some of the revenues of the Irish Church for the purpose of public education. The possible alternative of endowing the Catholic Church in Ireland as the Presbyterian Church was in Scotland he rejected, because of the nature of that church and its government. His mode of expressing this opinion was unfortunate, but not untypical; in part he said:

It has been but too evident of late years, that the Roman Catholic Church—looking to its proceedings in foreign countries—looking to its proceedings in this country—looking to that Church, acting under the direction of its head, himself a foreign Sovereign, has aimed at political power; and, having aimed at political power, it appears to me to be at variance with a due attachment to the Crown of this country—with a due attachment to the general cause of liberty—with a due attachment to the duties that a subject of the State should perform towards the State.

It is true that he did add a sentence or two to the effect that he was not 'saying that this character belongs generally to the lay members of the Roman Catholic Church', but the damage was done. Bright rebuked Russell for his speech, but the motion was easily defeated by a vote of 260 to 98.[1] The matter, however, did not stop there.

The three Irish Catholic members of the government, Monsell, Keogh and Sadleir, immediately submitted letters of resignation, politely but firmly phrased. Monsell's letter observed that Russell's slur was not on individual members but on the Catholic Church itself and he noted that 'no other Minister expressed dissent'. Therefore these would go out as the opinions of the government and of such a government he could not remain a member.[2] Monsell, in a private covering letter professing great personal esteem for the Prime Minister to whom he avowed he owed 'every sacrifice that man can make except that of [his] personal honor', said he had been particularly happy to accept office under Aberdeen because of the latter's attitude towards the Ecclesiastical Titles Bill, but now Russell had revived the policy of that bill. Russell's words 'were received with vehement cheering in the House of Commons', Monsell wrote, '& will give as great satisfaction at Exeter Hall as they will give pain to every Catholic in the dominions'.

[1] *Hansard*, CXXVII, 862–955.
[2] Add. MS. 43250, fols. 131–3, Monsell to Aberdeen, 2 June 1853; similar letters were received from Keogh and Sadleir (fols. 135–40), indicating their genuine regret at the step they had to take.

He said that he did not think the government would lose by his resignation, for he thought he might serve it better out of than he did in office
and thus in a small way show his gratitude for the many favours he had
received.[1]

Russell in turn wrote Aberdeen rather a huffy letter regretting Monsell's resignation and saying that his own speech had been made on the
spur of the moment without any consultation, following a very
vehement speech from an Irish member, Lucas. Russell disclaimed any
imputation on the loyalty of the Roman Catholics, but stood by his
remarks on the system of the Roman Church as represented by its
clergy. Rather unconvincingly, he concluded by offering his own
resignation, writing: 'But I feel so much the disadvantage to you of the
loss of Mr. Monsell, and other Roman Catholic Members of your
Government, that I think you had better, as an alternative, allow me to
retire, and retain their services.'[2] Here one detects the basic dissatisfaction of Russell in Aberdeen's government, grasping for a means of
getting out of it, supposing, no doubt, that it could not survive without
him.

In reply Aberdeen brushed aside Russell's offer of resignation, but
entreated him to consider what might be done to salvage the situation
on the eve of Wood's introduction of the government's important India
Bill. He indicated that Newcastle, who had some influence with the
Catholic party, would see Monsell. Russell replied: 'The Duke of
Newcastle's influence with the Roman Catholic gentlemen is the best, if
not the only, chance. On reflection, I am struck with the inconsistency
of Keogh's claiming a privilege to deny my Church of its revenue, and
not allow me to say what I think of his.' He remained quite obdurate in
his opinions, which he said were those of all continental liberals.[3]

In the meantime Graham had urged Aberdeen to put off any announcement until an attempt had been made to parley. 'Events stride on
with such rapidity', he added with his typical penchant for gloomy
exaggeration, 'that the crisis of one day is obliterated by the catastrophe
of the next.'[4] The affair coincided with the cabinet crisis over the India
Bill[5] and alarming developments in the Eastern Question.[6]

A little later in the same day Graham, now less despondent, wrote

[1] *Ibid.* fols. 127–30.
[2] *Ab. Cor. 1852–5*, p. 129, 2 June 1853.
[3] *Ibid.* p. 131.
[4] *Ibid.* pp. 129–30, 2 June 1853; 'I have no more work left in me today', he added.
[5] See above, pp. 82–4. [6] See below, pp. 151–2.

again to suggest that Russell might be persuaded to say something 'to satisfy the wounded feelings of the friendly Catholic members'. He continued:

Lord John's secession from your Government at this juncture, as a Martyr to his strong Protestant convictions, would convulse the country, and would overthrow your Administration.

On the other hand, the secession of the Catholic Members, on account of Lord John's speech, would endanger our position and render it scarcely tenable.[1]

Lord Clarendon made a similar suggestion, proposing that as the head of the government Aberdeen should write to Monsell expressing his dissent from what Lord John had said and indicating Russell's regret that he had used language offensive to the Roman Catholics. 'This would save Lord John from retracting his opinion, which he would probably not do', Clarendon concluded.[2]

In the end the crisis was resolved along these lines. Aberdeen wrote a letter to Monsell, which was subsequently published in the press, informing him that 'while the vote on that occasion had the sanction of the Government, the reason for that vote given by Lord John Russell and the sentiments of which you complain, are not shared by me, nor by many of my colleagues'. He added that Lord John Russell wanted him to say that he 'did not impute want of loyalty to the Roman Catholics'.[3] Having humbled the author of the Ecclesiastical Titles Act, the Irish members consented to remain in the coalition, but the incident was not calculated to make Russell an easier colleague.

Education

No subject was given more attention by Lord Aberdeen when making his original statement on forming his administration nor by Lord John Russell in his outline of the government's legislative programme than

---

[1] *Ab. Cor. 1852–5*, pp. 132–3.   [2] *Ibid.* p. 133, 2 June 1853.

[3] Add. MS. 43250, fols. 141–2, copy of letter to Monsell 3 June 1852; similar letters were sent to Keogh and Sadleir. See also *Annual Register, 1853*, pp. 120–2, and Whyte, *Independent Irish party*, pp. 99–100.

A few weeks later a motion was introduced into the House of Lords demanding an investigation of alleged seditious utterances by Keogh, but it came to nothing. 'The House was very full, and great exertions had been made to secure a large attendance against the Government', Aberdeen told the queen; 'but Lord Derby was afraid to divide the House, but recommended that the motion should be withdrawn.' R.A. A23, fol. 35, 27 June 1853.

that of education. Since the late 1830s successive governments had accepted some state responsibility for education, despite the thorny religious difficulties involved, in the belief that here was at least a partial solution to the great 'condition of England' problem.[1] More recently increasing attention was being given to proposals for a national system of elementary education aided by local rates, as was signalised by the formation of the National Public School Association in Manchester in 1850. Nevertheless, differences between the various religious denominations and particularly between the secularists and those who believed in the need for religious education continued to be a bar to effective action. In 1853 Sir James Kay-Shuttleworth, the leading expert in the field, published a book entitled *Public education* in which he sought to find a compromise between the Voluntaryists and the more extreme churchmen, along lines already indicated by the Committee of Council.[2]

On 4 April Russell duly asked for leave to bring in a bill based on Kay-Shuttleworth's suggestions and drafted with his aid that in many ways foreshadowed the great Act of 1870. He thoroughly reviewed the whole history of public education, with which he himself had had so much to do. His long speech was full of useful statistics on the number of different kinds of schools with and without public support and the number of children attending them. While applauding the progress that had been made, Russell emphasised that there was much still to be done. The question was in what way the government could give the greatest help, for he had no doubt that this was a government responsibility. The difficulties with respect to religion were fully and dispassionately explored. The proposal to secularise education was firmly rejected. His main recommendation was that corporate towns should under certain conditions be empowered to set up school committees and to levy an education rate to assist certain approved schools, with a conscience clause to protect children attending denominational schools. The borough school committees were to come under the supervision of the Committee of Council on Education, which would provide for inspection of the assisted schools. He also announced that the government was considering making additional building grants in some poor places where other money was not available.[3] Turning to the subject of higher

[1] J. W. Adamson, *English education 1789–1902*, p. 133.
[2] Frank Smith, *Life and works of Sir James Kay-Shuttleworth*, pp. 227–46; C. Birchenough, *History of elementary education in England and Wales from 1800 to the present*, pp. 103–6.
[3] See *P.P. 1852–3*, III, 235–46, for the text of the bill.

education he discussed the reports of the royal commissions on Oxford and Cambridge and their recommendations. He invited the universities to make proposals as to their implementation but promised that, if these were not forthcoming or not satisfactory, then the government would make its own proposals to parliament. He concluded his speech with a moving appeal, imploring the House to pay the most earnest attention to all these subjects and begging them 'to keep in view these great objects upon which the future happiness and welfare of this country must depend'.[1]

The debate that followed was mild and brief; Sir Robert Inglis said 'he must presume, from the state of the benches, that there was a silent contract that there should be no debate on the present occasion'. Inglis, himself, in a short speech made it clear he could accept none of Russell's proposals.[2] Several Radicals made minor criticisms while J. B. Blackett, a former tutor of Merton, regretted the government did not take immediate and resolute action with regard to university reform and that the royal commissions had been limited to the older universities, since he understood that the University of Durham 'had succeeded in a comparatively short period in attaining the same perfection of mismanagement which distinguished Oxford and Cambridge'.[3]

Gladstone was the only other minister to join in the discussion,[4] but he did so primarily as member for Oxford, disputing Blackett's strictures, yet taking the part of his ministerial colleague, Russell, against that of his fellow representative, Inglis. Reform must be undertaken, but patience must be exercised in the process. In part he said:

I hold that Parliament must, in the last resort, interfere to control, to regulate, and to manage the revenues of any public body. But before doing so, you must give them full time to produce these salutary changes themselves. These bodies are not bodies that are asleep, nor have they been asleep. They have done much, though it is true that much remains for them to do. But is there not also much for the House of Commons to do, though many reforms have been accomplished by this House in the course of the present century?[5]

Yet despite this auspicious beginning the Education Bill was dropped without explanation. Its first reading was passed without debate a few days later,[6] but no more was heard of it for the rest of the session. Kay-

---

[1] *Hansard*, cxxv, 549.
[2] *Ibid.* 559–61.
[3] *Ibid.* 568–73. The matter of university reform was taken up the following year. See below, pp. 332–44.
[4] *Ibid.* 573–9.
[5] *Ibid.* 577.
[6] *Ibid.* 722, 7 April.

Shuttleworth's biographer attributes the failure to the lukewarmness of the government,[1] and undoubtedly the exigencies of time and the poor prospects for success affected the cabinet's decision.[2] Evidence on the latter point is to be found in a comment by Milner Gibson on Russell's speech. While 'anxious that something should be done for education', he regretted that the government had not waited to hear the report of a committee of the House presently inquiring into the very matter of supporting denominational schools from local rates. 'He very much doubted whether two-thirds of a town council would be found to agree to teach all forms of religion in their respective towns, and to support such teaching out of the rates.'[3] This was undoubtedly the explanation and it was not the first or the last time that the cause of public education in England had suffered in the name of religion. All was not lost, however, for rural schools benefited from the attempt, since to balance the anticipated new rate for town schools a minute of the Committee of Council authorised a new capitation grant of 4s. 5d. a head for those in the country. This grant, which was made independent of local effort, increased the education vote in 1853 by more than one-half and in 1856 it was extended to all schools.[4] In addition to this increased estimate of £260,000 for Great Britain and £182,073 for Ireland there was a grant of £44,476 for the newly instituted Department of Science and Art set up in South Kensington. These estimates went through virtually without debate except for the objections of one member to the expenditure of £2,006 for professors at Oxford and Cambridge.[5]

Merchant shipping, pilotage and naval volunteers

The government had more success with two useful measures entrusted to Cardwell at the Board of Trade, a Pilotage Bill and a Merchant Shipping Law Amendment Bill. Cardwell's initial speech on 7 March, in which he outlined the background and general intentions of the government in this area, was well received on both sides of the House.[6]

---

[1] Smith, *Kay-Shuttleworth*, p. 246.
[2] At any rate the decision to abandon it was not taken until late in the session, for on 9 July Gladstone addressed a note to Russell which gives a clue as to its fate. 'Hopes have been audibly expressed today', he wrote, 'that if the Education Bill cannot go on you may be inclined to waive the second reading.' PRO 30/22/11/A, 9 July 1853.
[3] *Hansard*, cxxv, 552–3.
[4] Smith, *Kay-Shuttleworth*, p. 246; Birchenough, *Elementary education*, p. 106.
[5] *Hansard*, cxxvii, 417; Adamson, *English education*, p. 153.
[6] *Hansard*, cxxiv, 1227–67.

113

His proposals, which he modestly called unambitious, were the result of no political pressures; made in 'a time of unprecedented prosperity', he was hopeful that they would 'result in much practical good'. 'You are asked', he said, 'to take another step in the course begun by Huskisson, and continued by Peel; and in the name of British enterprise we defy competition, from whatever quarter it may come, believing, sincerely believing, that in proportion as you retain your place in the vanguard of commercial freedom, in that same proportion will you maintain the pre-eminence which you have earned both in mercantile prosperity and maritime power.'[1] This was the genuine voice of Peelism in action. The Pilotage Bill provided for the union of the Pilots of Trinity House and the Cinque Ports and considerably increased the overall control of the Board of Trade in the regulation of pilot services and dues. It generally aimed at providing a more economic system of pilotage and in order to secure the necessary information for further regulation in other parts of the country it required all pilots to make regular returns of their earnings and all pilotage authorities 'to make full returns to the Board of Trade of various particulars connected with Pilotage'.[2] On the motion to go into committee some opposition developed from certain vested interests, who sought a Special Committee, but a motion to this effect was defeated by 219–83.[3] The bill passed with no further opposition.[4]

The Merchant Shipping Law Amendment Bill was a rather wider measure, but with the same general purpose to bring the law up to date, to assist shipowners and increase the controlling authority of the Board of Trade where necessary. The bill laid down regulations with respect to the collection of light dues and other shipping dues (a long-standing grievance with the shipowners) and provided for the supervision and inspection of lighthouses by the Board of Trade. Other clauses dealt with desertion, contracts with Lascar seamen, volunteering into the navy, the law of salvage, and the abandonment of the old requirement that a proportion of the crew of all British ships should be British.

[1] Ibid. 1250. The debate on the second reading was very brief, in contrast to many longer discussions on less important topics. It is interesting to note that a dozen members expressed views within the compass of two or three pages of Hansard (ibid. CXXV, 579–85). See further A. B. Erickson, Edward T. Cardwell: Peelite (Trans. Am. Phil. Soc., new series, vol. 49, part 2, Philadelphia, 1959), pp. 16–17, who indicates that the Act was aimed at freeing the merchant marine from the outdated 'incubus of two ancient corporations'.

[2] Statutes, 1852–3, ch. 129, pp. 869–75.   [3] Hansard, CXXVI, 218–30.

[4] One amendment offered in the Lords was easily disposed of. Ibid. CXXIX, 1710–11.

Debate concentrated on these last two provisions, which were clearly in the tradition of the 'new commercial system' of free trade. Abandoning the requirement about the employment of British sailors was only the natural sequel to the repeal of the Navigation Acts. In respect to salvage, claims on the part of the Admiralty were now to be restricted to claims for personal services and no charge was to be made for wear and tear on naval ships involved in salvage operations.[1]

On the question of manning, Labouchere, former Whig President of the Board of Trade, expressed his opposition to the abandonment of the old policy. 'In objecting to the proposed change, he was actuated by no party feeling', *Hansard* reported him as saying. 'Ever since the formation of the present Government, he had given it his humble support, and he hoped to be able to continue so to do; but the question was of such vast importance that he felt bound to express his apprehension on the subject, even at the risk of appearing to act in opposition.'[2] In the end, however, the proposed amendment was rejected by 142 to 36 and the clause agreed to.[3]

The other measure of some importance affecting British seamen was a Naval Coast Volunteer Bill, which was passed late in the session without opposition. It provided for the setting up of a naval militia on terms very similar to the existing military militia and was no doubt inspired by the worsening foreign situation. Sir James Graham, in speaking briefly on the bill in committee, said that it was proposed to raise a volunteer force of 10,000 men whose period of training would be limited to 28 days a year, and who would serve at naval rates of pay, plus a bounty of £6.[4]

Home Office reforms

Lord Palmerston at the Home Office was also responsible for a number of useful measures that were enacted with little opposition.[5] A Factory Act was passed late in the session which put an end to the relay system

---

[1] *Statutes, 1852–3*, ch. 131; *Hansard*, CXXVIII, 1218–31; CXXIX, 101–25, 275–91, 1118–35. See also Erickson, *Cardwell*, pp. 17–18.

[2] *Hansard*, CXXVIII, 1228–9. This was not the first time that Labouchere had made trouble, for only a few days earlier Cardwell had addressed a note to Gladstone appealing to him to come and help them in committee where Labouchere was pressing them hard (Add. MS. 44118, fol. 57, 1 July 1853).   [3] *Hansard*, CXXIX, 101–25.

[4] *Ibid.* 1109–11. See also Erickson, *Graham*, pp. 332–3.

[5] See David Roberts, *Victorian origins of the British welfare state*, pp. 144–5, and his 'Lord Palmerston at the Home Office', *The Historian*, XXI (1958–9), 63–81.

by prohibiting the employment of children under twelve between six p.m. and six a.m.[1] The matter was first brought to the attention of the House by Cobbett, Feilden and Manners, who on 5 July asked permission to bring in a bill to ensure the better working of the Ten Hour Act of 1847. Lord Palmerston made no objection, but indicated his intention of bringing in a government bill. As a result the private bill was dropped and the government bill passed without debate, although, on the initial motion of Cobbett and Feilden, two former Whig ministers, Sir George Grey and Labouchere, expressed their opposition to the matter being opened up again.[2] Labouchere said that he joined with Grey in regretting that the Home Secretary had failed to resist the principle of curtailing the hours of adult labour 'under the plea of affording protection to others'.[3] Russell sought to bridge the gap between the present and the former Whig Home Secretaries by disclaiming any intention to impose restrictions on adult labour,[4] but this in fact was the effect of the Act of 1853.

Palmerston also tackled the perennial problem of sewage disposal, hoping, he said, to make the Thames 'as clear as the waters of Bandusia';[5] but he reckoned without the inveterate opposition of local ratepayers. A Greater London Drainage Bill never got past a Select Committee,[6] while in a bill to continue the Board of Sewers Commissioners, damned by the representatives of metropolitan ratepayers, he was forced to accept a limit of £300,000 on the borrowing powers of the commissioners. This was, however, some improvement over the previous law.[7]

Other Acts were passed governing the licensing and fares of hackney coaches in London,[8] providing for the licensing and regulation of common lodging houses,[9] extending and making compulsory provisions for vaccination,[10] for the suppression of betting houses[11] and providing for the abatement of smoke nuisance in London. In resisting an attempt to thwart the last mentioned measure Palmerston sounded quite the Radical when he said:

[1] Statutes, 1852–3, ch. 104.   [2] Hansard, CXXVIII, 1251–90.
[3] Ibid. 1285–6.
[4] Ibid. 1288. According to B. L. Hutchins and A. Harrison, A history of factory legislation, p. 111, 'this Act had the desired result of establishing by law a uniform working day, and the masters were now no longer able to work their mills for fifteen hours a day'.
[5] Hansard, CXXIX, 1587.
[6] Ibid. CXXIV, 1332–40.   [7] Ibid. CXXIX, 1571–91.
[8] Statutes, 1852–3, ch. 33.   [9] Ibid. ch. 41.
[10] Ibid. ch. 100.   [11] Ibid. ch. 119.

If ever there was a case in which, he would not say the interests, but the prejudices, of the few were opposed to the interests of the many, this was such a case. Here were a few, perhaps 100 gentlemen, connected with these different furnaces in London, who wished to make 2,000,000 of their fellow-inhabitants swallow the smoke which they could not themselves consume, and who thereby helped to deface all our architectural monuments, and to impose the greatest inconvenience and injury upon the lower class. Here were the prejudices and ignorance, the affected ignorance, of a small combination of men, set up against the material interest, the physical enjoyment, the health and comfort of upwards of 2,000,000 of their fellow-men. He would not believe that Parliament would back these smoke-producing monopolists, and he was ready, therefore, with great confidence to go to a division.[1]

He was sustained in a small House by a vote of 66 to 12.[2] Had Palmerston directed all his great abilities to Home instead of Foreign Affairs, his own reputation might have been the greater today and the record of mid-Victorian social reform more substantial.

Finally parliament was prorogued on 20 August, the same day on which the India Bill received royal assent.[3] In the queen's speech the government congratulated itself in particular on this measure, as well as on the various budget provisions and the Charitable Trusts Act. It also rejoiced at the conclusion of the wars on the frontiers of the Cape and in Burma and alluded to the efforts that were being made through the conference at Vienna to settle the differences between Russia and Turkey.[4] Before turning to these sombre events we shall attempt to make a more objective and detailed assessment of the coalition's first session than one might expect to find in a queen's speech.

[1] *Hansard*, CXXIX, 1496.   [2] *Ibid.* 1497.   [3] *Ibid.* 1823.
[4] *Ibid.* 1324–7. Following the conclusion of the Kafir War, the 1850 Constitution of Cape Colony was promulgated and the independence of the Orange Free State recognised.

6

THE COALITION TRIUMPHANT: AN
ASSESSMENT OF THE FIRST SESSION

Government strength and opposition weakness

Although as usual much time had been wasted in pointless debate on old questions, the legislative achievement of 1853 was a respectable one. In all, 136 Public Acts of parliament had been passed, a few of them initiated by the previous administration, as compared with 88 Public Acts in the short session of 1852.[1] Every year, of course, the greater part of the legislation is routine and not debated, but contemporaries attached importance to a number of the Acts of the 1853 session, especially those giving effect to the budget proposals. The biggest disappointments were the defeat of the Jewish Disabilities Bill in the Lords, the shelving of the Education Bill and the killing of the Registration of Assurances Bill. Consideration had also been promised to several Irish Land Bills that failed to survive.

Because of the budget innovations an abnormal amount of the time of the House of Commons—over thirty per cent—was given to the consideration of fiscal matters. About thirteen per cent was devoted to Indian affairs, mainly the India Bill, about ten per cent to Irish questions, about seven per cent to legal reforms, about five per cent to colonial matters, and another five per cent to election petitions and other electoral problems, about three per cent each to foreign affairs, to the Jewish Disabilities Bill, to the Pilotage and Merchant Shipping Bills and allied matters, and to religious questions in England.[2] On the whole, Whig and Peelite ministers shared the speaking burdens fairly evenly. Because of the extraordinary amount of attention devoted to fiscal matters Gladstone spoke far more than any other minister in either House, filling over 400 columns of *Hansard*, while Russell as leader of the House came next with some 286 columns.[3] Speaking burdens in the

[1] *Statutes, 1852–3.*,
[2] My percentages are based on a rough calculation of columns of *Hansard*.
[3] Palmerston was third (with about 124 columns), followed by Wood (109 columns), Graham (74 columns), Herbert (35 columns) and Molesworth (30 columns).

Lords were, of course, lighter, but it was a new experience for Aberdeen, usually taciturn, to have to take the lead, filling 105 columns, followed closely by the Lord Chancellor, responsible for the various legal bills, with 84 columns.[1] Of those outside the cabinet the law officers, Bethell and Cockburn, and Cardwell, President of the Board of Trade, spoke more than some cabinet ministers.[2] For a short time during the session following the death of Russell's mother, Palmerston substituted for him as House leader, and, according to Greville,[3] greatly pleased the House, who found him personally more acceptable than Russell.

Everyone was agreed that Gladstone had emerged as the strong man of the coalition, standing head and shoulders over his own contemporaries. Unexhausted by his labours in the fiscal field, he began to turn his restless, creative mind to other projects, a scheme for a decimal currency,[4] a project to bring the railways 'more immediately under the control of the Government',[5] university reform and civil service reform. These last two reforms in particular were engaging his mind in anticipation of the next session. Meanwhile, Russell kept his ideas on parliamentary reform to himself. Despite the darkening foreign sky, following the prorogation of parliament he went off with his family to Roseneath on the Firth of Clyde, loaned him by the duke of Argyll, where he proceeded to draw up his proposals. On this particular subject he could expect more sympathy from his Peelite colleagues, Aberdeen, Graham and Newcastle, than from Whigs such as Lansdowne and Palmerston,[6] but it remained to be seen whether Russell would stay in the cabinet long enough to bring in a Reform Bill.

It may be asked why in its first year the coalition survived so much

[1] Newcastle filled 71 columns, Granville 56 columns, Clarendon 34 columns, Argyll 29 columns, and Lansdowne was almost silent with 9 columns. Argyll's contributions were rather less than might have been expected, since in appointing him Aberdeen looked to his debating ability to strengthen the government in the Lords. He sometimes ran into trouble in crossing swords with some of the veteran members of that House. See *Greville Memoirs*, VI, 407.

[2] With 90, 55 and 54 columns respectively.

[3] *Greville Memoirs*, VI, 409–10.

[4] Add. MS. 44742, fols. 254–5, memo, n.d.; Add. MS. 44291, fol. 61, from Russell, 19 August 1853.

[5] *Ab. Cor. 1852–5*, pp. 66–7. 'This would be effected by a sort of joint ownership,' Aberdeen told the queen, 'but as the project is only in its infancy, it will require more communication with the Board of Trade, as well as with the Directors of the leading companies, before any decided opinion can be formed.'

[6] See Add. MS. 44262, fols. 125–30, Newcastle to Gladstone, 26 August 1852, and correspondence between Aberdeen and Graham in Graham papers and *Ab. Cor.*

more successfully than had been anticipated. This was undoubtedly to be explained in part by the solidarity shown by the cabinet, whose members worked together with much greater cordiality and understanding than had been expected. As we have seen, cabinet divisions, when they appeared, were never on party lines and were generally smoothed over with tact and good will, for which Aberdeen was largely responsible. Russell created difficulties from time to time, but on such occasions he never enlisted the sympathies of the majority of his old colleagues.

Charles Greville, basing his remarks on conversations with Graham, Granville and Clarendon, in his entries for 1853 frequently noted these good relations. 'The Cabinet is going on in the greatest harmony', he wrote on 30 May, 'and the men who were up to the time of its formation strangers have taken to each other prodigiously.'[1] On another occasion, recording a conversation with Graham, he wrote: 'Never was a Government so united and harmonious, and he [Graham] thinks their having been so divided in opinion on many subjects heretofore contributes to their harmony, as it makes them mutually tolerant and begets a spirit of concession and compromise.'[2]

Of the individual Ministers he commented:

Aberdeen unfortunately wants the qualities which made Lord Lansdowne so good a Leader, and is rather deficient in tact and temper in the H. of Lords... but in spite of these defects he has not done ill even there, and in the Cabinet he is both liked and respected, being honest, straightforward, and firm, very fair, candid, and unassuming. Granville tells me that of the whole Cabinet he thinks Aberdeen has the most pluck, Gladstone a great deal, and Graham the one who has least. He speaks very well of Molesworth, sensible, courageous, and conciliatory, but quite independent and plain-spoken in his opinion.[3]

In Graham's view (expressed to Greville) 'Clarendon was doing admirably'. Palmerston, he thought, was 'much changed and more feeble, his energy much less, and his best days gone by'! He expressed his regrets at Russell remaining without office, and thought that it impaired his influence. Discussing the question of a future leader, he rejected Greville's suggestion of Gladstone, saying 'it would not do'. He favoured Russell, but recognised the difficulties.[4]

[1] *Greville Memoirs*, VI, 425.
[2] *Ibid.* p. 423.   [3] *Ibid.* p. 425.
[4] *Ibid.* p. 423. Palmerston, it may be remarked, was still hale and hearty when Graham was laid to his final rest.

Outside the cabinet, among those whose way to higher office was blocked by the coalition, the relationships were probably less happy. For instance, a year later Granville met Cardwell on holiday at Carlsbad and wrote his impressions to Herbert:

I certainly never had an idea of what a Peelite was until I met Cardwell. He is much discontented with the present state of things, and his simple remedy seems to be to get rid of everybody in office except you, Newcastle, Gladstone, Lord Aberdeen and, perhaps, Graham.

Granville went on to ask: 'Is there much of this sort of old party feeling among the Government people who are not in the Cabinet?'[1] It may be presumed that the displaced Whigs held similar views.

In looking for an answer to the riddle of the government's surprising strength in its first year of office, obviously a very big factor was to be found in the disunity of the opposition following the collapse of Derby's government. Even before the opening of the session rumours were spreading about the unpopularity of Disraeli among his own followers, a handicap with which he had to put up for much of his long career as a leader. 'The principal occupation of the Derbyites at present is, I am informed,' Cornewall Lewis wrote to Graham, 'to vent maledictions agt Dizzy. Everybody disowns his budget & they complain of his first disgracing them & then turning them out.'[2] Nor did Disraeli make himself more popular in these quarters by flirting with the Manchester School and the ultras of the Irish Brigade. As Graham said to Aberdeen: 'This looks like Desperation.'[3] When Tom Baring expressed his disgust at Disraeli's speech on relations with France at the beginning of the session, Greville commented: 'It does not look as if the connexion between Dis. and the party could go on long. Their dread and distrust of him and his contempt of them render it difficult if not impossible.'[4]

During the session Disraeli's energies were largely absorbed in attacking the government from outside Westminster, by the launching of a new party weekly, *The Press*, for which he wrote anonymously, but frequently, at this period. It is doubtful whether it was worth the effort, for its circulation was only a few thousand and it was abandoned a few

---

[1] Stanmore, *Herbert*, I, 173.
[2] Graham Papers, Lewis to Graham, 4 January 1853.
[3] Add. MS. 43191, fols. 22–3, Graham to Aberdeen, 14 February 1853; cf. Monypenny and Buckle, *Disraeli*, I, 1328.
[4] *Greville Memoirs*, VI, 404. Cf above, pp. 56–7.

years later, but, as Buckle observes, it did outlast the coalition to oppose which it was founded.[1]

According to Greville the support of many opposition members for Gladstone's budget 'filled the Derbyites with rage and despair', and nothing could 'exceed their depression and their abuse of the Budget and its authors'.[2] 'What vexes and provokes them so much', he added, 'is the ascendancy and triumph of the Peelites.' The India Bill filled their cup to overflowing. Derby warned Disraeli against the amendment proposed by his own son in the Commons, saying that many of the party were restive and would not accept it. His letter to Disraeli on this occasion must be one of the sharpest ever written by an English party leader to his chief lieutenant. He told Disraeli that many of the party were dissatisfied because of 'a supposed understanding, and to a certain extent combination, between yourself and the Manchester School'. There was also suspicion of Disraeli's friendliness with the ex-Brigadier, Keogh, against whom he failed to protect the Derbyite Naas. Derby continued:

I have also heard strong comments on the fact of your having left the House the other night just before the division on the ballot, and upon your absence from any of the divisions or discussions which have taken place on the succession duty.

In short, I cannot conceal it from you that there is reported to me a growing fear, and the Government Press does its utmost to keep up the opinion, that you are gradually withdrawing yourself more and more from the Conservative portion of our supporters, and seeking alliances in quarters with which neither they nor I can recognize any bond of union.[3]

It may be noted that Disraeli's participation in debate after his India speech was very limited for the rest of the session. Indeed the India speech was his only major effort after the first week in May. 'His absence, however—& silence for the last few weeks,' Lewis wrote to Graham towards the end of August, 'will, after his former pugnacious & censorious habits, be taken by the public as indicating a consciousness of defeat.'[4]

---

[1] See Monypenny and Buckle, *Disraeli*, I, book III, ch. XIV.
[2] *Greville Memoirs*, VI, 421.   [3] Monypenny and Buckle, *Disraeli*, I, 1327–8.
[4] Graham Papers, 23 August 1853. Lewis went on: 'The idea of his forming a new party is, in my opinion, an absurdity—a party can only be formed by some strong interest or opinion—or by great personal popularity & qualities which inspire confidence. Disraeli has neither the one nor the other to trade upon. Nobody can say what his opinions are —& few believe he has any.'

The revelations of extensive corruption in the general election of
1852, which continued to come to light throughout the session on the
investigation of election petitions, were yet another factor affecting the
morale of the Derbyites. It is true that neither party had clean hands in
this respect and, as *The Times* said, the Carlton and the Reform Clubs
could scarcely throw stones at each other.[1] Indeed, according to this
authority, at no time since the Reform Act had electoral corruption
been so widespread. Following the election of 1852 there were a total of
109 election petitions[2] some of which were not settled until 1854. In all,
24 elections were declared void in England and one in Ireland. Ten of
these seats were held by Liberals and 15 by Conservatives.[3] Indeed, *The
Times* went so far as to assert:

With some few happy exceptions, every member of the Lower House knows
that, since last July, he has paid to somebody, on account of his election, a sum
very much larger than his legal expenses could possibly amount to. Indeed, he
has not ventured to ask what those legal expenses are. He shuts his eyes to the
expenditure as much as the miserable creatures who confess in the evidence
before us that they presented themselves at a bedroom door backwards, with
their hands behind them and received £2 without seeing the donor.[4]

The Times reckoned that there were not sixty members (out of 654)
who had not spent money in this way. On the whole the revelations of
the election committees seem to have reflected worse on the late
government and particularly upon Major Beresford, its Secretary at
War.[5] Some of the agents of the Carlton Club, such as a certain Mr Frail,
were becoming notorious by-words bandied about with great glee on
Liberal and Peelite platforms.[6] More light was thrown on the irregulari-
ties of the Derby government by the report of the 'Stafford Committee'[7]
in May, about which Greville wrote:

This affair has done great harm to them [the Derbyites] as a party, and served
to make them more odious and contemptible than they were before. They

[1] 9 March 1853.   [2] *Ibid.*
[3] *Return of members of parliament*, part II (1878), pp. 413–30. There were no elections
voided in Wales or Scotland.
[4] *The Times*, 10 March 1853.   [5] See *The Times*, 23 December 1852.
[6] See *The Times*, 3 January 1853, account of Graham's by-election address.
[7] See *P.P. 1852-3*, XXV, 'Report of the select committee on dockyard appointments',
23 May 1853, pp. 1–14 (appendices, pp. 15–529), which revealed the blatant misuse of
patronage for political purposes by Augustus Stafford, Secretary of the Admiralty
Board in the Derby administration.

are now irretrievably defeated, and although they may give much trouble and throw difficulties and obstructions in the way of the Government, it is all they can do. Every day adds to the strength and consistency of the Government, both from their gaining favour and acquiring influence in the country, and from the ruin in which the Tory party is involved, and the total impossibility of their rallying again so as to form another Government. This latter consideration has already produced the adhesion of some moderate and sensible men who take a dispassionate view of affairs and who wish for a strong and efficient Government, and it will produce still greater effects of the same kind.[1]

Graham confirmed Greville in these views a few days later. He 'considered Derby and the Tories irretrievably ruined, their characters so damaged by Stafford's committee and other incidents'.[2]

Analysis of the division lists indicates that there were over one hundred Derbyites who supported the government against the opposition leadership at least once, and fifty-eight or more who supported it more than once. In addition there was a hard core of forty-four Peelites, who regularly supported the government[3] and who now appeared lost to the Conservative party. On the other hand there were some thirty Irish Independents (Brigadiers), who would oppose the government on any issue where they thought Irish interests were being threatened. On other issues, however, most of these Irish members were quite ready to support a government led by Lord Aberdeen.

The Radical wing of the Liberal party was another uncertain factor in estimating the strength of the coalition government, for they were quite undependable on issues where their views went beyond those of the government. For this reason, as Russell told Aberdeen, the government was always in danger of defeat on minor questions.[4] In all, the government suffered seven defeats in the Commons in the course of the session,

---

[1] *Greville Memoirs*, VI, 422–3. He also made the interesting comment that Derby might have had the Peelites 'if he would have chosen to ally himself with them instead of with Disraeli; the latter had been the cause of the ruin of the party, and Derby had now the mortification of seeing his son devoted to him' (*ibid.* p. 424).

[2] *Ibid.* pp. 423–4.

[3] See Appendix A. Six had come in at by-elections since the general election, namely Lord Norreys, 3 December, H. A. Bruce, 16 December, E. Cardwell, 4 January, R. J. Phillimore, 26 February, T. Greene, 18 April, Roundell Palmer, 2 June, but one Peelite, C. B. Wall, died during the autumn recess and was replaced by a Liberal. Some of the Liberal Conservatives, such as Sir J. Owen, gave such frequent support to the coalition that they should perhaps be considered as Peelites, despite their support of the Disraeli budget. Unfortunately there is no indication on which side of the House they sat. See Appendix B for the voting records of thirty-six such independent Conservatives.

[4] Add. MS. 43067, fols. 9–10, 27 April 1853.

three of them in the week preceding the introduction of the budget. The first of these was not a party affair, but, in the view of *The Times*, an annual farce of no real significance. It occurred on 10 March on a motion introduced by Lord Robert Grosvenor, himself a Whig, to bring in a bill to repeal the solicitors' annual certificate duty.[1]

The defeats on the newspaper advertisement duty, of 15 April and 1 July, we have already noted, as well as on the salt clause amendment in the India Bill (28 July) and on the motion for leave to facilitate the recovery of personal liberty (10 May). Defeats were also sustained on a non-sectarian motion regarding Kilmainham hospital, pressed by the Irish Brigade, and on an opposition motion with regard to the Clithero election, supported by the Radicals, both on 12 April.[2]

Fortunately for the government, on no important issue were a majority of Derbyites, Radicals and Irish Brigade prepared to vote together, and so the coalition survived with no great difficulty, despite its lack of a clear majority in the House of Commons. That it was stronger than the Derby government may be seen in the greater amount of legislation that it was able to carry, for it will be remembered that the Peelites kept Derby in office on sufferance throughout the session of 1852 on the understanding that he would confine himself to essential measures prior to dissolution.

The queen and her ministers

In any assessment of the first session of the Aberdeen coalition a word should be said about the Prime Minister's exceptionally good relations with the Court.[3] Lord Aberdeen kept the queen fully informed of cabinet discussions by a series of memoranda and letters,[4] and she and Prince Albert never hesitated to present to him their views, which were always courteously received and listened to. In her correspondence with him the queen openly showed her partiality for his government, as for instance when she wrote on 4 May: 'The Queen always felt sure that *so* good a cause as that of the present Government—and such uprightness

[1] *The Times*, 11 March 1853. Two Peelites, H. Herbert and Sir J. Hogg, deserted the government on this occasion, but several Derbyites opposed the motion.
[2] *Hansard*, cxxv, 1074 and 1032.
[3] Graham told Greville that the queen was 'extremely attached to Aberdeen, more than to any Minister she had ever had'. *Greville Memoirs*, VI, 417.
[4] See Add. MS. 43046, but it may be presumed that the copies are not complete. The originals are in the Royal Archives at Windsor Castle.

and earnestness of purpose—*must* triumph.'[1] As always, however, she was watchful of what she considered to be her rights, as when Sir William Molesworth made an announcement with respect to the opening of Kew Gardens on Sunday. 'This ought not to have been done without the Queen's pleasure having been taken upon it,' she wrote to Aberdeen in an otherwise friendly letter, 'and, if granted, should have been announced as a favour conceded by the Crown, and not by a Department of Government.'[2]

On several occasions the prince advanced his views to the Prime Minister over his own name and when the queen was prevented from attending to her normal duties, in the spring by the birth of a son, and in July by an attack of measles, he was always there to look after her business.[3] In August, Aberdeen was anxious to have the queen prorogue parliament in person, but she begged off without difficulty, pleading that after the recent illnesses in the family she did not want the trouble of a special journey from Osborne prior to her impending state visit to Ireland.[4] It is of significance that one of the few such visits of her reign occurred during the Aberdeen ministry and from her account it was a great success. After it was over, however, one detects a sigh of relief in a note to her Scottish Prime Minister which she began: 'Arrived safely in *dear* Scotland.'[5]

The queen's good opinion of Aberdeen was in contrast to her dislike of both Russell and Palmerston. Indeed, she even neglected to answer Russell's letters written in his capacity as Leader of the House, until Aberdeen, at Clarendon's prompting, suggested she do so.[6] In September, Russell greatly annoyed the queen by excusing himself from attending her at Balmoral, because the dates she suggested were not convenient. In Russell's view, expressed frankly to Aberdeen, there was in fact 'no need for a Minister now a days at Balmoral, more than at Osborne or Windsor Castle'.[7] Aberdeen was 'disposed to agree', but thought the queen might have an opinion of her own.[8] At any event he

---

[1] *Ab. Cor. 1852–5*, p. 100. And again on 22 April regarding a government success in the House of Lords she writes: 'Altogether, thank God! the aspect of affairs is very cheering' (*ibid.* p. 94). [2] *Ibid.* pp. 110–11.

[3] *Ibid.* pp. 52–5, 172, Prince Albert to Lord Aberdeen: 'The Press rules the world in these days, and, as it decided yesterday that the Queen *should* have the measles, she got them accordingly yesterday afternoon.'

[4] *Ibid.* pp. 182–4, 5 August 1853.

[5] *Ibid.* pp. 203–6, 2, 4 and 5 September 1853.   [6] Maxwell, *Clarendon*, II, 11.

[7] Add. MS. 43067, fols. 146–7, 25 September 1853.

[8] *Ibid.* fol. 149, 26 September 1853 (copy).

had to turn from weightier affairs that kept him in London to arrange a suitable series of ministers to be in attendance; first Lord Granville, whom the queen found 'a most agreeable companion',[1] then Russell, who failed to go, then Palmerston, whom the queen took at Aberdeen's urging but on sufferance, then Graham, who had to cut short an official visit in Ireland but never questioned the inconvenience, and finally Newcastle, despite the growing international tension that forced Aberdeen to advise the queen to cut her holiday short.[2] When the queen showed some reluctance to invite Palmerston, Aberdeen pressed the political importance of her doing so:

The situation of Lord Palmerston is peculiar [he wrote]. Unless he should continue to be a cordial Member of Your Majesty's Government, he may very easily become the leader of the Opposition. Lord Aberdeen is, at this moment, ignorant of his views, and intentions. He has more than once, recently, been thwarted in his endeavour to press a warlike policy upon the Cabinet; and it has been reported to Lord Aberdeen, that he has expressed himself in terms of great hostility. This cannot, perhaps, be avoided, and is only the result of taking different views of the public interest; but it is very essential that Lord Palmerston should have no personal, or private, cause of complaint against Lord Aberdeen.[3]

Despite the inconvenience entailed in cutting short his Irish journey Graham appeared to enjoy the Balmoral visit, perhaps in part because in Aberdeen's absence he went there as the Prime Minister's private envoy, to represent to the queen and her husband the state of the cabinet. He and Aberdeen had for some time been discussing the future of the government. They had been aware of Russell's restlessness, and Aberdeen had intended, when the diplomatic skies appeared to clear earlier in the summer, to make way for Lord John. Indeed Russell had informed him that otherwise he would not remain a member of the government. In visiting the queen at Osborne during the summer

[1] *Ab. Cor. 1852–5*, p. 206, 5 September 1853.
[2] *Ibid.* p. 204, 4 September; p. 219, 8 September; pp. 251–2, 27, 28 September; pp. 262–3, 1 and 2 October 1853.
[3] *Ibid.* pp. 219–20, 10 September 1853. Aberdeen went on to refer to the excessive flattery offered Palmerston by the Tory Party. He hoped, however, that if Palmerston had any generous feeling he would respond (unlike Russell!) to 'a proceeding which cannot but afford him personal satisfaction'. According to Lady Clarendon's Journal, Aberdeen told her husband 'that when he announced to Lord P. that he was to go to the Queen, he thought that Lord P. looked rather sheepish, but said that he was of course at the Queen's orders' (Maxwell, *Clarendon*, II, 22).

Aberdeen had mentioned this situation, but it had been his intention to go after he had wound up his business in London. One cause for delay lay in his fear that Gladstone might refuse to serve under Russell and so break up the government. Consequently, before taking any action, he intended first to discuss the matter with Gladstone, but the latter fell ill, and the conversation was postponed. In the meantime the foreign crisis became worse and Aberdeen postponed the matter indefinitely. He kept Graham fully briefed as to his intentions and empowered him to discuss the matter at Balmoral, which Graham was glad to do, always relishing in his gloomy way anything that tasted of political crisis.[1]

En route to Balmoral, Sir James dropped a note to Aberdeen, still cooped up in London, that reveals the romantic soul that lay not far underneath his sombre exterior. He wrote from Braemar, 'having passed a romantic night at the Spittal of Glen Shee, amidst shepherds and drovers, the bleeting of sheep and lowing of cattle, all bound to the Tryst at Falkirk'. He continued:

I have passed this morning through snow and mist, but the grandeur of the scenery, and the solemn silence of the mountains are ample compensation for a journey of any distance; and the very recollection must make you sigh for one glimpse of Aberdeenshire...So adieu for this morning, with a kindly greeting from the hills.[2]

A few days later he told Aberdeen of conversations he had had with both the prince and the queen and said that he had prepared them both for the possibility of Russell and Palmerston breaking with the government on foreign policy. He told Aberdeen that he could rely on the full support of the Crown in any crisis:

While you are willing to fight the Battle, and to remain at the Head of Affairs, I am confident that the man does not live who can supplant you in Royal favour...She [the Queen] intimated to me distinctly that if Peel's friends remained united, Lord John and his friends must see the impossibility of power passing again into the hands of an exclusive Whig party; and she felt the force of my observation that Gladstone's signal success, and the abilities displayed by the Duke of Newcastle, Cardwell, Herbert, in high office, had rendered this position of your colleagues infinitely stronger than they were when Lord John could not exist without them. Whether *they* can exist without him, will depend very much upon the part which he now takes; and on the following which he can command:—the silent members of the Cabinet have hitherto been with you. I shall be surprised, if, satisfied with their own

[1] Graham Papers, 3 October 1853.   [2] *Ab. Cor. 1852–5*, p. 272, 4 October 1853.

position, they sacrifice themselves to his discontent. The reunion of Lord John and Palmerston is certainly formidable; but much will, after all, depend on the Righteousness of the Cause, and on the Purity of Motives and of Conduct.[1]

Problems of patronage

It is often supposed that one of the attractive features of the office of First Lord of the Treasury was the patronage that it commanded. Occasionally Aberdeen may have enjoyed the limited opportunities that he had to decide such matters, as when he offered a ribbon to Lord Haddington,[2] but with Russell breathing over his shoulder his opportunities were limited. Aberdeen regularly consulted Russell about appointments,[3] but Lord John was characteristically touchy and unpredictable on such matters, and there was a minor explosion late in the year. It started with a routine exchange of letters about the office of Secretary to the Master General of the Ordnance that had to be filled. One of Aberdeen's sons, who was a soldier, would have liked the appointment, but Lord Raglan, the Master General, was himself pressing for the appointment of his own son. A third candidate was a Captain Townshend, who had written an unpleasant letter on the subject. Aberdeen told Russell that the appointee should be a military man, but preferred to leave his son in the Prince's service, 'partly', he wrote, 'because I am reluctant to confer any office upon a person connected with myself'.[4] Russell, who had no illusions on such matters, answered Aberdeen:

Your son is fully qualified to hold the vacant office at the Ordnance, and no one would have a word to say. Why not, as well as Colonel Peel, who was appointed by Sir Robert Peel, his brother?[5]

It may be presumed, however, that he was glad to see that the office was left open for a Whig candidate. He acknowledged that Captain

---

[1] *Ab. Cor. 1852–5*, pp. 287–8, 8 October 1853. See also below, pp. 190–1.

[2] Add. MS. 43250, fol. 199, 17 June 1853, to whom he wrote: 'Lord Huntley is dead. His ribbon is the first I have had to bestow...You may think perhaps, it has come too late; but that is not my fault.' In answering, Haddington expressed his appreciation at this sign of old friendship. He admitted that he had been disappointed in 1846, but suggested, now that he was 73, Aberdeen might as well present it where it would do more good politically (*ibid.* pp. 200–1, 18 June 1853).

[3] See Add. MS. 43067 and PRO 30/22/11.

[4] *Ab. Cor. 1852–5*, p. 351, 12 November 1853.

[5] *Ibid.* p. 352, 14 November 1853. Russell had a way of spoiling nice gestures with some such cutting phrase.

Townshend's letter was 'ill-conditioned', but suggested he might be made a naval aide-de-camp to the queen. Since the Captain would succeed to the marquisate of Townshend, Russell thought 'it is in no way discreditable to do him a favour now'.[1] As for the Secretaryship, he suggested his friend, Colonel Romilly. 'I think,' he went on, 'in the new appointments to be made, some reparation should be made to the Whigs and Liberals for the very unequal share of office they obtained on the formation of the Government. Unless they are fairly considered, in proportion to their numbers and weight in Parliament, we must expect a good deal of discontent in the party in the next session of Parliament.'[2]

Aberdeen ignored this outburst and a week later offered a Garter to Lord Carlisle 'from a regard for his public and private character; and also, in consequence of his unavoidable exclusion from office'.[3] Russell expressed his gratification, but ten days later he was nagging again about letters from Lord Fortescue, Colonel Boyle and Colonel Tynte regarding places, that had to be answered. 'Old Whig friends are apt to write to me, imagining I have some influence in political and ecclesiastical appointments,' he wrote peevishly. 'It is a mistake.'[4] This was too much even for Aberdeen's patience. He wrote to say that there had been very few Crown livings vacant during the past year and that the one Lord Fortescue wrote about had already been granted. He reminded Russell that he had just given Carlisle a Garter and went on: 'To say the truth I thought that I had done very little else than comply with your wishes either at the formation of the Government or ever since; and I imagined that this was a matter of notoriety.' It had been pointed out to him, apparently by Argyll, that 32 out of 34 Scottish legal appointments had gone to Whigs. As for the Ordnance appointment, with Russell's agreement, he had turned down Raglan's son on the ground

---

[1] *Ab. Cor. 1852–5*, p. 352, 14 November. 'If the Duke of Atholl,' Russell continued, 'who is nearly mad, was entitled to a Green Ribbon for one Session's attendance and support, Captain Townshend, for many years attendance and support, may have a fair claim to some mark of favour.' The duke of Atholl was a Conservative, but Townshend, of course, a Whig.

[2] *Ibid.* p. 352, 14 November 1853.

[3] *Ibid.* pp. 362–3, 21 and 23 November 1853; R.A. A23, fol. 56, 22 November 1853. Only a few months earlier Aberdeen had offered another Garter to Lord Panmure, obviously to please Russell; at any rate in writing to Russell, Panmure attributed the gift to him, to whom, he said, he owed everything (PRO 30/22/11/A, fols. 195–7 and 200, 26 and 30 August 1853).

[4] *Ab. Cor. 1852–5*, p. 375, 2 December 1853.

that it must go to a military man. Consequently he ruled out Romilly; nor would he give it to his own son. So he offered it to a Colonel Lindsay,[1] who turned it down after consulting his family; 'but', Aberdeen added, 'I do not doubt that his future conduct in Parliament will be rendered still more friendly'. Of Tynte and Boyle he preferred the former, since the latter already had an office. As an afterthought, in a postscript, he asked Russell to recommend a successor to the duke of Norfolk, who was resigning the office of Lord Steward.[2]

Russell replied rather tartly that he did not understand why Aberdeen did not appoint his son to the Ordnance Office, but that as between Tynte and Boyle he preferred the latter 'as being a more respectable appointment'; his other office could easily be disposed of. He wanted a few days to think over the Lord Stewardship. As to the other matters he went on:

I know nothing of the thirty-two legal appointments in Scotland, but as the Tories are nearly all Derbyites, I think it fair that they should not fare equally well under you and Derby. They would all rally under him to-morrow.

I am sorry that Fortescue has missed his chance, but as the only ecclesiastical recommendation, and that on public grounds (Mr Edward Johnston), which I ever made, obtained no notice, I thought it of very little use to apply.

However, what you now say encourages me.[3]

Aberdeen welcomed Russell's choice of Colonel Boyle, for, in the meantime, he had discovered that 'Colonel Tynte is not in the army and I believe, never was'. His neglect of Russell's recommendation of Mr Johnston to the Canonry of Bristol was a source of embarrassment for he had to confess that his Secretary had neglected to show him the letter. So he had appointed a Mr Mosley on the recommendation of Lansdowne, Granville and Herbert. Had he known of Russell's wishes he would have appointed Mr Johnston 'with the greatest pleasure'. 'These, however, are comparatively minor matters,' he gravely concluded, 'and I wish to speak to you on a subject of much greater importance.'[4] He invited Russell to call on him on the following morning and so we have no written reply, but a letter to the queen later the same day

---

[1] Once classified as a Peelite, but more recently as a Derbyite, although he was one of those who had supported Gladstone's budget. The offer does not appear to have made him very much more friendly to the Government. See Appendix B.

[2] *Ab. Cor. 1852–5*, pp. 375–6, 4 December 1853.

[3] *Ibid.* pp. 380–1, 5 December 1853.   [4] *Ibid.* p. 381, 5 December 1853.

suggests that some time was taken up on such minor matters. Having consulted Lord John Russell, he told the queen, he recommended Lord Breadalbane as Lord Steward, Lord Bruce as Lord Chamberlain, and Colonel Boyle as Secretary to the Master General of the Ordnance.[1]

Before turning to Lord Aberdeen's graver business we may note one minor piece of patronage of interest to the Peelite historian. Shortly before the end of the session Graham wrote to Gladstone to say that he had heard from Newcastle that there was an opening in the tax office, 'which poor old Bonham might fill without any disadvantage to the public'. 'You, I know,' he added, 'esteem our Friend highly as I do; and a word from you would secure the appointment for him. I would not ask it if I did not believe he was competent to discharge the duties which are not onerous.' Gladstone gladly complied and on the following day offered Bonham the post, which was worth £600 a year and travelling expenses.[2] Bonham welcomed the offer provided he was able to cope with the work. A month later he was able to tell Gladstone with more confidence that the work was not beyond him.[3] The Peelite conscience was next best to a system of entrance by examination that Gladstone was already beginning to contemplate.

One other Peelite retainer, Abraham Hayward, leader writer for the *Morning Chronicle*, who thought his claims for an appointment were strong and well supported, was less successful. At the end of the session six commissioners had to be appointed under the new Charitable Trusts Act, three of whom were to be paid. On the advice of the Solicitor General, a Whig, Hayward applied for one of the paid commissionerships, aware that there was 'already a great rush for them' and that they were more likely to be carried by *interest* than *merit*'. Nevertheless, his chances seemed good since he could count on the support of all the Peelite ministers and he believed also of Lord Lansdowne, Molesworth and the Lord Chancellor. Leaving no stone unturned, he asked his Whig friend, George Cornewall Lewis, to do what he could for him with Palmerston, Clarendon and Russell. 'I have most reluctantly become a place hunter,' he told his friend frankly, 'but the plain matter of fact is, that I lost a considerable part of my small fortune on my brother's death.' And he added disingenuously, 'Few have really

[1] *Ab. Cor. 1852–5*, p. 382, 6 December 1853.
[2] Add. MS. 44163, fols. 96–8, 14 August 1853.
[3] Add. MS. 44110, fols. 253–60, 269–72, 15 and 23 August and 30 September 1853.

contributed more to the formation and success of the coalition than myself, with the exception, of course, of its more distinguished members; and I think no one has undergone a greater amount of personal insult and calumny for its sake.'[1] Yet Hayward's name was not among those which the Prime Minister submitted to the queen on 25 August.[2] Aberdeen, himself, wrote to the disappointed candidate regretting that it had not been found '*possible*' to include him. Hayward laid the blame squarely on Russell, who, he presumed, had taken umbrage at articles in the *Morning Chronicle*, which, actually, Hayward had not written. Looking at the list of 'unknown names' of the successful candidates, he wrote with some indignation to Sir John Young: 'I cannot admit that any Ministry have a right to give places to private friends from personal motives whilst their party obligations remain unsatisfied. When men work together for a party object, they are entitled, in their several ways, to a share in the advantage of success... But the truth is, Lord Aberdeen at once gave way to Lord John, and will probably do so whenever the same pressure may be put upon him.'[3]

The distribution of patronage was clearly not one of the pleasanter or more enjoyable tasks for the leader of a coalition government.[4] To a man of Aberdeen's sensitive and withdrawing disposition it was clearly a distasteful chore, but no colleague could have made it more difficult

[1] Henry Carlisle, *Correspondence of Abraham Hayward*, I, 185–6.

[2] R.A. A23, fol. 45, 25 August 1854. Appointment of the unpaid commissioners took more time. Aberdeen suggested Brougham's name to Russell, saying that Palmerston and the Lord Chancellor were favourable. He did not expect Brougham to accept, in which case he proposed Lord Harrowby. When the latter declined, Sir George Grey was appointed (*ibid.* fol. 53, 19 October 1853, and PRO 30/22/11/A, fols. 225–8).

[3] *Correspondence of Abraham Hayward*, I, 187–90. Poor Hayward was again disappointed the following year when he was promised the Secretaryship of the Poor Law Board on its being vacated by Lord Courtney, but the latter changed his mind at the last minute. See *ibid.* pp. 227–33.

[4] In actual fact the amount of patronage at the Prime Minister's disposal was fairly limited, to judge from the correspondence in R.A. A23. There were a number of Civil List Pensions, with a total value of only £1200 a year, 'which', Aberdeen wrote to the queen, 'is intended to include all cases connected with literature, science and art; as well as distress of every kind arising from exertion in the political service'. At the date of his letter, 30 August, five or six hundred pounds remained unappropriated (*ibid.* fol. 49). On 26 August, by way of example, he had recommended five pensions to widows of £50 to £100 each, and two literary pensions, one of £100 to Sir Francis Bond Head 'in consideration of the many useful contributions he has made to the literature of the country' (*ibid.* fol. 46). Head's writings are forgotten today, but his shortcomings as a colonial governor are still remembered in Canada.

than Lord John, who could not forget the day when he was the sole distributor and his supposed right to resume that role. Throughout the coalition the relationship between Aberdeen and Russell was a tenuous one, despite a certain mutual respect. Questions of patronage acted as grit to disturb the smooth running of the machinery of government; differences over policy, however, not domestic, but foreign, were to threaten its continued operation.

II

THE COALITION AND THE ORIGINS OF THE CRIMEAN WAR

7

THE EASTERN QUESTION: FROM
THE SEYMOUR CONVERSATIONS
TO THE VIENNA NOTE

Origins of the Eastern question, 1815–1852; the Seymour conversations,
January 1853

On domestic affairs the Aberdeen coalition had pulled together better
than expected and the future looked not unpromising. Unfortunately,
however, this government was formed on the eve of the gravest international crisis facing Britain and Europe between 1815 and 1914. No
account of the Aberdeen administration can avoid the tangled story of
the Crimean War and its causes.[1] Some narrative of events will be necessary to understand what happened, but our main concern will be to
trace the changing relationships between members of the cabinet as the
crisis developed, in order to determine what effect the war had on the
coalition, and indeed to what extent the coalition, as such, was responsible for the war.

The Crimean War has often and well been described as an unnecessary war. And yet it seemed to come about with the inevitability of a
Greek tragedy. Most of the chief actors on the stage, with the exception
of the extremists in the Turkish camp who played more the role of a
chorus in the wings, were clearly anxious to avoid a war which they did
not want. Over and over again a solution seemed to be forthcoming
but at the last minute some mischance destroyed it and war came a little
closer. Rarely was war approached more slowly or more hesitantly.
Prince Menschikoff presented his ultimatum in May of 1853. The
Principalities were occupied in July. The Turks decided on war on

---

[1] The fullest and most authentic account of British policy will be found in Harold
Temperley's *England and the Near East—the Crimea* and in his two articles, 'Stratford de
Redcliffe and the origins of the Crimean War', *E.H.R.* xlviii (1933), 601–21, and xlix
(1934), 265–98, but Temperley's interest centred in Constantinople, rather than London. In what follows on the background of the Eastern Question I have relied mainly
on Temperley. For a highly critical and uneven account, also based largely on original
sources, see V. J. Puryear, *England, Russia and the Straits question.*

4 October, but fighting did not begin until 23 October, and the Allies did not join until the following March. To add to the bizarre nature of the whole business, the Russian sinking of Turkish warships at Sinope after the initiation of hostilities by the Turks was condemned abroad as a 'massacre'.

The story is full of anomalies from beginning to end. Today the Crimean War seems one of the least justifiable in modern British history, yet it was declared by a government led by the most pacific of British Prime Ministers and containing in the person of Gladstone a minister who a generation later was to denounce a similar policy towards Russia and Turkey. Even after the Eastern Crisis of the 'seventies Gladstone continued to justify Britain's declaration of war against Russia in 1854.

From the beginning to the end two conflicting considerations present themselves in any analysis of the events leading up to this unhappy war. On the one hand there was the apparent threat to the balance of power in Europe presented by an ambitious Russia, anxious to supplant the Turks in the Balkans. This was the consideration always uppermost in the minds of Palmerston and of Russell. On the other was the fact of Moslem Turkish misrule over the Christian subjects of the Porte. Were the descendants of the crusaders in England and France to connive at the perpetuation of this situation? These were the considerations that weighed most heavily with Lord Aberdeen.

Basically, everything turned on the extent to which the Russians could be trusted. Aberdeen (and to a point Clarendon) was prepared to accept the good faith of the Russians; Palmerston and Russell were not. Here we are reminded of our own troubles in the twentieth century. Looking back with the detachment that a century affords, it is possible to say that Aberdeen's interpretation of Russian motives was fairer than Palmerston's, but, given our own experience, we can easily understand that Palmerston's was the more popular one in an England grown used to peace and imperial greatness.

The events of 1853 must be examined in the light of the history of the preceding four decades; and it is well to remember that many of the principals had been actively concerned in the so-called Eastern Question for all or most of that period, Aberdeen since he was Foreign Secretary in 1828, Palmerston since he first took over the Foreign Office in 1830, Stratford Canning since his first appointment to Constantinople in 1809, the Emperor Nicholas since his accession in 1825, Nesselrode since becoming Russian Chancellor in 1814, and Brunnow at least since his arrival in London as ambassador in 1839. Anglo-Russian relations had been chequered ever since the great alliance had brought victory in 1815. As in our own day, the Allies were faced with the fact that victory had left Russia the strongest military power on the continent of Europe. As the years passed English opinion became increasingly suspicious of Russian pretensions. Castlereagh's hopes in a Congress system waned in face of Alexander I's concept of a Holy Alliance. English opinion was repelled by the avowed opposition of the autocratic rulers of Russia, Austria and Prussia to liberalism wherever it might appear and their determination to defend the rights of legitimate rulers throughout Europe, and welcomed the stand that Canning took against them. Lord Aberdeen, a protégé of Pitt, whose personal European contacts went back to the days of the Grand Alliance which he helped Castlereagh to forge, sought to withdraw from Canning's advanced position when he became Foreign Secretary in 1828, for he remembered the Russians and the Austrians as Allies and numbered some of their statesmen among his friends. Aberdeen's tenure of the Foreign Office in 1828–30, however, was a brief interlude and it was Palmerston, the disciple of Canning, who shaped British policy throughout the 'thirties and again in the later 'forties. Palmerston embodied the growing British suspicions of Russia both as a reactionary autocracy and also as an imperial rival in Asia.

Even in 1828 Aberdeen had said that 'the existence of Turkey as a European power was essential to the preservation of that balance of power',[1] but Wellington's government was not prepared to press Turkey's defence beyond diplomatic means. As a result, after a short war, Russia was able to impose on Turkey the terms of the treaty of Adrianople, which gave Russia control of the delta of the Danube, certain opportunity to interfere in the semi-autonomous Principalities of Moldavia and Wallachia, and generally an increased control over the Christian subjects of the Porte, by extending and confirming the Russian claims embodied in the treaty of Kutchuk Kainardji of 1774.[2]

It may be noted that at this time it was not Nicholas's policy to partition Turkey, which would have brought strong rivals on to the scene. Rather, the new Russian policy was to preserve the *status quo*, but in fact to dominate a weak Turkey. This policy bore fruit in 1832–3,

[1] Temperley, *Crimea*, p. 54.
[2] For the significance of the Kainardji treaty see *ibid*. n. 445, pp. 467–9.

when Western Europe was more concerned with the Belgian question. Russia came to Turkey's aid against Mehemet Ali of Egypt and exacted from her the treaty of Unkiar Skelessi (1833) in which Russia promised to maintain the independence of Turkey and Turkey undertook to close the Straits to foreign warships in time of war. Stratford Canning, even then British ambassador in Constantinople, had called in vain for British help to Turkey in 1832. This treaty aroused all Palmerston's 'hatred and suspicion of Russia', which was to affect British policy for years to come. It is true, in 1839–41 he managed to undo the worst features of Unkiar Skelessi, replacing Russia's unilateral support of Turkey by a Four-Power guarantee against the renewed incursions of Mehemet Ali, but at the cost of alienating France. By the Conventions of 1840 and 1841, the latter grudgingly signed by France, the Great Powers collectively took Turkey under their protection and all agreed to the closing of the Straits to foreign warships in time of peace. Russian rights under the treaties of Kutchuk Kainardji, Adrianople and Akerman were not infringed, but the Treaty of Unkiar Skelessi, which expired in any event in 1841, was abrogated. Nevertheless, from the time of signature Russia and Britain were mutually suspicious of each other's intentions.

The years of the Peel ministry (1841–6), with Aberdeen at the Foreign Office, saw a general relaxation of tension as Britain cultivated better relations with both France and Russia. The visit of the emperor Nicholas to England was a great success and Nicholas was much pleased with his conversations with Aberdeen, recorded in the Nesselrode memorandum, for the accuracy of which Aberdeen was ready to vouch. The gist of this memorandum was to the effect that both Russia and England sought to maintain the integrity of Turkey as long as possible, and that in the event of anything happening to change that situation the two powers should consult on joint action. This memorandum was passed on to subsequent British Foreign Secretaries, but it did not bind them. Indeed, the events of 1849 seemed to remove its significance.[1]

These were years of reaction in Turkey despite the efforts of Stratford Canning to promote reform. In 1850 even Palmerston expressed his indignation at the cruelties perpetrated by the Turks on Christians in Bosnia, but this was incidental to his continuing policy of supporting Turkey against Russia. The events of 1848 resulted in an occupation by

[1] Puryear attaches an exaggerated significance to the Nesselrode memorandum in his *Straits question*, chs. I and III.

Russia of the Principalities under the terms of the treaty of Adrianople, but her action was a temporary one and her explanation apologetic.

In the affair of the Hungarian refugees, however, Palmerston took a strong line with Russia. He and Stratford Canning successfully supported Turkey in standing up to Russian demands. The fleet was called up to the Aegean, but war was averted, partly because of Palmerston's diplomacy in disavowing the action of the local British authorities in bringing British warships into the Narrows on a strained interpretation of the Straits Convention, and partly by the emperor's moderation in accepting the mission of the Turkish envoy Fuad, which settled the affair amicably. Britain and Russia, however, had come close to war and British public opinion was inflamed by the reactionary policy of the Austrian and Russian emperors in suppressing the revolts of 1848–9.[1]

With the temporary removal of outstanding differences in 1849 and the removal of Palmerston in 1851, Nicholas decided to make a renewed approach to Britain in December of 1852. By the time the famous Seymour conversations had begun in January Nicholas knew that the friendly Aberdeen had become Prime Minister. The importance of these conversations has often been exaggerated, but they did show that the emperor was anxious to reopen the Turkish question and to do so jointly with Britain. Nicholas told Seymour that he foresaw the imminent collapse of Turkey and suggested preparations for an 'ulterior system'. Seymour's reaction was negative, but he used the conversations to get information out of the emperor as to Russia's intentions, without giving any in return as to Britain's. Although himself quite unimpressed, Seymour faithfully reported the conversations to Russell, momentarily at the Foreign Office, and Russell wrote a friendly despatch in reply that, while leaving Britain uncommitted, pleased the emperor.[2]

The Menschikoff mission and the return of Stratford to Constantinople, March–May 1853

The Emperor Nicholas's timing of these conversations was governed by two developments, the revolt in Montenegro, which had resulted in successful Austrian intervention, and the dispute over the Holy Places in

---

[1] Puryear attaches great significance to this episode, but argues that it indicated that the so-called 'Anglo-Russian secret agreement of 1844' was still in force (*Straits question*, pp. 171–88).

[2] See G. Henderson, *Crimean War diplomacy*, pp. 1–14; Temperley, *Crimea*, pp. 272–9.

Palestine. Here the newly proclaimed Emperor Napoleon, recently snubbed by Nicholas, had appeared to outmanoeuvre the Russian champions of the orthodox clergy by the use of strong-arm methods—the despatch of the warship *Charlemagne* to Constantinople in violation of the Straits Convention.

Unduly reassured by the reception of his conversations with Sir George Seymour and placing unwarranted reliance on the accession of Aberdeen to office, Nicholas now began to plan a diplomatic offensive against Turkey in the shape of the ill-omened Menschikoff mission. Here was the second of a whole series of mischances that in the end made war inevitable. Prince Menschikoff was the worst possible choice for such a delicate operation. He was completely lacking in tact and in comprehension of the Oriental mind, and antagonised the Turks at every turn. He was even ineffective in his bribes. Another envoy, such as Prince Orloff, might have obtained the Russian demands through the exercise of diplomacy, or at least have left the way open for further discussions, which Menschikoff did not.[1] Indeed Menschikoff's initial steps at Constantinople were so disconcerting that the French fleet steamed to the Aegean and Colonel Rose, the British *chargé d'affaires* at Constantinople, vainly endeavoured to get the British Mediterranean fleet to do likewise.

From the beginning Rose was suspicious of the methods and intention of Prince Menschikoff's embassy. When Menschikoff gratuitously insulted the Turkish Foreign Minister, Fuad Effendi, by refusing to call on him, Rose concluded that the Russians were bent on a policy of intimidation and so to give the sultan confidence to resist such treatment he agreed with the French *chargé d'affaires* at Constantinople that they should summon the fleets at the request of the Turkish government.[2] The cautious Admiral Dundas (at Malta) wisely insisted on getting confirmation from the Admiralty, which was not forthcoming, but the great Eastern Crisis of 1853 had begun.[3]

The French government, not yet sure of itself, had obviously acted precipitately, as Walewski, the French ambassador in London, admitted.

[1] But Nesselrode's instructions to Menschikoff indicate that the Russian government intended him to be tough and peremptory (Temperley, *Crimea*, pp. 306–7). Cf. Puryear, *Straits question*, pp. 235–7, who plays down Menschikoff's violence.
[2] MS. Clar. Dep. C250, F.O. printed *Correspondence*, part I, nos. 171 and 172, 7 March 1853, pp. 155–9.
[3] For a timetable of the crisis, or succeeding crises, which continued for twelve months, see Appendix C.

Lord Cowley, the British ambassador in Paris, attempted to cool them down and was strongly supported in this by Clarendon,[1] who had just come into office on the eve of this initial crisis. At the same time Clarendon curtly told Rose that Admiral Dundas had been instructed not to comply with his request and reminded him that Russell had instructed him to ignore any Russian objections to Fuad Effendi.[2] Aberdeen was delighted with the peaceful tone of Clarendon's despatch to Paris, saying to him: 'We desire the preservation of Turkey but we must take special care to avoid entering into any engagement with France, either positive or conditional, upon the subject. We have a General Treaty to which all the Great Powers are parties. This is enough for the present.'[3] Aberdeen, who had not yet heard of Menschikoff's 'secret demands', sounded the same note in writing to the queen. He admitted that the Russian demands might be humiliating to Turkey but asserted, 'There is nothing whatever to justify the reproach of territorial aggression, or hostile ambition.' He recognised that if Turkey was obstinate, relying on the assistance of England and France, 'the affair might become serious', but he was sure that if Menschikoff could 'command himself sufficiently to wait for the arrival of Lord Stratford' the matter would be 'settled without coming to extremities'.[4] Two days later he told the queen that while Menschikoff's tone was peremptory his terms were 'reasonable, and moderate'. 'The departure of the French Fleet is the most alarming feature of the affair,' he added; 'but even this is rendered less important in consequence of the English Admiral not having left Malta.'[5]

Closely connected in time and probably in policy with the despatch of the French fleet to the Aegean was the warning of the French ambassador to Belgium on 22 March that, with the outbreak of war in the East, France would consider herself no longer bound by the treaties of 1815. The implication of this threat was that if Britain wished to preserve the neutrality of Belgium she must work more closely with France. Indeed two weeks earlier Drouyn de Lhuys, the French foreign minister, had warned Cowley that France had as much right to enter Belgium to rectify complaints as Austria had in Switzerland. Presumably Clarendon had these developments in mind when he wrote to

[1] MS. Clar. Dep. C250, no. 186, p. 174, 22 March 1853.
[2] Ibid. no. 187, p. 175, 23 March 1853.
[3] Ibid. C4, fol. 12, 21 March 1853.
[4] Letters of Queen Victoria, II, 537–8.
[5] Ab. Cor. 1852–5, pp. 70–1, 24 March 1853.

Seymour on 23 March regarding the government's conviction 'that no question can be agitated in the east without becoming a source of discord in the west'. But it would be a mistake to attribute the hardening of British policy against Russia in the months that followed entirely to this cause.[1]

Russell was not at the Foreign Office long enough to bring any very significant influence to bear on the course of events in the Near East. His two most important acts were the drafting of the despatch of St Petersburg commenting on the Seymour conversations and securing the re-appointment as British ambassador to the Porte of Stratford Canning, recently created Lord Stratford de Redcliffe. After many weary years of service at Constantinople Stratford had resigned his post while on leave in England in January, but the government, with some hesitation, now decided to ask him to return. 'Lord Stratford', Russell wrote to Aberdeen on 5 February, 'will go back to Constantinople for a short time, if we wish it, and for my part I think it very expedient.' He added that he thought Stratford was the only man who had much influence with the Turks.[2] Aberdeen agreed, reluctantly, perhaps, it has been suggested, for the bad reason that he did not relish having Stratford discussing Eastern affairs in the House of Lords.

Stratford's instructions were based on a memorandum he had himself prepared, but they did not give him the control of the fleet, which he wanted.[3] Aberdeen warned Russell that care must be taken in drawing up the instructions in view of this demand. 'The assurances of prompt and effective aid on the approach of danger, given by us to the Porte,' he wrote, 'would in all probability produce war. These barbarians hate us all and would be delighted to take their chance of some advantage, by embroiling us with the other powers of Christendom.' The Turkish government was to be warned that 'perseverance in their present course must end in alienating the sympathies of the British nation', and was to be encouraged to resume the course of reform. On this point Aberdeen observed that Stratford showed himself inconsistent in his recognition of the disordered state of the Turkish government and in his expressed belief in its powers of reform. The Prime Minister insisted that Britain

[1] Puryear, Straits question, pp. 242–55. Other historians tend to pass over this Belgian issue, but Puryear probably exaggerates its significance. [2] Ibid. p. 35.
[3] Eastern Papers, I, no. 94, pp. 80–2; P.P. 1854, LXXI (hereafter E.P. I). He might warn the fleet at Malta to hold itself in readiness, but was not to call it up to the Dardanelles 'without positive instructions from Her Majesty's Government'. The instructions were issued by Clarendon, who had just taken over the Foreign Office.

must retain its freedom of action. 'Above all,' he concluded, 'we ought not to trust the disposal of the Mediterranean fleet,—which is peace or war,—to the discretion of any man.'[1] These views characterised Lord Aberdeen's approach to the Eastern Question from beginning to end.

From that day to this, Stratford de Redcliffe has been the most controversial figure throughout the crisis. From the start he was suspected of secretly steeling the Turks to oppose all Russian demands and consequently regarded as bearing a large share of responsibility for the war. This myth, as Temperley calls it, was fully developed in Kinglake's famous history of the Crimean War[2] and not effectively dispelled by Stratford's official biographer, Lane-Poole. In the 1930s, however, Harold Temperley re-examined the historical evidence and largely exonerated Stratford from the charges made against him.[3] Temperley's case is convincing, but many contemporaries in high places both in England and abroad thought otherwise. There was no doubt about Stratford's ability, his great knowledge of the Near East and his extraordinary influence with the Porte, but Temperley makes it clear that this last point was much exaggerated, as was his alleged hatred of Russia. Certainly Russian diplomats did much to spread the stories about his supposedly sinister influence, and unhappily members of the cabinet were all too ready to believe them. Stratford was an extremely imperious man, who antagonised people too easily and so sowed the seeds of suspicion. When things began to go wrong the ministers at home instinctively tended to blame it on their proud ambassador. It is easy to say that the appointment should never have been made, but Stratford had served them all in the past at this outpost, and who was to foresee that the coming storm would be worse than those he had previously weathered. Yet the seeds of trouble may be seen in a casual note from Clarendon to Graham shortly after Stratford's return, in which he wrote:

Ld. Stratford is too bad—his temper is ungovernable & I believe that he is more often *in* a passion than *out* of one—he wd have quarrelled with me & thrown up the mission ½ a dozen times before he went if I had let him.

However he has done very well and quite changed the aspect of affairs since he arrived at Constantinople so we must bear with him & hope that his special mission will not be very protracted.[4]

[1] *Ab. Cor. 1852–5*, p. 41, 15 February 1853; *E.P.* I, no. 94, p. 82.
[2] A. W. Kinglake, *The invasion of the Crimea*, 9 vols.   [3] See above, p. 137, n. 1.
[4] Graham Papers, 9 May 1853. Temperley passes over this side of Stratford's character too easily.

These two sentences sum up well the ambivalent attitude of the Home government with respect to their representative in Constantinople. His first actions on his return were propitious, for the settlement of the dispute about the Holy Places is generally attributed to him. 'With the ulterior proposals it was otherwise,' as his biographer wrote.[1]

On the surface the new demands presented to the Turks by Menschikoff on 5 May in what amounted to an ultimatum did not look too impossible.[2] The Turkish ministers, however, and Stratford, whom they immediately consulted, considered that the implications of the Russian draft convention were quite unacceptable as they stood. The proposed convention, in Temperley's view, 'implied a political as well as religious protection, and carried with it the suggestion that Russia could interfere to enforce the guarantee'. Moreover, in the background lay the earlier Russian demand for a Russo-Turkish alliance, which the Turks only now revealed to Stratford.[3] Menschikoff, however, although he made some changes in the form of his demands and delayed his departure from Constantinople beyond 10 May, the date on which he had demanded Turkish assent, refused to consider the modifications in the convention proposed by the Turks. At the last moment Stratford sent a note to Reschid, the new Turkish foreign minister, suggesting a conciliatory reply to the latest Russian communication in order to further postpone Menschikoff's departure. Reschid did not take his advice, but in informing Menschikoff of Turkey's refusal he characteristically excused himself by putting the blame on Stratford.[4]

[1] Temperley, *E.H.R.* xlviii, 608; S. Lane-Poole, *Life of Stratford Canning, Viscount Stratford de Redcliffe*, ii, 250–1.

[2] *E.P.* i, no. 179, enclosure 2 (translation), pp. 169–70 (185–6). The first two articles of Menschikoff's project were as follows:

'Article I. No change shall be made as regards the rights, privileges and immunities which have been enjoyed by, or are possessed *ab antiquo* by, the Orthodox churches, pious institutions, and clergy in the dominions of the Sublime Ottoman Porte, which is pleased to secure the same to them in perpetuity, on the strict basis of the *status quo* now existing.

Article II. The rights and advantages conceded by the Ottoman Government, or shall hereinafter be conceded, to the other Christian rites by Treaties, Conventions, or special arrangements, shall be considered as belonging also to the Orthodox Church.'

The remaining articles dealt with Russian privileges in Jerusalem and the continuation of existing treaties between the two states. Temperley asserts that the term *les églises* in article I included the twelve million lay members of the Orthodox Church.

[3] Temperley, *Crimea*, p. 321.

[4] The Russian ultimatum had precipitated the resignation of two key Turkish ministers. The Russians mistakenly thought that the new Turkish foreign minister, Reschid, was their man. See Temperley, *Crimea*, pp. 323–32; and his articles in *E.H.R.* xlviii and xlix.

Stratford received full information about the Russian ultimatum of 5 May on the 6th and sent off a despatch with the text of Menschikoff's demands to London by special courier on the same day. This was received in London on 18 May, although presumably some telegraphic news had been received before that date.[1]

Indeed, on 16 May Brunnow, the Russian ambassador in London, showed the draft convention to Clarendon and wrote to Aberdeen to say that he thought he and Clarendon could settle the matter more easily than Stratford and Menschikoff. (This was possible since Menschikoff eluded Stratford's attempts to see him.) Brunnow thought that Clarendon would 'find it hardly worth while to involve Turkey into a quarrel about *so very little*'.[2] Clarendon, however, took a firm line in his conversation with Brunnow and defended Stratford's conduct, although he did not receive the ambassador's despatch until several days later.[3]

Different people reacted in different ways to the Russian draft convention. Walewski, who received the news from Constantinople before Clarendon, told him that the French and British ambassadors there were on good terms and both agreed that the convention 'would be fatal to Turkish independence'.[4] Brunnow, on the other hand, could see nothing in it that encroached on the independence or dignity of Turkey.[5] Clarendon thought that it would 'hardly justify an *European war*';[6] Russell considered the first article hard to swallow and did not blame the Turks for rejecting it,[7] but to Clarendon he admitted that he preferred the Russian proposals to war or the threat of war.[8] The queen was shocked and grieved by what she considered was the double-dealing of the Russians,[9] and even Aberdeen was driven to write his friend Mme Lieven: 'I hope you do not, at Paris, expect a European war quite as much as we do in London.'[10]

On 22 May Prince Menschikoff brought the first act of the drama to an end by sailing away from Constantinople. Clearly, at this point, the

[1] *E.P.* I, no. 179, pp. 164–5. Telegraphic communication did not extend beyond the Austrian frontier.
[2] *Ab. Cor. 1852–5*, pp. 102–3, 16 May 1853.
[3] *E.P.* I, no. 176, p. 163, Clarendon to Seymour, 16 May 1853. See also MS. Clar. Dep. C4, fol. 27.
[4] *Ab. Cor. 1852–5*, p. 104, 18 May 1853.
[5] *Ibid.* pp. 105–7, 21 May 1853.
[6] *Ibid.* p. 107, 22 May 1853.
[7] *Ibid.* pp. 107–8, 22 May 1853.
[8] MS. Clar. Dep. C3, fol. 298, 20 May 1853.
[9] *Ab. Cor. 1852–5*, pp. 110–11, 23 May 1853.
[10] *Ibid.* pp. 109–10.

major fault lay with the Russians, who had already begun warlike preparations in the Black Sea area. Their special envoy had been insolent and overbearing to the point of forcing the dismissal of Turkish ministers and his demands had been peremptory. It is true that he had postponed his departure, but he had turned down the alternatives offered by the Turks, he had refused the good offices of the ambassadors of the other powers, and in the end he had broken off his negotiations with the Porte. He had also made a fool of himself by forcing the appointment of Reschid Pasha, who had no intention of doing his bidding. During this period Stratford, working closely with the French ambassador, had advised the Turks against accepting the original demands of the Russians, but he had counselled moderation, had refused to encourage the Turks with any promises of naval aid, and had done his best to keep negotiations open. With the departure of Menschikoff, however, a serious crisis was clearly impending. The Russians, having broken off negotiations, had to resort to some more warlike action to emphasise their determination, and so on 27 May the Emperor made the crucial decision to occupy the Principalities, semi-autonomous Turkish provinces at the mouth of the Danube, where Russia had certain treaty rights. They were to remain occupied until full satisfaction had been received from the Porte. At the same time equally significant decisions were being made in London and in Paris.

The occupation of the Principalities and the summoning of the fleets to the Aegean, June–July 1853

Public opinion in England, whipped up by the press, was becoming markedly anti-Russian and taking a very belligerent tone. The Russian emperor replaced Louis Napoleon as the great anti-liberal in Englishmen's minds, an impression that had been fostered by the Hungarian refugee affair. Turkish misrule was overlooked on the empty supposition that the Turks were reforming themselves and needed help. The suggestion that the Christian subjects of the Porte would prefer Russian to Turkish rule was dismissed as propaganda.[1]

A cabinet with precarious support in parliament[2] could not ignore such opinion, especially when it was strongly held by two leading

[1] For all this see Kingsley Martin, *The triumph of Lord Palmerston* (London, rev. ed. 1963), pp. 110–17.
[2] It may be noted that this crisis coincided with the decision to introduce the India Bill and the resignation of the three Irish office-holders. Cf. p. 109 above.

ministers, Russell and Palmerston. In the March crisis these two had
unsuccessfully sought to persuade the cabinet to grant Colonel Rose's
request for the fleet.[1] Now again the same two were demanding action.
On 29 May Russell told Clarendon that it was time to assure the French
that the fleet would go to the Dardanelles,[2] and on the same day
Palmerston addressed a long letter to Sir James Graham for forwarding
to the Prime Minister, in which he urged that the fleet should be sent,
not just to the Dardanelles, but up to the Bosporus (in contravention of
the Straits Settlement of 1841). He said that the fleet at the Dardanelles
would annoy the Russians, but be of no use to the Turks, and went on
to argue in great detail the advantage of having it where it could
intervene to cut off a Russian attack on Constantinople. Palmerston's
case was impressive but overextended, and he weakened it by maintaining that Turkey was in many ways more civilised than Russia.[3]

Graham's reply was cautious. He was anxious not to 'give to Russia
prematurely any just cause of offence', and sounded the warning that 'a
false step might be almost fatal to our national greatness'. 'I place little
confidence in Princes', he wrote in the best Whig tradition; 'but I am
disposed to place more reliance on the honour of Nicholas than in the
broken faith of Napoleon, until I have distinct evidence that the Czar has
behaved treacherously.'[4] Aberdeen reacted much more strongly to
Palmerston's views and, in a letter to Graham,[5] he vigorously refuted
the Home Secretary's arguments on the basis of his own familiarity
with the area. Curiously, he termed Palmerston's proposals half
measures. He was against any precipitate action, but if the time came to
defend Constantinople, he said, then this would best be done by sending
the fleet right into the Black Sea. Half measures would merely release
the Russian emperor from his obligations. If Russia were to break her
engagements, then it would be more than a matter of half measures. As
for Palmerston's comparison of Russian and Turkish civilisation, Aberdeen here showed how different were his own sentiments. 'For my own
part,' he wrote, 'I should as soon think of preferring the Koran to the
Bible, as of comparing the Christianity and civilization of Russia to the
fanaticism and immorality of the Turks.' He had already told Graham,

[1] Bell, *Palmerston*, II, 85.
[2] MS. Clar. Dep. C3, fol. 306.
[3] *Ab. Cor. 1852–5*, pp. 119–24. For Palmerston's numerous letters to Clarendon about the
Eastern Question see MS. Clar. Dep. C3, fols. 9, 11, 28–31, 33–8, etc.
[4] MS. Clar. Dep. C3, fols. 48–51, 30 May 1853.
[5] *Ab. Cor. 1852–5*, pp. 125–6, 31 May 1853 (printed in Stanmore, *Aberdeen*, pp. 222–3).

however, that under certain circumstances he was prepared to give ✔ Stratford authority to call up the fleet.[1]

As always in diplomatic crises everything turned on the intentions of the suspected aggressor. For months Nesselrode in St Petersburg and Brunnow in London had been protesting the moderate and pacific nature of their requests, but Menschikoff's actions in Constantinople belied their mild language. When news of his departure from Constantinople reached London, Brunnow immediately wrote a personal note to Aberdeen quoting an old saying attributed to the duke of Wellington: 'Now, we have got into a mess; let us see how we shall get out of it.' He went on to examine the claims of the controversial Article I of the rejected convention and argued that it really amounted to nothing new. 'We do not ask for new powers of interference, we state only the existing law,' he pleaded. The phrase *comme par le passé*, he argued, 'excludes and resolves the whole difficulty'. It is significant that Brunnow made this approach to Aberdeen, so to speak, behind Clarendon's back. He had asked Clarendon for an interview, but indicated that Aberdeen's '*private* opinion' would carry particular weight with the emperor.[2]

In the meantime Walewski was pressing Clarendon in the opposite direction, urging the British government to summon its fleet. Clarendon told him that cabinet consent would be necessary, but he wished that they had already done it for he feared it might be too late to stop a *coup de main*.[3] He did not think that the Russian emperor had deliberately deceived them, but feared that hostilities against Turkey were imminent. 'Our position then will not be an enviable one', he told Aberdeen, 'and the contemplation of it, even, is painful.' He drafted a long despatch for Seymour,[4] which Aberdeen warmly approved, rehearsing the contradictions between the fair words of Brunnow and Nesselrode and the harsh actions of Menschikoff. Aberdeen admitted the difficulty regarding the first article, but thought that they were disposed to exaggerate the extent of the Russian demands as contained in

[1] *Ab. Cor. 1852–5*, pp. 125–6, 31 May 1853.
[2] *Ibid.* 29 May 1853, p. 117. Temperley maintains that in this article the Russians claimed to protect all Orthodox subjects of the sultan, not just clergy as the French had claimed (*Crimea*, pp. 320–1). He clearly regards this correspondence with Brunnow as rather incriminating to Aberdeen. See also R. E. Howard, 'Brunnow's reports on Aberdeen', *Camb. Hist. J.* IV (1934), 312–21.
[3] *Ab. Cor. 1852–5*, p. 116, 29 May 1853.
[4] See *E.P.* I, no. 195, pp. 200–4, 31 May 1853.

it. 'I am quite ready to admit that they are unreasonable', he wrote, 'and ought to be resisted. But I cannot yet believe that it will be necessary to do so by war if the Emperor should hitherto have been acting in good faith; if his whole conduct should have been a cheat, the case is altered.'[1]

When Clarendon saw Palmerston's letter on the 30th, he observed to Aberdeen that it was 'written under strong old feelings, but by no means in a bad spirit'. The Foreign Secretary himself was now prepared to send the fleet to the Aegean, arguing that Russia would have no right to take offence 'after the patience with which we have endured her enormous and unexplained armaments'. He recommended this 'as the least measure' that would 'satisfy public opinion, and save the Government from shame hereafter', if as he expected 'the Russian hordes pour[ed] into Turkey on every side'.[2] The reference to public opinion reflects the political weakness of the government's position.

The cabinet met forthwith and authorised the strong despatch which Clarendon had drafted for St Petersburg. Still more significantly, they approved the principle of entrusting Stratford with the power of calling up the fleet. On the 31st the Foreign Secretary sent Stratford a despatch to this effect, placing the fleet at Malta at his disposal in the case of an emergency such as a Russian declaration of war on Turkey, but warning him in no way to depart from a policy of moderation and conciliation.[3] The First Lord of the Admiralty issued his orders accordingly. 'Admiral Dundas', he told Prince Albert, 'will have under his command seven Sail of the Line, very powerful ships and 9 or 10 steamers of war.'[4]

After this fateful cabinet meeting Palmerston wrote to Graham about the attitude of the various ministers and to develop his own ideas as to resolute action. He claimed that the majority of the most experienced members of the cabinet, Lansdowne, John Russell and Clarendon, concurred in the same opinion; 'the Dukes of Newcastle and Argyll appear to be in the same way of thinking', he added, 'and the others seemed to agree with them there'. Palmerston went on to argue that, since they had come to the decision that Stratford should have the power, it would be far better to have the fleet close at hand, and he suggested to Graham, as First Lord, that it would be good for the sailors to

---

[1] MS. Clar. Dep. C4, fol. 38, 30 May 1853.
[2] *Ab. Cor. 1852–5*, pp. 126–7, 'Monday night' (30 May 1853).
[3] E.P. no. 194, p. 199. [4] Graham Papers, 2 June 1853 (copy).

have an Aegean cruise and get away from the mischievous idleness of a long sojourn in Malta. He thought it most unfortunate that orders had not already been sent to Admiral Dundas. 'I feel strongly', he added, 'that if we allow a long delay to intervene, circumstances may arise which make us the laughing stock of Europe.'[1]

Aberdeen persisted in believing that they should wait to hear Stratford's explanation of Menschikoff's departure, but on 1 June, the day on which they received a despatch from Stratford with this information,[2] he gave in to the combined demands of Palmerston, Russell, Lansdowne and Clarendon that the fleet should be directed eastwards.[3] At the same time he expressed the opinion that he was constantly to voice that the 'best prospect of success' was to be found 'in the union of the Four Powers and in their firm but friendly representation at St Petersburg'. He urged Clarendon 'to communicate frankly to Russia, the motive and spirit' that lay behind their fleet movement, hoping that it would not destroy Britain's 'salutary influence' as much as he feared. He continued:

The authority given to Lord Stratford to call up the fleet to Constantinople is a fearful power to place in the hands of any Minister, involving as it does the question of peace or war. The passage of the Dardanelles, being a direct violation of treaty, would make us the aggressors, and give to Russia a just cause of war. It is most important therefore that Lord Stratford should not have recourse to such a step except under the pressure of actual hostilities, or under circumstances fully equivalent to such a state.[4]

Clarendon, in transmitting the decision to the First Lord of the Admiralty, stressed the need for speedy action if they did not 'intend to remain passive spectators of the swallowing up of Turkey by Russia'.[5] It was a significant decision, as Greville observed, since, made jointly with France, it cemented the Anglo-French alliance so dreaded by the Russians. Temperley in his defence of Stratford says that Clarendon forced the decision in deference to public opinion,[6] but in a letter of 2 June Clarendon indicated that he considered the 'unpleasant communication' from Constantinople warrant for it.[7]

---

[1] Graham Papers, 31 May 1853 (copy). Likewise Russell wrote to Clarendon on the same day: 'I think it absolutely necessary that the fleet at Malta should go at once' (MS. Clar. Dep. C3).   [2] *E.P.* I, no. 196, pp. 204–5.
[3] Cf. MS. Clar. Dep. C3, fol. 312, from Russell, 1 June 1853.
[4] MS. Clar. Dep. C4, fols. 40–1, 1 June 1853 (Stanmore, *Aberdeen*, pp. 223–4).
[5] Graham Papers, 1 June 1853.
[6] Temperley, *Crimea*, p. 336.   [7] *Ab. Cor. 1852–5*, p. 128, 2 June 1853.

Another cabinet was held on 5 June, but Aberdeen found it difficult to give the queen 'any intelligent account of discussion so desultory'. He found his colleagues less inclined to rash action, but not sufficiently apprehensive of what was likely to happen.[1] On the same day news arrived of the Russian determination to occupy the Principalities.[2] Two days later he was wringing his hands again. 'As we are drifting fast towards war,' he wrote to Clarendon, using an oft-recurring phrase, 'I should think the Cabinet ought to see where they are going', but he despaired of calling them for lack of time for discussion.[3] He still professed to believe in the possibility of a pacific settlement and dwelt on the fact that no matter how important the integrity of Turkey might be they were 'under no obligation'.[4]

Brunnow continued his clever tactics of undermining the Prime Minister's resistance. On 6 June he told Aberdeen, more in sorrow than in anger, that 'it was *madness* on the part of Stratford to advise the Turks to reject this last note!'[5] On the 8th he dressed up the news of Russia's aggressive intentions in the Principalities by dwelling on the emperor's forbearance on receiving news of the Turkish rejection of Menschikoff's final proposal and dwelt on the unfortunate impression created in St Petersburg by Stratford's intervention. He announced that the Turks were to be given another chance to accept the proposal, which, he maintained, was a clear indication of the patient and pacific course of the Russian government. (It may be observed that there is some continuity in Russian methods of diplomacy.) If the Porte refused, however, then Russia would occupy the Principalities, he said, '*not with the view to make war*', but 'for the purpose of having a pledge'. He urged the British government to intervene to secure Turkish assent, despite the views of their minister in Constantinople. He concluded:

After all this is not a question of personal *amour propre*, but one in which the peace of the world is deeply involved.

I have nothing more to say on the subject. Remember, only, that the question of peace or war depends now mainly on the wisdom of Her Majesty's Government.[6]

[1] *Ibid.* p. 134, 5 June 1853.
[2] *Ibid.* p. 139, from Clarendon enclosing a despatch from Seymour.
[3] *Ibid.* p. 140, 7 June 1853.   [4] MS. Clar. Dep. C4, fols. 42–3, 7 June 1853.
[5] *Ab. Cor. 1852–5*, p. 139.
[6] *Ibid.* pp. 141–3, 8 June 1853. On the 24th he again wrote privately to Aberdeen in defence of Russian policy (*ibid.* pp. 153–5). He was clearly making the most of his personal friendship with the Prime Minister to supplement his formal communications with Clarendon.

This was certainly calculated to touch the peace-loving Aberdeen at his weakest point. And on the same day the king of the Belgians wrote to him urging that the Turks should be induced to make some nominal concessions and that some other English diplomat should join Stratford in Constantinople. 'The Emperor', he wrote, 'must be *assisted to help himself out of the scrape into which he has certainly got himself.*'[1] Two days later he wrote yet again to say that he had heard the Russians had praised the French ambassador in Constantinople 'and complain most bitterly of Lord Redcliffe'. Once more he stressed the necessity of giving the emperor a means of extricating himself ' *avec honneur* '.[2]

Aberdeen's inability to control the situation is seen in a report to Queen Victoria of a cabinet meeting on 11 June. Although he found the cabinet more favourable to peace and ready to acknowledge that they owed no treaty obligation to Turkey, he reported that it was unlikely that the Turks, 'acting under the direction of Lord Stratford', would accept the Russian terms. The result, he continued fatalistically, would be Russian occupation of the Principalities, which would probably lead to Stratford calling up the British and French fleets.[3] 'Pains have been taken to prevent this,' he added, which was an odd commentary on Clarendon's recent instruction to the ambassador. Actually, as early as 9 June Clarendon had suggested to Russell that, if the government did not want to make the occupation of the Principalities a *casus belli*, Stratford should be told so,[4] but instructions were not sent until 18 June. In these the Foreign Secretary, while roundly condemning Russia's action, indicated that Turkey should be urged not to make the proposed occupation a *casus belli*, but there is nothing in the printed despatch forbidding Stratford to call up the fleet.[5] This was followed on 24 June by a further despatch instructing Stratford to press reforms on the Porte with respect to its Christian subjects,[6] which again reflected the Aberdeen approach to the problem.

Strains now began to develop in the cabinet, according to Clarendon, who poured out his woes to Greville (little realising that this was the way to immortalise them). He dwelt on the task that he had in the cabinet 'mediating between Aberdeen and Palmerston, whose ancient and habitual ideas of foreign policy are brought by this business into

[1] *Ab. Cor. 1852–5*, p. 145. [2] *Ibid*. p. 146.
[3] *Ibid*. p. 144.
[4] PRO 30/22/11/A, fols. 85–6, 9 June. 'I wish I saw my way to putting the question back within the pale of negotiation', Clarendon added helplessly.
[5] *E.P.* I, no. 263, pp. 274–5. [6] *Ibid*. no. 282, pp. 293–4.

antagonism', and he said that the difficulty was made the greater by the unfortunate manner of Aberdeen, 'who cannot avoid some of that sneering tone in discussion which so seriously affects his popularity in the House of Lords'. Clarendon regarded himself as a buffer charged with the responsibility of preventing a collision between these two. As an example, he cited an occasion on 19 June when the majority of the cabinet, without bringing the matter to a vote, had sided with Aberdeen and himself against a proposal of Palmerston to make Russian entrance into the Principalities a *casus belli*.[1] Both Clarendon and Granville told Greville that on this occasion Palmerston had given way with good grace and 'behaved very well', but it remained to be seen how long it could last.

The situation was further aggravated by the growing hostility of the press to the government's foreign policy. Indeed the Tory *Press* and *Morning Herald* were demanding the impeachment of Aberdeen and Clarendon for aiding and abetting Menschikoff. Eventually the government was driven to persuade *The Times* to publish an inspired article answering the charges, which was done on 17 June, but this unfortunately contained an inaccuracy which displeased Brunnow; the latter remonstrated with Clarendon, who then had to secure the insertion of a second article to correct the first.[2] Further tension was created by a cabinet leak to the press, which was attributed to Palmerston, but which Greville thought was more likely the result of an indiscretion of Lady Palmerston's.[3]

On 13 June the British fleet arrived at Besika Bay on the Turkish coast close to the Dardanelles, and it was joined by the French fleet on the following day. Stratford, to the relief of Aberdeen and Clarendon, showed great restraint in the use of the powers entrusted to him. Indeed, even before he had been so directed by Clarendon, he had urged the Turkish government not to resist the occupation of the Principalities.[4]

[1] *Greville Memoirs*, VI, 430–1. Three days earlier Russell had explicitly written to Clarendon to say that entrance to the Principalities should not be considered a *casus belli* (MS. Clar. Dep. C3, fols. 334–5).

Palmerston continued his regular correspondence with Clarendon, plying him with scraps of intelligence, with proposals for effective action and with pungent comments on events as they developed with a Churchillian vigour that belied his years (see *ibid.* fols. 54–70).   [2] *Greville Memoirs*, VI, 429–30.

[3] *Ibid.* p. 431. Later in the summer an even more ridiculous situation occurred when *The Times* began to print conflicting leaders written by different members of the editorial staff representing the different points of view in the cabinet (*ibid.* p. 433).

[4] *E.P.* I, no. 308, pp. 317–18.

Nevertheless, on the 16th the Turks refused the most recent Russian ultimatum, this time from Nesselrode.

The rumblings within the cabinet continued and, as so often in the course of the protracted crisis, ministers gave expression to their views and sentiments in long memoranda, which they circulated among themselves. Russell set the ball rolling on 19 June with a paper in which he dwelt on the danger to England of a Russian control, direct or indirect, of Constantinople and argued that such an attempt 'must be resisted even by war on the part of England'.[1] Lord Lansdowne (the one survivor from another wartime coalition) was prepared to go further. He advocated a stiff protest against the occupation of the Principalities with 'a distinct intimation that any further invasion of territory under whatever pretence...would be considered as a ground of war by England and France'.[2] Graham professed himself in agreement with Lansdowne's views but warned against fixing 'beforehand a course of policy contingent on events which cannot be foreseen'.[3] Palmerston made his usual incisive contribution. 'My opinion', he wrote, 'is that if England & France stoutly support Turkey in this matter by negotiation, backing up their negotiation by adequate naval demonstration, they will ultimately succeed even if Austria & Prussia give them no assistance'. He professed to believe that, if the Allies took a strong line, then the Russians would eventually withdraw. 'I must say', he added, 'that I think that any other Result would be dishonourable to England & to France, and dangerous to the Balance of Power and to the security of the other States of Europe.' He thought any other Russian inroads would be out of the question once England and France had declared themselves. Indeed, he greatly belittled Russia's war potential and exaggerated Turkey's. He even suggested that Polish and Hungarian exiles might be enlisted to fight for Turkey.[4]

Lord Aberdeen concluded the discussion with a memorandum, in which he reminded the ministers that the cabinet had already agreed to advise the Porte not to meet the occupation of the Principalities with a declaration of war and to instruct the British ambassador not to make it the occasion of bringing the fleet to Constantinople. He presumed that

---

[1] Gooch, *Later correspondence*, II, 148–9, prints the first part of this long memorandum, and Walpole, *Russell*, II, 183, the second.

[2] Gooch, *Later correspondence*, II, 149.

[3] *Ibid.* p. 150.

[4] PRO/30/22/11/A, fols. 94–8, 20 June 1853 (partly printed in Gooch, *Later correspondence*, II, 150–1).

these decisions were taken to gain time 'for the employment of our endeavours to preserve peace', and this he argued must now be the government's main concern.[1]

Consequently Russell dropped his proposals for the time being and addressed a letter to Clarendon with suggestions that Aberdeen found much more acceptable. 'I liked your letter all the better', Aberdeen wrote, 'from the contrast exhibited by its spirit with the box of combustibles which I sent you yesterday morning.'[2] This presumably referred to the memoranda that had been circulating.

On 28 June Palmerston urged Clarendon that the Russians should be warned that the occupation of the Principalities would be considered an abrogation of the Treaty of 1841 and that England and France would consequently feel free to enter the Straits.[3] On 4 July (two days after the Russians had in fact crossed the Pruth) he addressed another letter, this time to the Prime Minister, urging that the British squadron be sent into the Black Sea in support of the Turks as soon as it was known that the Russians had entered the Principalities.[4]

Aberdeen offered strong resistance to Palmerston's suggestions. He complained that 'at present, we are drifting hopelessly towards war, without raising a hand to prevent it', and dwelt on the necessity of making some concrete proposals to Russia. If the Turks followed English advice and did not make the occupation of the Principalities a *casus belli*, he doubted whether under the treaty of 1841 the fleet could be allowed to enter the straits, and reminded Palmerston that in any event the cabinet had already made a contrary decision. He had no doubt, he said sarcastically, that the country and the opposition would welcome such a step, but it would not promote the cause of peace, 'which', he added, 'is that about which I am most interested'. 'In a case of this kind, I dread popular support', he continued. 'On some occasion,' he recalled, 'when the Athenian Assembly vehemently applauded Alcibiades, the latter asked if he had said anything particularly foolish!'[5] This may have been a clever sally, but it was not calculated to please his most formidable antagonist in the cabinet. That body, however, supported the Prime Minister for the moment and Palmerston once again accepted defeat, but he wrote to Russell, who apparently missed the cabinet meeting, saying:

[1] PRO 30/22/11/A, fols. 104–5, 21 June 1853.
[2] *Ibid.* fol. 106, 22 June 1853.   [3] MS. Clar. Dep. C3, fols. 85–7.
[4] *Ab. Cor. 1852–5*, pp. 157–8.   [5] *Ibid.* pp. 158–60, 4 July 1853.

I think our position waiting timidly and submissively at the back door while Russia is violently threatening and arrogantly forcing her way into the house, is unwise with a view to a peaceful settlement, and derogatory to the character and standing and dignity of the two powers.[1]

About the same time Russell suggested to Graham that the French and British should enter the Dardanelles, occupy the forts commanding the Straits, and proceed to the Bosporus if the Russians appeared in the Black Sea in force.[2] Recognising that both Graham and Stratford considered it would be dangerous for the British squadron to cruise in the Black Sea, he suggested that a small steamer or two might be used off the Turkish Black Sea ports to warn against any sudden attack.[3] Stratford had strongly opposed a French proposal to send a steamer to reconnoitre the Russian ports of Odessa and Sebastopol.[4]

Aberdeen opposed Russell's proposals and any enlargement of Stratford's powers, which in his view were 'already too great'.[5] In actual fact, up to this point Stratford's conduct had been beyond reproach from the point of view of the moderates in the cabinet. He had shown no inclination to abuse his powers with respect to the fleet and had warned the Turks not to place undue reliance upon it.[6] Stratford had also written to Graham about the relations between the French and British fleets and the proposal for reconnaissance in the Black Sea, which he had opposed. On the latter point Graham strongly supported Stratford, but on the question of strengthening the fleet to make it equal to the French he made it clear that he had strained every resource to bring it to its present strength, which was a maximum in the Mediterranean for the past thirty years; 'the union with our ally', he commented, 'is hollow, indeed, if our friendly relations are so balanced that a single Line of Battleship will turn the scale between confidence and distrust'. Referring to the reputed anti-English reputation of the new French admiral, who had been selected because he did not outrank Dundas, Graham suggested that the fleets might be separated rather than confined indefinitely in the close quarters of Besika Bay.[7]

[1] PRO 30/22/11/A, fols. 120–5, 7 July 1853 (partly printed in Walpole, *Russell*, II, 184).
[2] Graham Papers, 4 July 1853.　　　　　　　[3] *Ibid.* 3 July 1853.
[4] *Ibid.* from Clarendon, 3 July 1853.
[5] MS. Clar. Dep. C4, fols. 48–9, 5 July 1853.
[6] E.P. I, no. 299, pp. 312–13, 16 June 1853, regarding an audience with the sultan after the arrival of the fleet at Besika Bay.
[7] Graham Papers, to Stratford, 8 July 1853; Parker, *Graham*, II, 222, omits the important sentences regarding relations with the French, without any indication.

The Vienna note, June–July 1853; growing suspicions of Stratford

The crisis had now been dragging on for four months. Russia had thought the opportunity ripe to press her claims on Turkey, but had discovered both Britain and France hostile to her pretensions. Neither side desired war and so, despite the movement of the Allied fleets to the Aegean, the break in diplomatic relations between Russia and Turkey, and the occupation of the Principalities by Russia, the way was still left open to a settlement by diplomacy. No power was better situated than Austria to initiate an international settlement. She clearly had a vital interest in the area, but her friendly relations with Russia made her an acceptable intermediary in the eyes of the Czar, who undoubtedly relied too greatly on Austrian gratitude for assistance given in 1848–9. Consequently, on 16 June the British and French governments urged the Austrian government to summon a conference at Vienna to seek a solution to the problem. In the meantime both these governments proceeded to prepare draft conventions for the consideration of the interested parties.

On 7 July the cabinet approved such a draft submitted to it by Clarendon, which merely proposed the renewal by Turkey of the engagements of previous treaties with no extensions added to them.[1] A less satisfactory draft proposed by the French government was also accepted as an alternative.

Shortly after the Russian occupation of the Principalities Nesselrode circulated a memorandum announcing the action and attempting to justify it, a procedure which the Western Allies regarded as highly objectionable. Clarendon addressed a stiff remonstrance to St Petersburg,[2] but Palmerston made it the occasion for again demanding more militant action. Talk of 'la paix à tout prix' (a phrase attributed to Aberdeen),[3] he said, had misled the Russian government, which now presumed to lay down the law to France and Britain. 'It is the robber', he observed, 'who declares that he will not leave the house until the policeman shall have first retired from the courtyard.' The position of Britain and France, he claimed, was already humiliating, but Russia's announcement, published all over Europe before it was communicated to the British and French governments, made it no longer tenable.

[1] *Ab. Cor. 1852–5*, p. 161, 9 July 1853, to the queen; PRO/30/22/11/A, fols. 120–5, from Palmerston, 7 July 1853. [2] *E.P.* I, no. 346, pp. 364–7.
[3] See Add. MS. 43191, fol. 79, Aberdeen to Graham, 11 July 1853.

Consequently he urged that Russia should be notified of the despatch of the two squadrons to the Bosporus.[1]

Aberdeen immediately responded with a strong vindication of the existing policy. 'The conduct of the English Government', he wrote, 'has not only shown moderation and forbearance, but much wisdom. Any other course would have made war certain, or, at least, the continuance of peace extremely difficult.' While admitting the unsatisfactory nature of Nesselrode's circular and the necessity of making a firm diplomatic answer to it, he asked what was to be gained by such 'acts of bravado' as sending the fleets to the Bosporus or into the Black Sea. They had brought the fleets up to Besika Bay for the protection of Constantinople, but he reminded his colleagues that they were bound by no engagements to the Turks, that they had prepared a draft convention for consideration by the powers which in their view met the requirements of both parties, and he maintained that the time was propitious for a settlement 'unless we shall create fresh difficulties by our own imprudence'.[2]

Russell agreed with Aberdeen on this occasion, but warned that any Russian move beyond the Principalities must be regarded as a threat to Constantinople. Even Palmerston, although he did not accept all the points in Aberdeen's memorandum, saw the logic of the conclusion that the new proposals should not be endangered by premature action. Therefore he was 'prepared to share in the responsibility of submitting even to insult, rather than to afford the quibbling and pettifogging Government with which we have to deal, any pretext arising out of our course for rejecting terms of accommodation unobjectionable in themselves'.[3] Palmerston had perhaps been influenced by a note from Clarendon, who had argued that sending the fleet to Constantinople at this point would have been a disservice to Turkey since it might lose her the support of Austria.[4]

It may have been a temporary setback for Palmerston, but he con-

---

[1] *Ab. Cor. 1852–5*, pp. 162–3, 12 July 1853. This proposal had been turned down by the cabinet a few days earlier with the argument that Stratford had full powers to call up the fleet, but Palmerston put no stock in this assertion. 'This is no doubt stated in public despatches', he wrote to Russell, 'but we all know that he has been privately desired not to do so' (Walpole, *Russell*, II, 184).

[2] *Ab. Cor. 1852–5*, pp. 164–5, 13 July 1853 (partly reproduced in Stanmore, *Aberdeen*, pp. 225–7).   [3] *Ibid.* pp. 166–7, 15 July 1853; an excerpt is quoted by Stanmore.

[4] *Ibid.* pp. 169–70, 14 July 1853. Aberdeen seized on Palmerston's retreat as the occasion of a friendly note rejoicing that 'all *polémiques*' should cease between them on the matter (*ibid.* p. 167).

tinued to put steady pressure on Clarendon to induce him to take a stiffer line towards Russia. He did this subtly, for his tone was always friendly and intimate and the proposals casual as if to suggest there was no real difference between them. For instance, on one occasion he complimented Clarendon on a despatch to Stratford but suggested that it was 'rather a damper' for the recipient and objected to a phrase calling war 'the greatest of all calamities'. On another occasion he wrote more pointedly: 'I admired greatly your letter to Seymour but I did not like to say too much in its praise in the Cabinet for fear that by doing so I might lead others to think it was too strong.' He observed that Clarendon could say and do things that he [Palmerston] could not. 'I can assure you', he wrote, 'it is a great comfort and satisfaction for me to know that the Conduct of our Foreign Relations is in such able Hands as yours.'[1] In the long run Palmerston's friendly but constant pressure probably had its effect on Clarendon.

Meanwhile, on 9 July, after obtaining the approval of the French government,[2] Clarendon sent his draft project of a convention to Stratford in Constantinople, seeking the agreement of the Porte.[3] He also sent a copy to Seymour, to be shown unofficially to Nesselrode, who expressed no serious objection to it.[4] It was not, however, well received in Constantinople.[5] Indeed in a subsequent letter Stratford told Clarendon with extreme frankness that he did not consider it 'a desirable mode of arrangement' and that the French and Austrian ambassadors, he believed, agreed with him. With considerable insight he gave it as his opinion that 'if the Russian Government accept the project they will do so with the intention of giving it an interpretation that will leave them nothing to regret in the loss of Prince Menschikoff's note'. Stratford said he was sure that this was not Clarendon's intention and so did not commend it to the Porte.[6] Long before this, however, Clarendon's project had been superseded by the alternative proposal made by the French government. Clarendon, although preferring his own, offered no objection to this being presented at Vienna and St Petersburg.[7]

---

[1] MS. Clar. Dep. C3, fols. 102–3, 108–9, 28 and 31 July 1853.
[2] E.P. I, no. 365, pp. 391–2. [3] Ibid. no. 330, pp. 349–50.
[4] Ibid. no. 352, pp. 369–70; II, no. 28, pp. 22–3.
[5] MS. Clar. Dep. C10, fols. 256–60, 23 July 1853, from Stratford.
[6] Ibid. fols. 268–9, 4 August 1853.
[7] Temperley maintains that it was a tragedy that Clarendon's version was not adopted (E.H.R. XLIX, 270–1). According to Greville, Seymour told Clarendon that Nesselrode preferred his project and that he thought, if submitted from Vienna, it might be accepted (Memoirs, VI, 436–7).

The scene now shifted to Vienna, but unfortunately at the same time a side-show opened at Constantinople. The Austrian government had accepted the Anglo-French proposal that an ambassadorial conference in Vienna should mediate the dispute between Russia and Turkey. Initially Count Buol, the Austrian foreign minister, invited the Turkish government to propose, for the consideration of the conference, a note to be forwarded to St Petersburg with the backing of the Four Powers.[1] Eventually, under pressure from the four ambassadors in Constantinople, led by Stratford, the Turkish government produced such a note, which was unhappily dubbed the 'Turkish ultimatum'. Unfortunately, a Turkish government crisis had caused a week's delay in the production of this document.[2] Consequently, when Buol assembled the council of ambassadors in Vienna on 24 July, he proceeded to draft a note based on the French proposal,[3] which it was known had been well received in St Petersburg. On 27 July, after the ambassadors had been duly authorised to act, the conference proceeded to make some modifications to the French note, which were approved by the various governments, the British suggesting some very minor additions to ensure the adhesion of the Porte.[4] In the meantime the so-called 'Turkish ultimatum' was received by Count Buol, who communicated it to the council of ambassadors on the 29th with the observation that the Austrian government considered it unsatisfactory and proposed to proceed with the note that the conference had drafted.[5] As a result the 'Vienna Note' (with the British additions) was despatched to Constantinople and St Petersburg on 1 August. Within a week the assent of the Russian emperor had been obtained '*pure et simple*'.[6]

[1] *Hansard*, CXXIX, 1634–6, speech of Lord Clarendon.

[2] Temperley, *E.H.R.* XLIX, 266–9.

[3] *E.P.* II, no. 1, p. 1, telegraphic despatch, 24 July, Westmorland to Clarendon, received 25 July 1853.

[4] *Ibid.* nos. 2, 3, 4, 5 and 10, pp. 1–4, and 23, p. 20; Add. MS. 43047, fols. 176–7, Aberdeen to the queen, 30 July 1853.

[5] *Ibid.* nos. 40 and 45, pp. 35–7, 38–9. When Brunnow heard of this Turkish proposal he reminded Aberdeen of his old adage about 'too many cooks'. Believing that the Aberdeen–Clarendon proposal was still on the stove, he expressed a hope that their 'Scotch broth' would prove 'the most palatable'. It was not this Russian ambassador's fault that England finally declared war on his country (*Ab. Cor. 1852–5*, pp. 177–8, 29 July 1853).

[6] *E.P.* II, nos. 54–6, pp. 43–4. 'After an elaborate preamble the key passage of the proposed note ran as follows: "The undersigned has in consequence received orders to declare by the present note that the Government of His Majesty the Sultan will remain faithful to the letter and to the spirit of the Treaties of Kainardji and Adrianople relative

In a despatch on 2 August Clarendon informed Stratford of Britain's acceptance of the Vienna note since it was known to be acceptable to the Russian emperor and expressed the hope that 'before the receipt of this despatch' he would 'have found no difficulty in procuring the assent of the Turkish Government'.[1] In fact he was less sanguine, for on the 5th he wrote to Aberdeen: 'I shall write in strong terms privately to Stratford that the Vienna note *must* be accepted. I begin to think we shall have as much trouble with the Turks as with the Russians.'[2] One difficulty was that, while Paris and Vienna were within twenty-four hours of London by telegraph, it took at least nine or ten days to three weeks for letters and despatches to get to Constantinople and by the time they arrived they were generally out of date.

Stratford had worked very hard to secure a peaceful settlement, by restraining the Turks at the time of the occupation of the Principalities, by pressing the sultan to reinstate the moderate Reschid Pasha, who had fallen from favour after that event, and by extracting from the Porte with great difficulty the ill-fated 'Turkish ultimatum'. Thus he would have been more than human if he had welcomed the appearance of the Vienna note, and while, on instruction from London, he supported it, it was widely said that he did so without enthusiasm and that this encouraged the Turks to reject it, as they did on 20 August. At any rate the Turkish rejection of the Vienna note, which had been accepted by the Russians and approved by the other Powers, brought Europe a long step closer to the coming war. Indeed, by now, with the arrival of the Egyptian fleet, the war fever was mounting rapidly in Constantinople.[3]

Temperley claims that Stratford has been unfairly blamed for the Turkish rejection of the Vienna note and asserts that the Turks were now beyond his control. The Turkish grand council, which was more

to the protection of the Christian religion, and His Majesty considers himself bound in honour to cause to be observed forever, and to preserve from all prejudice now and hereafter, the enjoyment of the spiritual privileges which have been granted by His Majesty's august ancestors to the Orthodox Eastern Church, and which are maintained and confirmed by him; and moreover, in a spirit of exalted equity, to cause the Greek rite to share in the advantages granted to other Christian rites by convention or other special arrangement"' (*ibid.* no. 31, enclosure 10, translation p. 26).

[1] *Ibid.* no. 32, p. 27. See also MS. Clar. Dep. C3, fols. 55 and 61, 16 and 29 July 1853. He had expressed the same view when the convention was first under consideration (*ibid.* fol. 55, 16 July).

[2] *Ab. Cor. 1852–5*, p. 182, 5 August 1853.

[3] See Temperley, *Crimea*, pp. 347–8.

violent than the cabinet, was now beginning to dictate Turkish policy and the war party to get the upper hand. Nevertheless, there is no doubt that contemporaries tended to hold Stratford responsible, since in the past his influence with the Porte had been so great. It is quite extraordinary to find a Prime Minister and a Foreign Secretary writing to each other and to colleagues in such stringent terms about an ambassador whom they continued to employ. Clarendon is reported once to have said of Stratford: 'He is himself no better than a Turk, and has lived there so long, and is animated with such a personal hatred of the Emperor, that he is full of the Turkish spirit; and this and his temper together have made him take a part directly contrary to the wishes and instructions of the Government.'[1] On 18 August he told Graham that it was many weeks since he had received any letter or despatch from Stratford that he liked,[2] and on the same day he wrote to Aberdeen: 'I fear Stratford means to give us trouble—Reschid only speaks as he tells him.'[3] Aberdeen responded in similar terms.[4] On another occasion Clarendon told Aberdeen that De la Cour, the French ambassador at Constantinople, said that Stratford was all-powerful and could do what he pleased, but that he was not friendly to any arrangement not his own and that he spoke in strong terms about the convention.[5] The Foreign Secretary had this from Cowley in Paris, who wrote:

De la Cour asserts further that, to his *intimes*, Lord Stratford uses the most violent language, that he disapproves all the proceedings at Vienna, declares war preferable to such a solution, that the position of Turkey was excellent, etc. etc. Then he goes on to say that they shall know that his name is Canning, that he will resign, that he knows the government of England is not united on this question, and that a change must take place there which will bring into power the friends and supporters of his policy in Turkey.[6]

Why were the British ministers readier to believe the French ambassador than their own? Was it that they knew their man too well or that they subconsciously made him their own scapegoat? There is evidence to support both these views. They knew that Stratford was a proud, self-willed man, whose influence among the Turks was legendary, and who

[1] *Greville Memoirs*, VI, 445.
[2] Graham Papers. Stratford's letters of 23 and 25 July, 4 and 5 August had all been critical of Clarendon's proposals (MS. Clar. Dep. C10, fols. 256–75).
[3] Add. MS. 43188, fols. 217–18.
[4] MS. Clar. Dep. C4, fol. 16, 19 August 1853.
[5] Add. MS. 43188, fols. 219–20, 20 August 1853.
[6] Maxwell, *Clarendon*, II, 18–19.

had probably lived among them too long. When their own hard-pressed plans went awry they were too ready to suspect the worst, but it does not say much for them that they left a man they did not trust at this crucial post.

Indeed, they talked about replacing him, but only because they thought he might resign. Aberdeen told Clarendon he had prepared the queen for the possibility of Stratford's resignation, 'which I agree with you in thinking by no means improbable,' he wrote, 'and which she will not at all regret'. He advised Clarendon to have a replacement in mind and suggested Bulwer as probably the best man.

Stratford will have a bad case [he went on]. Had he resisted any concession on the part of Turkey, his course would have been intelligible, but having made himself the author of the Note of Reschid addressed to Nesselrode on 23rd July, it is impossible that he should with any reason reject the Note of the Four Powers, and already accepted by Russia, without having determined not to make peace. In fact his delay in obeying your instructions conveyed to him by telegraphic despatch, unless fully explained, would justify recall.[1]

Aberdeen made this judgment before receipt of Stratford's despatch of 23 August (which only arrived on 31 August) describing his vain efforts to persuade the Turks to accept.[2] Even after this explanation had arrived Stratford remained an object of suspicion although the shrillness of the criticisms was modified.

Stratford's bitterest critic was Graham, who seemed to harbour an almost pathological distrust of him. 'Stratford Canning', he wrote to Aberdeen, 'alone will be responsible for any disaster which may ensue; and I am afraid that he has deliberately calculated on the consequences.'[3] Graham told Greville that he was 'inclined to think not only that he [Stratford] has acted treacherously towards his employers, but that proofs of his treachery might be obtained, and he is all for getting the evidence if possible, and acting upon it at once, by recalling him'.[4] Clarendon, however, said it would be impossible to make out a case, for 'whatever his secret wishes and opinions might be, there was no official evidence to be had that he had failed in doing his duty fairly by his own Government; therefore it would be out of the question to recall him'.[5] Stratford remained at his post as long as the coalition was in office.

[1] MS. Clar. Dep. C4, fols. 68–9, 20 August 1853.
[2] E.P. II, no. 67, pp. 69–70. See below, p. 178.
[3] Ab. Cor. 1852–5, pp. 213–14, 8 September 1854.
[4] Greville Memoirs, VI, 447–8.   [5] Ibid. p. 449.

Parliamentary debates on foreign policy, July–August 1853

There were no great debates on foreign affairs in the session of 1853 despite the mounting tension in the East. From time to time the government was pressed for information, but for the most part ministers gave evasive answers or none at all on the grounds that they did not want to imperil negotiations under way. On 25 April Clarendon made a brief statement covering developments up to that date and assured the House that there was no danger of war over the Turkish situation. On 27 May, as the result of prodding from Lord Malmesbury, he gave some further account of the developments of the preceding month, but indicated his reluctance to say too much at that time. Lords Hardwicke and Beaumont criticised the government for not showing more vigour in resisting the pretensions of Russia. In the Commons, Russell made a discursive statement in reply to questions from Disraeli. On 30 May both Clarendon and Russell refused to answer questions regarding the departure of Menschikoff and British fleet movements.[1]

In early July, prior to the opening of the conference at Vienna, the ministers were apprehensive of joint motions threatened by Clanricarde in the Lords and Layard in the Commons (the latter a fanatical anti-Russian who had just returned from visiting Stratford in Constantinople), but after some difficulty they both were persuaded to agree to a postponement;[2] 'premature and imperfect Debate is pregnant with Evil and may lead to dangerous consequences *both at home and abroad*', Graham observed to Russell with typical foreboding.[3]

On 2 August Clarendon, in answer to a question from Clanricarde regarding the Russian assumption of administration in the Principalities, announced that the British ambassador in Constantinople had been authorised to withdraw British consuls from the area and that the British ambassador in St Petersburg had been instructed to demand an explanation from the Russian government.[4] Unfortunately the public interpreted these remarks as a warning that war was inevitable and for the following week, according to Greville, 'there was a great fall in the funds and the depreciation of every sort of security'.[5]

Members of both Houses who raised questions on these matters were

---

[1] For a summary of these discussions see *Annual Register, 1853*, pp. 179–83.

[2] See PRO 30/22/11/A, fols. 128–30, 8 and 9 July 1853, from Aberdeen; MS. Clar. Dep. C3 fols. 355, 357–8, 6 and 7 July from Russell, and Dep. C10, fol. 201, 7 July 1853, from Clanricarde.   [3] PRO 30/22/11/A, fols. 126–7, 8 July 1853.

[4] *Hansard*, CXXIX, 1138–9.   [5] *Greville Memoirs*, VI, 437.

usually strongly anti-Russian, as was Lord Clanricarde when he said on 8 August that the Russian occupation of the Principalities was either an act of war or of piracy, and he maintained that if the government had advised the Turks not to resist they had made themselves parties to the transaction.[1] The critics were especially annoyed by the Foreign Secretary's refusal to publish his reply to Count Nesselrode's insulting circular, which linked the Russian occupation of the Principalities with the arrival of the Allied fleets in the Aegean. Both Russell and Clarendon contented themselves with saying that it was not English practice to publish single documents, which scarcely satisfied their listeners, since the French had immediately published their rejoinder.[2]

On 14 August Lord Malmesbury formally moved for the production of papers on this subject and spoke at some length to Lord Clarendon's surprise. Malmesbury had made no great reputation as a Foreign Secretary, but some of the things he said in this speech are of interest, both for their political implications and as a reflection of the growing anti-Russian feeling in the country. He began by dwelling on his own success at the Foreign Office in cultivating good relations with France, in contrast with the injudicious speeches made by Graham and Wood at the time of their re-election in which they had spoken harshly of the French emperor. He noted the failure of the government to authorise the sailing of the fleet to the Aegean in the spring in company with the French fleet, despite the advice of Colonel Rose, the very experienced *chargé d'affaires* at Constantinople. He emphasised these points, he said, not to make political capital, but to suggest that they all led the Russians to suppose that the French and British would not cooperate in giving support to Turkey. He attacked the politicians who held that the integrity of Turkey was not worth a war and dwelt on the importance of the independence of that country to Britain.

It will be found [he said] that our trade with Turkey is two-thirds better and more important than that with Russia. Your Lordships will also see that if Constantinople, the great emporium of Turkish commerce, by any division of Turkey, should happen to fall into the hands of Russia, the Mediterranean will be in the possession of three great powers—France, Russia, and England. It is now in the possession of England and France.

He went on to show that any two of these powers coming together could virtually exclude the third.

[1] *Hansard*, CXXIX, 1418–22. [2] *Ibid.* 33–4, 89–92, 343–8, 1137–9.

I therefore cannot conceive any point in our foreign politics of more vital consequence to this country than the maintenance of the independence and integrity of Turkey; and I can hardly imagine a sacrifice too great to secure that independence, for it would not only be for the interests of this country, but for the interests of peace, and the maintenance of the territorial distribution of Europe, as arranged by treaty.

He derided the theory that Turkey was in a state of decay and had best be partitioned. Finally he analysed the events of the preceding four or five months to the great discredit of the Russians. He criticised the government for failing to move the fleets into the Dardanelles when the Russians crossed the Pruth. He protested that it was not his intention to make any factious motion against the government, but he did deplore the government's failure 'to furnish the country with some information on the subject, to state what line of policy they had adopted, and with what results, and to declare with what *animus* they entered into the affair'.[1]

Lord Clarendon expressed surprise that Lord Malmesbury, who had merely given notice of a question, had made so long a speech. He refused to be drawn into divulging information while negotiations were still in progress and answered Malmesbury briefly. Rebutting the latter's criticisms of the government, he did emphasise the fact they had worked very closely with the French government throughout the crisis. Colonel Rose himself had agreed when the initial alarm in March had passed that it was well that the British fleet had remained in Malta. On the other hand there was an advantage in having the French fleet at Salamis instead of Toulon. When it was eventually decided to send the two fleets to Besika Bay, he said, 'the instructions were agreed upon on the same day at Paris and in London, and despatched by the same telegraph; and within a few hours of each other the fleets arrived at Besika Bay, which could not have been the case if one fleet had been at Toulon and the other at Malta'. As for the occupation of the Principalities, the French and British governments, and Lord Stratford de Redcliffe, independently at Constantinople, were agreed upon the inexpediency of making it a *casus belli*. He then briefly gave the history of the Vienna note and announced the Russian emperor's formal acceptance of it.[2]

Lord Beaumont, the Earl of Hardwicke and the Marquis of Clanricarde all spoke briefly, expressing their indignation at Russia's action

[1] *Hansard*, CXXIX, 1605–24. [2] *Ibid.* 1624–36.

and their concern that the government was not taking a strong enough line in support of Turkey.[1] Only the Earl of Ellenborough warned his hearers not to embark too lightly on a policy that might lead to a war of the outcome of which he was apprehensive, but he fully endorsed the policy of friendship with France, which he associated with the name of his former chief, the duke of Wellington.[2] Lord Aberdeen was glad to take up the reference to the magic name of the great duke, whose Foreign Secretary he had been, and said he had always stood by a policy of friendship with France, whether the ruler be Charles X, Louis-Philippe or Napoleon III. Moreover, at the present moment, the four Great Powers of Europe were acting in concert and all were concerned to preserve the integrity of Turkey. He reiterated the point he made so often in the cabinet that Britain was not bound by any treaty with Turkey that required it to provide armed support for that country, but he assured the House that nothing would be proposed that could 'militate against the honour and the essential interests of the country'.[3] Lord Malmesbury, presumably satisfied with the airing of the subject, withdrew his motion and the debate terminated.[4]

On 16 August, in fulfilment of an earlier promise, Russell made a statement in the House of Commons which Greville described as 'tame, meagre and unsatisfactory'.[5] The redoubtable A. H. Layard[6] followed Russell with a speech that was most warlike and anti-Russian. He criticised the government for its failure to meet the Russian challenge, and its leader for proclaiming that its policy was based on peace, but in all his strictures he made a pointed exception of his friend the Home Secretary.[7]

After this blistering speech Sir John Pakington, speaking for the opposition, was mildness itself, for he had nothing to say. He complained of the lack of notice for the debate, which resulted in Disraeli leaving town the day before, unaware of what was to happen; but he excused himself from putting on his leader's mantle on the grounds that since the government refused to table any papers it was impossible to

---

[1] *Ibid.* 1636–47.   [2] *Ibid.* 1647–9.
[3] *Ibid.* 1649–51.   [4] *Ibid.* 1651–2.
[5] *Ibid.* 1760–9; *Greville Memoirs*, VI, 439.
[6] Layard had first been elected to parliament in 1852 and had been appointed Under-Secretary for Foreign Affairs in January of that year just before the fall of the Russell government. Unsuccessful efforts had been made to appoint him to minor office in the coalition. See above, p. 31. He was a close friend of Stratford, who had promoted his archaeological discoveries, and had accompanied the ambassador to Constantinople in the spring.   [7] *Hansard*, CXXIX, 1769–80.

make any judgment on their policy. He contented himself by professing to believe that all parties stood for the maintenance of the integrity of Turkey and of peace with honour.[1]

Lord Dudley Stuart, an advanced Liberal, emulated Layard in his criticisms of the government's policy and agreed with Pakington in complaining about their efforts to suppress discussion of it.[2] The only speaker not in office to speak sympathetically of the government's policy was the Peelite Monckton Milnes, who did not want to see the ministers give any pledge to Turkey 'because on the one hand they would have to contend with a Christian Power, and on the other to maintain the political relations of a European Power with a State with whose principles upon every point of religion and civilization they totally disagreed'. If he found any fault with the government it was they had gone too far in encouraging the Turks to resist.[3] Here was a speech that Lord Aberdeen must have welcomed, but it was not a popular theme.

Three other Liberal backbenchers, Muntz, Blackett and Danby Seymour, spoke briefly in favour of a more resolute policy against Russia. 'For instance,' said Seymour, who spoke last, 'we had annexed Burmah, because a petty officer was kept waiting for half an hour in the sun; while, on the other hand, we forbore from any interference with powerful nations which had committed the most wanton aggressions.'[4]

The most interesting, if not the most useful, contribution to the discussion came from Cobden; while professing no great love for the Russians he found them distinctly less distasteful than the Turks, who inhabited a country without roads, who tolerated the buying and selling of slaves, and whose capital, Constantinople, despite its fine location, compared most unfavourably with St Petersburg. He did not approve of Russian encroachment on Turkey, but he found Russian policy here no different than British policy in India and more recently in Burma. He admitted that the future of the Turkish empire posed a problem that required study, but he proposed no solution beyond affirming that the wishes of the inhabitants should be taken into consideration. He thought Russia's strength greatly exaggerated, and refused to believe that she

---

[1] *Hansard*, CXXIX, 1780–3. Russell reminded him that he had promised a statement before prorogation and said he supposed Disraeli had correctly assumed that it was not his intention to enter into any general discussion (*ibid*. 1793).

[2] *Ibid*. 1783–90.

[3] *Ibid*. 1790–3. [4] *Ibid*. 1810–11.

presented any threat to England, but he vigorously protested against any policy that might lead to war. His conclusion was enigmatic:

I have nothing to say to the Ministers. I do not blame them because they have taken up a position to defend the Turkish Empire. It is a traditional policy they have followed, which has been handed down to them by previous Governments, and unless they had public opinion with them no Government could avoid doing so. All I say is, that I have no doubt they will soon get rid of the difficulties regarding the Wallachian provinces; and I congratulate them on having been as peaceable as the people would allow them to be.[1]

This was too much for Lord Palmerston, who rose to speak, not so much for the government, as for those former ministers whose policy Cobden had castigated. Palmerston refused to accept praise for the present government from such a source and in such a speech, which he said was riddled with contradictions. He maintained that the maintenance of the integrity of Turkey was not only a desirable but a perfectly feasible object. He assured Cobden that he was quite misinformed as to the state of that country, which he said had made greater progress than any other country in the preceding thirty years. That progress had been aided by British help and advice.

If that system is pursued [he concluded]; if England, united with France, determine that Turkey shall not belong to Russia or to any other Power, and if that doctrine is enforced in practice, I am convinced that if no foreign Power endeavour to destroy Turkey, our policy, so far from being ridiculous, as the hon. Gentleman endeavoured to represent it, will prove a sound policy —a policy which deserves the approbation of the country, and which it will be the duty of every future British Government to pursue.[2]

Greville says 'the discussion would have ended languidly and ill for the Government but for this brilliant improvisation, which carried the House entirely with it'. He recognised, however, that it was not really a defence of the government's foreign policy. Fortunately no one dwelt on this point and Greville concluded that 'on the whole his speech did good, because it closed the discussion handsomely, and left the impression of P.'s having cast his lot for good and all with his present colleagues, as is really the case'.[3] He was of course unaware that Palmerston would attempt to leave the government before parliament met again.

[1] *Ibid.* 1798–1806.
[2] *Ibid.* 1806–10.   [3] *Greville Memoirs*, VI, 439.

Graham also saw the clash between Cobden and Palmerston as the highlight of the evening, so describing it in a letter to Clarendon in which he commented on its significance, saying:

We have [had] a stand up fight between Cobden and Palmerston; the former the Champion of Russia and Christianity; the latter the sworn ally of Turkey and Mahometanism. Both made very able Speeches in opposite senses; but both pushed their doctrines to an extreme. Cobden in the long run will have England with him; but the Derbyites were enchanted with Palmerston and cheered him to the Echo; so did young India, who were most offensive in their language towards Aberdeen. Fortunately it is the last night of the Session; and before we meet again the Turkish affair, at least for the present, will probably be adjusted; otherwise the Breach on our side of the House would soon spread into a rupture.[1]

It was an odd debate in that there was no participation from the opposition side of the House apart from the one negative contribution of Pakington.[2] But the growls of discontent from a wing of the Liberal party were warning of the storm that would eventually bring the government down. The ministers had not relished the debate, which was calculated to further arouse public opinion, but which also revealed different shades of opinion within the cabinet. Clarendon told Graham that he was 'sorry to hear the turn things took in the H. of C^s', but said that he was not surprised. 'We are lucky that this is the last night of the Session,' he agreed. 'Otherwise we shd have a series of such debates.' He feared that Brunnow would report Cobden's opinion to be that of the country and that the result would be continued pressure by Russia on Turkey and a disinclination to evacuate the Principalities.[3]

When parliament was prorogued the diplomatic situation looked reasonably bright from London. The Four Powers and Russia had agreed on the Vienna note and as yet no word of its rejection had come from Constantinople. Consequently ministers quickly dispersed with the labours of their first parliamentary session at an end.

The Prime Minister summed up the situation with pardonable pride in a letter to his old friend Madame Lieven:

We have brought the Session of Parliament to a triumphant close [he wrote]; we have carried many useful and important measures; our majorities were

[1] MS. Clar. Dep. C4, fols. 199–200, 16 August 1853.
[2] Thus Kingsley Martin is inaccurate with respect to the Commons when he asserts that 'Clarendon and Lord John were severely handled by Tory opponents' (*Triumph of Lord Palmerston*, p. 123). [3] Graham Papers, 16 August 1853.

numerous; and although a coalition of very different materials, we have adhered well together. For my part, I think I have done quite enough, but when *chained to the oar* it is difficult to escape.[1]

At this point Lord Aberdeen's prestige was at its highest. His ministry had survived its first session far more creditably than was expected and now the line of moderation in foreign policy that he had consistently pressed on his colleagues appeared to be paying dividends. Granville told Greville that this anticipated success would 'be principally owing to Aberdeen, who has been very staunch and bold in defying public clamour, abuse, and taunts, and in resisting the wishes and advice of Palmerston, who would have adopted a more stringent and uncompromising course. He says Clarendon without Aberdeen's support would not have been able to fight the battle against Palmerston in the Cabinet with success.'[2]

Gladstone said much the same thing in a letter to Aberdeen on the eve of parting for his vacation. Referring to the Eastern Question he wrote:

Whatever be its final issue you are the person to whom we owe its present state. There is clearly no other man in the Cabinet who combined calmness, solidity of judgement, knowledge of the question, and moderation of views, in a manner or degree (even independent of your personal and official authority) sufficient to have held the country.

He emphasised the consequent importance of Aberdeen keeping his post and dwelt on 'the embarrassments and dangers that, however cordial may be the internal relations of the government, could not fail to come into view were [he] to think of its abandonment'.[3]

As we have seen,[4] Aberdeen in consultation with Graham, had come to the conclusion that the hour was approaching when he should step down in favour of the restless and ambitious leader of the House of Commons. Graham and perhaps most of the other Peelites in the ministry would have accepted the change on Aberdeen's recommendation,

---

[1] *Ab. Cor. 1852–5*, pp. 217–18, 8 September 1853.

[2] *Greville Memoirs*, VI, 438.

[3] Add. MS. 43070, fols. 372–5, 12 August 1853. In the same letter Gladstone very oddly warned Aberdeen that he had heard 'that another Papal Aggression was contemplated' and urged that they should avoid getting into the false position in which they found themselves last time. He expressed the belief that British policy in the Eastern Question had favoured the Church of Rome and suggested that since their attitude to that church must, he feared, be one of 'unalterable antagonism', it might be well to adopt a more friendly attitude to the Orthodox Church, which would involve some respect for the secular position of the Czar.   [4] See above, pp. 137–8.

but clearly Gladstone was likely to be a formidable obstacle to its completion. Aberdeen hoped to persuade his younger colleague during a contemplated visit of the latter to Haddo, but the meeting never took place. Gladstone fell ill unexpectedly and was laid low until the end of September. By this time the international situation was much graver, and indeed the Prime Minister had had to abandon his plans for a holiday in his Scottish retreat.

8

THE EASTERN QUESTION: THE FAILURE OF NEGOTIATION— AUGUST TO DECEMBER 1853

The failure of the Vienna note and the excitement of the English press,
September 1853

With the prorogation of parliament most of the ministers quickly dispersed, for the most part to relax in the country after the toils of the session. The queen with Prince Albert, as we have seen, departed on an official visit to Ireland, one of the few of her long reign, accompanied by Lord Granville, the perfect courtier. Sir James Graham combined business with pleasure, plunging into a strenuous tour of the dockyards and naval defences along the south coast, in the Channel Islands, and at Queenstown, Pembroke and Holyhead. He found naval affairs in Portsmouth in a state of turmoil, but expressed great satisfaction with the progress of defence works in the Channel Islands, which seemed to be a case of preparing for the last war rather than the next. 'These works in combination with the breakwaters at Dover and Portland are well worthy of a great maritime power', he wrote enthusiastically to Wood, 'and will, I am persuaded, increase our strength in the Channel in defiance of all the outlay at Cherbourg,'[1] a rather anomalous statement in view of the alliance that was already being forged between England and France.

Soon Aberdeen and Clarendon were the only ministers left in London, although the Prime Minister spent a few days on a busman's holiday at Osborne, prior to the queen's departure. It had been his intention to leave for Haddo, where he had hoped to welcome both Graham and Gladstone in September, as soon as more reassuring news came from the East. When this failed to happen he remained in London, unwilling to desert Clarendon. 'Clarendon is alone in London, and is naturally desirous of having advice,' Aberdeen explained to Gladstone. 'To say the truth, I am anxious to be on the spot as

[1] Graham Papers, 19 September 1853; see also *Ab. Cor. 1852–5*, pp. 213, 223–4, 8 and 19 September 1853.

I know not what may take place in my absence, under the influence of other opinions...It is the more essential that I should be here at this crisis, as I have never known the danger of an irreparably rash division more imminent.'[1] It is unlikely that Clarendon would have objected to the desertion, for as the crisis worsened and the despatches poured in thick and fast, all requiring answers, he complained to his wife about the inordinate amount of time that he had to waste chatting with the chief.[2]

Russell left for his holiday in a pacific frame of mind, hoping with the rest that the Russian emperor's acceptance of the Vienna note had settled the crisis. With Aberdeen he insisted that positive orders should be given to Stratford to push the Turks into acceptance. He professed his confidence that these would have their effect.

If not they must be repeated and enforced [he wrote to Clarendon]. The Turks must be told that if they will not make this moderate concession, which is after all scarcely more than their own last Note, they must be prepared to see the Principalities occupied all the winter. For we cannot abet them in their obstinacy.

On the other hand the Emperor of Russia must not be permitted to go beyond his present positions...If he crosses the Danube, our fleet must go to the Bosphorus...The only danger is that the war party in Turkey may bring on a war by some imprudence...In that case Russia can hardly be kept in a leash—and we must take fresh counsel with our three Allies.[3]

With that he retreated to Scotland to brood over a new Reform Bill, sending occasional messages to Aberdeen about patronage and his disinclination to visit Balmoral. The Prime Minister was well satisfied to hear his unpredictable lieutenant express such moderate views on foreign affairs[4] and glad to know that he was turning his restless mind to less controversial domestic matters, for on Reform Aberdeen was prepared to go every step as far as Russell. The latter's reference to the war party in Turkey, was, however, all too perceptive. They made the

---

[1] Add. MS. 44088, fols. 195–6, 7 September 1853.
[2] See Maxwell, *Clarendon*, II, 26–32, for extracts from Clarendon's letters and Lady Clarendon's diary. Clarendon's patience grew thinner as the months wore on, to judge from a letter of 30 December, when he wrote: 'As I gave old Aberdeen an hour and a half of my company as I came into London this morning, I thought he would have spared me this evening; but not a bit of it! He came at 7 and staid till 8.'
[3] MS. Clar. Dep. C3, fols. 382–3, 20 August 1853 (Walpole, *Russell*, II, 185–6).
[4] Add. MS. 43188, fols. 225–6, 21 August 1853, Aberdeen to Clarendon from Osborne (copy).

acceptance of the note impossible. Clarendon had sent off a strong despatch to Stratford,[1] but all to no avail. He blamed the delay in the Turkish Divan's consideration of the note on his ambassador, but the Turks were beyond control.[2]

By 26 August news had arrived (apparently via Paris) of the Turkish proposals for the modification of the Vienna note. 'The Turks seem to be getting more stupid and obstinate every day', Clarendon wrote to Aberdeen. 'This despatch shews that they are determined not to come to an agreement, for, in the proposed Note that they sent to Vienna last month, there was not a word about the Principalities, or guarantees for the future; but now their object is evidently to make arrangements impossible.'[3] 'The Turkish modifications, although not absolutely altering the sense of the Note, are not insignificant', Aberdeen admitted. He maintained that the 'Turks had no right to ask the emperor to accept them after what had already been done and concluded that the conduct of the Porte was suicidal'. 'I always expected difficulties at Constantinople', he added; 'but this cannot be made in good faith. Had they rejected the Note altogether, it would have been intelligible, and they might have been sincere; at present it is impossible.'[4] Sending Russell a copy of the telegraphic despatch from Constantinople, Clarendon vented his spleen against the unfortunate ambassador. 'I have all along felt sure that Stratford would allow of no plan of settlement that did not originate with himself.'[5]

Russell agreed with Aberdeen that while it was to be hoped the emperor might accept the Turkish modifications he could not be pressed. Russell maintained that both parties should be urged to maintain the *status quo* for the winter. 'Of course', he added, 'we shall not think now of advancing to the Bosphorus.'[6] Within a few days, however, he was becoming more belligerent. Although agreeing that the proposed modifications were calculated 'to insense the Emperor', he was unwilling to desert the Turks.

Hitherto we have shown great forbearance to Russia under much provocation [he wrote], and have permitted her unmolested, to seize her neighbour's provinces, & occupy them as an Enemy. It now becomes us to show a similar

---

[1] *Ibid.* The despatch is not printed in the *Eastern Papers.*
[2] Add. MS. 43188, pp. 227–8, 22 August 1853.
[3] *Ab. Cor. 1852–5*, p. 197, 26 August 1853.
[4] MS. Clar. Dep. C4, fols. 70–1, 26 August 1853.   [5] Walpole, *Russell*, II, 186.
[6] Add. MS. 43067, fols. 109–10, 27 August 1853; cf. a similar letter to Clarendon, Walpole, *Russell*, II, 188.

indulgence towards Turkey, when she becomes in her turn wilful & wrong headed.

I do not see that we can retire with our fleet, while the Russian armies occupy the Principalities.[1]

To Clarendon, Russell was more outspoken. He was prepared to promote further negotiation; 'but if that cannot be done', he wrote, 'I am for the Turk against the Russian'.[2] Aberdeen, in writing to Russell, was more critical of the Turks, and could only express the hope that the emperor would be magnanimous.[3]

Finally, on 31 August, they received Stratford's letters and despatches of 13 to 20 August explaining the course of events in Constantinople.[4] While their tone indicated his lack of confidence in the Vienna note, Stratford made it clear that he had urged it on the Porte, and Clarendon admitted to Aberdeen that the ambassador's private letter was 'far less sulky' than he expected.[5]

In view of the controversy regarding Stratford's part in the matter, this letter deserves some consideration. He began by declaring his weariness of the whole endless affair, but he was particularly irked by the rejection of his own plan (the so-called 'Turkish ultimatum'), which he had 'sent home in full reliance of its usefulness'. 'I have not even the consolation of thinking that it gave way to a more successful invention,' he added.

'I was not aware until the arrival here of the latter that a regular conference was established in Vienna', he went on. 'My impression was that the occasional meetings of the Four were similar to those which have been held here, neither more formal nor more authorized.' In a postscript, in which he claimed Clarendon's indulgence for what he had written, he recurred to the matter of the note, saying: 'I feel confident that you will give me credit for having done my *official* best in support of the Vienna Note. Reschid told me candidly the last time I saw him that no formal influence could have induced the Porte to give way.'

Stratford also complained about the attitude of *The Times* (which he described as a government paper) towards him, and remarked on the lack of cordial relations with his colleagues in Constantinople, saying that

---

[1] Add. MS. 43067, fols. 114–15, 31 August 1853. Walpole's quotation from this letter is incomplete and misdated (*Russell*, II, 188).

[2] MS. Clar. Dep. C3, fol. 392, 29 August 1853 (Walpole, *Russell*, II, 188).

[2] Gooch, *Later Correspondence*, II, 152–3, 30 August 1853.

[4] *E.P.* II, nos. 67–73, pp. 69–82.

[5] *Ab. Cor. 1852–5*, p. 201, 31 August 1853.

there was 'a kind of *inconsequence*' in the language of the French ambassador, 'which puzzles at times both Turk and Christian'. He concluded by urging Clarendon to 'approve and second the suggestions of the Porte', warning that Russian acceptance of the note might 'have raised an additional difficulty'. 'The Porte', he wrote, 'is, to all appearances, ready for anything. Even Reschid...talks of shouldering his pipe-stick and going to the wars, if no arrangements on his terms can be obtained.'[1]

This letter reflects both Stratford's strength and his weakness. He knew and understood the Turks and how to get the most out of them, but his proud and imperious character made him a difficult colleague and almost an impossible subordinate. He acted as if he was born to rule rather than to serve, and here lay his failing as an ambassador. Although, according to his own lights, he worked towards the common goal of peace, his frank statement that he had done his '*official* best' reveals the limits of his service to the government that commissioned him.

Graham, who had received Admiral Dundas's account of developments in the East, remained unimpressed and as suspicious of Stratford as ever. 'I only hope that you will not allow Europe to be involved in War', he wrote to Clarendon, 'because Canning thinks he can write better than anyone else; and because he is resolved to embroil matters both at home and abroad, in the hope of obtaining a triumph for his own morbid vanity and implacable antipathies.'[2]

By the beginning of September the situation had become so serious that Russell was recalled to London, where on the 3rd he met with Aberdeen, Clarendon and Palmerston, who happened to be in town. Aberdeen, who called the meeting a 'rather warlike Council',[3] gave the following description of it to Graham, who was unable to attend:

The present state of Eastern Affairs was fully discussed, as well as plans for the future. There was no very great difference of opinion, except a strong desire on the part of my three companions to come to a decision that we should enter the Dardanelles, as soon as the state of the weather rendered it necessary to leave Besika Bay. I rejected this suggestion, partly as being premature, and partly because it was a measure of too great importance to be taken without the consent of the whole Cabinet.

Palmerston was not so warlike as Lord John; but neither of them was very unreasonably pugnacious.

[1] MS. Clar. Dep. C10, fols. 277–80, 20 August 1853.
[2] MS. Clar. Dep. C4, fols. 204–5, 3 September 1853.
[3] *Ab. Cor. 1852–5*, p. 204, to the queen, 4 September 1853.

It was also decided that if the emperor refused the Turkish modifications the Turks must be pressed to accept the original note.[1] Russell had reservations on this last point, or developed second thoughts after the meeting, for that evening he produced a memorandum[2] in which he argued that Turkey was quite entitled to make some modifications to demands put to her so brusquely and that, if the emperor refused these modifications, then he should be presented with the Turkish note of 23 July. 'If the Emperor of Russia rejects both,' Russell continued menacingly, 'we must conclude that he is bent on war, and prepare our measures accordingly.' He proposed that when the time came the fleets should move up to Constantinople on the invitation of the sultan. This was a view with which both Palmerston and Louis Napoleon concurred.[3] Clarendon had been worried about this problem for some time. As early as 28 July he had said to Aberdeen: 'They can't remain much longer in the open Bay of Besika, and however bold you may be in the cause of peace, I don't think you would have the courage to order the British fleet back to Malta, before the Russians have re-crossed the Pruth.'[4] Now that looked a long way off. The council of four presumed that the fleet could ride out the weather in the Bay for at least another month, recalling that Admiral Parker on an earlier occasion had entered the Dardanelles under supposed stress of weather on 1 November. Consequently Aberdeen told Graham he thought it desirable 'to have some naval authority to sanction this decision', and said he would be obliged if Graham would 'procure some statement to this effect'.[5] Temperley rather implies that this was an attempt to cook up evidence. It may be supposed, however, that Aberdeen believed that the information would be forthcoming and simply wanted it to be available for the record. At any rate Graham lost no time in providing the necessary naval opinions that indicated the ships would be safe where they were, at least until November, and he denied that the weather had been responsible for Parker's moving in at that time in 1849. It was also decided, subject to the agreement of the French, that detachments of the fleet should take

---

[1] Graham Papers, 4 September 1853.

[2] MS. Clar. Dep. C3, fols. 400–2, memo. dated 3 September; the covering letter (*ibid.* fol. 399), dated 4 September, makes it clear the memorandum was written after and not before the meeting as Walpole indicates (*Russell*, II, 188–9).

[3] Temperley, *Crimea*, pp. 352–3. On hearing of the French emperor's views Russell wrote to Clarendon: 'Bravo Louis Napoleon! He is a much better fellow than Louis Philippe' (MS. Clar. Dep. C3, fols. 397–8, 3 September 1853).

[4] *Ab. Cor. 1852–5*, pp. 176–7.

[5] Graham Papers, 6 September 1853.

turns in cruising in the Aegean to improve the health and morale of the men.[1]

The duke of Newcastle entered the discussion on 6 September with a letter to Clarendon saying that he could not understand what all the fuss was about with respect to the fleets remaining at Besika Bay into the winter. 'I was myself in my Yacht with the English fleet under Sir W. Parker at the anchorage in 1849 at *Christmas*', he wrote, 'and the winter that year was unusually inclement.'[2]

On 9 September, conscious that the other three had only postponed the question of bringing the fleet through the straits, Aberdeen prepared a memorandum setting forward his objections. Russia, after all, had accepted the peace terms presented by the Four Powers. To send the fleet forward now would only provoke her and unduly encourage the Turks. Rather, he suggested, the fleet should withdraw to Mytilene, not 50 miles away, or to wherever the nearest safe anchorage might be. The men, he added, were sickly and in need of a change.[3] 'Nothing shall be decided on this subject', he told Graham, 'without the Cabinet being summoned.'[4]

When their meeting was over and decisions made, Russell returned to Scotland, where he was reported by his brother to be in good spirits and working on his Reform Bill. Once again Aberdeen and Clarendon settled down to their lonely vigil in deserted London, waiting to hear the worst from St Petersburg, and carrying on occasional correspondence with their colleagues. If Russia rejected the Turkish amendments, then, the ever hopeful Prime Minister wrote to Graham, 'we must begin again; and', he added, 'I still think that we shall be stronger than Lord Stratford, and that we shall be able to prevent war'.[5]

Palmerston as usual was more bellicose; 'if matters were to end in war', he wrote to Clarendon, 'the Turks with the assistance of skilful officers, English, French, Polish and others and with the cooperation of our squadron in the Black Sea would make an example of the Red haired Barbarians, or as Gray politely called them 'the blue eyed

---

[1] Graham Papers, from Aberdeen, 7 September, to Aberdeen (copy), 8 September 1853 (*Ab. Cor. 1852–5*, p. 207).

[2] MS. Clar. Dep. C4, fols. 335–6.

[3] MS. Clar. Dep. C4, fols. 75–88, 9 September 1853.

[4] Graham Papers, 12 September 1853.

[5] *Ibid*. He wrote in much the same vein to Russell on the same day, saying he saw 'no greater danger of war, unless the Turks, acting under evil advice, should seek a collision' (*Ab. Cor. 1852–5*, pp. 222–3) and to the queen (*ibid*. pp. 221–2).

myriads of the Baltic Coast!'[1] The duke of Argyll took quite the opposite point of view. While he admitted that the Turks had a grievance
against Russia he saw no reason why Britain should abandon the Vienna
note, pointing out that the Christians in the Principalities would not
side with the Turks and there was no reason to force Turkish rule upon
them. Scoffing at the idea of real Turkish independence, which he called
pure nonsense, he opposed any commitments to Turkey and upheld the
principle of a collective European right as opposed to a Turkish protectorate.[2] The duke of Newcastle feared that the emperor of Russia
wanted war and that the Turks had played into his hands.[3]

Aberdeen continued to receive pressing notes from Brunnow, who
wrote on the 8th to say the Turks *must* adhere to the Vienna note. He
said it was 'preposterous' to answer that 'the Ulemas will not sign', for
they were 'ignorant brutes, stubborn, arrogant and *cunning*, deeply
impressed with the fixed idea that England and France must come to
their assistance'. Even Stratford was deceived by them. 'Put a stop to all
this deceit,' he implored. 'Tell them they are at liberty to accept or
reject proposals but not to involve Europe in war.'[4]

On receipt of Russia's refusal of the Turkish amendments, Count
Buol informed the Vienna conference that he was pressing the Turkish
government to accept the original note as it was.[5] Although Aberdeen
seemed to think that the meeting of 3 September had agreed to a similar
policy, Clarendon now criticised it as useless.[6] On the following day (the
15th), however, he discussed the matter further with Aberdeen and
Palmerston and it was agreed (on the latter's suggestion) 'to propose at
Vienna that the four powers should declare that they adopted the
Turkish modifications as their own interpretation of the original
Note'.[7] Russell again began to grow belligerent. On hearing the news
he wrote to Aberdeen saying he concluded the emperor sought to sub-
jugate Turkey. 'If that is the case', he added, 'the question must be
decided by war, and if we do not stop the Russians on the Danube, we
shall have to stop them on the Indus.'[8] Two days later he was even more

---

[1] MS. Clar. Dep. C3, fol. 132, 12 September 1853.
[2] *Ibid.* C4, fols. 365–9, 26 September 1853.
[3] *Ibid.* fols. 355–8, 15 September 1853.   [4] *Ibid.* Jols. 209–18.
[5] *E.P.* II, no. 95, pp. 106–7, from Westmorland, 14 September 1853.
[6] *Ab. Cor. 1852–5*, pp. 224, 13 and 14 September 1853.
[7] PRO 30/22/11/A, fols. 225–8, Aberdeen to Russell, 16 September 1853 (Walpole, *Russell*, II, 190).
[8] *Ab. Cor. 1852–5*, p. 230, 15 September 1853.

hostile. 'All this makes me very uneasy,' he wrote, referring to Clarendon's despatch, 'and if the Austrians agree to Clarendon's terms, and forward them to Constantinople, I do not see how I can remain a Member of your Government.'[1] He remonstrated with Clarendon even more strongly. 'I must say I much lament the step you have taken,' he wrote. 'I am vexed about the last move, and you must not be surprised, if it is accepted at Vienna, if I were to decline any responsibility.'[2] In a further letter he pointed out that Clarendon's despatch ran counter to the spirit of his own memorandum of 3 September.[3]

Clarendon objected vigorously to Russell's carping attitude, saying rather sharply: 'Your first thought seems to have been declining to share responsibility with me.'[4] This infuriated Russell, who quoted and underlined the sentence in his reply, saying he presumed it was written in haste. He complained bitterly of the degradation of his position, where he was expected to defend in the House of Commons decisions which he had no share in making and of which he had recorded his disapproval. 'It was impossible that I could so lower myself', he wrote, 'or that I should not feel the blow you had inflicted upon me more than all the other humiliations I have endured.'[5]

Clarendon replied in more conciliatory tones, admitting that he had forgotten Lord John's memorandum, and that if he had looked at it he would not have felt surprise at Russell's reaction. 'The scramble & pressure of this office at times prevents things being done with all the reflection they require', he concluded, 'but I adhere to my own view of the 4 Powers giving the interpretation of the Note.'[6] The breach was soon healed, although the two continued to refer to the difference half apologetically in their correspondence for some time to come. On 2 October Russell wrote that he was sure that Clarendon, Palmerston and Aberdeen thought their action honourable, but luckily it had failed. 'I believe it is our first and I hope our last difference', he wrote. 'While the matter has been in your hands it has been conducted in a way that I shall be proud to defend in the House of Commons.'[7]

[1] *Ab. Cor. 1852–5*, pp. 235–6, 19 September 1853.
[2] MS. Clar. Dep. C3, fols. 417–18, 17 September 1853; cf. Walpole, *Russell*, II, 191–2.
[3] MS. Clar. Dep. C3, fols. 421–4, 22 September 1853.
[4] PRO 30/22/11/A, fols. 229–30, 20 September 1853.
[5] MS. Clar. Dep. C3, fols. 425–9, 23 September 1853; cf. Walpole, *Russell*, II, 193.
[6] PRO 30/22/11/A, fols. 247–8, 24 September 1853.
[7] MS. Clar. Dep. C3, fols. 441–2, 2 October 1853.

A few days later Aberdeen gave Graham an account of these developments:

I fear that I must now renounce the sanguine view that I have taken of the termination of the Eastern Question; for nothing can be more alarming than the present prospect. I thought that we should have been able to conquer Stratford; but I begin to fear that the reverse will be the case, and that he will succeed in defeating us all. In fact the war frenzy at Constantinople is now at such a height as to be beyond his control. Although at our wits end, Clarendon and I are labouring in the cause of peace, but really to contend with the pride of the Emperor, the fanaticism of the Turks, and the dishonesty of Stratford, is almost a hopeless attempt.

He then went on to relate Russell's latest tantrum, which he saw as very significant. Describing the proposals that had been made to Vienna and Russell's reaction to them, he continued:

Now the comical part of this affair is that we caught Palmerston on his way to Balmoral, and the proposal which has so much excited Lord John's indignation, not only had Palmerston's concurrence, but was in great part his own work ! ! !

Clarendon has been greatly annoyed by this affair, and has written very strongly to Lord John. I shall laugh a little at him. But I told you it was significant; and it seems to me pretty clear that Lord John is determined to go.

Aberdeen went on to say that these unforeseen developments in the Eastern Question affected his own position a good deal. He had wanted to retire but he was reluctant 'to give the appearance of running away from an unfinished question'. He dwelt on his excellent relations with Clarendon, whose views he considered sound although he was 'a little too much afraid of the Publick and the Press'. He only wished that Graham himself was there.[1]

In reply Graham expressed his distress at this news: 'I am grieved', he wrote, 'on the public account; and still more because I deeply regret the numerous annoyances, to which you are subjected.' He offered to return immediately, if necessary, and added: 'I have long suspected the intentions of our little Friend at Roseneath to break away from us on the first opportunity, which he considered favourable.'[2]

To make matters worse, at about the same time news came of a leak to a German newspaper which disclosed that Nesselrode had put an unacceptable interpretation on the Vienna note that seemed to justify the proposed Turkish amendments. This marks one of the many turning-

[1] Graham Papers, 22 September 1853.
[2] Add. MS. 43, 191, fol. 108, 24 September 1853.

points on the long road that led down into the abyss of war, for henceforth English opinion, and Clarendon in particular, ceased to put any trust in the Russians. Temperley suggests that Clarendon simply made Nesselrode's 'violent interpretation' an excuse for his change of attitude and that it was really dictated by the growing hostility of English public opinion. It is very difficult to sort out the relative influences of various events that bear on an individual's actions and there is no doubt that Clarendon was impressed by the public outcry against Russia, but there seems to be no reason to believe that he was not persuaded that it was now proper to take a course compatible with public demand.

The news of Nesselrode's 'violent interpretation' of the Vienna note, which came just after the British proposal had been sent to Vienna, virtually invalidated it, since it was quite clear that the Russians refused to put the same interpretation on it that the British were proposing to the Four Powers. Consequently Russell's immediate pretext for resignation was lost and in informing him of the new turn of events Aberdeen could not resist twitting him on the fact that the proposal which he had found so objectionable had been drafted by Palmerston.[1] The result of it all was the abandonment of the Vienna note by Britain and France and the closing of the Vienna conference by Buol on 20 September. Again Temperley insists that this *volte-face* was occasioned by popular outcry against Russia in England and that the Nesselrode interpretation was a mere pretext, but the two factors are too closely intertwined to be separated.[2]

Clarendon told Graham that he was 'in despair' and that everything tended towards war. Russia's reasons for rejecting the proposed modifications justified the Turkish demand for them and, given the excited state of the Turkish army, it would be impossible for the Turkish ministers to accept the note now. There was little room for further negotiation since 'Russia insists on [getting] what Turkey won't concede'. Moreover, he feared that Russian views prevailed in the Austrian cabinet.[3] Palmerston wrote from Balmoral to say that if the news was true he saw 'no peaceful solution', and that the time had come to send the fleet through the straits.[4]

[1] PRO 30/22/11/A, fols. 235–7, 22 September 1853.
[2] Temperley, *E.H.R.* XLIX, 274–5.   [3] Graham Papers, 20 September 1853.
[4] MS. Clar. Dep. C3, fols. 145–7, 22 September 1853. The previous day he had written to suggest a new note, making the shrewd observation that there were too many centres of decision, to which he added the more controversial assertion: 'No conference has yet come to good result which was not held in London' (*ibid.* fols. 141–4).

Greville testifies to 'the violence and scurrility of the Press' at this time, which he said exceeded 'all belief'. 'Day after day', he noted, 'the Radical and Tory papers, animated by very different sentiments and motives, pore forth the most virulent abuse of the Emperor of Russia, of Austria and of this Government, especially of Aberdeen.'[1]

Actually, according to Kingsley Martin, while the attack on the government was unceasing in July and early August, after the prorogation of parliament there was a lull, except for the *Morning Advertiser*, which continued to publish the hysterical outpourings of David Urquhart, who denounced *The Times* and the whole Aberdeen cabinet, including Palmerston, as being the tools of Russia.[2] But in September the Peelite *Morning Chronicle* began to desert the government and speak of the shabby treatment being given to Turkey. As early as 2 September Aberdeen was writing to Newcastle in some alarm over this development. He enquired whether Newcastle was in a position to interfere, saying that the 'extraordinary articles' which had recently appeared were 'as bad as possible' and calculated to encourage the war frenzy to the utmost. He went on to point out that 'as the paper is supposed to speak the sentiments of the Peel party, we are liable to much misrepresentation'. Worse still, the paper was attacking their (Whig) Chancellor personally, which, he thought, 'in a paper which is supposed to support the Government is surely unusual'.

'It is very well for The Times to take its own course, as it thinks proper, however annoying to the Govt; because as it is perfectly independent, we must be thankful for its support when we receive it, but for a paper that is so much indebted as the Chronicle to some of you it does seem an extraordinary course, to oppose the policy of the Government, & personally to attack one of its principal members.'[3]

Newcastle replied that he had asked Herbert to see the editor on his way through London, since he disliked writing on such a matter if it could be avoided. Herbert told him that 'the Chronicle people had been very angry at an important communication made to The Times by Clarendon some 2 or 3 weeks ago'. The Chronicle had gone to a great deal of expense to get a certain scoop, only to be beaten by *The Times*, which received the news *gratis* from the Foreign Office. Newcastle recognised that this could not be helped 'because The Times is so much

---

[1] *Greville Memoirs*, VI, 450.
[2] Kingsley Martin, *Triumph of Lord Palmerston*, pp. 128–32.
[3] Newcastle Papers, 2 September 1853.

more valuable an ally than *all* the other Papers', but he pointed out that it was naturally irritating to a struggling competitor. He had learnt that the attack on the Lord Chancellor had been instigated by Brougham, and promised to do his best to see that it was not repeated, 'for whatever may be our own opinion of the Chancellor's efficiency', his 'feelings of loyalty to a colleague as well as a sincere respect for the Chancellor as a man', made him anxious to stop it.[1]

There must have been some improvement, for late in October Graham was writing to Herbert saying that he was anxious that no injustice should be done to the *Chronicle*, which had done the government good service. He also spoke of his concern to see that there was a more even distribution of government advertising among the newspapers. He had his own worries, for on 27 September Clarendon wrote to him that there was a traitor in the Admiralty, who had presented to the *Morning Herald* the government's instructions to Admiral Dundas and Graham's orders respecting reinforcements.[2] Some weeks later Graham appealed to Clarendon to help him find out the traitor who was leaking information, saying despairingly, 'I am surrounded by Spies and Informers'.[3] Later he told Herbert that anything he said or even thought was liable to be printed in the *Morning Herald*, which indicated a leak in the Admiralty which alarmed him.[4] The publication of the Nesselrode interpretation aroused the press generally. The *Daily News* wanted to know whether Aberdeen was merely stupid or a 'willing dupe'. 'Even *The Times* admitted that Turkey had, after all, been justified in rejecting the Note'. But *The Times* alone took the government's line that any action must be by the Four Powers.[5]

---

[1] *Ibid.* (copy), 4 September 1853. In 1848 Newcastle (then Lord Lincoln), Herbert and some other younger Peelites purchased the *Morning Chronicle*, previously a Palmerstonian paper, to promote their political and ecclesiastical views and in general the political fortunes of the Peelite party, but it is doubtful whether the investment was worth the time and money put into it, for the circulation was low and eventually the paper was resold in 1855. See H. R. Fox Bourne, *English newspapers*, II, 153–9; James Grant, *The newspaper press*, I, 310, who includes Gladstone among the purchasers; Carlisle, *Hayward*, I, 224, who includes Cardwell.

[2] Graham Papers.

[3] MS. Clar. Dep. C4, fols. 221–2, 20 October 1853.

[4] Herbert Papers, 29 October 1853.

[5] Martin, *Triumph of Lord Palmerston*, pp. 134–5.

*Deterioration of the situation in Constantinople and the Olmütz
proposals, September–October 1853*

In the second week of September there was also a grave deterioration in
the situation at Constantinople as the war party began to get out of hand
and to whip up a series of riots and demonstrations to warn the sultan
against any further concessions to Russia. On 12 September the British
and French ambassadors called up four small steam warships to protect
the persons and property of their nationals in Constantinople, but
Stratford resisted the demand of his French colleague to summon the
whole fleet.[1]

Oddly enough, the pacific ministers in London were more disturbed
by the telegraphic news of these Constantinople riots (supplied from
French sources) than was their supposedly warlike ambassador on the
spot, who refused to take them too seriously. Aberdeen and Clarendon,
despite all previous talk of making the summoning of the fleet a cabinet
matter, decided on their own on 23 September to instruct the ambassador to call up the fleet to Constantinople, since it appeared that the
lives and property of British subjects were exposed to serious danger
that the Turkish government was unable to avert. This, of course, was
arranged in conjunction with the French government, which actually
had initiated the proposal and issued similar instructions.[2]

Aberdeen explained to Clarendon the grounds on which he assented
to this important decision:

We have *nothing* to do with the *authority* of the Sultan [he wrote], but only
his personal safety. Our main object in going to Constantinople is for the
protection of British life and property, and if necessary, of the person of the
Sultan.

The Whigs formerly used to object to our saving a Prince even from the
hands of the Mob; but we never pretended to interfere further between a
Sovereign and his People, than to protect his life.

I think it very essential that information should forthwith be given to
Russia, through Seymour, of our proceeding; with an explanation that [it] is
not intended as a menace, or hostile movement directed against Russia.[3]

[1] Temperley, *Crimea*, pp. 350–2.
[2] *E.P.* II, nos. 108, and 109, pp. 114–16. The French government appeared to be able
regularly to receive information from Constantinople and to transmit it to London
before the British government had heard anything from their ambassador. This
may have been partly because they controlled the lines of communication east of
Marseilles, partly because their ambassador was readier to make use of the incomplete
telegraph system.   [3] MS. Clar. Dep. C4, fol. 94, 23 September 1853.

Aberdeen hastened to explain his action to Russell, Graham and Gladstone, as well as to the queen.[1] 'Unwilling as I have always been to do anything approaching to a violation of the Treaty of 1841,' he wrote to Gladstone, 'I have had no difficulty in this case as the emergency is sufficient to dispense with all such formal obligations.' He denied an allegation in the *Morning Post* (which he told Graham 'sent down the funds more than two per cent') that this action indicated the intention of Britain and France to intervene in the inevitable war between Russia and Turkey. 'I have been most careful', he protested, 'to avoid taking part in anything which could tend to war, and deprive the Cabinet of perfect freedom of judgement in these matters.'[2]

By persuading themselves that calling up the fleet in this situation would only be a defensive measure, as Temperley suggests,[3] Aberdeen and Clarendon overlooked the real significance of their action. Indeed, in his letter informing Graham of what they had done Clarendon continued to regard Stratford, who unknown to him had resisted French pressure regarding the fleet, as the dangerous element. 'Adml Dundas seems almost as warlike as Stratford,' he wrote, 'tho he only looks how best to make war while the latter has been bent upon causing it. He will be gratified I suppose now for I don't see how it is to be averted.' He bitterly criticised the Russian emperor, who in giving his reasons for rejecting the Turkish modifications 'thereby falsified his declarations that he wanted no new rights in Turkey'.[4] Commenting on the death of a dear relative, he concluded: 'If it were not for my children I shd now envy him his repose, for this Eastn Question, its responsibilities and its consequences almost make my life unendurable.' The Foreign Secretary was showing the signs of strain and for the moment seemed near the breaking point. His next letter was equally gloomy. The leak in the Admiralty that had resulted in the publication of the government's orders to Admiral Dundas had produced consequent bad effects in the City. 'Rothschild tells me he never remembers such a day', Clarendon reported. Worse still, intelligence reports revealed that the Russian navy in the Baltic was much stronger than had been realised.[5]

Graham expressed his concurrence under the circumstances in the decision to call up the fleet to Constantinople, but suggested that a part

---

[1] For the letters to Russell and the queen see *Ab. Cor. 1852–5*, pp. 240–1 and 243–5; to Graham, Graham Papers, 24 September 1853.
[2] Add. MS. 44088, fols. 197–8, 24 September 1853.   [3] *E.H.R.* XLIX, 276–7.
[4] Graham Papers, 22 September 1853.   [5] *Ibid.* 27 September 1853.

of it should be left in the Dardanelles to ensure that the rest were not cut off. 'Your decision with respect to the fleet does not surprise me', he wrote. 'I regret the necessity which abrogates the Treaty of London and which opens both the Dardanelles and the Bosphorus to rival Maritime Powers, but every effort of amicable negotiation having been exhausted, the defence of British interests demands the presence of a British Force in the centre of this great movement which is the prelude to the fall of the Ottoman power in Europe.'[1]

Russell did not dissent, but took the opportunity to express his sur-prise that Aberdeen and Clarendon had acted before seeing the emperor's answer (and, he might have added, Stratford's despatches). He hoped that no attempt would be made to resurrect the Vienna note without his hearing of it. He urged that for all his faults Stratford should be supported as no one else could succeed in prolonging the life of Turkey. He foresaw further difficulties in the coming month, but comforted Aberdeen by reminding him that he would 'have Gladstone at hand'.[2]

To Clarendon, Russell wrote in much more belligerent tones: '*We must not retire till the Russians leave the Principalities.*' 'It seems to me', he continued, 'that the only safe course for the Porte at present would be to declare war.' He argued that it was impossible to let the Turks down now. 'I know something of the English people', he concluded, 'and I feel sure that they would fight to the stumps for the honour of England.'[3]

Russell's intentions were temporarily frustrated, but he remained an undependable colleague. He told his brother that 'matters could go on no longer as they were...and that very soon he could no longer act without being primarily responsible for the policy of the Government'. On his return to London Russell (pushed by his wife and her clique in Greville's opinion[4]) was anxious to bring about the proposed succession, but, as we have seen, Aberdeen was now reluctant to leave while the crisis lasted. Moreover, it appears that when Gladstone at last returned to London he indicated that he would not remain in a Russsell government. Therefore, Aberdeen pointed out to Russell that if he pressed the matter now he would only break up the government and have 'to encounter

[1] MS. Clar. Dep. C4, fols. 210–14, 25 September 1853.
[2] *Ab. Cor. 1852–5*, pp. 246–7, 24 September 1853.
[3] MS. Clar. Dep. C3, fols. 431–4, 27 September 1853.
[4] *Greville Memoirs*, VI, 454–6. Greville had it direct from the duke of Bedford.

the odium of doing so'.[1] Up until now the public was unaware of how
badly Russell had behaved on the formation of the government and of
the difficulties that he had made behind the scenes. Indeed, according to
Greville he had regained some of his lost popularity by accepting the
duties of leading the House without receiving the emoluments of
office, and would have gained more 'if he had not chosen to quit the
House early every afternoon, and go down to his wife and his nursery
at Richmond, leaving Palmerston to do the work, and ingratiate himself
with the House'.[2] Greville's characteristically catty remark may be
exaggerated, but there is little doubt that Palmerston by his diligence,
moderation and good humour was building up far more credit in the
coalition than his little rival.

Realising that neither his Peelite nor his Whig colleagues were prepared for the change at that time, Russell eventually told Aberdeen that
he had given up the idea, but the Prime Minister had no doubt that he
was only looking for 'an opportunity to break up the Government on
some popular ground'. When Aberdeen told him that as leader of the
House of Commons 'he had the most powerful and honourable position of any man in England', Russell answered, 'Oh, *there* I am quite
happy!' The two were not beyond joking about Russell's ambitions:
when Russell said he had his Reform measure ready but did not think
the time opportune, Aberdeen shot back, 'You mean unless you sit in
the Chair which I now occupy?', at which Lord John laughed.[3]

From October onwards British policy seemed to be more than ever
at the mercy of events over which the government had no control.
Increasing differences among the ministers further paralysed the
country's capacity to act. Two developments now began to operate in
opposite directions. The Turkish grand council sat from 26 September
to 4 October and determined on a policy of declaring war, but Russia
was given fifteen days to evacuate Turkish soil.[4] In the meantime the
Czar and Nesselrode travelled to Olmütz to discuss new proposals
for peace with the Austrian government and the Allied ambassadors.

---

[1] *Ibid.* p. 455. Clarendon filled in the details when he learnt that Greville knew part of the
story.   [2] *Ibid.* p. 457.

[3] *Letters of Queen Victoria*, II, 557–8, memo. of Prince Albert, 16 October 1853. Aberdeen
told the queen that Graham had indicated that if Russell left the government he
recognised that there were objections to his (Graham) succeeding, but that 'he himself
could not well sit in the House of Commons under so much younger a man as Mr Gladstone as Leader'. He would, however, be glad to join Aberdeen in the Lords. So
Graham's pride was almost as prickly as Russell's.

[4] Temperley, *E.H.R.* XLIX, 281–3.

Nicholas said 'he looked to nothing but the maintenance of treaties and the *status quo* in religious matters', thus apparently repudiating Nesselrode's 'violent interpretation', and he offered to withdraw from the Principalities as soon as the Vienna note was signed *pur et simple*. This was to be accompanied by a project drawn up by Buol which would convey Russian assurances witnessed by the four Powers.[1]

The coincidence of these two events was dramatically illustrated in a letter from Aberdeen to the queen on 3 October in which he described the alarming state of Turkey and the promising developments in Austria: 'Last night', he wrote, 'despatches were received from Olmütz, which give an account of a very strong declaration on the part of the Emperor of Russia, of his desire to obtain nothing in Turkey beyond the actual *status quo* in religious matters.' The letter ended with the ominous postscript: 'P.S.—3 o'clock—a telegraphic message from Constantinople, just arrived, announces that the Turkish Divan has declared war.' In the same letter the Prime Minister urged the queen to hasten her return to London since a state of war would face the government with grave decisions that might 'very materially affect the Government itself'.[2]

The news from Constantinople tended to cancel out that from Olmütz. In any event Clarendon was not prepared to accept the Olmütz proposals, partly because the Turkish decision seemed to make them inoperative, partly because he no longer trusted the Russians since Nesselrode's 'violent interpretation' had been divulged. Napoleon also turned them down on 5 October, although he had been initially favourable. Russell supported the Foreign Secretary, writing on 5 October: 'Of course the proposition from Olmütz is intended only to deceive.'[3] This was tragic, since it now seems pretty evident that the Russians genuinely wanted to find a way of avoiding war, and were prepared to evacuate the Principalities if they were given some face-saving opportunity to do so. As usual the violence of English public opinion and the

[1] Temperley, *E.H.R.* xlix, pp. 284–7. On 20 September Westmorland wrote from Olmütz: 'His Majesty asks only for a general guarantee of the immunities already granted to the Greek Church, and for nothing which could in any way prejudice the independence or rights of the Sultan, or which would imply a desire to interfere with the internal affairs of the Porte' (*E.P.* ii, no. 122, p. 129).

[2] *Ab. Cor. 1852–5*, pp. 264–5, 3 October 1853. Actually the Turkish council decided in favour of war, but left the declaration to the sultan and his ministers. *E.P.* ii, no. 123, p. 130, 26 September 1853, from Stratford, received 3 October.

[3] MS. Clar. Dep. C3, fol. 454. See also Temperley, *E.H.R.* xlix, 386–7; *Crimea*, p. 355.

divisions within the cabinet were factors that prevented the right decision being taken.

Part of the trouble lay in the government's lack of confidence in their ambassador at Vienna, whom (unlike Stratford) they regarded as incompetent and who, they thought (in Russell's words), had been 'bamboozled' by the Russians and the Austrians. Indeed, Clarendon suggested sending Granville to Vienna 'as coadjutor to our faithful but feeble Westmorland', but Aberdeen parried this by saying he could see no point in sending him to Vienna and would prefer to see Granville at Constantinople or St Petersburg. Consequently Granville stayed in London and the situation continued to deteriorate.[1]

On hearing of the news of the Turkish decision for war Palmerston wrote to Aberdeen saying that this made it easier to pass off the Allied decision about the fleets. He suggested that Clarendon should keep a 'mysterious indefiniteness' and uncertainty as to the manner and degree of assistance which England and France might deem it right to give to Turkey.[2] Clarendon acted on this suggestion, telling Aberdeen that he hoped the despatch to Stratford calling up the fleet was not '*too much* in contradiction with the Note to Brunnow'.[3] In his reply to Palmerston Aberdeen said that he looked upon war with Russia 'with the utmost incredulity' and that Brunnow was frightened out of his wits at the prospect. He assured Palmerston that when he saw Brunnow he did nothing to diminish his alarm and expressed a hope that the fear of war with Britain and France might exercise a salutary influence on the Emperor.[4] This was no doubt a factor in the Czar's conciliatory attitude at Olmütz about which news reached London on the 2nd. But it was in fact too late.

'In truth', Aberdeen wrote to Graham, now at Balmoral with the queen, 'matters are in that state, both at home and abroad, that I have written to the Queen today pretty strongly, in order to hasten her return.'[5] The following day he wrote again saying, 'But the plot thickens apace, and, if we do not take care we may have war in a

---

[1] MS. Clar. Dep. C4, fol. 101, 11 October 1853.

[2] *Ab. Cor. 1852–5*, p. 261, 2 October 1853. Stratford's telegraphic despatch of 26 September containing this news only arrived on 3 October. Consequently it would appear that Palmerston's letter is misdated or he had received prior intelligence from his friend Walewski.

[3] *Ibid.* pp. 261–2. Palmerston in the meantime was plying Clarendon with comment and advice regarding these various communications. MS. Clar. Dep. C3, fols. 150–60, 26, 29 and 30 September 1853.

[4] *Ibid.* p. 272, 5 October 1853.   [5] Graham Papers, 3 October 1853.

week'. He hoped Graham could get back to a cabinet meeting that had been called for Friday. 'I greatly desire to see you', he wrote, 'not only on publick, but, perhaps, still more on private grounds.'[1] On both grounds he needed moral support for the expected onslaught when the ministers met. The canny Graham, however, refused to be hurried, arguing that his sudden departure from Balmoral might 'create needless alarm'. 'Moreover,' he added, 'my absence may prevent any hasty *irrevocable* decision.'[2] Aberdeen agreed to the wisdom of this argument. 'In fact,' he admitted, 'it is more for my personal comfort than anything else that I long to see you.'[3] As to the cabinet that was to meet on the 7th, he wrote: 'As far as I can understand, it will be proposed by Lord John, and I believe by Palmerston, to engage as Auxiliaries on the side of Turkey, but not as Principals in the War.' He continued: 'The fleets will now come without any objection up to Constantinople. The declaration of war by the Turks has opened the Dardanelles. But an entrance into the Black Sea would be war with Russia.' He went on:

I cannot entertain a doubt that Lord John will seek, and of course, will find, an opportunity of breaking off on a popular ground, instead of one ridiculously untenable. Palmerston most undoubtedly will do the same. Indeed, I feel that, very possibly, I may stand alone. I am almost inclined to hope so.[4]

Aberdeen had, however, talked at length to Gladstone and found the Chancellor of the Exchequer as pacific as himself. Writing to Queen Victoria, Aberdeen said that they should follow a policy of neutrality, seeking to mediate the quarrel. The French, he believed, would follow the same course as England, 'for the English alliance is more valuable to himself [Napoleon], personally, than all other considerations'. Aberdeen's main fear was a demand for immediate English participation. 'No doubt', he said, 'it may be very agreeable to humiliate the Emperor of Russia; but Lord Aberdeen thinks that it is paying a little too dear for this pleasure to check the progress and prosperity of this happy country, and to cover Europe with misery, confusion, and blood.'[5]

On 4 October Russell suggested that if Russia would not make peace on fair terms, then the least that England and France could do was to support Turkey as auxiliaries, scouring the Black Sea of Russian ships.

[1] Graham Papers, 4 October 1853.   [2] *Ab. Cor. 1852–5*, pp. 273–4, 5 October 1853.
[3] Graham Papers, 6 October 1853.
[4] *Ibid.*   [5] *Ab. Cor. 1852–5*, 6 October 1853, pp. 275–6.

Recognising the problem of thus supporting a barbaric power with a bad record of mistreatment of Christian subjects, he maintained that if they were to act in conjunction with France, as principals in the war, they must act 'not for the Sultan, but for the general interests of the population of European Turkey'.[1] Just before the cabinet met, Palmerston made two practical proposals: one, that any Russian ships found cruising in the Black Sea should be detained, and two, that a convention should be concluded with Turkey, promising naval assistance and allowing the enlistment of British nationals in the Turkish forces. In return Turkey was to agree to consult regarding the conditions and terms of a new treaty to govern its relations with Russia.[2] Aberdeen refused to accept that the present state of affairs would justify such proceeding.[3]

In view of the development Aberdeen was doubtless more concerned to combat the danger of aggressive action in the Black Sea than to attempt a defence of the Olmütz proposals, which obviously would not be accepted by the cabinet. He sent Graham the following account of the fateful cabinet meeting, the first that had been held since the prorogation of parliament under such different circumstances six weeks earlier:

When we met Clarendon made a sort of *résumé* of what had taken place since we all separated, but ended with no specific proposal. After a few interlocutory remarks from different quarters, Palmerston proposed his plan. Lord John faintly supported it in general terms; but did not seem much in earnest about it. I said that it appeared to involve the necessity of a declaration of war against Russia, and the calling together of Parliament forthwith. Gladstone strongly argued against the proposal. Clarendon then read an outline of his proposed instructions, which were a great abatement from Palmerston's plan. We came at last to a sort of compromise; our great difficulty being how to deal with the question of entering the Black Sea. I consented to this being done, provided it was strictly in defence of some point of attack on Turkish territory. I have no fear that this will take place; and as long as we abstain from entering the Black Sea, peace may be possible between us and Russia. We have thus assumed a strictly defensive position, which for the moment may be sufficient, and will enable us to carry on negotiations; but this cannot last long. Under the character of a defensive war we should inevitably become extensively engaged. Should the Turks be at all worsted,

---

[1] *Ab. Cor. 1852–5*, pp. 268–71 (Walpole, *Russell*, II, 193–6); see also PRO 30/22/11/B, 265–72.
[2] *Ab. Cor. 1852–5*, pp. 380–1, 7 October 1853; so also to Clarendon, MS. Clar. Dep. C3, fols. 171–3.   [3] *Ibid.* p. 281.

which is probable, of course we must increase our assistance. We should have a French Army, and put up English money,—all for defence.

The aspect of the Cabinet was on the whole good. Gladstone active and energetic for peace. Argyll, Herbert, Ch. Wood and Granville all in the same sense. Newcastle not quite so much so, but good. Lansdowne not so warlike as formerly. Lord John warlike enough, but subdued in tone. Palmerston urged his views perseveringly, but not disagreeably.

The Chancellor said little, but was evidently peaceful.[1]

It is strange that Lord Aberdeen should have written so complacently about this fateful cabinet meeting that failed to do anything about the Olmütz proposals, which offered the best chance of peace between the failure of the Vienna note and the outbreak of war. At least one of his younger colleagues was more perceptive as to the true significance of the meeting.

That evening Herbert wrote a long letter to Clarendon expressing his great uneasiness at what was happening. He granted the necessity of keeping Russia out of the Bosporus, but argued that if the Turks were to receive British assistance it must be on British terms. He accepted the necessity for the defensive naval measures that were being taken, but feared that the government was open to criticism for its failure to do something about the Olmütz proposals. He did not overrate those proposals, but he thought the government was bound to try to acknowledge the spirit in which they appeared to have been made, to propose a new form acceptable to both parties, and to restrain the Turks from beginning hostilities. If not, England would be held responsible for the failure.[2]

On the same evening the duke of Argyll addressed a similar long letter to Lord John Russell, with whom he often corresponded about the Eastern Question. 'Approving as I quite did of our decision today,' he wrote, 'I cant [sic] help seeing that it borders very closely upon some other decisions which I shd deem very dangerous.' What Argyll feared was that the Turks might misinterpret the Allied decision as backing them in their declaration of war. 'In short,' he went on, 'let our

---

[1] Graham Papers, 8 October 1853. A shorter account of the cabinet meeting is to be found in *Letters of Queen Victoria*, II, 551–2, where part of the letter to Graham is printed in a footnote. Molesworth's view is not recorded since he missed the meeting through a mistake.

[2] MS. Clar. Dep. C4, 8 October 1853 (Stanmore, *Herbert*, I, 204–8). Herbert's warning perhaps bore some fruit in the note which Clarendon drafted the following week. See below, p. 202.

Instructions show that our Fleets are to act strictly on the defensive—and that, too, defensive against Cis-Danubian aggression, aiming at the heart of the Turkish Empire. I will not conceal from you my great fear that we are getting into a *drift* of circumstances which will place our action in the great cause of European Peace or War at the mercy of the Turkish Muftis—and of the Army on the Danube.' He reiterated a point made in other letters that Turkey was not a real power by European standards, as could be seen from the language in which the British Foreign Office and embassy constantly addressed her.[1] Argyll also addressed an almost identical letter to Clarendon, using many of the same phrases, in which he expressed his disinclination to their taking 'any active part in a war which the Turks seemed disposed to undertake on their own responsibility'.[2]

Nevertheless, at a second meeting on 8 October the cabinet gave final approval to Clarendon's fateful despatch to Vienna and on the same day it was sent off to Lord Westmorland. In it the Foreign Secretary said that in view of Nesselrode's interpretation of the Vienna note, which the present project failed to neutralise, the Turks could not be expected to accept it. He claimed that Count Buol's project of a note appeared to adopt the Russian interpretation of the Treaty of Kainardji as assuming 'a protectorate over the Greek subjects of the Sultan'. The British government regarded this as a demand for a new right which the sultan 'with due regard to his independence', could not be expected to concede. 'The Emperor of Russia, however,' the despatch continued, 'disclaims all desire of acquiring any new right, and it is impossible therefore to comprehend why a point that could so easily be made clear should so perseveringly be left in doubt.' After further arguments against the form of the project Clarendon concluded by saying: 'If Europe is for such a cause to be exposed to the calamities of war, they will be without parallel in history;' and urging the Austrian government to so persuade the Russian emperor.[3]

Aberdeen had said nothing to Graham in his letter of the 7th about this decision, but on the 8th he told Queen Victoria that he 'was not satisfied with the tone or substance of the answer to the Olmütz proposal'. Although it was not possible to adopt it in the manner recommended by Austria, like Herbert he thought that it would have 'furnished a

[1] PRO 30/22/11/B, fols. 273–8, 7 October 1853; see also fols. 241–6, 304–5, 309–16 and 317–18 for other letters of Argyll to Russell on the subject.

[2] MS. Clar. Dep. C4, fols. 389–92; dated 'Friday night', i.e. 8 October.

[3] *E.P.* II, no. 135, pp. 143–5.

very useful element in any future proceedings'. Rightly, however, he feared that the despatch sent to Lord Westmorland would 'not advance the work of conciliation'.[1]

At the second cabinet meeting on the 8th, which, Aberdeen declared, despite differences of opinion was 'carried on amicably, and in good humour', the terms of the instructions to be sent to Constantinople with regard to the disposition of the fleet were finally settled.[2] Again one gathers the impression from his account of the meeting that the Prime Minister was more concerned with maintaining cabinet solidarity than with getting the right decisions made.

Both the queen and Graham expressed misapprehensions over these cabinet decisions. Graham acknowledged that Aberdeen had to make some concessions to keep the cabinet together and only hoped they might 'prove harmless'. He thought that the contingent decision on the Black Sea was premature. 'Peel's general rule is strictly applicable in this case,' he wrote; 'weigh every possible contingency, but never decide until the last moment, when all the facts and circumstances are before you.'[3]

The other point of view was expressed in a letter from Palmerston to Clarendon a few days after the meeting, in which he deprecated the opinion voiced at the recent cabinet 'that our support of Turkey would depend upon whether the Porte takes our advice'; as Molesworth said to him after the meeting, he added: 'We have gone too far to draw back.'

I hate war [he continued] but I am perfectly willing to incur the responsibility of war with Russia if Turkey can be saved by no other means. That war, however, is not so near as some of the Cabinet anticipate, and if near it is not so dreadful a calamity as they imagine...I will confess to you in confidence that the language I have heard on this matter in some of our Cabinet Discussions has often tried my patience, and led me to the conclusion that we are in one Respect at least like Turkey, & have also our 'wretched' Pasha.[4]

The queen herself wrote to Clarendon, commenting on the various despatches that had been sent off 'without receiving her sanction'. She

---

[1] *Ab. Cor. 1852–5*, pp. 285–6 (partly printed in Stanmore, *Herbert*, I, 209).

[2] *Ibid.*; *E.P.* II, no. 133, pp. 142–3. The cabinet was very emphatic that Stratford should summon the fleet immediately (with the sultan's concurrence), if he had not already done so.

[3] *Ab. Cor. 1852–5*, pp. 289–92, from Graham, 9 October, and from the queen, 10 October 1853.

[4] MS. Clar. Dep. C3, fols. 187–92, 14 October 1853.

congratulated him on his able despatch to Vienna explaining why the government could not accept the Olmütz proposals as they stood, but severely criticised the vague instructions that had been sent to Lord Stratford. 'As matters have now been arranged,' she scolded, 'it appears to the Queen, moreover, that we have taken on ourselves in conjunction with France all the risks of a European war without having bound Turkey to any conditions with respect to provoking it. The one hundred and twenty fanatical Turks constituting the Divan at Constantinople are left sole judges of the line of policy to be pursued, and made cognizant at the same time that England and France have bound themselves to defend Turkish territory ! This is entrusting them with a power which Parliament has been jealous to confide even to the hands of the British Crown.'[1]

Evidently fateful decisions had been taken at the cabinet meetings of 7 and 8 October about which at least three ministers were distinctly uneasy and with which one who was not present disagreed. Had Graham attended the meeting as Aberdeen had wished and had the other three stood up more boldly to Russell, Palmerston, Lansdowne and Clarendon, the Crimean War might have been averted, but Aberdeen was afraid, with some reason, of breaking up his government, and Herbert and Argyll alone were scarcely in a position to offer effective opposition by themselves to such a formidable quartet; yet they might have obtained support from Wood and Granville, who were peacefully disposed. Had Gladstone been more in the picture he might have taken the lead, but since the formation of the ministry his mind had been preoccupied with domestic questions, and he had, moreover, just returned to London on recovering from a long and severe illness. The decisions of these cabinets, however, must be remembered as crucial when any estimate is made of England's degree of responsibility for the war. What was worse, in his account Aberdeen clearly sought to deceive himself by minimising the significance of the decisions taken.

The explanation of the cabinet's action may be found in a letter of Clarendon's to Cornewall Lewis (which also illustrates how lightly the rules of cabinet secrecy were observed, at least by the Foreign Secretary). After summarising the decisions Clarendon explained: 'With reference to public feeling in England, we could not well do less...I see little chance of averting war, which, even in the most sacred cause, is a horrible calamity; but for such a cause as two sets of Barbarians

[1] *Letters of Queen Victoria*, II, 554–5.

quarrelling over a form of words, it is not only shocking but incredible.'[1]

The queen and her husband were much distressed by the letters which the Prime Minister had sent to Balmoral, describing the decisions of the cabinet, especially because of their constitutional implications. After discussing the situation thoroughly with Graham, Prince Albert prepared a memorandum[2] in which he wrote: 'It was evident that Lord Aberdeen was, against his better judgment, consenting to a course of policy which he inwardly condemned, that his desire to maintain unanimity in the Cabinet led to concessions which by degrees altered the whole character of the policy, while he held out no hope of being able permanently to secure agreement.' Prince Albert pointed out to Graham that this put the queen in a 'very painful' position, since the most important decisions were being taken by the Cabinet without her being able to take any part in them and with evidence that the minister in whom she placed chief reliance disapproved of them. He proceeded to make a strong claim for the Crown's rights. 'The position was morally and constitutionally a wrong one', he wrote. 'The Queen ought to have the whole policy in spirit and ultimate tendency developed before her to give her deliberate sanction to it, knowing what it involved her in abroad and at home.' He continued: 'Lord Aberdeen renounced one of his chief sources of strength in the Cabinet, by not making it apparent that he requires the sanction of the Crown to the course proposed by the Cabinet, and has to justify his advice by argument before it can be adopted, and that it does not suffice to come to a decision at the table of the Cabinet.' Graham might have pointed out, as Palmerston did to Clarendon, that events could not 'be kept waiting for the goings and comings of Messengers from the Highlands',[3] but according to the prince he agreed with their views, which he undertook to take to Aberdeen in London forthwith. The queen was to follow on Friday, 14 October.

When the Prime Minister finally saw the queen on the 15th he made some rather lame excuses for the cabinet decisions that had been taken in her absence, and professed to see some rays of hope. 'The French', he said, 'were ready to do anything we pleased'; and Lord Stratford himself was 'thoroughly frightened' and proposing a peaceful solution—

[1] Maxwell, *Clarendon*, II, 26.
[2] *Letters of Queen Victoria*, II, 552–4.
[3] MS. Clar. Dep. C3, fols. 187–92, 14 October 1853.

not that he placed any trust in Stratford, who had to his certain knowledge 'called "the conduct of the Government infamous" and declared
"he would let the world know his name was Canning"'.[1]

Continued search for a diplomatic solution: Turkish declaration of war

The Eastern Crisis had reached another turning-point that seemed to
lead directly to war. It is true that war had appeared imminent in the
early summer when the Russians had decided to occupy the Principalities and the Western Allies to send their fleets to the Aegean. Two
months later the production of the Vienna note and its acceptance by
the Russians raised hopes for a peaceful solution. Thereafter, the situation deteriorated as the Russians rejected the Turkish demand for
modifications, the Turkish grand council decided on war, and the Allies
ordered their fleets to Constantinople. The meeting of the Austrian
and Russian emperors at Olmütz presented an opportunity to stop this
rot, for the Russians were still looking for a means of averting a war
they did not want, but suspicion of Russian intentions had blinded
Western statesmen to the possibilities of the situation. They seemed to
have reached the point of no return, and yet, shocked by the consequences of their own actions, at the eleventh hour they once more
began to look for peaceful solutions.

In actual fact nobody appears to have been working harder for peace
at this stage than Stratford. Twice he managed to persuade the sultan to
postpone the outbreak of hostilities, even after the decision to declare
war had been made, and he postponed to the last moment calling the
fleet up to Constantinople, although pressed by the sultan and instructed
by the despatch of 23 September, which he acknowledged on 6 October.[2] Stratford's delaying tactics and the Olmütz negotiations gave
the ministers in London an opportunity that they failed to utilise
satisfactorily for the unfortunate reasons given by Clarendon to Lewis.

[1] *Letters of Queen Victoria*, II, 555–8.
[2] Temperley, *E.H.R.* XLIX, 280–3. See *E.P.* II, nos. 183, 6 October; 185, 15 October;
186, 17 October 1853. Puryear, *Straits question*, pp. 278–9, 292–301, charges the Allies
with numerous infractions of the Straits Convention since the arrival of the fleets at
Besika Bay in June, but Temperley has rebutted these at length in 'The alleged violations of the straits convention by Stratford de Redcliffe between June and September
1853', *E.H.R.* XLIX (1934), 657–72, and in his *Crimea*, appendix IV, pp. 499–506.
Although he received Clarendon's order to call up the fleet on 4 October, Stratford did
not pass it on to the Admiral until 20 October and the fleets did not pass the Dardanelles
until the 22nd. The Allied fleets did not arrive at Constantinople until 24 November.

Clarendon does not seem to have seen the distinction, clear to Stratford, that the declaration of war (4 October) and the commencement of hostilities were two different things.

Stratford also produced a new proposal, which sought to modify the Vienna note in such a way as to meet the Turkish objections, but which, in Aberdeen's view, was also framed to meet all reasonable Russian demands.[1] On receipt of this proposal Clarendon drafted a note based on it, which was considered by the cabinet on 10 and 12 October,[2] but several more days were spent in discussing amendments. Aberdeen, who had little hope that these proposals had any chance of success, suggested an additional clause rehearsing what had already been done for the Porte and expressing the expectation that the Turks would now acquiesce. 'Should this unfortunately not be the case,' the proposed clause declared, 'they [the British Government] feel it to be their duty to declare that they cannot permit themselves, in consequence of unfounded objection, or by the declaration of war which they have already condemned, to be drawn into the adoption of a policy inconsistent with the peace of Europe, as well as with the true interests of Turkey itself.'[3]

'It appears to me that common sense requires that we should make some such explanation,' Aberdeen wrote in making his proposal to Clarendon, 'unless we are to be dragged in the wake of a barbarous Power, whose movements we are not able to regulate or control.'[4]

'Clarendon at first totally agreed with me', Aberdeen told Gladstone, 'but at present seems rather doubtful. Palmerston certainly and Ld John probably will be against it. Newcastle approves of it and Graham thinks it indispensable. My own opinion is that it can only be objected to by those who want to make peace impossible.'[5] On the other hand Aberdeen was also ready to tell the Porte that, if they accepted the note and the Russians did not, this was bound to bring more decided support.[6] Throughout the week Graham kept Herbert, who was in Ireland, briefed on the developments. 'You know that my gloom is proverbial', he wrote on the 14th, with the news that Clarendon was moving over

---

[1] *Ab. Cor. 1852–5*, pp. 291–2, 10 October 1853, to Queen Victoria.
[2] *Ibid.* pp. 294–5, 12 October 1853.
[3] Add. MS. 44088, fols. 201–3, Aberdeen to Gladstone, 17 October 1853, enclosing a copy of his proposed clause (Stanmore, *Aberdeen*, pp. 232–3).
[4] MS. Clar. Dep. C4, fol. 102, 12 October 1853.
[5] Add. MS. 44088, fols. 201–2.
[6] MS. Clar. Dep. C4, fol. 110, 17 October 1853.

into the camp of Palmerston and Russell and that the latter was urging an early meeting of Parliament.[1] On the 15th he reported that Lord John was remaining in London and had recalled Lady John from Roseneath, which he considered a bad omen. On the 16th he thought that the note, as amended by Aberdeen, would probably be submitted to the cabinet, and on the 17th he feared Palmerston would make objections, but on the 18th he reported: 'things look better', because Palmerston has agreed to the substance, if not the words. On the 20th: 'The Question has now assumed a new shape. The recast Note has become so Turkish in its fresh attire that there is little danger of its rejection at Constantinople, but much less chance of its acceptance at St Petersburg.' The war party were pressing for an early assembly of parliament; 'the Friends of Peace a more distant one'.[2] On the 22nd he hoped the matter might be settled without a cabinet, 'but Palmerston and Lord John are somewhat jealous of each other; and when one makes a concession the other is disposed to hang back'. Graham also expressed suspicion of the intentions of the French emperor, who, he feared, looked to the defeat of the Turks and the occupation of Constantinople and the Dardanelles by a French army. 'The verge, on which we stand, is slippery and the staff, on which we rest, is broken,' he concluded with a characteristic flourish. The next day, however, he was able to report that 'the Note and the course of proceeding [had] been settled *without* a Cabinet, by the concurrence of Lord Aberdeen, J. Russell and Palmerston'.[3]

As usual Aberdeen surrendered part of what he considered necessary to avoid a break-up of the government. He justified his concession in a letter to Gladstone in which he wrote:

Reasonable as it [his proposed amendment] was, I have not thought it prudent to adhere to it. I found that both Palmerston and Ld John were determined to resist it to the utmost extremity; and I had to consider how far I should be justified in creating a breach on such grounds...To those who did not know all that had passed, such a condition would have appeared harsh, and unjust;

[1] Herbert Papers; these letters are printed in Stanmore, *Herbert*, I, 209–13.
[2] When Russell made this suggestion Aberdeen said it was meant to break up the cabinet. 'I hope not', was Lord John's laughing reply (*Letters of Queen Victoria*, II, 557).
[3] For the text of the note and despatch of 24 October to Stratford see *E.P.* II, no. 164, pp. 173–7. For the original draft and the proposed addition see *Ab. Cor. 1852–5*, pp. 309–11. See also PRO 30/22/11/B, fols. 325–6, Aberdeen to Russell, 22 October 1853, saying that he had suspended the cabinet since there did not seem to be sufficient difference of opinion between them to render it necessary.

and I felt that it could not properly be made the ground of an irreconcilable difference in the Cabinet.[1]

Aberdeen did, however, insist that Stratford should be directed to extract from the Turks a suspension of hostilities while negotiations were in progress. Unfortunately the phrase 'for a reasonable time' was added at Russell's insistence.[2]

At the last moment Palmerston made fresh objections, to a paragraph in the proposed despatch warning Turkey that the rejection of the note would influence Britain's future action. 'I wish to state on my Part, distinctly and formally to Lord Aberdeen,' he wrote to Clarendon, 'that I am no Party to that sentence, that I protest positively against it.' 'If we are now laying the ground for the abandonment of Turkey', he concluded, 'it is high time that another Government was formed.'[3] Queen Victoria, now back in London, advised Clarendon to ignore these bullying tactics, which she recognised of old, and to send the despatch as it was. This Clarendon did, sending it by the *Fury* on the 24th and at the same time despatching special messengers to Berlin and Vienna asking for the assent of the Central Powers. Palmerston accepted the *fait accompli* with good humour, for was it not the way that he would have acted as Foreign Secretary?[4] Graham suspiciously attributed Palmerston's *volte-face* to a private letter he believed that the latter had received from Stratford 'by the French mail', and he thought that the leading article in Palmerston's *Morning Post* of 26 October confirmed this hunch.[5]

It will be noted that these proposals were sent direct to Constanti-

---

[1] Add. MS. 44088, fols. 204–6, 20 October 1853 (Stanmore, *Aberdeen*, p. 233). On 17 October Arthur Gordon had written to Gladstone saying that his father was most anxious that Gladstone should return to London since the cabinet was in danger of breaking up. Aberdeen feared that Clarendon would join the seceders, although originally he had supported Aberdeen's addition. Gladstone, of course, fully endorsed it (Add. MS. 43070, fol. 390; *Ab. Cor. 1852–5*, p. 311).

[2] Stanmore, *Aberdeen*, p. 234, who suggests this was a fatal weakness. For Russell's views see MS. Clar. Dep. C3, fols. 473–81.

[3] MS. Clar. Dep. C3, fols. 206–8.

[4] *Ibid.* fol. 209, 27 October 1853. 'As your despatch is gone, it is gone,' he wrote, 'and I dare say no harm will come of it...I can quite imagine that you must have had a hard time of it to get a team which is disposed to go so many different ways to agree to any common pull together. If we can bring the contending Parties to Peaceful ends well & good, but the Emperor is so much in the wrong & the Turks so much in the right that it is hard to find a middle term for them to meet upon.' See *Greville Memoirs*, VI, 459; *E.P.* II, no. 164, pp. 173–7.

[5] MS. Clar. Dep. C4, fols. 225–8, 25 and 27 October 1853.

nople and not for consideration of the conference of ambassadors at Vienna, in which Russell, Lansdowne and Palmerston had no faith. Palmerston put his views on the subject in characteristically blunt terms when he wrote to Russell:

That Conference is dead. Peace to its remains—no good can come out of a Conference at Vienna on these matters and at the present time. A Vienna Conference means Buol, and Buol means Meyendorff, and Meyendorff means Nicholas...Westmorland and Bourqueney are good men in their way, but neither of them up to the mark for Conference functions. Moreover the very atmosphere of Vienna is unhealthy, and I doubt whether even you or I should not find ourselves paralyzed by the Political Miasma of the Place. If the machinery of the Conference is to be set up again, and it may be very useful to reorganize it, we ought to make a sine qua non of its being held in London.

It is indeed doubtful whether the Gold & Silver age of Notes has not gone by and whether when the Fury gets to Constantinople she will not find the age of Brass and Iron already begun, but we are quite right in making the attempt.[1]

The suggestion of a London conference first came from Prussia and was taken up enthusiastically by Russell.[2] Aberdeen strenuously objected to all suggestions of bringing the conference to London, which remained a subject of difference for some time to come.

Clarendon saw little prospect for the success of his endeavours for, as he said to Aberdeen, he thought that the Turks were driven 'to their own destruction by fatalism, fanaticism, and that spirit of Musselman exaggeration'.[3] His fears were well founded, for when his despatch arrived on 5 November, Stratford, despite great efforts, was unable to persuade the Porte to accept it. Two months previously they would have done so, but now it was too late. Omer Pasha was already conducting skirmishes across the Danube to the annoyance of the Russians, and had claimed two minor victories.[4]

Up until this time Gladstone, many years later to be so deeply involved in the Eastern Question, had taken little part in the discussions

---

[1] PRO 30/22/11/B, fols. 329–32, 24 October 1853.
[2] MS. Clar. Dep. C3, fols. 461–4, and 471, 16 and 19 October 1853.
[3] *Ab. Cor. 1852–5*, p. 318, 22 October 1853. Graham, on the other hand, told Herbert that he was 'certain that, if Stratford Canning only runs honest, peace is secure' (Stanmore, *Herbert*, I, 214). Stratford, as usual, was to be the scapegoat.
[4] Temperley, *Crimea*, pp. 368–9.

and decisions. Shortly after the close of the session he had fallen ill and, as we have seen, only returned to London early in October to assist in restraining the war party in the cabinet meetings of the 7th and 8th. He then left London for a visit to Manchester to participate in the unveiling of a statue erected in Peel's memory. In the speech that he was called upon to make, he took the opportunity of the friendly reception he enjoyed to say 'more on the war question' than he had intended. From the reaction of the audience he found evidence of the existence of a peace and a war party, but he judged the former to be the stronger. He emphasised his distaste for the anomalous situation in which millions of Christians in this corner of Europe were under Moslem rule, but he said that intervention by one power was unacceptable.[1] Aberdeen professed to believe that the speech produced a great and, he hoped, beneficial success.[2]

Despite the despatch of Clarendon's peace proposals on 24 October the ministers continued to exchange memoranda expressing their different points of view, stimulated in part by Prince Albert, who offered his own ideas on England's position *vis-à-vis* Russia and Turkey, which corresponded closely with those of the Prime Minister.[3] Russell responded by proposing a policy of intervention on the Black Sea very similar to that adopted by the Allies two months later.[4] Palmerston was equally resolute. The maintenance of the Ottoman empire he considered 'more valuable than peace', the occupation of Turkey by Russia 'worse than war'. He argued that the Allies had crossed their Rubicon when they called up their fleets. 'The Government[s] of the two most powerful Countries on the face of the earth must not be frightened.' He pooh-poohed stories of Turkish fanaticism as 'fables invented at Vienna and St Petersburg' (in the way that Disraeli was to dismiss the Bulgarian massacres of 1876 as 'coffee house bauble') and treated Prince Albert's proposals to turn the Turks out of Europe as impracticable. He professed to have 'no partiality for the Turks as Mahometans', and claimed he would be 'very glad if they could be turned into Christians', but suggested that many Christian subjects of Russia, Austria, Rome and Naples would like to be as well treated as the Christian subjects of the Sultan.[5]

[1] *Ab. Cor. 1852–5*, pp. 297–8, 12 October 1853; Morley, *Gladstone*, I, 483–4.
[2] Add. MS. 44088, fols. 201–2, 17 October 1853.
[3] *Ab. Cor. 1852–5*, pp. 315–17, 21 October 1853.
[4] *Ibid.* pp. 304–5, n.d.
[5] *Ibid.* pp. 326–30, 1 November 1853.

Aberdeen could not let Palmerston's views pass without comment. In his rejoinder he frankly expressed his own opinion of the Turks:

Peace is still our object [he wrote]; and we surely have a right to expect that the Turks should do nothing to counteract the endeavours we are making on their behalf...If the Turks should reject our advice, and should be ostensibly bent on war, when we are labouring for peace, I confess that I am not disposed to sacrifice our freedom of action, and to permit ourselves to be dragged into war by a Government, which has lost the requisite control over its own subjects, and is obliged to act under the pressure of popular dictation... I have no belief whatever in the improvement of the Turks...Their whole system is radically vicious and abominable. I do not refer to fables which may be invented at St Petersburg or Vienna, but to numerous despatches of Lord Stratford himself, and of our Consuls, who describe a frightful picture of lawless oppression and cruelty.

I have no wish to abandon Turkey; on the contrary I fully concur in the policy which seeks to preserve it; for whatever may be the opinion that I entertain of the Government and the people, I believe that its preservation, at this moment, is a European necessity. I would, however, endeavour rather to preserve it by peace than by war.[1]

The last paragraph quoted sums up the points on which these two men (who for a quarter century had represented the opposite poles of British foreign policy) both agreed and differed. The restricted area in which their views coincided was just large enough to make it possible for them both as men of good will to work together, but it was clear that the one was indifferent where the other was enthusiastic, and vice versa. The resulting compromises tended to make the overall policy of the government ineffective. Both were counting on events to turn things their way, and in the end they went in Palmerston's direction, although by himself he might have avoided a war, as he did on other occasions in his career when he came close to the brink.

Clarendon as good as said this to Aberdeen in commenting on Palmerston's memorandum and Aberdeen's rejoinder, which he feared was not likely to abate discord in the cabinet. He thought Palmerston had made out a strong case. 'We are now in an anomalous and painful position,' he wrote, 'and although I shall admit it to no one but yourself, I have arrived at the conviction that it might have been avoided by firmer language, and a more decided course five months ago. Russia

---

[1] *Ibid.* pp. 334–7, 6 November 1853 (printed, less the first twelve lines, in Stanmore, *Aberdeen*, pp. 235–8).

would then, as she is now, have been ready to come to terms, and we should have exercised a control over the Turks that is now not to be obtained.' And he concluded: 'You cannot be more adverse to war than I am, but if our pacific determination is too securely reckoned upon, we may render war inevitable.'[1]

A week later Gladstone joined the memorandum writers, with a carefully reasoned paper in twenty-two numbered paragraphs, impartially weighing the pros and cons of the Russian and Turkish cases. The evidence led him, however, to oppose British support for Turkey. He argued that there should be no change in British policy as a result of the Turkish declaration of war. 'It is intolerable', he wrote, 'that the arm of England should be wielded by the brains of Turkey or that we should become parties to the operations of a war which we disapprove & have dissuaded.' 'It is not to be thought of', he continued, 'that England should aid the Ottoman power in keeping or in putting down its Christian subjects.'[2]

Wood also put himself in the peace camp (along with Aberdeen, Graham, Herbert, Argyll and Gladstone) in a long letter addressed to the Foreign Secretary in which he said: 'Whatever outcry there may be for war the general sense of the country is against it; &...we shall be held responsible if any even unguarded step is taken, or word used. I say nothing of the probable schism in the Government, & its consequences.[3]

This lull also saw an exchange of letters between the emperor of Russia and Queen Victoria. Nicholas addressed a strange epistle to the queen on 30 October couched in friendly tones, referring sadly to their differences, but expressing anxiety to clarify his position before all the English cabinet.[4] The queen was uncertain whether it was merely the farewell of an old friend before the beginning of a desperate struggle, an attempt to vindicate his personal honour, or an actual effort to find an understanding by appealing directly to her.[5] When Clarendon saw the letter he was unimpressed. 'Such communications are irregular, and

---

[1] *Ab. Cor. 1852–5*, pp. 331–2, 4 November 1853.
[2] Add. MS. 44742, fols. 186–90, 11 November 1853. It is not clear whether Gladstone wrote this for circulation, since his papers are full of such memoranda, often written presumably to clarify his own thinking on important and less consequential subjects. This memorandum and a note on church fees, for instance, are squeezed between lengthy papers on the Kensington estates and Metropolitan sites and buildings (*ibid.* fols. 170–92).
[3] MS. Clar. Dep. C4, fols. 393–6, 19 October 1853.
[4] *Letters of Queen Victoria*, II, 559–60.   [5] *Ab. Cor. 1852–5*, p. 345.

generally useless,' he told Aberdeen; 'for the Emperor does not probably *realize* the difference between the Queen's position and his own.'
He thought the emperor's primary object was 'to set his word of
honour right with the Queen', but he also saw the letter as a warning.[1]
Nevertheless, he thought it provided a good opportunity for the queen
to put the views of the British government directly to him and sent the
Prime Minister some headings for such an answer.[2] The queen followed
this advice,[3] although Aberdeen needlessly feared that such a letter
might sound too much like a despatch.[4]

Meanwhile, in Constantinople, Stratford was continuing his efforts
for peace. Encouraged by the cabinet's reception of his earlier proposals
of 28 September (which in turn were the basis of Clarendon's proposals
of 24 October), he prepared the draft, in conjunction with the French
ambassador, of a new note, which he sent on 22 October 'as a forlorn
hope' to Lord Westmorland in Vienna.[5] Haste was essential, since he
had only succeeded in persuading the Turks to make a brief postponement of hostilities, which, of course, had broken out by the time
Stratford's despatch regarding these developments reached London.
Clarendon's reaction was mixed. 'We shall probably have the same
embarras de richesses over again at Vienna that we had in the summer,' he
commented on first hearing of Stratford's intentions. When the proposals arrived, however, he pronounced them 'good', since they were
similar to those contained in his own despatch of the 24th; 'but his
letters are terrible', Clarendon told Aberdeen, 'and make me quite
despair of maintaining peace'.[6] The queen was highly suspicious of
Stratford's private letter to Clarendon, believing that it indicated 'a
desire for war, and to drag us into it', for he wrote as if war was
inevitable and openly said that to be successful it must be '*very comprehensive*'. Consequently she urged his recall.[7] Nevertheless, with the
agreement of the cabinet Clarendon magnanimously gave official
approval to Stratford's action and indicated to the other powers that he
was willing to withdraw his own laboriously drafted note in favour
of his ambassador's.[8] The outbreak of hostilities, however, led the

[1] *Ibid.* pp. 343–4, 9 November 1853.   [2] *Ibid.* p. 349, 11 November 1853.
[3] *Letters of Queen Victoria*, II, 561–4.
[4] *Ab. Cor. 1852–5*, p. 349, 12 November 1853, to Clarendon.
[5] *E.P.* II, no. 189, pp. 199–203, 22 October, received 31 October 1853.
[6] *Ab. Cor. 1852–5*, pp. 325–6, 28 October and 1 November 1853.
[7] *Ibid.* p. 333, 5 November 1853.
[8] *E.P.* II, no. 215, p. 219, 8 November 1853, Clarendon to Stratford.

Austrian government to reply that in their view 'the time for notes was passed, and that the differences between Russia and the Porte could only be settled by a Treaty'.

At the cabinet of 8 November, which approved Stratford's note, a Turkish proposal regarding fleet operations in the Black Sea was rejected, and it was decided that the Turks should be pressed to agree to an armistice prior to the negotiation of a treaty. Aberdeen strongly resisted the proposal to transfer the Vienna council to London as unrealistic. He feared that for all their deliberations they had made 'no real advance' towards peace. He told the queen: 'It will always be in the power of those at Constantinople who desire war, with a certain support in this country, to render abortive all attempts at negociation.'[1] Both he and Clarendon remained sceptical of Stratford's activities. Showing Aberdeen a private letter to accompany the despatch, Clarendon observed: 'As we cannot quarrel with him, I must adopt a style that will not excite his infernal temper.'[2] Aberdeen described Clarendon's letter as 'quite excellent', but commented that unless they could obtain an armistice they would be defeated, 'for he will render peace impossible'. He referred to an article in that morning's *Times*, 'which', he said, 'clearly enough describes the absurdity of our present position'. 'We are entirely at the mercy of Stratford,' he wrote; 'and although none of your arguments may produce an effect, I fear we cannot expect much from his co-operation.'[3] Again these two frustrated ministers in London seemed unwittingly to be making a scapegoat of their ambassador in Constantinople.

On 25 October Count Buol (who a few days later dismissed Stratford's proposals as invalidated by the outbreak of hostilities) called together the ministers of Britain, France and Prussia to inform them that he had received a communication from the Russian government indicating its willingness to enter into peace negotiations with Turkey. Buol suggested that this proposition should be forwarded to Constantinople with a collective note from the Four Powers urging Turkey to accept it under certain conditions. On 9 November he recalled the ambassadors and told them that since time was of the essence he proposed to transmit the Russian message to Constantinople forthwith and read to them the draft of the note he was sending.[4] Clarendon threw

[1] *Ab. Cor. 1852–5*, pp. 341–2, 8 November 1853.   [2] *Ibid.* p. 340, 7 November 1853.
[3] MS. Clar. Dep. C4, fols. 120–1, 8 November 1853.
[4] *E.P.* II, nos. 182 and 236, pp. 186 and 234–6.

cold water on this news in a reply to Lord Westmorland in which he said that there was nothing new in Buol's despatch to Constantinople and that the British government could not have supported the proposals being made to the Turkish government without their concurrence, and considered that any such offers would only irritate the Porte.[1]

In a separate despatch of the same date, however, Clarendon indicated the willingness of the British government to participate in a collective note to be presented to the Porte from the Four Powers, which would seek the re-establishment of friendly relations between Russia and Turkey and express the willingness of the Four Powers to mediate in view of assurances from Russia of her readiness to treat. He also sketched the heads of an answer that the four representatives in Constantinople might propose to the Turkish government in the event of their being asked for advice.[2] In a further despatch on 19 November Clarendon indicated that the British government deemed it useless to prepare a draft treaty at that moment.[3]

On 20 November Buol concurred in Clarendon's proposals of the 16th.[4] Clarendon replied to this enquiry (by telegraph) on the 22nd, saying that the draft of the note would be sent as soon as it was agreed upon with the French.[5]

A series of cabinet meetings was held throughout November to settle British policy. On the 10th, Aberdeen told the queen 'symptoms of great differences of opinion were apparent'. Palmerston made proposals for an armistice and the drafting of new treaties, apparently at a conference to be held in London rather than Vienna. Clarendon expressed sympathy with these ideas, which Aberdeen considered ridiculous unless Russia were to be defeated in war.[6] He still professed a hope of preventing hostile measures for the present but told the queen that 'with the determination of Lord Stratford, and the cunning of some of the Turkish Ministers, it is vain to hope for much progress at Constantinople'. On the 12th the cabinet discussed the Austrian proposals for an armistice, but Aberdeen continued to argue that it was impossible to consider new treaties as Palmerston proposed.[7] A further meeting on

---

[1] *Ibid.* no. 241, p. 239, 16 November 1853.
[2] *Ibid.* no. 240, 16 November 1853, pp. 238–9.
[3] *Ibid.* no. 257, pp. 255–6.   [4] *Ibid.* no. 265, p. 258.
[5] *Ibid.* no. 266, p. 259.
[6] *Ab. Cor. 1852–5*, p. 347, exchange between Clarendon and Aberdeen, 9 November 1853; pp. 348–9, Aberdeen to Queen Victoria, 10 November.
[7] *Ibid.* pp. 348–9, 351, to Queen Victoria, 10 and 12 November 1853.

the 16th he pronounced as on the whole 'satisfactory', for the rather negative reasons that it refused to support Russell's demands for an early meeting of parliament and ceased to discuss the objectionable topics of a new treaty or a London conference. The Turks were to be invited to indicate armistice terms, but Aberdeen considered success to be unlikely.[1]

The cabinet of 19 November considered despatches between London and Paris, and then turned to the subject of Russell's Reform Bill, which they continued to discuss on 22 November.[2] The nerves of the Prime Minister and his Foreign Secretary were beginning to wear thin as the crisis seemed to continue indefinitely. Evidently conscious of the differences that were growing between them, Aberdeen went off on the evening of 22 November to call on Clarendon and speak to him 'very seriously'. On his return he told his son that on the whole the conversation had gone well. According to Arthur Gordon, Aberdeen had argued that the only chance of peace lay in the supposition that the emperor of Russia was sincere. He probably was not, but they must appear to believe him. One can imagine that Clarendon was unimpressed. Aberdeen again objected to Lord Cowley's proposal for a London conference, on which point he said Clarendon was silent.[3]

It is presumably of this meeting that Greville (who was in Clarendon's confidence) has left a very different account. Clarendon said that he had had a scene with Aberdeen, who had been objecting to the new note after it was agreed upon, saying, 'Really, this is too bad. You come now after it has been settled in the Cabinet where you let it pass, and make all sorts of objections. And this is the way you do about everything; you object to all that is proposed and you never suggest anything yourself. What is it you want? Will you say what you would have done?' According to Greville, Aberdeen had no reply to make.[4] There are some experiences that it is difficult to share with a young son.

A few days later there was some difference or misunderstanding over an action of Lord Cowley's in discussing with the French government the possibility of renewing or modifying the existing treaties between Russia and Turkey. Aberdeen complained that Cowley had led the

[1] *Ab. Cor. 1852–5*, pp. 354–5, 1 November 1853.
[2] *Ibid.* pp. 355–6, 19 November 1853; p. 364, 22 November 1853.
[3] *Ibid.* pp. 363–4. Extracts from Arthur Gordon's Journal, 22 November. Aberdeen also told his son that some time ago he had explained to Clarendon that his real objection to a London conference lay in the fact that the negotiations would not be 'in *his* hands'.
[4] *Greville Memoirs*, VI, 466.

French government to believe that the British cabinet had come to a decision on the matter, which was not the case. Rather tartly he wrote: 'If therefore, it should be thought desirable to make any proposition to the French Govt. which should appear to have the sanction of the English Cabinet, it ought previously to be called together, and the question fairly submitted to it. Any other course, I must say, seems to me not to be fair either to the French Government, or to the Cabinet, or, I will add, to myself. . .; but in a matter of this importance, you will probably think that the Cabinet ought to pronounce some opinion.'[1]

In the meantime the French government had approved the form of a note proposed by the British government and had submitted a draft of instructions which was approved by the British cabinet on 26 November.[2] The combined Anglo-French proposals were finally sent to Vienna on the 29th, and on 3 December the conference of ambassadors was resumed in Vienna under the presidency of Count Buol. The Anglo-French note and draft protocol were initialled, and it was agreed that they should be transmitted by Lord Westmorland to Lord Stratford, who was to use his judgment as to how best they should be presented to the Porte.[3]

As usual all this diplomatic activity came to nothing. The note arrived in Constantinople after news of the Battle of Sinope and after the four ambassadors had made other proposals to the Porte. Under the circumstances Stratford put the note aside.[4] Count Buol was so annoyed at this reversal that he proposed the note should be given to the Turkish ambassador in Vienna, but the British government declined to authorise this until more was heard from the ambassadors in Constantinople.[5]

On 5 December, Aberdeen addressed a long letter to Gladstone welcoming news of his early return to London, for 'the state of matters', he said, 'is daily becoming such as to render personal communication more and more desirable'; and divisions in the cabinet were to be anticipated. He went on to review the position as he saw it, rehearsing all the familiar arguments that he had been pressing on Clarendon and Company for the past two months. He feared pressure for more active participation in support of Turkey. 'But, after all,' he concluded, 'it is

[1] MS. Clar. Dep. C4, fols. 131–2, 25 November 1853.
[2] *Ab. Cor. 1852–5*, p. 366, to Queen Victoria, 26 November 1853.
[3] *E.P.* II, no. 301, pp. 277–9, 3 December 1853.
[4] *Ibid.* no. 350, p. 325, 19 December 1853.
[5] *Ibid.* no. 358, p. 35, 28 December; no. 361, p. 331, 30 December 1853.

the exclusion of Russia, rather than the preservation of the Turks, that we ought to have in view.'[1]

Serious differences remained within the cabinet. Russell told Aberdeen he did not understand what he intended. 'I say the same of him,' Aberdeen wrote to Clarendon on 3 December. 'The only real explanation is that which I have already given you, viz: that he intends war, and I intend peace.'[2] Three days later he talked the matter over fully with Russell,[3] 'and he knows how entirely I differ from him', Aberdeen reported to Clarendon. The Prime Minister's confidence in his Foreign Secretary now seemed to be quite restored.

The arrival of the Allied fleets at Constantinople at the beginning of November was a development bound to influence the course of events in that area, by increasing both Turkish confidence and Russian annoyance. Allied ambassadors and admirals working under none too clear instructions from home had to decide under what circumstances they should send their ships into the Black Sea. Stratford opposed Admiral Dundas's proposal to send six Allied ships there in November (although at home Aberdeen was blaming naval activity on the ambassador), and resisted a Turkish move to send a strong naval force cruising in the Black Sea, but he did not object to a small detachment of six Turkish warships being sent to the harbour of Sinope.[4] On 30 November an overwhelming Russian force entered that Turkish port and sank the ships anchored there with considerable loss of life. It was a normal act of war, but its consequences were fateful. The news greatly aroused the war feeling in both camps and acted with electric effect in England and France. It arrived in England on the eve of a cabinet crisis over parliamentary reform.

[1] Add. MS. 44088, fols. 215–18; the letter is printed by Stanmore, *Aberdeen*, pp. 238–40, who misdates it 3 December.
[2] MS. Clar. Dep. C4, fol. 135, 3 December 1853.
[3] *Ibid.* fol. 139, 6 December 1853.
[4] See Temperley, *Crimea*, p. 370; *E.H.R.* XLIX, 292.

9

A DOMESTIC INTERLUDE—THE CABINET CRISIS OF DECEMBER 1853

The resignation of Lord Palmerston

Although war was more than likely, it was as yet by no means certain, and consequently the government had to prepare for the next session of parliament, assuming peace until war became inevitable. This meant the production of the long-promised Reform Bill and so it was that at this point the cabinet, for so long concerned exclusively with foreign affairs, became embroiled in a reform bill crisis. When the ministry was formed Russell was determined on another measure of parliamentary reform to fulfil a promise made to the radical wing of his party a year before, but some of his Whig colleagues, particularly Lansdowne and Palmerston, were notably cool to the idea and encouraged its postponement for a year. Aberdeen, as we have seen, had all along been ready to accept a Reform Bill; although, as a peer with no Commons experience, he was less familiar with the details, he was quite ready to accept as liberal a measure as Russell was likely to produce. Graham, who with Russell had been one of the committee which drafted the First Reform Bill, took a particular interest in the subject and was fully prepared to talk to Lord John about details. Of the younger Peelites Newcastle was the most interested. Although a peer, most of his parliamentary experience had been in the House of Commons and he had some definite ideas on the subject, which he had expressed to Gladstone at some length in the previous year. He refused to be frightened by parallels with France, for he considered that country was suffering from her present fate because there had been 'too great and obstinate resistance to a fair and necessary expansion in the democratic element in her Government'. He thought that the franchise should be both extended and lowered, although he admitted that the latter was 'both a difficult and a dangerous operation'. At the same time he wrote, 'I believe that the fears of many as to the stronger revolutionary tendency of the working class as compared with the middle class (the present elective body) are much exaggerated.' He was ready to accept the idea of fancy

franchises, but he did not favour the idea of 'Double Election', 'though
if we are driven to Universal suffrage', he added with equanimity,
'this will probably be found the best, if not only, mode of mitigating its
evils'. Newcastle thought that the 'disfranchisement of the decayed &
corrupt Towns' lay at the root of any measure which could 'be success-

THE MINISTERIAL SPLIT
Palmerston. 'I'll just frighten them a little.'
(reproduced from *Punch*)

ful popular & conclusive'.[1] Gladstone, although largely responsible for
the Second and Third Reform Acts, was not as yet much interested in
the subject.

Early in November the cabinet appointed a committee, consisting of
Russell, Graham, Newcastle, Granville, Palmerston and Wood, to
consider Russell's proposals. In the view of the hostile Greville these
ministers took up the cause for different reasons: 'John from old

[1] Add. MS. 44262, fols. 125–30, 26 August 1852.

prejudices and obstinacy, Graham from timidity, Newcastle because he has espoused Liberal principles.' 'Granville', Greville added, 'will be inclined to go with John, and Palmerston alone is likely to stand out against a democratic scheme, unless C. Wood should go with him.'[1] Graham told Greville that he fully approved of Russell's scheme, that the first meeting of the committee had gone well, and that Palmerston was making less objection than had been anticipated.[2]

Russell's original proposals envisaged a redistribution of seventy seats taken from boroughs with less than 300 electors (500 in the case of two-member constituencies), and the extension of the borough franchise either to a six-pound rating or to the existing municipal household franchise.[3] Newcastle, who was the most advanced member of the Reform committee, wrote to Russell after one of its meetings about his slight differences of opinion, which he said were all 'in a somewhat more *Radical* sense'. He questioned the proposal to give a majority of the disfranchised seats to the counties and proposed, with Graham's support, to give seats first of all to such constituencies as the Universities and Inns of Court, then to divide the remaining seats between the counties and the large towns.[4] He also thought the disfranchisement was too limited, 'but in this as in some other respects', he told Herbert, 'I found myself too radical for my colleagues'. He was prepared to go further with the lowering of the franchise, but admitted 'that at present the Country is against any *lowering*', and that the proposed bill probably went as far as their support in the House would allow.[5]

On the subject of university representation the duke of Argyll, who wrote frequently to Russell on the Reform Bill as on other matters, declared that he could not show his face north of the Tweed if representation was given to London, but not to the Scottish universities.[6]

Despite Graham's initial optimism it was not long before Palmerston began to make trouble. He addressed a strong letter to Russell arguing that there was no public demand for Reform at that time; 'the necessity arises primarily if not solely from declarations made by you in the House of Commons in former years, without any previous concert or agreement with the other members of your Government,' he asserted

---

[1] *Greville Memoirs*, VI, 461, 12 November 1853.
[2] *Ibid.* p. 464, 15 November 1853.   [3] Walpole, *Russell*, II, 198.
[4] PRO 30/22/11/B, fols. 372–5, 21 November 1853.
[5] Herbert Papers, 16 December 1853.
[6] PRO 30/22/11/B, fols. 396–9, 26 November 1853.

bluntly. What was demanded, he said, was 'a remedy for those abuses of Bribery & Corruption which were exposed by the proceedings of Election Committees last Session'. Russell's proposals, he said, would upset 'the existing Balance of Legislative and Political Power' to the disadvantage of the aristocracy and gentry, giving it over to the 'Manufacturing, Commercial and Working Classes', which he considered to be 'uncalled for and unwise'. The working classes, he said, were already well represented, but he objected to their becoming the majority and so 'the paramount masters of the destinies of the Country'. Rather naïvely he suggested that the working classes were represented by the employers as well as by the members for the boroughs in which they lived.[1] The recent strikes, he added, were a proof that the working men were not free agents. Russell responded with a warm denial of the charges.[2] From Graham, however, he received the fullest support and assistance in a correspondence begun in September. 'It is a great pleasure and satisfaction to me to work with you in this matter so cordially, happen what may', he wrote in one of these letters. 'I know not who in the end will be found to agree with you and me: but it is enough for me that we are at least of one mind in this matter.'[3]

The subject was broached in the cabinet of 22 November and Russell felt they had 'every reason to be satisfied with the general result'.[4] Lansdowne, who took copious notes, made most objection, but Palmerston was 'more amenable than had been anticipated'. Aberdeen told Russell that he would like to have seen a more liberal bill extending the county franchise to £10 instead of £20, but he objected to the proposal of a seat for Scottish universities.[5] Gladstone suggested that every voter in a three-member constituency should have three votes, but be at liberty to give two to one candidate. Russell, in commenting on these suggestions to Graham, quoted Lord Grey's objection to a £10 county franchise, that it would lead country gentlemen to 'split their farms to the great injury of agriculture'. He said he would 'yield to the

[1] PRO 30/22/11/B, fols. 354–8, 14 November 1853.
[2] This is reproduced in Walpole, *Russell*, II, 198–9. It is interesting to note that mill-owner Bright wrote to Russell to refute the argument that the strikes proved these men undeserving of the franchise. 'It is a very unfair thing to be very harsh with our working men', he wrote, 'because they do not fully understand the laws of political economy!' This was magnanimity indeed. (PRO 30/22/11/C, fols. 417–18, n.d.)
[3] Graham Papers (copy), 23 October 1853.
[4] *Ibid.* from Russell, 24 November 1853.
[5] *Ab. Cor. 1852–5*, p. 364, A. Gordon's Journal, 22 November 1853, recording his father's account of the meeting; also Aberdeen to the queen, 22 November 1853.

opinion of the Cabinet', although he thought the change a more radical one than any yet adopted.[1]

In his reply Graham supplied figures to defend the proposed limitation of plural votes to two in three-member constituencies, but he admitted that Russell had shaken him on the £10 county franchise, which he had originally approved with the rest of the cabinet except Palmerston and Russell. Typically, he sought to turn their retreat here to advantage by making it ground for a deal with Palmerston. 'Some consideration is due to Palmerston', he wrote. 'If Palmerston concede to us the addition of the Municipal Franchise in cities and towns, we may well hesitate before we press him against his will to adopt a £10 occupation Franchise in Counties.' 'In the meantime', he concluded, 'I should say, hold your Ground; and keep every one steadfast to the provisional Engagements without wavering...you can always make the Concession at the last moment with good grace, if you think it just and expedient, or necessary to secure the success of the entire measure.'[2]

The trouble with Palmerston came to a head early in December. On the evening of the 3rd he called on the Prime Minister to state his decided objections to the bill, and Aberdeen told the queen that he anticipated Palmerston would resign 'in order to take the lead of the war party and the Anti-Reformers in the House of Commons', who were essentially the same. Aberdeen appeared remarkably sanguine as to the government's ability to cope with such opposition. 'At all events', he concluded, 'it would tend greatly to the improvement of Lord John's Foreign Policy.'[3] The queen was delighted with the news and urged Aberdeen 'to let him go at once'. 'He will be a source of mischief to the country as long as he lives', she observed, but she thought the mischief he could do in office would be greater than in opposition. And she added shrewdly: 'If he is to go, as he most probably will, anyhow, let it be on the *Reform question*, which is unpopular ground.'[4] A few days later Prince Albert wrote to Aberdeen on the queen's behalf, urging that Palmerston's objections 'should be obtained *in writing* so as to make all future misrepresentation impossible', and that 'no attempt should be made to damage the character of the Measure in the vain hope of propitiating him'.[5]

---

[1] Graham Papers, 24 November 1853.
[2] PRO 30/22/11/B, fols. 384–91, 25 November 1853 (printed in part in Parker, *Graham*, II, 207–8). [3] *Ab. Cor. 1852–5*, pp. 382–3, 6 December 1853.
[4] *Ibid.* pp. 384, 7 December 1853.
[5] *Letters of Queen Victoria*, II, 568–9, 9 December 1853.

On 8 December Palmerston wrote to Lord Lansdowne, seeking to enlist his support in opposition to the Reform Bill. He had three main objections; first, the extent of disfranchisement; second, the increased representation to metropolitan boroughs and great towns; third, the extension of the franchise downwards. With these feelings he did 'not choose to be dragged through the dirt by John Russell'. He went on:

I have thought a good deal on this matter; I should be very sorry to give up my present office at this moment; I have taken a great interest in it, and I have matters in hand which I should much wish to bring to a conclusion. Moreover, I think the presence in the Cabinet of a person holding the opinions which I entertain, as the principles on which our Foreign Affairs ought to be conducted, is useful in modifying the contrary system of policy which, as I think, injuriously to the interests and dignity of the country, there is a disposition in other quarters to pursue; but, notwithstanding all this, I cannot consent to stand forward as one of the authors and supporters of John Russell's sweeping alterations.[1]

In his reply Lord Lansdowne criticised the bill, but not as sharply as Palmerston. He took the orthodox position of an 1832 Whig, that there was no question of a new Reform bill, but that it was merely a matter of a bill to remedy defects in the original Reform Act. The main defect in that Act had been the prevalence of bribery, which the present proposal did not seem to meet. He agreed to the £20 county franchise, however, and did not particularly object to the increase of the municipal franchise. He did object to a redistribution favouring the boroughs.[2]

Palmerston then sent this exchange of letters to Aberdeen saying that it was not the occasion for the surrender of a private opinion in face of a great public demand. 'The great mass of the intelligent portion of the nation', he wrote, 'deprecate any material change in the organic arrangements of the House of Commons, though their wishes are strongly set upon some measures which shall prevent the bribery and corruption which have, of late, so flagrantly prevailed at elections.' Having said this, he turned abruptly to reiterate his views on the Eastern Question. Britain and France could not afford to see Turkey defeated by Russia and so he urged that the Allies should bring their superior naval power to bear on Russia in the Black Sea.[3] Any final

---

[1] *Ab. Cor. 1852–5*, pp. 389–91 (partly printed in Bell, *Palmerston*, II, 96).
[2] *Ab. Cor. 1852–5*, pp. 291–3, 9 December 1853.
[3] *Ibid.* pp. 387–9, 10 December 1853.

treaty settlement on the outstanding issues should be between Turkey and the five Powers and not Russia alone.

Aberdeen immediately showed this correspondence to Russell and Graham, writing to the latter: 'This is a very dextrous move. P. has stolen a march, by combining the Eastern Question with Reform. I am at a loss what to do...Truly he is a great artist.'[1]

Graham was harsher in expressing his views on the matter. 'We have a crafty foe to deal with,' he wrote; 'but these very clever men sometimes outwit themselves. The letter to Lord Lansdowne contains nearly all we want, or that we could have hoped to extract in black and white.' He urged Aberdeen to have the correspondence copied before returning it to Palmerston, thus showing he was just as clever as the other.[2] Graham wrote to Russell in the same tone, saying that Palmerston had 'stolen a march' in addressing this letter to Lord Aberdeen. 'Love of War and Hatred of Reform are mingled in equal proportions very much as you anticipated', he wrote. Obviously Palmerston hoped to kill reform by raising a war cry.

This is the Game which has been played before [Graham continued characteristically]...but there is a nobler and a better one quite open; and be it yours.

Propose a sound, but popular measure of Parliamentary Reform; and, without making any undue concessions to Russia, cement the union of the Four Powers, maintain the integrity of Turkey and preserve the peace of Europe.

Cordial concord and co-operation between you and Lord Aberdeen may secure both objects, to the great advantage of the nation and to your own immortal honour.

But cordial concord is necessary; and those, who agree as to Reform, must not quarrel on the Eastern Question.[3]

Russell told Aberdeen that he had heard similar objections from Wood and Clarendon to the proposals of Newcastle, Graham and himself. (It is interesting to notice that Russell's main support on Reform was from the Peelites.) He thought they could survive Palmerston's opposition, provided they presented a firm line to parliament on the Eastern Question.[4]

---

[1] Graham Papers, 10 December 1853. Presumably Graham meant that Palmerston was using current hostility to a pacific foreign policy to undermine the government's Reform plans.   [2] *Ab. Cor. 1852–5*, pp. 393–4, 10 December 1853.

[3] PRO 30/22/11/B, fols. 454–7, 11 December 1853.

[4] *Ab. Cor. 1852–5*, pp. 394–5, 10 December 1853 (Gooch, *Later Correspondence*, II, 124–5).

On 11 December Aberdeen returned the correspondence to Palmerston saying that he had kept a copy of the letter to Lansdowne to obtain a detailed statement of Palmerston's objections to the Reform Bill with a view to seeing what modifications might be arranged.[1] Aberdeen at first intended to call the cabinet together to consider the crisis, but after consultation with Russell, Graham and Clarendon he decided that this was unnecessary and wrote a rather abrupt letter to Palmerston to tell him that his objections were too fundamental to make useful alterations possible.[2] Palmerston took this brusque letter as an invitation to resign and, despite his wife's pleas for delay, he immediately wrote to ask Aberdeen to tender his resignation to the queen.[3] H. F. Bell, who discusses Palmerston's 'resignation' at length, quotes Lord Stanmore to prove that it 'was not voluntary, and that he was in fact extruded', because he 'had given great offence to the queen'.[4] This version perhaps makes too much of a martyr out of Palmerston. He probably thought he could scare the others by a threat of resignation, but in fact the Prime Minister, fully supported by the queen and his principal colleagues, was quite ready to call the old war-horse's bluff. At the same time they were anxious to keep Lansdowne in the cabinet and the queen agreed to help them by appealing to him not to take any hasty step before seeing her.

The Times announced Palmerston's resignation on the 16th in, for those days, extremely sensational headlines. The account, which was remarkably accurate, emphasised that it was entirely because of Reform and that, contrary to the suppositions of some of his Radical admirers, he was opposed to the bill. Nevertheless, The Times regretted his departure in view of his efficient administration of the Home Office and his experience in foreign affairs, which had been of value to the government in its deliberations. 'There is something in the month of December', the leader writer commented archly, 'which seems uniformly to make Lord Palmerston unmanageable.' The paper picked Russell as the obvious choice as a successor in the Home Office. 'The gauntlet is

---

[1] *Ab. Cor. 1852–5*, pp. 397–8, to Palmerston, 11 December 1853.

[2] *Ibid.* p. 404, 13 December 1853.

[3] *Ibid.* p. 405, 14 December 1853; Maxwell, *Clarendon*, II, 36.

[4] Bell, *Palmerston*, II, 95–100, and *J.M.H.* IV (1932), 193–204. See also B. K. Martin, 'The resignation of Lord Palmerston in 1853' (*Camb. Hist. J.* I (1923), 107–12), for a discussion of Palmerston's reasons for resigning. Mr Martin argues that Palmerston chose to resign over Reform rather than the Eastern Question in order to separate himself from Russell, trusting that 'the public, aided by the *Morning Post*', would 'form a different conclusion'.

thrown down', it said, 'and Lord John Russell is challenged to pick it up.'[1]

Aberdeen and Graham pressed Russell strongly to take the Home Office, but after consulting with Lady John (always a thorn in the side of the coalition), he declined and urged that the seals should be offered to Sir George Grey.[2] He had no objection to a suggestion now made by Aberdeen that Cardwell should enter the cabinet.[3] At a cabinet meeting on the 17th Aberdeen read the correspondence with Palmerston to his colleagues, who gave general assent to the invitation to Grey. Apparently they made objection to Cardwell's entrance, however, for Aberdeen was forced to ask the queen, who had already sanctioned the promotion, to regard it 'as only in contemplation'.[4] (At the same time Argyll, who was not present, sought to make this the occasion of Canning's entrance to the cabinet.)

The cabinet was prepared to get along without Palmerston, but there was a general feeling that every effort should be made to keep Lansdowne. Wood, who had done his best to persuade Palmerston to stay, wrote to Russell as early as the 9th, warning him that the Palmerstons were off to Bowood for a visit. He said that it was most undesirable that Palmerston and Lansdowne should offer opposition 'in concert', but he thought Lansdowne's objections were not insuperable and suggested that Russell might anticipate Palmerston at Bowood. He thought that if Russell made some concessions Lansdowne would act, he would 'not say *cordially*, but steadily', with Russell.[5] Argyll expressed a similar view when he wrote:

You know better than myself how great is his [Lansdowne's] influence with the old Whig party, and from my own observation during several years when I sat opposite to him in the House of Lords, I know also his great influence with the more moderate & liberal Conservatives. I feel sure that if

[1] *The Times*, 16 December 1853.

[2] PRO 30/22/11/C, fol. 486, 14 December 1853; Graham Papers, 16 December (copy). See also Russell's correspondence with Grey, PRO 30/22/11/A, fols. 161–2 and 171–80, 2 and 9 August 1853, regarding Grey's choice of a seat, and his letter urging Grey to accept Aberdeen's offer (Gooch, *Later Correspondence*, II, 128).

[3] *Ab. Cor. 1852–5*, p. 407.

[4] *Ibid.* p. 409, 17 December 1853. The queen expressed her 'great satisfaction' at Lord Aberdeen's report on the cabinet's quiet reception of the news of Palmerston's resignation and asked the Prime Minister to warn Palmerston that he was expected to give up the seals in person, which he had failed to do in 1851 (*ibid.* p. 412, 18 December; p. 416, 20 December 1853).

[5] PRO 30/22/11/B, fols. 446–9, 9 December 1853 (Gooch, *Later Correspondence*, II, 123–4).

I were an independent member of the House at the moment, Ld Lansdowne's opposition wd go very far to awaken my alarm.[1]

Russell wrote to Graham about his worries concerning Lansdowne,[2] to which Graham replied:

There is no chance of any difference between you and me on a Reform question; let us in a friendly spirit carefully avoid difference on every other matter so much as possible... I am most anxious that Lord Lansdowne should be propitiated. It would be grievous to part company with him: and no loss that the Government can sustain would be greater than his secession.[3]

An exchange of letters with Lansdowne did nothing to reassure Russell, who felt himself in a very awkward position, isolated from Palmerston and Lansdowne on Reform and from Aberdeen and Graham on foreign policy.[4]

Actually Russell was far from satisfied with the cabinet's policy on Eastern affairs at this time, but Graham on learning of his objections managed to obtain some changes in an important despatch that helped to meet them.[5] In the meantime Russell himself took the Lansdowne bull by the horns by visiting Bowood, where he effected an understanding. 'Lord Lansdowne is quite ready to stay for the present', he told Graham. 'He does not wish to be identified with Palmerston, but is not convinced with regard to Schedule C.'[6]

Meanwhile Lord Aberdeen invited Sir George Grey to come up to town and accept the Home Office.[7] Grey answered promptly from his home in Northumberland to the effect that he was anxious to give the

---

[1] PRO/30/22/11/B, fols. 89–91, 18 December 1853 (partly printed in Gooch, *Later Correspondence*, II, 128).

[2] Graham Papers, 16 December 1853.

[3] *Ibid.* 19 December 1853 (copy).

[4] See Walpole, *Russell*, II, 202, PRO 30/22/11/B, fols. 500–4, 16 December 1853; also Gooch, *Later Correspondence*, II, 125–7, for an earlier exchange. Cf. Clarendon's laconic comment about the first cabinet meeting after Palmerston's resignation (which Lansdowne did not attend): 'Cabinet harmonious—regretting P.'s resignation, but not appearing much alarmed at it. His absence seemed to make J.R. more reasonable upon Eastern affairs' (Maxwell, *Clarendon*, II, 31).

[5] See below, pp. 237–41.

[6] Graham Papers, 20 December 1853. In a similar letter to Clarendon (MS. Clar. Dep. C3, fols. 569–72, 19 December 1853), Russell wrote: 'He [Lansdowne] is very eager upon Eastern affairs, and anxious that we should not fall off in vigour in consequence of Palmerston's resignation.' See also PRO 30/22/11/B, fols. 509–11, Russell memorandum, 17 December 1853 (typed copy).

[7] *Ab. Cor. 1852–5*, p. 410, 17 December 1853.

government his sincere support, but he said that he had reasons that made him feel unwilling to take office at that time. He agreed, however, to see Aberdeen and promptly set out for London.[1] He arrived on the 20th and immediately called upon the Prime Minister. While ready to overcome his private objections if convinced that his acceptance of office was for the public good, he expressed the view that Palmerston's resignation was a great misfortune and that he could not 'supply his loss in the House of Commons'. Indeed, he doubted the government's ability to survive, but promised to see Russell before he made a final decision.[2] He sounded like Graham declining to enter Russell's rickety administration a few years earlier.

The return of Lord Palmerston

In the meantime Palmerston began to have second thoughts, prompted by colleagues and others who regretted his departure. The initiative came from two separate elements in the cabinet, the Whig Wood and the Peelites Newcastle and Gladstone, but paradoxically it was the Peelites who played the major role in the reconciliation. Indeed, poor Wood only succeeded in arousing the ire of Russell, his avowed leader, who apparently at one stage accused him of 'truckling and unworthy concessions'.[3] These three ministers were all concerned with the bad effect that Palmerston's resignation would have on the House of Commons, but at first did not see that anything could be done about it; 'it was not till I found from Fitzroy & Lady Palmerston herself that Palmerston had no wish or intention of going out', Wood wrote to Russell later, 'that it seemed to me to be possible to repair the evil'. He became convinced that there was a genuine misunderstanding, or so he said, since Aberdeen and Russell were convinced 'that Palmerston intended from the first to go out', while Palmerston believed that Aberdeen had tried to force him out. Within a day or two of the cabinet meeting both Wood and Gladstone had called on Aberdeen to discuss the situation with him.[4]

[1] *Ibid.* p. 415, 19 December 1853. At the same time Grey wrote to Russell urging the latter to take the Home Office. He said he thought Russell should have remained at the Foreign Office and that this was an opportunity to rectify that mistake that was not to be missed (PRO 30/22/11/B, fols. 518–19, 19 December 1853).

[2] *Ab. Cor. 1852–5*, pp. 418–19, Aberdeen to Russell, 20 December 1853 (partly reproduced in Gooch, *Later Correspondence*, II, 129). See also Wood to Russell, 19 (?) December, PRO 30/22/11/B, fols. 528–9.

[3] PRO 30/22/11/B, fol. 550, 25 December 1853.   [4] *Ibid.* fol. 546.

On the 18th, before Grey's arrival, Gladstone sent a mysterious note to Aberdeen urging him to hold up any new appointment since he had heard something to suggest that Palmerston felt he had put himself in a false position and since theirs was *not wholly sound*'.[1] Gladstone said he expected to hear more later that evening. The news came from Monckton Milnes, who opened the subject in a letter to Newcastle, which was passed on to Aberdeen and Russell. Russell presumed that Palmerston now thought his action hasty, but refused to agree with the implication in Milnes's letter that the queen should 'appoint her Secretaries of State to suit the suspicions of Louis Napoleon', or that Palmerston had 'ever been the victim of personal injustice'. 'But I have always liked him', Lord John added, magnanimously, 'and I have always a leaning to his policy.' He refused, however, to surrender any essentials of what he called 'my—or rather our,—Reform Bill'. If the cabinet preferred Palmerston's plan, then he, Russell, would resign.[2] Aberdeen told Newcastle that he would be the last person to stand in the way of reconciliation, but was sceptical as to its success.[3]

On the 20th Wood saw Lady Palmerston and heard from her how much she desired to see a reconciliation. He pointed out the difficulties 'and the necessity for Palmerston making up his mind to go much further than he had done, if he wished to come back'.[4] The matter was discussed in the cabinet on the 22nd and Clarendon told his wife it 'was pretty well in train'. 'J.R. and Aberdeen', he wrote, 'both behaved well, but Graham was most *tantankerous* [sic] and ill disposed tho' of course affecting great candour and great regard for P. The matter ended by its being put in Newcastle's hands.'[5] And so the nobleman who a year earlier was the proudest of the Peelites set out to win back the boldest of the Whigs to the coalition craft. According to Prince Albert, Gladstone and Sir Charles Wood participated in the operation,[6] but the main work was done by Newcastle. Gladstone wrote to Herbert:[7] 'I was rather

---

[1] Add. MS. 44088, fol. 219, 18 December 1853 (my italics).
[2] *Ab. Cor. 1852–5*, pp. 421–2, 21 December 1853, from Bowood.
[3] Newcastle Papers, 22 December 1853.
[4] PRO 30/22/11/B, fol. 550, 25 December 1853.
[5] Maxwell, *Clarendon*, II, 30.
[6] *Letters of Queen Victoria*, II, 574. Stanmore (*Aberdeen*, p. 273) says that Newcastle and 'another member of the Cabinet' (presumably Gladstone) set themselves to work to induce Palmerston to return, but from different motives: 'for the Duke, like Palmerston, desired that strong measures should be taken against Russia, which his colleague did not; and the latter felt some sympathy with Lord Palmerston as to Parliamentary Reform, while the Duke was an ardent reformer'.   [7] Herbert Papers, 23 December 1853.

stunned by yesterday's Cabinet. I have scarcely got my breath again. I told Lord Aberdeen that I had had wishes today that P. was back again on account of the E. question.'

Aberdeen had warned the queen of what was afoot, asking her to postpone the council at which Palmerston was to have handed over his seals. He too was having second thoughts and apologetically explained to her that 'the effect of Lord Palmerston's secession may be very serious in the House of Commons and, perhaps, very materially affect the stability of the Government'. He thought to ease the reversal by noting that the Home Secretary's resignation had not yet been officially accepted.[1] The queen was not impressed by this argument and postponed the council very reluctantly. She thought Palmerston had attempted to break up the government and, having failed, realised that he had put himself in an awkward position from which he now sought to extricate himself. She doubted whether 'any useful end' could be served in bringing him back, and feared that with his 'unscrupulous dexterity' he would succeed in making himself the injured man, 'whose traducers had been finally obliged to beg him on their knees, to come back'.[2] She thought his power with the opposition unduly exaggerated.

Now Aberdeen had to tell her that the cabinet were anxious to get Palmerston back, all the more so in view of Grey's reluctance to join. He promised that no important concessions would be made to him and tried to cheer the queen by expressing doubts whether Palmerston would be prepared to make such a sacrifice. 'At all events', he wrote, 'it may be considered a matter of necessity to effect the reconciliation, if possible, but it is a little like what has already been done to secure the French Alliance.'[3]

On the evening of Friday, 22 December, Wood, after consulting Newcastle, again called on Lady Palmerston and at her request saw Palmerston himself, impressing upon him, so he told Russell, that there must be no more differences, that he must make up his mind to a much larger disfranchisement than he had been prepared for, and that Russell considered it important 'not to exclude the working classes'.[4]

The more important part, however, was played on the following day by Newcastle, who had a three-hour talk with Palmerston, making him

---

[1] *Ab. Cor. 1852–5*, pp. 422–3, 21 December 1853.
[2] *Ibid.* pp. 423–4, 21 December 1853.
[3] *Ibid.* p. 426, 22 December 1853.   [4] PRO 30/2/11/B, fols. 550–1.

understand: '(1) that the first move must come from him and (2) that he must come back, not on terms, but on the basis of the status quo with the right to discuss and object but no more'. In giving this news to Herbert, Gladstone wrote: 'It is obvious that coming back thus he will have lost pretty nearly his right of individual & sole action.'[1]

After their meeting, Palmerston wrote a letter which he asked Newcastle to convey to Lord Aberdeen.[2] In this letter Palmerston dexterously climbed out of the hole into which he had fallen. He said that he gathered from several members of the government that he had misinterpreted Aberdeen's letter of the 14th as meaning that there was no room for discussion of the details of the Reform Bill.

Under these circumstances [he continued], and acquiescing, as I have all along done, in the leading principles on which the proposed measure has been founded, I cannot decline to comply with the friendly wish expressed to me on the part of many members of the Government, that I should withdraw a resignation which they assure me was founded upon a misconception upon my part; and, therefore, my letter to you on the 14th may be considered as cancelled, if it should suit your arrangements so to deal with it.

He added that the cabinet's decision made in his absence to send the fleet into the Black Sea greatly entered into his decision.[3] Lord Granville was evidently not one of the colleagues who are alleged to have urged Palmerston to return, for in sending the news to Herbert he said that the letter 'was not quite as satisfactory as he had hoped, inasmuch as it gave a reason for the withdrawal of the resignation, the wish expressed by *some* of his colleagues that he should remain'. Granville nevertheless expressed himself as satisfied.

The splicing of the Cabinet [he wrote] is a very good thing. The public how-ever will never believe but that Pam has had his own way, that his objections to the Reform Bill have been met and that the vigorous measures at length adopted by the Cabinet in the Eastern Question have induced him to remain. It will make it impossible for him to fly again, it would be too ridiculous.[4]

---

[1] Herbert Papers, 23 December 1853.

[2] *Ab. Cor. 1852–5*, p. 428, Palmerston to Newcastle, 23 December 1853.

[3] *Ibid.* pp. 427–8, 23 December 1853. To Clarendon, who had welcomed his return, Palmerston wrote: 'I too am very glad that matters have ended as they have done for I should have been very sorry to have felt myself obliged to separate from friends with whom I am desirous of remaining united' (MS. Clar. Dep. C3, fol. 252, 27 December 1853).

[4] Herbert Papers, 24 December 1853.

Aberdeen answered Palmerston's letter, saying that he readily agreed to consider his letter of the 14th 'as cancelled', but he expressed surprise at the alleged misconception of his own letter. He was glad to hear that Palmerston approved of the government's decisions taken in his absence regarding the Eastern Question. 'I feel assured you will have learnt with pleasure', he wrote with ironic humour, 'that, whether absent or present, the Government are duly careful to preserve from all injury the interests and dignity of the country.'[1] Sir George Grey, glad to be released, hastened back to Northumberland that same night (Christmas eve) exchanging greetings of mutual respect with the weary Prime Minister,[2] who was spending his second Christmas in London in an atmosphere of crisis. The storm created by Lord Palmerston was over, but the odious Eastern Question remained. On the day after Christmas Aberdeen received a note from Palmerston about the next cabinet as if nothing had ever happened.[3]

The sequel to the Reform crisis was anti-climactic. Some concessions had to be made to Lord Lansdowne by giving a little more weight to the country representation and a little less to the towns.[4] 'It is somewhat hard after 34 years labour in this cause to have my proposals thwarted by those who have been always adverse, or are new to the work', Russell wrote to Graham,[5] presumably referring to Lansdowne and Argyll. Graham was not happy about the redistribution of borough seats, but was ready to forgo his objections if unanimity could be obtained in the cabinet for the entire plan.[6] Lord Lansdowne, however, was satisfied and told Russell that he had heard from more than one quarter how much satisfaction Lord John's conduct had given; 'I am

[1] *Ab. Cor. 1852-5*, p. 429, 24 December 1853.
[2] *Ibid.* pp. 429-30, 24 and 25 December 1853. Grey also received an odd note from Russell, who wrote: 'I think considering your disinclination to come into office, the state of your health, the animosity your taking Palmerston's place would be sure to provoke, and your views for the future which might be destroyed, you will do right to decline. I do not put among these motives any external danger by which the Ministry may be threatened, as I am sure your courage would make that danger a temptation, nor do I put internal danger for I am sure you would wish to stand by me in the difficult position in which, unfortunately for myself, I am placed' (Gooch, *Later Correspondence*, I, 129, but the date of 24 December seems incorrect).
[3] *Ab. Cor. 1852-5*, p. 434.   [4] Walpole, *Russell*, II, 204.
[5] Graham Papers, 24 December 1853. In another letter (Graham Papers, 23 December) Russell wrote: 'I am glad to find we agree so well, and think everything will turn out well in the end, if we real Reformers keep together.'
[6] Add. MS. 43191, fols. 183-5, to Aberdeen, 28 December 1853. Graham also sent his statistical tables to Aberdeen, fols. 186-93.

convinced', he wrote, 'you will not have occasion to repent of it here-after—of course radicals & Tories will disapprove because they will be disappointed.'[1] Aberdeen, Graham and Newcastle, who were no longer Tories, had apparently become Radicals.

On 27 December Russell presented to Aberdeen the amended pro-posals which he intended to lay before the cabinet at its next meeting. 'I think it is wise, politic, and just, after an interval of more than twenty years,' he wrote by way of introduction, 'to review the details of the Reform Act, to amend its provisions where they have been found defective, to improve its machinery, where it may be done with advantage, and to enlarge its basis where growing intelligence, and independent action, point out fit elements for an extended franchise.' He went on to indicate the details of the bill, which, with some minor changes, he was later to introduce in the House. By and large he pro-posed to redistribute 66 seats, including the 4 seats already taken away from Sudbury and St Albans. At this stage he intended to allot 51 of these seats to the counties and only 11 to the boroughs, with the 4 remaining seats going to the Inns of Court and the Universities. Eighty boroughs with a population over 10,000 were still left unrepresented.[2] The county franchise was to be extended to the £10 and the borough franchise to the £6 householder.

Forwarding the memorandum to Newcastle, Aberdeen commented:

The Proportion of seats attached to counties is inordinately large, & will give rise to much complaint.

The part about which I feel most doubt is the franchise in towns.

I think the great distinctive feature of our bill is the admission of working classes to the provision of electoral franchise—and we ought to take care that this admission is really and liberally granted, avoiding everything like mere pretence. Now I do not know to what extent the six pound qualification will admit the best of the class whom we desire to see. I am assured the number will be considerable and if this be correct all is well.[3]

He said much the same thing to Russell, telling him frankly that the bill as a whole was less liberal than he expected. 'I hope we shall get rid of the freemen at once', he wrote. 'They are become odious in the sight

[1] PRO 30/28/11/B, fols. 560–3, 27 December 1853.
[2] *Ab. Cor. 1852–5*, pp. 436–43. For the details of his proposals in their final form see below, pp. 294–5. At this stage Russell preferred a long residence qualification to fancy franchises as a means of giving the vote to the better sort of working man.
[3] Newcastle Papers, 30 December 1853. Aberdeen also indicated that he had shown the memorandum to Gladstone and Herbert, who had made no objections.

of the public, and generally exhibit the most disgraceful feature in all our elections.' The Scottish university graduates he considered a poor constituency since they had no continuing connection with their universities.[1] In some respects the old Tory showed himself more liberal than the old Whig; and his younger Peelite colleague's views were very similar.

Although highly critical of 'the preponderance given to Counties', Newcastle wrote:

The measure however is as a whole a good measure—above all it is an honest measure, & if it succeeds in its object of admitting a sufficient number of the best of the Working Classes to the Franchise (and of its success in this respect I confess to some misgivings) it will do credit to its author and confer a great *future* benefit upon the Country.

I feel very confident that, like the Budget it will be carried—that is if War does not interfere & prevent its consideration or perhaps even its proposal.[2]

Herbert's views were detached but penetrating and sympathetic, the genuine liberal conservative view of Reform. He wrote to Gladstone:

The disfranchisement is I think right in principle & in amount but it tends rather to the diminution of rotten than of corrupt boroughs. When there is nomination, there is of course no corruption for there is no struggle. The popular demand is for the suppression of corrupt boroughs, but that is merely an impossibility and nomination boroughs are no longer maintainable as a part of the constitution & as they were argued before the Reform Bill. I think we can fight all this pretty well.

The redistribution is more difficult. I regret it for the small amount given to learning or learned professions. The number of counties gaining seats will look more agricultural than it really is, for Yorkshire, Lancashire, parts of Cheshire, Staffordshire & Middlesex are rather an aggregate of towns than counties in the ordinary sense.

He said that if the towns of Birkenhead, Burnley and Stalybridge were to be put on the same footing as Honiton, Tiverton or Devizes with only one member each it would be a blot on the bill. 'As regards suffrage on the whole I am for an extension & a considerable one', he continued. 'If we open this question it ought to be so dealt with as to be closed.' Noticing the anomalies in the franchise proposals, he confessed

[1] *Ab. Cor. 1852–5*, pp. 445–6, 31 December 1853.
[2] Graham Papers, 1 January 1854. Graham sent the letter to Aberdeen with the cynical comment: 'He shows a desire to leave no mistake on the subject of his reforming tendencies. Otherwise the object of sending it now is not very apparent.'

that he liked 'inequalities & varieties in the suffrage because the society to be represented is composed of unequal & various materials'. 'The £10 has already too much power', he wrote. 'You will not now gain in real uniformity by admitting them to the County Franchise unless you admit the £6 man too which nobody proposes.' Finally, he favoured retention of the Savings Bank franchise because it was a conservative one. 'The greater numbers you can include without danger', he concluded, 'the greater is your safety.'[1]

The duke of Argyll, the most conservative of the Peelites, confined his criticism to a vigorous demand for increased Scottish representation, especially for Glasgow and Edinburgh and the Scottish universities.[2] Gladstone supported the bill, but his mind was already preoccupied with the problem of the civil service. In writing to Graham he said that he was anxious to see the spirit of reform turned to the introduction of the principle of competition as against private favour in the civil service.[3]

The Reform Bill was fully considered by the cabinet on 3 January and received general support. Lord Lansdowne gave his consent with some reluctance. Palmerston made some objections but did not press them in view of Lansdowne's decision.[4] In a second session on 12 January the bill was finally settled 'without any change or material opposition in any quarter'.[5]

It was a curious interlude on the eve of war, which demonstrated that most of the Peelites were to be found in the liberal wing of the cabinet, but that divisions on policy were not taken along party lines. The ministers still hoped that war would be averted and that they could proceed with such major legislation, but this of course was not to be, and when war came the bill had to be shelved.

[1] Add. MS. 44210, fols. 112–15, to Gladstone, 1 January 1854.
[2] PRO 30/22/11/C, fols. 594–7; Graham Papers, 2 and 3 January 1854.
[3] Graham Papers, 3 January 1854; for Graham's long and sympathetic reply see Parker, *Graham*, II, 210–15.
[4] *Ab. Cor. 1852–5*, Aberdeen to the queen, p. 448, 3 January 1854.
[5] *Ibid.* pp. 456–7, 12 January 1854. *Ibid.* pp. 456–7, 12 January 1854. There were some changes between the plan proposed by Russell on 27 December and the bill introduced on 13 February, but these may have been settled before the cabinet meeting. See below, pp. 292–3. Even after the cabinet approval of the bill the doubters continued to press their views on Lord John. See PRO 30/22/11/C, fols. 736–45, 9 February, from Argyll.

10

THE DRIFT TO WAR FROM DECEMBER 1853 TO MARCH 1854

The battle of Sinope and the Anglo-French response, December 1853

In the last two months of the year, November and December, operations of war overshadowed negotiations for peace. The so called Massacre of Sinope of 30 November was one of the last turning-points on the long road leading to war. In London and Paris discussions now turned more on fleet movements than on further peace overtures, although Stratford continued to press these in Constantinople.

On 8 October, assuming that war had by then been declared by Turkey, the cabinet had ordered Stratford to call up the fleet to Constantinople, if he had not already done so under previous instructions, and had authorised him in conjunction with Admiral Dundas and the French ambassador (who received identical orders from his government) 'to employ the combined fleets in whatever manner or at whatever place' he might 'think necessary for defending the Turkish territory against direct aggression'. He was told that if the Russian fleet was to come out of Sebastopol the Allied 'fleets would then, as a matter of course, pass through the Bosphorus'. In view of the circumstances the government left the ambassador and the admiral in conjunction with their French colleagues 'to determine upon the best mode of giving effect to their views for the defence of the Ottoman dominions against direct aggression'. It was also suggested that Admiral Dundas should warn the Russian admiral at Sebastopol that in the event of Russian aggression his orders were 'to protect the Sultan's dominions from attack'.[1]

With the opening of hostilities on land at the end of October the Turkish navy became anxious to cruise in the Black Sea and it was only with great difficulty that Stratford deterred them from doing so. He did not object to a small detachment going to the Turkish port of Sinope, but the French admiral blocked his efforts to send Allied ships in to

---

[1] *E.P.* II, nos. 133 and 134, pp. 142–3, 587–9. On 18 October it was explained that this order did not apply to troop movements between Russian ports, no. 152, p. 607.

233

protect the Turkish littoral under the instructions of October.[1] Nevertheless, on hearing of these efforts Aberdeen and Graham were highly critical of the ambassador and held that he was exceeding his instructions.[2] In contrast the French government quickly rebuked their admiral for his backwardness when they heard of the incident.[3]

On 30 November a superior Russian force entered the harbour of Sinope and sank eleven or twelve Turkish ships anchored there with great loss of life.[4] Since the Turks had declared war and begun hostilities on land more than a month earlier, the Russian action was surely justifiable, but it had tremendous repercussions, in Turkey and in Russia, where it raised the war spirit, and in England, where, quite inaccurately described as a massacre, it aroused all the latent hostility towards Russia. Members of the cabinet themselves responded to public opinion and hardened their hearts towards the Czar, presuming they could no longer put any faith in his peaceful intentions.[5] The sharpest reaction, of course, came from Palmerston, who told Clarendon that the news made him ashamed both as an Englishman and as a member of the government. 'But the fact is,' he wrote, 'our Chief has allowed himself to be bullied by Brunnow, who has threatened his own recall if squadrons entered the Black Sea.' He insisted that something should be done 'to wipe away the stain' and suggested that the Russian fleet should be requested to keep within the port of Sebastopol.[6]

For the past two months the bulk of the English press had been growing more and more anti-Russian and pro-Turkish and critical of their own government for its cautious and detached approach to the problem. Following the news of Sinope the demand for war against Russia became unanimous, as even moderate papers such as the *Manchester Guardian* and the *Morning Chronicle*, and to a lesser extent *The Times*, joined the hue and cry. The resignation of Lord Palmerston, ever increasing in popularity, redoubled the criticism of the government, although his return came as a jolt to the opposition press.

The Times, while moving beyond the position of Aberdeen, continued to present a balanced picture of events. Early in December it reported

---

[1] Lane-Poole, *Stratford Canning*, II, 328; *E.P.* II, no. 310, pp. 292–3.
[2] Graham Papers, from Aberdeen, 1 December 1853; MS. Clar. Dep. C4, fols. 249–52, from Graham, 1 December 1853.   [3] *E.P.* II, no. 295, p. 276.
[4] *E.P.* II, no. 320, pp. 300–1 and no. 331, pp. 305–6.
[5] For an account of the war fever in England aroused by this incident see Martin, *Triumph of Lord Palmerston*, pp. 170–8.
[6] MS. Clar. Dep. C3, fols. 240–2, 11 December 1853.

and welcomed the news of renewed action by the Four Powers in Vienna in producing a new collective note,[1] but at the same time it asserted that in view of the war situation on land and sea the British fleet was now justified in cruising in the Black Sea and even suggested ships of the royal navy might visit Sebastopol as some Russian warships had recently visited Portsmouth.[2] When the first official news of Sinope arrived *The Times* commented: 'War has begun in earnest...The Emperor of Russia has thrown down the gauntlet to the Maritime Powers.' *The Times* did not regret that it had hitherto preached a policy of peace, for it had also warned of the necessity of being ready for an emergency. Now it had come. Russia had achieved naval superiority over the Turks, and so it was now up to the maritime powers to give Turkey naval protection. The news, it feared, dispelled hopes for pacification.[3] The next day, however, it had a most perceptive leader on the problem of the Christian subjects of Turkey. 'The difficulty lies in satisfying the Christian populations that, although we support the sovereignty of the Porte, we are not less anxious to obtain for them a complete reform of their condition', the leader ran. 'In this position, while we are equally interested in supporting Turkey against Russia, and the claims of the Christian races against the ascendancy of the Turk, there seems to be but one course to pursue, and it is that marked out by Lord Stratford de Redcliffe.'[4]

In actual fact the toughening of British policy following the news of Sinope occurred during Palmerston's absence from the cabinet, although, before leaving, he had addressed words of warning both to Aberdeen and to Clarendon. On the 10th, even before hearing of Sinope, he had recommended prohibiting Russian ships on the Black Sea, and on hearing of Sinope he advocated either invasion or the blockade of Sebastopol.[5] When the first rumours arrived on 11 December Clarendon thought 'they must be false',[6] but on the next day the news was confirmed by telegraph from Paris.[7] On the 10th he had also received letters and despatches from Stratford telling of his fruitless efforts to persuade the Turks to accept Clarendon's note of 24 October.[8] In view of the

---

[1] *The Times*, 6, 7, 9, 10 December 1853.
[2] *Ibid.* 1 December 1853.
[3] *Ibid.* 13 December 1853.
[4] *Ibid.* 14 December 1853.
[5] *Ab. Cor. 1852–5*, pp. 387–9, 399.
[6] *Ibid.* p. 397.
[7] *E.P.* II, no. 317, p. 299.
[8] *Ibid.* nos. 304–8, pp. 280–91. This illustrates the frustrating nature of the time lag in Crimean War diplomacy; the Clarendon note had been superseded by the collective note but only now, two weeks after he had sent off the draft of the collective note, did

most recent developments Clarendon had no difficulty in approving Stratford's efforts to send the fleet into the Black Sea to protect the Turkish littoral and in regretting the failure of the French admiral to agree.[1] Had this been done, Sinope might have been averted, or the Crimean War might have begun three months earlier. He also indicated that he recognised his note of 24 October was no longer applicable, but expressed a hope that the collective note (that had only just been despatched from Vienna) might still be accepted by the Turks.[2]

At the same time that Aberdeen and his colleagues were standing up to Palmerston on the Reform question to the point of forcing his resignation, they had to face up to the implications of Sinope. Gloomily Graham feared that it might lead to full-scale war under the naval instructions of 8 October.[3] Aberdeen continued to hope for peace, but Clarendon was pressing for some positive action. On 13 December they had an important discussion, which Aberdeen told Graham was incomplete but 'not unsatisfactory'.[4] To Russell he wrote: 'I cannot say my conscience is perfectly at ease in consequence of sacrifices I have made to the opinions of others;' but he was most anxious to remove differences and placed great hope in a recent assurance of Russell that his policy was '*a policy of peace*'.[5] 'My policy is assuredly one of peace', Russell answered. 'The question is, how to attain it.'[6] This was the crux of the matter. On sending Russell news of Palmerston's resignation next day, Aberdeen appealed to him for close cooperation. 'There can be no real difference or difficulty', he wrote, 'where the object is the same, and the parties act in good faith.'[7] In his reply Russell recommended 'that, upon the Russians crossing the Danube, hostilities should be carried out against them in every part of the Black Sea'; he said he agreed with Aberdeen that 'open war is better than war in disguise'.[8] To Graham, Russell wrote: 'I hope we may be able, at the next Cabinet, to decide upon such a course as I urged in my room the last day we met. I own I feel

Clarendon learn the fate of his earlier note; and at the same time he received the news of Sinope, which puts all diplomatic activity in a new light.

[1] *E.P.* II, no. 322, p. 301, 12 December 1853.
[2] *Ibid.* no. 329, pp. 303–4. By the time this advice had reached Constantinople, of course, Stratford and the ambassadors had set aside this note in favour of their own, which was receiving serious consideration from the Porte.
[3] *Ab. Cor. 1852–5*, p. 399, 13 December 1853.
[4] Graham Papers, 13 December 1853.
[5] *Ab. Cor. 1852–5*, pp. 402–3, 13 December 1853.
[6] *Ibid.* p. 403, 13 December 1853.
[7] *Ibid.* pp. 405–6.   [8] *Ibid.* p. 407, 14 December 1853.

deeply humiliated, as an Englishman, at the affair of Sinope, & I trust we may not have to blush for such another disaster.'[1]

For some time before news of Sinope, Russell had been urging a more forward policy in the Black Sea on Clarendon.[2] His discontent with the government's policy or lack of one was doubtless fomented by the letters he received from his father-in-law, Lord Minto, always a critic of the coalition, who told Russell that he felt 'mortified & humbled by the want of honest energy in our govt', which he blamed on Lord Aberdeen, and he warned Russell that when parliament met the government must be prepared with 'an elaborate defence of their conduct'.[3] Russell passed these letters on to Clarendon, whom he criticised for not standing up to the conflicting views of his colleagues. 'Surely it is time', he wrote on 8 December, 'to act on your own views & not to bend the twig a little one way, & a little another so as to have a crooked staff to lean on.'[4]

Graham, anxious to prevent a breach between Aberdeen on the one hand and Clarendon and Russell on the other, wrote to the Foreign Secretary pointing out that their differences were not really very great.

Lord Aberdeen is ready to declare War [he wrote], if Russia crosses the Balkan; and I think he would consent to make the Danube the Rubicon, if the Four Powers were so minded...The passage of the Danube does not necessarily portend a march on Constantinople; the passage of the Balkan does; and therein is the difference. Turkey declared War: and tho' Russia was the Aggressor and first Wrong-doer, yet in opposition to the advice of her Allies Turkey appealed to arms and made the first onslaught.

In these circumstances to declare war with Russia because we cannot control Turkey, and because Russia prefers fighting on one side of a River rather than on the other, that River having been first crossed by the Turkish Army, would appear a strong measure.

Continued agreement between the Four Powers will solve every difficulty. Recurrence to separate action with France alone will not be safe.

I wish you were better served both at Vienna and at Constantinople; but the most important negotiation is now in your own hands; and if this succeed, everything will follow.[5]

---

[1] Graham Papers, 15 December 1853.
[2] MS. Clar. Dep. C3, fols. 519–23, 524–7, 4 and 5 December 1853.
[3] *Ibid.* fols. 524–42, Russell to Clarendon, 5 December, enclosing Minto's letters of 10, 16 and 18 November 1853. On 18 November Minto went so far as to say: 'The Turks up to the present time have shown themselves superior to the Christians in diplomacy & war, in moderation & in courage.'
[4] *Ibid.* fols. 536–45 (Maxwell, *Clarendon*, II, 32–3).
[5] MS. Clar. Dep. C4, fols. 270–3, 13 December 1853.

At the same time Wood was pressing Russell to continue a policy of peace and forbearance. 'The Emperor [Napoleon] is clearly very peacefully inclined', he wrote; '& will probably not be well pleased if we drag him into war.' Arguing that Napoleon might desert them if they went to war, he said: 'I would not be driven into war till I could honestly say that I had not an alternative to propose.'[1]

Clarendon, on the other hand, now seemed to be moving into Russell's advanced camp. On the 14th he told Russell that he had obtained Lord Aberdeen's agreement 'that if the Russians pass the Danube in force we shd intercept their ships, etc. in the Black Sea', but for diplomatic reasons he advised against any official announcement. He wrote to Seymour in St Petersburg to make this policy known unofficially, but significantly he asked Russell not to allude to this letter in conversation with Aberdeen.[2]

Meanwhile, Clarendon drew up a memorandum of agreement to which both Aberdeen and Graham gave their assent, but Graham again reminded Clarendon that it was the Turks who started the fighting and wrily observed that it would be a strange thing for Britain and France to fight under the banner of Mahomet.[3] That evening Aberdeen, Newcastle and Gladstone met with Graham at the Admiralty, where he was temporarily laid up following a brief trip to the North Sea,[4] and, according to Gladstone,[5] went over the late events and the course to be taken at the next day's cabinet. This was one of the few occasions, if not the only one, on which the Peelite ministers, or most of them,[6] met separately to discuss cabinet business, and it is an indication of how close the coalition was to breaking up at that moment.

At the cabinet of the 17th, which received the news of Palmerston's resignation, there was an important discussion on Eastern affairs, which, Aberdeen told the queen, went 'much more agreeably than he expected'. 'Some rather strong measures', he continued, 'were adopted in consequence of the catastrophe at Sinope, by directing the presence of the English and French fleets in the Black Sea; but no violent or very

---

[1] PRO 30/22/11/B, fols. 472–7, 13 December 1853.
[2] *Ibid.* fols. 482–3 and 484–5, two letters dated 14 December 1853.
[3] MS. Clar. Dep. C4, fols. 274–5, 16 December 1853.
[4] *Ab. Cor. 1852–5*, p. 408, Graham, 16 December 1853, saying that despite his illness he would attend the cabinet.
[5] Morley, *Gladstone*, I, 490, quoting Gladstone's diary.
[6] *The Times*, 17 December 1853, reported this meeting, giving the number of ministers in attendance as six, but Gladstone's diary may be regarded as more accurate evidence.

hostile decision was taken. Lord John Russell was decidedly conciliatory and considerate.'[1] Russell was less satisfied with the meeting, for he felt that Aberdeen had gone back on his agreement to the Black Sea proposal.

> I expected Clarendon to have the despatch for this purpose to France ready [Russell wrote], but [not] only was not this done, but when the proposal was made every sort of cavil was raised & Lord Aberdeen instead of supporting me said but a few words, & those in discouragement, & with a view to postponement.
>
> I confess I was surprised & mortified…it is obvious I cannot trust to any compromise, & I must henceforth state fully my own views in the Cabinet and press for a positive decision. If it is against me I must consider what is due to my own character & the reputation of the country.

Referring to the 'disaster of Sinope', which he believed 'would tarnish the British name throughout the East', he said: 'I do not blame the Russians; they are fighting for Empire, & they do it boldly—But we must not be conniving parties to the subjugation of Turkey, either morally or physically.'[2]

Graham told Aberdeen he read this 'incomprehensible letter' with 'astonishment'. 'I am at a loss to conjecture what are his real intentions', he wrote. 'Why fill up the Home Office with the friends of his own nomination, if he really foresees the necessity of breaking up the Government within a fortnight?' He expressed himself as 'bewildered by the uncertainty of the tone and temper of John Russell' and was uncertain whether he was working to a fixed object or 'driven to and fro by discontent and caprice'. He queried Aberdeen's alleged agreement with Russell and said he was at his wit's end and knew not what to advise or suggest.[3]

The French proposals referred to by Russell were described by Clarendon as very similar to those decided upon by the cabinet on the 17th except that they included a warning to the Russian admiral at Sebastopol of Allied intentions and that they proposed to require all Russian ships on the Black Sea to return to Sebastopol. The difference which Clarendon sought to minimise in presenting them to the Prime Minister was the difference between peace and war, but the Foreign Secretary was growing more warlike after almost a year of fruitless

---

[1] *Ab. Cor. 1852–5*, p. 409, 17 December 1853.

[2] Graham Papers, 18(?) December 1853.

[3] *Ab. Cor. 1852–5*, pp. 410–11, 18 December 1853. Graham appears to be referring to the letter from Russell just quoted, although it was only one of several received during these few days.

diplomatic probing for peace. 'You think I care too much for public opinion,' he told Aberdeen, 'but really when the frightful carnage of Sinope comes to be known we shall be *utterly disgraced* if, on the mere score of humanity, we don't take active measures to prevent any more such outrages.' He argued that the vast scale of Russian preparations indicated they had no intention of peace 'even if the Turks propose reasonable terms, so that by the time Parliament meets we shall find ourselves bamboozled, and in a worse position than ever'.[1]

Aberdeen had to admit to Graham that he had agreed to Russell's proposal, but said he wished to see first the result of their last proposal at Constantinople (the collective note). To meet the demands of Russell and the French, however, he was ready now to agree to the immediate declaration, but he wondered what the British fleet was to do to protect the Turkish fleet should it enter the Black Sea.[2]

At this moment Wood entered the picture, much upset at the way in which his chief was rocking the boat. Later he gave a retrospective account of the affair to Russell[3] in which he wrote:

It seems that Lord Aberdeen had promised to support in the Cabinet on Saturday [the 17th] your view that we should announce the occupation of the Black Sea on the Russians crossing the Danube and that he did not do so. Now so little did you apparently press this, at the Cabinet, or he oppose it, so little difference was apparent that Graham and I who happened to be left in the room, after everybody else had gone, remarked to each other how much of one mind the Cabinet had been, that Aberdeen and you had been very conciliatory to each other, and we augured better than we had done of concord on foreign affairs.

On Sunday evening I was surprised by your note telling me to warn George Grey that the Govt might break up on foreign affairs and I went to Clarendon on Monday. He had received a letter from you saying that if matters went on, as at the Cabinet on Saturday, you could not remain in the Government;[4] and Lord Aberdeen arrived in Grosvenor Crescent with a similar letter from you to Graham in his pocket. Aberdeen and Clarendon began discussing how far the former had promised to concur in your view.

Clarendon then read out a draft despatch to Paris, and Wood proposed an additional paragraph purporting to contain Russell's views which was incorporated.

---

[1] *Ab. Cor. 1852–5*, p. 413, 18 December 1853.   [2] *Ibid.* pp. 414–15, 19 December 1853.
[3] PRO 30/22/11/B, fols. 544, 25 December 1853.
[4] See MS. Clar. Dep. C3, fols. 567–8, 18 December 1853.

In the end Graham wrote a reassuring letter to Russell, and the next cabinet on the 20th went much further in the direction he desired. Russell expressed satisfaction with these developments, but told Graham that he was still unhappy at 'the want of a clear understanding in the Cabinet with regard to our Eastern policy in general'.[1] In reply Graham testified to Aberdeen's 'constant and anxious desire to act in concert' with Russell in foreign affairs, 'to the utmost limit consistent with his strong sense of Public duty'. 'It would be a great calamity if there was any serious misunderstanding in spite of such friendly disposition,' he wrote; 'I cannot believe that it will occur.'[2]

To Graham and Aberdeen, humouring the little man was one of the occupational hazards of the coalition, but to Sir Charles Wood the vagaries of his chosen leader were becoming a little too much to bear. He had thought the whole thing over throughout his long night-time journey down from London in the dark, and on Christmas day he sat down to pen a 3,500-word letter to Russell going over the events of the past week and remonstrating with him for his unfairness and ingratitude. He wrote, he said, because Russell, and especially Lady John, seemed to have misunderstood his role in recent events, which made him 'surprised and sorry'. All he had done, Wood protested, was for the good of the government and of Lord John himself. 'How indeed could I act from any other motive?' he asked. 'I am little likely to acknowledge any other leader than yourself. I have not yet contemplated the state of politics in which I should be in a Government in which you were not.' He indignantly rejected the charges of 'truckling and concession' and warned Russell of his concern for the prospects of the government. 'The principle of cohesion must be stronger than it has seemed to be for a fortnight', he concluded, 'to afford a fair prospect of going on.'[3]

Important decisions were taken at the cabinet meeting of 20 December, which Aberdeen hoped would meet Russell's difficulties, but which left him still with feelings of apprehension.[4] Despatches to Stratford were agreed to, approving his decision to send the Allied fleets into the Black Sea 'as, in fact, it is only by obtaining the complete command of the Black Sea', the despatch ran, 'that the policy of the English and French Governments can be effectually carried out'. At the same time

---

[1] Graham Papers, 20 December 1853.
[2] *Ibid.* 20 December 1853 (copy). [3] PRO 30/22/11/B, fols. 543–52.
[4] *Ab. Cor. 1852–5*, pp. 416–17, to the queen, 20 December 1853.

he was instructed to keep up his efforts to persuade the Porte to accept a policy of peace.[1]

Still more significant was a despatch received from Paris, which Aberdeen told the queen was 'pressed by the French Government with a degree of vivacity' which was 'not very promising for the future cordiality of the alliance'.[2] Clarendon said that the eagerness of Napoleon was because public opinion was getting excited at the inactivity in the East.[3] A similar explanation may be offered for the British cabinet's readiness to agree to the French proposals on the 22nd.

The cabinet met from 2 to 7.30 p.m. on the 22nd to consider the latest French proposals, which Aberdeen told the queen would 'doubtless very effectively check all military operations of the Russians' in the Black Sea area.[4] According to Wood he and Newcastle argued strongly for accepting the French proposals without qualification, but Gladstone stoutly resisted any outright engagement and insisted on conditions, namely that Turkey would be required to refer any terms of peace to England and France. 'Gladstone said he could be no party to unconditional occupation,' Wood reported; 'so it ended in our telling France that we would occupy the Black Sea, that is, prevent the passage of any ships or munitions of war by the Russians, but that we trusted she would join us in enforcing the above conditions on the Turks.' With this the French ambassador professed to be satisfied.[5]

Aberdeen admitted that the decision might provoke a declaration of war from Russia, but he professed to believe that the danger was no greater than before. He justified the decision on the unhappy grounds that the French alliance depended upon its acceptance. Indeed the whole tone of the French communication had been 'exacting and peremptory', apparently because of the state of French public opinion on receiving the news of Sinope; 'and, unfortunately,' he continued, 'public opinion in this country would not permit the risk of dissolving the alliance at this juncture by the assertion of a little independence. It is a proof, however,' he added with bad grace, 'that little reliance can be placed upon such a connection.'[6] It was not for this that he had sought an *entente* with the France of Louis Philippe a decade earlier.

A despatch accepting the French proposals was sent off to Paris on

[1] E.P. II, nos. 339–42, pp. 319–20. [2] Ab. Cor. 1852–5, pp. 416–17.
[3] Ibid. pp. 419–20, 20 December 1853. [4] Ibid. pp. 425–6.
[5] Morley, Gladstone, I, 491, quoting a paper by Wood.
[6] Ab. Cor. 1852–5, pp. 425–6, 22 December 1853.

Christmas eve, the day upon which Palmerston returned to the cabinet that had made these significant decisions without him. It was explained that in order to preserve unity the British government was prepared to go beyond the instruction issued on 20 December, but it was suggested that the Turks should be required not to act independently and that no support should be given to Turkish acts of aggression.[1] Because the course now adopted might lead to war between the Allies and Russia, it was most important to ensure that they did not become the agent of Turkish nationalism. Consequently, assurances should be obtained from the Porte that the terms of a treaty of peace should be left to the decision of the English and French governments. The French agreed to these stipulations to the relief of at least one English minister. 'God grant these may be the means of preventing the worst extremities', Gladstone wrote to Herbert on hearing of the French reply to Clarendon's despatch.[2]

Needless to say, Aberdeen was filled with foreboding. On the 20th he wrote despondently to Russell saying that they were now so deeply committed in this unhappy business, that there was scarcely anything except the declaration of War itself, which could give them cause for much hesitation. After reminding Russell of his assurances that his policy was peace, Aberdeen continued: 'For myself, I confess that I feel like King David, when he said, "I labour for peace; but when I speak unto them thereof, they make them ready to battle".'[3]

Russell for once expressed sympathy with Aberdeen's views on eastern affairs, observing that the Czar and the Sultan wished to fight and who was to stop them.

All we can do [Russell continued] is to offer some inducements to peace to both sides.

To the Turks we may say, 'Until the Russians cross the Danube we shall not intercept their vessels going from one port to another. So that we shall not help you to get back the Principalities unless you agree to reasonable terms of peace.'

To the Russians we may say,—

'If you cross the Danube we shall occupy the Black Sea, and if you attempt to acquire, directly, or indirectly, Turkish territory, we shall call upon Austria and Prussia to act up to their engagements.'[4]

[1] *E.P.* II, no. 344, pp. 321–2.   [2] Herbert Papers, 27 December 1853.
[3] PRO 30/22/11/B, fols. 532–5; Gooch (*Later Correspondence*, II, 129) omits most of the letter including the sentences quoted.
[4] *Ab. Cor. 1852–5*, pp. 421–2, 21 December 1853.

The failure of diplomacy, December 1853–February 1854

Ironically, as the governments in London and Paris, influenced by the rising tide of public opinion, took decisions leading to war, Stratford, the supposedly warlike ambassador, was still striving for peace in Constantinople with some promise of success. With the outbreak of hostilities towards the end of October the time for a settlement by notes was passed and it was gradually recognised that one could now only be reached by treaty. On 25 October Count Buol had announced Russia's willingness to enter into peace negotiations. Anglo-French proposals to be submitted to the Turkish government were sent to Vienna on 29 November and forwarded as a 'Collective Note' from the Four Powers to Constantinople on 3 December. As we have seen, however, by the time it arrived it was already out of date.[1] On 12 December Stratford had persuaded his colleagues to support his proposals for an armistice on the basis of a renewal of existing treaties and the despatch of a Turkish representative empowered to treat with the Russians. Because this was already being pressed on the Turkish government, Stratford and the ambassadors, as we have seen, had set aside the collective note as less likely to succeed. Their decision was a wise one, for by the end of the month the Porte finally agreed to Stratford's proposals, which were now forwarded to Vienna.[2]

The Vienna conference not unnaturally had been annoyed at the setting aside of the collective note and had proposed to transmit it to the Turkish government through the Turkish ambassador in Vienna, but Britain and France fortunately put a stop to this.[3] When news arrived of the likelihood of Turkish acceptance of Stratford's note, the Allies approved of it; indeed Clarendon went so far as to say that it seemed 'about the best thing that had yet been concocted'. Final confirmation of the Turkish approval was slow in coming, however, and old suspicions of Stratford were revived. 'There is evidently some hitch at Constantinople,' Clarendon commented on 8 January 1854; 'and I shall not be at all surprised if Stratford, on hearing that Palmerston was out, had become less urgent for the adoption of his own scheme.'[4] This, of course, was unfair, because the Turkish government had by this time

---

[1] See above, pp. 211–13.   [2] Temperley, *E.H.R.* XLIX, 294.

[3] Clarendon, as yet unaware of Stratford's success, commented sourly to Aberdeen, 'It appears the conference proposes to make the botch at Constantinople worse by another botch at Vienna' (*Ab. Cor. 1852–5*, pp. 435–6, 28 December 1853).

[4] *Ibid.* pp. 444, 30 December 1853, and 454, 8 January 1854.

agreed and the note had been forwarded to Vienna, where it received the approval of Buol and his conference of ambassadors on the 13th, and was thereupon transmitted to St Petersburg.[1]

Clarendon quickly agreed to Buol's proposed course of action, saying to Russell: 'I am afraid of delay for the Czar won't accept and the sooner he puts himself in the wrong the better for us.'[2] By this time the Foreign Secretary had given up any hopes for peace. Indeed on 2 January he wrote to his wife: 'For my part, I am getting *in favor of war*.' A 'patch up' would 'only be playing the Emperor's game'.[3] Aberdeen welcomed the news more hopefully. 'Most welcome intelligence has arrived from Vienna by telegraph,' he wrote to the queen; 'the objections of the Emperor will apply more to the proposed form of proceeding, than to the substance of the proposal itself. He will probably resist the notion of being summoned like a criminal before what he calls *La Police Correctionelle* of Europe. Should a real desire exist to arrive at peace, on both sides, these difficulties of form may be overcome.'[4]

These last moves for peace, however, were overshadowed by more warlike actions of the Allies in the Black Sea. As we have seen, the news of Sinope had led the French and British governments to order their fleets into the Black Sea to protect the Turks. Under his instructions of 8 October Stratford had the power to do this himself, but he did not decide to act until mid December and the actual order was postponed to the 26th, three weeks after the news of Sinope. He made this decision in conjunction with the French ambassador, but bad weather put off its execution and it was not until 3 January that the Allied fleets had completed their passage into the Black Sea. By that time Clarendon's despatch of 20 December ordering this very action had been received.[5]

Stratford in his imperious way had issued orders sending the whole fleet into the Black Sea, despite the remonstrances of Admiral Dundas, who considered this dangerous in view of the weather, but the ambassador refused to take his advice, to the annoyance of Graham and other ministers at home, who held that on tactical questions of this sort the ambassador should have deferred to the admiral.[6] 'Stratford writes in a

---

[1] *E.P.* II, nos. 398, 403, pp. 365, 368–70.
[2] PRO 30/22/11/D, fol. 23, 12 January 1854.   [3] Maxwell, *Clarendon*, II, 37.
[4] Add. MS. 43048, fols. 135–6 (copy), 12 January 1854 (Stanmore, *Aberdeen*, pp. 244–5).
[5] Temperley, *Crimea*, pp. 380–1.
[6] See Add. MS. 43048, fols. 118–19, 5 January 1854, Aberdeen to the queen (copy); Graham Papers, 16 January 1854, from Clarendon; PRO 30/22/11/C, fols. 638–9, 15 January 1854, from Graham.

very improper tone to Dundas,' Clarendon wrote to Russell. 'Dundas is luckily a good-tempered man & will obey and do his duty, but his co-operation with such a dictator cannot be cordial.'[1] Graham was much annoyed at Stratford's 'harsh rejection' of Dundas's advice and wrote to the admiral expressing full confidence in him.[2] The feud continued, however, for many months, but the outbreak of war eventually made the admiral's position more independent of the ambassador.[3]

On 27 December, following the cabinet decisions of the previous week,[4] Clarendon had instructed Stratford to arrange that the Allied admirals should warn the Russian naval commander in the Black Sea of the Allied determination to prevent a second Sinope and the consequent requirement 'that every Russian ship of war [would] henceforth be required to return to Sevastapol, or the most neighbouring port; and that all aggression against the Ottoman territory or flag would impose upon the Admirals the painful necessity of repelling force by force'.[5] Stratford had already anticipated this instruction but on receipt of it a more precise warning was sent to the Russians.[6]

On 6 January 1854 the British warship *Retribution* steamed into the harbour of Sebastopol, saluted the Russian flag with 21 guns and the Russian rear-admiral there with thirteen, and delivered the letter containing the first warning, which the Russians insisted on forwarding unopened to Prince Menschikoff, who was absent in Kherson.[7] Since no answer was received to this communication, the second warning was sent to Prince Menschikoff via the British consul-general in Odessa.[8]

When Brunnow heard of the message that had been sent to the Russian authorities in Sebastopol he not unnaturally expressed himself as 'much disturbed'.[9] Meanwhile Seymour had been informed of the instructions sent to the naval commanders in the Black Sea and was given the delicate task of making them known to Count Nesselrode. It was emphasised that these instructions were consequent upon the 'disastrous affair' of Sinope, that the British government had not

---

[1] PRO 30/22/11/C, fols. 636–7, 14 January 1854, from Clarendon.

[2] *Ibid.* fol. 638, 15 January 1854 from Graham; Graham Papers, 9 January 1854 from Clarendon.

[3] There are numerous letters on this subject in the Graham, Clarendon and Russell Papers.

[4] See above, pp. 272–3.   [5] *E.P.* II, no. 346, pp. 323–4.

[6] *Ibid.* no. 414, pp. 375–6, 3 January 1854; VII, no. 13, pp. 6–8.

[7] *Ibid.* VII, no. 15, pp. 9–11, 11 January 1854.   [8] *Ibid.* no. 26, p. 17, 16 January 1854.

[9] *Ab. Cor. 1854–5*, p. 2 (there is no title to this volume, which runs from 7 January 1854 to 23 January 1855).

abandoned the hope of peace, and in taking this action in the Black Sea had no hostile intention against Russia.[1] On 11 January Seymour had a painful interview with the Russian chancellor. Nesselrode, who had risen from a sick bed to see him, had already received the news from Brunnow, who had been briefed by Clarendon in London. He regretted that the British government should have taken such drastic action just as strenuous efforts were being made in Vienna to arrange a peaceful solution.[2] On the following day the indignation of the Russian government was aroused by the news that the French government had broadcast their instructions to the Black Sea fleet in the official newspaper, *Le Moniteur*. At the same time Russian preparations for war proceeded apace.[3]

The proposals sent from Constantinople via Vienna reached St Petersburg on 20 January, but the Russian government, doubtless influenced by Allied action in the Black Sea, did not respond to them. Instead Count Orloff was sent off to Vienna with counter-propositions which the Vienna conference considered but found to be incompatible with those they had already transmitted from Constantinople. Consequently Orloff departed from Vienna on 8 February without any settlement, but left the door just slightly ajar by having some verbal discussion with Buol as to yet another basis of settlement.[4] The most striking feature of this phase of the revived Vienna conference was the unanimity of the Four Powers and the strong line that Austria took against the Russian proposals, a stand that she reinforced by strengthening her army on the eastern frontier.

When Clarendon first heard of Orloff's mission he feared that 'Buol was being bamboozled', but on hearing the Austrian ambassador's account of what happened in Vienna he expressed his satisfaction.[5] Aberdeen considered the news the best he had heard for a long time, for it showed that Austria was firm and that the initiative for peace came from Russia. 'I still say that war is *not inevitable*,' he wrote to Clarendon, 'unless indeed', he added, ironically, 'we are all determined to have it, which perhaps for aught I know *may* be the case.'[6] The final Buol–Orloff conversation again aroused the suspicion of the Foreign Secretary, who thought it might be used to gain time, but not as a basis of peace. He

[1] *E.P.* II, no. 345, pp. 322–3, 27 December 1854.
[2] *Ibid.* no. 412, pp. 374–5.   [3] *Ibid.* VII, no. 1, p. 1; no. 3, p. 2; no. 4, p. 2.
[4] *Ibid.* nos. 31 and 32, p. 19; no. 41, pp. 28–9; no. 58, pp. 38–9.
[5] Add. MS. 43188, fols. 403, 405, 10 and 12 February, from Clarendon.
[6] *Ibid.* fol. 407, 12 February 1854.

considered the cabinet should be consulted, 'because if the proposals lead to the mischief I anticipate,' he told Aberdeen, 'we shall be criticized for not having frankly declared our opinion of them'.[1] By this time, however, the government had settled on a course that was bound to lead to war.

Before this happened, however, the French emperor made one last attempt to cut the Gordian knot by a personal appeal to the Czar. Clarendon looked upon this move with suspicion, but it appears to have been a perfectly genuine attempt to avoid war on the basis of an honourable peace. The fact was that, in contrast to the situation in England, the French government was in advance of public opinion, which was cold to the idea of war with Russia.[2] Nicholas, however, rejected the offer with a taunt, and the fears of the more warlike English were again dissipated.[3] A little earlier Nicholas had written in more friendly terms to Queen Victoria, again justifying Russia's course, but the English ministers had advised the queen to make a polite reply.[4]

On Sunday evening 22 January 1854 the peace of Lord Clarendon's family fireside was invaded by a despatch-box bearing news that the Russian government was about to force a show-down.[5] A few days later Brunnow placed in the Foreign Secretary's hands the copy of a stiff despatch from Nesselrode, complaining bitterly of the Allied action in the Black Sea. Brunnow followed this by a pointed query as to whether policy towards Russia and Turkey was to be reciprocal, that is to say, whether the same restrictions were being required of the Turks in the Black Sea. On failing to receive satisfactory assurances on this point in either London or Paris, the Russian ambassadors in both capitals were then (on 4 February) required to ask for their passports.[6] On

---

[1] Add. MS. 43188, fols. 409–10, 20 February 1854. The last member of the cabinet to speak for peace was Gladstone, who on 26 January addressed a long and involved letter to Lord Aberdeen proposing a reciprocal attitude toward the Russian and Turkish navies that might be acceptable to Russia. The time for such proposals, however, was passed (*Ab. Cor. 1854–5*, pp. 18–20).

[2] Indeed on 30 January Clarendon was writing to Graham saying that 'the unpopularity of the war in France is to me alarming' (Graham Papers).

[3] See F. A. Simpson, *Louis Napoleon and the recovery of France 1848–56* (1923), pp. 242–7; PRO 30/22/11/C, fols. 744–5, 17 February 1854, from Clarendon, who said to Russell they had reason to complain of Napoleon's letter but supposed they had better not.

[4] *Ab. Cor. 1852–5*, pp. 432–3, 453–4.

[5] Maxwell, *Clarendon*, II, 39, quoting Lady Clarendon's Journal.

[6] *E.P.* III, nos. 1–6, pp. 1–8; VII, no. 33, p. 25.

7 February the British and French ambassadors were recalled from St Petersburg.

A few weeks later the British and French governments agreed to present joint summonses or ultimata to the Russian government, requiring the evacuation of the Principalities. Both the Austrian and, after some hesitation, the Prussian governments gave diplomatic support to this step, but the initiative was left to the two western powers.[1] Clarendon addressed a letter, dated 27 February 1854, directly to Count Nesselrode, advising him that if Russia did not announce her intention of completing the evacuation of the Principalities by the end of April, the British government would consider the silence or refusal of the Russian government as equivalent to a declaration of war. Aberdeen informed the queen of the cabinet's decision on 26 February with a heavy heart as he knew that war must be the result. He said he would have preferred to wait in the hopes of obtaining Austria's participation in the ultimatum, but the cabinet were in no mood to wait for Austria, of whom they were always suspicious, and determined to proceed alone with France.[2] The queen also advised the government to await a reply from Austria. On the 27th Aberdeen told her that 'highly satisfactory intelligence' had been received from Vienna that morning and that consequently there was no further reason for delay. He reported that Westmorland had sent an amended form of convention, which assured 'the concurrence of Austria in the summons made to the Russian Government' and which contained terms that could 'mean nothing but cooperation in war'.[3]

To the great indignation of the ministers a fully accurate account of the government's decisions and of the terms of the ultimatum appeared in *The Times* on 28 February. 'Now, this is really too bad, and is highly discreditable to the Government', Aberdeen wrote to Clarendon in the tone of a headmaster reprimanding a prefect for failing to keep discipline. He continued:

At a time when I was protesting in the House of Lords against revealing the intentions of the Government, our most secret decisions are made public!

Unfortunately it is believed the 'Times' is especially my organ; although in fact there is very seldom an article in it from which I do not entirely dissent. It can only be from the Foreign Office that the information was obtained; and it seems to me very essential that the practice should be entirely discontinued.

[1] *Ibid.* VII, nos. 91 and 92, p. 57; nos. 106 and 107, p. 64; no. 127, pp. 72–3.
[2] *Letters of Queen Victoria*, III, 15–16.   [3] Add. MS. 43048, fol. 272.

I hope you will exert yourself to correct this evil which has become a scandal not to be endured.[1]

This was too much for Clarendon, who answered:

The newspapers are among the many curses of one's official existence & I never was more disgusted than in reading the article in the Times this morng but I am at a loss to imagine why you say that it can only be from the F.O. that the information is obtained unless you suspect that *I* furnished it. I really don't believe there is anyone base or stupid enough in the F.O. to commit such an outrage & the art. moreover contains an announcement of our naval operations in the Baltic about wh nothing is known in the F.O. I have not much doubt however as to how the information was obtained & before I got yr note I determined to bring the matter before the Cabt to-morrow tho of course without saying on whom my suspicion falls. I met Delane in Westr Hall...and asked him where he got his information. He wd not tell me but he promised that the subject wd not be adverted to again.[2]

The courier, Captain Blackwood, who brought the British communication to St Petersburg, picked up a similar letter from the French government in Paris for simultaneous delivery. At the same time the Austrian and Prussian governments were informed of the action taken by the two allies,[3] by despatches dropped off by the same messenger, who took a circuitous route to the Russian capital from Paris via Berlin and Vienna. He did not arrive at St Petersburg until the 13th and on the following day the British and French consuls, still in the city, presented their summonses to Count Nesselrode. Following the emperor's return to the capital on the 17th, the consuls were recalled by the chancellor, who said: 'L'Empéreur ne juge pas convenable de donner aucune réponse à la lettre de Lord Clarendon.'[4]

In a not unfriendly conversation that followed this formal reply, the British consul asked Nesselrode as to the consular arrangements in the event of a war. 'That will entirely depend upon the course Her Britannic Majesty's Government may adopt,' the Chancellor answered; 'we shall not declare war.'[5] Two months earlier Clarendon had broached the question to Russell, saying, 'I don't suppose we can leave our consuls or that they would be permitted to remain in the event of war'! Claren-

[1] Add. MS. 43188, fol. 412, 28 February 1854 (copy).
[2] *Ibid.* fols. 414–15, 28 February 1854.
[3] *E.P.* VII, no. 101, p. 61; no. 112, p. 64.
[4] *Ibid.* no. 137, pp. 1013–16.   [5] *Ibid.* p. 1016.

don suggested that in such an event English nationals in Russia might be placed under Swedish protection,[1] but it was later arranged that the Danish embassy would assume this responsibility.[2]

Preparations for war

After the decision had been made to send the Allied fleets into the Black Sea at the end of December, the British ministers' thoughts turned more and more to war. Indeed it is very striking how warlike preparations began to dominate their correspondence. As early as Christmas day 1853, even Lord Granville, one of the more pacific members of the cabinet, was writing to the Foreign Secretary, urging that they should be prepared to act in the event of a Russian declaration of war. He even raised the question at this early date whether the destruction of Sebastopol was the 'only or the best thing to be done'.[3]

On 7 January 1854 Newcastle was already writing to Graham about 'the enormous estimate for the transport of troops' which had come from the Horse Guards, although in Peelite fashion he was hopeful of reducing it.[4] On the 14th he was in touch with Russell about the preparation of the army estimates, proposing that an increase of 10,000 to 12,000 men could be effected merely by bringing the regiments up to strength at a cost of not more than £350,000. At this early date he, too, mentioned the possibility of an expedition against Sebastopol, but hoped that 5,000 British troops would suffice. He was already regulating 'the reliefs in the Mediterranean to meet such an emergency'.[5]

A few days later Graham told Russell he thought that the Allied fleet already in the Black Sea was sufficient to confine the Russians in Sebastopol, but that that base could not be attacked without an army. He feared, however, that the French had other plans. 'The Emperor Napoleon', he wrote enigmatically, 'prefers the West to the East and reserves his Troops for operations on the Rhine rather [than] in the Crimea.' He proposed that a force of 20,000 men should be sent to secure the European side of the Dardanelles as a protection to the fleet in the Black Sea.[6] He had already obtained from the cabinet authorisation

[1] PRO 30/22/11/C, fols. 650–1, 17 January 1854.
[2] E.P. VII, no. 110, pp. 65–6, Seymour to Consul Michele, 19 February 1854.
[3] MS. Clar. Dep. C4, fols. 442–4.   [4] Graham Papers.
[5] PRO 30/22/11/C, fols. 634–5, 14 January 1854.
[6] PRO 30/22/11/C, fols. 638–9, 17 January 1854.

THE ORIGINS OF THE CRIMEAN WAR

to send a detachment of engineer officers to Constantinople to direct new works at Sinope and to assist in improving the defences of the Bosporus and the Dardanelles.[1]

Graham also circulated a memorandum prepared by Sir John Burgoyne, a senior engineer officer. Burgoyne's arguments, he observed, clearly demonstrated 'that Sebastopol was not open to attack by Sea, unless the land Defences be taken by an Army equal to cope with the Russian garrison'.[2] Palmerston in returning the memorandum expressed the opinion that Burgoyne underrated the value of Turkish troops, whom Palmerston considered would be sufficient to accompany an expedition against Sebastopol. He suggested, however, that sweeping away Russian forts and establishments on the coast of Circassia would be an easier operation. 'Something too might be done in the Sea of Azoph', he added.[3]

Russell proposed sending 5,000 English and 5,000 French troops to the Bosporus, to be used either for the defence of the Dardanelles or for operations in the Black Sea. While recognising that the French army was larger he argued that the English were 'more accustomed to move troops by sea'.[4] He was less certain about the wisdom of an attack on Sebastopol, which might be defended by 40,000 or 50,000 Russian troops. 'The Emperor of the French', he observed, 'will not risk the reputation of the French Army in such an enterprise.' Graham himself composed a memorandum[5] considering the naval aspects of war with Russia. 'Before the commencement of a great conflict', he began, 'it is prudent to count the cost and to weigh well the chances of failure and success', sound advice to which the cabinet might have paid more heed in the months to come. He pointed out that war with Russia was bound to take on a naval character in both the Black Sea and the Baltic. 'It is not in the power of England to strike a decisive blow to the heart of Russia in either of these seas', he warned. As yet, he considered the capture of Sebastopol impossible, but recognised that only a temporary supremacy could be maintained in the Black Sea without it, and this was dependent upon the retention of Constantinople. Should the Russians manage to reach Constantinople and the shores of the Darda-

---

[1] Graham Papers, to Newcastle, 11 January 1854, asking for a detachment of sappers to go with the party.
[2] Graham Papers, to and from Raglan, 12 January 1854; also correspondence with colleagues of 14, 18 and 19 January.
[3] *Ibid.* 19 January 1854.   [4] *Ibid.* 19 January 1854, memo initialled by J. R.
[5] Graham Papers, 22 January 1854.

nelles, then the Allied fleets in the Black Sea would be trapped. 'How then is this inglorious termination to our Naval Defence of Turkey to be prevented?' he asked. So he concentrated his attention on the defence of Constantinople by the preparation of a strong base on the Dardanelles along the lines proposed in Burgoyne's memorandum.

Graham warned against the expectation of easy victories in the Baltic, where the Russians had thirty sail of the line and fortified ports. It would be difficult to get large screw-steamers into that sea and to keep them coaled there. The Kattegat might be blockaded but this would be 'no very brilliant operation' and was bound to lead to angry disputes with neutrals, raising the old danger of a hostile northern alliance or a quarrel with the United States. In conclusion Graham said he was 'anxious to abate any extravagant expectation' that by naval means England could 'humble the pride of Russia, or strike any decisive blow'. 'In concert with France', he wrote, 'she can confine the Russian fleets within the Baltic and the Euxine, but Prussia and Austria must co-operate to compel the evacuation of the Principalities and to prevent the sure success of the passage of the Danube and of the march on Con-stantinople.' In the light of these gloomy prognostications Allied suc-cesses against Russia in the Crimean War were more creditable than historians have generally allowed.

Newcastle fully agreed as to the prime importance of protecting the Dardanelles and announced that he was holding up all reliefs of garrisons except to the Near East in order to have the maximum number of troops available.[1]

All the evidence indicates that in January 1854, three months before the declaration of war, British ministers were awake to the necessity of making preparations for that eventuality. Lord Lansdowne only expressed the general view when he wrote to Russell on 22 January that they must show they were 'ready for war at a moment's notice'.[2] On 21 January Aberdeen told the queen that the cabinet had decided to ask parliament for an increase of service expenditures to provide 10,000 additional seamen and 3,000 marines for the navy, and 12,000 additional men for the army.[3]

When the English commander of the Turkish fleet, Admiral Slade, asserted that Sebastopol could be taken, Burgoyne wrote to Graham maintaining 'the thing was impossible'. He asserted that even 30,000 or

[1] *Ibid.* 20 January 1854.
[2] PRO 30/22/11/C, fols. 661–4.   [3] *Ab. Cor 1854–5*, pp. 11–12.

40,000 of the best British troops would not have a chance in face of the 30,000 or 40,000 Russian troops reported available to oppose a landing. 'The finest feat of landing in an enemy's country was by the British in Egypt,' he asserted, 'and it was esteemed a great achievement, between 5,000 and 6,000 landing in face of 2,000 Frenchmen.' On the other hand 'to attempt to enter the Port with shipping', he said, 'would be madness'.[1]

Clarendon fully supported Graham's proposals for the defence of the Dardanelles and suggested that 10,000 English and 15,000 French troops should be sent: 'but what is to be done if the Emperor adheres to his determination of not sending a single soldier?' he asked. 'If we go to war and the Russian fleets won't come out of Sebastopol and Cronstadt', he added, 'we have no means of hitting Russia except in Georgia and Circassia...but what will that do towards the evacuation of the P[rincipali]ties?'[2] In the meantime, however, it was agreed, on his volunteering to go, to send Burgoyne to Constantinople to inspect the defences of the Bosporus and of the Dardanelles. He left without delay, stopping over in Paris to discuss matters with the French authorities.[3]

For the next few months Graham was extremely busy with naval preparations, gathering a fleet to send to the Baltic, victualling it, making coaling arrangements, training pilots, obtaining maps and other intelligence information, and discussing with Clarendon the government's policy with respect to privateering and blockade and relations with the Scandinavian countries.[4] Clarendon believed that the best way to meet the Russian threat of issuing letters of marque was to modify British law respecting neutrals. He argued that it was impossible to expect to enforce the maritime law of the Napoleonic period without incurring the hostility of the whole world. Thus it would be best to change voluntarily and graciously. He preferred to quarrel with their own lawyers rather 'than disagree with France or get into war with America'.[5]

Graham and Clarendon worked closely together to produce a declaration of policy towards neutrals designed among other things to put an end to privateering, a practice in Clarendon's view comparable to that of private war on land, which, he observed, 'was left off with other barbarisms of the middle ages'.[6] He reported that the American

[1] Graham Papers, 20 January 1854.   [2] Ibid. 22 January 1854.
[3] Ibid. 26 January 1854 to Raglan, from Raglan 27 January, and passim. See G. Wrottesley, Life and correspondence of Field Marshal Sir John Burgoyne, II, 1–12.
[4] See the extensive correspondence in the Graham Papers on the subject.
[5] Graham Papers, 16 February 1854.   [6] Ibid. 16 March 1854.

ambassador greeted the declaration as a noble and manly document, 'going much further than he expected but not a bit further than he desired'.[1] He was less sanguine as to the chances of a convention being signed, but this did not worry Graham, who wrote complacently: 'But probably we shall stand on higher ground, if on this occasion also, as with respect to Free Trade and the Navigation Laws, we are content to lead the way, and to set a noble example, demanding nothing in return for the bold assertion of right Principles and for the promotion of the Commercial interests of the civilised World.'[2] Eventually, but with some reluctance, the French government was persuaded to issue a similar declaration of neutral rights.[3]

Graham did a good job in preparing the navy for war. In the Black Sea he produced a force of 32 ships, mounting 1,282 guns and manned by 12,740 men. A second fleet of ultimately 44 ships, 2,200 guns and 22,000 men was formed for service in the Baltic. In the case of the navy difficulties lay not so much in faulty administration as in a lack of able commanders. Admiral Dundas proved incompetent to meet the demands of operations of war, but fortunately Graham secured the services of Sir Edward Lyons, a former admiral, now withdrawn from the diplomatic service, as Dundas's second in command. Lyons proved to be the one really competent senior British service officer in the Crimean War and eventually took over full command from Dundas.[4]

The appointment of an admiral to command the Baltic fleet was particularly difficult under the prevailing rules of seniority. The size of the fleet and participation with the French, according to Graham, made the appointment of an admiral or a vice-admiral 'indispensably necessary'. Lord Dundonald at seventy-nine was not to be trusted and Sir William Parker's health was failing. These were the only two admirals available and of vice-admirals there were only Sir George Seymour, who was absent in North America, and Sir Charles Napier, who consequently was the only possible candidate.[5] The ministers were none too happy in the appointment, for Napier had a reputation as a difficult man, but in the event they hoped for the best, which was not good enough. The situation called for the bold promotion of a more capable junior officer, but Graham and his colleagues did not have this sort of courage and imagination.

---

[1] *Ibid.* 16 March 1854. [2] *Ibid.* Graham to Clarendon, 16 March 1854.
[3] *Ibid.* 21 and 31 March 1854.
[4] See Erickson, *Graham*, pp. 336–9. [5] See Parker, *Graham*, II, 227–9.

The Baltic fleet was sent off several weeks before war was declared and as soon as news came that that sea was clear of ice. 'I am anxious to get Napier under weigh', Graham wrote to Clarendon on 8 March. 'He is too fond of demonstrations on shore, of Dinners and Speechifying. We must now get to work in earnest.'[1]

By this time Sir James appears to have joined the militants and thrown himself wholeheartedly into the preparations for war. Developing his earlier plans for the defence of the Dardanelles, he wrote to Clarendon on 1 March in favour of more aggressive operations, saying:

but *the* operation which will be ever memorable and decisive, is the capture and destruction of Sebastopol. On this my heart is set: the eye tooth of the Bear must be drawn: and until his Fleet and Naval Arsenal in the Black Sea are destroyed there is no safety for Constantinople, no Security for the Peace of Europe.

On the back of his own copy of this letter he jotted the caption 'delenda est Sevastapol'.[2]

This was mild, however, in comparison to a memorandum penned by Lord Palmerston a few weeks later in which he proclaimed his 'beau ideal' of a war with Russia as one which would lead to the transfer of some of Russia's German provinces to Prussia, of Finland to Sweden, of Georgia and the Crimea to Turkey and the resurrection of an independent Poland![3] About the same time Russell produced some notes and queries of more practical value which showed some realisation of the very real problems facing the Allies when war came, and dwelt on the necessity of inducing Austria, and if possible Prussia, to join them.[4] Lord Lansdowne, commenting on these two memoranda, agreed with Russell as to the importance of enlisting the participation of Austria, but dismissed Palmerston's ideas as day-dreams.[5]

There was general indignation at the reluctance of Prussia to join a proposed convention against Russia. 'If Austria holds firm,' Clarendon wrote to Russell, on 5 March, 'I think that miserable K of Prussia will not venture to betray the interests of his country.'[6] On the 11th he told

---

[1] Graham Papers. See below, p. 280.
[2] Graham Papers, 1 March 1854, partly printed in Parker, *Graham*, II, 242.
[3] Gooch, *Later correspondence*, II, 160–1.
[4] See *ibid.* pp. 159–60; Gooch omits the final important point, the necessity of drawing up instructions for Dundas, Raglan and Napier to be presented to the cabinet. PRO 30/22/11/C, fols. 815–16, March 1854.
[5] PRO 30/22/11/C, fols. 869–70 (Gooch, *Later correspondence*, II, 161).
[6] PRO 30/22/11/C, fol. 837.

Aberdeen: 'The news from Berlin is as bad as possible,' and said he feared that Austria would not sign the proposed convention without Prussia.[1]

Poor Lord Aberdeen looked upon all these preparations with distaste, grasping at any straw that might appear to promise some possibility of peace. A little heartened by the increasing firmness of Austria, he wrote to the queen on 8 February saying that 'on the whole, the appearances in the Cabinet today were favourable to peace. No rash or hasty determination was proposed.' But he had to admit that 'in the meantime, active preparations, both naval and military', were in progress. 'By the end of the present month, ten thousand men will be embarked for Malta and the naval recruiting is going on most prosperously,' he added. 'These, as well as other preparations, are undoubtedly wise and prudent; but Lord Aberdeen cannot abandon the hope that they may still turn out to be unnecessary.'[2]

A few days later he gave her details of the expedition to Malta and announced that the French would have 20,000 men ready by the end of the month, but he warned that 'both these corps can only be considered as preliminary to a much larger force being employed in the event of actual war'.[3]

The queen soon began to catch the fever, writing to Aberdeen on 24 February urging 'in fairness to our potential German allies', an increase of 30,000 rather than a mere 10,000 men, which would do no more than bring the army up to peacetime establishment. Showing her distaste for the French alliance she could not help adding: 'Who can say it is impossible that our own shores may be threatened by Powers now in alliance with us?'[4] Aberdeen answered to the effect that another addition of 15,000 would be announced soon, bringing the total increase to 25,000 men for the army. If war came, further increases would probably be needed, making a total augmentation of 50,000, but this, of course, would entail the creation of new units.[5] On 4 March he told her that the cabinet had considered Gladstone's plans for war finance which visualised the doubling of the income tax.[6] All the fine plans of 1853 had now to go by the board.

---

[1] *Ab. Cor. 1854–5*, p. 66; even the queen deplored the vacillation and weakness of the king of Prussia (*ibid.* p. 68).
[2] Add. MS. 43048, fol. 235, 8 February 1854.
[3] *Ibid.* 11 February 1854, fols. 241–2.
[4] *Ibid.* fols. 259–62, 24 February 1854.
[5] *Ibid.* fol. 263, 24 February 1854.   [6] *Ibid.* fols. 289–90.

Some reflections on the question of responsibility for the Crimean War

As war came closer, Aberdeen's conscience continued to bother him. Looking back over the events of the previous year he told Russell he felt that war might have been averted had he stood out for keeping the fleet at Malta and counselling the Turks to accept the Russian demands. 'But that was a course to which Lansdowne, Palmerston, Clarendon, and Newcastle, and I, would not have consented,' Russell replied; 'so you would only have broken up your Government, if you had insisted upon it.'[1] Aberdeen refused to be consoled. 'On the contrary,' he replied, 'I believe there were in the course of the negociations, two or three occasions when, if I had been supported, peace might have been honourably and advantageously secured.' He referred in particular to the Olmütz proposals. 'But', he continued, 'I repeat that the want of support, although it may palliate, cannot altogether justify to my own conscience the course which I pursued.'[2]

On 22 February Aberdeen asked Gladstone whether he did not think that he might withdraw from office when it came to a declaration of war. He said that 'all along he had been acting against his feelings, but still defensively'; when it came to the offensive he felt he must withdraw. Gladstone dissented from this view and avowed that the war would be a defensive one. They would not be fighting for Turkey, as Aberdeen objected, but 'warning Russia off forbidden ground'. Gladstone's account of the conversation continues:

He said that if I saw a way for him to get out he hoped I would mention it to him. I replied that my own views of war so much agreed with his and I felt such a horror of bloodshed, that I had thought the matter over incessantly for myself. We stand, I said, upon the ground that the Emperor has invaded countries not his own, inflicted wrong on Turkey and what I feel much more, most cruel wrong upon the wretched inhabitants of the Principalities; that war had ensued and was raging with all its horrors; that we had procured for the Emperor an offer of honourable terms of peace which he had refused.

Gladstone's earnest arguments evidently persuaded Aberdeen to remain, perhaps unfortunately.[3]

It is easy to imagine the poor man's feelings a few weeks later when he received a long and moving letter from John Bright urging that he

---

[1] *Ab. Cor. 1854–5*, pp. 61–2, 3 March 1854.   [2] *Ibid.* p. 62, 3 March 1854.
[3] Add. MS. 44778, fols. 167–74, memo. III, 22 February 1854 (Morley, *Gladstone*, II, 491–2).

make a last-minute effort to avert war. Bright said that the conversation that they had had when they dined together at Lord Granville's,[1] and Aberdeen's moderate speeches in the House of Lords (which contrasted with those of some of his colleagues in the Commons) gave him courage to make this appeal. If there was truth in the report that Austria and Prussia had brought forward new proposals for a mutual withdrawal of forces by both sides and a multilateral settlement, then he thought war could still be averted. Bright shrewdly observed that he did not believe that Aberdeen shared the views of those who sought the abrogation of all existing treaties, which would make peace impossible until Russia had been defeated. He did not think that the English people had made up their minds for war, which was advocated by a portion of the London press. He was confident that the House of Commons was not warlike and on both sides of the House had found dissatisfaction with Disraeli's position. On the government side, with the exception of a few extremists, he maintained the feeling was 'strongly in favour of peace'. 'The nearer we approach war', he said, 'the more I dread it. Familiarity with it only makes its dangers more grave, and its features more terrible to my mind.' He saw dangers everywhere, the possibility of dispute with France, of Austria and/or Prussia joining Russia, of difficulties with Sweden and Denmark over neutrality. 'And perhaps before all, and above all, I dread the almost inevitable quarrel with the United States', he added.

He went on in words that must have touched the unhappy Aberdeen to the quick:

I need not tell you that *you* have more interest in preserving peace, in one sense, than any man in this Kingdom. Your administration will not be known in our Annals as the *Russell*, or the *Palmerston*, but as the *Aberdeen* administration, and as Prime Minister, on you will mainly rest the praise or blame.

He recognised Aberdeen's difficulties in the cabinet, but reminded him: 'An honest conscience and a strong will in behalf of that which conscience approves, will go far to break down unreasonable opposition, and even in case of failure, it were more glorious to fall in defence of humanity and peace, than to reign through the growing and deepening calamities of war.'

He said that he had written unknown to anyone and expecting no answer, but that he believed his motives would be understood. 'If I have

---

[1] See G. M. Trevelyan, *The life of John Bright*, p. 230.

said a word that may encourage a thought of peace,' he concluded, 'I shall not repent having written...I pray that God may give you both wisdom and firmness, now when the lives of thousands and the fortunes of millions are at stake.'[1]

Bright's hopes that a new basis of peace had arisen were groundless, yet much of what he said reflected all too clearly what Aberdeen had been unsuccessfully maintaining with his own colleagues for the better part of the last year, and it was not calculated to make him accept the final declaration of war which Clarendon was now about to prepare any more easily.

In response to a friendly reply[2] Bright called on the Prime Minister at Argyll House on 22 March. Aberdeen told him that he feared hostilities were now unavoidable. He said that he had accepted the premiership reluctantly, 'sensible of his deficiencies', but that he consoled himself with the thought 'that at least he could preserve peace, and yet, step by step we had approached the verge of war: *his grief was such that at times he felt as if every drop of blood that would be shed would rest upon his head*'. Bright concluded his account of the meeting with the observation: 'I left Lord Aberdeen with the belief that he is sincerely anxious to avert the horrible calamity impending over Europe, but I suspect that he is not sufficiently master of his own Cabinet, and has been dragged by his colleagues into a course which is entirely opposed to his own convictions.'[3]

The king of the Belgians made a similar final appeal, saying that he was sure that the Czar wanted to get out of the difficulties and that this might be done by Aberdeen securing the complete emancipation of the Christian subjects of Turkey. Aberdeen could only answer that Russia must first evacuate the Principalities but that unfortunately the Czar did not know how to back down 'with a due regard for his honour'.[4]

A more personal *cri de cœur* came from his old friend Mme Lieven, who had kept up a correspondence with Aberdeen for many years. She found it hard to believe that events could have turned out as they did with Aberdeen governing England. She wrote to say that she had fled Paris—she knew not where she would go, probably to Brussels.

[1] *Ab. Cor. 1854–5*, pp. 72–6, 16 March 1854 (partly quoted in Trevelyan, *Bright*, p. 232).
[2] 'There is much frankness and simplicity in the language and correspondence of the Prime Minister', Bright recorded in his journal (Trevelyan, *Bright*, p. 232).
[3] Trevelyan, *Bright*, pp. 232–3.
[4] *Ab. Cor. 1854–5*, pp. 78–9, 17 and 20 March 1854.

'Vagabond! — à mon age! Adieu mon cher Lord Aberdeen, mon cher ami, mon cher ennemi.'[1]

The sands had run out. When news arrived of the Czar's refusal to answer the Allied summons, nothing remained but to frame a declaration of war, and this was issued by France on 27 March and by Britain on the 28th, although the British declaration, in the form of a royal message read to both Houses of Parliament by the Lord Chancellor, managed to avoid the use of the word 'war'.[2]

The Crimean War has inspired few historians to defend it, for it has generally been considered an unnecessary war, the result of blundering and hesitation among the statesmen who avowedly sought to avert it. Lord Aberdeen carried his sense of responsibility, even guilt, to the grave. His son tells a pathetic story about his leaving the rebuilding of a little church on one of his estates to his successor, bearing in mind the biblical injunction: 'thou shalt not build an house unto my name, because thou hast shed much blood upon the earth in my sight' (1 Chron. xxii. 7, 8).[3] None of his colleagues, however, shared this sense of compunction. Even those who had originally belonged to the peace wing of the cabinet, such as Gladstone, Argyll and Granville, persuaded themselves of the justice of the war as it finally came about and two of them defended their views in print, Argyll anonymously in the *Edinburgh Review* of that year and Gladstone many years later in a signed article in the *English Historical Review*. Clarendon also made his contribution in after years by assisting Reeve to write a critical review of Kinglake's first volumes for the *Edinburgh*.[4] He was particularly concerned to refute Kinglake's slanders of Britain's French ally and to deny that the British government had been the dupe of Louis Napoleon, as Kinglake suggested. Britain's decision to intervene, this joint article maintained, was 'determined not by the importunity and example of France, but by the increasing violence, menace and aggression of Russia'. The reviewers continued:

England has no call to throw off the responsibility of the measures taken on any other Power. Those measures were taken because they were demanded by her own conception of the duty she had to perform; and by far the largest share of that responsibility rests with this country. We see no reason to deny it; and if the case occurred again, we should see no reason to act with less

[1] *Ibid.* p. 1, 7 January 1854.
[2] *Annual Register, 1854*, pp. 54–5, and appendix, pp. 531–2.
[3] Stanmore, *Aberdeen*, p. 303.   [4] *Edinburgh Review*, CXVII (1863), 307–52.

determination. With singular inconsistency, whilst Mr Kinglake ascribes to the British Cabinet this mean and unworthy part, he lauds to the sky the wisdom and firmness of the British ambassador. Who sent out Sir [sic] Stratford Canning? Who instructed, supported, and approved him?...No man ever took upon himself a larger amount of responsibility than Lord Stratford, when he virtually overruled the decision of the four Powers, including his own Government, and acquiesced in—not to say caused—the rejection of the Vienna Note by the Porte, after it had been accepted by Russia. The interpretation afterwards put upon the Note by Count Nesselrode showed that he was right; nevertheless, that was the point on which the question of peace and war turned. We shall not enter in the wearisome detail of the successive diplomatic propositions, because one fatal vice pervaded them all. Russia had formed the design to extort from Turkey, in one form or another, a right of protection over the Christians. She never abandoned that design. She thought she could enforce it. The Western Powers interposed, and the strife began.[1]

There is a fatalistic element in Clarendon's analysis and it may be noted that he continued to exaggerate Stratford's influence with the Turks, although his tone is more charitable than of yore.

Argyll's essay was a skilful piece of special pleading written even before the war had actually begun.[2] It provided a very competent summary of the diplomatic events leading up to the war, based upon a careful analysis of the blue-books, which he was reviewing ostensibly as a detached outsider, but he slid rather too easily over the Olmütz proposals, which the Allies refused to consider. Argyll concluded his analysis with some general comment justifying the government's course. While not subscribing to the view that the Czar was bent upon war from the start, he maintained that 'pride and obstinacy' prevented his retreat when he found his plans opposed. Argyll continued:

All that we contend for on behalf of the policy of France and England is, first, that it was the policy best adapted to turn aside the current which, through so many channels, was setting irresistibly to war; and, next, that it was the policy best adapted to strengthen, in the meantime, the lines of European defence whenever diplomacy should give place to arms.[3]

He treated with respect the arguments of those who objected that England should have had nothing to do with the quarrel in the first place, but he pointed out that the maintenance of the Ottoman empire against external aggression 'had long been an admitted principle of policy among the European Powers', which indeed had been asserted in

[1] *Edinburgh Review*, CXVII (1863), 331.   [2] *Ibid.* C, no. 203 (1854), 1–43.
[3] *Ibid.* p. 39.

the preamble to the Treaty of 1841. 'To have evaded it', he claimed, 'would have been injurious to our influence and derogatory to our honour. Geographically Russia held a commanding position *vis-à-vis* Prussia and Austria, but her approaches by sea to the rest of the world were at present circumscribed. Thus it was obvious that her power would be greatly and dangerously increased by the occupation of Constantinople.' He reinforced these arguments by dwelling upon the despotism and intolerance of Russian rule, the extension of which 'threatens at once the progress of political freedom and of religious truth'. The objections of Bright and Grey to the corruption of the Turkish government he dismissed as irrelevant.

Like Argyll, Gladstone justified the course taken by the government in steering between the two extremes of those who would have offered no opposition to Russia and those who would have resisted from the beginning.[1] He vigorously denied that the country had drifted into war, maintaining that Clarendon's famous phrase to that effect only related to the last few weeks while they were waiting for the ultimatum to expire.[2] In rejecting the criticism that Britain should have taken a firmer stand at an earlier date, he pointed out that if she had done so she would have been isolated and as ineffective as in 1863, when she was unable to make good her assurances to Denmark. He acknowledged that there were differences, mainly in emphasis, among those who were making day-to-day decisions on foreign policy (Aberdeen, Clarendon, Russell and Palmerston), but he firmly denied that the cabinet was torn with divisions, asserting that he had never served in a cabinet where there was less dissension. Gladstone maintained that Aberdeen had been mistaken in admitting blame for the war. It resulted, he argued, from the natural working of the concert of Europe as it operated in those days, seeking to restrain one of its members who had transgressed the law of nations. Unfortunately Prussia had failed to play her part and Austria had feared to go the whole way with the Allies in view of the exposed

---

[1] *E.H.R.* II (1887), 'The history of 1852–60 and Greville's latest journals'. The article is actually a very good review of the last Greville volumes.

Morley records that in 1881 Gladstone said to him: 'As a member of the Aberdeen Cabinet I never can admit that divided opinions in that cabinet led to hesitating action, or brought on the war' (*Gladstone*, I, 495). Actually this charge is more applicable to decisions made or not made in the summer and autumn of 1853 when the cabinet did not meet and Gladstone was out of London.

[2] Nevertheless, the phrase or variations of it was used more than once and by more than one minister in the course of the twelve months preceding the declaration of war. See above, pp. 153, 157, 197, and below, p. 277.

position of Vienna. Like Argyll, Gladstone also tended to glide over the failure to respond to the Olmütz proposals; and he rather exaggerated the significance of the final abortive negotiations in Vienna in February of 1854.[1]

Now, more than a century later, it is possible to take a more dispassionate and objective view than could be expected of those who were involved in the fateful decisions of 1853–4.[2] No account of the Aberdeen coalition can evade making some estimate of its degree of responsibility for the Crimean War. It was formed as the result of a domestic political crisis arising from the prolonged disturbance of normal political connections that followed the repeal of the Corn laws in 1846, but the greatest challenge to confront it lay in the field of foreign and military policy. It was primarily not a party issue, for some of the sharpest critics of the coalition's policy in this sphere sat on its own benches.

Differences among the ministers with regard to foreign policy began to develop at an early date, which is not surprising when it is remembered that Aberdeen and Palmerston had been mutual critics of each other's methods in this sphere for almost a quarter of a century. Their ultimate objectives may have been similar, but their methods were as different as those of their respective mentors, Castlereagh and Canning. Nevertheless, the ministerial differences were regularly patched up because of the reluctance of the majority of the cabinet, indeed of all except Russell, to see the existence of the coalition threatened. In terms of foreign policy the result was unfortunate.

It has been said that either Aberdeen's or Palmerston's policy undiluted might have preserved the peace, but that the attempt to combine them led to war. It is most unlikely that a European war would have broken out had Lord Aberdeen been allowed to have his way, but the price of peace was more than the majority of his colleagues, or at any

---

[1] For a penetrating, if partisan, critique of the government's policy, see John Bright's letter to Mr Absalom Watkin of 3 November 1854, quoted in Trevelyan, *Bright*, pp. 220–3.

[2] For a judicious summing up of the responsibility of all the powers for the war see Temperley, *Crimea*, appendix v, pp. 507–13. See also his bibliographic note, pp. 455–6. For a very different interpretation, more sympathetic to Russia and more critical of Britain, see V. J. Puryear, 'New lights on the origins of the Crimean War', *J.M.H.* III (1931), 219–34. For valuable bibliographical discussions of the subject see B. Schmidt, 'Diplomatic preliminaries of the Crimean War', *A.H.R.* 25 (1919), 36–67; and B. D. Gooch, 'A century of historiography on the origins of the Crimean War', *A.H.R.* 62 (1956), 33–58; and 'The Crimean War in selected documents and secondary works since 1940', *Victorian Studies*, I (1958), 271–9. There is also an extensive bibliography in Puryear, *Straits question*, pp. 450–68.

rate the militant minority, were prepared to pay. Had he been free, Aberdeen would have insisted that the Turks accept the Vienna note or take the consequences; to say that this was impossible was to deny the Western Allies any freedom of action. Turkey might still have gone to war and been defeated as she had been in 1829 and was again in 1877, but the Powers could still have placed limits on Russia's pretensions as they did in 1878. The Olmütz proposals presented a second opportunity which Aberdeen failed to grasp. Unfortunately the majority of the cabinet were no longer prepared to put any trust in Russian promises at this point, disillusioned by Nesselrode's so-called 'violent interpretation' of the Vienna note. The Prime Minister should have made a greater effort to persuade his colleagues to give these proposals more serious consideration or at any rate to have used them to keep the door open. Their rejection brought war much closer and it is hard to see that the 'preservation of Turkish integrity' was worth the bloody price that the Crimean War proved to be. The failure of the Russian armed forces in that war against both the Turks and the Western Allies indicates that the Russian danger was greatly exaggerated.

The fact that all the Powers were really reluctant to resort to war may be deduced from the surprising number of efforts to find a settlement even after the failure of Olmütz. These projects collapsed partly because of the slowness in communications, which over and over again resulted in laboriously drafted projects being out of date by the time they reached their destination, partly because the diplomats on the one side, then as now, failed to envisage the inevitable response of those on the other side to a particular course of action. Thus it was scarcely realistic to expect the Russian government, after it had agreed to the Vienna note, to turn round and accept the Turkish modifications. Again, if Clarendon was serious, as he undoubtedly was, about his proposals of 24 October, it is difficult to understand how he could dismiss the Olmütz proposals so brusquely only a few weeks earlier. The labour that went into the preparation of his own proposals and of Stratford's project that coincided with them indicates the willingness to seek a solution quite contrary to the spirit, almost of contumely, in which the Russian proposals were rejected. Finally, it was surely inconsistent to support Stratford's eleventh-hour bid for peace and at the same time make demands of Russia in the Black Sea that no great power could have been expected to accept. Both sides wanted a peaceful settlement, but they were too suspicious of each other and too sensitive of their dignity to bridge the gap of words that divided them. The Russian demands on Turkey were not entirely justifiable, but the Western Allies were perhaps too inclined to read more into them than would have been the case had they been accepted by Turkey. After all, the terms of the Treaty of Kainardji, which was the stumbling-block, do not appear to have been implemented in any way particularly prejudicial to Turkish sovereignty. It is true that no European power would have tolerated this sort of infringement on its sovereignty, but Turkey was a backward and semi-barbaric empire and treated as such by Britain and France. Thus, it is difficult to see why the British and French governments were prepared to go to war to resist the Russian demands for the implementation of old treaties; the distrust of Russia was evidently as great in the middle of the nineteenth century as it is today.

Palmerston and Russell, of course, from the beginning considered it essential to stand up to Russia and were prepared to pay the cost, but they appear to have developed their views independently and not in collaboration. Indeed, Russell, who was always self-centred, never thought in terms of supporting Palmerston's policy, but rather of developing his own, which in general, but not entirely, coincided with Palmerston's. His approach was more impetuous and he was capable on occasion of expressing much more exasperation with the Turk (and with Stratford) than Palmerston was ever prepared to do. Lansdowne took less initiative than either of these two, but his views were just as militant.

The majority of the cabinet gradually swung around behind this formidable trio, as the impression gained ground that it was impossible to come to an understanding with the Czar. In the early stages they had been peacefully inclined and closer to Aberdeen, especially Graham, Gladstone, Argyll, Wood, Granville and Herbert. During this period Clarendon worked genuinely for peace and seemed reasonably in agreement with Aberdeen. Palmerston, Russell and Lansdowne were the hard core of the anti-Russian or war party from the beginning and at some point they probably began to draw support from Molesworth and Newcastle; there is little evidence of the Lord Chancellor's disposition beyond one observation of Aberdeen's to the effect that it was peaceful. The key figure was that of the Foreign Secretary, for in the autumn he shifted from the camp of Aberdeen to that of Palmerston and Russell. Nesselrode's 'violent interpretation' was the turning-point for him, but his growing indignation with Russia was clearly stimulated by the swelling roar of public opinion. Clarendon was an able Foreign Secretary in the technical sense that he stuck to his desk and wrote a good despatch; he was also a shrewd observer of events; but he lacked the strength of character and determination of a Palmerston. Once he had moved over to the advanced party, the majority of the remainder, most of them younger members of the cabinet, swung into line, influenced no doubt by the tough-minded trio of senior ministers, now become a quartet. Eventually Aberdeen was isolated and even Gladstone accepted the argument that wanton aggression must be resisted, forgetting (or in spite of) the opportunities that had been neglected over the preceding year.

Whether the Palmerston–Russell approach would have avoided war had it been pressed resolutely from the beginning is more difficult to say. Had the Czar of Russia known from the start that Britain and France were prepared to fight to defend Turkey against him, he might have avoided going out on the limb from which he saw no retreat, but the Palmerston policy was always a risky one, a gamble that might or might not have paid off. One may agree that in terms of results, if not morally, it was preferable to the compromise policy which was substituted and which did result in war. The policy of Aberdeen, however, had it not been compromised, was the only one that would have guaranteed peace, and at this distance the price seems reasonable weighed against the heavy cost in blood and treasure the Crimean War was to exact.

A complicating factor throughout the whole tortuous business was the strange relationship with France, for centuries the traditional enemy. Indeed, even as the Eastern Crisis loomed on the horizon, Britain was strengthening her coastal defences against the renewed threat (supposed) of a Napoleonic invasion. There had been various attempts at a French *entente* since 1815 but none had been too successful, and the advent of a new Napoleonic empire did not look propitious. Thus the alliance was not an easy one and the British were always inclined to watch the French suspiciously. It was difficult to say which government took the lead in the policy that led to war, for sometimes it was the one and sometimes the other; it was the British who insisted on rejecting the Olmütz proposals in October, the French who pressed for decisive measures in the Black Sea in December; and yet in February when the British ministers, with the partial exception of Aberdeen, took war for granted, Napoleon III attempted a last-minute overture to the Czar.

The fact is that the new French emperor was feeling his way. There was less popular support for the war in France than in England and less substance to France's anti-Russian policy. Louis Napoleon, in his insecurity, felt more dependent on the British alliance than did the British feel the need of a French alliance. On the whole, however, the relationship worked better than might have been expected. Occasionally the British ministers were annoyed by French precipitancy, as in December, but generally the two governments worked together with remarkable cohesion, receiving each other's proposals in the spirit of understanding and cooperation. In the case of Britain this readiness to accept French proposals, generally in a forward direction, may be in part accounted for by the fear of unilateral action by France. This was undoubtedly one of the many factors that helped to lead Britain into this 'unnecessary war'.[1]

[1] The economic factor, to which British diplomatic historians have paid little attention, has been developed by V. J. Puryear in chapter II of his *England, Russia and the Straits question* and more fully in his *International economics and diplomacy in the Near East*. British trade in the Black Sea area increased greatly with both the Russian and Turkish empires in the quarter century preceding the outbreak of the Crimean War. Trade with Turkey, however, was better balanced and, relatively speaking, grew more rapidly after the signing of the treaty of Balta Liman in 1838, while Russia continued to keep out British exports by her protectionist policy. These factors undoubtedly had some bearing on Britain's attitude to the two countries, but it is more difficult to relate them directly to the events of 1853–4. Cobden, spokesman for the Manchester School, was obviously unimpressed by such arguments.

11

PARLIAMENT, PUBLIC OPINION AND THE OUTBREAK OF WAR

The attack on Prince Albert

There is no more depressing aspect of Britain's involvement in the Crimean War than that presented by the attitude of the popular press and of public opinion, whipped up by unscrupulous journalists.[1] The hysteria of the press is seen at its worst and in its most ridiculous form in the attack on Prince Albert that developed in the month that followed the news of Sinope. The most extraordinary stories were circulated accusing him of unpatriotic and unconstitutional activities. Inevitably the queen took into her confidence a husband whom she loved and respected, and shared with him her thoughts and even her duties. Inevitably the prince, from his very nature, took a deep interest in all the public affairs that concerned his wife and made it his business to become fully informed on all the matters that were officially brought to her attention. Inevitably he acted as a sort of special private secretary, saw all her papers,[2] helped her to form her opinions, prepared memoranda for her and attended meetings with her ministers, indeed often saw them alone. Both the queen and the ministers (in and out of office) took this for granted, although occasionally there might be raised eyebrows if the prince considered extending the sphere of his activities in public, as, for instance, when it was proposed that he might succeed Wellington as commander-in-chief.

The public, looking for a scapegoat, were quick to denounce all this and to imagine the prince's influence to be a nefarious one. The admirers of Palmerston had long suspected Albert, as the tool of the Austrian and

---

[1] See Kingsley Martin, *Triumph of Lord Palmerston*, pp. 178–86.

[2] See *Greville Memoirs*, VII, 10–11. Melbourne and Russell (and, Russell thought, the whole cabinet) had agreed it would be quite proper for the prince to see and know everything. His presence at interviews with her ministers began in Peel's ministry. On this occasion the queen told Russell that if she had had the prince to talk to at the time of the Bed-chamber crisis it would never have happened. Russell said he had always assumed she had acted on advice, to which the queen answered: 'No, it was entirely my own foolishness.'

Russian emperors, to have been responsible for the dismissal of Palmerston in 1851 and they now blamed him for their hero's resignation in December. An aroused English nationalism distrusted him as a foreigner and indeed rumour went so far that it is said one day a crowd gathered to see him committed to the Tower of London as a traitor![1] To comprehend this hostility it must be remembered that the monarchy had only recently become respectable and that the conventions which have protected it for the past century were only slowly taking root. It was of course a passing storm in a teacup, but painful for the royal couple while it lasted. This sort of situation Lord Aberdeen handled well and to the satisfaction of the queen. On 5 January 1854 she wrote a pathetic letter to him appealing for his help against these most infamous attacks, saying that 'in attacking the Prince who is one & the same with herself, the Throne is assailed'.[2] Answering the queen on 6 January, the Prime Minister pointed out that the attacks were 'not sanctioned by the most respectable portion of the Press' and he undertook to see that they were dealt with in parliament. He discussed the prince's position sympathetically but frankly, writing:

It cannot be denied that the position of the Prince is somewhat anomalous, and has not been specially provided for by the Constitution; but the ties of Nature, and the dictates of common sense are more powerful than Constitutional fictions; the Lord Aberdeen can only say that he has always considered it as an inestimable blessing that Your Majesty should possess so able, so zealous, and so disinterested an adviser. It is true, that Your Ministers are alone responsible for the conduct of public affairs, and although there is no man in England whose opinion Lord Aberdeen would more highly respect and value; still if he had the misfortune of differing from His Royal Highness, he would not hesitate to act according to his own convictions, and a sense of what was due to Your Majesty's service.[3]

The queen was much relieved by Aberdeen's letter and wrote to him saying:

She is anxious to express *how much* his kind letter on the subject of her most dearly beloved and adored Husband has gratified and pleased her. The Queen's feeling for the Prince is of so strong a nature that she can only describe it by saying that *he* is the life of her life![4]

[1] Stanmore, *Aberdeen*, pp. 255–6; Martin, *Triumph of Lord Palmerston*, pp. 178–9.
[2] Add. MS. 43048, fols. 120–3.
[3] *Letters of Queen Victoria*, III, 3–4.
[4] Add. MS. 43048, fol. 126, 6 January 1854.

On 16 January she was writing in better spirits to enquire who had written an excellent article in the *Morning Chronicle* which took 'quite the *right line* on the infamous and *now* almost ridiculous attacks'.[1] Aberdeen replied that he thought the author was Mr Gladstone and told the queen she would be shocked to hear that Sir Robert Peel was likely to raise the matter in parliament, adding that 'as he is half mad, it is difficult to know what he may not do'.[2]

Unfortunately, before he could make any statement in parliament *The Times* published an article, supposedly answering the criticisms, but the tone of which greatly annoyed the queen. She wrote to the Prime Minister in great excitement:

If the *country really has* such incomprehensible and reprehensible notions, there is no remedy but the introduction of the *Salic Law*, for which *she* would *heartily* vote. A *Woman must* have support and an adviser; and *who can* this *properly* be but her husband, whose *duty it is* to watch over *her interests private and public*. From this sacred duty NO EARTHLY POWER can absolve him! Were it not for the Prince, the Queen's health would long since have sunk under the multifarious duties of her position as a Queen, and the mother of a large family.[3]

Aberdeen had been put in a quandary when Delane had proposed to write on this controversial subject. 'I dare say we should have well written and powerful articles,' he told Graham; 'but as *my organ*, the discussion might assume a more inconvenient character.' 'At the same time', he added, 'I hesitate to reject the aid of so formidable an ally.'[4] He assured the queen that *The Times* was 'under no control'; indeed the editor had raised the matter with him, he said, and ignored his injunction;[5] but the next day he sent her a letter from Delane which appeared to mollify her somewhat.[6]

Shortly afterwards the queen, unknown to her husband, wrote to Aberdeen regarding the 'expediency of settling some day *by law*, the

---

[1] *Letters of Queen Victoria*, III, 7–9.

[2] *Ab. Cor. 1854–5*, p. 4, 17 January 1854; *Letters of Queen Victoria*, III, 9–10, omits the bit about Peel, which is quoted by Martin, *Triumph of Lord Palmerston*, p. 185. There is a draft of Gladstone's article published as a leader on 16 January in Add. MS. 44743, fols. 121–6, dated 15 January 1854.

[3] *Ab. Cor. 1854–5*, p. 6, 18 January 1854 (cf. Martin, *Triumph of Lord Palmerston*, p. 184).

[4] Graham Papers, 6 January 1854. The reference to '*my organ*' is of course ironic.

[5] Add. MS. 43048, fol. 163, 19 January 1854.

[6] *Ibid.* fol. 168; Martin, *Triumph of Lord Palmerston*, p. 185.

position of the *Consort* of the *Queen Regnant* which (strange to say)', she noted, 'has been entirely overlooked by the Constitution'. Recent events, she argued, had shown 'how dangerous it is to leave things *undefined*'.[1] Several times the queen reverted to this matter, but Aberdeen, while promising to look into it, preferred to postpone action for the present,[2] and it fell to his successor, and the queen's old enemy, to settle the matter.

After some hesitation the queen, accompanied by the prince, opened parliament on 31 January and was well received by the public, 'but all the *enthusiasm*', according to Greville, 'was bestowed on the Turkish Minister'.[3] *The Times* correspondent heard the cheers for the Turkish minister, but also reported that the queen was greeted with much cheering and that the prince only received a few solitary hisses and groans. Interruptions from noisy and quarrelsome members crowding in to hear her threatened to drown out the queen's speech, but according to this observer her 'sweet, clear and persuasive voice' was distinctly heard over the hubbub.[4] In the debate on the speech from the throne that followed, both Aberdeen and Russell took the opportunity to vindicate the conduct of the prince, whom they highly praised. Derby made what Greville called 'a slashing speech', but he added that it was 'very imprudent, and played into Aberdeen's hands'. He attributed stories and opinions in *The Times* to the ministers, which enabled Aberdeen to say to his great annoyance that the disgraceful stories in the Tory press might just as well be attributed to the Tory leaders. Derby indignantly replied to the effect that these absurd charges were started in the papers of extreme Liberal opinions such as the *Morning Advertiser*.[5]

Both Aberdeen and Russell alluded to the prince's decision against the suggestion that he might succeed Wellington as commander-in-chief on the grounds that it would not be compatible with his role as consort. He had developed this opinion in a letter to Aberdeen a week earlier, quoting his original letter to the duke in which he had described the position of consort as follows:

This position is a most peculiar & delicate one. Whilst a female sovereign has a great many disadvantages in comparison with a King, yet if she is married, & her husband understands & does his duty, her position has, on the other hand, many compensating advantages. But this requires that the husband

[1] *Ab. Cor. 1854–5*, pp. 20–1.   [2] *Ibid.* pp. 26–8, *et passim*.
[3] *Greville Memoirs*, VII, 11.   [4] *The Times*, 1 February 1854.
[5] *Hansard*, CXXX, 86–108, 182–92; *Greville Memoirs*, VII, 11.

should entirely sink his own *individual* existence in that of his wife—that he should aim at no power by himself or for himself, should shun all ostentation, assume no separate responsibility towards the Public, but make his position entirely a part of hers, fill up every gap which as a woman she would naturally leave in the exercise of her less Regal functions, continually and anxiously watch every part of the Public business, in order to be able to advise & assist her in any moment, in any of the multifarious and difficult questions or duties, brought before her, sometimes international, sometimes political, or social or personal. As the natural Head of the family, superintendent of Her House-hold, manager of her Private Affairs, sole *confidential* adviser in politics, and only assistant in her communications with the Officers of the Govt, he is, besides the husband of the Queen, the Tutor of the Royal Children, the Private Secretary of the Sovereign, and her permanent Minister.[1]

Both the Prime Minister and the royal couple were well pleased with the way in which the air was cleared by the parliamentary denouement. Aberdeen told the queen that there was cordial unanimity in the House of Lords on the subject of the odious calumnies and that she might forget it 'although it will always remain as a disgraceful example of the audacity of Party Spirit, and of the credulity of the people'.[2] A few days later he wrote to the prince saying: 'Fortunately, the whole edifice of falsehood and misrepresentation is entirely overthrown; and we may trust that a great reaction will now take place.'[3] The queen and the prince expressed their satisfaction at the way in which the matter had been settled and with Aberdeen's judicious manner in handling it.[4]

Public and parliamentary opinion, January–March 1854

The session of 1854 opened under the shadow of war and this considera-tion necessarily dominated everybody's thoughts and actions. Critics of the government had been complaining of the lack of official informa-tion available since the prorogation of the previous summer, a long period during which so much had changed for the worse. Lacking information as to what the government had been doing, they were ready to believe the worst. The government now met this charge by tabling

---

[1] Add. MS. 43048, fols. 178–9, 184–6, memorandum of Prince Albert, 22 January 1854, and copy of his letter to the duke of Wellington, 6 April 1850. In the latter the prince acknowledged his particular interest in the army, in which, he said, the queen, as a lady, would have less interest.

[2] Add. MS. 43048, fol. 217, 1 February 1854 (copy).

[3] *Ibid.* fol. 222, 3 February 1854 (copy). [4] *Ibid.* fols. 224–5 (copy).

two volumes of blue-books giving in detail despatches between the Foreign Secretary and H. M. ambassadors in the capitals concerned with the Turkish question, and other relevant documents.[1] Professor Temperley has criticised this collection[2] on the ground that there was some editing (i.e. omissions) for diplomatic or political purposes, and of course it does not include the private correspondence between Clarendon and the ambassadors, especially Stratford, which is often more revealing than the official despatches. Nevertheless, there is a great deal of pertinent information in these documents, which run to more than 1,000 closely printed pages, and they were pored over with interest by members of Parliament and the public, as we may judge from Greville's comment:

The publication of the Blue Books has relieved the Government from a vast amount of prejudice and suspicion. The public judgement of their management of the Eastern Question is generally very favorable, and impartial people applaud their persevering efforts to avert war, and are satisfied that everything was done that the national honour or dignity required...As Lord Ellenborough said in the H. of Lords, the case has been most ably conducted, both by the Government and its Agents. Clarendon's despatches are exceedingly good, and in one respect greatly superior to Palmerston's when he was at the Foreign Office; they are very measured and dignified, and he never descends to the scolding and taunts, and sarcasms in which the other delighted...Stratford's despatches are very able, and very well written, but they leave the impression (which we know to be the truth) that he has said and done a great deal more than we are informed of; that he is the real cause of the war, and that he might have prevented it, if he had chosen to do so, I have no doubt whatever. His letters have evidently been studiously composed with reference to the Blue Book, and that he may appear in a popular light.[3]

The immediate effect of the crisis and of the publication of the blue-books was to rally both Houses behind the government, which had turned out to be firmer than its critics had anticipated. There were of course questions and criticism, particularly in the House of Lords. An unusually long debate on the address occurred there on the very first night of the session, before the Foreign Secretary had time to table his papers, and some of the most persistent criticism came from Whig peers. Lord Clanricarde, one of the sharpest critics, started the attack on the

[1] *Eastern Papers*, parts I to XII, *P.P. 1854*, LXXI, 1–1007 (referred to as *E.P.*).
[2] Temperley, *E.H.R.* XLVIII (1933).
[3] *Greville Memoirs*, VII, 15–16. Thus the myth of Stratford de Redcliffe's responsibility for the Crimean War was spread and accepted.

first night by criticising the government for its vacillation and inconsistency and charged that the country was left uncertain whether or not it was at war.[1] Lord Grey, another Whig critic, took the opposite line, but with more forbearance and restraint. Like Lord Aberdeen he viewed 'with horror and apprehension the breaking out of war', and professed himself to be of the opinion that the country ought not to have interfered at all in the quarrel.[2]

Lord Malmesbury, postponing a full-scale attack until later, contented himself with some general criticisms, alluding to his own success in forging the *entente* with France despite criticism from the present ministers and their press.[3] Both he and Lord Derby complained of the way in which parliament was ignored and news revealed to *The Times*. Indeed to Aberdeen's indignation Derby charged that *The Times* was informed of Palmerston's resignation before the queen or the cabinet. Derby warmed to Clanricarde's theme that they did not know whether or not the country was at war. 'It is intimated to us, however,' he said, 'that a state of warfare has ensued from the failure of all our negotiations. A state of warfare; with whom are we engaged in that warfare? are we belligerents? are we partisans? are we carrying on war openly and boldly, or are we carrying on that which is tantamount to war, but a war carried on in a pettifogging manner, and, I might almost say, in a manner discreditable to this great country?'[4]

Lord Aberdeen expressed his well-known detestation for war, saying that he thought it was 'the greatest proof of the depravity and corruptness of human nature that anything so horrible as war should ever be just and lawful', and repudiated the suggestion that he was either pro-Russian or pro-Austrian, maintaining that he had no more personal contacts with the Austrian cabinet than with the cabinet of Japan.[5] Greville maintains that Aberdeen had the better of the exchange, but Greville's opinion was coloured by Aberdeen's handling of the prince consort affair, in which Greville himself had been involved in the prince's defence through a celebrated letter to *The Times*.[6]

On 2 February Lord Lyndhurst, after studying the blue-books, pressed the Foreign Secretary with some questions regarding the Vienna note, suggesting that Turkey had not been consulted in advance as had Russia,[7] but the brunt of the questioning came from the government

---

[1] *Hansard*, cxxx, 19–35.
[2] *Ibid.* 56–65.
[3] *Ibid.* 46–56.
[4] *Ibid.* 65–86.
[5] *Ibid.* 86–94.
[6] *Greville Memoirs*, VII, 11–12.
[7] *Hansard*, cxxx, 207–12.

side of the House and from the crossbenches. On 6 February Lord Clanricarde agreed to postpone a motion to precipitate a foreign affairs debate, since the last negotiations in Vienna had just been reopened.

Ellenborough and Fitzwilliam again pressed Clarendon with searching questions on the 10th,[1] and Lord Grey questioned the wisdom of embarking on parliamentary reform on the eve of war.[2] In justifying the government's course on this last question Lord Aberdeen was so bold as to say:

Noble Lords seem to think that we are actually at war; but I must say that not only is this not the case, but I, for one, deny (although it has been asserted in this House by various noble Lords) that war is inevitable. On the contrary, although I admit that the case is such as to require ample preparations to meet the dangers of war, yet I will not abandon the hope of maintaining peace.[3]

Clanricarde pounced on this statement by asking if any negotiations were going on that might put an end to hostilities, to which Aberdeen gave an evasive answer.[4] This was too much for Lord Clarendon, who whispered to the Prime Minister that he was humbugging the country by talking about peace when negotiations were over. Clarendon threatened to get up and say as much, but Aberdeen is reported to have said to him, 'No, no, I will do it.'[5] At any rate he took advantage of a supplementary question from Lord Beaumont to say that there were no more negotiations proceeding.[6] According to Lady Clarendon 'the appearance of vacillation produced an unpleasant laugh in the House'.[7]

Lord Granville sought to come to the Prime Minister's rescue by protesting the irregularity of the questions being asked, which brought a sharp retort from Earl Grey, who said he believed 'that from a false point of honour, and to redeem a pledge which they believe they have given, Her Majesty's Government are about wantonly and deliberately to risk the welfare, and perhaps the safety, of the country, by bringing forward at an inexpedient moment the subject of Parliamentary Reform'.[8]

On 14 February, with the final negotiations in Vienna over, Lord Clanricarde brought forward his motion requiring further information on the disruption of diplomatic relations with Russia, which produced a full-dress debate. The government was attacked by two Whig peers, by

[1] *Hansard*, cxxx, 389–92. [2] *Ibid.* 392–5.
[3] *Ibid.* 395–6. [4] *Ibid.* 398.
[5] Maxwell, *Clarendon*, II, 40; *Greville Memoirs*, VII, 17. [6] *Hansard*, cxxx, 399.
[7] Maxwell, *Clarendon*, II, 40. [8] *Hansard*, cxxx, 400–2.

Clanricarde, who criticised the government's whole conduct of the affair, but especially their failure to join the French in sending the fleet to the Dardanelles in the previous March when it had been called for by Colonel Rose, and by Grey, who criticised them for allowing the country to be dragged into the quarrel at all.[1] Malmesbury and Derby joined in the attack, while the government was defended by Clarendon, Aberdeen, Argyll and Glenelg, the latter rather ineptly comparing their policy to that of Sir Robert Walpole.[2] Clarendon defended his policy vigorously, but used an unfortunate phrase in trying to describe the intermediate state of relations with Russia at that moment. 'I must say', he told the House, 'that our hopes of maintaining it [peace] are gradually dwindling away, and that we are drifting towards war.'[3]

Derby, in contrast to Grey and following the lead of Clanricarde, attacked the government for failing to take a strong line against Russia from the beginning, made sport of the comparison of Aberdeen to Walpole 'without his little peccadilloes', and chaffed Clarendon for inventing a new state of diplomatic relations.

He says, we certainly are not at war—we certainly cannot be said to be at peace, says my noble Friend; and he says that, when we consider...what has taken place in the Black Sea...we cannot be supposed to be entirely neutral. I want to know what is the state of the country, when we are neither at peace, nor at war, nor neutral? My noble Friend has given us a new phrase in Parliamentary or diplomatic language; we are not at war, nor at peace, and we are not neutral, but we are drifting towards war.[4]

The subject was reopened on 24 February by Lord Beaumont, who demanded immediate measures against Russia in a hostile speech of inordinate length,[5] which according to *The Times* tried the tempers of his fellow peers by its triviality. Clarendon's reply was comparatively brief, but, according to *The Times*,[6] it was the best speech that had been made on the Eastern Question; indeed in Greville's view[7] it was the best speech Clarendon had ever delivered. He made it clear that it would have been madness to precipitate the breach with Russia in the previous year, with the British fleet dispersed all over the world and the way to Constantinople wide open, and in complete disregard of the views of the vitally interested central powers of Prussia and Austria. Instead they acted as any responsible men would have acted, with the result that

[1] *Ibid.* 545–63.   [2] *Ibid.* 595.   [3] *Ibid.* 568.
[4] *Ibid.* 627–8.   [5] *Ibid.* 1201–24.   [6] 2 February 1854.
[7] *Greville Memoirs*, VII, 20.

now a powerful Turkish army faced the Russians and they had earned the good will of the Central Powers. Indeed that very day he had learned that Austria had sent 25,000 men to the frontier; and England and France had both mobilised strong forces. Lord Beaumont did not need to fear that they would back down in their demands on Russia, but England was not acting alone and must keep in step with her Allies. A convention was even then being negotiated with Turkey; it would not be right to send troops there until this was done. It would be impossible to satisfy the noble lord's demands regarding the terms of a final peace settlement before the war had yet begun. It might be well to abrogate all existing treaties between Russia and Turkey, but there were great misapprehensions as to the nature of those treaties. He assured his hearers, however, that it was the purpose of Her Majesty's Government, so far as the course of events would permit, to do that which was 'necessary for the future security and tranquillity of Europe—to check the aggressive and ambitious powers of Russia'. And he concluded:

I say it will be necessary to take solid guarantees that Europe shall not be again deprived of the great blessings of peace; but I say also that neither this country nor the other Christian Powers would fulfil the great duty that has devolved upon them, nor, indeed, would they consult the best interests of the Sultan himself, if they did not take this opportunity to secure equal rights and equal justice to the Christian subjects of the Porte, and to pave the way for that progress and prosperity which Christian civilization would bring about in that empire.[1]

In the House of Commons there was some desultory discussion of the government's foreign policy in the debate on the speech from the throne,[2] but no regular debate until 17 February, when Layard forced one on the motion that the Speaker leave the chair. In what Greville described as a 'bitter and impertinent speech',[3] he attacked the government strongly on the basis of what he found and did not find in the blue-books, which he had studied closely.[4] He was answered most effectively by Sir James Graham in a good fighting speech, which was frequently applauded. Graham dealt with Layard's charges systematically, the refusal to grant Colonel Rose's demand for the fleet, the alleged inadequacy of the Vienna note, the failure to prevent the disaster of Sinope; and he dwelt upon the government's success in isolating Russia and on

[1] Hansard, CXXX, 1224–32.
[2] See Annual Register, 1854, pp. 12–15, for a summary.
[3] Greville Memoirs, VII, 19.   [4] Hansard, CXXX, 831–60.

the magnitude of the war preparations already under way. He roundly asserted that the government had no apologies to make and challenged its critics to make a direct attack with a motion of confidence rather than waste parliament's time with a trifling motion that the Speaker do leave the chair. 'We ask for great sacrifices on the part of the country', he said. 'And is this an occasion on which you should potter over blue books—on which you should indulge in miserable carping at petty details, and endeavour to sow the seed of disunion between us and our ally?'[1]

After a critical speech from Lord Jocelyn, and comments from two Radicals, who sympathised with the government but disliked the tone of Graham's reply to their friend Layard, Russell rose to make a further defence of government policy. He covered much the same ground as Graham, although his tone was less contentious, and he concluded with a spirited appeal for full support in the struggle to come, which was loudly cheered.[2]

On a motion for adjournment of the debate Disraeli cleverly intervened to say that his party was not responsible for the debate, that they had no intention of holding up supply, but that he thought it reasonable to take another night to complete the debate once begun. He rapped Graham over the knuckles for the tone of his speech, which he contrasted with the more statesmanlike contribution of Russell. 'We are told by the First Lord of the Admiralty that the House of Commons is not to potter over blue books', he said. 'But why sir are there such things as blue books? What is the intention of those state secrets and those important documents being placed upon our table, and being submitted for consideration, if, on the first occasion that presents itself to offer an opinion, a Minister of the Crown rises and tells us that we are not to potter over blue books?'[3] Welcoming Disraeli's assurance that there would be no delay in the granting of supply, Russell offered no objection to the adjournment of the debate.[4]

When the debate was renewed on the 20th Cobden raised a lone voice against war with Russia, Lord John Manners continued the criticism of Clarendon's diplomacy, Horsman and Herbert defended the government against both these attacks, and Drummond made a long speech blaming the whole mess on the Pope. Disraeli made a strongly pro-Turkish speech, attacking Clarendon for his softness towards the

[1] *Hansard*, cxxx, 869.   [2] *Ibid.* 870–910; *Annual Register, 1854*, pp. 32–5.
[3] *Hansard*, cxxx, 910–13.   [4] *Ibid.* 912–13.

Russians, and ended on a patriotic note, telling Russell in taunting tones that *this* opposition would not be responsible for holding up any measures for the effective prosecution of war.[1] Palmerston wound up the debate for the government in a speech that can have given Lord Aberdeen little consolation, for it outdid Disraeli in its praise of the Turks and condemnation of the Russians.[2]

In the five weeks that still intervened before the actual declaration of war the subject of relations with Russia came before both Houses from time to time, mainly as a result of questions, and on the debate on supplementary estimates. In all these discussions the anti-Russian tone of the majority, including government spokesmen, was very pronounced, but some voices were raised to question the position of the Christian subjects of the Turks. In the Upper House Lord Shaftesbury could find little sympathy for these people because he saw them as the anti-Protestant pawns of the Orthodox Russians, but in the Commons Monckton Milnes expressed his concern over the treatment of Christian insurgents in Macedonia. There were also critical questions raised about alleged understandings between Britain and Russia that led to the publication of Nesselrode's memorandum of 1844 and the correspondence regarding the Seymour conversations of early 1853.[3]

One storm in a teacup arose from newspaper reports of the imprudent farewell dinner given at the Reform Club in honour of Sir Charles Napier.[4] Three ministers, Palmerston, Graham and Molesworth, had attended and made warlike speeches of more levity than suited the occasion, and as a result were roundly lectured by Bright for their misconduct. Graham, to the amusement of the House, doubted whether he should be held responsible for what he might have said after dinner at the Reform Club, and Palmerston indicated that he received the censure of the 'hon. and reverend Gentleman' with 'the most perfect indifference and contempt',[5] while Molesworth, to the surprise and sorrow of Cobden, repudiated the connection with Bright, whom he now found 'full of illiberal and narrow-minded prejudices'.[6] The palm for this miniature debate went to Disraeli, who greatly enjoyed the mutual

---

[1] *Annual Register, 1854*, pp. 36–42.   [2] *Ibid.* p. 42.
[3] See *Ibid.* pp. 42–52.
[4] *Hansard*, cxxxi, 674–88. The queen disliked the boasting tone of the speeches and told Aberdeen that she did not favour 'partaking of that swaggering which our French Allies are so famous for'. The Prime Minister himself considered it an 'affair in bad taste' (*Ab. Cor. 1854–5*, pp. 70–1 and 77–8; see also Erickson, *Graham*, p. 346).
[5] *Hansard*, cxxxi, 680.   [6] *Ibid.* 683.

recriminations flowing on the other side of the House, and in mock sympathy he set out to exonerate the three ministers who had feasted well but not wisely. On reflection he was not worried at the orders so injudiciously issued by the First Lord to his septuagenarian admiral because it was 'a matter of considerable notoriety that Sir Charles Napier never obeys orders'. Nor was he worried about the noble baronet sounding his admiral's praises as an old Reformer, because everybody knew 'that a sound Reformer means a gentleman who does not Reform', indeed a sort of Conservative and 'the most harmless animal going'. As for Palmerston's hostile language towards the Russian emperor, this must not be taken too seriously when one remembered that it was only a year since he had been delivering his invective against another emperor.[1]

The declaration of war, 27 March 1854, and its parliamentary sequel

Eventually the long period of doubt and uncertainty was brought to an end when on 27 March a royal message was sent to parliament proclaiming the formal commencement of hostilities. 'On that day', commented the staid *Annual Register*, 'both Houses of the Legislature presented a scene of unwonted excitement; and the solemnity of the incident, recurring after an interval of more than forty years, gave rise to varied emotions amongst the assembled Members, who awaited the anticipated announcement of a war, which may change, ere it closes, the destinies of the civilized world.'[2] In the House of Lords, where the royal message was read, the floor was full of peers and the galleries of peeresses and other ladies, while many visitors thronged the bar, anxious to witness the proceedings. Actually these were something of an anti-climax, for the Prime Minister merely handed the message to the Lord Chancellor, who read it and handed it to a clerk, who read it again in an 'utterably inaudible' voice. As *The Times* observed, there was 'nothing in the form of this communication, or in the manner in which it was made to parliament, to bring forcibly before the minds of the hearers and spectators of the scene the magnitude and importance of the occasion'.[3] It was noted that the actual declaration of war did not once mention that ominous word. Indeed its main concern was to justify the action taken. It emphasised the deceit of the Russian government,

[1] *Ibid.* 683–5.
[2] *Annual Register, 1854*, p. 54.   [3] *The Times*, 28 March 1854.

pretending that its objects were peaceful at the time of the Menschikoff mission, when in actual fact inadmissible demands were being pressed on Turkey and preparations for war initiated in Russia. It was pointed out that the Russian decision to occupy the Principalities was taken before the Allied fleets were ordered to the Dardanelles. The efforts of the Powers to restore peace between the contending parties had been unavailing, and it was clear from the scope of Russia's military preparations that she was bent on a course that must lead to the destruction of Turkey. Consequently Her Majesty felt called upon 'to take up arms, in conjunction with the Emperor of the French, for the defence of the Sultan'.[1]

For the moment public opinion was intensely warlike and patriotic, but Greville in the private pages of his Journal predicted that before long they 'will be as heartily sick of it as they are now hot upon it'. He commented on their ignorance of Russia's resources and power for war, on the reluctance of Austria and Prussia to engage, and on the uncertainty as to where the Allied fleets and armies were to operate. He continued:

The Government here is in a very weak unsatisfactory state. They are supported in carrying on war, but in every other respect they are treated with great indifference, and appear to have very little authority or influence either in Parliament or in the country. Nobody seems to have risen in estimation, except perhaps Clarendon, who has done his work well and got credit for it. Palmerston and Graham have positively *disgraced* themselves by their dinner to Napier, and the foolish speeches they made both there and in the House of Commons afterwards.[2]

The debate on the special message from the queen was introduced in the House of Lords, not by Aberdeen, but by Clarendon. Dwelling upon the anxieties and burdens that war must bring, he declared: 'These considerations—presenting themselves, and weighing heavily, as they must do, upon every reflecting mind—have not proved sufficient either to abate the determination or to damp the ardour—I would rather say the enthusiasm—with which this country has risen, as one man, at the sacred call of duty to defend the national honour in a holy, just, and righteous cause.'[3] The language of statesmen on such occasions changes little over the years.

[1] *Annual Register, 1854*, p. 532.　　[2] *Greville Memoirs*, VII, 27–8.
[3] *Hansard*, CXXXII, 141.

He announced the signing of a convention with France for the defence of Turkey and expressed his satisfaction with the conduct of Austria. Although there was some difference of opinion between Austria and Prussia as to the course which they should pursue, he was hopeful that they would eventually come to agreement and accede to the policy adopted by the Western Powers. Answering Lord Derby's challenge to the Prime Minister to assert the 'object of the war', he said: 'We enter on the war for a definite object; it is to check and repel the unjust aggression of Russia. In what manner that will be carried out, and to what consequences it may lead, must depend entirely upon the proverbial chances of war, upon the success which may attend our arms, and upon the activity of our allies.'[1]

Lord Derby promised the support of his party for the war, but the tone of his speech, as Greville said, was bitter towards the ministers, whom he compared unfavourably to the rulers of Russia and France. In particular he went after Lord Aberdeen for misleading the Russians and for his silence now.[2] His speech at least elicited an answer from Aberdeen, but the Prime Minister was more concerned to defend his character than the policy of the government. He also repudiated with indignation falsehoods contained in the latest number of Disraeli's paper, *The Press*. He made no apologies for having tried to avoid war, reminding his hearers that the 'most virtuous character in our civil war . . . even when arming himself for the combat, still murmured, "Peace! Peace!"'[3]

Malmesbury jeered at Aberdeen for wasting their time reading extracts from what he himself called a 'scurrilous paper' (contributed to by Disraeli) and ignoring the weighty arguments in Derby's speech. He then proceeded to reiterate the criticisms of the Seymour conversations and the Nesselrode memorandum of 1844, which he identified closely with Aberdeen.[4] He was answered briefly by Granville,[5] who was followed shortly afterwards by Grey, the Cassandra of the debate, the one peer who voiced regret at the declaration of war, although accepting it, and who warned of financial embarrassments to come.[6] Lord Hardwicke warned against a niggardly use of money and urged higher pay for the navy to ensure the enlistment of the best seamen; he expressed apprehension as to the strength of the Baltic fleet.[7] The

[1] *Ibid.* 149–50. [2] *Ibid.* 153–74. [3] *Ibid.* 174–80.
[4] *Ibid.* 180–4. [5] *Ibid.* 184–5. [6] *Ibid.* 187–91.
[7] *Ibid.* 191–2.

debate was concluded by Lansdowne, who joined Hardwicke 'in imploring the House and the country not to expect too much from the gallant men who have gone forth so nobly at the first call in the cause of their country'. He continued:

Whatever defects may exist in our preparations, I must say that no blame can attach to the Government—no blame to any of the establishments. All that man could do had been done by every individual in the Horse Guards and Admiralty, and in every department and nothing had tended so much to excite the universal admiration of Europe as the manner in which that splendid fleet has been equipped, which I trust will soon vindicate the honour of this country against her enemies.[1]

In the House of Commons, Russell made a statement very similar to Clarendon's, although spending rather more time in going over the history of the question. He explained the necessity of tabling the Nesselrode memorandum of 1844 and the correspondence regarding the Seymour conversations to refute irresponsible charges made in St Petersburg; he spoke of the conventions being negotiated with France and Turkey, of the satisfactory attitude of Austria and the less satisfactory attitude of Prussia, who did not seem to realise her position as a European power. Russell laid great stress on Britain's policy being a European one and part of a long tradition associated with his great hero of the seventeenth century. In one long and characteristic sentence he said:

But we, Sir, who are following the maxim which, since the time of William III. has governed and actuated the councils of this country—we, who have believed that we have a part in the great question of the liberties and the independence of Europe—we who believe that preponderance cannot safely be allowed to any one Power—who believe it is our duty to throw our weight into the scale in these conflicts—we who have seen our country rise to power, rise to reputation, rise, I may almost say, in moral greatness, by the assertion and maintenance of these doctrines...we are not prepared to abandon our position in Europe, and we ask you, by agreeing to the address of tonight, to be firmly prepared to maintain it.[2]

As so often was the case, the main criticism came from the government side of the House, but in speeches expressing opposite points of view, namely those of the Turcophile Layard and the pacific Bright. In

[1] *Hansard*, CXXXII, 196.   [2] *Ibid.* 213.

a long harangue, which Greville described as bitter and rabid because he had been disappointed in not receiving office when the ministry was formed, Layard attacked their past policy and especially that of the Foreign Secretary. Layard indicted the government for having two policies, that of Russell's speech with which he agreed, and that of other ministers, notably Clarendon and Aberdeen, as revealed in the various papers that had been tabled, which he denounced in the strongest language. Layard spoilt his case by exaggeration and his arguments were dismissed very coolly by both Palmerston and Russell, the two ministers with whose views he was clearly in sympathy. If there was any truth in his charges of divisions in the cabinet, at least these ministers were not going to be trapped into substantiating them, especially now that their policy had won out over that of Aberdeen.

Bright, of course, criticised the government from the opposite point of view. This was a needless war, the Turks were not worth fighting for; they should not have been encouraged to resist all Prince Menschikoff's proposals and allowed to reject the Vienna note; the Czar should have been listened to at Olmütz. Bright made telling use of former Whig pronouncements on foreign policy by Burke, Whitbread, Fox and Lord Holland to the effect that there was no point in propping up such a barbaric country as Turkey against Russia and denying that the 'balance of Power' entered into this situation.[1]

The marquis of Granby, a Conservative, expressed sympathy with Bright's point of view, but Palmerston wasted little time in demolishing it. Answering Bright's rhetorical question about the meaning of the phrase 'the balance of power', he said:

Now, the Hon. Member for Manchester and I differ so much upon almost every question involving great principles that I am afraid I shall be unable to gratify him by complying with his request to explain the meaning of the expression 'the balance of power'. I think, however, that a man of his un-questioned ability, of his extensive knowledge, who has arrived at the age which he has attained, and who has not by his intuitive perception acquired a knowledge of the meaning of the words 'balance of power', is not likely to be greatly enlightened by any humble effort of mine. Why, Sir, call it what you like—'balance of power', or any other expression—it is one that has been familiar to the minds of all mankind from the earliest ages in all parts of the globe. 'Balance of power' means only this—that a number of weaker States may unite to prevent a stronger one from acquiring a power which should be

[1] *Ibid.* 243–67.

285

dangerous to them, and which should overthrow their independence, their liberty, and their freedom of action. It is the doctrine of self-preservation. It is the doctrine of self-defence.

Palmerston then proceeded to contrast his views on peace and war with those of the member for Manchester in a passage that has been often quoted:

The hon. Member, however, reduces everything to the question of pounds, shillings, and pence, and I verily believe that if this country were threatened with an immediate invasion likely to end in its conquest, the hon. Member would sit down, take a piece of paper, and would put on one side of the account the contributions which his Government would require from him for the defence of the liberty and independence of the country, and he would put on the other the probable contributions which the general of the invading army might levy upon Manchester, and if he found that, on balancing the account, it would be cheaper to be conquered than to be laid under contribution for defence, he would give his vote against going to war for the liberties and independence of the country, rather than bear his share in the expenditure which it would entail.[1]

As so often happens, this pronouncement revealed more of Palmerston than of Bright, who dismissed it in his diary with the observation: 'Palmerston spoke later in the evening, flippant and superficial as usual in his attack on me.'[2]

The main, indeed the only, speech for the official opposition came from Disraeli, who expressed the full support of his party for the address in reply to the royal message, which he seconded, but who, nevertheless, proceeded to criticise the past policy of the government as reflected in its blue-books.[3] He was answered briefly by Russell and the debate was closed the same evening after a brief interposition by Colonel Sibthorp, who expressed his pity for the poor ministers after the drubbing they had received from the member for Buckinghamshire, and who announced that 'for his part his humble services were at the disposal of the country'.[4]

Although the war with Russia overshadowed all other business in 1854, it took remarkably little of parliament's time. Once war was

---

[1] *Hansard*, CXXXII, 279–80. [2] Trevelyan, *Bright*, p. 234.
[3] *Hansard*, CXXXII, 281–301.
[4] *Ibid.* 307. The imagination boggles at the idea of the worthy colonel sharing responsibilities in the field with the other charlatans who masqueraded in the Crimea as military men.

declared, the country and both Houses of Parliament rallied behind the government in its prosecution, but the main work was administrative rather than legislative. Parliament was prepared to pass any measures required for the prosecution of the war, but the members had to wait until the session was over before they could see any results. In the meantime they fell back on the old routine in a frustrated spirit that boded ill for the coalition's second instalment of reform.

III

REFORM AND FRUSTRATION

12

LORD JOHN RUSSELL'S PARLIAMENTARY REFORM BILL OF 1854

The scope of the bill and its introduction in the Commons

The main public interest in the queen's speech of 1854 lay in what it had to say about the developments in the Eastern Question and the preparations for the coming war with Russia. Nevertheless, in the speech the ministers made it clear that they intended to continue with their programme of moderate reform. The three most important measures forecast were for the reform of parliament, the reform of Oxford, and the reform of the Civil Service. Further measures of commercial and legal reform were also promised and a liberalisation of the laws of settlement.

In Russell's eyes the main measure for the session was to be his Reform Bill and so he objected to its being placed last in the queen's speech.[1] Aberdeen, however, defended the order in which he had placed it, saying: 'It is the subject for which people will wait with most interest and curiosity, and I think will form the most striking conclusion. If we begin with Foreign Affairs and Reform all the rest will be flat and uninteresting as scarcely to secure decent attention.'[2] And so reform remained the last but most prominent item in the speech forecasting new legislation.

The persistence of Russell in pursuing the Reform Bill in spite of the likelihood of war is puzzling, but he seemed to feel that his honour would be compromised if he did not go ahead with it. Undoubtedly he was sensitive to the criticisms of the left wing of the Liberal party, and the doctrinaire radicals continued to demand further parliamentary reform in season and out.[3] Only a week before the meeting of parliament they had held their annual Reform Banquet in Manchester, where in the words of *The Times* 'the principal teachers of the famous "school" established in that town laid before the world their peculiar views on the political questions of the day'. On the platform there were

[1] Add. MS. 43067, fols. 267–70, 27 January and fols. 271–2, 28 January 1854.
[2] PRO 30/22/11/C, fols. 692–3, 28 January 1854.
[3] See Charles Seymour, *Electoral reform in England and Wales*, pp. 234–42.

ten members of parliament, including Cobden, Bright and Gibson, who all spoke, and George Wilson, who was in the chair. The speakers not unnaturally turned to the great Eastern Question, which was dominating men's minds, and Gibson 'observed that a taunt was now thrown out that instead of a new reform bill we were to have war and no reform, that instead of retrenchment we were to have increased taxation'.[1] A day later *The Times* commented editorially: 'The speeches at the Manchester Reform Meeting entirely bear out our observation, that Parliamentary Reform is not demanded as a means to better government, or a more liberal, popular, or economical policy, but simply for its own sake as a purer, more symmetrical, and better looking system of representation.'[2]

On 16 January Lansdowne informed Russell that he had been looking more closely at the statistics and urged him to consider increasing the redistribution to the counties from 45 to 52. Arguing the case for North Wiltshire among other counties, he observed, 'Tho' Calne may be called my borough, North Wiltshire certainly is not, & I have nothing to say to its election politics.'[3]

Palmerston, however, remained the main opponent. On 22 January he reiterated his old arguments against large numbers of electors 'necessarily low in the scale of Intelligence and political knowledge' and open to intimidation and bribery. Politicians, like actors, would play to the shilling gallery and as a result the tone of the House would be lowered to that seen in the U.S.A.[4] Palmerston circulated his letter among the cabinet. Graham told Russell that it made no great impression on him: for no new arguments were advanced, and old ones, which he considered refuted, were again brought forward. He suggested a civil answer, saying, 'He can hardly hope to convince you, and his unavailing protests are somewhat stale'. He demonstrated his own soundness by concluding: 'My consolation is the Certainty that our Proposal is at all events no Sham.'[5] A week later Palmerston was writing again at even greater length about the undependability of the working classes. Expressing himself with the candour that he always enjoyed displaying to John Russell, he said:

Your measure may possibly give you some small & fleeting Popularity among the lower Classes, though there seems good Reason to doubt whether the

---

[1] *The Times*, 25 January 1854. [2] *Ibid.* 26 January 1854.
[3] PRO 30/22/11/C, fols. 642–5, 16 January 1854. [4] *Ibid.* fols. 665–8.
[5] *Ibid.* fols. 671–2, 23 January 1854.

Balance of Feeling would not be against you for not giving to all that which you would grant to a few. But your intended course is openly disapproved by all intelligent & respectable classes whose good opinion is most to be valued, & you can hardly be aware of the feelings of personal hostility towards you which are daily spreading through all the Party which has hitherto acknowledged you as their Leader...Some few of your intimate Friends may lead you to think that your measure will gain you good opinions, but if you ask those who know more about the general feeling of men I think they will give you a different view of the matter.[1]

This line of attack was not calculated to arouse any sense of appreciation in its recipient. Argyll developed the same point, but in friendlier fashion. 'I dined last night', he wrote on 9 February, 'where I met a lot of Liberal M.P.s and they were all joining in a loud & general chorus against the *time* for introducing the measure. Whether right or wrong, this feeling seems almost universal.' He acknowledged the point that there was no opportune time in the view of those opposed to Reform. 'But at the same time', he added, 'it is right to consider the undeniable force of *some* of the objectors.'[2]

On 12 February, the day before Russell was to introduce the bill in the Commons, Palmerston switched his attack to Aberdeen, saying that the length of the discussion on foreign affairs in recent cabinets had prevented him again bringing up objections to the proposed extensions of the franchise. Of the new voters he wrote: 'They will be comparatively poor, ignorant, and dependent. Their ignorance will prevent them from exercising a sound judgement, their poverty will make them accessible to bribes, their dependence will make them victims of intimidation.' Men who will murder their children for £9, argued the Home Secretary, will undoubtedly sell their votes. 'Wise statesmen', he went on, 'don't make great and sweeping changes in the constitutional organization of their country without some adequate necessity.' He pointed out that a Reform Bill would unite the hitherto divided opposition and divide the government supporters already bound by very loose ties.[3]

Aberdeen not unnaturally complained at this broadside being delivered so late in the day when the subject might have been introduced at

[1] *Ibid.* fols. 694–7, 29 January (partly reproduced by Gooch, *Later correspondence*, II, 130–1).

[2] *Ibid.* fols. 736–41, 9 February 1854. See also *ibid.* fols. 742–5, 9 February 1854 (partly printed in Gooch, *Later correspondence*, II, 132).

[3] *Ab. Cor. 1854–5*, pp. 32–5, 12 February 1854.

three or four cabinet meetings. He forwarded the letter to Russell, but saw no likelihood of changes at this date, unless amendments in the House forced a reconsideration.[1] To Russell he wrote on the same day: 'Only let us have peace, which I persist in saying is *not hopeless* and we may defy all opposition, or intrigue.'[2] Russell, of course, refused to consider any changes and indignantly rejected Palmerston's slanders of the English working man. He hoped for peace, but doubted that it could be obtained.[3]

The meeting of the Commons on 13 February opened with ticklish questions on foreign policy, which Russell disposed of with finesse. A few minutes later he rose to ask leave to introduce his Reform Bill. Noting that the papers of the day were by contrast filled with news of war, *The Times*[4] gave the following description of the occasion:

Yet on the evening of that day Lord John Russell introduced, not only with his customary *sang-froid*, but also with the intimation that he thought it a very slight affair, a measure of Parliamentary Reform not much less sweeping than that which some twenty years since brought us to the eve of a revolution and anarchy itself...At the very time when he and his colleagues were sending two immense fleets to the Mediterranean and the Baltic, and immediately after Lord John had explained the conduct of the Admiral in command, he rose again to invite the House of Commons to the work of its own reconstruction.

Considering the importance of the measure, Russell's speech was surprisingly short (less than eleven pages of *Hansard*) and in Greville's view 'very tame'. He wasted little time with arguments as to the necessity of the Reform, treating the bill as one designed to correct some imperfections in his original measure of 1832. He justified bringing it in under the shadow of war with references to the attempts of Pitt and Grey in 1782, 1793 and 1797. He professed his belief in the merits of the small borough, which was independent both of the county or agricultural interest on the one hand and the commercial interests of the large towns on the other, but he recognised that some of these were too small and so proposed to take away representation from the 19 boroughs (returning 29 members) that had either less than 300 electors or a population of less than 5,000, and one of two members from the 33 boroughs with less than 500 electors or 10,000 inhabitants. Adding the four vacant seats

[1] *Ab. Cor. 1854–5*, pp. 35–6, 12 February 1854.
[2] PRO 30/22/11/C, fol. 756, 12 February 1854.
[3] *Ab. Cor. 1854–5*, p. 37, 13 February 1854.   [4] *The Times*, 14 February 1854.

arising from the disfranchisement of Sudbury and St Albans, he proposed to redistribute the 66 seats made available as follows:

Counties & divisions of counties	38
West Riding of Yorkshire	4
South Lancashire	4
3 new boroughs (Birkenhead, Burnley and Stalybridge)	3
Borough of Chelsea & Kensington	2
Additional seats to 9 boroughs over 100,000 population	9
Inns of Court	2
London University	1
Scotland	3

Since only three new boroughs were being enfranchised, he justified extending the £10 household franchise to the county seats to give representation to £10 householders in unrepresented towns who would vote for the country member. He would have liked to extend the borough franchise to £5 householders, but, yielding to that opinion which considered this too great an extension, he proposed a £6 franchise with two and a half years residence. He also proposed a wide range of fancy franchises for both county and borough seats (votes for certain categories of taxpayers and fundholders, for men on salaries of at least £100 a year, for university graduates, etc.). The freeman vote was to be abandoned in the future. Minorities were to be given representation by the device of some three-member constituencies in which the voters would have two, not three, votes. It was also proposed to abolish the requirement that members appointed to office should seek re-election.[1]

After a variety of short comments and questions, mostly critical, Russell was given leave to bring the bill in but it never reached its second reading. The Times[2] took the bill seriously and welcomed its provisions, suggesting that Russell underestimated its significance, but there is no

[1] Hansard, cxxx, 491–512. (Cf. above, pp. 230–2.) It may be noted that of the seats which it was proposed to abolish outright 13 were held by Liberals, 10 by Conservatives and 6 by Peelites, and in the constituencies which were to lose one member there were 34 Liberal, 29 Conservative and 3 Peelite members. Consequently the bill was in no way a partisan measure, but the high number of Liberals affected undoubtedly helped to explain the coolness towards the bill on the government benches.

[2] The Times, 14 February 1854.

evidence that it made any great impression on either the House or the public.[1]

Two Whig peers, Lord Panmure and Lord Fortescue, congratulated Russell on fulfilling his Reform pledge and forecast support in the country, but this was the extent of the favourable response in his mailbag.[2] Another Whig friend, Cornewall Lewis, writing to Graham, also anticipated ultimate success, but warned that 'the accidents of party divisions, and the creation of enemies by disfranchisement', might raise obstacles that session.[3]

The postponement of the bill

Opposition soon appeared, however, in the form of a notice of motion from Sir E. Dering (an independent Conservative) that he would move an amendment at the second reading of the bill, scheduled for 13 March, 'to the effect that it was inexpedient to discuss the question of Reform in the present state of our foreign affairs'.[4] Sir John Young reported that all the Irish members who supported the government and all members of the 'Peelite section (that was)' favoured postponement.[5] Russell wrote to Aberdeen about this development and Young's misgivings. It appeared that Dering was likely to have a majority of 40 or more on the 13th when the lawyers would be absent from the House; yet to postpone it to the 27th, which would make it coincide with the declaration of war, was to play into Dering's hand. Russell was prepared to postpone the reading until after Easter provided this would not throw a doubt on their sincerity. 'If not,' he went on in a way that must have been offensive to the Prime Minister, 'it would have the great convenience of keeping the Ministry together at the outset of the contest, —enabling them to prepare all the means, military, naval, and financial, of carrying on a vigorous war, and then handing over to their successors a well equipped fleet, a powerful army, and a full exchequer.'[6]

Aberdeen was more resolute and refused to admit any case for postponement, saying that they would stand 'self-condemned by proposing delay'. Even though Dering be successful, he said, 'I think a regard for

---

[1] *Greville Memoirs*, VIII, 18.   [2] PRO 30/22/11/C, 15 and 26 February 1854.
[3] Graham Papers, 13 February 1854. 'Come what may I am satisfied', Graham replied. 'Lord John and I', he added unctuously, 'are true to our plighted faith' (*ibid.* copy, 14 February).   [4] *Annual Register, 1854*, p. 115.
[5] Add. MS. 44778, fols. 165–6, memo. 110.
[6] *Ab. Cor. 1854–5*, pp. 45–6, 25 February 1854.

our honour and consistency demands that we should persevere'. The second reading would create no inconvenience to public business and the committee stage could be postponed to whenever was convenient.

The Bill will have been for a month before the Country [he wrote]. It has found favour with the public as a liberal, wise and honest measure; and I think that the people may fairly expect to see its principle affirmed by the House of Commons without delay.

He made his own position clear:

I have never been a great Parliamentary Reformer; but having conscientiously adopted the principle of Reform, and believing that the present measure is perfectly safe, and likely to be generally advantageous, I am clearly of opinion that we ought not to give way to a combination of persons, many of whom we may believe to be prompted by very questionable motives. Should we postpone the Bill it would be a virtual defeat, and we shall not be long in experiencing its effects.[1]

Graham also told Russell that he was opposed to postponement, but Russell was not prepared to consider the possibility of a dissolution as Graham suggested. On the other hand, Gladstone, to Russell's surprise, was adverse to going on with the bill while the country was at war. Worse still, Wood was reported to be making excuses for delay; and Russell said it appeared to him to be 'inconsistent with his character and honour'.[2]

Russell indicated his appreciation of Aberdeen's reaction, but said he would take another day to reflect on the matter. He reported that it was Lord Robert Grosvenor's intention to gather a number of friends of the government together and then to come to the ministers to induce them to withdraw the bill: 'What folly!' Russell commented angrily.[3]

Meanwhile the ground swell against Russell's persistence in pressing Reform was growing. Edward Ellice, the elder, wrote to Aberdeen about 'the obstinacy of John Russell, in insisting upon forcing this Reform Bill under the grave circumstances of the moment'. 'Edward [his son] brings me an account from the Clubs, and the House,' he continued, 'of a general explosion of feeling against the course he persists in. It was proposed at Brooks's to sign a round robin of remonstrance

---

[1] *Ibid.* pp. 46–7, 26 February 1854 (partly reproduced in Gooch, *Later correspondence*, II, 132–3, and partly in Stanmore, *Aberdeen*, p. 274).
[2] *Ab. Cor. 1854–5*, pp. 47–8, Graham to Aberdeen reporting a conversation with Russell, 26 February 1854. Cf. Add. MS. 44778, fols. 167–74, memo. 111).
[3] *Ab. Cor. 1854–5*, p. 50, 27 February 1854.

against the Government.' Russell and Graham should heed his warning, he said, for they must realise that they could rely little on this occasion on the old cry, 'the Bill, the whole Bill, nothing but the Bill'.[1]

His colleagues now began to press Russell to reconsider. Sidney Herbert wrote an extremely persuasive letter, for he emphasised his own genuine admiration for the bill and realisation that any later measure might be too democratic. Recognising the merits of the bill he went on:

But it's [sic] honesty is the cause of its weakness in a Parliament where local & traditional if not selfish interests are attached, & in which the Government has no strong party following to set against their interests. The Government have hitherto stood solely by the excellence of it's measures, that is, the external support of the country has overborne the hostility of the opposition and the indifference or jealousy of our supporters. The budget was so carried last year. Had this Reform Bill been brought in last year it wd have been carried in the same way. But the prospects of the measure in this session are entirely changed. For the first time in nearly forty years we are about to engage in a European war. The people are so possessed by the gambling excitement of the chances of war that they will listen to nothing else. So far as they can be got to attend to it, they approve of the measure, but they had rather not hear of it and will not give themselves the least trouble about it.

We have therefore in Parliament a large array opposite to us leagued against the bill. Behind us many opposed to it because it struck a blow at their own interests, some because they fear the measure itself & many more who approve of the measure but are unwilling to see it brought before Parlt at a moment when it has no fair chance of success.

At the same time we have not out of Parlt any feeling wh can be brought to bear against the hostility within.

He argued that the measure could only be carried by ministerial pressure threatening resignation or dissolution. The first course he ruled out as 'impossible for any men of character and honour to take' in that moment of public danger. The prospects of dissolution, however, would be doubtful, for 'all moderate & sound thinking men' would be against it. Thus by bringing Reform on when they could not push it through would be to set the Reform cause back for years.

Surely this will not be redeeming our pledge [he continued]. It will rather be treason to the cause we profess to serve. The country cannot entertain two such subjects as war & reform simultaneously. Its capacity for excitement is not large enough.

[1] *Ab. Cor. 1854–5*, pp. 54–5, 'Friday' (?24 February 1854).

The only safe and honourable course for the Government therefore appears to me to be an immediate postponement of the measure, coupled with the strongest assurances of its unchanged intentions with respect to it & a frank statement of the reasons which have induced the postponement.[1]

Sir Charles Wood wrote to Russell in still stronger terms, stressing party implications that did not concern Herbert. He started his sixteen-page letter by saying that he did not want to enter into any correspondence on the subject, and then proceeded to spell out the disadvantages of going on. 'You must know', he argued, 'that except a small body of the H. of C. the general opinion of the steadiest of our friends, of our late colleagues, and others (strong Whigs) is against proceeding with the measure in present circumstances.' He saw no hope in dissolution since 'there is no such feeling for the bill in counties and large towns as will ensure a countervailing return of reforming members'. Like Herbert he said: 'The country seldom entertains two ideas at the same time. It is now bent on war, & will not trouble itself about Reform.'

He and Herbert had gone over the lists the previous night and had come to the conclusion that at the best they could only expect a small minority against Dering's motion. He went on to spell out the implications 'as regards the position of the country & the liberal party by whose aid you must in the end hope to carry reform'. He maintained that the government had acquired the confidence of the country. 'The country doubted our foreign policy,' he wrote; 'it is satisfied, & more than that, is surprised & pleased at the extent of our warlike preparations.' Having brought the country to the verge of war, the government would sadly disillusion it by raising such an issue as Reform now. Palmerston would lead the opposition, the war party would triumph, and the Whig party would fall to pieces. He continued:

I do not think that you are sufficiently alive to the consequences possible to your own character by the course which Aberdeen & Graham & yourself seem disposed to adopt. The first, I think, is anxious to be relieved from his position. I have no great confidence in Graham's judgement; and I fear that you may find yourself in a different position from what you anticipate & *with you* in great measure the fortunes of the Whig party, & of the cause of Reform.

[1] PRO 30/22/11/C, fols. 797–802, 28 February 1854; partly reprinted in Gooch, *Later correspondence*, II, 134–5, who leaves out several important paragraphs in the middle of the letter without any indication of the omission.

As a political follower, an old friend and a colleague, Wood told Russell that he felt he had to speak out in this way. 'Personally I am very indifferent to the result...', he added. 'I am very willing to be out of office, but I cannot look with indifference at the breakup of the ablest Govt the country has had for some time at such a crisis & the disorganization for a considerable time, at least, of the old party.'[1]

Apparently all this was too much for Russell, although he was not yet ready for final surrender. On the same day he wrote a second letter to Aberdeen to say that he had reflected on Aberdeen's arguments, which were of great weight with him, but he had come to the conclusion that the government's first duty was 'to obtain sanction of the House of Commons to all the preparations for war necessary, to place the Country in a strong position'. The estimates would not be voted before the following Friday and the Income Tax Bill would take another ten days or a fortnight. After that he was ready to risk a decisive battle in the House of Commons and to take any course that might seem necessary in the event of defeat.[2]

Aberdeen replied the same day to the effect that he could not pretend to be a greater reformer than Russell and so could follow Russell's advice with a clear conscience. 'We must not, however, deceive ourselves,' he wrote. 'It is an indefinite postponement which is desired, and nothing short of this will satisfy the most active of those who are pressing for such a decision.' Saying that in all matters connected with parliamentary reform he was disposed to place himself entirely in Russell's hands, he added:

I wish I could feel as much at ease on the subject of the unhappy war in which we are about to be engaged. The abstract justice of the cause, although indisputable, is but a poor consolation for the calamities of all war, or for a decision which I am not without fear may prove to have been impolitick and unwise. My conscience upbraids me the more, because seeing, as I did from the first, all that was to be apprehended, it is possible that by a little more energy and vigour, not in the Danube, but in Downing Street, it might have been prevented.[3]

Gladstone has left us a record of what took place in the cabinet on 3 March. Russell was willing to postpone the second reading to 27 April,

[1] PRO 30/22/11/C, fols. 805–12, 28 February 1854 (partly reproduced in Gooch, *Later correspondence*, II, 133–4, without any indication of omissions).
[2] *Ab. Cor. 1854–5*, pp. 51–2, 28 February 1854.
[3] PRO 30/22/11/C, fols. 803–4 (typed copy), 28 February 1854.

while Palmerston recommended 'postponement altogether'. Aberdeen and Graham were 'averse to any postponement', the latter with particular vehemence.

Of the rest of the Cabinet [Gladstone continued] Molesworth and I expressed decidedly our preference for the more decided course of at once giving up the Bill for the year—as did the Chancellor...Lord Lansdowne, Wood, Claren-don, Herbert were all with more or less decision of phrase in the same sense. Newcastle, Granville & Argyll were I believe of the same mind. But all were willing to accept the postponement until Ap. 27 rather than the very serious alternative.

Molesworth and Gladstone urged the danger of this course.[1]

And so it was decided to postpone the second reading of the bill until the end of April. Aberdeen told the queen that this decision became inevitable, since defeat seemed certain if it was attempted on 13 March 'and as the state of public business at that time would have fettered the free action of the Govt'.[2] He showed Russell's letters to Queen Victoria, who returned them with the sharp comment that there were hints in them which gave her great uneasiness. She obviously was referring to Russell's cryptic remarks about the future, for she urged the 'paramount importance' of maintaining the stability of the government at the commencement and throughout the war.[3]

That the crisis was only postponed was indicated by Palmerston in a letter to Aberdeen expressing the hope that Russell would be guarded in announcing the postponement to 27 April. He feared that those who sought the government's defeat might try to pin Russell down to an express engagement when in actual fact he, Palmerston, had agreed to the arrangement 'on the clear understanding that the question as to the postponement of the Bill over the end of this session should be as open to discussion and consideration on the 25th of April as it was yesterday'.[4] On the following day he wrote again to complain that Russell was reported to have said to Walmsley (a Radical), 'If you want the Reform Bill, now is your time to get up an agitation for it in the Country'. This was too much for Palmerston, who said that the cabinet had postponed

---

[1] Add. MS. 44778, fols. 175–80, memo. 112, 3 March 1854. According to Gladstone, the next day Russell suggested dividing the bill in half and going on with the enfranchise-ment clauses. Gladstone had an open mind on this but did not think it would satisfy Graham, who was more interested in the redistribution.

[2] Add. MS. 43048, fol. 277, 1 March 1854.

[3] *Ibid.* fol. 278, 2 February (March) 1854.   [4] *Ab. Cor. 1854–5*, p. 56.

the bill to 27 April rather than for the whole session out of consideration for the feelings of Russell and Graham, but not to give them an opportunity to create 'an artificial excitement in the Country'.[1]

When shown this letter Russell said that withdrawal of the bill on the 27th of April would be the equivalent of defeat or worse. He allowed, however, that the cabinet might have a different opinion and that he might change his. 'Pray explain this to Palmerston', he added. 'I shall not pin down the Government in any way.'[2] Both he and Graham assured Aberdeen that they had never spoken to Walmsley in the sense indicated.[3]

On 3 March Russell rose in the House to propose the postponement of the second reading to 27 April, the day immediately following the Easter recess. He claimed that it was always within his discretion to change the day of the second reading and that, in view of developments in the country's foreign relations which seemed to make war with Russia inevitable by the end of the month, and since priority must be given to the budget, which would be introduced the following week, postponement seemed to be required. He warned the House, however, that while he hoped the time assigned would be opportune, he could not promise that further postponement might not be necessary.[4] It was not a very satisfactory explanation and, as Greville pointed out, it gave Disraeli ample opportunity for a philippic.[5] Sir John Shelley, 'in the name of the Reformers of England', expressed his great sense of shock on learning of the decision to postpone this bill, which they had hailed with satisfaction because it had taken a long stride in their direction; 'but should the noble Lord persist in breaking all the promises he had made to the House and to the country,' Shelley warned, 'it would be difficult to believe that the whole thing had not been a sham from the beginning to the end, and that the Reformers of England had not been completely bamboozled by Her Majesty's Ministers.'[6]

Joseph Hume expressed his regrets more mildly, for he refused to doubt Lord John's good faith. He said that 'every communication he had from the country spoke favourably of the Bill as a whole', and he questioned Shelley's right to speak for 'the Reformers of England'.[7] Sir Edward Dering, to whose notice of motion Russell had made a cryptical allusion, protested that he was a believer in parliamentary

---

[1] *Ab.Cor. 1852–5*, p. 63, 3 March 1854. [2] *Ibid.* pp. 63–4, 3 March 1854.
[3] *Ibid.* p. 64, 4 March 1854. [4] *Hansard*, CXXXI, 277–81.
[5] *Greville Memoirs*, VII, 23. [6] *Hansard*, CXXXI, 281–3.
[7] *Ibid.* 292–3.

reform and he wished it to be understood that he brought this motion forward 'upon public grounds alone' and 'as an independent Member, totally unconnected with either of the great political parties in that House'.[1]

From the opposition benches Colonel Sibthorp delivered one of his usual devastating contributions, saying the measure was a hoax in the first place, that Lord John was now afraid to bring it forward and 'no one as yet had ever witnessed anything he had done which had been of the slightest good'.[2] Sir John Pakington bluntly told the House that 'he thought the explanation they had that evening heard from the noble Lord was humiliating and discreditable'. He did not object to the government's postponement of the bill, 'but he could not refrain from expressing his strong and emphatic condemnation of their conduct in bringing forward a measure which, if it ought not to have been persevered in, ought never to have been introduced'.[3] Disraeli was a little more subtle in his criticism, exploiting the differences between the government's supporters and exposing the weakness in Russell's case for postponement, which was just as pertinent when the bill was first introduced.[4]

Russell was warmly defended by two former colleagues, Sir George Grey and Labouchere,[5] and appeared quite at ease in making his own rebuttal, chiding Shelley for his pretensions as a spokesman for the Reformers and against Disraeli quoting the lines of the poet who wrote:

> He fagotted his notions as they fell,
> And if they rhymed and rattled, all was well.[6]

The abandonment of the bill

Three weeks later the crisis was renewed. Russell wrote a long letter to Aberdeen saying that he recognised that the great majority of both Houses wanted postponement until another year. He had considered every possible course and had come to the conclusion that it would be best for him to resign and let the government give up the bill for the present.[7] Aberdeen replied to the effect that he would not object to

---

[1] *Ibid.* 283–4. Although once classified as a Peelite, Dering generally voted against the coalition. [2] *Ibid.* 287–8.
[3] *Ibid.* 290–2. [4] *Ibid.* 295–304.
[5] *Ibid.* 285–7, 293–5. [6] *Ibid.* 304–7.
[7] *Ab. Cor. 1854–5*, pp. 82–4, 23 March 1854 (Walpole, *Russell*, II, 208–9).

postponement if there was an earnest desire to get the war over quickly and then to tackle the work of domestic reform. 'But instead of this', he continued sarcastically, 'we have a plan sketched out of a thirty years' war; and even if we could dictate peace at Moscow, we have the certainty of our colleagues undertaking Parliamentary reform with indifference, if not with reluctance.' He expressed his own regret that they had not gone ahead with the second reading on 13 March as originally proposed. 'Both you and I have said that we did not think war ought to impose any insuperable obstacle to the progress of reform,' he reminded Russell; 'and you have declared that increased taxation furnished a claim for extended franchise.' He appealed to Russell 'to consider the state of the Cabinet & the effect of that decision at which we must arrive'.[1]

To this Russell replied rather tartly that if the majority of the cabinet objected to going on with the Reform Bill he could only object on his part 'to going on any longer with them'.[2] Wood heaped more coals on the fire with two more long letters marshalling all the arguments in favour of postponement, while protesting his personal loyalty to Russell as his political leader.[3]

Aberdeen now began to weaken, perhaps under pressure from the queen, who, he told Russell, was very upset. On 3 April he sent the correspondence with Russell to her,[4] outlining possible courses of action. Temporary postponement with a pledge for next session, he thought, now seemed the only solution, if Russell would accept it, as he himself, Aberdeen, was prepared to do, although with misgiving. (He feared that it would make a continuation of the war tolerable to anti-reformers!) On the next day Aberdeen broached this possibility to Russell, saying that he thought that no other course would be 'compatible with the existence of the Government'.[5] At the same time the gloomy Graham told the queen that he was of the opinion, which 'the experience of every night' confirmed, that the present House of Commons and the present government could not long exist.[6]

Russell told Graham that he considered Aberdeen's proposal the worst of all, which led Aberdeen to write to Prince Albert suggesting a

[1] PRO 33/22/11/C, fols. 879–80, 24 March 1854 (partly printed in Stanmore, *Aberdeen*, p. 275).   [2] *Ibid.* fol. 883, 25 March 1854 (copy).
[3] PRO 30/22/11/C, fols. 885–94, 26 March, and fols. 908–13, 28 March 1854.
[4] *Ab. Cor. 1854–5*, pp. 91–2, 3 April 1854.
[5] *Ibid.* pp. 92–3 (partly printed in Gooch, *Later correspondence*, II, 135–6).
[6] *Ab. Cor. 1854–5*, p. 90, 4 April 1854, Graham to Russell.

little royal pressure might be put on Russell via the duke of Bedford![1] On 6 April Russell wrote to Aberdeen saying: 'The more I think of the *alternative* the less I like it.' Contrary to the majority of the cabinet he believed a dissolution necessary, 'for, if none of the measures mentioned in the Queen's speech are carried, it is obvious there should either be a new Parliament for the present Ministers, or new Ministers for the present Parliament'.[2]

Two days later he wrote to say that in view of Palmerston's uncompromising opposition it would be impossible to pledge the government to produce a bill at a later date. Therefore he asked Aberdeen to place his resignation before the queen, promising to state his case before the cabinet that evening. 'Your personal kindness to me on all occasions', he added, 'and the sense of justice and honour which guides you in the direction of public affairs would make me wish that this conclusion had been different.'[3]

By this time, according to Greville, Russell had got himself into a terrible state of 'vexation and perplexity', that made him ill and unable to sleep.[4] A cabinet was held on Saturday, 8 April, at which Aberdeen made his proposal of postponement with a unanimous pledge to go on with it at some indefinite time in the future, but Palmerston and Lansdowne refused to be pledged. Both Palmerston and Russell offered their resignations, which their colleagues refused to accept. In the end it was settled that Russell should announce the postponement of the bill for the present session 'with the understanding that it would be brought forward again whenever the state of affairs would admit of its being fairly and calmly considered by Parliament'. Lord John was to make the best statement that he could, not pledging the whole cabinet as he had hoped to do.[5]

After the cabinet meeting of 8 April Wood wrote to express what he thought was the general feeling of gratification among his colleagues at the sacrifice which Russell was prepared to make: 'So far from having impaired your character or means of usefulness,' he assured Russell, 'you will have raised both most essentially by the course which you have taken.' He now looked forward to 'a comfortable talk over these matters' with Russell.[6]

---

[1] *Ibid.* p. 93, 4 April 1854.
[2] *Ibid.* pp. 94–5, 6 April 1854 (partly in Walpole, *Russell*, II, 210).
[3] *Ibid.* p. 96, 8 April 1854.   [4] *Greville Memoirs*, VII, 30.
[5] *Ibid.*; *Letters of Queen Victoria*, III, pp. 25–6.
[6] PRO 30/22/11/C, fols. 947–8, 10 April 1854 (Walpole, *Russell*, II, 211).

When the queen was informed of this decision she immediately wrote to Russell to express her satisfaction and the belief that 'the sacrifice of personal feelings' on Lord John's part would be compensated by the knowledge of the service that he had done by avoiding a dissolution.[1] But the matter was not to be settled that easily. 'On Sunday', according to Greville, 'John's doubts and fears returned, his mind became unsettled again, and he was inclined to withdraw from his agreement and to go on.'[2] He answered the queen's letter in terms she can scarcely have anticipated, dwelling on 'the deep feelings of mortification' which affected him in reviewing the cabinet's proceedings. 'Lord Aberdeen', he wrote, 'was the only person who behaved with due regard to the honour of the Administration. The rest appeared ready to sacrifice everything to keep the Ministry together.' He concluded that he must reflect further on the subject before he came 'to a final determination'.[3]

The queen told Russell she was sorry to hear of his feelings of mortification, but assured him that all the ministers, other than Palmerston, were quite prepared to take the Reform Bill up again, and that he, Lord John, had misjudged them.[4]

Nevertheless, Russell persisted in concluding that the cabinet had preferred Palmerston's views to his and that consequently he could no longer remain in the cabinet.[5] He thereupon wrote to Palmerston to this effect and received a generous letter from the latter in return. He urged Russell to reconsider his intention saying, 'It really seems to me that there can be no Reason why Two Colleagues should separate because they think that at some future Time they might not agree as to such matters of Detail'. He argued that Russell's resignation would inevitably upset the government and that this would not be in the public interest. He went on to say that if Russell continued to feel that their difference of opinion regarding Reform made it impossible for them to remain together in the same cabinet he was the one who should resign, since the majority of their colleagues inclined more to Russell's views than to his, and since his part in the government was not indispensable.[6]

On Monday Russell saw Aberdeen and Graham and told them that he

[1] *Letters of Queen Victoria*, III, 25–6.　　[2] *Greville Memoirs*, VII, 30.
[3] *Letters of Queen Victoria*, III, 26.　　[4] *Ibid.* p. 27.
[5] Walpole, *Russell*, II, 211.
[6] PRO 30/22/11/C, fols. 949–54, 10 April 1854; the first half of this letter is printed in Gooch, *Later correspondence*, II, 136–7, with no indication of omissions, the second half in Walpole, *Russell*, II, 211–12.

could not deceive the House by making his proposed statement and so must resign after all. Aberdeen said that this was 'really too monstrous' after all the assurances that had been given him by the queen, the Prime Minister and all his colleagues except Palmerston. Nevertheless Lord John continued to object 'with the greatest bitterness'. While they were talking, Palmerston's letter arrived, but, on being asked by Aberdeen whether Palmerston's resignation would satisfy him, Russell answered that he did not believe it 'would mend matters'. 'Lord Aberdeen's opinion, however,' wrote Prince Albert in an account of the meeting, 'is that it is what Lord John, and still more what Lady John, wants.'[1]

Aberdeen was most upset, for, if Russell went, Palmerston would expect to lead the House, which he termed 'perfectly ludicrous'. This, he thought, might lead to the formation of a new government, perhaps under the duke of Newcastle and Mr Gladstone, whom he would see that evening with Sir James Graham, prior to a meeting with Palmerston and Russell the next morning. (The government seemed to be falling into its original constituent parts.) 'This is really very bad!' the prince wrote in concluding his memorandum.[2]

When Russell failed to make his expected statement to the House on Monday, it became generally known that something was wrong and according to Greville 'the curiosity and excitement were very great'. 'All Monday and Tuesday mornings were passed in conferences and going backwards and forwards,' Greville continued, 'the Duke of Bedford being called in to work upon John.'[3]

At this point Sidney Herbert made a special effort to break the impasse by addressing a most moving letter to Russell, in which, in part, he said:

I have now served under your lead for sixteen months, and I have learnt to take a strong interest in whatever concerns your political & personal position ...I endeavour to place myself in your position & view it, if such a thing is possible, irrespective of my relation to the Government & to your Colleagues.

The whole Cabinet are agreed that the Reform bill must be postponed. To bring the measure forward wd be to incur certain defeat & under our present circumstances a defeat wh could not be repaired or avenged. In the interests of Reform, therefore, postponement is inevitable.

---

[1] *Letters of Queen Victoria*, III, 27–8, memorandum 10 April 1854.
[2] *Ibid.*
[3] *Greville Memoirs*, VII, 30. The duke first sent his brother a note referring to conversations with Lansdowne and Clarendon but not to the prompting from the palace. PRO 30/22/11/C, fols. 945–6, 10 April 1854.

So far we are unanimous.

One man in the Government dislikes the bill & thinks the measure a bad one. One is perhaps luke-warm, but still assenting, and being a man of honor beyond suspicion his assent is sincere. All the rest of the Govt are hearty supporters of the Bill wh embodies the policy of which by your previous services you are the recognized champion.

In postponing the measure it is agreed that we mean to declare our adherence to the principles of reform & hold ourselves in honor bound to the same engagements with respect to it with which we entered office.

Here is a great difficulty for Ld Palmerston but none it seems to me for you and for us.

There can be no doubt that if in Febry next circumstances are such that we can go on with the Bill Palmerston must go.

But is the prospect of his being obliged to retire under certain circumstances next year a justification for your resigning now?[1]

Herbert went on to assure Russell that no one would question the rectitude of his motives but urged that at such a time he ought not to evade 'great difficulties and great responsibilities', but rather that he ought to be prepared to render a service to the country. He reminded Russell that he had 'the unanimous support' of the cabinet on every other measure that could come under discussion that year. He hoped Lord John would not abandon the position that he occupied 'under engagements not only to party but to the Country'. 'It will be a great political error and a great public misfortune,' he wrote, 'and I doubt whether the Country, on whom the loss will fall, will think your course justifiable.' Excusing himself for writing so freely, he concluded on a most friendly note saying: 'Whatever course you take, I shall recollect with pleasure the period during which I have served under you, and learned to know the many noble qualities of one to whom I was once politically opposed.'

Under the impression that Russell would resign, Aberdeen held his proposed meeting with his friends on Monday night and it was decided that since it was still a Reform government, Palmerston could not be asked to lead it in the House of Commons, but that it was hoped he would consent to serve under Gladstone as his contemporary Sir James Graham was prepared to do![2] It never became necessary to make this

[1] PRO 30/22/11/C, fols. 955–8, 11 April 1854; Walpole, *Russell*, II, 212, quotes part of this letter, but omits all but the first sentence of the passage quoted above. The sentiments expressed by a man not given to dissimulation indicate the strange hold that Russell exercised over his associates, despite his many exasperating characteristics.

[2] *Letters of Queen Victoria*, III, 30.

proposal, however, for on the next morning Russell submitted to the weight of opinion marshalled against him.[1] That afternoon, although he almost broke down in the course of it, he made a most effective speech to a surprisingly sympathetic House of Commons, which recognised his emotion as genuine and reciprocated it. 'The eyes of young men and of old were brimming with tears of sympathy, and almost affectionate respect', one member told him afterwards.[2] 'His emotion was sincere', Greville commented coldly, 'because he is no actor, but it was in my opinion completely uncalled for; and as there is but a step between the sublime and the ridiculous, it might just as well have appeared ridiculous; but fortunately for him his audience were disposed to take it au grand sérieux.'[3] Even the duke of Bedford told Greville he thought John had been overpraised.

Actually Russell's speech[4] was better than his previous explanation of postponement. He first made it clear that it was not himself alone but the whole government that was committed to Reform. It was readily understandable that it could not be pressed the first session, when the problem of the income tax and the government of India had to be settled. It had to be brought in this session, however, despite the unsettled state of foreign affairs, and so the ministers had made their preparations and persisted with them as long as possible. But it had to be admitted that any Reform Bill must stir up the opposition of vested interests and it had to be asked whether under the new situation of war the government could carry the bill 'in the present state of public opinion both in the House and in the country'. Russell said that he had recognised an indifference to their proceeding with the bill because of preoccupation with the war and this was reflected in the lack of petitions supporting it. He spelt out to the House as it had been spelt out to him the implication of defeat at this time, and the adverse effect that would have on the conduct of the war. He made it clear that the government was still committed to the measure and would bring it forward again when the opportunity presented itself, although they would be ready to accept such modifications as might be required. He concluded by saying a few words about his own position. He recognised that he was fair game for 'all those weapons of taunt and sarcasm which the right hon. Gentleman opposite [Mr Disraeli] knows so well how to

[1] *Ibid.* p. 29.
[2] PRO 30/22/11/C, fol. 962, from G. A. Vernon, 11 April 1854.
[3] *Greville Memoirs*, VII, 31.   [4] *Hansard*, CXXXII, 836–44.

use', but it was different with respect to members on his own side. The *Hansard* version of his speech continues:

With respect to them, I must say, that when the statement I have made is held to be open to suspicion, such suspicion can hardly be entertained without weakening and destroying my utility and my position as the organ of the Government in this House. If I have—[The noble Lord appeared now to be affected by deep emotion, and paused. Meanwhile he was loudly and repeatedly cheered from both sides of the House.]—If I have done anything in the cause of Reform, I trust that I have deserved some degree of confidence, but at all events, I feel that, if I do not possess that confidence, I shall be of no use to the Crown or to the country, and I can no longer hold the position I now occupy.[1]

A very moderate debate followed.[2] Grey and Labouchere repeated their expressions of warm satisfaction with the course Russell had chosen, Hume and Bright accepted it and Russell's good faith, although Hume denied there was a lack of support in the country, while Bright, less satisfied with the bill in the first place, explained why there was. From the other side of the House Dering and Jocelyn welcomed the decision, but took the opportunity to suggest that the bill scarcely reflected the former views of some of the Peelite members of the government. This point was briefly rebutted by Sidney Herbert. Disraeli made one of his mildest speeches, renewing the charge that what was obvious now was obvious when the bill was brought in, but he eschewed the sarcasm which Russell expected of him.

The atmosphere of the House was reflected in a letter to Russell from Sir Denis Le Marchant, who wrote to congratulate him on his success, saying:

There were some moments, when I thought you had never occupied a prouder position—certainly never a more enviable one. I saw Spooner and many of the Tories cheering, & the Liberal benches for once all of one mind. Disraeli, I was told, (from a Tory quarter) had prepared a speech of no friendly tenor, but after Bright, he felt it would not do. It was altogether a scene that I shall never forget. I felt that I was sitting in an assembly of *gentlemen*, & whatever may be said about the tone of the Reformed House as distinguished from the Unreformed, no one after last night can fairly dispute their pretensions to a high standard of feeling as has been witnessed in the best periods of our history.[3]

---

[1] *Hansard*, CXXXII, 843–4.   [2] *Ibid.* 844–72.
[3] PRO 30/22/11/C, fols. 959–60, n.d.

The congratulations that showered in on Russell were in marked contrast to the silence that had greeted his original introduction of the bill. The most significant of these letters came from the Peelite G. E. H. Vernon, who wrote:

As a very humble member of a party which has now become intimately associated and indeed amalgamated with the great party of which you have been so long the leader, I beg to assure your lordship that the magnanimity which you have displayed on this as on so many other occasions gives to you additional claims on the confidence of those who like myself are sincere well wishers of a Government based on liberal and yet conservative principles.[1]

A few days later Russell gave his own assessment of the situation to Cornewall Lewis, saying that a minister had to consider whether he should insist on the Reform Bill at the expense of putting a retrograde party in power. He continued:

For the question with the people again is whether they will have the liberal party or the Tories. The Tories no longer offer to the country the abilities of Sir R. Peel and his followers as a compensation for the liberal principles of Whigs & Radicals. It is a choice between liberal principles with the present Ministers or a narrow obsolete policy with Derby & Disraeli. Such being the case I consider the matter as very hopeful...But it may take two years to complete the building which 22 years ago I took so much pains to erect.[2]

For the time being the little man had recovered his equanimity, but not for long.

[1] PRO 30/22/11/C, fols. 961–2, 11 April 1854. There were also letters from Palmerston, fol. 967, 11 April, the Lord Advocate, fol. 31, and Lord Normanby, fol. 1003–4, 19 April 1854. See Walpole, *Russell*, II, 213–14, for quotations from Aberdeen, Sir Francis Baring, Clarendon, and Lord Oranmore.
[2] PRO 30/22/11/C, fols. 989–90, 15 April 1854.

13

THE PEELITE CONTRIBUTION TO
REFORM IN 1854

Civil service reform

The queen's speech of 1854 had forecast two other reforms, embracing the civil service and the universities, that were much closer to the heart of the Chancellor of the Exchequer than the ill-fated bill for improving the representation of the people. Indeed, while Graham was busy assisting Russell in the preparation of that measure, Gladstone told him that the reconstitution of the civil service was to be *his* 'contribution to the picnic of Parliamentary Reform'.[1]

Radical reformers of an earlier generation had thought of such reform merely in terms of retrenchment, the abolition of redundant offices and the curtailment of extravagant salaries, but as the role of government expanded, this approach was clearly outdated. A series of departmental inquiries were already in progress under the superintendence of the Treasury. These were examining the establishments of various departments to determine among other matters where increase of staff or of salary might be required, or conversely where abolition or consolidation of redundant offices was desirable; also to consider the introduction of simpler and more efficient methods of transacting business, and especially the establishment of 'a proper distinction between intellectual and mechanical labour'.[2] Two men played a leading role in many of these investigations, Sir Charles Trevelyan and Sir Stafford Northcote.

Trevelyan was a hard working, aggressive and extremely opinionated public servant. After fourteen years of distinguished service in India, he had been appointed Assistant Secretary to the Treasury, the senior permanent official in that office, where he remained until he returned to India as Governor of Bengal in 1859. At the Treasury he had served five successive administrations, Whig, Tory and coalition, but his connections and outlook were primarily Whig or Liberal. As we have seen, he was the friend and brother-in-law of Macaulay and his views on

---

[1] Graham Papers, 3 January 1854. [2] *P.P. 1854–5*, xxx, 375.

economy and *laissez-faire* were strong enough to endear him to the hearts of the Manchester School, but equally to make him forever a villain in the eyes of the Irish, whose starvation he seemed prepared to accept, almost with complacency, at the time of the Great Famine.[1] No man did more to place the Treasury in its modern role of watchdog of the whole government service.

Northcote was a Devon landowner of Tory stock, who had trained as a barrister and had a reputation for great industry. As a young man he had become greatly attached to Gladstone while serving as his private secretary at the Board of Trade. Although suspicious of the coalition with the Liberals he had been very active on Gladstone's election committee for Oxford at all the elections. Even before the Aberdeen government had been formed, Gladstone asked him in December of 1852 whether he would be available for some form of official work. Northcote expressed an interest, providing his doctor gave him a clean bill of health (he had been nursing a weak heart for the past eighteen months that was to lead to his death in Lord Salisbury's waiting-room thirty-seven years later); but he warned Gladstone: 'I am rather a stiff Conservative, and I do not feel at all sure that the next Administration will be one that I can work under.' He took the starch out of his stiffness, however, by declaring that if Gladstone were to 'form a leading element in it' he could scarcely imagine having any doubts.[2]

Three days later he announced that he was free of the doctors[3] and on Christmas day he wrote again saying, 'I have heard of a piece of work, which, if it is to be carried out, would suit me exactly.'[4] This was a commission proposed by the outgoing government to inquire into the possible reorganisation of the Board of Trade. He also volunteered to help Gladstone's private secretary, Lawley, to get started. For the better part of the next month, however, he was kept busy with Gladstone's re-election.[5] When the by-election was over he moved into the Treasury and seems to have performed numerous jobs for Gladstone, even to representing him in police court.[6] He was appointed not only to the commission to investigate the Board of Trade, but to eight others as well, which kept him busy for the best part of the next year.[7] His

---

[1] See Cecil Woodham-Smith, *The Great Hunger*. For a critical appraisal of Trevelyan see Jennifer Jones, 'Sir Charles Trevelyan at the Treasury', *E.H.R.* lxxv (1960), 92–110.   [2] Add. MS. 44216, fols. 185–7, 18 December 1852.
[3] *Ibid.* fol. 191.   [4] *Ibid.* fols. 192–3.
[5] *Ibid.* fols. 196–203.   [6] *Ibid.* fol. 207.
[7] See *Reports of committees of enquiry into public offices*, P.P. 1854 (1715), xxvii, 1–363.

colleague on all these commissions was Sir Charles Trevelyan, and in a few cases they were joined by one or more other senior civil servants. The report on the Board of Trade was signed on 20 March 1853,[1] and it was followed in quick order by reports on the Science and Art Department (25 May), the Poor Law Board (20 July),[2] the Privy Council Office (6 August),[3] Copyhold, Enclosure and Tithe Commutation (16 August), the Colonial Land and Emigration Office (10 August),[4] the Board of Ordnance (17 December),[5] and the Office of Works (20 January 1854). 'As regards the Treasury,' Trevelyan wrote to Gladstone at the end of March 1853, 'I should be disposed to be content *for the present* with the degree of improvement which has been obtained, on the ground of the recency of that Reform, of the *disproportionate* expenditure of time & feeling necessarily incident to the revision of *one's own* office, and of the fact that there are several other Offices which stand more in need of Enquiry, and therefore require our *earliest* attention.'[6] In actual fact a report had been done on the Treasury, in which Trevelyan had participated,[7] in 1849, and since then he had himself carried out a series of reforms in that department.[8]

While most of these reports were still in the course of preparation or not yet begun, Northcote and Trevelyan were instructed by a Treasury minute of 12 April to draw up a general report on the civil service. 'In connection with these inquiries into each particular establishment', the minute ran, 'it is highly necessary that the conditions which are common to all the public offices, such as the preliminary testimonials of character and bodily health, the examination into their intellectual attainments, and the regulation of the promotion, should be carefully considered' to ensure that the best candidates should be selected. The minute touched upon the qualifications of Northcote and Trevelyan for the task and provided that the former 'should give up his whole time to it and be paid at the rate of £1000 per annum'.[9]

[1] With J. Booth.
[2] With T. P. Courtney.
[3] With C. Greville.
[4] With T. W. C. Murdoch.
[5] With W. G. Anderson and E. A. Hoffay.
[6] Add. MS. 44333, fols. 30–3.
[7] *P.P. 1854* (1715), XXVII, 3–46.
[8] E. Hughes, 'Sir Charles Trevelyan and civil service reform, 1853–5', *E.H.R.* LXIV (1949), 58.
[9] *P.P. 1854–5*, XXX. Return to an address of the House of Commons, 16 July 1855, pp. 1–2. In all Northcote was paid £875 for the period 15 February–31 December 1853. *Ibid.* cf. E. Hughes, 'Civil service reform, 1853–5', *History*, XXVII (1942), 51–83, and reprinted 'with minor corrections and additions' in *Public Administration*, XXXII

By November the report was finished and on the 28th Trevelyan sent Gladstone two copies with a covering letter in which he said:

The political bearing of these proposed changes will, I think, strike you as extremely important. The Government Patronage is habitually employed in influencing, or, according to a stricter morality, corrupting, Representatives & Electors at the expense both of their independence and of the public interests...It is time that the Government should rest its claim to support upon simply & directly consulting the public good. The experience of last session shows that this is quite practicable. The Government, which began with a narrow majority, acquired, by the general approbation with which its measures were regarded, a strength & stability exceeding what has been known for many years. Following out this principle, we cannot doubt that no distribution of the Government Patronage would benefit the Government so much as the general confidence that all appointments to the public service were made solely with a view to the public good, without any indirect personal or interested motives whatever.[1]

For such a famous state paper, the Northcote-Trevelyan Report is surprisingly short.[2] There is no indication of a thorough and laborious investigation of the whole service, no appendices of evidence, no statistical tables (although a few were added), in short, none of the trimmings that would accompany a modern report of such significance. Professor Hughes, noting the lack of information on method of procedure, has said that the report leaves the impression of being 'a brilliant airing of preconceived ideas' with no obvious relation to the facts.[3] It must, however, be taken in relation to the other reports that the commissioners were preparing at the same time. Indeed its major ideas are to be found in them, and in its first sentence we see the close relationship it bore in their minds to the other reports.[4] The commissioners

(1954) along with the Northcote–Trevelyan report on the reform of the civil service. Professor Hughes appears to overlook the above return when he says that there is no information regarding the terms of reference of the commissioners.

[1] Add. MS. 44333, fols. 65–6. This and other letters from Trevelyan to Gladstone on the subject in Add. MS. 44333 are printed by Professor Hughes in *E.H.R.* LXIV, 67–88 and 206–34, to which all further references will be made. See also Trevelyan's memorandum entitled 'Thoughts on patronage', *ibid.* pp. 69–70.

[2] *Report on the organization of the permanent civil service...*, *P.P. 1854* (1713), XXVII, 1–31.

[3] *History*, XXVII, 65.

[4] 'We now proceed to comply with that part of our instructions which states that, in connection with the enquiries which we were directed to make into each particular office, it is highly necessary that the conditions which are common to all the public establishments...should be carefully considered.' 'Report on the organization of the permanent civil service', *P.P. 1854* (1713), XXVII, 3.

may have had preconceived ideas, but they did take a number of
sample departments and offices, and investigate them thoroughly, to
judge from the detail of the reports, and here they considered that they
had ample evidence to support their views.[1] Unfortunately none of the
great departments of state were included among those investigated,
perhaps because of the susceptibilities of their chiefs who were cabinet
ministers.

The findings of the Report itself and its recommendations are well
known.[2] It began with a scathing indictment of the existing patronage-
ridden service, although paradoxically admitting that 'with all its
defects' it 'essentially' contributed 'to the proper discharge of the
functions of Government'. It was suggested that the civil service was
the home of the misfits from the upper classes, for the most part
indolent fellows, quite untrained for their jobs, prone to ill health and
very lightly worked. The commissioners admitted that there were
'numerous and honourable exceptions' and that 'the trustworthiness of
the entire body' was 'unimpeached', but they observed that the
existing members were much better than the public had any right to
expect from the system under which they were appointed and promoted. The Report dwelt upon the evils of promotion by mere seniority
through all steps from the very bottom and the consequent necessity of
making important staff appointments (such as Trevelyan himself) from
the outside. It also condemned the fragmentary nature of the service,
which considered each department as completely self-contained.

To overcome these serious defects the commissioners recommended
that a fixed number of appointments should be made each year not on
the basis of patronage, as formerly, but by the results of open competitive examinations which would be relevant to particular categories
of openings, whether for 'mechanical' or 'intellectual' work. Examinations would be supervised by an independent examining board for the
whole service, and departments would merely make selections from
the list of successful candidates, whose number would be the same as
the number of vacancies. It was also proposed that promotion should be
based upon merit and might be from one department to another, thus
overcoming the evil of fragmentation.

The Report was shown in draft to the Reverend B. Jowett of Balliol

[1] Professor Hughes recognises this connection in his later note in E.H.R. LXIV, 61.
[2] See *Public administration*, vol. 32, where it is reprinted; see also E. W. Cohen, *The
growth of the British civil service, 1780–1939* (1941); Robert Moses, *The civil service in
Great Britain*.

College, whose comments, in the form of a letter, were published as an appendix to it. In his letter Jowett warmly supported the recommendations of the commissioners and proceeded to sketch out in more detail both the type of references that should be required of all candidates and the nature of the examinations which they would be required to take.

Gladstone immediately set about enlisting the support of his colleagues to the proposed reforms. He had no difficulty with the younger Peelites, who responded naturally to such ideas so well calculated to appeal to their way of thinking and their outlook on public life. Newcastle told Gladstone that the object of the reform had his hearty concurrence. 'I have long been convinced', he wrote, 'that the days of government by patronage having passed away, every remnant of the system should if possible be removed.—Patronage is one of the greatest impediments in the way of an honest Government.'[1] Cardwell, too, whose Board of Trade had been investigated, expressed his sympathetic interest, promising to hold up pending appointments until a decision was made. He advised against making too rigid barriers between the two classes of appointment, made some suggestions about examiners, and concluded by saying: 'It would be a great thing to establish at the same time a greater degree of strictness in the service; & to this the abolition of patronage would tend.'[2]

Aberdeen also gave the proposals his warm support, which was to be expected after his championship of similar proposals for the Indian service. Few Prime Ministers have had less *political* experience, and consequently the political implications of the reform did not worry him. Graham, on the other hand, although an administrative reformer, had too long an experience as a politician to welcome the proposed changes. He was one of the first colleagues with whom Gladstone discussed the subject.[3]

Early in January Gladstone sent Graham a copy of the Northcote–Trevelyan Report, seeking his support to the principle of a measure to open the public service to personal merit, which he proposed to place before the cabinet. He said that he had already spoken to Aberdeen and proposed to speak to Newcastle and perhaps Molesworth before taking any other step. He himself wrote with great enthusiasm of the proposed assault on the citadel of patronage, seeing it as part of a larger campaign

[1] Add. MS. 44262, fols. 144–5, 3 January 1854.
[2] Add. MS. 44118, fols. 60–3, 13 January 1854.
[3] Add. MS. 44163, fols. 101–4, 3 December 1853.

which began with the India Reform of the previous year and which would be extended by a pending measure he proposed for Oxford.[1]

Graham replied in a long and sympathetic letter, but he had been steeped for too long in the old system to be fully convinced. He recognised the merits of the examination system in principle and in particular favoured promotion on merit, but he went on to point out the political considerations with considerable acumen:

Before the Revolution [he wrote], the Crown struggled to maintain supreme power by prerogative; since the Revolution it has succeeded in upholding supremacy by Influence. This Influence is mainly dependent on Patronage, and is brought to bear on the Parliamentary System of Government by its double action, both on the constituent and the representative Body; and the House of Lords itself is not elevated above the Sphere of this great attraction. The plan proposed at one stroke abolishes the civil patronage, and leaves only the naval and military at the free disposal of the Crown as a matter of Grace and Favour. I am not certain that Parliamentary Government can be conducted on such principles of purity.

He admitted that 'a sounder public opinion' was gaining ground and that in time the old system would fall into disrepute.

Still [he continued], it must not be dissembled, that this is an immense stride towards Self-Government in the democratic sense; that it is pregnant with indirect consequences, which cannot be exactly estimated or foreseen; for it leaves the House of Commons—that mighty engine—without its accustomed regulator, at the very moment when you are about to increase its power.

This proposal, if made by the Ministers of the Crown, and with the consent of the Crown, will eclipse all other reforms, and will be regarded as the greatest boon conferred on the Nation, since Bread was freed from Taxation.

Graham concluded by indicating his desire to consult Lord Aberdeen and to discuss the matter further with Gladstone before it was 'launched into the whirlpool of the Cabinet'.[2]

The more Sir James turned the matter over in his gloomy mind, however, the more his doubts began to grow. A week later he wrote again dwelling upon the magnitude and difficulty of the proposed reform, saying in part:

[1] Graham Papers, 3 January 1854 (Parker, *Graham*, II, 209–10).
[2] Add. MS. 44163, fols. 111–15, 4 January 1854 (Parker, *Graham*, II, 211–15). In a postscript he approved the section of the report dealing with superannuation since he agreed that 'the root of the evil' was 'promotion by seniority'.

Tho' the Civil Service ought by no means to be exclusive, and is not so at the present moment; yet in some branches, where great trust is reposed, it is a Qualification to be a Gentleman: and no other attainments can compensate for the want of this inestimable merit...I remember asking the Duke of Wellington whether he advised me to send my son, whom I destined for the Army, to Sandhurst or to some Military Academy, where he might acquire scientific knowledge and technical training; his answer was,—'send him to Eton and *make him a Gentleman*'; a significant maxim from a great Master, who had tried every class of our Fellow-Countrymen in every circumstance of difficulty and danger.

He alluded to the system of nominations for naval and military commissions by the First Lord and the Commander-in-Chief which were considered by an independent Board of Examiners and asked:

Why should not the Great Officers of State nominate to civil appointments of the lower Grade on like conditions? The harmony, for which I contend, would thus be maintained; Gentlemen in confidential departments would still have a preference; and the connexion between the Crown and the Civil Service would not be entirely dissolved. This competition would indeed be restricted, but the examinations would be central and manageable; the larger measure might ultimately be adopted.[1]

Gladstone expressed his appreciation of Graham's letters, but stuck to his guns. He claimed that the system of examination was likely to favour the gentleman, since the narrowness of the poor man's background was likely to tell against him. Examination experience in Oxford, he said, bore this out. Arguments emphasising the trustworthiness and the fidelity of the civil service he thought were true only in the negative sense. There were exceptions, but on the whole he felt that the civil service was not remarkable for zeal, energy, cheerfulness, contentment or a lively sense of obligation. The case of the military, he felt, was 'plainly and broadly different'. He continued:

Let me now advert to a distinction which I think vital. When you speak of the connection between the Civil Service & the Crown, you mean I apprehend by the Crown the Ministry & the Parliamentary majorities which have a determining influence over its existence.

Presuming however that due powers of promotion & dismissal are secured to the Heads of Departments I find a difficulty in saying what other relation of dependence I should wish to preserve between the Civil Service & the political

---

[1] *Ibid.* fols. 117–19, 11 January 1854; this letter is not printed in Parker, who consequently leaves a false impression regarding Graham's attitude.

party in power. When *you* are in doubt on such a question, I must speak with deference: but my opinion is that we have lived into a period in which upon the whole the principle of Government, as respects our country, is weakened & not strengthened by the operation of the system of patronage in the Civil Service. This opinion implies I admit a great faith in the good sense of the community: but after all we have seen, I cannot refuse it this much of my confidence.[1]

Graham's doubts, nevertheless, continued to grow and in his next letter he deplored the premature publicity of the Northcote–Trevelyan Report. Anything short of the full thing would now be a disappointment, but he counselled a step-by-step approach, since withdrawal was now impossible. He went on to elaborate his former thesis in reply to Gladstone's arguments:

I cannot separate the Crown from the Ministry in considering Patronage. The appointments in the Army, Navy, Church, and Civil Service, all flow equally from the Crown and thro' the same channels. The First Lord of the Treasury makes Deans and Canons and appoints Treasury Clerks...The whole Patronage, Civil, Naval and Military, is exercised by responsible Ministers in the name of the Sovereign, and often under the Sign Manual: and in this respect the Civil Service is not distinct from the Military. Open competition will draw the distinction for the first time.

Graham cited the Engineer and Artillery services as examples of the satisfactory combination of the nomination and competitive systems. 'I am the warm Advocate of searching and Impartial Examinations,' he added; 'indeed I adopt your Plan in all its Parts, saving only doubts on the question of unrestricted Competition at the first Entrance.' (But this was the key proposal.) He concluded his letter, however, on a generous note, saying that he left the matter with entire confidence in Gladstone's hands; 'when it has been decided I shall not look back,' he promised; 'and you may rely on every assistance, which I can give.'[2] This was perhaps as much as Gladstone could hope for from that generation, although it is interesting to speculate how Peel would have reacted to the Report in view of his known distaste to the distribution of patronage.

[1] Add. MS. 44163 fols. 120–4, 14 January 1854 (copy).
[2] *Ibid.* fols. 124–7, 16 January 1854. In the previous session Graham had defended government patronage in dockyard appointments provided they were subject to examination and that promotion was by merit alone (G. Kitson Clark, 'Statesmen in disguise', *Hist. J.* II (1959), 21).

Gladstone met Graham's arguments with the paper supplied by Jowett and reminded him that they had experience of the competitive system at the universities. He avowed that some of his more timid constituents objected to the proposed reform as destroying the poor man's chances and giving everything to the gentleman.[1] He agreed with Graham in deploring the premature publicity.

The opposition from Lord John Russell was more formidable. On 20 January he wrote to Gladstone:

I hope you are not thinking seriously of the plan of throwing open to competition the whole civil service of the country... [In the case of the Indian Civil Service he allowed there was some excuse.]

But I am convinced such a plan introduced into our civil service would make it worse instead of better...It is proposed to substitute talent & cramming for character...I confess I don't see much evil in that patronage which Mr Jowett says makes a change necessary. No man changes his politicks on account of this patronage. But an adherent of the Ministry attends more constantly, & is less flighty in his votes when his interest in his vanity or borough may be promoted by the Minister.

When a superior man is wanted, you look elsewhere for him—Stephen, Merivale, Waddington & Trevelyan himself are instances. But the service itself has produced excellent men. The Foreign Office is very good. I hope no change will be made, & I certainly must protest against it.[2]

Opposition only whetted Gladstone's enthusiasm. He replied with a twenty-two page letter in which he presented a striking case for the proposed reform. He began on a gentle note, saying that he hesitated to argue with one of Russell's experience; that the matter was more one for a Prime Minister or leader of the House. However, he rejected Russell's claims as to quality. There were exceptions, but by and large the country was not getting value for its money in the case of others who were a dead weight, lowering the morale and efficiency of the whole machine. There was a case for improving the salaries and superannuation benefits of the service, but its efficiency must first be improved before this could be legitimately granted. He went on to discuss ten major evils to be found in the existing system of patronage. For one thing, he said, it produced 'an actual class of the community... who spend a large and often the best part of their days in a worse than worthless expectancy'. As to Russell's remark that it was possible to bring in good men from outside, he maintained that this simply

[1] Graham Papers, 17 January 1854.   [2] Add. MS. 44291, fols. 91–2, 20 January 1854.

emphasised the evil, that it was necessary to look outside for good men. He agreed that men did not change their party politics on account of patronage, 'but looking calmly around', he said, 'I cannot for one deny that it in very many cases is, and that by its nature tends to be, a mild form (in Ireland not at all a mild form) of corruption. In Parliament I think notoriously the bad men get the greater share of it. The good deal with it as little as they can, or shrink altogether from touching it.'

Moving over to the offensive, Gladstone gave it as his opinion that the reform would tend 'to strengthen and multiply the ties between the higher classes and the possession of administrative power'. 'As a member for Oxford', he said, 'I look forward eagerly to its operation.' He continued:

I have a strong impression that the aristocracy of this country are even superior in natural gifts, on the average, to the mass; but it is plain that with their acquired advantages, their *insensible education*, irrespective of book-learning, they have an immense superiority.

He reminded Russell that it was an important feature of the plan to separate the mechanical and intellectual work wherever possible, which would, he maintained, 'open to the highly educated class a career, and give them a command over all the higher parts of the civil service', which up to that time they had never enjoyed.

As for the effect of the reform on the carrying on of the business of the House of Commons, he argued that it was a matter of adjustment, a development following naturally from the other changes produced by the Reform Bill.

I speak with diffidence [he wrote]: but remember that at the Revolution we passed over from prerogative to patronage, and that since the Revolution we have also passed from bribery to influence. I cannot think that the process is to end here; and after all we have seen of the good sense and good feeling of the community, though it may be too sanguine, I cherish the hope that the day is now near at hand, or actually come, when...we may safely give yet one more new and striking sign of rational confidence in the intelligence & character of the people.[1]

'I am sorry to say I remain quite unconvinced,' Lord John replied, and proceeded to refute Gladstone's various arguments in a letter of

[1] Add. MS. 44291, fols. 93–103, copy in Gladstone's hand, 12 January 1854. He added that he regretted the publicity that had been given the report and was shocked that Northcote had written an article for the *Quarterly* which was already set up. Part of this letter is printed in an Appendix in Morley, *Gladstone*, I, 649–50.

eight pages.[1] He said that in his view 'the worst and most important consequence' of the proposed reform would be that favours would 'no longer flow from the Queen'. 'Our institutions', he warned, 'will be as harshly republican as possible...I cannot say how sincerely I feel all this.'[2] He proposed the circulation of their letters. In agreeing to this proposal Gladstone contented himself with saying: 'I assure you that I have no such idea as that the country can be governed without party; but I incline to believe that party can be maintained without patronage of the kind which would be abolished by throwing open first appointments to the Civil Service.'[3]

In the meantime Trevelyan had written to Gladstone on 20 January saying: 'I do not know that anything more can be done at present except to draw up a short Act of Parliament authorizing the formation of an Establishment for the purpose of testing the qualifications of Candidates for Civil Employment, and directing that the rules under which it is to act shall be sanctioned by Order in Council, and be submitted to Parliament.'[4]

The plan was considered by the cabinet on the 26th, supported by all the Peelite ministers plus Granville and Molesworth, but opposed by Russell, Lansdowne, Clarendon, Wood and the Lord Chancellor. Palmerston, according to Gladstone, had not spoken decidedly before leaving for Windsor.[5] In the end, however, Gladstone's proposals were adopted.[6] He described them in a memorandum for the queen, which indicated that the proposed bill would provide that:

(1) Candidates for those grades in the Civil Service to which appointment takes place in youth with a view to succession, will be examined in groups; the examinations being open to all qualified persons.

(2) A number corresponding with the number of vacancies will be selected by the examiners according to merit.

(3) The Chief of each Department will fill the vacancies in his office by choice from among the successful candidates.

(4) First appointments to offices being thus regulated, promotion will thereafter be given by the Chiefs of Departments according to merit, as estimated by them, not as usually now by the dead rule of seniority.

---

[1] Morley, *Gladstone*, p. 511, quoting his earlier letter, misleadingly asserts that Russell replied 'curtly'.   [2] Add. MS. 44291, fols. 117–19, 20 January 1854.
[3] PRO 30/22/11/C, fol. 669, 23 January 1854.
[4] *E.H.R.* LXIV, 71.   [5] Add. MS. 44778, fol. 157, memo. 107, 26 January 1854.
[6] *Ab. Cor. 1854–5*, p. 17, Aberdeen to Queen Victoria, 26 January 1854.

The examination, which was for the first grade, was to carry a right of succession to higher grades. Examinations would be held 'for groups of vacancies, having duties of an homogeneous character'. Heads of Departments would select the man they wanted from among the successful candidates.[1]

The queen, although expressing misgivings, gave her sanction to the plan, 'trusting that Mr Gladstone will do what he can, in the arrangements of the details of it, to guard against the dangers' which were inherent in it. Gladstone assured Her Majesty that in the nature of things the diligent student was normally one of character and virtue, but he promised that the strictest enquiries would be made as to character in the selection of candidates.[2]

As soon as he heard of the cabinet's approval, Trevelyan proceeded to draw up a bill which he sent to Gladstone on 10 February, and at the same time, with Gladstone's approval, he prepared for publication a volume of reports on public establishments, including their own general report together with Jowett's proposals for its application.[3]

In anticipation of the publication of the report Trevelyan wrote to Delane of *The Times* enclosing a copy of it. He said that they must expect opposition since 'there can be no doubt that our high aristocracy have been accustomed to employ the Civil Establishments as a means of providing for the waifs and strays of their Families—as a sort of Foundling Hospital, 'where those who had not energy to make their way in the open professions...might receive nominal office, but real Pension, for life, at the expense of the Public'.

The Dukes of Norfolk, for instance [he continued], have provided for their illegitimate children in this manner generation after generation. There are still several of them in the Public Service, & one of them is the most notorious idler and jobber in it.

I trust to your discretion and good feeling to respect the line I have hitherto taken on this subject; and although it is right that you should know these things, I hope that you will handle them delicately, so as not unnecessarily to wound private feeling.

He also argued that the proposed reform would improve the character of the House of Commons 'both by the diminution of interested motives to get into the House and by the great curtailment afterwards of the

[1] Add. MS. 44743, fols. 132–5 (*E.H.R.* LXIV, 63–4).
[2] *Letters of Queen Victoria*, III, 12–14, 17 February 1854.
[3] *E.H.R.* LXIV, 81–3, 208.

interested motives which at present induce members to give a blind support to the government, and the consequent necessity governments will be under of purchasing support by the excellence of their measures'.[1]

The impropriety of a civil servant communicating in these terms to a newspaper editor apparently did not occur to this self-opinionated man. There is no indication that Gladstone had released him from his promise of 18 January to take the most effective steps in his power 'to prevent any further discussion of the *plan* in the newspapers'.[2] At any rate Delane wasted no time in producing a leader on 9 February that showed he was fully in the confidence of the government, for he wrote in the most categorical terms about what the proposed reforms would do. His tone was quite as scathing as Trevelyan's own. While he admitted that the worst sinecures had disappeared, he asserted that the civil service was 'a relic of the world which preceded the Reform Bill'. The leader continued:

Incapacity, indifference, and idleness are reported to be the characteristics of a body appointed chiefly through private interest or political venality...; whether so corrupt a tree is likely to bear good fruit we leave to common sense to determine.

It is one of the greatest evils about this system that its defects do not attract observation...; it vegetates under the deadening influence of seniority.

Nothing less is purposed than the creation of a new liberal profession, as freely opened to all, as the church, the bar or the hospital.[3]

One senior officer in Trevelyan's own department, George Arbuthnot, auditor of the civil list, strongly protested to the Chancellor about *The Times* leader, saying that the editor in answer to an inquiry alleged that the words 'incapacity, indifference, neglected duties & supercilious demeanors' used to describe the attitude of existing civil servants were Trevelyan's and not his. Arbuthnot strongly criticised Trevelyan's action, saying:

I wish that, instead of beginning with the external agitation, the internal organization of the Departments had first been looked into in an impartial manner, and with the aid of those who have had long experience of the working of the details of the public Service. Our own office needs such a

[1] Add. MS. 44333, fols. 138–41, 6 February 1854 (*E.H.R.* LVIV, 84–6).
[2] Add. MS. 44333, fol. 97, 18 January 1854. This was not the first time that Trevelyan had been guilty of such indiscretion. See G. Kitson Clark, *Hist. J.* II, 30–1.
[3] *The Times*, 9 February 1854.

revision more than any other, and I have no hesitation in saying that whatever 'incapacity, indifference and idleness' may be found among the Clerks of the Treasury is due rather to the inherent vices of our departmental system than to defect in the mode in which selections for first appointments are made.[1]

On the next day Gladstone granted Arbuthnot an interview and, according to the latter, told him that he had disapproved the agitation in the public press in favour of the report.[2] A month later Arbuthnot complained again to Gladstone, indicating that Trevelyan had broken the Chancellor's injunction by printing and distributing a pamphlet containing insulting remarks with respect to all civil servants whose views differed from his, 'and thus', Arbuthnot wrote, 'the Officer who undertakes the work of reforming the Civil Service sets the example of violating the first duty of a Servant of the Crown—obedience'.[3] It is unknown whether Gladstone expostulated with Sir Charles, but he remained in sympathy with his views.

The report was presented to parliament on 24 February as well as the reports of the committees that had enquired into the various public offices.[4]

The Times welcomed the report with another friendly editorial,[5] but elsewhere the reaction was unfavourable. Macaulay found opinion very hostile at Brooks's and, indeed, was much alarmed on his brother-in-law's account. 'He has been too sanguine', Macaulay recorded in his diary. 'The pear is not ripe. I always thought so.' Trevelyan's son (and Macaulay's biographer) writes that his father was much mortified and had cause to be alarmed, for his career was seriously threatened, but in the end he weathered the storm. He was not the man easily to give into the storm and canvassed with Gladstone ways and means of cultivating public opinion.[6] He made the best of it, observing to Gladstone that the opposition came for the most part from 'the existing corps of civil servants' and 'the old established Political Families'.[7] There was, of course, some support from individuals whose opinions were of signifi-

---

[1] *E.H.R.* LXIV, 207–8. [2] *Ibid.* p. 222. [3] *Ibid.*

[4] *P.P. 1854* (1713) (1715), XXVII, 'Report on the organization of the permanent civil service; together with a letter from Rev. B. Jowett', pp. 1–31; 'Reports of committees of inquiry into public offices and papers connected therewith', pp. 1–363. The main report was reprinted in the latter collection.

[5] *The Times*, 24 February 1854.

[6] G. O. Trevelyan, *Life and letters of Lord Macaulay* (London, 1908 ed.), p. 612.

[7] *E.H.R.* LXIV, 210–11.

cance, such as the Dean of Hereford, Dr Jeune and Professor Thompson of Oxford, John Ball, M.P. for Carlow, John Wood, Chairman of the Board of Inland Revenue, Major Graham, Sir James's brother and Registrar General, and others.[1]

The project was evidently still alive on 4 March when Northcote wrote to ask Gladstone when he wanted a draft of the Civil Service Bill. Gladstone asked to have it the following week, but that is the last we hear of the matter in 1854. The opposition was too strong to press it under the circumstances of the moment, and Northcote, for one, was all against any compromise measure.[2]

The question was first raised in parliament by Lord Monteagle, who moved in the House of Lords for a copy of the instructions given the commissioners and of the evidence taken before them.[3] In speaking to the motion he vigorously attacked the report. He claimed that the members of the English civil service had been grossly and unjustly maligned and that no evidence had been produced to substantiate the charges in the report, other than a letter from a Balliol tutor who could not be expected to know much about the duties of 16,000 civil servants, a number which the speaker considered grossly inflated.[4] With some reason Monteagle denounced the inquiry as incomplete, since there was no evidence that the major departments of state had been examined. He also scoffed at the proposed system of entrance by examination, wittily comparing it to the Chinese system, which he described at length. 'Do not, then, let this Report go forth uncontradicted,' he appealed to his hearers; 'not merely because it is an attack upon the Gentlemen of the Civil Service of England, but because it is an attack, also, upon the social state of our country with which that Civil Service is connected, and of which, to a certain extent, it may be considered as the representative.'[5]

Lord Granville made a lame reply, acknowledging that no written evidence was taken by the commissioners, mildly repeating their case, and citing the support of such eminent public servants as Sir James Stephen, Mr John Wood and 'Mr John Mill, of the India House, who was not only a great philosophical writer, but one of the most able administrators of the day'. He concluded by arguing that the proposed

---

[1] *Ibid.* pp. 206–34.

[2] Add. MS. 44216, fols. 224–5, 23 January 1854; fols. 250–1, 4 March 1854; fols. 254–7, 10 November 1854.

[3] *Hansard*, CXXXI, 640–55.

[4] A subsequent return showed that half of them were post office employees.

[5] *Hansard*, CXXXI, 654.

reform would only 'do justice to some of the best members of the Civil Service', and that it would give 'a most powerful stimulus to education in all classes of the community'.[1]

Lord Brougham said that he had met no one except Lord Granville who took the proposed reform seriously and he did not think that they were 'likely to hear much more about it'. He was particularly sarcastic at the proposal to interpose an independent examiner between a head of a department and his clerks. On this point he concluded:

It was his wish that the schoolmaster should be kept to his own proper functions; and, although he had at some former time and somewhere else expressed his high gratification 'the schoolmaster was abroad'—a phrase that had become somewhat popular—yet he was afraid he should now, if plans like this for making the schoolmaster depart from his proper province, and encroach upon provinces with which he had nothing to do, were to be adopted, feel inclined to wish that the schoolmaster might go home again.[2]

Lord Harrowby thought that 'the plan, so far as it had been indicated, was based upon a noble and generous principle' and 'he did not think his noble and learned Friend, who had contributed so largely towards sending the schoolmaster abroad, should, after having seen the proofs of his labours, wish to call him back to his home again'.[3] Lord Clanricarde briefly protested against what the report said about the civil servants and claimed that in his experience at the Foreign Office he did not think 'a more able, a more efficient, or a more honourable body of men' were to be found anywhere in the world.[4] He denied that there was any comparison between the cases of the Indian and the English civil services, but the duke of Argyll insisted that there was an analogy. The duke knew the plan 'would be received with very great reluctance by powerful parties—by those who had been, or those who hoped to be, connected with public office and with the exercise of patronage...; but against the reluctance of official people he believed it would force its way on its own merits, and, either under the auspices of this Government or of some future Government, some such plan would be adopted'.[5] No Derbyite participated in the debate.

Nothing was said on the subject in the House of Commons until 5 May when in answer to a question Gladstone announced that the

[1] *Hansard*, CXXXI, 655–62. A few days later, unfortunately, he had to admit that he was mistaken as to Stephen's opinion (*ibid.* 764).　　[2] *Ibid.* 662–5.
[3] *Ibid.* 665–6.　　　　　[4] *Ibid.* 666–7.　　　　　[5] *Ibid.* 668.

government had abandoned the hope of introducing a bill that year since it had become clear that there would not be the opportunity of giving it proper consideration. He assured the House, however, that the government had by no means abandoned its plans as announced in the speech from the throne.[1]

For the present the Treasury contented itself with gathering opinions of various experts in the field of public service and of education, which were ultimately published in a blue-book, along with the original report, some further comments of Northcote and Trevelyan on the proposed examination system, a statistical table indicating the numbers presently engaged in various categories of the public service, and a letter of protest from George Arbuthnot, auditor of the civil list, to the Lords of the Treasury.[2]

In all thirty-nine people responded to the requests for comments and it may be said that some of their observations were as interesting and deserving of attention as the original report. Edwin Chadwick characteristically wrote his own report of eighty-five pages (compared to the twenty-one of the original) plus seven pages of appendices, but it was a turgid and obscure paper compared with some of the others which rivalled the original in clarity of expression and sharpness of ideas.[3] The

---

[1] *Ibid.* CXXXII, 1305–7.

[2] 'Papers relating to the reorganization of the civil service', *P.P. 1854–5*, 1870, XX, pp. 1–474. Appendix I (p. 439) includes the following information taken from the 1851 census:

Heads of Departments	105	⎫
Secretaries & Chief Clerks	190	⎪
Officers employed in special capacities	378	⎬ 6,500
Heads of subordinate divisions, librarians, etc.	1,893	⎪
Clerks, on establishment	3,476	⎪
Clerks, extra or temporary	506	⎭
Others employed on special duty	11,267	
Office keepers, messengers, porters, etc.	3,867	
Inferior revenue officers, postmen, etc.	17,465	
	39,147	
Workmen in dockyards & naval arsenals	14,531	
	53,678	

Of the 'others employed on special duty' 7,892 were postmasters, etc., many of whom were part-time employees. The figures include some 4,000 postal and revenue officers residing in Ireland.

The original report was included as Appendix no. 2 with the original pagination.

[3] Especially those of R. M. Bromley, James Booth, J. S. Mill and the Dean of Carlisle.

papers of Edward Romilly, chairman of the board of audit, and Sir Thomas Fremantle, chairman of the board of customs, were also longer than the original, although Romilly's contribution consisted of a collection of papers on the subject written by him on earlier occasions and now briefly brought up to date. There is no indication in the blue-book as to the basis on which the contributions were invited and it may be noted that they were not all solicited at the same time.[1] Some of the later papers comment on the earlier ones. Eleven of the commentators may be described as academics or educators, i.e., university dons, school headmasters and in one case, a school inspector, Canon Moseley. The remaining twenty-eight were civil servants, active or retired, with the exception of William Spottiswoode, the queen's printer, and John Stuart Mill of the East India Company, who were both men of great practical experience in this field. Sir James Stephen is included with the civil servants although he was now retired from the Colonial Office and Professor of Modern History at Cambridge. The academics, who were all clergymen, were without exception in favour of the report, although expressing occasional differences of opinion on details. Canon Moseley, for instance, did not think the report went far enough. Of these comments perhaps the most notable was from the Dean of Carlisle, a former headmaster of Rugby and fellow of Balliol, who with others dwelt on the great stimulus the proposed reforms would have on both elementary and higher education. Of the others, if we include Spottiswoode and Mill with the civil servants, twelve were generally favourable,[2] eight expressed mixed views,[3] and only eight were distinctly

[1] Two are dated January 1854, three February, fourteen March, three April, two May, two June, one July, seven August, two September, three November, one December 1854, and the rest are undated.

[2] Shaw Lefevre, Clerk Assistant of the House of Peers; Lieutenant-Colonel Larcom, Under-Secretary of the Lord Lieutenant of Ireland; Alfred Power, Chairman of Irish Poor Law Commission; John Stuart Mill; Major Graham, Registrar General; W. G. Anderson, Principal Clerk at the Treasury; R. Griffith, Chairman of the Public Works Board, Dublin; Rowland Hill, Secretary of the Post Office; John Wood, Chairman of Inland Revenue; Henry Cole and Dr Lyon Playfair, Joint Secretaries of the Science and Arts Department.

[3] R. R. Lingen, Secretary of the Committee of the Council on Education (who feared the recommendations were not compatible with the facts of political life); Sir G. C. Lewis, former Poor Law Commissioner and now editor of the *Edinburgh Review*; James Booth, Secretary to the Board of Trade (who wrote an excellent paper, favouring more discretion to the Department); Edwin Chadwick (who strongly supported the principle of competitive examination, but suggested that it had been largely adopted in the new branches of the service, where patronage no longer governed);

hostile.[1] Only five took objection to the strong indictment of the existing service. Those expressing mixed views tended to agree with the general aim of the Report, but expressed doubts or objections with regard to the idea of open competitive examinations. They would prefer a system of closed examinations to test those who had been nominated in the usual way. Some of the critics pointed out that there was much more of this actually in practice than the Report allowed, while the sympathisers to the Report argued that such limited examinations were unrealistic. One of the most devastating criticisms came from Sir James Stephen and this must have been a great shock to Trevelyan, who on 10 March told Gladstone he had spoken to Stephen and found him 'entirely in accordance' with their views.[2] Stephen Merivale, Murdoch and Spearman all made the point that there were not sufficient opportunities in the service to induce the best university graduates to compete for entrance. One unsolicited, but vehement, criticism of the Report (and of its being divulged to the editor of *The Times* before publication) came from George Arbuthnot. This letter was published with the others on Arbuthnot's agreeing to withdraw a demand for a committee to inquire into the allegations made in the Report.[3] Northcote and Trevelyan answered it with a joint letter in which they expressed their regret that the language of their Report had occasioned any painful feelings and even admitted that it was an error on their part that they had not expressed more distinctly their awareness of the merits of the service, which they had tended to take for granted, since their commission was rather to discover and propose remedies for its defects. The charges about *The Times* were brushed aside rather unconvincingly.[4]

The coalition had fallen before any action was taken on the Report; by that time Sir George Cornewall Lewis, one of the compromising commentators, had succeeded Gladstone as Chancellor of the

---

Edward Romilly, Chairman of the Board of Audit; Sir Thomas Fremantle, Chairman of the Board of Customs; Rt. Hon. H. H. Addington, late Under-Secretary of State for Foreign Affairs (who suggested some interesting alternative proposals based on practice in the Foreign Office).

[1] Sir James Stephen (who held that the indictment only applied to half the civil service); Sir T. Redington, Permanent Secretary of the Board of Control; T. W. Murdoch, Chairman of the Emigration Board; Herman Merivale, Under-Secretary of State for the Colonial Department; Benjamin Hawes, Deputy Secretary of War; H. Waddington, Under-Secretary for the Home Department; Sir A. Y. Spearman, Comptroller General of the National Debt Office.

[2] Add. MS. 44333, fol. 264.

[3] *E.H.R.* LXIV, 216.

[4] *P.P. 1854-5*, XX, 413-22.

Exchequer, and so the proposals for open competitive examinations were then abandoned until fifteen years later, when they were eventually adopted, with Gladstone First Lord of the Treasury.[1]

The Oxford University Reform Bill

Gladstone's other major attempt at reform in 1854 was more successful and indeed absorbed far more of his energies than the abortive civil service scheme. Although the latter had his full blessing and support, its real inspiration came from Trevelyan and to a lesser extent Northcote, but the Oxford Reform Bill, while introduced by Russell, was mainly Gladstone's handiwork. He had not, however, always been the champion of reform at Oxford, where the work had been begun by others.

The movement went back more than a decade. Indeed Jowett's biographers and C. E. Mallet[2] trace it back to the publication of articles by Sir William Hamilton in the *Edinburgh Review* in the year 1831. Several proposed reforms were brought before the oligarchic Hebdomadal Board, but without success. Pamphlets on the subject were published in 1839 by the senior tutor of Balliol, A. C. Tait, the future archbishop (with the help of A. P. Stanley, fellow of University College, and later dean of Westminster), and in 1848 by Jowett, who had followed Tait as a tutor at Balliol. In 1847 Jowett wrote to Roundell Palmer (whom he considered 'half an M.P. for the University of Oxford'), telling him of the interest of men such as Clough, Lake, Lingen, Temple, Stanley, Arnold and himself in the subject of university reform and their desire that Palmer should take the matter up in parliament. 'They seemed to think,' Jowett wrote, 'and I heartily agree, that for many reasons, the subject would be far better in your hands than in those of Gladstone.'[3]

Palmer was sympathetic, but declined on the grounds that the oath he had once taken as a fellow of Magdalen precluded his doing so. A Radical, Heywood, however, raised the matter in the Commons in

---

[1] For some penetrating comments on the historical significance of the Northcote–Trevelyan report see G. Kitson Clark, 'Statesmen in disguise', *Hist. J.* II (1959), 19–39.

[2] *A history of the University of Oxford* (London, 1937), III, 290–2. For a full account of the background of the Oxford Reform Bill see Ward, *Victorian Oxford*, chs. V to VIII, published since this section was written.

[3] E. Abbott and L. Campbell, *Life and letters of Benjamin Jowett* (London, 1897), I, 188–92; see also 172–7.

1850 and Russell's subsequent appointment of a royal commission of enquiry was welcomed by the Oxford reformers. Although distinctly liberal in complexion and opposed by the old guard of heads of colleges who dominated the Hebdomadal Board, the commission was a strong one calculated to inspire respect. It included such men as Dr Hinds, bishop of Norwich (the chairman), Tait, now dean of Carlisle, and Dr Jeune, the master of Pembroke; and had for its secretaries Arthur Stanley and Goldwin Smith.[1]

Gladstone made an unhappy attack in parliament on the appointment of the commission. Of his speech on that occasion Morley has commented:

In truth no worse case was ever more strongly argued, and fortunately the speech is to be recorded as the last manifesto, on a high theme and on a broad scale, of that toryism from which this wonderful pilgrim had started on his shining progress.[2]

When the commission reported two years later Gladstone was shaken by its arguments, but even more by the evidence supporting it. He urged his Oxford friends to begin immediately to set their own house in order, but another year passed by with nothing done. Gladstone was now in office and the government committed to the cause of educational reform. The issue was no longer to be shirked and what member of the government was better equipped to undertake it than himself, a representative of the university in parliament and one of its most brilliant and devoted graduates.

It was Russell, of course, who had first appointed the commission in 1850, which Gladstone had opposed, and it was not unnaturally in Russell's name that the Oxford bill was introduced. From the beginning, however, the real inspiration came from Gladstone, and the bill was his handiwork. As early as 2 April 1853 while in the midst of preparations for his great budget—he produced a memorandum on wine duties on the same day—he listed what he considered were the main objects that the government should pursue in respect to Oxford Reform. These were: provision for the adequate representation of the teaching body as distinct from the colleges, the opening of fellowships, etc.,

---

[1] For its work and reaction to it see R. T. Davidson and W. Benham, *Life of Archibald Campbell Tait* (London, 1891), I, 158–74; Mallet, *University of Oxford*, III, 298–317; Ward, *Victorian Oxford*, ch. VI; A. I. Tillyard, *A history of university reform* (Cambridge, 1913), ch. VI.

[2] Morley, *Gladstone*, I, 498.

to more effective competition, provision of college endowment for university instruction, and the 'further introduction of students into the University'.[1]

In December in the midst of the Cabinet Reform Bill crisis and with Eastern affairs at a crucial stage Gladstone wrote to Russell on the subject of Oxford Reform. He dwelt on the undesirability of compulsion and the difficulty of working out all the details of Reform in a parliamentary bill. On the other hand he recognised that the proposals of the Hebdomadal Board (heads of colleges and proctors) were quite unacceptable. Instead he proposed the appointment of a statutory commission with considerable powers of calling for information and sanctioning university enactments or proposals of colleges for modifications of their statutes. He suggested some names of men who would both be in general agreement with the government programme and inspire confidence in residents and fellows of colleges. As to his own position he went on:

My own personal difficulties in the matter are very considerable. One of the first & weightiest things to be done is greatly to narrow the powers of the Board of Heads—but the majority of the Heads have been the nucleus and the soul of the opposition to me at three contests during the last six years. It ill becomes me therefore to be their executioner. But these are not matters with which the Government need be troubled.[2]

On this personal question as to whether he should resign his Oxford seat in view of the anticipated legislation he consulted the faithful Northcote. The latter responded with strong reasons against resignation. Gladstone was doing what he considered best for the university and there was no reason to think that his clients would not take the same view. The subject of university reform had been under discussion for some time and was indeed a factor in Gladstone's election. The reformers looked upon Gladstone as their champion and his return was due to their efforts. They were powerless to bring the matter to a head in the university because the initiative lay in the hands of their opponents. Northcote dismissed Gladstone's scruples in acting against the heads of colleges. 'A member elected by the anti-hebdomadal interest, need not

[1] Add. MS. 44742, fols. 3-4, 2 April 1853.
[2] PRO 30/22/11/B, fols. 488-92, 14 December 1853. For the development of the views of the tutors on the one hand and the heads of colleges on the other see Ward, *Victorian Oxford*, ch. IX.

quit his post because he takes part in an anti-hebdomadal measure', he wrote. University Reform was of such paramount importance to Gladstone and his constituents that Northcote assured him that they would stick by him even if the government also brought in some unpopular measure such as Parliamentary Reform. By 'they' he meant those who like himself had 'had uncomfortable crotchets about Conservatism and the Coalition, and cannot clear their minds of them'. Personally, however, he had such strong confidence in Gladstone that he was prepared to prefer Gladstone's judgment to his own.[1]

In the meantime, Gladstone had proceeded with the sketch of a bill,[2] which he sent to Russell on 19 December, saying that the names of the commissioners would be all-important. 'It would be a very mild and with the bulk of the University a very acceptable measure', he wrote, 'were you *simply* to appoint a Commission with power to inquire, & to sanction schemes for the improvement of College Statutes; & to let other matters stand over would certainly relieve me personally from an invidious position.' But he reluctantly had to admit that duty required that they do something to settle the two questions of '*University Government* and *University Extension*, both of which', he said, 'I believe are perfectly ripe and require little of detail'.[3]

A few days later Gladstone discussed his ideas with Jowett, who produced a draft bill of his own, which was centred on a reorganisation of the Hebdomadal Board; it was to consist of the Vice-Chancellor and twenty-four members, eight elected by heads of colleges, eight by professors, and eight by tutors. The main power of government would remain with this reorganised Board but other clauses provided for the reform of regulations governing fellowships and scholarships and the abolition of clerical sinecures.[4] Gladstone sent both Jowett's draft and his own to the Solicitor General and proposed to circulate them to members of the council committee on education, but he told Russell that he stuck to his own draft.[5] Gladstone also circulated letters from Jowett defending his own plan and criticising Gladstone's. The latter refuted the objections to a commission on the grounds that it was a question of necessity rather than policy to soften parliamentary opposition.

[1] Add. MS. 44216, fols. 210–13, 18 December 1853.
[2] Add. MS. 44742, fols. 199–233.
[3] PRO 30/22/11/B, fols. 520–1.   [4] Add. MS. 44743, fols. 1–18.
[5] PRO 30/22/11/C, fols. 614–15, 7 January 1854.

He argued that according to the opinion of all Oxford men whom he had consulted, the oaths against changing statutes would inhibit certain colleges from taking any initiative.[1] Gladstone also showed his proposals to Northcote, who commented on them at length, but rather critically. He regarded the commission as an evil, but possibly a necessary one, and urged that its powers should be restricted as much as possible.[2] Gladstone forwarded the letter to Russell, magnanimously calling it 'an acute and helpful discussion of our Oxford schemes'. He doubted whether the Crown should be substituted for a commission as Northcote suggested, but agreed that the commission's discretion should be carefully restricted.[3]

On being informed of the government's intention to bring in an Oxford bill, the authorities of the university finally bestirred themselves to take action that they had neglected for the past four years. The Chancellor, Lord Derby, wrote to the Home Secretary asking the government to suspend action pending the presentation of counter-proposals. An emergency meeting of convocation was called at five days notice and by a majority of 373 to 212 approval was given to these proposals, which envisaged the repeal of three Caroline statutes and the setting up of a new Hebdomadal Board. This action was strenuously opposed by the majority of the resident fellows, but the outside voters carried the day. Eighty of those opposed publicly proclaimed their dissent.[4]

The Times sharply criticised this attempt to block reform, pointing out that the very authorities who needed to be reformed were those responsible for the opposition to it. 'Both Oxford and Cambridge are now governed by "Heads of Houses"', the leader asserted. 'The main object of the proposed reforms...is the substitution of a constitutional or representative government for government by Heads.'[5]

The government firmly resisted the Oxford proposals. Gladstone drafted a reply to be sent by the Home Secretary to Lord Derby's letter in which he said that the government was reluctant to entrust 'all administrative and interpretative functions' to the present Board, 'which is composed in the proportion of 24 members to 2 of a single

[1] Add. MS. 44743, fols. 119–20, 12 January 1854.
[2] Add. MS. 44216, fols. 214–21, 13 January 1854.
[3] PRO 30/22/11/C, fol. 640, 16 January 1854.
[4] The list of names is published in *The Times*, 25 February 1854, with an account of the meeting.
[5] *Ibid.* 27 February 1854.

though justly respected & highly important class'. Lord Derby was told that the government conceived it 'absolutely essential' to obtain 'a substantive and considerable share of representation' for professors 'who may be held as a body to represent the University as apart from the Colleges'.[1]

Gladstone carried on an extensive correspondence about details of the bill with many of his constituents and with his old friend Heathcote, a moderate Conservative who had now succeeded Inglis as the other member for Oxford University.[2]

The bill in its final form was an extensive measure, which may be summarised thus:

It was proposed to replace the old Hebdomadal Board, which the evidence presented to the royal commission demonstrated to have been most unsuitably constituted, by a new Hebdomadal Council of 24 or 25 members. These were to include the Vice-Chancellor, the two proctors, six heads of colleges, six professors and six tutors elected by the congregation, as well as a seventh head and a seventh professor appointed by the Vice-Chancellor and the retiring Vice-Chancellor when not otherwise elected. Congregation itself was to be reconstructed to include all resident members of the teaching staff and given increased powers. The extension of the student body of the university was to be provided for by the establishment of private halls, which it was hoped might effect some economy for prospective new students. Outdated restrictions on fellowships and scholarships had often resulted in very ordinary men being preferred to others more distinguished, and many fellowships had been held by men no longer in residence. Consequently fellowships and scholarships with a few exceptions were to be thrown open to competition and in all cases examinations were to precede appointment. Normally fellows would be required to reside at Oxford. The bill sought to combine the advantages of the tutorial system associated with the colleges with that of the professorial system under university guidance by providing for additional contributions to professorial stipends from college funds. It also prohibited the imposition of oaths on fellows which inhibited their freedom to initiate changes in their statutes. Finally, it provided for the appointment of

[1] Add. MS. 44743, fols. 143–9, 16 February 1854, a draft in Gladstone's hand of a letter from the Home Secretary to Lord Derby, with a covering note initialed W.E.G.
[2] Add. MS. 44208, fols. 49–109. The frequent interchange of letters with Heathcote reveal some differences of opinion, but a basic understanding.

parliamentary commissioners for fixed terms of office with powers to assent to and to frame statutes.[1]

On 17 March Russell introduced the bill in the House of Commons with acknowledgment of Gladstone's assistance in its preparation. In his speech he made a good case for the necessity of reforming what was a national institution. Some 300 halls of an earlier day had closed their doors and the student population declined to 1,300, which he thought a very insufficient number 'for a great national institution with a revenue of 150,000 l. a year'. Attendance at lectures languished and indeed some endowed lectureships were reduced to the perfunctory reading of one lecture a term, which clearly was not the intention of the founder. In their proposed reforms they would not depart from the spirit of the founders, but changes must be made *pro ratione temporis* just as they had been made in the sixteenth and seventeenth centuries. He then proceeded lucidly to outline and explain the scope of the bill and concluded by saying that the question of admitting Dissenters, to which he was personally favourable, was best left to separate consideration.[2]

Although this was only the first reading and consequently not contested, ten members rose to speak on the general principles of the bill.[3] While some were critical, nevertheless the general tone of the debate was highly satisfactory, at any rate in the view of the Chancellor of the Exchequer, who made a special plea that the subject should not be treated 'as a question of mere party politics'.[4] Several speakers on the government side (Blackett, Heywood and Miall), while not criticising the bill, regretted that it made no provision for allowing Dissenters to enter Oxford. Several on the opposition side[5] rather deprecated the need for compulsory legislation, but their tone was not unreasonable, given the sensitive nature of the topic. Roundell Palmer, a former fellow and a strong churchman, welcomed the bill, especially the proposals with respect to the revision of the university constitution, which he defended against the arguments of the critics.

According to *The Times*, which itself welcomed the bill, it was well received outside parliament as well as in. Noting that the existing authorities at Oxford had promoted a petition against the bill, *The Times* derided the idea of these oligarchs reforming themselves and

---

[1] PRO 30/22/11/C, fols. 843–6, 9 March 1854—a précis of the bill prepared by Gladstone, which was developed by Russell in the House of Commons, *Hansard*, CXXXI, 892–911.

[2] *Hansard*, CXXXI, 892–911.   [3] *Ibid.* 911–55.

[4] *Ibid.* 943.   [5] Walpole, Henley, and Heathcote.

pronounced that the government had acted wisely in interfering to promote the good government of the university, which was 'now monopolized by a certain class of College officers, to the utter exclusion of every other academical element, and to the destruction of all those principles on which constitutional administration is based'.[1]

When the bill came up for a second reading before a small house on 7 April, the debate remained on a high plane. Sir William Heathcote set the tone by announcing that he accepted the principle of the bill and consequently would vote for its second reading in the hope that in committee he might obtain alterations to those features of it to which he objected. He was acutely aware of the necessity of a speedy settlement of the matter and he admitted that the names of the commissioners announced by the government 'were, in his opinion, a guarantee not only that the powers to be entrusted to them would be administered in a friendly spirit; but also that the Bill conferring those powers had been framed with no hostile disposition, and that it ought to be criticised in a spirit of fairness'.[2]

Sir John Pakington was rather more critical, but said that after considerable doubt and hesitation he had decided not to oppose the second reading. He abstained from making the measure one of party conflict and hoped that the government would accept criticism in fair part.[3] Henley took a somewhat similar tone,[4] but more outright opposition was expressed by Lord Robert Cecil, making his maiden speech in the sharp, uncompromising manner that was to characterise his orations for the rest of the century.[5] Five of the fourteen members who participated in the debate were Peelites. Of these Roundell Palmer, R. J. Phillimore and G. E. H. Vernon were all sympathetic, Palmer at considerable length;[6] old Goulburn contented himself, as member for Cambridge, with arguing that the proposals were not applicable to Cambridge.[7] Gladstone again expressed his satisfaction with the tone of the discussion. 'Without a single exception', he said, 'that discussion has been conducted on the part of those belonging to Oxford in a tone of affectionate attachment and veneration for the place which is well deserved; and with respect to those who do not belong to Oxford, with a seriousness and calmness of consideration, and an entire freedom from any reference to party politics, which likewise eminently distinguished

---

[1] *The Times*, 30 March 1854.   [2] *Hansard*, CXXXII, 673.
[3] *Ibid.* 682–94.   [4] *Ibid.* 742–9.   [5] *Ibid.* 711–14.
[6] *Ibid.* 723–42.   [7] *Ibid.* 749–53.

other speakers.' Complimenting Cecil on his maiden speech, he gently reprimanded him for lacking faith in the Commons whom he had just joined:

For when the noble lord speaks of the levity and precipitancy with which majorities of this House deal with great interests and great institutions of this country—when he tells us we have one year a Ministry of the highest Toryism, and another year a Ministry of the lowest point of Radicalism— when he says that the majority of this House is no more than a weathercock, swayed by every passing breeze—I venture to promise him that his future practical acquaintance with the constitution conducted within these walls, where I trust he will long remain, will give him in a short time, I doubt not, a better opinion of the British House of Commons.[1]

And so, it may be observed incidentally, the tone of the debate between these two great Englishmen was set for the next forty years.

The subsequent stages of the bill presented heavier going. A motion to send it to a select committee, which would probably have meant its postponement for at least another year, received support from both Radicals, who thought it did not go far enough, and Tories, who wanted no change. The debate on this motion was notable for a bitter attack by John Bright, speaking as one of those classes 'who have been purposely excluded from any enjoyment of the advantages of the institution to which this Bill refers', a bill which he described as of a 'pusillanimous and tinkering character'.[2] Disraeli, who showed no great interest in an institution that he had never attended, did his best to belittle the bill.[3] In particular, he made fun of the attempt to blow up the office of the professor in the German pattern, saying that the only reason that professors were such great people in Germany was that the Germans had no such beneficent an institution as the British parliament to attract the first-class brains of their country and that the professorial chair was the only goal for the gifted German citizen to aim at. The man who in Germany would hold a professorial chair in England would occupy a cabinet post.

Why, Sir [he continued, warming to the theme], you had the whole ability of the country devoted to politics; and if we have not these profound professors in England, it is because the character of this country is different; the character of our life is contrary to it. We are a nation of action, and you may depend upon it that, however you may increase the rewards of professors—

[1] *Hansard*, CXXXII, 755.   [2] *Ibid.* 978–83.   [3] *Ibid.* 967–77.

though you may give them 2,000 l. instead of 200 l.—ambition in England will look to public life—men will look to the House of Commons, and not to professors' chairs in the universities.[1]

Nevertheless the government survived this division with a majority of 82 in a House of 262.[2] The bill was less fortunate in committee, for the detail of its many clauses was subject to endless debate and the possibilities of amendment seemed inexhaustible. A great many of the amendments were proposed by two friends of Gladstone, like him intensely interested in the fortunes of the university, of whom one was a representative and the other a former fellow. Both Heathcote and Roundell Palmer were independent Conservatives; indeed Palmer, as we have seen, may be described as a Peelite; and neither pressed his endless arguments for mere purposes of party politics. The debate between them on the one hand and Gladstone on the other remained on a high level, but harsher opposition was also raised by more straight-laced Tories.

The committee stage lasted for nine sittings between 1 May and 22 June with the result that on 1 June, with only 28 out of 58 clauses passed, the government announced its intention of reducing the remaining 30 clauses to 14, abandoning some of the controversial clauses designed to reform the colleges but giving the commissioners powers to institute such reforms.[3] Several amendments were accepted by the government and several more withdrawn or negatived without a formal vote, but fifteen were pressed to divisions, of which the government survived eleven and was defeated on four. One of these hostile amendments, moved by Walpole from the opposition front bench, provided for sectional election to the Hebdomadal Council (i.e. heads to elect heads, professors professors, etc.); this severe restriction was passed by 162 to 149,[4] but was reversed in the House of Lords, and when the bill came back to the Commons the government managed to maintain the Lords' reversal. Another hostile amendment, moved by Heathcote, broadening the membership of Congregation by extending it to all resident members of the university, was passed by 138 to 104,[5] while another, moved as an additional clause by Palmer designed to protect

[1] *Ibid.* 970.   [2] *Ibid.* 987. There is no division list.
[3] *Ibid.* CXXXIII, 1212–13.
[4] *Ibid.* CXXXII, 1163–5. The 24 Peelites in the House supported the government, as did 15 independent Conservatives including Heathcote. Three ministers, Graham, Herbert and Wood, were absent.   [5] *Ibid.* CXXXIII, 199–200.

scholarships awarded from certain schools, was passed by 160 to 108.[1] These amendments were all conservative in that they were designed to limit or restrict the scope of the bill, but one most important change was forced from the government side of the House when the Radical Heywood moved that Dissenters should be allowed entrance into the university by abandoning the requirement of assenting to the Thirty-nine Articles on matriculation. Herbert and, later, Russell and Gladstone all opposed this amendment, not on principle—Herbert made it clear that he was sympathetic to the claims of the Dissenters and Russell that he strongly supported them—but on the grounds that such an addition would endanger the whole bill in the Upper House. It was argued that under its new constitution the university would have the opportunity to initiate this reform itself and that if this was not done it might be made matter for later legislation. The Conservatives were now on the defensive and had to fall back on the arguments that religion could not be divorced from education, that the Anglican church was still the national church, and that to allow in Dissenters was to expose young men to the dangers of Romanism, which would then be preached with impunity. Nevertheless, the liberal spirit on this occasion carried the day: the government's backbenches, plus Irish and independent Conservative votes, defeated the ministers and the Tories by a decisive vote of 252 to 161.[2] With such a majority under his belt Heywood then proceeded to move a second clause waiving any oaths or subscriptions to any persons taking degrees in arts, law or medicine at Oxford, but this was defeated by a vote of 196 to 205.[3] Those who changed their vote apparently did so because the second clause would have the effect of making Dissenters full members of the university and consequently participants in its government. On the third reading, however, Heywood introduced a modified version of this clause simply admitting Dissenters to the degree of B.A. and this was passed with the support of the government by a vote of 233 to 79.[4] A government amendment on the third reading was defeated by 139 to 129 and the bill was finally passed in its truncated form on 29 June.[5]

Many of the proposed regulations governing college fellowships and the diversion of revenues to university professorships contained in earlier drafts of the bill were left to the new university government to

---

[1] *Hansard*, CXXXIV, 303.
[2] *Ibid.* 585–8. There were seven Peelites in the majority.
[3] *Ibid.* 590–2. [4] *Ibid.* 891–3. [5] *Ibid.* 909–11.

inaugurate under the supervision of the commissioners, whose powers, guarded as they were, became the saving grace of the bill as a reform measure.

The bill fared well in the House of Lords, despite continuous criticism from Lord Derby, speaking both as leader of the opposition and as chancellor of the university.[1] The government's case was admirably presented by Lord Canning,[2] assisted by the duke of Newcastle, and the divisions all went in the government's favour. Only two clauses were pressed to division, clause 27 authorising the opening of private halls, which was sustained by 109 to 76,[3] and clause 45, waiving the oaths that had debarred Dissenters from the B.A. degree, which was passed by 73 to 47.[4] Two opposition amendments were defeated by votes of 77 to 64 and 99 to 72.[5] Several minor amendments were accepted without a vote and Lord Ward's amendment restoring the power of Congregation to elect the Hebdomadal Council, which received government support, was passed by 103 to 87.[6] The third reading was passed on 13 July without a division and the bill returned to the Commons on 27 July. The rest of the Lords' amendments were accepted, with one exception objected to by the government, on which it was sustained by a vote of 130 to 70.[7] The rejected amendment was not insisted upon by the Lords and so the bill became law, receiving the royal assent on 7 August.[8]

The significance of the reforms that it initiated has been evaluated by Oxford's historian, C. E. Mallet, as follows:

The effect of these comprehensive proposals was to inaugurate a quiet revolution in Oxford life. The old oligarchical monopolies in the University and in the Colleges began to disappear. The government of both became really representative. A new vigour was infused into teaching and administration. The Professorial system was reorganized and strengthened, and to some extent endowed from College funds. The prizes of academic life were set free for competition. Vested interests, obsolete regulations, encumbering restraints were swept aside, and endowments too long indifferently applied were made available for wider uses. New University Statutes affecting some of the Professorships received the Commissioners' assent. Certain Colleges, Exeter, Queen's, Lincoln, Corpus, took the opportunity to recast their Statutes and secured for them the Commissioners' approval. But in most

---

[1] *Ibid.* 1212.　　　　　　　　　　　　　　[2] *Ibid.* 1186–1212.
[3] *Ibid.* 1351.　　　　[4] *Ibid.* 1365.　　　　[5] *Ibid.* 1312, 1330.
[6] *Ibid.* 1322.　　　　[7] *Ibid.* cxxxv, 859.　　　　[8] *Ibid.* 1318, 1361.

cases the Commissioners framed Ordinances, issued in 1857 and 1858, embodying reforms which without some measure of compulsion the Colleges might have proved unwilling to adopt.[1]

These reforms, for the most part, followed the lead given in the abandoned clauses of the bill, annulling ancient oaths, removing preferences and inequalities in the awarding of fellowships and scholarships, placing the election to fellowships on the basis of merit, in many cases removing the obligation of fellows to take orders and so on.[2] Such reforms would have made little headway under the rule of the old Hebdomadal Board, but were the natural consequence of the new system of university government instituted by the Act of 1854.

The bribery bill and other legislation

One other government measure rivalled the Oxford University Bill in time and energy consumed in debate, namely Russell's bill for the prevention of bribery and treating at elections. The survival, even the increase, of electoral corruption after the Reform Act of 1832 had been a great disappointment to parliamentary reformers and indeed a matter of some anxiety to all members of the House of Commons concerned with its integrity. In the years since 1841 various bills had been introduced on both sides of the House of Commons to meet the problem. Some had been defeated by the anti-reform majority in the House of Lords; a few had been passed, generally in an amended form, but had proved largely ineffective.[3] Thus when Russell introduced a new bill on 10 February[4] most of the speakers on that occasion expressed themselves in favour of legislation, although some felt that the proposed measure did not go far enough.

The only outright opposition came from the redoubtable Colonel Sibthorp, who denounced the measure as 'a manoeuvre got up by the Government to screen their base and cowardly policy'. He promised to 'tear away the flimsy veil, and expose them in their true colours', charging that 'the Treasury bench stunk of bribery'. He expressed his indignation at this attempt to stop him 'from performing the common

---

[1] Mallet, *History of the University of Oxford*, III, 327–8; cf. Ward, *Victorian Oxford*, chs. IX and X. [2] Mallet, pp. 328–30.
[3] See Seymour, *Electoral reform*, pp. 215–27.
[4] A second bill provided for an amendment to the law for the trial of election petitions. For Russell's speech see *Hansard*, CXXX, 412–19.

Christian duties of life', i.e. by saving a fellow creature from starving as he had done in the past and as he would do again. As for the ballot advocated by the member for Manchester (Milner Gibson), all he could say was that 'of all the dirty things in this world, of all the un-English, disgraceful things the ballot was the worst. He hoped that no constituent of the city which he represented would consent to screen himself under such a mean cloak; he certainly would not thank such a man for his vote.'[1] Nevertheless, leave was given without a division and there was no debate on the second reading. When the committee stage was moved on 3 April the government with the support of Walpole on the other side of the House, who was himself an advocate of anti-bribery legislation, resisted a motion to refer all the pending bribery and election bills to a Select Committee.[2] Once again Colonel Sibthorp expressed his indignation, saying that he had been in parliament for six and twenty years and 'was still unable to understand what bribery really and truly was'; he denounced the bill as 'an attempt to prevent a humble individual like himself from doing that which it was his duty to do in the station in life in which he was placed'. He particularly regretted the 'kind of understanding which he did not understand between the Tory and the Radical bench'. While the government were spending the whole of the secret service money in bribes a poor candidate was to be barred from the House of Commons for life for offering a glass of wine to an elector. 'Talk of the cruelty and oppression of the Emperor of Russia!' he exclaimed. 'Why the Emperor of Russia would never oppress anyone so much as the noble Lord proposed to oppress the poor voter.'[3]

The debates in committee and on the third reading were prolonged and the bill did not finally pass the House of Commons until the end of July. In all some 22 amendments were proposed and 9 additional clauses were added.[4] In the course of these protracted debates there were some 26 divisions. On the last night of the debate the government was defeated on the 37th clause, which sought to impose a very demanding declaration on every parliamentary candidate, but the bill as amended was then finally passed by 107 to 100.[5] It was necessary to obtain a

---

[1] *Ibid.* pp. 422–3.   [2] *Ibid.* cxxxii, 336–48.   [3] *Ibid.* 343–4.
[4] *Ibid.* cxxxiv and cxxxv, *passim*; see index in cxxxv.
[5] *Ibid.* cxxxv, 941–2. Commenting on the attitude of the House in passing the early readings with little opposition and making such difficulty on the third reading, Russell observed to the queen: 'The whole proceeding only shows what an uncertain body the present House of Commons is' (RA B 13, 137, 29 July 1854).

suspension of the Standing Orders of the House of Lords to have the bill considered so late in the session. To avoid controversial amendments the duke of Newcastle accepted the deletion of a clause regarding the payment of travelling expenses.[1] The bill was then returned to the Commons, where, to get acceptance of the Lords amendments, Russell was forced to agree to putting a limitation of one instead of two years on its operation, after which it was to be reconsidered.[2]

The Act as passed provided 'the first exact and complete definition of bribery'. Its most important contribution was the institution of election auditors 'to receive and scrutinize all accounts payable by candidates'.[3] Russell's original intention had been to exclude candidates found guilty of bribery from parliament for life and to disfranchise all voters found guilty of accepting bribes,[4] but the law as passed only kept such candidates out of the existing parliament; the voter found guilty of accepting a bribe was liable to a £10 fine and his vote was made void.[5] Although only of limited effect the Act was an important step towards the elimination of electoral corruption and the basis of further legislation.[6]

It is not generally realised how much relatively uncontroversial legislation parliament passes every year and this was true also for the session of 1854 when, despite sensational setbacks on certain measures, some 125 Public Acts were passed (not to mention 222 local and personal Acts of a public nature and 41 Private Acts).[7] The majority of these bills, as always, were passed with little or no debate. In this category there were two valuable measures introduced by Cardwell to extend his reforms of the previous year, a comprehensive Merchant Shipping Act, and an Act putting a final end to the old Navigation Code by opening the coastal trade to foreign ships.[8] The Merchant Shipping Act, which

---

[1] *Hansard*, CXXXV, 1370–5. He expressed his own personal dislike of the clause, which allowed some payment for travel; this understandably led one noble Lord to note the differences of opinion between cabinet ministers in the two Houses.

[2] *Ibid.* 1411–32. Lord Hotham, abetted by a Mr Hillyard, was so opposed to the acceptance of the amendment that even after it had passed he threatened to hold up the bill indefinitely by a series of motions for adjournment, but the limitation compromise was finally accepted.

[3] Seymour, *Electoral reform*, pp. 227–30. [4] *Hansard*, CXXX, 412–19.

[5] Seymour, *Electoral reform*, pp. 228–9.

[6] *Ibid.* pp. 231–3. See also G. M. Young and W. P. Handcock (eds.), *English historical documents, 1837–1874* (London, 1956), pp. 114, 145–8.

[7] See *Annual Register, 1854*, Appendix to Chronicle, pp. 441–61; *Hansard*, CXXXV, list at end of volume.

[8] There were no divisions on either bill in the Commons and only some brief discussions; see *Hansard*, CXXX, 223–55; CXXXI, 462–6; CXXXIII, 571–85; CXXXIV, 744–8.

contained 504 clauses, was a 'masterful blending of exacting detail and sound principle',[1] revealing Cardwell's great talent for minute planning that would one day produce his famous army reforms. Other legislation included an Act to enable the Canadian legislature to amend its own constitution, Acts respecting burials, public libraries, episcopal estates, local boards of health, cruelty to animals and the suppression of gaming-houses, as well as several law reforms. There were also, of course, numerous measures occasioned by the war, such as a Manning Act for the navy, an Act Governing Prizes and Bounties (that involved Graham in much correspondence with Clarendon), and an Act regulating the purchasing of clothing in the army (putting an end to the old abuse of giving the regimental colonel the profitable monopoly of outfitting his men).[2]

Unfortunately it was the legislation that failed that tended to gain more public notice and that undermined the strength of the ministry.

---

[1] Roberts, *Victorian origins of the British welfare state*, p. 147. For a summary of Cardwell's measures see Erickson, *Cardwell*, pp. 18–19.

[2] *Hansard*, cxxxv, end of volume, See above, pp. 254–5.

14

FRUSTRATION: THE FAILURE OF THE LEGISLATIVE PROGRAMME OF 1854

The settlement bill, the Scottish education bill and the oaths bill

Parliamentary Reform and Civil Service Reform were only the most important of a longer list of reform measures which the coalition government was forced to abandon in the session of 1854. One of these was a Settlement and Removal Bill introduced on 10 February by M. T. Baines, Chief Commissioner of the Poor Laws, a highly respected minister of middle-class Liberal background. The bill was designed to abolish the archaic and illiberal provisions of the old Law of Settlement, which empowered parishes to return applicants for Poor Relief to their parish of last legal settlement. It also provided 'for the more equitable distribution of the charge of relief in Unions'.[1] Opposition to it centred on two points, the threat of higher poor rates in some areas entailed in the equalisation proposals, and the failure to include in the scheme the case of the Irish poor in England. Baines only proposed to legislate for England and Wales since Scotland and Ireland had their own separate Poor Law systems, but Irish members immediately became concerned that Irish poor in England would be placed at a disadvantage in comparison with English poor. On the eve of the second reading some of them appealed to the Home Secretary, who had jurisdiction over the Irish Poor Law. At the time Palmerston was confined to his home by illness, but after communicating with the cabinet he gave the Irish members a sympathetic answer. Unfortunately this news got out before Palmerston had the opportunity of explaining the cabinet's attitude to Baines, who seems to have heard of the matter for the first time on 24 March when the debate on the second reading of the bill was begun in Palmerston's absence. Consequently, in a very brief speech he confined himself to maintaining his original position that the measure applied only to England and Wales. Russell in an equally brief inter-

[1] *Hansard*, CXXX, 443–61.

vention said that he favoured a separate bill for Ireland. The ensuing debate reflected a wide range of opinion, but there was a general tendency to regard the issue as a non-party one. On the advice of Graham the debate was adjourned until the return of Palmerston the following week. When it was resumed on 27 March, the day on which war was declared, Baines stuck by his original position and opposed a motion to adjourn the debate for a month. Palmerston, now returned to the House, likewise opposed adjournment, but, asking only for approval of the principle of the bill, he left the door open for its later extension. The government was defeated on the motion for adjournment by 208 votes to 183, with the result that the bill was subsequently abandoned.[1]

Baines was not unnaturally 'hurt and mortified' by the action taken by Palmerston and the cabinet without consulting him. Moreover, he did not consider that it would be feasible to extend the bill to Ireland and Scotland, for lack of the necessary information. Consequently, he tendered his resignation to Lord Aberdeen, who in 'a very kind letter' begged him to reconsider his decision, or at any rate to remain until it was seen whether anything could be done to remove the difficulties. On consulting some friends Baines agreed to this last suggestion with the warning that he must renew his resignation if unable 'to acquiesce in the ultimate decision of the Government with regard to the Settlement and Removal Bill, and the other questions connected with it'.[2] Whether it was on account of these difficulties or because of the setback on the motion of adjournment, the government ultimately abandoned the bill, but Baines retained his office until the fall of the coalition.[3] The incident was one of several contributing to the decline in the ministry's reputation, and Disraeli seized the opportunity of rubbing this in. While congratulating Baines on his decision to return to office, he could not help but note the 'very remarkable circumstance' that within a period of much less than twelve months five members of the administration had 'felt it to be their duty to resign their offices', and had 'almost immediately returned to their posts'. Facetiously he suggested that the government should set up some internal machinery to

[1] *Hansard*, CXXXI, 1274–1336; 1353–71; *The Times*, 28 March 1854. No division list was published.

[2] *Hansard*, CXXXII, 72–5; *The Times*, 30 and 31 March 1854.

[3] Correspondence between Palmerston and Graham in the Graham Papers (10 and 12 April 1854) indicates that Palmerston sought to obtain a settlement with Baines by appointing a committee to inquire into and report on the general subject of the Removal Bill, which for the time being was to be shelved.

deal with these 'internal bickerings'. He proposed, for instance, that the services of the youngest bishop or of a retired diplomatist might be enlisted by way of arbitration. 'I make this suggestion in the most friendly spirit', he added, 'and, if acted on, it might prevent the repetition of scenes which all must deplore, and which the Government must feel at this moment, notwithstanding their strength, to be rather awkward.'[1]

Education was another knotty subject on which the government sought to legislate in vain. It will be recalled that Russell had attached much importance to the promotion of a national system of education on the formation of the coalition, but that the bill to this purpose drafted in 1853 had been dropped. In 1854 it was decided to bring in a Scottish Education Bill, which had been under consideration since the preceding year.[2] It was introduced into the House of Commons on 12 February, but like so many other bills of its kind it foundered on the rocks of religious susceptibilities.

Scotland had long had a superior system of elementary education, with schools in every parish supported by public funds, but it had become archaic in two important respects: the salaries of the teachers were tied to the price of grain and as a result had become quite inadequate; and the legal stipulations tying the system to the Established Church of Scotland took no cognisance of the divisions that had recently taken place among Scottish Presbyterians. Consequently the bill proposed greatly to increase the teacher's stipend, to abolish all religious tests for schoolmasters, to remove the superintendence of the presbytery over parish schools and to provide certain hours for religious instruction at which children would not have to attend if their parents objected.[3] The bill initially had a good reception, but on the second reading, which did not take place until 12 May, opposition from members of the Established Church of Scotland hardened.

The Lord Advocate, the only member of the government to speak in the debate on the second reading, which took place on 12 May, warned his hearers 'that the vote the House was about to give involved a question of much more serious importance than the success or failure of this particular Bill, for that vote would in fact decide whether or not

---

[1] *Hansard*, CXXXII, 79–81.
[2] Smith, *Kay-Shuttleworth*, pp. 246–7. The duke of Argyll, who was initially critical of the project, played an active role in framing the bill. See PRO 30/22/11/D, fols. 12–14, 4 January, and fol. 63, 31 January 1854.   [3] *Hansard*, CXXX, 1151–73.

a national system of education was possible, not only in Scotland, but also whether a system of national education was possible in Great Britain'.[1]

Nevertheless, the bill was debated on the whole as a Scottish measure; most of the speakers (12 out of 16) were Scottish members. More than one claimed that this was not a matter of party politics and indeed no leader of the opposition and no member of the government, other than the Lord Advocate, participated in the debate. In the end, however, the government experienced a further setback when an adverse motion to adjourn the debate for six months was passed by a vote of 193 to 184.[2]

Two weeks later the government suffered yet another reversal. For years Lord John Russell had sought the admission of Jews into the House of Commons. With the help of his Peelite partners in the coalition he had obtained the passage of a Jewish Emancipation Bill in the previous session, only to see it defeated once again in the House of Lords. Now he attempted to eliminate a variety of grievances of Presbyterians and Roman Catholics, as well as Jews, by introducing a bill designed to abolish all the archaic oaths required to be sworn by members of parliament of that day and substituting in their place a single inoffensive oath of allegiance, omitting the phrase 'on the true faith of a Christian', which had hitherto precluded the admission of Jews. When the second reading of the bill was moved on 25 May it was immediately attacked on narrow sectarian ground by such religious bigots as Thesiger and Newdegate, who protested that the bill surrendered the royal supremacy to the susceptibilities of Roman Catholics and 'Romanizing pseudo-Protestants'. For this reason Disraeli found it possible to oppose the bill, while protesting his belief in the cause of Jewish emancipation, which he claimed did not require the sacrifice of cherished and historic oaths on the part of other members of parliament. Noble speeches from Russell and Gladstone were of no avail.

[1] *Ibid.* cxxxiii, 283.

[2] *Ibid.* 232–98; three Peelites, T. Greene, H. Herbert and A. E. Lockhart, voted in the majority; of 27 Conservatives voting who had been friendly to the government in the previous session 21 now voted against it, but six supported it (J. Baird, H. A. Bruce, C. R. Colville, J. Johnstone, W. B. Hughes and A. Smollett).

A few weeks later the Lord Advocate introduced a temporary measure to provide for the salaries of Scottish schoolmasters, which was passed without opposition. On this occasion he took the opportunity to deny that the government had had any prior consultation with leaders of the Free Church party before the introduction of the ill-fated Scottish Education Bill (*Hansard*, cxxxiii, 1132–5; cxxxv, 1501).

In the early morning hours of 26 May the government was defeated by a vote of 251 to 247 and the bill was killed by a six-month adjournment.[1]

The bribery prevention bills

A fourth upset followed quickly on 29 May when the Attorney General announced that the government felt it necessary to withdraw some bills that had been introduced earlier in the session with a view to disciplining five corrupt constituencies censored in the reports of recently appointed election commissioners. The law officers had come to the conclusion that undertakings given to witnesses at the investigations into these cases rendered the punitive legislation proposed open to question. Moreover, some of the reports on which the legislation was based were found to be inaccurate. Unfortunately the government only recognised these difficulties as a result of public protests after the legislation had been first introduced and so it faced the ignominy of having to abandon its own handiwork. The purpose of the bills was good, but the method was not feasible.[2]

Sir Frederic Thesiger, who had promised to oppose the bills, contented himself with a mild and brief 'I told you so' speech, but Disraeli saw and seized the opportunity for a scathing broadside attack on the coalition. He noted that there were seven important measures of which the government had given notice that session, three of which had been defeated, the Settlement Bill, the Scottish Education Bill and the Oaths Bill, and three of which had been withdrawn, the present measures, the Reform Bill and the proposed change of the civil service, which he suggested 'would have altered the character of the country and the whole spirit of our administration'. The seventh measure, the Oxford Reform Bill, remained to be decided, although the government had already sustained 'considerable, though partial, defeats' on it. He then proceeded to emphasise the radicalism of the government and his own conservatism by analysing the common characteristics of these proposals as he saw them:

These measures [he said], whatever different opinions may be entertained as to their expediency and policy, have all one characteristic in common—all these seven measures are either assaults on the rights of the subject or upon the

[1] *Hansard*, CXXX, 272–89; CXXXIII, 870–974. Four Peelites opposed the Oaths Bill (Goulburn, Greene, Legh, and Lockhart), while 31 supported it. See Appendix A.
[2] *Hansard*, CXXXIII, 1064–8.

institutions of the country. That no one can deny. You met here tonight with the intention of disfranchising a considerable number of Her Majesty's subjects, and you were to proceed, after having read these Bills a second time, to a Bill which attacks the rights of the University of Oxford. You may, some of you, be of the opinion that in both instances such violent measures ought to be had recourse to; but nobody can deny that one is an attack upon the rights of the electors of the country, and the other an attack upon the rights of the Universities of the country. No one can deny that the scheme of Parliamentary Reform which the noble Lord introduced was an attack upon the institutions of the country...No one who has given any consideration to the subject but must feel that the measure relating to the Civil Service—which, by the by, was announced in Her Majesty's gracious Speech—was a measure which probably would have effected a greater alteration in the whole habits and character of the nation than any other change which has been proposed. Abolishing, as it did, the present parochial system of education in Scotland, no one will pretend that the measure for Scottish education was not an assault upon an institution of that country.

Saying much the same of the other measures under review, he added, 'And, if my view with respect to them be a correct one, it is in my opinion highly impolitic in any Government to bring forward measures of such a character, which they have not a fair prospect of carrying, and carrying them in the Session in which they were introduced'.[1]

Disraeli's arguments were exaggerated, but the line of attack was a shrewd one in a parliament where Liberal Conservative voters often held the balance of power. Had he left the matter there, his speech would probably have been passed over as a clever comment at the end of a debate, but he had to go further. Here was an opportunity to wound the kingpin of the coalition in a peculiarly sensitive area, and indeed to expose the whole coalition to ridicule. He continued:

It is of importance to impress these circumstances on the attention of the House and country, because we must never forget we enjoy the inestimable fortune of having our affairs administered by men remarkably distinguished for their abilities—men who have made enormous sacrifices for their country —and for themselves. No man has made greater sacrifices than the noble Lord himself; for he has thrown over his old Friends and Colleagues, and connected himself with a coterie of public men who have passed a great part of their lives in depreciating his abilities and running down his eminent career.

[1] *Ibid.* 1075–6.

And yet, Disraeli asked, what had Lord John to show for it? What was there to show for the price that had been paid in the breaking up of parties and the 'departing from the spirit and genius of our Parliamentary constitution'? He complained that they had not been given what had been promised:

In short [he continued] when we were told that though the Government, to be sure, was to have no principles, it was to have 'all the talents', we had a right to expect that the noble Lord would at least have done something—that, at least, he would have achieved something as compensation for this remarkable state of affairs, which has banished from him all his natural Colleagues to invisible positions in the House, and left him on that bench surrounded by those who have been decrying his career for the last quarter of a century.[1]

Since procedure required that each of the five bills should be discharged separately Russell had the opportunity on the motion for the discharge of the second bill to reply to this onslaught.[2] He began quietly in response to the charge that no government should introduce measures it does not expect to carry by saying that in the reformed House of Commons there could never be that certainty of carrying measures that there had been in the unreformed House, where the ministers could rely on their influence through the control of rotten boroughs. But he reminded the House that on the great questions of peace and war and of paying for the war the government had enjoyed strong support in the House and that the leader of the opposition had not dared to divide the House on the former ground, and that on the matter of Ways and Means his challenge had been defeated by a majority of more than a hundred. Again this was a fair political rejoinder to a political attack, but Russell, too, had to press it further to the point of personalities. He could not resist twitting Disraeli for his betrayal of the cause for Jewish emancipation in opposing the Oaths Bill. 'Still,' he said, 'notwithstanding his great anxiety to see the Jews in possession of those privileges [enjoyed by other subjects of the Crown], the right Hon. Gentleman sometimes stays away, and sometimes votes against them; the political convenience of the hour always seems to overcome his attachment to the cause.'[3]

Since they were debating a fresh motion this gave Disraeli the opportunity to come back, and like Gladstone he could be terrible on the rebound. As a result he treated Russell to eight more columns of

[1] *Hansard*, CXXXIII, 1077.   [2] *Ibid.* 1079–82.   [3] *Ibid.* 1082.

sarcastic invective[1] of the kind with which he used to enjoy making Sir Robert Peel wriggle in former days. This time he dwelt upon the unfair treatment which Russell, aided and abetted by the present Chancellor of the Exchequer with all his 'sanctimonious rhetoric', had given him (Disraeli) when their positions were reversed two years earlier. Lord John was now defended by Sir George Grey and by Colonel Peel, an independent Conservative, who made one of his few interventions in debate to protest Disraeli's line of attack.[2] Clearly, by indulging in personalities Disraeli had lost much of the advantage gained in his initial attack on the anti-Conservative nature of the government's reform programme.

On the motion for the discharge of the third bill Russell returned to the fray with a stout defence of the coalition and the liberal principles on which it was formed. He acknowledged that the government had suffered reverses in its reform programme, but justified its continuance on its record in the conduct of the war. He reiterated this position in terms of future significance:

But, Sir, considering that this is the immediate, the great and the pressing question of the country, no taunts of the right hon. Gentleman would make me leave the Government with which I am connected—a position, God knows, one of far more labour and anxiety than of any pleasure, profit or emolument. I repeat that, unless I were convinced that the present Government is not more likely than any Government which could be formed to carry on the war successfully, and to conclude it by an honourable peace, I should cease to be one of its Members; but so long as I have that opinion, I shall trust to the House and to the country for putting a fair interpretation upon my conduct.[3]

In the midst of these altercations John Bright introduced a fresh note in a speech equally distributing sympathy and criticism between both parties to the debate.[4] He fully accepted Lord John Russell's case for joining the coalition and he readily approved of the record of the coalition government, and especially of its Chancellor of the Exchequer with respect to free trade and related matters.

But on all other matters [he continued] the Government appears to be unable to advise, or to lead, or to control the House. It is clear that the noble Lord who by courtesy is called the leader, does not lead this House, and the House

---

[1] *Ibid.* 1082–90. [2] *Ibid.* 1090–3.
[3] *Ibid.* 1097. [4] *Ibid.* 1103–7.

does not follow him. The legislative measures which the Government has offered to the House have not been accepted in a friendly spirit;—though many of them are good measures, they have, unfortunately, been kicked overboard in a very unceremonious manner.[1]

Consequently Bright suggested that it might be best for the ministers to abandon their attempt at coalition, which had failed, in order to seek some more successful combination. Bright's real complaint, of course, was the government's responsibility for getting the country into war and he was indignant at Russell's argument that this was a reason for their staying in office.

But see what a pernicious principle that is to advance in the House of Commons [he argued]. Because, let a Minister be ever so reckless, ever so unprincipled, ever so unpatriotic, yet by a course of concealed and mismanaged diplomacy, let him involve this country in difficulties with a foreign country, and then we are told that the majorities of this House go for nothing —that reform Bills, corruption Bills, oaths Bills, settlement Bills—all that in ordinary times were thought necessary for the welfare of the country, and for our Parliamentary system—all these are to go for nothing now—we may not be able to pass a single measure except those which have reference to the imposition of taxes—but as we have led this country into a war, Parliament must support us, and all other measures must be deferred.[2]

He asserted his right to criticise in this way since from the beginning he had denounced the policy of Lord John and Lord Stratford de Redcliffe. But rather oddly he went on to say:

I do not want the noble Lord to resign. I do not want Lord Aberdeen to resign. No man has ever heard me say a single word depreciating the character of Lord Aberdeen. I believe that if that noble Lord had been at the head of a Cabinet partaking his own views upon the questions of foreign policy, we should have had no war. And from all I have seen of Lord Aberdeen since he took office, I have never seen but that he is as liberal in all matters of internal policy...as any other Member of the Cabinet.[3]

Thus he concluded that the question which had been raised between the leader of the House and the leader of the opposition was not as one-sided as some members had suggested; but Bright's own views as to what should be done were far from clear. Presumably he meant that while he had no personal wish to see either Russell or Aberdeen leave office, on constitutional grounds he felt the resignation of the govern-

[1] *Hansard*, cxxxiii, 1104.   [2] *Ibid.* 1106.   [3] *Ibid.*

ment was called for. It was impossible to imagine, however, any possible alternative government that Bright would have been any more friendly, indeed as friendly, towards than this one, and this no doubt he knew himself. It was the privilege of the independent Radical in those days to tell everyone what was wrong without having any responsibility for putting things right.

Before this curious debate closed one final and inevitable contribution was made by the Chancellor of the Exchequer, whose name had been mentioned in various contexts by several of the preceding speakers. He vindicated his own conduct towards the late administration of Lord Derby, upheld the legislative record of the government, and defended Russell against the absurd proposition advanced by Bright that the leader of the House was using the war to prevent a vote of confidence.[1]

Shortly afterwards another crisis suddenly arose that almost upset the government. On 13 July the House of Commons heard a strongly voiced complaint from Napier, member for Dublin University, at the failure of the government to promote some Irish bills in which they had professed to be sympathetic. These had been held over from the previous session and now appeared likely to be shelved again. Disraeli took the opportunity in the debate that followed to chafe the ministers again for their alleged incapacity.

What have Her Majesty's Ministers been doing the last six months [he asked] that we have not had this question fairly considered and ably arranged? I want to know what is the catalogue of their legislative exploits which may be an excuse for the period of time which has been thus employed or thus wasted? I want to know, if they have been at war, what conquests they have achieved? I want to know, if they have been at peace, what beneficial arrangements—what advantageous legislation—they have accomplished? Have they reformed Parliament? Have they revised Parliamentary oaths? Have they educated the country? Have they even educated Scotland? What corrupt constituencies have they punished? What have they done which may be a valid excuse for not having dealt with this all-important measure?...Report the progress of these two Bills! Why, Sir, it's too derisive a proposition to be made. Report the progress of the Ministry! Tell us what they have done. Make a Motion to that effect. Report the progress of Her Majesty's Government. Come forward to the table to tell us what Her Majesty's Ministers have done.[2]

---

[1] *Ibid.* 1110–15.
[2] *Hansard*, CXXXV, 207. He went on in this vein for another ten columns of Hansard.

Russell replied briefly, reminding the House that when Lord Derby was in office he had been adverse to passing these same measures. He made the mistake, however, of adding some derogatory remarks about Disraeli's leadership, comparing it unfavourably with that of Peel and denouncing the new mode of merely opposing for the sake of opposing, when no party principle was at stake. He observed that as a result the leader of the opposition could not rely on his troops following him and that as a result he could not take the normal course of attempting to turn the government out of office.[1]

This was an invitation to Disraeli to return to the fray, which he did with alacrity, dealing out even more of the same sort of abuse and cleverly turning Lord John's observations against him. He concluded his remarks in a vein of high sarcasm, saying:

I do not wish to disturb the Government. I admire their powers of sufferance. I am willing, as one of a grateful community, to do justice to their patriotism. Sir, when the Coalition Government was formed, I was asked how long it would last, and I ventured to reply, 'Until every Member of it is, as a public character, irretrievably injured.'[2]

All this was too much for the thin-skinned Lord John. The next day he wrote to Lord Aberdeen asking to be relieved from his duties as leader of the House of Commons in view of the existing state of parties there. 'The frequent defeats we have sustained, the number of measures we have been forced to withdraw, and the general want of confidence which prevails among the Liberal party, form a sufficient motive and justification for the step I now take,' he wrote. He contrasted the weakness of the government in the Commons with its strength in the Lords and suggested that a change of leader in the former House might 'remedy the defect'.[3]

Aberdeen's son, Arthur Gordon, warned Gladstone of the gravity of the situation.

We have arrived at another crisis [he wrote]! During the past ten days Lord John has said & done things that were neither very agreeable nor very intelligible; he has now today resigned his position as Leader of the House of Commons, on the grounds that he cannot carry the measures of the Govt:, *at any rate not in his present position.*

[1] *Hansard,* CXXXV, 217–23.
[2] *Ibid.* 230.
[3] *Ab. Cor. 1854–5,* p. 170, 14 July 1854; Walpole, *Russell,* II, 229.

He went on to say that with the additional anxiety caused by the serious illness of his eldest son, Lord Haddo, Lord Aberdeen seemed 'inclined to let the Government break up'.

Hitherto these *crises* have been surmounted owing very much to Ld A's patience & moderation [he continued]. On this occasion, however, I do not believe that he will exert himself, or take any trouble to prevent a catastrophe. I therefore think we at last are approaching the end.[1]

Nevertheless, Aberdeen, although declaring himself 'surprised and distressed' at Russell's letter, wrote to urge the latter to reconsider his decision.[2] He later called on Russell, telling him (to quote the prince's account of the interview)

he did not see how Ld John could justify or even reasonably explain his steps; there he had been sitting, submitting to a great many defeats certainly, but remaining in office, & now that a disagreeable speech had been made by Mr Disraeli, for the purpose of wounding him, he should run away?—It ended by Ld John agreeing to remain.[3]

The queen added her own plea to Lord John.[4] As a result it was decided to hold a special meeting of the government's supporters in Downing Street on 17 July. Russell addressed the meeting telling them of the difficulties facing the government and of the necessity of its receiving better support if it was to continue.[5] 'Many hostile speeches were made and much confusion prevailed', Aberdeen told the queen, but on the whole he thought the results of the meeting were favourable.[6] He said that Herbert made 'a very good impression' when he spoke, explaining the functions of the office of Secretary at War, which had been under attack; he had maintained that these functions were indispensable, but acknowledged that in the future the office was not likely to carry a seat in the cabinet. According to Greville, Vernon Smith and Horsman spoke bitterly against the government, but Bright, although hostile, 'alluded to Aberdeen in a friendly spirit', as did Hume.[7] 'Such a party as appeared yesterday in Downing Street form[s] a strange basis for a Government to rest upon', Russell told the queen.

[1] Add. MS. 44319, fols. 56–7, 14 July 1854.
[2] Walpole, *Russell*, II, 229; cf. PRO 30/22/11, where the letter is misdated 24 July 1854.
[3] R.A. G15, fol. 21, 15 July 1854, memorandum of Prince Albert.
[4] Walpole, *Russell*, II, 229.   [5] *Greville Memoirs*, VII, 47.
[6] R.A. [?G15] 17 July 1854; misdated 7 July in *Ab. Cor. 1854–5*, pp. 172–3.
[7] *Greville Memoirs*, VII, 47.

'But at the present moment', he continued, 'it is doubtful whether any Government would obtain more support than the present.' In reply he emphasised the importance of the government giving the impression that it was united.[1]

Throughout the session of 1854 Greville was constantly noting the weakness of the government in contrast to its strength and success of the previous year. Graham, Wood and Gladstone all agreed with him on this point in private conversation.[2] Wood declared that a private revolution had 'silently been effected'. He and Greville agreed that 'parties were at an end, and the House of Commons was no longer divided into and governed by them'. Every government they thought would be faced with the same predicament and so 'business could no longer be conducted in parliament in the way it used to be'. Greville himself added:

It is evident that the Government is now backed by no great party, and that it has very few independent adherents on whom it can count. It scrambles on with casual support, and its continuing to exist at all is principally owing to the extreme difficulty of forming any other, and the certainty that no other that could be formed would be stronger or more secure, either more popular or more powerful.[3]

He was critical of Disraeli's tactics in turning so vehemently on Russell in the debate over the withdrawal of the bribery bills, saying:

D. seems inclined to have recourse to his old tactics against Peel, and to endeavour to treat J. Russell (and Gladstone when he can) in the same way, hoping probably to re-ingratiate himself with his own side by giving them some of those invectives and sarcasms against their opponents which are so congenial to their tastes. This course will not raise him either in the House or in the country, and he will not find in John a man either so sensitive or so vulnerable as Peel.[4]

The abandonment of the Home Office Reforms and the end of the session

The worst of the reverses were over, but embarrassments would not cease until the session had come to an end. On 1 July Aberdeen nonchalantly told the queen that the cabinet had agreed to abandon some more bills.[5] These were the Divorce Bill and the Testamentary Jurisdic-

---

[1] *Ab. Cor. 1854–5*, pp. 173–4, 19 July 1854.   [2] *Greville Memoirs*, VII, 35–6, 38.
[3] *Ibid.* pp. 35–6.   [4] *Ibid.* p. 39.
[5] *Ab. Cor. 1854–5*, pp. 160–1.

tion Bill, which had already passed through the House of Lords, but the withdrawal of which the Lord Chancellor announced on 10 July in view of the anticipated opposition.[1]

Lord Palmerston at the Home Office was likewise forced to make a number of strategic withdrawals, although he always seemed to carry them off in an inconsequential and jaunty manner that involved the minimum loss of credit. He would take the line that he was sorry to drop such a useful measure, but after all they were all men of the world and if the House did not want it then he would not be so uncivil as to force it on them. On occasion he might also adopt these tactics in reverse to accept a proposal from the floor of the House without appearing to lose face. For instance, on 10 May in Gladstone's absence, Milner Gibson renewed the attack on the sore spot of the newspaper stamp duty, by moving a resolution to the effect the laws were 'ill-defined and unequally enforced'. The Attorney General met the challenge with a conciliatory speech, but sought to avoid a head-on clash by moving the previous question. When Palmerston saw that this would not be acceptable to the House, he suggested a modified form of the resolution, but Gibson refused to be drawn. Therefore, Palmerston good-humouredly said he had no objection to the resolution, providing it was understood that no reflection was meant on the Board of Inland Revenue. Gibson agreed to this much, and an open break between the government and their restless allies on their own side of the House was averted.[2]

On 12 June Palmerston suffered a more obvious upset when he endeavoured to include an item of £550 for Roman Catholic chaplains in a vote of £371,383 for the upkeep of government prisons and convict establishments. That inveterate pair of Protestant watchdogs, Messrs. Spooner and Newdegate, pounced on this insidious attempt on the part of the government to propagate error, and forced an amendment deleting the £550, which was passed by a triumphant Protestant majority of 158 to 136.[3]

Palmerston was also forced to abandon some Police Bills that merited more attention than the House was prepared to give them. On 2 June he obtained permission to bring in a bill 'to render more effectual the police in counties and boroughs in England and Wales', but even at this

---

[1] Hansard, CXXXIV, 1436–40. [2] Ibid. CXXXIII, 419–60.
[3] Ibid. 1388–1422. Twenty-two Peelites supported the government and seven independent Conservatives. Two Peelites, Wortley and Wickham, followed Disraeli into the opposition lobby.

stage he was warned of trouble ahead. With the polite moderation that characterised his handling of Home Office business, he assured members that he would listen to the advice of those 'whose local knowledge must necessarily be greater than his own'.[1] Opposition quickly developed with respect to some portions of the bill. On 27 June, in response to a question from John Bright, he said that 'he attached very great value to the principle of local self-government' and that while he did not think the present bill infringed that principle, he would not press it if others thought so.[2] Consequently he proposed to withdraw the bill and replace it with another, which would be confined to the subject of county constabulary.[3]

On 10 July he moved for leave to introduce such a modified bill dealing with rural police, but once again numerous objections were made on the floor of the House. Palmerston said he only wished to do what was best. He thought postponement until the following session, as Pakington suggested, would be inconvenient, but he would not persist if the House wished him to withdraw in the knowledge that he had done his duty.[4] (This perhaps implied that only duty forced him to trouble with such matters when his mind was preoccupied with the sterner stuff of war.)

On 24 July the Home Secretary accepted yet another reversal. Objections were being made to a bill to consolidate and amend the Nuisance Removal and Diseases Prevention Acts, which had already been passed by the House of Lords. Palmerston informed the House 'that no one was less desirous than himself to give unnecessary trouble' and so he undertook not to press the second reading of the bill, although he admitted that he personally thought it a beneficial measure.[5] The bill was then condemned to oblivion by a three months' adjournment.

More serious was the failure of the Public Health Amendment Bill introduced by Palmerston on 10 July for the purpose of extending and reorganising the Board of Health under the control of the Home Secretary. In the debate on the second reading on 31 July he made an eloquent plea, that might have come from the mouth of his son-in-law, Lord Shaftesbury, for those who by their poverty were unable to look after their own welfare.[6] Making it clear that he was not concerned with the health of the well-to-do who could look after themselves, he said:

[1] *Hansard*, CXXXIII, 1266-8.   [2] *Ibid*. CXXXIV, 750-51.
[3] *Ibid*. and 957 answering a further question from Mr Palk on 30 June.
[4] *Ibid*. 1073-5.   [5] *Ibid*. CXXXV, 689-90.   [6] *Ibid*. 967-80.

I speak of those humbler and poorer, but much more numerous members of the community, who by their calling are fixed to spots from which they cannot fly—who by their poverty are precluded from having recourse to the aids of art and science...Health to the lower classes is life—it is existence itself—it is the very breath they breathe. As long as they have health, so long are they able to labour and to apply their industry to purposes useful to themselves and beneficial to others; but when sickness oppresses them, they are cast down into helpless poverty, and either they themselves, with their families, or their families if they should die, probably become burdens to that community of which they ought to be the mainstay and support.[2]

He went on to dwell on the blessings that Providence had showered on their country and even extolled the English climate as one of their greatest benefits, but argued that all was to no avail without health. The Home Secretary's case was a good one and well expressed, but it made no impression on the enemies of the Board and, especially, of its most active member, Edwin Chadwick. A few weeks earlier they had already forced a postponement of a vote of supply for the Board and on that occasion the debate was notable for the vehemence of the attack on Chadwick and all his works, by a metropolitan Liberal member, Sir Benjamin Hall.[2] Another inveterate foe of Chadwick, Lord Seymour, an arrogant and reactionary Whig aristocrat and former member of the Board of Health, immediately sought to block Palmerston's bill. He maintained that the issue was not a party one and indeed in the main it revolved around the controversial figure of Chadwick, who was regarded as the epitome of that bureaucracy and centralisation which was anathema to so many members, including Liberals. Despite the fact that Palmerston had the resignations of the old Board in his pocket, and in defiance of strong speeches by Russell and Monckton Milnes, the bill was killed in a small morning House by the representatives of London's threatened interests, who, in Professor Finer's words, 'had, silently, taken their places', and produced a majority of nine in a House of 139.[3]

[1] *Ibid.* 968.   [2] *Ibid.* CXXXIV, 1295–1309.

[2] S. E. Finer, *The life and times of Sir Edwin Chadwick* (London, 1952), p. 471; *Hansard*, CXXXV, 967–1005. The incident is primarily a chapter in the life of Chadwick and as such is told with gusto by Finer, who quotes Palmerston as quipping that the vote was 'the foulest' he had known in his parliamentary experience. See also J. L. and B. Hammond, *Lord Shaftesbury* (London, 1936), p. 167, who note the curious nature of the division list, which is not printed in *Hansard*. Radicals such as Hume, Fox and Brotherton supported the ministers; Bright and Disraeli voted in the majority.

Before introducing the bill, Palmerston had made it clear to Russell how seriously he took the matter, saying:

To watch over the health of the country is surely part of the higher functions of the Home Secretary and to create for that purpose a separate and independent department like the Poor Law Board would be to reverse that course which has been pursued with success by Graham in the Naval Department... Matters of public Health are so interwoven with the ordinary business of the Home Office that it is impossible thus wholly to separate them.[1]

On this occasion he told Russell that if the House of Commons did not think him competent to organise this Board he would resign. He did no such thing, however, and the day after the defeat of his bill, his colleague, Sir William Molesworth, brought in a second Public Health Bill that proposed to set up a new and independent Board of Health with a president, who would sit in the House. Provision was made to pension off poor Chadwick, unless some other job could be found for him, and with this *bête noire* out of the way, the opposition faded and the bill was passed unopposed.[2]

It is not easy to assess Lord Palmerston's success at the Home Office. His biographers say little about his tenure of this office; indeed one significantly entitles the chapter dealing with it 'The Home Secretary and Foreign Affairs',[3] but a more recent authority is generally complimentary to Palmerston's efforts in this capacity.[4] It is pointed out that he spoke some eighty times in the session of 1854 and his office had responsibility for or some interest in 48 of the 125 Public Acts of parliament passed in that session. His correspondence and his speeches suggest that he expended much energetic activity on all fronts, demanding higher efficiency of his staff and his inspectors, lecturing local authorities on their responsibilities, enforcing regulations prohibiting intramural interments and governing the production of smoke, and so on. On the other hand, he was frequently defeated by the resistance of vested interests, and sometimes, perhaps, he accepted these defeats too easily. Greville complained that he would not trouble himself with the details

[1] PRO 30/22/11/D, 7 July 1854, fols. 1128–30 (copy).
[2] *Hansard*, cxxxv, 1138–42, 1142, 1144, 1347, 1404, 1501. Ironically, Sir Benjamin Hall was appointed first president of the new Board, but he responded to his new responsibilities, under Palmerston's guidance, better than might have been expected.
[3] Bell, *Palmerston*, ii, 81–103.
[4] David Roberts, 'Lord Palmerston at the Home Office', *The Historian*, xxi (1958–9).

of his office,[1] but Greville was generally critical of Palmerston and this criticism seems contradicted by the evidence. His son-in-law, Lord Shaftesbury, was more appreciative when he said that Palmerston had 'done more than ten of his predecessors'.[2]

THE HOLIDAY LETTER

Royal Mistress (*writes*). 'In the case of Masters Aberdeen and Russell, I regret to say that the most extreme idleness has characterised the whole half-year.'
(reproduced from *Punch*)

Parliament was prorogued on Saturday 12 August with a queen's speech that dwelt on the strong support that had been forthcoming for the prosecution of the war and the successful course of operations to that date. 'The engrossing Interest of Matters connected with the Progress of the War', the queen was made to say, 'has prevented the due Consideration of some of those Subjects which at the opening of

[1] *Greville Memoirs*, VII, 32.
[2] Finer, *Chadwick*, p. 457. Finer calls Palmerston 'an astonishingly able Home Secretary', p. 456.

the Session I had recommended to your Attention.' Through the queen, however, the ministers expressed their satisfaction with such measures as the Coasting Trade Act, the Merchant Shipping Act, the Oxford University Reform Act, the Bribery Prevention Act, and 'the Act for establishing the direct Control of the House of Commons over the charges incurred in the Collection of the Revenue', which it was anticipated would 'promote Simplicity and Regularity in our System of Public Account'.[1] In fact, of course the coalition government was fortunate to have survived the session; its legislative record for 1854 compared poorly with that of 1853 and its future was obviously less certain.

Charles Greville, a candid friend, took the occasion of the prorogation to write in his Journal a long assessment of the coalition since its formation and its prospects as he saw them. 'But though all immediate danger is removed from the Government, and, unless they fall to pieces during the recess by any internal dissensions, they will probably go on unscathed, the state of affairs is very unsatisfactory, and pregnant with future troubles and difficulties,' he wrote. 'The condition of the Government in its relations with the H. of Commons, throughout the past session,' he continued, 'has been extraordinary, and I believe unprecedented.' He proceeded to give an interesting account of the evolution of party cabinet government based on the possession of majority in the House of Commons by the party in power, and to trace the recent disintegration of that system. In particular he gave a very full résumé of the circumstances under which the Aberdeen coalition had been formed and of its fortunes in its first two sessions. From the end of the first session dissatisfaction with the government's supposed handling of the Eastern Question had led to a serious decline in its prestige, but the publication of the blue-books on the eve of the war had cleared the air in this respect. He continued:

Clarendon's despatches were highly approved of, and all fair and candid observers, including many who had found fault with the Government before, declared that they were perfectly satisfied that our policy had been wise and proper, and the whole of the negotiations very creditable to all who had been concerned in carrying them on. So little did the events correspond with the general expectation, that the Eastern question, which had been considered to be the weak part of the Government, turned out to be its great strength; and

[1] *Hansard*, cxxxv, 1551–3. For the parliamentary debate on the conduct of the war see the next chapter.

the war which eventually broke out has been the principal cause of their being able to maintain themselves in power. It is now fashionable to say that if it were not for the war, they would have been turned out long ago.

He went on to emphasise at great length the miserable weakness of the government in the House of Commons with respect to everything other than the war. At the same time he observed that it was evident that the House was determined to keep them in office, for whenever a vital question of confidence arose they were always sure of a majority, with the result that the Derbyite opposition, while able to harry them unmercifully, were themselves 'baffled whenever they attempted anything which had a tendency to place the Government in serious embarrassment'. He continued:

The whole conduct of the Session and the relations of the Government with the H. of Commons, presented certainly something very different from what had ever been seen before in the memory of the oldest Statesman, implied a total dissolution of party ties and obligations, and exhibited the Queen's Government and the H. of Commons as resolved into their separate elements, and acting towards each other in independent and often antagonistic capacities...At present it is difficult to see how this state of things is to be altered, and time alone can show whether great parties will again be formed, and Governments be enabled to go on as in times past.[1]

Superficially one may be struck by the similarity of the situation here described by Greville, with some exaggeration, to the American system, but a dozen years later Walter Bagehot, a more profound observer, was able to dwell on the fundamental differences which remained with respect to the relationship between the executive and the legislature. Despite Greville's forebodings, as Bagehot emphasised, this close relationship continued to be a cardinal feature of the British system.

The Prime Minister and the queen; further patronage problems

As usual prorogation was followed by the rapid dispersal of the cabinet from London, for by this time the major decisions of policy had been taken and there was little that most ministers could now do, either

---

[1] *Greville Memoirs*, VII, pp. 55–7. A year later Gladstone wrote in equally gloomy terms about the breakdown of the party system in a long unpublished paper entitled 'Party as it was and as it is', Add. MS. 44745, fols. 173–222 (see my 'Peel and the Peelites', *E.H.R.* LXXIII, 432), and in an anonymous article in the *Quarterly Review*, XCIX (1856), 521–70, entitled 'The declining efficiency of parliament'.

individually or collectively, to influence the course of events in the next few months.[1] As in the previous year, the Prime Minister and the Foreign Secretary remained to hold the fort in London, now reinforced by the Secretary for War, the duke of Newcastle, who this year bore the heaviest load, both of responsibility and of detailed administration. Toward the end of September Newcastle, writing to Gladstone about office matters, commented: 'My life for 6 weeks has been a strange mixture of excitement and intense dullness.' Ten days later, with the strain beginning to tell, he wrote: 'I have been for seven weeks *entirely alone* in London, and it begins to be more than the spirit will bear.'[2] A few months later Hayward heard that Newcastle was suffering from the recurrence of an old heart disease. 'He is killing himself with work and anxiety', Hayward wrote to Young. 'The fact is the rest of the Cabinet left him alone during the greater part of the vacation.'[3] Hayward and Newcastle appear to have overlooked the fact that Aberdeen and Clarendon were spending their second vacation period in London.

Actually, on 23 September Lord Aberdeen got away for a fortnight in Scotland, part of which he had to spend in attendance on the queen at Balmoral. His departure had been delayed by the ill health of his son, Lord Haddo, whom he had sent off to Egypt for a rest cure, never expecting to see him again.[4] The poor man was in a state of great dejection, burdened by these private worries and smarting under the neverending personal attacks made on him in the press, which he took too much to heart.[5]

While Lord Aberdeen's relations with Queen Victoria remained

---

[1] R.A. A 23, fol. 135, 12 August 1854. On the very day of prorogation the Prime Minister supplied the queen with full information regarding his colleagues' movements. Sir Charles Wood had already left for Yorkshire and Scotland. Sir George Grey was going that day to Northumberland, and Lord Granville and Sir William Molesworth were reported to be leaving immediately, the one for Carlsbad, the other for Scotland. Sidney Herbert was off to Ireland and then to Wilton, where he was to be joined by Gladstone, who would first bring his family for a two-week holiday to Broadstairs. The Lord Chancellor would be at Holwood and Lord Palmerston was thought to be going to Broadlands. The following week Lord John Russell would go to the lakes of Cumberland for a fortnight and then for a fortnight to Minto, his wife's family home; at the same time Lord Lansdowne would go to Bowood and the duke of Argyll to Scotland. Sir James Graham would get away from London on Admiralty business, again visiting the Channel ports.

[2] Newcastle Papers, 27 September and 6 October 1854.

[3] Carlisle, *Hayward correspondence*, I, 228.

[4] R.A. A 23, fols. 143–4, 31 August 1854.   [5] *Greville Memoirs*, VII, 65.

excellent as long as he continued to be her Prime Minister, she could at times be difficult. For instance, when, following the declaration of war, Aberdeen responded to a proposal in the House of Lords by stating that the government had under consideration the proclamation of a day of humiliation and prayer,[1] she expressed herself as startled by his assertion. She preferred the adoption of an appropriate prayer to the proclamation of a day of humiliation, for she was sure that the bishops would select some totally inapplicable chapter from the Old Testament and the Psalms. 'Moreover,' she continued in her letter to Aberdeen, 'really to say (as we probably should) that the *great sinfulness of the nation* has brought about this War when it is the selfishness and ambition of *one* man and his servants who have brought this about, while our conduct has been throughout actuated by unselfishness and honesty, would be too manifestly repulsive to the feelings of everyone, and would be a mere act of hypocrisy.'[2]

On 12 April she wrote again urging that it should be a day of 'prayer and supplication', not of 'fast and humiliation', as, she said, might be expected after a calamity. She told the Prime Minister that she had spoken strongly to the archbishop of Canterbury, urging '*no Jewish imprecations against our enemies, &c*', but rather suggesting a 'beautiful prayer' in the Prayer Book 'to be used before a Fight at Sea'.[3] Aberdeen replied to the effect that 'fasting and humiliation' was the usual term, but he agreed that there was no reason for proclaiming a general fast which would not be followed. 'Humiliation', he reminded her on the other hand, 'must always be a duty.'[4]

Lord Aberdeen in the end persuaded the queen, with some difficulty, that there was a public demand on the part of what Greville called 'the religious part of the community' for such an expression of public sentiment and that there was precedent for it in George III's reign. It was agreed, however, to meet her objections, that the day in question should not be made a day of fast, as had been proposed. At the last minute, nevertheless, the government had to reverse its decision and proclaim the day of humiliation a fast day in order to comply with the law under which the proclamation was to be issued and prevent confusion in the business community. Greville was scathing in his comment both on what he regarded as the ridiculousness of the proceeding and

---

[1] *Hansard*, CXXXII, 139.

[2] R.A. A23, fol. 85, 1 April 1854; *Letters of Queen Victoria*, II, 24–5.

[3] *Ab. Cor. 1854–5*, pp. 100–1, 12 April 1854.   [4] *Ibid.* p. 101, 12 April 1854.

the mismanagement of it. 'In Peel's time this never would have happened,' he wrote, 'but with a nominal Premier, a Home Secretary who will give himself no trouble about the details of his office, and an Attorney-General who does nothing, knows nothing of law and won't attend to anything, it is no wonder that such things (and many others) occur.'[1] As Clerk of the Privy Council, of course, Greville was directly involved in the issue of such proclamations, and he was in a bad temper with the ministers because of their fumbling the question of the issue of trading licences following the declaration of war.[2]

Some months later the queen exploded again when the archbishop of Canterbury proposed a special prayer against cholera. She pointed out the Liturgy provided for prayers against calamities generally. 'The Queen must repeat', she wrote, 'what she has frequently done, that she strongly objects to these *special* prayers which *are*, in fact, not a sign of gratitude or confidence in the Almighty.'[3]

The queen also made difficulties about a proposed visit to Paris by the duke of Cambridge on his way to Constantinople, where he was going in March in his capacity as commander-in-chief. The emperor was anxious that the duke should stay with him in the Tuileries, and Clarendon had pressed this on the queen lest any offence be given to their ally. The queen was very annoyed at this pressure and plied Aberdeen with precedents to show that visiting royalty did not normally stay at Buckingham Palace unless it was 'a near relation or particular friend'. She betrayed her real feelings about the upstart who ruled France, saying:

The Queen must say that every time she shews the Empr or Empress any civility with a *sincere* wish to give satisfaction, & the sincerest desire to *do* everything consistent with her dignity—to strengthen this alliance wh is now of so much importance to this Country—something more is pressed in so strange a manner as to take away all the grace of the intended compliment & to oblige her to resist advances wh shd never have been made. Instead of doing therefore good the very result intended is destroyed. Against this the Queen must & *will* protest—for she cannot mix up personal friendship &

---

[1] *Greville Memoirs*, VII, 31–2. [2] *Ibid.* p. 31.

[3] R.A. A23, fols. 139–41; *Letters of Queen Victoria*, III, p. 51. On 11 September Aberdeen ventured to recommend yet another special prayer, this time in thanksgiving for the abundant harvest. He was aware of the queen's objections on principle, of which he approved, but as the blessing was so great and 'at such a crisis', he somewhat illogically recommended it (R.A. A 23, fol. 146).

intimacy with a Political Alliance. The former is the *result* of the experience of years of mutual friendship, & cannot be *carried by storm*.

She went on to describe a similar experience of the king of the Belgians, who made the mistake of receiving the Prince Napoleon only to become more involved than he had intended and forced to sanction the visit of the duke of Coburg to Paris.

As soon as the Duke of Cambridge will have been recd the *screw* will be put on again [she continued] to make us receive a Counter visit, & the Duke's going to the Tuileries will be attempted to be made the reason for forcing Prince Napoleon into the Queen's House. As the Queen is *determined not* to have him thrust into the privacy of her Family—by avoiding one affront we shall only bring on another.[1]

Clarendon professed his concern at having so annoyed the queen and promised that she would hear nothing more from him on the question of civilities to the emperor. He pointed out, however, that England was embarked on war with France as an ally 'or rather with the Emperor of the French;—who is—a Parvenu' whose '*amour propre* is excessive'. He thought it a convenience that the duke of Cambridge should go to Turkey via Paris and that it was an ordinary courtesy for the emperor to invite him to stay at the Tuileries no matter what the custom might be at Buckingham Palace. He observed that a refusal would injure the emperor in public opinion and said he thought it 'not worth while to mortify a vain man for such a cause'.[2] When it was suggested that the duke might also go to Vienna Clarendon said 'he wd not do much good but still he might bring some information'. He warned that Lord Raglan should not accompany the duke since it would be impossible for the former to go without Marshal St Arnaud, commander of the French force.[3] In the end all went well. The queen wrote a polite letter to the Emperor Napoleon addressed '*Sire et mon bon Frère*' and signed '*la Bonne Sœur, Victoria R.*', accepting the emperor's kind invitation on behalf of the duke of Cambridge.[4] The duke's visit to Paris was pronounced a complete success,[5] and the emperor removed all fears of

---

[1] Add. MS. 43048, fols. 280–5, 2 March 1854. Only part of this letter is reproduced in *Letters of Queen Victoria*, III, 17–18.

[2] *Ab. Cor. 1854–5*, pp. 60–1, 2 March 1854.

[3] PRO 30/22/11/C, fols. 853–4, 13 March to Russell.

[4] *Ab. Cor. 1854–5*, p. 97, 9 April, a draft sent by the queen to Aberdeen.

[5] *Ibid.* p. 103, Clarendon, 14 April 1854.

jealousy by himself suggesting that the duke should also visit Vienna on the way.[1]

The Prime Minister had other worries as well, apart from the conduct of the war and of parliamentary business. The queen had to be humoured, ministers had to be comforted, scandals had to be cleared up, and patronage had to be distributed, as vacancies occurred. On church appointments the susceptibilities of the queen and the recommendations of colleagues, especially Lord John, always had to be kept in mind.[2] For instance in March the see of Salisbury fell vacant and on the recommendation of the bishop of London the Prime Minister proposed the name of Professor Blunt. The queen approved this recommendation but reminded Aberdeen how very strong her feelings were 'against Puseyite tendencies', since she considered them 'as *fatal* to the Church'. She professed herself as unimpressed by the bishop of London's views on church affairs as by those of the king of Prussia in political affairs.[3] As it turned out, Blunt declined the offer and in his place Aberdeen recommended Canon Hamilton of Salisbury.[4] The queen approved, trusting that his views were acceptable, but a few days later wrote in great alarm to say that she heard the canon was a high churchman.[5] Lord Aberdeen defended his recommendation. He explained that he only recommended men of known 'moderate character and opinion'. His letter continued:

Provided these qualifications exist, Lord Aberdeen is indifferent to what party in the Church such persons may incline. He thinks it would be unwise and unjust to exclude good men in consequence of a tendency either to High Church or to Low Church; although he would at once equally reject High Church doctrines that lead to Popery, and Low Church opinions tending to fanaticism, and to bring the Church of England into contempt.[6]

[1] *Ab. Cor. 1854–5*, pp. 104–5, 17 April 1854. See *Letters of Queen Victoria*, III, 30–2, for a report of the duke's visit to Vienna, 28 April 1854.

[2] Aberdeen's initial appointment to the bench of bishops, and the only one in 1853, was that of John Jackson, rector of his parish church in Piccadilly, who was made bishop of Lincoln. On this occasion he told Russell that he intended to decide the matter himself, but his choice of a broad churchman was unlikely to give offence to either Lord John or the queen. It did upset the high churchmen and especially Bishop Wilberforce, who had hoped to influence the Prime Minister's choice through his son, Arthur Gordon, who was an ardent Anglo-Catholic. See John Kenyon, 'High churchmen and politics, 1845–65', a Ph.D. thesis in the University of Toronto Library, which quotes from the Wilberforce–Gordon correspondence in the Stanmore Papers.

[3] Add. MS. 43048, fols. 299–302, 10 and 11 March 1854.

[4] *Ibid.* fol. 308, 16 March 1854.   [5] *Ibid.* fols. 310–11, fol. 313, 17 and 21 March 1854.

[6] *Ibid.* fols. 315–16, 22 March 1854.

Canon Hamilton, whose claims had been warmly, if unorthodoxly, urged by the late bishop on his deathbed, was in the end appointed to the vacant see, to the chagrin of the low churchmen. Some of these urged Edward Horsman, Whig member for Stroud, to attack the appointment in parliament. Horsman told Gladstone that, 'looking to the composition of the present Government and wishing to support it,' he had determined 'to refrain altogether from agitating religious questions'. 'But', he added, addressing Gladstone as a cabinet minister, 'I beseech you to be careful what you do in ecclesiastical patronage.' In reply Gladstone disclaimed any attempt on his part 'to meddle in matters of church preferment', and defended Aberdeen's policy of choosing men irrespective of the complexion of their opinions, providing they were known to be moderate. In writing to Aberdeen[1] about this conversation Gladstone professed the hope that the Prime Minister would continue to act on his 'own conscience and judgement', in the tradition of Sir Robert Peel. Gladstone suggested to Aberdeen that he might expiate 'the sin of Sarum' by appointing the low-church Whig clergyman, the Rev. C. Baring, to the recently vacated see of Bath and Wells. Baring, he said, was an Oxford man and a double first for whom he had a high regard twenty-five years ago, although he was a political opponent. He greatly preferred him to another low churchman under consideration, whom Gladstone considered to be quite unfit.[2] This may have been Lord Wriothesley Russell, of whom Gladstone wrote the next day to say that he was a member of the Christian Alliance, which Gladstone described as 'a new form of the Christian Church, founded on confusion',[3] or it may have been Lord Auckland, who was subsequently appointed to the see to the gratification of the queen.[4]

In June the dean of Windsor died and Lord Aberdeen proposed to appoint Lord Wriothesley Russell to please Lord John. The queen, on the other hand, wanted the appointment of Mr Wellesley, her favourite chaplain. She professed to believe that Lord W. Russell would not accept, and in any event argued that the office was so closely connected with herself she thought 'her *claims* ought to take precedence of Lord John's'. Moreover, she pointed out, Lord Wriothesley was already

---

[1] *Ab. Cor. 1853–4*, pp. 124–6, 17 May 1854.

[2] *Ibid.* In a semi-facetious tone Gladstone concluded a letter to Arthur Gordon with some more down-to-earth reasons for appointing Baring. 'Lastly,' he wrote, 'I believe he never bullied his bishop; and he is the brother of an ex-Cabinet Minister, and thoroughly Whig!' (*ibid.* pp. 123–4, 16 May 1854).

[3] *Ibid.* p. 126, 18 May 1854.   [4] *Ibid.* p. 133, 25 May 1854.

Deputy Clerk of the Closet. Aberdeen passed this on to Lord John, saying that he had no option but that Wellesley's appointment would be a good one.[1]

There were of course many other ecclesiastical preferments of a more routine nature to be determined. And there were always a variety of civil offices and honours to be disposed of, but the demand from office-seekers tended to outrun the supply. Among several recommendations for lord-lieutenancies, one for Cardiganshire was hastily withdrawn when the Prime Minister discovered that the gentleman in question lived 'in a state of such frequent intoxication, as is almost unknown in these days'.[2] With some uneasiness the Prime Minister reported to the queen the cabinet's views that the three children of Lord Nelson's adopted (but really illegitimate) daughter should be placed on the Pension List. This was to forestall a numerous party in the House of Commons who favoured a special vote which the cabinet feared 'would give rise to much scandal and a disagreeable debate'.[3] With much less hesitation he proposed to make Sir Robert Inglis a Privy Councillor on the occasion of his retirement after long service in the House of Commons. 'His political conduct has always been distinguished by devotion to the *throne*,' Aberdeen wrote to the queen; 'and although his opinions may have frequently been tinctured by prejudice, he is a man immeasurably respected, and is a sort of representative of a numerous class in this country.' Aberdeen concluded on a political note by observing that the appointment would 'conciliate the good opinion of many towards Your Majesty's Government'.[4]

This was a fairly innocuous award for an old man, even though he had been a narrow partisan all his life, but a Garter was another matter. In the spring of 1854 there was a vacancy. Aberdeen first thought to humour Lord John by offering it to him and even discussed it with the queen. But when Russell began to press for the division of the War Office and the Colonial Office,[5] he asked the queen's permission to offer it to the duke of Newcastle, after first ascertaining that no word of the previous idea had been breathed to Russell. On receiving the queen's

---

[1] *Ab. Cor. 1854–5*, pp. 150–1, from the queen and to Russell, 11 June 1854; R.A. A23, fols. 110 and 112, 11 June 1854, from Aberdeen.

[2] R.A. A23, fol. 137, 19 August 1854.

[3] *Ibid.* fol. 145, 1 September 1854. It is doubtful whether Hayter would have agreed with Aberdeen's conclusion.

[4] *Ibid.* fol. 129, 7 August 1854.

[5] See the next chapter.

permission[1] he wrote to Russell, whose approval he regarded as necessary. Realising that a case must be made, he said:

It is perhaps not very usual to select a colleague; but in the present case I think there are circumstances which justify it. His rank under ordinary circumstances would render such a choice perfectly natural; but his official exertions at this moment have been so great, as seem to call for some acknowledgement. An attempt is made to disparage these services, which cannot but give additional value to any mark of confidence. It will prove to him also, that the proposal to withdraw from under his charge a large portion of the duties of the Colonial Office, does not arise from any deficiency of personal regard.[2]

Russell, however, refused to agree. 'The Duke of Newcastle is a fit person to have the Garter,' he wrote, 'but I think not yet.' He argued that Newcastle reaped the harvest sown by Lord Grey, who had held the office for six years in face of much unjust obloquy. Getting more to the point he continued:

Lord Grey is the son of our Whig Prime Minister. I do not know that he would accept the Garter at this time, but I think to pass him over for his successor would be an affront to the Whig party who support your administration.[3]

On receiving this reply, which a less charitable man might have considered political blackmail, Lord Aberdeen returned to his first idea and offered the Garter to Russell, saying:

The case would not be without precedent, and it would be infinitely more agreeable to me. I think too, it would be advantageous to the Government.

The Duke of Newcastle is a young man who can afford to wait, and whose station and merits will obtain for him the distinction in no long time.[4]

Lord John declined Aberdeen's 'kind proposal' and renewed his recommendation of Lord Grey, saying that he did not think Grey would decline 'unless he thinks that he is not rich enough for the expense'.[5] Aberdeen said he was agreeable, but that he thought Grey would refuse and might even resent it. Again he urged Russell to reconsider,[6] but to no avail.

[1] *Ab. Cor. 1854–5*, pp. 115–16, to Queen Victoria, 29 April; from Queen Victoria, 29 April 1854.
[2] *Ibid.* p. 117, 30 April 1854. [3] *Ibid.* p. 118, 30 April 1854.
[4] PRO 30/22/11/D, fols. 1047–8, 1 May 1854.
[5] *Ab. Cor. 1854–5*, p. 119, 1 May 1854.
[6] PRO 30/22/11/D, fol. 1049–50, 1 May 1854.

Early the following year the queen herself settled the question of the vacancy by conferring the award on the Prime Minister. Aberdeen at first demurred and he even made the ridiculous proposal that the honour should be conferred on Lord Cardigan. In the end, however, on the very eve of the government's downfall, he acceded, not without pleasure, it would appear. Both Russell and Newcastle in congratulating him indicated that they were glad they had made the award possible by their own refusals.[1]

One colonial appointment had embarrassing consequences. Francis Lawley, Liberal member for Beverley, and for two years Gladstone's private secretary, was appointed Governor of South Australia and accordingly resigned his seat, which was thereupon successfully contested by Aberdeen's son, Arthur Gordon. Then just before Lawley was to leave for Australia, it developed that he had participated in questionable transactions on the stock exchange, while private secretary to the Chancellor of the Exchequer. It appeared, however, that he did not actually make use of official information, and indeed that he lost on the transaction. Since he lost his appointment as well as his money, and made a clean breast of what had happened, he perhaps gained some sympathy. At any rate, to Aberdeen's relief, the affair passed off in the House of Commons 'better than could have been expected'. 'Much good feeling was shown by the House', the Prime Minister told the queen.[2] He had feared that the opposition would try to link his son's name with the case, 'however groundless' the insinuation.

Greville made a similar comment, saying that 'there was no personal animosity and no coarseness or inhumanity displayed, but, on the contrary, forbearance and good nature towards Lawley. Any expectation of being able to wound Gladstone through Lawley has quite failed.'[3] Although it fell to Sir George Grey, who had just taken over the Colonial Office, to make the painful explanation of what had happened, the appointment had been initiated by the duke of Newcastle on the recommendation of Gladstone, who took full responsibility for doing so because of his very high opinion of Lawley's ability and accomplishments while acting as his secretary. The poor man's difficulties stemmed from his long-standing 'connection with the turf', which in fact he had been attempting to break since entering public life, but this in itself,

---

[1] *Letters of Queen Victoria*, III, 83–5; *Ab. Cor. 1854–5*, pp. 316–17. Neither Grey nor Newcastle ever received the Garter, but Russell did in 1862.
[2] R.A. A23, fols. 125–6, 3 and 4 August 1854.   [3] *Greville Memoirs*, VII, 48.

Grey pointed out, should not have shocked the party of Derby and Bentinck. Indeed, the ensuing debate[1] turned much more on the general principles regarding the appointment of colonial governors and here the leading criticism came from men like Bright on the government side of the House. Gladstone, a former Colonial Minister, took this point up with alacrity, reminding the House of the great difficulty in finding a distinguished man willing to go to these remote parts of the earth, 'placing himself in a society often comparatively rude, in a climate frequently insalubrious, with a great risk of not maintaining his popularity for any lengthened period' and with remuneration which 'in most instances is miserably low'.[2]

Another embarrassment arose in January when John Sadleir, one of the three Irish Catholic office-holders, had to resign office when it was discovered that he had been responsible for the wrongful imprisonment of a political opponent in the election of 1852.[3] Aberdeen, on the advice of Newcastle and Young, then told Russell that he first intended to offer the post to Henry Herbert (a Peelite) and if he refused, as was expected, then to approach Chichester Fortescue (a Liberal), whose seat was more in doubt.[4] In the end Fortescue accepted the offer and was re-elected.

The Kennedy case

One case involving personnel overshadowed all others and, indeed, might have brought down the administration had not a more serious crisis intervened. This was the so-called 'Kennedy case', which Russell's biographer, Spencer Walpole, dismisses in a brief footnote.[5] Kennedy had first been appointed to office by Lord John Russell as long ago as 1837, and in 1850, after the Whigs' return to power, had been made a Commissioner of Woods and Forests. He had taken some high-handed action against several employees in this department, who had in turn complained to the Treasury. On the report of two Treasury officials,

---

[1] *Hansard*, cxxxv, 1225–59. This short discussion deserves the attention of colonial historians.

[2] *Ibid.* 1255.   [3] Whyte, *Independent Irish party*, pp. 161–2.

[4] Newcastle Papers, Young to Newcastle, 6 January 1854; Newcastle to Aberdeen, 7 January 1854; Add. MS. 38080, fol. 96, Aberdeen to Russell, 7 January 1854.

[5] Walpole, *Russell*, II, 243 n. Morley, *Gladstone*, I, 520, summarises the whole dispute brilliantly in a paragraph, but perhaps fails to recognise the full significance of the dispute, which might have given Russell his pretext for resignation had it not been for the Roebuck resolution, since the Kennedy affair was still unsettled when the government fell.

who investigated the case, Gladstone as Chancellor of the Exchequer wrote to the Prime Minister on 1 May informing him of the necessity of dismissing Kennedy.[1] Following his dismissal Kennedy proceeded to draw up a petition to the House of Commons, which Gladstone regarded as 'somewhat sharp practice'.[2] In June Kennedy appealed to Russell on learning that Gladstone had caused his dismissal without consulting Lord John. Russell expressed his concern, but upbraided Kennedy for appealing to the House of Commons before approaching him.[3] Russell forwarded Kennedy's letter to Gladstone, who said in reply: 'If I have done injustice to Mr Kennedy, either in substance or in form, no consideration of consistency or selfish feeling will restrain me from concurring in any step which may repair it.' He went on, however, to give his reasons for feeling confident that his action was just.[4]

Seven weeks later Russell wrote again to Gladstone endeavouring to force him to reverse his decision. In part he said:

Lord Fortescue spoke to me the other day on the subject of Kennedy. He thinks you have been misled by Treasury officials, & that Kennedy has been ill used.

My own impression is that Kennedy has been harshly used. Vernon Smith gave him the consolation that if he had been harshly used it was no more than happen'd to all old Whig public servants!

In the meantime he is forced to refuse to his only son the education of a gentleman.

All this occurring to a man whom I have known all my life—whose integrity & veracity I highly respect—& whom I placed in what I thought was a permanent office affects me very painfully.

I hope you will be induced to reconsider the whole matter.[5]

In a courteous reply Gladstone stuck to his guns. He expressed his regret at the pecuniary injury done to Kennedy and made no objection to his being placed elsewhere provided he had no responsibility over other people. 'I am bound to state my conviction', Gladstone wrote, 'that he [Kennedy] could not be allowed to continue in the administration of that Department.' He was willing, however, to submit the

[1] *Ab. Cor. 1854–5*, p. 118, 1 May 1854; see also lengthy correspondence between Gladstone and Aberdeen in Add. MS. 44089.
[2] PRO 30/22/11/D, fols. 1069–70, 9 May 1854. At this point Gladstone expressed his regret that he had not known of Russell's interest in Kennedy.
[3] *Ibid.* Kennedy, fols. 1154–8, fols. 1175–6 (copy), 5 June, and Russell, 11 June 1854.
[4] *Ibid.* fols. 1177–8, Gladstone, 7 June 1854.
[5] Add. MS. 44291, fols. 202–5, 27 July 1854.

whole affair to the judgment of their colleagues. Three months had now passed since the dismissal and it was time to settle on Kennedy's successor.[1]

From this point the situation between Russell and Gladstone seriously deteriorated. Russell wrote a lengthy and stiff reply condemning the way in which Kennedy had been treated and the action taken on behalf of the Prime Minister without his knowledge.[2]

Gladstone replied: 'I am afraid I must answer your [?] remarks on Mr Kennedy's case by simply demurring to the whole of them. I do not think you are informed of the facts.'[3] And so he proceeded to reiterate them, but of course to no purpose. Here in a concrete case of flesh and blood were reflected the two diametrically opposite views of the civil service and the rules governing its functioning that Gladstone and Russell had argued in more theoretical terms earlier in the year. Russell stood by the old-fashioned view that a politician must stand by his friends, whatever their merits. Gladstone, in advancing a more modern ideal, perhaps showed some naïvety as to the political realities of that day.

In November Aberdeen offered the vacant post to Russell's friend Colonel Romilly without consulting Gladstone but, as he told Russell, 'not without some apprehension that he might not like it'.[4] Romilly wrote in some embarrassment to Russell explaining his difficulty since he had expressed the view that Kennedy had been ill treated. He decided to rely on the opinion of his brother and of Lord Dunfermline.[5] The latter also wrote to Russell regarding his difficulty in advising Romilly.

You and I who know Kennedy are aware how impossible it is that he should have done anything that was inconsistent with the loftiest and strictest principles of honour. He may have been too unbending in enforcing what he thought was right, he may have been too hasty in temper, his manner may not have been conciliatory, but that he has ever been activated by any other motives than an honest and earnest desire to do his duty to the public I know to be impossible.[6]

[1] PRO 30/22/11/D, fols. 1286–7, 28 July 1854.
[2] Add. MS. 44291, fols. 206–13, 29 July 1854.
[3] PRO 30/22/11/D, fols. 1288–9, 29 July 1854.
[4] *Ibid.* E, Aberdeen to Russell, fol. 1592, 21, and fol. 1596, 23, October 1854.
[5] *Ibid.* Romilly to Russell, fols. 1580–3, 18 October 1854, and fols. 1584–7, 26 October 1854.
[6] *Ibid.* 31 October 1854.

He proposed that Lord Aberdeen should rectify the harsh wording of the Treasury report on Kennedy and that the latter should receive a suitable pension.[1]

On 17 December Gladstone produced a memorandum setting forward his views of the case.[2] On the same day Aberdeen wrote to Russell:

From personal regard to you and compassion to Kennedy, I have been willing to agree to any arrangement by which the matter could be satisfactorily terminated; but I have invariably declared that I could do nothing which should in any degree injure the position of Gladstone in the transaction...it seems to me that Gladstone's memorandum places the subject on the only footing consistent with justice, and a due regard to the character of the Government.[3]

Russell wrote a huffy reply expressing his dissatisfaction with Aberdeen's attitude and adverting to Sir John Shelley's motion for a parliamentary enquiry which he, Russell, would refuse to oppose.[4] Gladstone argued the constitutional impropriety of Shelley's notice of a motion. If such a case were to be investigated by the Commons then every single act of the sort by the Executive would be liable to such an investigation. Only a specific accusation brought against the minister in question could justify such an investigation. 'So far as poor Kennedy is concerned,' Gladstone wrote to Aberdeen, 'I shall be very glad if any good comes to him out of this business; and if the decision of competent authority shall be that my act was unwarrantable, the consequence that it will carry of removing me from the public service will cause me no regret, for I have no desire to continue in a service where tyranny and injustice are to enjoy a licenced impunity.'[5]

Aberdeen had already told Russell that Shelley could have no grounds for demanding a commission unless he had direct charges to bring against the Treasury.[6] Russell replied:

The charge I understand to be this—that some subordinate officers of the Woods and Forests found themselves incommoded by Kennedy's prying enquiries into abuses—that they soon discovered that they had at the Treasury the valuable support of Wilson & Mr Arbuthnot. That a Committee was appointed by the Treasury unfavourable to Kennedy—that Gladstone com-

[1] PRO 30/22/11/E, fols. 1622–3, 31 October 1854.
[2] Add. MS. 43068, fols. 233–4.
[3] *Ibid.* fols. 231–2 (copy).   [4] *Ibid.* fols. 235–9, 18 December 1854.
[5] Add. MS. 44089, fols. 69–71, 26 December 1854.
[6] Add. MS. 43068, fols. 240–1, 18 December 1854.

mitted an *error of judgment* in relying upon the report of this committee without hearing Kennedy. That you adopted this error and thereby injustice was done to Kennedy.

Russell reiterated Dunfermline's proposal of a Treasury minute clearing Kennedy's name and a pension of £1000, concluding with the warning: 'If the enquiry goes on, it must be a most unpleasant one.'[1] Aberdeen made no objection to a minute to clear Kennedy's character, but refused to grant a pension, fully trusting Gladstone's judgment in the case.[2] Russell continued to grumble, saying that while he did not think Vernon Smith's charge about the fate of Whig public servants was true, the Kennedy case gave 'currency to it'.[3] Gladstone, not unnaturally, was much annoyed by Russell's attitude and urged an independent inquiry by a cabinet committee.[4] When Aberdeen suggested this to Russell, Lord John replied:

I am surprised at your answer about Kennedy. I thought that I had complied with Gladstone's proposal and that he would feel no further difficulty.

I must decline to submit to the decision of the Cabinet on questions regarding my personal honour in respect to which I may appear to have been already too tame.[5]

There the matter lay, set aside by the rush of events that filled the New Year and led to the overthrow of the administration. It is a tale without an end; whether Russell would have backed down, as on other occasions in the face of a united front from his colleagues, or whether it would have been the final straw had not the more dramatic occasion of the Roebuck motion intervened, can only be a matter of conjecture. The story, here told in detail for the first time, I believe, does reveal some of the special problems involved in a coalition government, especially when one of the party leaders was a man of the temperament of Lord John Russell. His inclination to treat these matters on personal terms was clearly wrong, but Gladstone was too inflexible and understandably exasperating to the older man, who was his House leader. Lord Aberdeen's part throughout was typical, the peacemaker's, but he stuck by the colleague whom he judged to be in the right.

About the same time Gladstone wrote to Newcastle giving his

---

[1] *Ibid.* fols. 244–9, 21 December 1854.   [2] *Ibid.* fols. 250–1, 29 December 1854.
[3] *Ibid.* fols. 252–5, 30 December 1854.
[4] Add. MS. 44089, fols. 80–1, 5 January 1855.
[5] Add. MS. 43068, fols. 262–3, 4 January 1855.

reasons for resisting the demand for a parliamentary enquiry, which he thought struck at 'the whole principle of ministerial responsibility and at the whole system on which civil administration' was based. 'The question has grown to an unnatural magnitude by the manner in which it has been handled by the leader of the House of Commons,' he said, 'and I feel I am drawing near a formidable issue.'[1]

Gladstone's determination to take a firm stand when he judged that considerations of justice required him to do so were also illustrated in a row he had with the Bank of England at the same time that the Kennedy case was brewing. He had come to the conclusion that it was pointless to raise more money through the issuance of deficiency bills than experience showed would actually be needed for the current quarter and so he notified the Bank of England of his decision to reduce quarterly payments into the bank accordingly. The Bank questioned the legality of Gladstone's action and urged him to obtain the opinion of the law officers of the Crown. The Attorney General and the Solicitor General supported Gladstone's view, whereupon to his indignation the Bank turned to private counsel to obtain a contrary opinion. This, Gladstone told Aberdeen, made it a cabinet matter.[2] Aberdeen approved of Gladstone's actions, but did not see what the cabinet could do. 'However right you may be, is it not doubtful how far you may be able to coerce the bank? I apprehend that Lord Monteagle holds in his hands the means of resisting you, which he will probably not be slow to employ.'[3]

Likewise, when the Bank proposed that its discretionary powers with respect to the issue of bank-notes should be increased, Gladstone raised objections and began to devise further schemes to revise the banking relations between the Bank and the state, and the governance of savings-bank finance. The fall of the government precluded further action and the Bank found his successor easier to deal with.[4]

All parliamentary governments face the same sort of problems and endure the same sort of frustrations to a greater or lesser degree as did the administration of Lord Aberdeen. Such experiences provided a searching test for the viability of the coalition, and despite the strains it continued to survive. The problems produced by war, however, proved to be too intractable, and to these we must now turn.

[1] Add. MS. 44262, 5 January 1855.
[2] Add. MS. 44089, fols. 52–4, 8 September 1854.   [3] *Ibid.* fol. 55, 16 September 1854.
[4] Add MS. 44744, fols. 85–118.

IV

THE CRIMEAN WAR AND THE
FALL OF THE COALITION

THE CONDUCT OF THE WAR—THE DEBATE IN PARLIAMENT, APRIL–AUGUST 1854

War estimates and war finances; first questions and criticisms

The prosecution of the war against Russia was, of course, the most pressing task facing the coalition government throughout 1854. From the beginning of the year preparations were under way and military as well as naval forces were already mobilised in the Black Sea area when war was declared at the end of March. Serious fighting did not begin, however, until the early autumn, after the prorogation of parliament. The military crisis of 1854, therefore, developed while parliament was not sitting, as had the diplomatic crisis of the preceding year.

Initially both the ministers and the public at large were unduly complacent respecting the efficiency and preparedness of the armed forces for the struggle that lay ahead. All too long the old duke of Wellington's tremendous prestige and influence had dominated British military policy. It is quite extraordinary how right up to his death in 1852 at the age of eighty-three everybody deferred to his military opinions. The result was that nothing changed. For forty years the Peninsular mentality remained supreme. The appointment and promotion of officers were governed in the main by two factors: money, which determined the purchase of commissions up to the rank of colonel, and seniority, which was normally the determining factor in the appointment and promotion of officers above that rank. Thus the men chosen to direct this war on the distant shores of the Black Sea in the middle 1850s were almost all veterans of the Peninsular War of four decades earlier. Fitzroy Somerset, first Earl Raglan, born in 1788, who had been Wellington's aide-de-camp in Spain and wounded at Waterloo, and who for a quarter of a century had been secretary at the Horse Guards until he was made Master General of the Ordnance in the coalition government, was the inevitable choice as commander of the expeditionary force. Raglan's qualities as a gentleman made him highly respected by all who had contact with him, but in retrospect it is perfectly clear that his age and the long years of routine in Whitehall did not qualify him for the exacting task now assigned to him, which in the end cost him his life.

For reasons already noticed the war took a surprisingly small proportion of parliament's time in the session of 1854, despite general preoccupation with it. Once the die had been cast there was little that parliament could discuss until the campaign had begun. The months in which parliament was in session were the months of preparation during which the country's forces were taking the field, and it was difficult for the opposition leaders or private members to raise matters of general war policy at this stage.

The naval and military estimates were passed with very little debate. With a certain irony in view of the outcome, in introducing these estimates on the eve of the war Sidney Herbert chose to dwell on a series of reforms that had been initiated in recent years, provision for the education both of officers and other ranks, arrangements for the training of army surgeons, improvements in the system of discipline, of pay, of accommodation on transports, the introduction of a much more accurate rifle (the Minié), the provision of an adequate shooting range at Hythe, and the reduction of colonial garrisons.[1]

Herbert had taken an active interest in the experiments at Enfield on the new French rifle designed by Captain Minié and according to Lord Stanmore its early adoption throughout the Army was 'largely due to his insistence'.[2] Herbert was also largely responsible for the opening of an experimental military camp at Chobham, the precursor of Aldershot, where troops could be trained for field service.[3] Another reform undertaken at this time was the abolition of the colonel's clothing privilege. Under the old system colonels of regiments were given a fixed allowance for clothing from which they furnished their men. According to Herbert the system was inefficient and expensive, but the colonels did not make big profits.[4] *The Times*, which denounced the system as 'disgraceful and unbecoming', thought otherwise. It pointed out that Prince Albert made a profit of £1,840 for clothing the Grenadier Guards in addition to his pay as Colonel of £1,200. This reform was clearly long overdue.[5]

---

[1] *Hansard*, CXXX, 1283–92. [2] *Herbert*, I, 177. [3] *Ibid*.
[4] 'The army before Sebastopol', fourth report, pp. 161–97, *P.P. 1854–5*, IX, 184–5.
[5] *The Times*, 27 February 1854.

A further important military reform initiated by Herbert in the course of the year 1854 was the abolition of the archaic brevet, whereby from time to time wholesale and artificial promotions were made to army officers. On the recommendation of a special commission on promotions and retirements it was now proposed to base promotion on the principle of reward for service, but since this change would affect the vested interests of existing field officers, it was proposed that a final brevet should be granted which would cost the Treasury £18,550. Herbert assured the Chancellor of the Exchequer that the cost of the brevet and of the addition to the retired list would be met approximately by the savings effected by the new clothing arrangements, which provided for fixed pay to the colonels in lieu of the profits they formerly derived from sale of clothing.[1]

Sir James Graham in introducing the naval estimates dwelt in particular on the important change in progress 'caused by the application of screw power as an auxiliary to sailing power'.[2] Debate on these estimates was very brief and for the most part limited to questions and suggestions made by members with military experience. Sir John Walsh drew attention to the incongruity of a great power such as Britain proposing to fight a European war with what amounted to a peace establishment, and that distributed all over the world. 'But why should England have an army only of 40,000 men available for foreign service?' he asked. 'Why...with 27,000,000 inhabitants, with the richest country on the face of the globe, and with soldiers who had never been surpassed by any troops in the world, should we not be a military nation if an European war should occur?'[3] The question was not answered until the twentieth century.

The army estimates only came to six and a quarter million pounds, but supplemental votes brought them to over ten million. Ordnance estimates, including supplemental, came to over three million, while the naval estimates were £7,480,000, with another £1,457,000 supplementary, making a total of just under nine million.[4]

To meet these increased expenditures Gladstone brought in a budget early in March before war was declared and a supplementary budget in May when it was clear that further increases in expenditure were necessary. Although the exigencies of war required the Chancellor to find a great increase in revenue, the budget of 1854 was a simpler and more

[1] Herbert Papers, to Gladstone, 5 June 1854; see also Stanmore, *Herbert*, I, 232–3.
[2] *Hansard*, CXXX, 1310–13.   [3] *Ibid.* 1268.   [4] *Annual Register, 1854*, pp. 149–52.

straightforward affair than that of the preceding year, on which it was built. Gladstone refused to touch any of the remissions of indirect taxation that he had made in 1853, but he had to forgo the plan of reducing the income tax. Indeed this 'mighty engine' was to be made the main means of financing the war, for the Chancellor strongly asserted the principle that a country bent on war must endeavour to pay its way and not put the burden on posterity, as had been done so disastrously in the early stages of the French Revolutionary Wars.[1] Consequently he asked for doubling of the income tax, initially for half a year, to help meet the deficiency created by increased military expenditures, a deficiency that would have been greater had it not been for the surplus resulting from last year's budget. He also proposed to obtain additional revenue from a revised stamp tax.[2] In the supplementary budget produced on 8 May he extended the increase of the income tax from half to the whole year and he proposed to obtain additional revenue from increased duties on spirits, malt and sugar.[3]

With the exception of the succession duty the returns from the 1853 budget had been very favourable,[4] but the plans for conversion had been upset by an adverse turn in the money markets under the shadow of war, which had not been anticipated when the budget of 1853 was introduced. Gladstone had used up a large part of the existing exchequer balances in the execution of his conversion programme and as a result he now had to ask for authority first to issue exchequer bills and later exchequer bonds in anticipation of future revenue.[5] This did not add to the permanent indebtedness, which he was determined to keep to a minimum, but it did give the opposition an opportunity for criticism of his lack of foresight in his conversion plans.

As one who had accepted the necessity of war reluctantly, Gladstone took some relish in telling those who had clamoured for it that they must be prepared to pay the bill. Developing his argument in favour of taxation as against borrowing, he said:

[1] For a criticism of Gladstone's views on war loans see Northcote, *Financial Policy*, pp. 258–64.
[2] *Annual Register, 1854*, pp. 153–9.
[3] *Ibid.* 172–80. See also Appendix D below; Add. MS. 44778, fol. 181, Gladstone memo. of 3 May 1856; Northcote, *Twenty years*, pp. 243–51.
[4] Income exceeded expenditure by £1,035,000 (Add. MS. 44743, fol. 159, table I, 6 March 1854), whereas expenditure was £1,012,000 less than expected (*ibid.* fol. 160, table II). Customs duties to the amount of £1,483,000 had been repealed in the 1853 budget, but customs revenue rose £204,000 (*ibid.* fol. 161, table IV).
[5] See further Northcote, *Twenty years*, pp. 251–7.

The expenses of a war are the moral check which it has pleased the Almighty to impose upon the ambition and the lust of conquest that are inherent in so many nations. There is pomp and circumstance, there is glory and excitement about war, which, notwithstanding the miseries it entails, invests it with charms in the eyes of the community, and tends to blind men to those evils to a fearful and dangerous degree. The necessity of meeting from year to year the expenditure which it entails is a salutary and a wholesome check, making them feel what they are about, and making them measure the cost of the benefit upon which they may calculate.[1]

Disraeli accepted the necessity of increased revenues, but took Gladstone to task severely for the failure of his debt conversion and for his depletion of exchequer balances.[2] In a second speech on 21 March[3] he broadened his attack to the more general subject of the government's war policy or policies, for he maintained that the pronouncements of various ministers were contradictory. He developed this theme of differences among the ministers with some effect, saying:

I would like to know how the war is to be carried on with efficiency and success by men who have not settled what the object of the war is. The war has been brought about by two opposite opinions in the Cabinet. These conflicting opinions have led to all the vacillation, all the perplexity, all the fitfulness, all the timidity, and all the occasional violence, to which this question has given rise; and I must say that if the noble Lord the leader of this House—I speak my solemn conviction—had remained Prime Minister of this country, or if the noble Lord the Secretary of State for the Home Department, who is not here, had been minister of this country—or if Lord Derby had continued Minister of this country—nay, if Lord Aberdeen—I wish to state the case fairly—had been Minister of this country, with a sympathizing Cabinet, there would have been no war. It is a coalition war. Rival opinions, contrary politics, and discordant systems have produced that vacillation and perplexity, that at last you are going to war with an opponent who does not want to fight, and whom you are unwilling to encounter. What a mess for a great country! And all brought about by such distinguished administrative ability! And then they say if we criticise their policy, we are bound immediately to come forward, and propose a vote of no confidence in them. I tell them again I will not propose a vote of no confidence in men who prove to me every hour that they have no confidence in each other.[4]

It was a smart speech calculated to raise the morale of his followers, but one which Gladstone had no great difficulty in answering. In the

[1] *Hansard*, CXXXI, 376.   [2] *Ibid.* 408–21.   [3] *Ibid.* 1124–61.   [4] *Ibid.* 1156–7.

debate on the supplementary budget Disraeli began to question the policy of pay-as-you-go, chiding Gladstone for his strictures on Pitt, and Russell for breaking with the principles of Whig finance, 'principles', he cried, 'which Mr Fox never deserted nor relinquished, and which, notwithstanding the comparative degradation of the office which the noble Lord now fills, I did not believe that he, in deference to the Chancellor of the Exchequer and Lord Aberdeen, would have relinquished in the House of Commons'. (Loud cries of 'Oh!' from the ministerial, and cheers from the opposition, benches.[1])

The two income tax bills and the bills authorising the issuance of exchequer bills and exchequer bonds were passed with little debate. An amendment by T. Baring at the committee stage of the Exchequer Bonds Bill on 22 May was defeated by a vote of 290 to 186. The majority included the 39 Peelites in the House and at least 23 Derbyites.[2]

There were also divisions on a Malt Tax Bill and an Excise Duties Bill in which the government was sustained by votes of 224 to 143 and 303 to 195 respectively. On the former vote, rejecting a hostile amendment, the 28 Peelites in the House supported the government, as did at least 13 independent Conservatives, while on the latter the 37 Peelites in the House supported the bill, and some 25 independent Conservatives.[3] The general lack of divisions on financial measures was in marked contrast with the preceding year.[4]

In the House of Lords the government was subject intermittently to prodding questions from such independent critics as Clanricarde, Hardwicke and Ellenborough, who pressed for information about relations with the German Powers and criticised the failure to prevent Russian demolition and evacuation in Circassia. They also raised critical questions about the administrative arrangements for the troops arriving in Gallipoli, the cost of transporting troops to the East, the method of paying them, and the provision of baggage horses. The brunt of the

---

[1] *Annual Register, 1854*, p. 185.

[2] *Hansard*, CXXXIII, 777–80. See Appendices A and B.

[3] *Ibid.* 49–52, 393–7. See Appendices A and B.

[4] Gladstone also instituted an important reform of the public accounts in 1854. Hitherto the cost of collecting the revenue and some other miscellaneous expenses had been paid out of the gross revenue on collection and not shown on the national balance sheet of revenue and expenditures. Gladstone transferred these charges, except for a few that he extinguished, to the consolidated fund, which of course produced an equivalent increase in the annual revenue, amounting to some £4,000,000 per annum. See Northcote, *Financial Policy*, pp. 237–9.

answers to these questions of course fell on Clarendon and Newcastle, but on occasion the Prime Minister became involved.[1]

The publication of a joint memorandum on the Eastern Question by the Austrian and Prussian governments provoked a remarkable speech from old Lord Lyndhurst on 19 June. With much documentation he developed the thesis of Russia's long-planned encroachment in the Middle East and he demanded the prosecution of the war to destroy Russian power in that area. Lord Clarendon defended Austria against Lyndhurst's criticisms, pointing out that, with Prussia, she had summoned Russia to withdraw from the Principalities and that in anticipation of a refusal she had concluded a military convention with Turkey.[2] He said that it was premature to talk about peace terms, but he did not hesitate to assert that it was in the interests of Europe to curtail Russia's power and ambitions. Lord Derby developed Lyndhurst's argument that the Austro-German memorandum envisaged German withdrawal once the Principalities had been evacuated, which would have left Turkey still open to Russian threats. He warned that, after such great expenditure as had been made, the country would not be satisfied unless it was assured that the danger of further Russian aggression was removed. Lord Aberdeen made an unfortunate intervention in the debate, going further than it was politic for a wartime Prime Minister to do in exonerating Russia from Lyndhurst's charges of long-term aggression. This speech was badly received both by the House and by the public.

Indeed some of Russell's own constituents in the city were so annoyed by the Prime Minister's remarks that they presented an address to the Lord Mayor condemning the speech and in contrast praising the manly declarations of Russell and Clarendon; they called on the Lord Mayor to preside over a meeting to be held at the Guildhall to declare the country's determination not to make peace with Russia without satisfaction. 'The position of the Government has become precarious', Russell commented in passing this news on to Aberdeen.[3] Arthur Gordon wrote indignantly to Gladstone on this occasion, saying:

The plot thickens—Lord John with an exceedingly dry note, has sent my father a requisition to the Lord Mayor to preside at a public meeting at the Guildhall to thank Lord John and Clarendon for their 'English' speeches, & to record their 'indignation' at my father's speech on Monday last. Lord John

---

[1] See *Hansard*, CXXXIII–CXXXV, and the *Annual Register, 1854*.
[2] See below, p. 434 n. 3.
[3] *Ab. Cor. 1854–5*, p. 152, 23 June 1854.

cooly informs my father that *he* (Ld A.) has brought the Govt. into a very precarious position.[1]

Gladstone expressed his vexation, comparing the requisition to that of Canning to Pitt under the Addington government, and intimated his anxiety to be of some use to Lord Aberdeen.[2]

In the meantime Layard gave notice of a motion in the House of Commons with a view to denouncing Aberdeen's speech. The government took alarm and proposed to meet this challenge with an amendment. 'After the various defeats of the Government', Aberdeen wrote to the queen, 'it is most essential that an opportunity should be found of testing the real feelings of the House of Commons.'[3] At the same time, with the queen's approbation,[4] he took what Greville considered 'a step of questionable prudence and dignity', namely the tabling of a memorandum on the Treaty of Adrianople which he had written in 1829 as Foreign Secretary, in order to give himself the opportunity of explaining his previous remarks. Then on 26 June the Prime Minister delivered a long and vigorous speech in which he made it clear that he had no illusions about the danger of Russian aggression, although he did note a change in Russian policy since the days of Catherine the Great. Now that war was declared he recognised that everything depended on its outcome, but the independence and integrity of Turkey were essential war aims. He reiterated his well-known love of peace and detestation of war, but avowed that no one had been more urgent than himself in insisting on a speedy concentration of forces in support of Turkey.[5] Aberdeen's speech was given a good hearing, but it was followed by 'a violent personal attack' made on him by Clanricarde, which the Prime Minister told the queen was 'very coldly received throughout'.[6] The queen expressed her sympathy with him over the public misunderstanding of his position, which she attributed to his candour and courage in expressing his opinions, but she shrewdly warned him not to attempt any further vindications of the emperor of Russia.[7]

Clarendon told Aberdeen that he thought the speech had been 'quite

[1] Add. MS. 44319, fols. 54–5, Friday [23 June 1854].
[2] *Ab. Cor. 1854–5*, p. 153, 23 June 1854.   [3] R.A. G14, fol. 28, 24 June 1854.
[4] *Ab. Cor. 1854–5*, p. 154, 26 June 1854. Nevertheless, the queen and Clarendon (*ibid.* p. 155, 26 June 1854) both warned him of the necessity of recognising the state of public opinion.   [5] *Hansard*, CXXXIV, 640–50.
[6] *Ibid.* 650–65; R.A. G14, fol. 37, 26 June 1854.
[7] R.A. G14, fol. 36, 26 June 1854; *Ab. Cor. 1854–5*, p. 156, 26 June 1854.

successful' and that he believed it had 'a very good effect below the bar'. He said that the general opinion was that Clanricarde had damaged no one but himself.[1] To the king of the Belgians who wrote to congratulate him on the speech,[2] Aberdeen revealed his real feelings. He remarked on the serious state of affairs since the French emperor had determined to carry on the war to the extremity. He was not afraid of Russian power in the west of Europe, but he observed that his ally seemed to be generally regarded with as much alarm and hate as was the first Bonaparte. Aberdeen thought that notwithstanding the vigour of their warlike operations they would 'do well not to lay aside altogether a spirit of moderation and forbearance which must ultimately be to our own advantage'.[3]

On hearing of Aberdeen's intention to debate the matter in the Lords, Layard withdrew his motion in the Commons, but expressed the opinion that that House should have an opportunity for a general discussion on foreign affairs before the session was concluded. This never took place (except for incidental comment in other debates) but in the course of the session critical questions were raised by various members, which were answered generally by Russell, Graham or Herbert, who all vigorously defended the government's conduct of the war. In the criticism that was made, on the basis of *The Times* reports, of the administrative arrangements for the reception of British troops in Gallipoli, we may see the beginnings of a wave of public opinion that was to overwhelm the government in the following year. But at this stage the first charges were dismissed by Herbert in the Commons, as they were by Newcastle in the Lords, as unfounded, and Herbert in particular took the *Times* correspondent to task for his unjust criticism of Sir John Burgoyne, the general whom the government had sent out to reconnoitre the situation in the East.[4]

There was also an attempt to reflect on the failure of British naval activity in the Black Sea or the lack of it. 'It is quite clear', Clarendon wrote to Russell in regard to a question from Layard on this theme, 'that Stratford means to run down Dundas through Layard upon whose spite (particularly against myself) he can reckon...I can't see how *war* is to be carried on agst the enemy & at the same time agst the Govt by its own agents.'[5]

[1] *Ab. Cor. 1854–5*, p. 156, 26 June 1854. [2] *Ibid.* p. 159, 30 June 1854.
[3] *Ibid.* pp. 161–2, 4 July 1854. [4] *Hansard*, CXXXII, 999–1003.
[5] PRO 30/22/11/C, 28 April 1854.

It was more difficult for Russell to defend the actions of the Turkish government in suppressing the insurrection of its Greek subjects against the criticism of Cobden and Bright. Here, it may be noted, the warlike Layard joined Russell in defending the Turks against the spokesmen of the Manchester School.[1] On 29 June Graham replied to a criticism from Milner Gibson objecting to the naval bombardment of undefended towns and villages in the Baltic. In Palmerstonian language that he was capable of using on occasion, he bluntly asserted the navy's right to go after the enemy in their harbours if they refused to fight at sea. 'I for one', he concluded, 'am not prepared to check the pursuit of such a course; and I hope and believe that in so acting I and my Colleagues will not violate either the feeling or the sentiments of the people of England.'[2]

Problems of military organization — the separation of the War Office from the Colonial Office

Early in the struggle men began to ask whether Britain's military constitution, which had hardly changed since the days of Marlborough, could be good enough to win a modern war. Inevitably this debate touched the delicate ground of the royal prerogative, which in the duke of York's administration of the army had proved its value.[3] Naturally, too, proposals for modernisation came more easily from men out of office, who, because they were not immersed in the task of administration, had time to think the problem through; men in office were more than fully employed in the attempt to make antiquated machinery work and consequently flinched from the task of simultaneously reconstructing it. Moreover, this machinery, much of it dating from the time of Marlborough, had worked reasonably well in the Napoleonic Wars, during the latter part of which the British army had operated with notable success. The two chief protagonists in this debate were the duke of Newcastle and Earl Grey, who had been Secretary at War from 1834 to 1839 and Secretary for War and Colonies from 1846 to 1852. The latter's position was, however, weakened by his own failure when he was in office in peacetime to make the changes he now demanded in

---

[1] Hansard, cxxxii, 1003–17; Annual Register, 1854, pp. 72–3. For the Greek crisis see below, pp. 420–1.
[2] Hansard, cxxxiv, 915–21. For operations in the Baltic, see below, pp. 427–8.
[3] See Richard Glover, Peninsular preparation. I am indebted to Dr Glover's kind assistance in the composition of this paragraph.

the opening months of a new war of his successor, who bore the main responsibility of organising the campaign.

Early in May Grey alarmed the prince consort by telling him that the army should be placed 'under a Civil Board and under the control of the House of Commons'. 'My protest that this would be destroying the prerogative of the Crown, &c., &c., did not make the slightest impression upon him,' the prince wrote indignantly to Aberdeen; 'he continued eagerly to decry the present system, the gross ignorance of military men, their incapacity to reform the Army, and his hope to bring forward facts that would startle the world.' Prince Albert told the Prime Minister that he regarded this as the 'gravest constitutional question' and hoped that the government would give it careful consideration.[1] Lord Aberdeen tried to reassure the prince, saying that the motion for papers which Lord Grey had subsequently made in the House of Lords was 'fairly harmless'. He thought that it would familiarise the public with the question and that some reform might be 'requisite'.[2]

On 7 April Grey spoke to his motion for papers in the House of Lords in a long and well-informed speech[3] in which he vividly described the faults of the existing system as he saw them from his own experience and sketched out possible reforms to place the command of the army on a more rational basis. His speech may be quoted at some length since it provides such a telling description of the patchwork arrangement that passed for a military system on the eve of the war and the problems that it entailed.

My Lords [he said], these important duties are divided amongst a great number of entirely independent departments. The Commander in Chief has the command of the troops—except of the Artillery and Engineers, which are not directly under his orders—but he has no authority whatever to adopt measures involving any expense without the consent of other Departments of the Government. On the other hand, it is the duty of the Secretary at War to submit to Parliament the estimates for the Army, and to see that the money devoted is duly applied to the intended objects. He is always expected to answer in Parliament all complaints which are made as to the misapplication of that money or the mismanagement of the service for which it was intended to provide. But, while he has this duty, he has no right, officially and properly,

[1] *Ab. Cor. 1854–5*, pp. 88–9, from prince consort, no date. Grey further damned himself in the prince's eyes by saying that with his ministerial experience he would show Cobden and Bright how an attack on the army should be made.
[2] *Ibid.* p. 89, 2 April 1854.   [3] *Hansard*, CXXXII, 606–39.

to interfere in the slightest degree in any one of the measures of the Commander in Chief, even those which most materially in their consequences affect the expenditure of the Army, unless they involve some immediate outlay. No money is required for carrying into effect the measures of the Commander in Chief. The Secretary at War, according to the theory of the service, has no right to interfere. Then, again, the Master General of the Ordnance has personally the command of the Artillery and the Engineers. Without the assistance of any board, he performs, with respect to those two corps, the duties which, with regard to the rest of the Army, appertain to the Commander in Chief. In conjunction with the Board of Ordnance, the Master General has a very great variety of duties to perform, connected not only with the Ordnance and Engineer Corps, but also with the general management of the Army...The Master General and the Board of Ordnance have to attend to the barracks, the fortification, and some of the arms; but nothing can be more capricious than the rule; for instance, the Board of Ordnance provides the cavalry with carbines, not with swords...Lastly the Board of Treasury, in addition to having a general control over all matters relating to expenditure, keeps directly in its own hands all that relates to that important branch of military arrangements which consists in providing the troops with provisions, at least on foreign stations.[1]

Lord Grey failed to add that the Home Secretary had responsibility for the militia and for the use of troops in the United Kingdom in aid of the civil power. He went on to emphasise, however, that with the exception of the Treasury, which was completely independent, all the other offices and authorities, which he described, were in theory under the control of the Secretary of State for War and Colonies, who was supposedly responsible for their coordination. Actually, in practice, this was not possible, he argued, for a minister who was responsible for the detailed administration of all the colonies.[2]

He proceeded to give a harrowing account of the high mortality rates that the army had suffered in tropical stations because of improper rations and insufficient barrack accommodation. The failure to remedy these conditions sooner he attributed to the division of authority between the War Office and the Treasury. He pointed out that as long ago as 1810 Sir Willoughby Gordon[3] had urged the consolidation of the various authorities responsible for the army into one great office; that he

---

[1] *Hansard*, CXXII, 608–9.
[2] *The Times*, 27 February 1854, made the same point.
[3] Sir James Willoughby Gordon (1773–1851) had been military secretary to the duke of York and from 1811 to 1812 Quartermaster General in the Peninsula under Wellington.

himself had been chairman of a royal commission that had reported to parliament in 1837 recommending extensive changes in the organisation of the army which had not been adopted.

Grey urged the necessity of withdrawing the War Office from the jurisdiction of the Secretary of State for the Colonies, and the consolidation of the financial and military administration of the army in one office, preferring the creation of an Army Board under a responsible minister, comparable to the Admiralty Board, to the creation of a fourth Secretary of State, which he thought would lead to anomalies. He vigorously rebutted the argument, for which he could see no grounds, that his proposed reform would interfere with the prerogative of the Crown. Shrewdly he observed:

Upon this subject I will remark that it is quite true the Crown ought to have sole and exclusive command of the Army; but the Crown ought equally to have the full and exclusive command over every other branch of the Executive Government; and if either House of Parliament were to attempt to take any branch of the executive power out of the hands of the responsible servants of the Crown—if Committees were appointed to execute administrative duties, as in the time of the Great Rebellion—that, I say, would be a very dangerous invasion of the Royal prerogative, and a departure from the principles of the constitution. But there is no distinction, that I am aware of, between the military and any other branch of the executive authority of the Crown; and if the rule I have mentioned holds good in all cases, there is also another rule which holds equally good, and that is, that none of the powers of the Crown are to be exercised except at the hands of some responsible Minister, and that Parliament is perfectly free to tender advice to the Crown as to the manner in which any powers vested in the Crown should be exercised.[1]

He pointed out how inconvenient it would be if the Crown was to be held personally responsible for any mistakes in the conduct of a war. Nor was it possible for the Crown to shelter behind any imaginary independent authority of the Commander-in-Chief. 'How can the Government, being responsible to Parliament for the amount of the estimates, and for the economy with which the public service is conducted, be irresponsible for the manner in which the most public money is expended upon the Army?' he asked. 'If responsibility to Parliament means anything', he continued, 'it implies a responsibility that the greatest possible amount of efficiency shall be obtained for a given

[1] *Hansard*, CXXXII, 634.

397

outlay; but if they have no control over the organisation and administration of the Army, how can the Government be held responsible for its efficiency?'[1]

After such a wide-sweeping attack the earl's motion asking for papers regarding any change in the administration of the army or of the department of the Secretary of State for War and Colonies seemed anticlimactic. The duke of Newcastle, answering on behalf of the government, made no objection to accepting the motion for papers, but he denied the validity of much of Lord Grey's argument. He did not rule out the possibility of some changes, but he maintained that in fact the system did work; that the shortcomings Grey had referred to had been righted; that the various authorities responsible for the army all worked very closely together. Considering the various proposals for reorganisation that had been made, Newcastle admitted the strength of the argument against the commissariat being under the control of the Treasury, but fatally he rested his case for the *status quo* in the arms of the dead duke. 'I am sure my noble Friend behind me (Lord Panmure) is not ignorant of the fact that this is a subject upon which the duke of Wellington—and to his opinions we ought to bow in such matters—felt very strongly, and I have myself seen in the handwriting of the duke of Wellington the strongest possible assertion of his conviction that it was most desirable that the Commissariat should remain in the hands of the Treasury.'[2] So did the unfortunate influence of the Iron Duke live after him. Against Lord Panmure's known views to the contrary Newcastle argued for the necessity of maintaining a permanent commissariat. He pointed out that with forty or fifty colonies 'this country is really very seldom free from some military undertaking or other'. He asked how the Kafir War could have been carried on efficiently without the able body of commissariat officers who accompanied the army. Then, in no position yet to judge what the future held in store, he went on to say: 'I should look with much less confidence than I do to the departure of that force which is about to be despatched to the East if it were not possible to send with that army, I believe, as capable, as intelligent, and as able a body of Commissariat officers as ever accompanied an army into the field.' (This unqualified assertion is a fair example of how unprepared the poor duke was for the disasters that were to come.) Turning to Lord Grey's observations regarding the lack of harmony between the various authorities responsible for the

[1] *Hansard*, CXXXII, 635.   [2] *Ibid.* 646.

army, Newcastle commented: 'I will only say that the noble Earl has been unfortunate in his experience; I cannot, from my own, corroborate the statement of the noble Earl.' And a little later he continued:

I can only say, and I say it with the greatest sincerity, that having in the last two months been engaged with the whole of the military and naval departments—having had daily, almost hourly, communications, verbally in the first instance, and subsequently in writing, with my noble Friend the Commander in Chief, with my noble Friend the Master General of the Ordnance, with my right hon. Friend the Secretary at War, with the heads of the Commissariat Department, and, as an important element in the matter, with my right hon. Friend the First Lord of the Admiralty, and those of his department who are more immediately connected with transports—there never has been the slightest want of harmony amongst us—there never has been the slightest difference of opinion—and there never has been the slightest hesitation, after the instructions to carry out the directions of the Government have been received...I say the experience of the last two or three months does not lead to the belief that any very great evil is to be apprehended in consequence of the present system. I admit that there may be improvements, but what I want to prove is, that the existing system is not so radically and essentially vicious as the noble Earl wished to represent.

Adverting to the fears expressed by Lord Ellenborough regarding the magnitude of the operations under way, Newcastle went on to give further hostages to fate:

I have a right to say that, under the circumstances, and at this time, the fact of having sent a large body of men to the East in better condition, in more admirable order, and with greater expedition than we had formerly any idea of, either in this or in any other country, does reflect the highest credit upon the efficiency of every department engaged in the undertaking...I believe that such careful preparations never were made before, whether I look to the food which has been provided for the men, to the arrangements for their comfort and convenience, or even to the indulgences, in the shape of beverages and matters of minor importance, which have been supplied to them.[1]

The duke of Newcastle maintained that he himself frequently intervened in these arrangements to ensure central control, and that, despite the gossip of the clubs to the contrary, the machinery to date had run smoothly. Consequently he would be very loath to accept any of Grey's proposals for major change in time of war for fear of dislocating the machinery already effectively in operation. He quoted Grey's different

[1] *Ibid.* 649.

opinion on the desirability of dividing the War Office from the Colonial Office when the matter was raised in 1850 and argued against the proposal of placing the army under the control of a Board and of placing its patronage in the hands of a minister at the head of such a Board. 'My Lords,' he concluded, 'however inefficiently I have replied to the very elaborate speech of one, on these matters, of the most experienced Members of this House—I am bound to say, on behalf of the Government, that though not repudiating alterations, much less improvements, we do deprecate any attempt to make at this juncture, extensive changes in the existing system, and still more do I deprecate an attempt to dislocate the important joints of a machinery which, if put out of gear, cannot readily be replaced, and may lead, at the present time of war, to most disastrous consequences.'[1]

Newcastle was strongly supported by the commander-in-chief, Lord Hardinge, a man of long experience, both on active duty in the field and in various high offices connected with the army.[2] Hardinge sharply defended the reputation of Wellington against supposed slurs cast on his memory by Lord Grey and then proceeded to testify to the smooth and efficient working of the existing system. He allowed that there might be room for some improvements in the Ordnance Department, but warned against any attempt to limit the powers of the commander-in-chief that might restrict his effectiveness in time of war. Alluding to the expedition recently sent to Turkey, he said that 'the whole of the forces sent out had embarked with an alacrity, a readiness, and a discipline which did them the greatest possible honour'. He also heaped praises on his friend the duke of Newcastle, saying that 'never had he known less alterations made in the orders when once issued, than had been made in the last two months', and 'from no Secretary of State had he ever received more satisfactory assistance than from the noble Duke'.[3]

Lord Ellenborough, another former Governor General of India, and briefly First Lord of the Admiralty in Peel's reconstituted ministry of 1846, admonished the House, or rather members not there, for the small attendance to debate such an important subject. He supported Lord Grey's advocacy of the principle 'that the military should be entirely

[1] *Hansard*, cxxxii, 654.
[2] Sir Henry Hardinge, first Viscount Hardinge of Lahore (1785–1856), served under Moore and Wellington in the Peninsular Wars and under Gough in India. He was Secretary at War in 1828–30 and 1841–4, Governor General of India, 1844–7, and Master General of the Ordnance in 1852 before succeeding Wellington as Commander-in-Chief.　　　　[3] *Hansard*, cxxxii, 654–7.

subordinate to the civil authority', but he strongly disagreed with the proposal to entrust any authority to a Board, citing his own limited experience at the Admiralty. He gave it as his opinion that the overall direction of the war should be in the hands of the Prime Minister, although doubting that the present Prime Minister with his well-known hatred of war would show an aptitude for such work. With gloomy reference to the failure of that great minister in peace, Mr Pitt, as a war minister, he solemnly warned the government of the great dangers and difficulties that lay ahead of them, and of the necessity of securing early victories if the public were to remain in support of what he described as a 'statesman's war'.[1]

Lord Panmure, who had been Secretary at War in the Russell administration, while asking for no sudden and violent change, warmly supported Lord Grey's advocacy of a policy of centralisation, and especially insisted on the necessity of withdrawing the commissariat from the control of the Treasury.[2] In winding up the debate Lord Grey expressed his scepticism regarding Newcastle's claims as to the harmonious working of the present system. He hoped that everything had been as well managed as was claimed, but he reminded the noble duke 'that the time for boasting was not when the harness was put on, but when it was taken off'.[3]

Lord John Russell listened with sympathy to the proposals of his former colleagues. With all hope of his Reform Bill now abandoned, he turned his attention more fully to the problems connected with the prosecution of the war. On 24 April, he produced an important, if badly written, memorandum on the subject of the command of the army. He rejected the idea of transferring all the powers of the Secretary of State to the Secretary at War, both because of the relationship of that minister to the commander-in-chief, and because he was primarily a financial officer in the House of Commons. He also rejected Grey's proposal of vesting the control of the army in a Board as unsuitable. He therefore proposed to give the existing Secretary of State for War control over all the other authorities, the commander-in-chief, the Board of Ordnance, the Secretary at War and the commissariat, and to relieve him of responsibility for the Colonies, which would pass to a fourth Secretary of State. The Secretaries of State for the Colonies and for Home Affairs would indicate their military requirements to the Secretary of State for the War Department, who would settle the overall

---

[1] *Ibid.* 657–62.   [2] *Ibid.* 662–5.   [3] *Ibid.* 665–9.

disposition of the forces with the cabinet.[1] On 27 April Aberdeen replied saying that he considered Russell's proposed division 'not only practical but highly advantageous'.[2] For the moment, however, the cabinet was busy with other plans.[3]

On 5 May Russell wrote again to Aberdeen complaining of the failure of the cabinet to deal with the proposed division of the War and Colonial Departments. Aberdeen had suggested in conversation that in the event of a division Russell should take one of the two offices. Russell now wrote:

I think the time has arrived when I ought either to take office or to cease to be a member of your Government.

Had I full confidence in the Administration, of which you are the head, I should not scruple to take office under you.

But the late meetings of the Cabinet have shown so much indecision, and there is so much reluctance to adopt those measures which would force the Emperor of Russia to consent to a speedy peace, that I can feel no such confidence.

Indeed, the sooner I can be relieved of my share of the responsibility the better.[4]

Normally such a letter from a cabinet minister to a Prime Minister could have meant nothing but resignation, but by this time Aberdeen was fully familiar with Lord John's eccentricities. He wrote to Russell on the same day, saying that he had taken the division of the Colonial Office for granted since it had been highly approved by Graham, Gladstone and Newcastle. He agreed, however, to submit the matter formally to the cabinet, saying that it had escaped him at the last meeting.[5]

Two weeks later Russell circulated another memorandum[6] on the separation of the War Office from the Colonial Office in which he said:

This is not the moment for consolidating & rearranging departments which have at least practice & experience in the conduct of military affairs. But

[1] *Ab. Cor. 1854–5*, pp. 107–8, partly reproduced in Walpole, *Russell*, II, 218–19.
[2] PRO 30/22/11/C, fol. 1034 (copy).
[3] See below, pp. 449–52.
[4] Walpole, *Russell*, II, 220–1. On the same day Lord Minto had advised his son-in-law that he might be best out of the government (PRO 30/22/11/D, fols. 1061–2).
[5] PRO 30/22/11/d, fol. 1053, 5 May 1854.
[6] *Ibid.* fols. 1099–1102, 20 May 1854. Gooch, *Later correspondence*, II, 165, omits the latter part of this passage from his text, without any indication.

neither is it the moment for heaping upon one man the conduct of an arduous war in addition to an office, which in itself is one of the most laborious in the service of the State. A Secretary of State for War while he directed the operations at home necessary to give effect to the operations abroad, might survey and examine the working of the Horse Guards, Ordnance, Sec at War's Office & Commissariat with a view to simplify and consolidate according to the report of the Committee of the House of Commons.

He argued that 'in practice the proposed division would be easy', pointing out the precedent of 1794 when the War Office was separated from the Home Office.

At last the matter was ripe for cabinet agreement. On receipt of Russell's memorandum Aberdeen acknowledged that for some time he had thought the proposed division desirable and that it should be done without delay. In view of the precedents, he said, parliamentary authority was unnecessary.[1] Wood expressed his concurrence and Clarendon was equally emphatic.[2] Even Gladstone gave a categorical assent. 'Though reluctant to see the Duke of Newcastle's connection with the Colonies brought to an end,' he wrote, 'I cordially concur in Lord John Russell's first proposition.'[3] Herbert, who was more closely affected by the change, likewise agreed, saying:

What is wanted in the military Department is not consolidation, but the supervision of one recognized authority over the whole. Indeed they suffer in some respects from over-consolidation, the Ordnance being an overtasked Department.

The Secretary at War cannot in my opinion be that authority without destroying his authority as a financial check upon the army.

A Secretary of State should supervise the whole.[4]

Aberdeen reported the subsequent cabinet discussions to the queen, saying that there was a growing desire for great changes, 'but it may be hoped', he added, sounding a different note from that in his letter to Russell, 'that it will be possible to make them innocent, if not greatly advantageous'. He warned her that the mere separation of the Colonial

---

[1] *Ibid.* fols. 1097–8, 20 May 1854.
[2] *Ibid.* fols. 1121–2, n.d., and 1113–16, 22 May 1854.
[3] *Ibid.* fols. 1119–20, 23 May 1854. For Gladstone's comments on Russell's other proposals see below, pp. 424–6.
[4] *Ibid.* fols. 1123–4, 23 May 1854. It might have been better if he, rather than Newcastle, had been made the new Secretary of State.

and War Offices would not satisfy the military reformers, 'but', he told her, 'it would remove the evil which really exists and would probably prevent any serious pressure'.[1]

When notice was given of a question in the House of Commons on the subject on 29 May, the queen wrote to the Prime Minister cautioning the government not to allow any discussion of army reform in parliament. She asked them to investigate but not to prejudge the question, and promised to give full consideration to any proposal brought before her.[2] Russell answered the question cautiously, but told Aberdeen that the sentiment of the House was clearly with the questioner. He went on to suggest possible allocations of the two offices when the division was made, proposing that either Newcastle or Palmerston might take the War Office and Sir George Grey be brought in to take either the Colonial Office or the Home Office, depending upon which was vacated.[3]

Aberdeen answered, saying that he trusted the queen would be satisfied with the proposed division 'and that this arrangement might be the means of preventing any changes, for the present at least, in the general administration of the army'. He thought it would be unjust to remove Newcastle from the War Department 'under present circumstances', and while welcoming the suggestion of Sir George Grey for the Colonies expressed a hope that Russell would revert to his earlier intention and take that department himself. 'It will be indeed a great disappointment if you should persevere in abandoning this intention', he concluded. 'But the fact of the division of the office I consider as now being finally settled.'[4]

Russell replied:

> With regard to the personal part of the question, I entirely agree with you that it would be unjust to the Duke of Newcastle under present circumstances to remove him from the War Department. But I rather gathered from what he said at the Cabinet that it was indifferent to him which office he took, & that of the two he rather preferred the Colonies.

He suggested that Newcastle should be asked directly and intimated that when the duke had chosen then they should discuss who should

---

[1] R.A. G 13, fol. 61, 28 May 1854.   [2] *Ab. Cor. 1854–5*, pp. 133–4.

[3] *Ab. Cor. 1854–5*, pp. 134–5; Walpole, *Russell*, II, 222–3. Aberdeen assured the queen that despite the attitude of the House the government had no intention of adopting Grey's proposals (R.A. E 3, fol. 88, 30 May 1854).

[4] *Ab. Cor. 1854–5*, pp. 135–6, 30 May 1854; Walpole, *Russell*, II, 223.

take the other office.[1] On the same day he produced another memorandum developing his previous ideas as to how the division should be effected. The new Secretary of State for War in charge of the War Department would fix the number of land forces, exercise control over the commander-in-chief and the Master General of the Ordnance, and be responsible for the preparation and direction of military expenditure. He should start to consolidate and simplify the military departments, but the Secretary at War should remain as he was. Gibraltar, Malta and the Channel Islands should be assigned to the War Department.[2]

In reply Lord Aberdeen maintained that the only change was in the division of duties of the Secretary of State, which had become too multifarious, and that no immediate change in the military departments was contemplated. In his view the Secretary of State kept the same powers and privileges as when the office was a joint one, although no doubt he would examine any imperfections and bring the necessary measures to correct them to the cabinet.[3] The duke of Newcastle contented himself with saying that the question of change involving consolidation might be left without prejudice, but that the new department might absorb the military functions of the Home Office.[4] Gladstone expressed himself as disposed to concur, while Wood was content to leave further changes to the War Secretary.[5] Palmerston regarded the division as a parliamentary necessity.[6] On 2 June Aberdeen authorised Russell to announce the division in the House of Commons if he thought it necessary, but suggested waiting until it was completed.[7]

The only thing that remained to be settled was the appointment of a new Secretary of State for the Colonies.

On 4 June, Wood wrote to Russell saying that he would like to see Lord John take the Colonial Office himself, but deferring to Lady John's judgment as to his health. He thought that Sir George Grey should be appointed to the Colonial Office, and that Russell should become President of the Council. 'Your taking office & his coming into the Cabinet will give us the consistency and character of permanency which your not being in office deprived us of,' Wood wrote, '& the counter-action of the Puseyite tendency which prevails to a considerable extent and which certainly weakens us in all matters into which religion

---

[1] Add. MS. 43068, fols. 72–3, 31 May 1854.
[2] *Ab. Cor. 1854–5*, pp. 136–7, 31 May 1854.
[3] *Ibid.* pp. 137–8, n.d.   [4] *Ibid.* pp. 138–9.
[5] *Ibid.*   [6] *Ibid.*   [7] *Ibid.* p. 140, 2 June 1854.

extends.' Wood said he would have preferred to see Grey at the Home Office, where he did not trust Palmerston, but recognised that it was best to leave well enough alone, since, if Palmerston was moved, there would be a demand for him to take the War Office. Sir Charles was one Whig who had little faith in Palmerston and by his account neither Grey nor Fitzroy, Palmerston's under-secretary, had any more.[1]

On Aberdeen's request Russell himself approached Grey about taking the Colonial Office. Grey told Lord John that he would 'strongly object' to taking an office 'vacated expressly' for him. He thought Lord John himself should take it, but if on the grounds of health or any other reason he declined, then he (Grey) would take it providing Russell at the same time would become President of the Council.[2] Russell passed on this information to Aberdeen, but he made it clear that he himself would only accept office (i.e. the Presidency of the Council) on the understanding that in the future the cabinet should be more ready, or rather 'more pressed, to clinch matters of urgent importance', than had hitherto been the case.[3] Aberdeen expressed his satisfaction at Grey's response, but put some reservations on the question of consolidation. He professed his readiness to consider any proposals for improvement in the cabinet. 'But if it should be proposed to place the whole administration of the Army, including military patronage, in the hands of a Board, or of one person and that person a civilian,' he wrote, 'I can be no party to any such a project.' He agreed to approach Granville about making the Presidency available for Russell, 'but it is not without some misgiving or the sense of novelty that I look to the arrangement,' he added. He felt that the reign of Henry VIII was a long way to go back for a precedent.[4] He also insisted that Granville, whom he regarded as 'indispensable in the House of Lords', must have another office and asked Russell to speak to Strutt, Chancellor of the Duchy of Lancaster, since he was a Whig appointment.[5] Later the same day Aberdeen thought of another solution to the problem—perhaps inspired by Gladstone, who had been corresponding with Arthur Gordon on the subject. Aberdeen now suggested that, since Sir George

[1] PRO 30/22/11/D, fols. 1144–9, 4 June 1854.
[2] *Ibid.* fols. 1160–3, 5 June; and Walpole, *Russell*, II, 223–4 for an incomplete quotation.
[3] Walpole, *Russell*, II, 224; another letter in the Russell Papers dated 6 June puts this more emphatically, but there is no evidence that it was sent, PRO 30/22/11/D, fols. 1167–8.
[4] I.e. for a member of the House of Commons holding the office.
[5] PRO 30/22/11/D, fols. 1171–4, 7 June 1854, partially reproduced in Walpole, *Russell*, II, 224.

Grey evidently did not desire to come into office, his entry might be postponed to the end of the session and Granville made Colonial Minister, thus rendering it unnecessary to disturb Strutt. 'I think this might offer a better appearance in the eyes of the public', he wrote, 'than the complicated arrangement now proposed.' His main concern was doubtless the reaction of the Peelites to the addition of another Whig to the cabinet, for he added: 'I do not for a moment look to anything like Party in the Cabinet; but, if a new Member should be introduced, I am not certain that Cardwell and Canning might not feel aggrieved.' The poor man evidently realised that he was caught between two conflicting forces and he was most loath to arouse a storm, for he concluded rather weakly: 'I only throw this out for consideration, and am quite ready to abide by what you finally decide; but the suggestion had not previously occurred to me, and it certainly gets rid of many difficulties.'[1] Russell of course, would have nothing of the new proposal. He pointed out that it would result in three of the four Secretaries of State being in the Lords with a corresponding extra burden placed on himself in the Commons, and moreover that there would be no advantage, but much disadvantage, if a further change were to be made at the end of the session. He said that Grey and Granville were fully prepared for the original arrangement and that he would write to Strutt. He did not think that Canning or Cardwell could object and pointed out that Grey's accession to the cabinet would 'go but a small way to compensate the partiality of the original distribution of offices'. 'I could tell you much in conversation on this subject, but it is not worth writing', he added. 'It was borne with good humour at the time [!], but, as I told you would be the case, the Session has not shown the same acquiesence as the last did.'[2]

The reaction of one stout Peelite, the Chancellor of the Exchequer, who was commissioned to explain these developments to Lord Canning, illustrates the emotions that seethed under the surface. Gladstone wrote to his friend on 8 June:

I have obtained Lord Aberdeen's permission to make known to you certain changes that are in contemplation—changes much more worthy in my opinion of a set of clowns at Astley's or mountebanks on a village stage than of an English Cabinet: but which, bad & discreditable as I think them in every

---

[1] *Ab. Cor. 1854–5*, pp. 145–6, 7 June 1854, partly reproduced in Walpole, *Russell*, II, 225.
[2] *Ab. Cor. 1854–5*, 8 June 1854, pp. 146–7, only partly reproduced in Walpole, *Russell*, II, 225.

way, distress me particularly with reference to you (I must say also to Cardwell but in regard to him I have no personal responsibility) when I remember what passed between us at the time of the formation of the Government & when I consider I have been in some part the means of drawing you into a position which you may find fettering your liberty of action.

He went on to spell out the proposed arrangements including (as he wrongly thought) the inevitable dropping of Frederick Peel as Under-Secretary for the Colonies since Grey would be in the Commons. 'I shall be most ready to see you', he concluded in a burst of emotion, 'and indeed *happy* to see you for I feel very keenly my position in regard to you: & my only excuse is that I had at the time not sounded the depths of a certain woman's restlessness & folly, or the amount of influence it might exercise on the man who for the country's misfortune is her husband, in bringing him both to a pitch of wilfulness & to an abyss of vacillation & infirmity of purpose, which are in themselves a chapter in the history of human nature.'[1] To Aberdeen, Gladstone wrote: 'I have seen Canning, and I think he will submit, & without a word. That he does not feel I am unable to say; but not a word escaped him, questioning either your motives or your conduct, and I am sure he is sensible of the difficulties in which you are placed.'[2] To Aberdeen's son Gladstone was more outspoken when he wrote: 'I doubt if there is any man in England, except Lord Aberdeen, who could have borne what he has had to bear during the last seventeen months from *Lady* John.'[3]

Meanwhile the reorganisation proceeded along the lines desired by Lord John. On 9 June he told Aberdeen that he thought Grey would accept Aberdeen's views regarding reorganisation. As to the shuffle of offices he wrote: 'I should be glad if there were any other arrangement possible than that of Strutt's giving up his office. If any other occurs to you or to Granville I shall be glad to dispense with asking Strutt to retire. The precedent of Henry VIII is, I think, quite sufficient.'[4] Lord Granville was more than accommodating; 'the pleasure which I felt at contributing to an arrangement which I think very desirable', he wrote to Russell a few days later, 'has not been diminished by anything that I have heard.'[5]

[1] Add. MS. 44778, fols. 183–4, 8 June 1854 (presumably a copy, although possibly the letter was never sent).
[2] *Ab. Cor. 1854–5*, p. 148, 8 June 1854.   [3] *Ibid.* p. 142, 6 June 1854.
[4] *Ibid.* pp. 144–5.   [5] PRO 30/22/11/D, fols. 1189–90, 12 June 1854.

When parliament resumed its sitting after the Whitsuntide vacation on 8 June, Russell took the opportunity of a question previously addressed to him by Hume regarding the administration of the army to announce the government's decision to divide the War Office from the Colonial Office. As to further proposals for consolidation he emphasised the difficulties and objections to any precipitate and mechanical unification in terms that must have been highly pleasing to the court. In particular he emphasised the undesirability of taking military patronage out of the hands of the commander-in-chief and placing it in the hands of a political officer. As to consolidation he said: 'It appears, therefore, to the Government better to allow the Secretary of State, who is to be placed at the head of this Department, to consider from time to time what is the best arrangement, and how improvement can be carried out.'[1] The announcement was generally well received, although Hume, Ellice and other advocates of military reform, urged the necessity of the Minister for War taking control of the various separate military authorities.[2] Nothing was said by Russell about the impending ministerial shuffle, although he promised that the new minister would be in the Commons.[3]

On the following day, 9 June, the War Office and the Colonial Office were divided by order in council and the duke of Newcastle and Sir George Grey were sworn in as the Secretaries of State responsible for these two offices respectively. At the same time Lord John Russell was sworn in as the new Lord President of the Council, but Lord Granville was not sworn in as Chancellor of the Duchy of Lancaster until 21 June.[4] No allusion to these changes was made in either House by the leaders of the government, but on 19 June the unfortunate Strutt made a somewhat embarrassing statement to allay false rumours about the reason for his resignation. He made it quite clear that on finding that all the arrangements for the shuffle had been made before he was approached he did not consider that he had any alternative but to comply with the request made to him and place his office at the disposal of the Prime Minister unconditionally. He also indicated that he had not been too happy in holding what amounted to a sinecure without any special duties allotted to him as was often the case with the holder of this office. Finally he declared that he was 'most anxious not to say one single word

---

[1] *Hansard*, CXXXIII, 1268–72.   [2] *Ibid.* 1272–6.   [3] *Ibid.* 1276.
[4] *Annual Register, 1854*, Appendix to Chronicle, pp. 383–4. Russell was sworn in to the House of Commons on re-election on 15 June, Grey on 20 June. *Hansard*, CXXXIV, 181 and 385.

or utter one single observation with reference to the conduct of any other person in these transactions'.[1] Although Lord John was in the House and indeed immediately afterwards introduced the next business, he said never a word to acknowledge his own debt to the minister whose exclusion he had so selfishly engineered.

The only other parliamentary comment came from the maverick Liberal member, Lord Dudley Stuart, who in a speech on 29 June about the recent changes managed to step on everybody's toes. He welcomed Russell's appointment to office, but regretted that he had not become Prime Minister. He expressed surprise at a man in the prime and vigour of life such as Lord Granville being content to step down to what was virtually a sinecure office 'and thereby to elbow out the right hon. Gentleman the Member for Nottingham (Mr Strutt)'; he hoped 'that in going to Lancaster he [Granville] might only be on his way to a better place'. He gave it as his opinion that 'the House and the country had a right to expect some explanation why the right hon. Gentleman who had always discharged his duties satisfactorily had been treated with so little consideration and in a manner which was very discouraging to those who placed their services at the disposal of the Government, for he thought it would be admitted on all hands that the right hon. Member for Nottingham had received what in common parlance might be described as very scurvy treatment'. Lord Dudley thought that for all his ability Sir George Grey was misplaced in the Colonial Office. 'On the contrary, he saw in it an illustration of the truth of the saying, that, in the present Government, the parts had been so cast that all the square men were in round holes, and all the round men were in square holes.' He pointed out that the creation of a Minister for War made the office of the Secretary at War rather anomalous. He also remarked that the whole conduct of the war was in the hands of the Prime Minister's Peelite colleagues, and, while recognising the merits of the duke of Newcastle, he expressed his great disappointment at the failure to take this opportunity to put the War Office in the hands of Lord Palmerston; such an appointment, he claimed, would have been welcomed by the whole country and recognised abroad as proof of the government's determination. He proceeded to develop this theme with great gusto:

Did anybody tell him of the number of years that had passed over the noble Lord's head? He replied that the noble Lord was an extraordinary man; he

---

[1] *Hansard*, CXXXIV, 335–9. Strutt warned Russell that he intended to make this statement. PRO 30/22/11/D, fols. 1205–6, 19 June 1854.

united with the experience of age the vigour of youth. There were few men who at his time of life had the same physical strength, and very few indeed who had equal mental powers. He did not find that age was considered an objection in the case of naval and military commanders. Admiral Dundas was, he believed, pretty well contemporary with the noble Lord; Lord Raglan was not much younger, and Old Charley himself, though he might perhaps have the advantage of one or two years, was not half so active. And a man like that, with all his capacity, with all his reputation, with his political experience of half a century, was wasted in labours about common sewers, boards of health, and county rates, and the armies which he had to regulate were armies of policemen.

'Something must be done if the government intended to re-acquire the confidence of that House and of the country,' he concluded. 'That confidence, long declining, was now pretty well lost. . . The government were not in the position that they ought to be. All that they could carry was taxes—taxes for the war. . .But neither the people nor the House were for half-and-half measures, and they did not want a half-and-half Ministry.'[1]

The ministers preferred to ignore this strange outburst, but behind the scenes discussion continued regarding the extent of the reorganisation. On 4 July the duke of Newcastle wrote to the Prime Minister referring to a previous conversation they had had regarding the commissariat and the Ordnance, saying that a more delicate matter was the disposition of those military responsibilities coming under the Home Office, namely, the militia, the yeomanry, home fortifications and barracks.

You are aware of the objections which I always entertained to the change now carried into effect [he wrote]; but the moment the change is made, the leading principle of which is the concentration under one Civil Head of all matters connected with the army except its military discipline, organization, and patronage, there remains less justification, both theoretically and practically, for any military functions attaching to the Home Secretary than to the Colonial.

But Newcastle was unwilling to appear to be encroaching on Palmerston. 'The public, I know, think I ought not to be War Minister,' he added. 'On the other hand I cannot but believe they desire an arrangement complete in itself, and it is on this ground alone, apart from my

[1] *Hansard*, CXXXIV, 921–6. 'Old Charley' was presumably Sir Charles Napier.

want of ability or its possession by others, that I ask you to consider what ought to be done.'[1]

For the time being no attempt was made to reduce the military responsibilities of the Home Office, but it was decided to transfer the commissariat to the War Department and to consider ways in which that department might take over non-military functions of the Ordnance. These decisions were alluded to by Lord John Russell on 17 July in a speech introducing the estimates for the new War Department. He again referred to previous proposals for consolidation and to the difficulties which resulted in their not being acted upon. If any further changes were needed then his noble friend, the duke of Newcastle, who was 'an active man of business', would propose in due course what might be required.

Sir John Pakington, speaking for the opposition, criticised the government for reversing its earlier decision with regard to splitting the Department of War and Colonies without first of all settling on the duties of the new department and without making any provision for settling the anomalies of divided authority within the army which had been pointed out so often in both Houses. He chided Russell, who had himself been a member of one of the earlier commissions recommending consolidation of authority, for accepting the duke of Wellington's objections as sufficient for abandoning them.[2] He also took the occasion to question the wisdom of maintaining the office of the Secretary at War and of including that minister in the cabinet.

In replying to these charges Sidney Herbert contented himself with making the point that the various changes to be made were a matter of timing and that there was plenty of financial supervision for a Secretary at War which was quite distinct from the work of the Secretary for War. As for his being in the cabinet, he hoped that with his considerable experience in the business of the War Office his services 'might be of great value to assist not only in promoting the efficiency, but also in assisting the Government in arranging in a final and satisfactory manner the various duties of the War Department'. 'Give us time', he concluded, '—that is only fair—and I am satisfied that we can introduce into the military department changes which will promote the efficiency of the service, and which will enable the Government and people to look with perfect confidence, as to efficiency in every respect, upon those

[1] *Ab. Cor. 1854–5*, pp. 162–3, 4 July 1854.
[2] *Hansard*, cxxxv, 327–34.

forces upon whom now the honour and safety of this country depend.'[1] After a couple of brief comments from private members the estimate was passed, much to the ministers' relief, without a vote. For the moment the Downing Street meeting of 17 July[2] seemed to have some effect.

Debate on a special vote of credit—further attacks on Lord Aberdeen

The following week, however, saw the debate on the special vote of credit in which the Prime Minister was bitterly attacked by two members on the government benches. A royal message was sent to both Houses on 21 July requesting the authorisation of additional expenditures for the war, which amounted to £3,000,000. This provided the opportunity for debate on the war in each House on the following Monday, 24 July. In the Lords, Aberdeen introduced the address with a very brief speech, indicating that they were only asking for approval for additional expenditures, hitherto unappropriated but already provided for by vote of parliament. After some growls from Ellenborough, Hardwicke, Fitzwilliam and Clanricarde and a short response from Clarendon defending the position of Austria, the address was passed in the House of Lords without opposition.[3]

In the Commons the debate on this royal message was more protracted. Russell, in asking the House to support the proposed vote of credit, was more communicative than Aberdeen had been. He acknowledged the good sense of the House in refraining from attempts to embarrass the government by pressing for information about proposed plans at the commencement of hostilities and proceeded to give some brief résumé of what had been done. With obvious reference to Aberdeen's despatch of 1829 he emphasised the point that long experience of Russian aggression in this area would prevent the Allies accepting any peace settlement based on the *status quo ante bellum*. And he made it pretty clear that they were not prepared to tolerate the continued existence of a great fortress and naval base in the Black Sea (Sebastopol) as a continuing menace to Turkish security.[4]

In the ensuing debate[5] various speakers on the side of the government criticised it for failing to prosecute the war 'with becoming vigour'.

[1] *Ibid.* CXXXIV, 915–31.   [2] See below, p. 459.
[3] *Hansard*, CXXXV, 535–50.
[4] *Ibid.* 598–613. For his references to Austria see below, pp. 429–44.
[5] *Ibid.* 613–90.

Hume, however, dismissed these criticisms as groundless, extolled the ministers for all they had done and defended the coalition against its critics, saying 'he was very glad to see the followers of Sir R. Peel joining the old Liberals in that House, who received them with great pleasure'.[1] Some welcomed Russell's allusion to the Crimea, but Cobden warned of the folly of attempting to occupy such a place where the climate held great danger of fever for an occupying army. Cobden's arguments were strongly attacked by the warlike Layard, who criticised the administrative arrangements for the reception of the expeditionary force in the East and the failure to send out properly qualified leaders or to draw on the advice of men of experience (such presumably as himself). He made a sustained and violent attack on the inadequacy of Lord Aberdeen as a wartime Prime Minister and urged the desirability of making Palmerston Minister of War. Lord Dudley Stuart continued the same theme, saying that 'the very name of Palmerston carried with it an amount of moral force equal to a whole army'.[2]

The debate had gone on for almost six hours, with all the criticisms made from the government side of the House. Disraeli, who now rose to speak, was not slow to point this out, but he really had little to add. His speech was clever, but very party-political, while pretending to be the reverse. He joined most of the preceding speakers in urging the necessity of an autumn session, about which Russell had refused to make any commitments. But the greater part of his speech was an extempore comment on a chance intervention of Russell's, or had the artful Dizzy purposely set the trap producing the intervention he wanted? At any rate he drew the House's attention to the very important announcement that Russell had made with the full support of the cabinet that the destruction of Sebastopol was part of the government's war policy. Russell then intervened to say that he had merely 'thought Russia could not be allowed to maintain the menacing attitude which she had so lately done by keeping so large a fleet at Sebastopol'. This produced an incredulous reaction from Disraeli. For six hours the House had been carrying on a debate on a mythical speech that the House leader now said he had never made. What enthusiasm he had produced by apparently promising a dramatic war objective was now evaporated, for, shorn of this proposal, the government's plans were no more than those always associated with the insipid leadership of Lord Aberdeen. And so ironically he came to his conclusion:

[1] *Hansard,* cxxxv, 613–90.   [2] *Ibid.*

We have not a divided Cabinet. We hear at last as the Session closes, that they are in unison upon one subject; and, so far as the conduct of the war for small purposes, so far as having for the great object of their policy a mean and insignificant end, Her Majesty's Ministers, though they are a Coalition Ministry, appear to be unanimous.[1]

Palmerston wound up the debate for the government in a very brief and thin speech that gave no indication that he was the obvious war leader. Lord Dudley Stuart, Layard and other Liberal critics insisted, however, that in view of Russell's alleged retraction of the promise to destroy Sebastopol, and in view of unsatisfactory reports of what had passed in the other House, they should have opportunity for further discussion. Several Conservatives came to Russell's support to say that they had understood him to say no more than he claimed in his second statement, but the critics would not be appeased. In the end it was agreed that they would have their chance by bringing the resolutions up for report on the following day.[2]

Consequently when this was done Lord Dudley moved an amendment, seconded by Sir John Shelley, to the effect that parliament should not be prorogued until the government had been able to make a full report 'with respect both to Her Majesty's relations with Foreign Powers and to Her views and prospects in the context which Her Majesty is engaged in'.[3] Once again he attacked Russell bitterly for deliberately misleading the House with a statement that most members took to promise a military operation against the fortress of Sebastopol but which later in the debate he admitted referred only to a proposed provision in the final peace settlement. He further twisted the sword in Russell's wound by suggesting that Lord John's unsatisfactory explanation had been made as a result of 'some hints from his Colleagues as to what the head of the Government had said in another place'.

He went on to deplore the lack of firm and resolute leadership, which in fact was responsible for the present war. To a cry of 'Hear, hear!' he added that 'he believed that if they had had any other Minister than Lord Aberdeen, this war would not have occurred; but the fluctuating and pusillanimous conduct of the Premier—unworthy as it was of a great country like this—rendered war inevitable'.

Lord Dudley was followed by Sidney Herbert, who in a vigorous speech spent most of his time refuting the charges made by Layard on the previous evening with respect to the state of the commissariat and

[1] *Ibid.* 680. [2] *Ibid.* 684–90. [3] *Ibid.* 709–16.

the medical services. As for achievements he chided the naïveté of critics who supposed that great battles could be fought and won on distant fields in the first four months of a war, and reminded them rather sombrely that Waterloo was not won in the lifetime of Pitt. He made much, however, of the effectiveness of the blockade of Russia, reminding his hearers that much of Nelson's career was spent on the unexciting business of blockade, and that expensive Russian fortresses had been evacuated in Circassia.

Lord John Russell spoke briefly at the end of the debate,[1] standing by his original statement as reported in the press and maintaining that there was nothing inconsistent between it and his subsequent elaboration. His speech was notable for its outspoken vindication of Lord Aberdeen. His own statement on the previous evening had only been longer than that of the Prime Minister because supply was primarily the business of the House of Commons. He strongly objected to 'the attempt to separate the Cabinet from the noble Lord who is at the head of it, and to make him alone responsible for that in which all his colleagues must share his responsibility'. 'With regard to the general measures of the war,' he said, 'those measures have been considered step by step by those advisers of Her Majesty who are usually called the Cabinet, and for the decisions which have been adopted all the colleagues of Lord Aberdeen are alike responsible.'

The attack was renewed by Layard, who denied that the blockade was effective, by Sir John Shelley and one or two others, but it is clear from the reports that the House was small and apathetic to the motion. In the end Lord Dudley expressed himself as satisfied with Lord John's speech and withdrew his amendment.[2] Thus, although some wounding remarks had been made, the government had reason to be satisfied with their position.

For once Lord Aberdeen's apparent equanimity was upset as the strain of the preceding twelve months began to show. He evidently felt chagrined at the failure of any of his Peelite colleagues in the Commons to come to his defence, for on the following day he wrote a letter to Graham in which he said: 'And it will require a little time for me to recover my equanimity, after having been made the subject of repeated attack during a long debate, without a single syllable being said in defence...I should have no pleasure in meeting the Cabinet today at

[1] *Hansard*, CXXXV, 716–66, for the debate.
[2] *Ibid.* 766.

dinner.'[1] This was perhaps not entirely fair to Russell, who had emphasised the doctrine of the collective responsibility of the cabinet in his rebuttal at the end of the debate, but it is true that no Peelite spoke in Aberdeen's defence, although Herbert in a speech mainly confined to repelling criticisms levelled at the government's war effort did make the point that there was no difference in substance between the speeches of the Prime Minister in the Lords and the government leader in the Commons in introducing the special vote.

Graham had evidently seen Aberdeen the previous day and was much disturbed to find his chief so upset, for on the 26th he wrote saying:

My interview with you yesterday grieved me very deeply, and your note of this morning has not diminished the painful impression.

If you think I have not been true to you, or have failed in any one duty on any one occasion, as a colleague or as a friend, I am sure that the error is mine; for you are just and forbearing and I regret the error from my heart. Since the death of Peel I have regarded you as my most faithful and familiar friend, and I have endeavoured always to act in conformity with these feelings.

I was quite ready to have spoken on Monday night but the brunt of the attack fell on Lord John himself, in consequence of an imprudence; and, not knowing what had taken place in the House of Lords, I found that I might do more harm than good in critical circumstances.[2]

It was not in Lord Aberdeen's nature to hold a grudge against a friend and he immediately responded warmly to Graham's letter:

You may be assured I blame no one except myself. I ought to have acquired sufficient philosophy to meet an occurrence like that of Monday without repining. Fortunately, I have expressed my feelings to no one but yourself, and, in a much less degree, to Gladstone; neither shall I say anything more on the matter.

Believe me I am fully sensible of your friendship, upon which I have always felt I could securely reckon.[3]

In his reply Graham said that he hoped the ludicrous termination to the assault on Tuesday evening might provide 'some relief to the pain which the event of Monday night could not fail to occasion'.[4]

[1] *Ab. Cor. 1854–5*, p. 177, 26 July 1854 (copy). There is what appears to be a copy of this letter in the Graham Papers with a note by CSP (Graham's biographer, C. S. Parker) saying that Lord Stanmore preferred not to have this letter published and that consequently Mrs Baring (Graham's daughter) agreed that Graham's of the same date should not be published.   [2] *Ab. Cor. 1854–5*, p. 178.
[3] *Ibid.* p. 178, 27 July 1854.   [4] *Ibid.* p. 179, 28 July 1854.

Gladstone had been kept informed of the situation by Arthur Gordon, who had sent him a note on the afternoon of Monday 24 July, saying: 'If my father is personally attacked tonight he is very desirous that *you* should speak in his defence. I am very anxious about it too, for I have heard him say that you have never done so yet—not of course that he doubts your willingness.'[1] Gladstone replied by saying that since he was 'commonly supposed to be tarred with the same stick' he feared this weakened his ability to defend Lord Aberdeen effectively.[2]

Three days later Arthur Gordon wrote again, expressing his regret at Gladstone's inability to speak, 'because', he said, 'I know how restless my father feels about it believing as he does that a defence from you *coming from the heart as it would do*, would go much further to set him right with the public than a few conventional proprieties from Lord John about the whole govt being responsible &&. Pardon my freedom in saying all this.'[3]

One can imagine how uncomfortable Gladstone felt on receiving this letter. He immediately replied explaining his difficulty in intervening after Herbert's 'excellent' speech; he had intended to follow Disraeli, but the latter did not speak and so Russell closed. Otherwise he would have put aside his natural diffidence about speaking on the Eastern Question, of which he did not feel himself a master. He assured Gordon that his father's reputation remained high with the public.

No one I think can fail to see [Gladstone continued] that, whoever has lost, Lord Aberdeen has not lost by the formation of the present government. That act itself was an achievement which no other man could have accomplished. Before he became Minister, it might be said that his reputation was more continental than British: but he has now become a great historical figure in domestic politics. By the errors, losses and defeats of the Government, which have been too many, he remains unscathed.[4]

On 12 August, two days before the session ended, Lord Clanricarde, moving for the production of an Austro-Turkish Convention of

---

[1] Add. MS. 44319, fol. 58, 'Monday 3 p.m.'

[2] *Ibid.* fols. 60–1, 24 July 1854.   [3] *Ibid.* fols. 62–3, 27 July 1854.

[4] Add. MS. 44319, fols. 66–9, 28 July 1854. Gordon wrote to express his thanks from Beverley, where he was contesting a by-election. He feared the Tories would vote against him for he found them 'most venomous' against his father. As a result he went rather far in the other direction. 'I am much afraid of your deeming me too liberal', he wrote in a postscript, 'for I wish to take you for my guide, & had I been prudent I would not have said so much' (*ibid.* fols. 70–1, 29 July 1854). Nevertheless, he won the election and asked Gladstone to introduce him in the House (*ibid.* fol. 72, 1 August 1854).

12 June, made one final onslaught on the government's conduct of the war. He repeated charges regarding the inefficiency of the blockade and the failure to provide light-draft warships for operations in the Baltic. He expressed much suspicion of the intentions of Austria, especially with respect to her proposed occupation of the Principalities, and alleged that too much had already been sacrificed for this alliance. In conclusion, however, he did welcome reports that an expedition was being undertaken against the Crimea. Clarendon, who was the only other speaker on this occasion, made no objection to tabling the required convention, but he sharply rapped Clanricarde for discussing information of value to the enemy. He vigorously rebutted most of his critic's charges and in doing so took the last opportunity of the session to outline what had been done in the first four months of the war. In conclusion he assured the House that France and England would not relax their efforts until they had obtained a just and lasting peace and that while they welcomed the cooperation of other powers, they would not be dependent upon them.[1]

The session of 1854 came to an end before the heavy fighting had begun, but the tone of the critics in parliament, especially on the government's side of the House of Commons, gave ample warning that if things went wrong in the East there would be a reckoning to settle at Westminster. Before turning to the Crimean operations, however, we may first consider some of the other problems alluded to by Lord Clarendon.

[1] *Hansard*, CXXXV, 1522–33.

16

THE CONDUCT OF THE WAR—
SOME DIPLOMATIC PROBLEMS

Trouble in Greece and in Greytown

In the early stages of the war diplomatic problems continued to over-shadow purely military ones; indeed throughout the war attempts to reach a diplomatic settlement were made intermittently. From the beginning Britain and France were anxious to ascertain the intentions of the German powers and in particular to seek the support of Austria; they were also anxious to explore the possibility of an alliance with Sweden, to curb the hostility of Greece towards Turkey, and to devise means of giving financial as well as military support to the Turks in an acceptable form.[1] In the background there were also several rather serious differences with the United States to worry the British government during much of the war. It will be convenient to consider some of the more incidental problems first before turning to the central problem of the German Powers and especially of Austria.

Ever since the beginning of the Eastern crisis the Greeks, both those in the independent state of Greece and those still under Turkish rule, had inevitably been in a state of great excitement. Early in 1854 an insurrection had broken out in the Turkish provinces across the Greek frontier and its leader was none other than a General Grivas. There is little doubt that men and arms poured across the border from free Greece, but the Greek government denied all knowledge of these charges and ignored appeals from the Allied governments to put an end to the intervention. In April the Allied ambassadors were empowered to blockade Athens and in May the British government reluctantly agreed to the joint occupation of the Greek capital, rather than allow the

---

[1] Space precludes the development of this last theme, but it was a not infrequent item on the cabinet agenda. In July it was decided to guarantee a Turkish loan, in conjunction with the French government, but much time was lost because of the sensitivity of the Turks on the question of supervision. See correspondence in *Ab. Cor. 1854–5*; PRO 30/22/11/D; MS. Clar. Dep. C 14 and 15. See also Olive Anderson, 'Great Britain and the beginning of the Ottoman public debt, 1854–5', *Hist. J.* VII (1964), 47–63.

French to do so alone. Some 8,000 French and 1,000 British troops were landed on the Piraeus on 25 May but met no resistance. Instead, the Greek government resigned and left the king with no alternative but to give in and promise complete neutrality. It was surely an historical irony that a government headed by Lord Aberdeen should have been responsible for treatment of the Greeks even more high-handed than that of Lord Palmerston in the celebrated Don Pacifico case four years earlier. The Allies did, however, with some success, insist on the Turks making some concessions to their Christian subjects.[1]

Further from the scene of war, British foreign policy in 1854 was also complicated by a number of differences with the United States that created a tense situation between the two countries in the later part of the year. The perennial fisheries question was settled for the time being as part of a reciprocity treaty respecting trade between the United States and British North America which was negotiated and signed in June by Lord Elgin, the Governor General of Canada.[2] Difficulties over neutral rights were also largely averted by the new British policy, which the Americans regarded as a great improvement over that of the Napoleonic Wars.[3] A crisis threatened in September when an American annexation of the Sandwich Islands was feared, but this soon evaporated.[4] There were also various rumours of an intended American seizure of Cuba that proved equally groundless, but which raised apprehensions while they lasted.[5] The most serious differences, however, were in Central America, despite the signature of the Clayton–Bulwer treaty a few years earlier. Britain did not consider this treaty applied to British Honduras or its dependencies, including the Bay Islands south of Belize, which, to the indignation of the United States, were constituted a colony by the Colonial Office in 1852. Britain also claimed an historic protectorate over the Indians of the Mosquito Coast and the settlement of Greytown at the mouth of the San Juan River, which was inhabited mainly by Englishmen, Americans and Nicaraguans and which was

---

[1] See *Correspondence on relations between Greece and Turkey* (7 April 1853–6 May 1854) in *P.P. 1854*, LXXII, 1–273, and *Annual Register, 1854*, pp. 380–9.

[2] It is curious that there are no more than one or two passing references to this treaty in the British ministerial correspondence consulted.

[3] E.g. see PRO 30/22/11/D for a letter of 8 June 1854 from E. Everett, former American ambassador in London, congratulating Russell on the Allied policy toward neutrals.

[4] See R. W. Van Alstyne, 'Great Britain, the United States and Hawaiian independence, 1850–1855', *Pacific Historical Review*, IV (1935), 15–24.

[5] E.g. see Graham Papers, Graham to Clarendon, 4 January and 11 May 1854.

virtually self-governing. A state of undeclared war developed between the Greytowners and the inhabitants of a rival American community that had sprung up across the river on land originally leased from Greytown by an American transit company. This eventually culminated in the intervention of the American minister to Central America and the despatch of an American sloop of war, the *Cyane*, to Greytown which bombarded and destroyed the place. The issue was taken up by the two governments in the latter part of 1853 and discussions dragged on throughout 1854. The administration of President Pierce, represented in London by James Buchanan, attempted in the name of the Monroe Doctrine to force the British government to abandon all territorial claims in the area, while the British sought satisfaction for the Greytown outrage. The matter was frequently discussed in the cabinet and was the subject of a good deal of correspondence between the various ministers, some of whom, and especially Palmerston, did not rule out the possibility of war. On one occasion he criticised Clarendon for failing to demand satisfaction and an apology from the Americans. 'In dealing with vulgar minded Bullies,' he wrote, in his most outrageous manner, 'and Such unfortunately the People of the United States are, nothing is gained by Submission to Insult & wrong... Such people are always trying how far they can venture to go, and they generally pull up when they find they can go no further without encountering Resistance of a formidable Character.' Arguing that Britain held all the cards in her hand he went so far as to say: 'The United States have no Navy of which we need be afraid, and they might be told that if they were to resort to Privateering we should however reluctantly be obliged to retaliate by burning all their Sea Coast Towns.'[1]

As the Allies became more deeply involved in the Crimea, however, British policy became more restrained. In November Clarendon admitted to Graham that his object was 'to get out of the Central American mess as soon as we can with honour', but he continued to take a firm line in his despatches with the full support of the cabinet.[2] In fact, by the end of the year the differences had reached an impasse and were simply let lie by the two governments, neither of which really wanted to pick a quarrel with the other. They were eventually settled in 1860 when Britain concluded treaties with the Central American

[1] MS. Clar. Dep. C15, fols. 187–90, 10 September 1854.
[2] Graham Papers, 1 November 1854.

Republics concerned that resulted in her complete withdrawal from the Bay Islands and the Mosquito Protectorate to the complete satisfaction of the United States.[1]

The proposed Swedish alliance

Napoleon III also took the initiative in attempting to open up the war against Russia in another theatre by pressing Sweden to join the Allies in the Baltic. On 17 April Clarendon complained to Aberdeen that the French government had acted imprudently in approaching the Swedish government in this way without any previous communication with its British ally.[2] Failing to bring the matter before the cabinet at its next meeting, he wrote to Russell in disgust: 'What you said last week about the cabinet never coming to a decision was well exemplified today & there was no use in mentioning Sweden.'[3] Nevertheless, he warned the British minister in Stockholm that the 'French move was evidently premature'. In the meantime the Swedish Crown Prince enquired about the possibility of a British subsidy. Initially the British ministers approached the matter cautiously. Russell was prepared to grant a subsidy provided Aberdeen and Gladstone were agreeable and the French were consulted, but he warned against any commitments to Sweden with regard to Finland and the peace treaties. 'I believe we never bound ourselves to Frederick of Prussia, who was the best ally we ever had', he observed with his characteristic *penchant* for historical precedents.[4] He returned to this point a few days later writing: 'If the Swedes come to us & propose to join us I shd be glad to accept their aid, but they must take the fortune of war, & I wd not promise them Finland, or even Aland as a bribe.'[5] Even Palmerston agreed to the proposal with reservations. He warned that the contest they had entered into with Russia was 'not Child's Play' and that it would be difficult for Britain to supply troops in force in addition to those committed to Turkey. He thought the Swedes were asking for too much, but

---

[1] See further M. W. Williams, *Anglo-American isthmian diplomacy 1815–1915* (Washington, 1916); R. W. Van Alstyne, 'British diplomacy and the Clayton–Bulwer treaty, 1850–60', *J.M.H.* XI (1939), 149–93, and his documents on 'Anglo-American relations, 1853–57', *A.H.R.* XLII (1937), 496–7; R. A. Humphries, *The diplomacy of British Honduras.*

[2] *Ab. Cor. 1854–5*, p. 105; cf. PRO 30/22/11 Clarendon, 17 April 1854.

[3] PRO 30/22/11/C, fols. 1013–14, 22 April 1854.

[4] MS. Clar. Dep. C15, fols. 445–8, 13 April 1854.

[5] *Ibid.* fols. 457–9, 16 April 1854 (postscript).

recognised that the loss of Finland would be a good way of weakening
Russia 'for the future security of Europe'. 'On the whole', he concluded,
'I should say that if the money difficulty can be got over, the offer is
one that ought not lightly to be declined.'[1] Aberdeen and Clarendon
expressed themselves in general agreement with Russell, but both
doubted whether Sweden would join under acceptable conditions.[2]

For some weeks the matter remained in abeyance, but in the middle of
May it was brought before the cabinet. Gladstone, who was unable to
attend the meeting, wrote a long letter to Graham expressing his views.
He recognised the military objective and did not question it on financial
grounds, but he saw moral difficulties, pointing out that England and
France had gone to war to protect Turkey against aggression.

> Turkey is at war for self defence [he wrote]; we are at war for the tranquillity
> of Europe; on what footing is Sweden to go to war? I feel then that our invit-
> ing Sweden to go to war as an independent power for objects of her own tends
> greatly to lower our present very high moral position; and I dread the politi-
> cal implications to which this will lead...To hire Sweden outright and in
> plain terms would it seems to me be better. He that is hired, when he is paid,
> has no more to say.[3]

By this time Russell's interest in the Swedish project had warmed. He
raised it again in his memorandum of 20 May regarding the division of
the War and Colonial Offices, arguing that immediate action was necessary if Sweden was to get an army into the field that year. A mere
Baltic blockade, he maintained, was not enough, for Russia was not
greatly dependent on her mercantile power and could fall back on other
routes.

> It becomes therefore of more importance [he concluded] to strike military
> and naval blows with a view to put an end to the war. A land force is essential
> in the Baltic, and no force so ready, so cheap, and so likely to be efficient as a
> Swedish force can be had. I therefore propose that official instructions be sent
> at once to Mr Grey [British minister to Stockholm] empowering him to sign:
> 1. A Treaty of Alliance without guarantee of conquests. 2. A Treaty of
> Subsidy, half the subsidy to be paid by England and half by France.[4]

---

[1] MS. Clar. C15, fols. 109–10, 27 April 1854.
[2] *Ibid.* C14, fol. 37, 23 April 1854; PRO 30/22/11/C, fols. 1015–16, 23 April 1854.
Clarendon was also doubtful whether Gladstone would 'venture to propose or the
H of C to sanction a monthly £100,000', which was apparently the amount for which
the Swedes were asking.
[3] Graham Papers, 17 May 1854; copy in Add. MS. 44163, fols. 137–40. Cf. p. 431 below.
[4] Gooch, *Later correspondence*, II, 165–6.

Ironically, Russell, the great upholder of Whig traditions, indicated that the Swedish king favoured the idea and that if his present ministers did not he could find others who would. This was scarcely a document for Queen Victoria's eyes, since it seemed to undermine what Russell liked to tell her about the Revolution of 1688.

Aberdeen immediately objected to Russell's proposals as likely to embarrass England's future freedom. If any subsidy was to be paid it would be better to Austria, but he feared it might derange the country's financial operations.[1] Clarendon was more favourable, observing that Swedish support was desirable since little or nothing could be effected in the Baltic without land forces. He thought it would be good economy to subsidise Sweden provided no guarantee was made for the future. If Britain and France could send 60,000 or 70,000 men to assist the fleets it should be done.[2] Lansdowne was cautious, suggesting that Admiral Napier should be asked whether land forces would be effective. He gave it as his own opinion (and his experience went back to the Napoleonic Wars) that the capture of Cronstadt would be more significant than the occupation of Finland.[3] Wood expressed 'great doubts'. He pointed out that Sweden sought the recovery of Finland, which Russia would only give up as a very last resort. He did not think that the Allies could match Russia in that area and warned that the result would be a long-drawn-out war. On the other hand, if the recapture of Finland was not the objective, then he did not think it would be fair to involve Sweden. He also queried the proposal of a subsidy and suggested it would be better to give it to Turkey.[4]

Palmerston took a contrary view, going even beyond Russell in his proposals.

It would be taking a very narrow & imperfect view of the causes and objects of the war in which we are engaged [he wrote] to think that the great and only thing to be aimed at is to drive the Russians out of the Principalities, and that this once accomplished the Sword may be returned to the scabbard. We are pledged by national interest, by European interest, and by our Convention with France to prevent the Recurrence of the Causes which have brought the war on, and this can be accomplished only by weakening Russia for a Time at least, if we cannot do so permanently, in some material point.

[1] *Ab. Cor. 1854-5*, pp. 130-1, 20 May 1854.
[2] PRO 30/22/11/D, fols. 1113-15, 22 May 1854.
[3] *Ibid.* fols. 1043-4, n.d.
[4] *Ibid.* fols. 1121-2, n.d.

The best security, he argued, was to deprive Russia of some of her recently acquired provinces such as Finland, Georgia, Crimea, Poland and so on. As for a plan of campaign in the Baltic, he proposed the destruction of the naval bases of Sveaborg and Cronstadt and of the Russian fleet, which would offer great security to Sweden. The capture of the bases would require troops and he suggested that the Swedish army with some French assistance would be well suited to this purpose. He concluded with this remarkable observation:

Successful operations of this kind in the Baltic would enable us greatly to diminish our Naval force in that sea and thus to reduce our expenses, or else to detach a larger force to the North American station to support our negotiations with the United States Government, and to prevent a Rupture with the Americans.[1]

Herbert expressed the opinion that while Turkey must be their first concern a strong diversion in the north would weaken Russia in the south. He thought the occupation of Finland was pointless, but asserted that the destruction of Sveaborg or Cronstadt and their fleets would be second in importance only to the destruction of Sebastopol, and that it would take Russia years to recover from such a blow. He would accept the proposed Swedish alliance providing there were no political conditions.[2] Gladstone stood by his previous opinion that it would be 'attended with very great and peculiar difficulties' and that it did 'not bear to the greatest advantage *materially* upon the main purpose of the war, while it has some tendency to lower the very high moral position of the Powers opposed to Russia'. While he did not object to sending a land force to the Baltic, he thought it much more important to bring Austria into the war.[3]

The cabinet debated the proposal on 24 May, but considered the French memorandum on it unsatisfactory. It was impossible to come to any decision, Aberdeen told the queen, 'more especially as the Swedish Government has made no official request for a subsidy'. He said that hitherto all the negotiations had been conducted with the Crown Prince 'without the knowledge of the Swedish Minister, and not

[1] PRO 30/22/11/D, fols. 1129–32, 26 May 1854.
[2] PRO 30/22/11/D, fols. 1123–4, 23 May 1854. Herbert's views are of particular interest since his mother was a Russian and he had relatives in high positions in Russia. See Stanmore, *Herbert*, I, 181.
[3] *Ibid.* fols. 1119–20, 23 May 1854.

always with that of the King'.[1] The discussion was resumed on 27 May, by which time news had been received indicating that the king of Sweden appeared to have decided to follow the example of Austria.[2] Nevertheless, the French government continued to press the matter and on 8 July persuaded the British cabinet to agree to some terms proposed by Sweden providing Austria took the field.[3] Throughout July negotiations were carried on behind Britain's back in Paris, Stockholm and Vienna, and the terms of a treaty were drawn up to which Britain was invited to accede at the price of paying half the proposed subsidy to Sweden. The latter was to provide 6,000 troops and a naval force of 10,000 men with a substantial complement of ships. The Swedes, however, asked for too much—the immediate entrance of Austria into the alliance and the annexation of Finland after the war.[4]

By mid August Aberdeen was advising the abandonment of the project, about which he had never been enthusiastic. 'The King of Sweden appears to be rather shy of our Ministers and entirely to distrust his own', he wrote to Clarendon. 'The whole affair seems to have arisen from a masonic friendship between the Crown Prince and Grey.'[5] Even Russell was turning against the idea, which he had been the first to support, since it was apparent that it would involve more troops and money than had been anticipated and Sweden was insisting on a pledge regarding Finland.[6] By this time the Allies were becoming fully engaged in the Black Sea theatre and the project of a land campaign in the north faded from view.

The naval effort in the Baltic was, however, continued, although with very limited success. It will be recalled that Admiral Napier had sailed for that theatre in March with a strong fleet and promise of great achievement. Following the declaration of war he was ordered to blockade the Gulf of Finland and the Gulf of Bothnia and to reconnoitre the fortresses of Cronstadt, Sveaborg and Bomarsund. The British fleet was soon joined by a French squadron of twenty-three ships and in the course of the summer by a French landing force of 10,000 men. The Allied fleets cruised extensively, fired on some Russian shore

---

[1] R.A. G13, fol. 48, 24 May 1854.
[2] *Ibid.* fol. 61, 28 May 1854, Aberdeen to the queen.
[3] *Ab. Cor. 1854–5*, p. 167, to the queen, 8 July 1854.
[4] R.A. G14/66, memorandum of the prince, Osborne, 3/7/1854. The address and context show the month is August, not July. For the Austrian negotiations see below, pp. 429–44.   [5] MS. Clar. Dep. C14, fols. 71–2, 16 August 1854.
[6] Gooch, *Later correspondence*, II, 169.

establishments, captured some Russian ships and succeeded in enforcing the blockade, but they had relatively little to show for the large naval and military establishments at their disposal. Throughout the summer Napier showed himself extremely hesitant in carrying out his instructions, although in August, on direct command of the Admiralty, and in conjunction with the French, he eventually attacked and captured Bomarsund and the Åland Islands, where it was situated, along with 2,000 Russians, with inconsiderable losses. Nevertheless, to the indignation of Graham and of the public he refused to take chances in attacking the other fortresses and in December, after some unseemly bickering with the Admiralty, he returned home with his fleet in disgrace and was ordered to strike his flag. Napier was a cantankerous old man and sought to make a public quarrel out of this affair, but by that time the ministers concerned were out of office and refused to be drawn.[1]

The capture of Bomarsund led to a long and weary discussion as to what should be done with it. Some, including Palmerston,[2] suggested that Sweden should be invited to take it over and repair the fortifications. Clarendon thought the Swedes should at least be consulted as a courtesy.[3] Aberdeen and Newcastle were agreeable to its destruction, unless the French were willing to occupy it, but Aberdeen did not think it was a matter to discuss with Sweden unless the Swedes immediately entered the war.[4] In the end the Swedes declined to come into the matter (or the French to stay) and so the demolition was carried out.[5]

The Baltic campaign of 1854 may have been disappointing to a public looking for great and decisive victories over the enemy, but at least it had one real achievement and no great disasters.

[1] For a contemporary account of these operations see *Annual Register, 1854*, pp. 398–402, and for a modern account, Erickson, *Graham*, pp. 346–53, who deals with the quarrel between Graham and Napier. According to Prince Albert 'the enlightened British public' attributed lack of success in the Baltic to Lord Aberdeen, who actually was critical of Napier's failure to attack Sveaborg (R.A. G17, fol. 89, memorandum of 7 October 1854; Graham Papers, from Aberdeen, 9 September 1854).

[2] MS. Clar. Dep. C15, fols. 165 and 170, 23 and 27 August 1854.

[3] *Ab. Cor. 1854–5*, p. 197, 25 August 1854.

[4] *Ibid.* p. 198, Newcastle, 25 August 1854; MS. Clar. Dep. C14, fols. 76–7, Aberdeen, 25 August 1854; Graham Papers, Newcastle, 22 and 26 August, and Aberdeen, 23 August 1854.

[5] Graham Papers, Clarendon, 28 August 1854; *Annual Register, 1854*, p. 402. A small British squadron also invaded the White Sea and successfully demolished a number of Russian shore establishments. A small Allied fleet cruising in the Pacific made similar hit-and-run attacks on Petropaulowski in the Russian province of Kamchatka. See *Annual Register, 1854*, pp. 402–5.

The problem of the German Powers—the search for an Austrian alliance

It had been a great disappointment to Lord Aberdeen that the German Powers, especially Austria, had not been prepared to go as fast or as far as Britain and France in resisting Russian aggression. Under pressure from the majority of his own cabinet, from public opinion in parliament and the country, and from their French ally, he had reluctantly assented to a separate declaration of war by the Western Allies on Russia. The Four Powers, however, did not immediately abandon the principle of joint action, even after this declaration. Indeed, on 9 April their representatives at Vienna signed a joint protocol (sometimes called the Quadruple Convention) binding themselves 'to remain united in the double object of maintaining the integrity of the Ottoman Empire, and of providing, by every means compatible with the Sultan's independence and sovereignty, for the civil and religious liberties of the Christian subjects of the Porte'. The Four Powers also engaged not to enter into any treaty with Russia or with any other power 'at variance with the principle laid down in the protocol', without previously deliberating on the matter in common.[1]

This protocol was followed on 20 April by the signature of a treaty of alliance between Austria and Prussia guaranteeing their mutual territories and 'the rights and interests of Germany against every species of attack'. In an 'additional article' these two Powers deplored the continued occupation of the Danubian Principalities by Russia as a threat to the material interests of the whole German Confederation and urged that the concessions recently made to the Christian subjects of the Porte

---

[1] *Annual Register, 1854–5*, p. 281, text in Appendix to Chronicle, p. 525. The agreement on and publication of this protocol were long delayed by the hesitation of the Prussian government, and the British ministers, suspecting the worst of Prussia, were apprehensive that Austria would not sign alone (R.A. G 10, fol. 105, Aberdeen, 4 March 1854; *Ab. Cor. 1854–5*, p. 66, Clarendon, 11 March 1854). During March a General von der Grüben made a mysterious visit to England carrying a letter to Queen Victoria from the king of Prussia. The general said that the king of Prussia was deterred from signing the protocol because he was shocked by a French attempt to bribe him with a promise of territory. Therefore he was determined to do nothing which could indicate a desire to profit by the defeat of Russia. General von der Grüben maintained that the king was as much opposed as ever to the policy of Russia, and if not pressed would ultimately be compelled to take a part against her (R.A. G 11, fol. 17, Aberdeen, 12 March 1854). The duke of Argyll received a more disquieting explanation of 'the real position of things at Berlin' from a private source there, indicating that a weak monarch was under the influence of a pro-Russian Court party. This informant hoped, however, that 'the feelings of the Country' would 'prevail against this infamous party' (MS. Clar. Dep. C 14, fols. 594–5, 22 March 1854).

should lead to Russian withdrawal from these territories. An '*article unique*' provided that Austria would seek an assurance from Russia that no further forward movement into Turkish territory was intended, and the Prussian government on its side undertook to back up this proposition. It was indicated that an unsatisfactory answer on the part of Russia might be expected to lead to the implementation of the treaty.[1] No answer, however, was made by the Russian government to the Austrian and Prussian notes until late July, by which time the Russians were on the point of withdrawing from the area.[2]

Aberdeen set great store on the possibility of the German Powers forcing Russia to evacuate the Principalities as a result of this treaty and urged that the Allied military policy should be governed accordingly.[3] Wood agreed with Aberdeen on the importance of getting Austria involved in the Principalities, but rejected the suggestion of an Austrian subsidy on the ground that it was bound to be unpopular in the House of Commons.[4] Gladstone also welcomed all efforts to bring Austria 'into the field in strength'. In a letter to Graham reflecting nicely his attitude to the war, he wrote: 'England and France are at present acting as the armed constabulary of Europe against the wanton destruction... of its peace. We hope to see Austria in the same really Holy Alliance: and Prussia though with an ill grace keeping guard at the back door.'[5] In fact, on 23 May Prussia refused to attend further ambassadorial conferences in Vienna, but discussion between Austria and the Allies continued.

On 24 May Aberdeen told the queen that the Austrian government was friendly and cordial but evidently 'unwilling to take any decisions before the Allied forces [had] made their appearance in the field'.[6] In reporting a Cabinet meeting on 28 May Aberdeen wrote again to the queen, saying that the question now was how to push Austria and 'whether the application of a subsidy as a *mise en campagne*, might not be attended with good effect'. He recognised, however, that a certain time was indispensable to Austria to prepare her north-eastern defences before she took any warlike action. He also noted that some members of the cabinet were unwilling to embark on the subsidising of foreign powers 'as being fatal to the financial principles recently established,

---

[1] *Annual Register, 1854*, pp. 281–2. See also PRO 30/22/11/C, fols. 1017–19, Clarendon to Russell, 25 April 1854.　　　　[2] *Annual Register, 1854*, p. 283.
[3] *Ab. Cor. 1854–5*, p. 121, memo, 5 May 1854.
[4] PRO 30/22/11/D, fols. 1071–4, 9 May 1854.
[5] Graham Papers, 17 May 1854.　　　　[6] R.A. G 13, fol. 48.

and to the commercial prosperity of the country'.[1] Nevertheless, the Chancellor of the Exchequer did not appear to be among these, for while opposing the proposal to subsidise Sweden he said of Austria that he preferred to 'subsidize the power which is going to join in the war on the same principles as our own, namely for the vindication of the public law of Europe'.[2] In opposing the subsidisation of Austria we may suppose that Palmerston was expressing a view on political rather than economic grounds.[3] Russell, although aware of the objections, was prepared to offer Austria the guarantee of a loan or the grant of a subsidy if she would join in the war against Russia.[4]

On 3 June Austria sent a summons to Russia to withdraw from the Principalities. Although the demand was not cast in the form of an ultimatum, by this action Austria clearly ran a real risk of becoming involved in the war. Consequently she became interested in negotiating a treaty of alliance with the two Western Powers with a view to protecting her own interests and limiting the scope of the war. The French government, quick to capitalise on this situation, immediately began to discuss the basis of an agreement with Austria from which the famous 'Four Points' began to emerge. The subsequent negotiations were almost as protracted as those of the previous summer, but it is unnecessary to follow them in detail.[5] The British government was less inclined to take the lead than formerly. Initially the ministers welcomed the increased activity of Austria, but they were loath to curtail their war effort in any way in the interests of diplomacy. Commenting on an Austrian communication about possible peace terms, Russell wrote: 'The only answer we can give is that having sent at a vast cost our fleets & armies to Turkey we cannot withdraw them without the signature of preliminary articles of peace.'[6] Aberdeen was naturally delighted with Austria's new course of action and was confident that the Austrians were 'bound to get the Russians out of the Principalities by negotiation,

---

[1] *Ibid.* fol. 61, 28 May 1854.

[2] Graham Papers, Gladstone, 17 May 1854.

[3] PRO 30/22/11/D, fols. 1129–32, 26 May 1854. 'If Austria wants money to carry on war for her own interests,' he wrote, 'she must raise what she wants in the money markets of Europe.'

[4] MS. Clar. C15, fols. 499–502, 26 May 1854.

[5] See G. B. Henderson, 'The diplomatic revolution of 1854', reprinted from *A.H.R.* XLIII (1937), in his *Crimean War diplomacy*, pp. 153–89.

[6] MS. Clar. C15, fols. 536–7, 14 July 1854. See also his memorandum of 5 July commenting favourably on Austria's new course and laying down the essential requirements for ensuring the security of Turkey (*ibid.* fols. 517–20).

or by force'.[1] Prussia, however, refused to join the negotiations that were now resuming at Vienna.[2]

On 19 July at a meeting that lasted from 12 to 5 p.m. the British cabinet heard the news of Russia's rejection of the Austrian summons and first considered the French proposal for a protocol in which the Conference of Vienna would enumerate the principal conditions upon which the Allies would treat. While ready to accept the principle of the French-Austrian proposals the cabinet at this stage was not prepared to agree to precise terms of peace.[3] Palmerston, especially, was leery. 'It seems to me that Austria wants to get Russia out of the Principalities but does not wish Russian Power to be much crippled', he commented to Clarendon.[4] He himself outlined the heads of a proposed treaty by which Austria, France and Britain should 'mutually agree to employ military & naval Forces for the attainment' of their common object, the maintenance of the independence and integrity of Turkey.[5] At one stage the more warlike British ministers feared lest the Austro-French proposals might interfere with the Crimean operation which had already been decided on by the Allies.[6] In his speech of 24 July moving the special vote of credit,[7] Russell spoke briefly of Austria's peculiar position. He informed the House of the demands that Austria had made on Russia and of Russia's answer to the effect that she declined to evacuate the Principalities while still engaged in hostilities with England and France, but that she was ready to accept the protocol of Vienna of 9 April. Russia, however, ignored the Allied proposals regarding Turkey; and Britain and France, Russell said, were no longer content to recognise any claim of Russia to exercise special privileges with regard to the Christian subjects of Turkey. Thus the matter remained at an impasse. He was unable to say whether Austria would hesitate any longer or make any further attempt to gain better assurances from St Petersburg, but he did not believe that she would break her engagements with the Western Powers and with Turkey.[8]

At a meeting on 29 July the cabinet gave approval to a tripartite agreement presented by the French government with only some slight modifications.[9]

[1] MS. Clar. Dep. C14, fol. 61, 21 July 1854.   [2] Ab. Cor. 1854–5, p. 176, 20 July 1854.
[3] Ibid. pp. 174–5, 19 July 1854.   [4] MS. Clar. Dep. C15, fols. 138–9, 25 July 1854.
[5] Ibid. fols. 140–1.   [6] Ibid. fols. 550–3, Clarendon and Russell, 24 July 1854.
[7] See above, pp. 413–16.   [8] Hansard, CXXXV, 598–613.
[9] R.A. G15, fol. 82, Aberdeen, 29 July 1854. See also MS. Clar. C15, fol. 555, Russell, 31 July 1854; C14, fol. 651, Lansdowne, 2 August 1854.

News of a Russian withdrawal from Wallachia, however, began to threaten the whole project. On 2 August Clarendon received an urgent appeal from Drouyn to accept some proposed Austrian modifications in the treaty and protocol without delay in order to pin Austria down. He was particularly concerned to do this since his Swedish plans depended on the Austrian alliance, but by this time Clarendon was aware of and highly indignant at all that was going on in Paris and Vienna behind his back.[1]

Some of the British ministers were soon beginning to make reservations. Palmerston and Herbert were disturbed by the provision for a 'suspension of hostilities', and Clarendon agreed that there was 'nothing more usual than to negotiate during the continuance of hostilities', noting that this was the case in 1763, 1799 and 1803, but he was prepared to retain the phrase rather than sacrifice the whole affair.[2] Palmerston continued to voice his concern: 'To agree to a Suspension of Hostilities now', he wrote to Clarendon on 3 August, 'would be to lose all the Fruits of our Exertions, & to expose ourselves to the Derision of Mankind. I do hope that this may not be done.'[3]

Russell, too, sounded the same note as complications began to arise, comparing the situation to the previous summer when 'everything went wrong'. 'The French are too clever by half, as Disraeli said of Gladstone last night', he wrote on 4 August. 'What with projects, notes, and projects of Treaty, I hardly know what we are doing.' Like Palmerston he now expressed dislike for the suggestion of an armistice unless some success such as the capture of Sebastopol had been obtained. 'But it would be fatal to leave our armies to rot of a Walcheren fever in the Crimea', he wrote. 'The place has to be taken in a month, or the expedition abandoned.' 'I hold the diminution of the Russian fleet at Sebastopol to be quite essential,' he continued; 'knowing Aberdeen's readiness to make peace in season & out of season, I thought it necessary to pledge myself to that at least in the H. of Commons.'[4] Palmerston also expressed his old distrust of the Prime Minister, writing to Clarendon:

Aberdeen evidently wants to make Peace *without* attaining the objects stated in Article No. 1 of the Heads, (outlining the objective of the Allies with

---

[1] See R.A. G14, fol. 66 (1–4), memorandum by the prince of 3 August 1854 (misdated 3/7); cf. above, p. 427.
[2] MS. Clar. Dep. C14, fols. 652–3, n.d.
[3] MS. Clar. Dep. C15, fols. 144–5, 3 August 1854.
[4] *Ibid.* fols. 561–3, 4 August 1854.

433

regard to the security of Turkey) and *without* weakening Russia anywhere or at all & therefore it was that he wished our Troops to die of Fever in the Marshes of Wallachia rather than that they should wrest Sebastopol & the Black Sea Fleet from Russia; but such an infatuated Policy cannot & must not prevail.[1]

By this time, however, the wind was taken out of the sails of the projected tripartite alliance by the dramatic withdrawal of the Russians from the Principalities. As soon as the Austrian government became aware of this development, its interest in a treaty of alliance cooled. The result was that the Western Powers for the time being had to be satisfied with an exchange of notes and the treaty had to wait until a further change in the international climate again swung Austria towards the Allies. Nevertheless the exchange of notes signed by the Allied ambassadors in Vienna on 8 August was important as containing the Four Points on which peace with Russia was finally to be reached almost two years later. It was agreed (1) that the Russian guarantee of the Principalities should be replaced by a European guarantee, (2) that the Danube should be made a free river, (3) that the Treaty of 1841 should be revised in the interests of the balance of power and (4) that the Christian peoples of the Porte should be placed under European rather than Russian protection.[2]

The treaty negotiations were not entirely abandoned, but for the time they languished as the Allies became preoccupied with the expedition to the Crimea and Austria with the occupation of the Principalities in the wake of the withdrawing Russians. This was done with the agreement of the Allies and of Turkey,[3] but not without some apprehension on their part. Indeed, as Russell pointed out to Clarendon, if the Austrians had made this move at an earlier date they would have done the Allies a great service. 'As it is, they are rendering a great service to Russia,' he continued. 'Had the Russians remained in possession of the Principalities I should have had little doubt of the success of the expedition. As

---

[1] MS. Clar. Dep. C 15, fols. 146–8, 10 August 1854.

[2] See Henderson, *Crimean War diplomacy*, pp. 165–8, who emphasises the lead taken by France and Austria in these matters and the listlessness of the Aberdeen ministry.

On the last day of the session, in answer to a question, Russell informed the House of Commons of Russia's announcement of withdrawal from the Principalities and of Austria's agreement with Britain and France that there could be no mere return to the *status quo ante bellum* (*Hansard*, CXXXV, 1554–6).

[3] Austria had concluded a convention with Turkey on 14 June which provided for the possible use of Austrian troops in the Principalities to free them from the Russians. For the text see *Annual Register, 1854*, Appendix to the Chronicle, pp. 537–8.

it is, time may defeat us.'[1] In Russell's view the interposition of a still neutral Austria into the Principalities between the Turks and the Russians released large Russian forces for the defence of the Crimea.[2] On the other hand the Russians now had reason to distrust the Austrians and so were bound to keep troops to guard themselves on that flank against possible Austrian attack. Moreover, the interposition of Austria into the Principalities relieved Turkish troops for fighting in the Crimea if they were wanted.

No matter how annoyed the Russians might have been over the unfriendly course of the Austrians, it was obviously in their interests to keep Austria neutral. Nevertheless, in mid August they indignantly rejected Austria's peace proposals. Palmerston was delighted when he heard the news that Nicholas had rejected the Four Points:

If he had nibbled at them we should have been embarrassed [he wrote to Clarendon] though not actually hampered. If Austria now takes her time with Decision, Prussia must follow her, and if Austria & Prussia take the Field in good earnest against Russia they *must* restore a substantive Kingdom of Poland...when once they draw the Sword they must for their own Sakes throw away the Scabbard.[3]

Palmerston was always allowing his enthusiasm to run away with him and on the subject of Poland he was quite unrealistic, but most suspicious of Aberdeen:

Is it *possible* [he had written in an earlier letter] that Aberdeen can have discouraged the idea of the Reestablishment of a Kingdom of Poland!! I hope & trust that this cannot be but it would be well to enquire about it because we well know that his private & verbal Communications with Brunnow last year were not at all in accordance with the opinions of many of his Colleagues & that irreparable mischief was thereby occasioned.[4]

The coalition ship was no tighter than it had been.

Russell likewise greeted the news of Russia's rejection of the Four Points with satisfaction, presuming that it would induce Austria to sign a treaty and enter into active operations.[5] A week later, however, the

[1] MS. Clar. Dep. C15, fols. 576–8, 16 August 1854.
[2] Cf. MS. Clar. Dep. C15, fols. 630–2, Russell, 15 September 1854, saying that the Austrian occupation of the Principalities allowed Russia to transfer 50,000 men to the Crimea.
[3] MS. Clar. Dep. C15, fols. 174–7, 3 September 1854.
[4] *Ibid.* fols. 163–4, 22 August 1854.
[5] *Ibid.* fols. 596–9, 4 September 1854.

Austrian ambassador, Colloredo, informed Clarendon that his government refused to do anything further since in their view two of the four points had been virtually obtained, 'viz. the evacuation of the Principalities and the navigation of the Danube, *with the exception of the mouth*'. The third point would be settled by the Allied expedition to the Crimea and the fourth could be assured by the action of the Turks, which would make the protection of Russia '*superfluous*'.[1]

The British ministers were naturally indignant and Clarendon sent a strong despatch to Vienna.[2] Even Aberdeen did not object to Clarendon's remonstrance, but observed that Austria had less reason to go to war with the Russians out of the Principalities. Nevertheless, he looked with growing apprehension at their worsening relations with Austria and Prussia, observing: 'For all this may at last end in a revolutionary war, greatly to the delight of many here, and elsewhere. It may suit the French well enough; for they would see the Rhine in perspective.' He urged Clarendon in his communications with Vienna to leave an opening for future negotiation. 'If we succeed at Sebastopol, as I feel confident we shall,' he concluded more cheerfully, 'the whole question will assume a new character, and we shall be able to do much, both with Austria and Prussia, which is now impossible.'[3]

Russell took a surprisingly moderate view, saying that although Austria had disappointed them he thought she was more for than against them. 'If she chooses to be neutral, neutral let her be', he commented philosophically; and, sounding an almost Aberdonian note, he continued: 'We ought to avoid altogether if we can allowing this war to degenerate into a revolutionary war...If we succeed in the Crimea and send a right man to Vienna, I still think Austria will be with us in the spring.'[4] Russell, as always, was critical of Westmorland and anxious to replace him.

Aberdeen continued to be apprehensive of a split with Austria whom he still regarded as 'perfectly honest, and even without war' as likely to be of great service.[5] He strongly demurred to a French suggestion that Britain and France should send commissioners to the Principalities to participate in their administration as being calculated to lead to estrange-

---

[1] *Ab. Cor. 1854–5*, p. 211, Clarendon, 10 September 1854 (Clarendon's italics).
[2] *Ibid.* p. 218, 18 September 1854; cf. MS. Clar. C15, fols. 633–6, 16 September for Russell's views.
[3] MS. Clar. C14, fols. 85–6, 19 September 1854.
[4] MS. Clar. Dep. C15, fol. 619, (?) September 1854.
[5] *Ibid.* C14, fol. 88, 25 September 1854.

ment with Austria. 'You cannot possibly desire this, although others may,' he wrote to Clarendon; 'but to this I think we are drifting, and that it will only be averted by your prudence, conciliation and forbearance.'[1] He wrote thus with good reason, for Clarendon was losing all patience with Austria, whose policy he declared to be only one degree better than that of Prussia.[2] He agreed with Aberdeen about the undesirability of sending British and French commissioners into the Principalities, but he continued to be suspicious about Austrian policy and more concerned about keeping some check on the Austrian authorities. 'Unadulterated selfishness is the policy of Austria,' he wrote, 'for which I don't the least blame her, but I contend that it is no part of our policy to promote her objects at the expense of our own interests.'[3]

By this time Austria was becoming alarmed at her isolated position and aware of the discontent of France and Britain, who were now seriously threatening the Russians in the Crimea. Consequently Buol offered the allies 'a sort of offensive and defensive Treaty, which', Clarendon wrote, 'I am very sorry for'. While anxious to be on good relations with Austria he shied off a resumption of the Vienna conference with interminable discussions about the Four Points. He continued:

Austria never will take the ball at its bound, she is always too late, and things which might have been practicable or desirable six weeks ago, have been put out of the question by the march of events...Would the people of this country endure anything that savoured of negotiation, at a time when English blood is flowing in torrents in the Crimea, and thousands of English families are execrating the obstinacy of the Czar?

He confessed he did not know what to say to Colloredo because he did not wish 'to offend or even to annoy Austria', and proposed to stall for time until the cabinet could be assembled. He assured Aberdeen that there was no plan to his knowledge for estranging England from Austria as Aberdeen had alleged.[4]

The queen also urged on Clarendon 'a temperate consideration of the Austrian proposals...and the avoidance of anything which could weaken the accord Européen'. She recognised that, as they stood, the Austrian proposals were too limited but she shrewdly asked how England and France could bring the war to an end single-handed,

---

[1] Ab. Cor. 1854–5, pp. 232–4, 5 October 1854.
[2] Ibid. pp. 241–2, 5 October 1854.
[3] Ibid. pp. 249–51, 8 October 1854.   [4] Ibid.

reminding the Foreign Secretary that their army in the Crimea was the only one they had.[1]

Clarendon was not unaware of the importance of an Austrian alliance, although lacking Aberdeen's confidence in Austria. He claimed to have been successful in moderating the French government's reactions to the original Austrian proposals, which they considered '*détestable*'.[2] At a cabinet meeting on 17 October there were differences of opinion,[3] but Clarendon did not propose to reject the Austrian overture altogether. 'I think of telling Colloredo frankly, but in the most friendly way, what our difficulties are about the renewed Conferences, &c,' he wrote to Aberdeen the next day, 'and that we don't see our way out of them *at present.*'[4] At a second cabinet meeting on 20 October Clarendon, according to Aberdeen, pressed strongly for an Austrian treaty 'having for its object more definite understanding with a view to future cooperation'. 'Notwithstanding any bitterness of feeling which may exist in the Cabinet,' Aberdeen told the queen, 'the communication to the Austrian Government is intended to be of the most conciliatory and friendly description'. He believed that Austria was 'really anxious for a closer understanding with the Western Powers', but he found the conduct of the French government 'inconsistent, and not very intelligible'.[5]

Nevertheless, the Prime Minister was not satisfied with Clarendon's subsequent despatch to Vienna; 'as, although we profess to desire a Treaty, we neither propose one ourselves, nor desire them to do so', he complained. 'We ought not to lose time in placing our relations with Austria on a perfectly clear and definite footing, which can only be done by a Treaty.'[6]

At this point European diplomacy suddenly emerged from the doldrums in which it had been drifting since mid summer. The French government, alarmed by a 'very active intrigue' centred in Berlin for the purpose of detaching Austria from the Western Powers, on 1 November proposed a new form of a treaty to bind Austria by military engagements. Clarendon, himself concerned by the situation

---

[1] *Letters of Queen Victoria*, III, 61–3, 10 October 1854. See also *Ab. Cor. 1854–5*, pp. 240–1, to the queen, 6 October, and from the queen, 7 October 1854.

[2] *Ab. Cor. 1854–5*, pp. 256–7, 14 October 1854.

[3] R.A. G18, fol. 29, Aberdeen, 17 October 1854.

[4] *Ab. Cor. 1854–5*, p. 259, 18 October 1854. As proof of his distrust of the Austrians he cited their peremptory veto of a Turkish sally against the Russians from the Principalities.

[5] R.A. G18, fol. 35, 20 October 1854.   [6] *Ab. Cor. 1854–5*, p. 260, 23 October 1854.

developing in the Crimea, welcomed this proposal.[1] Russell expressed his approval,[2] but Palmerston was more critical. He warned that the only thing that was really to be feared from Austria, was that she would 'endeavour craftily to entangle England & France in the Intricacy of Negotiations', which would paralyse their action in wars and bring them to a point at which they would be forced to choose between unacceptable alternatives.[3] When Aberdeen urged some modifications to make the draft more acceptable to Austria,[4] Clarendon answered:

It is rather difficult to reconcile opinions upon such a matter as this Treaty. You think it does not go far enough for Austria; Lord John approves; Palmerston objects; and I must say that Westmorland's letter this morning justifies his notion that we may be entangled in negotiations, if we don't take care.[5]

The French draft treaty was approved by the British government and forwarded to Vienna, where the Austrians proposed some modifications. In the meantime news arrived that Russia had accepted the Four Points, stimulated perhaps by an Austrian mobilisation and diplomatic pressure from Prussia. The British cabinet met to consider the Austrian revisions in the shadow of harrowing news from the Crimea. Under pressure from the French and without enthusiasm, they agreed to instruct Westmorland to sign the revised treaty.[6] According to Aberdeen the British despatch was 'founded upon an excellent memorandum sent by the Prince'.[7] Palmerston for once had no objections because at the time of the meeting he was in Paris, where he was well received and pleased to find that both Louis Napoleon and Drouyn held views similar to his own about pressing the war hard against Russia. Obviously influenced by his conversations with the French foreign minister, he wrote:

My impression is that Austria wants to engage us in premature negotiation to make Merit with Russia for having moderated our Demands, to make Merit with us for having brought Russia to make concessions the value of which She

[1] PRO 30/22/11/F, fols. 1626–9, Clarendon, 2 November 1854.
[2] *Ibid.* fols. 1532–5, 4 November 1854.
[3] MS. Clar. Dep. C15, fols. 225–30, 2 November 1854; on the following day he sent Clarendon the sketch of heads of a treaty (fols. 231–3).
[4] *Ab. Cor. 1854–5*, p. 266, 2 November 1854.
[5] *Ibid.* p. 267, 3 November 1854.
[6] Henderson, *Crimean War diplomacy*, pp. 182–3; PRO 30/22/11/F, fols. 1715–17; *Ab. Cor. 1854–5*, p. 299, Clarendon, 19 November 1854.
[7] *Ab. Cor. 1854–5*, pp. 279–80, Aberdeen to the queen, 21 November 1854.

will greatly Exaggerate and thus she hopes to avoid war...If this Plan can be defeated by a cautious & guarded acceptance of her Treaty with suitable Reservations, we may avoid the appearance of rejecting her overtures, and at the Same Time keep ourselves out of the Pitfall if she is trying to lead us into one.[1]

The Treaty was finally signed in Vienna on 2 December. Professing to seek the re-establishment of peace on a solid basis and citing the protocols of 9 April and 23 May and the exchange of notes of 8 August, it provided that Austria should guard the Principalities against any return of the Russians, but not interfere with the military movements of the Allies or Turkey against Russia and that a commission should be formed at Vienna by the three Powers, with Turkish participation invited, to deal with questions that might arise in that area; in the event of hostilities between Russia and Austria the three Powers mutually promised to each other their offensive and defensive alliance; it was further agreed that none of them would enter into peace negotiations with Russia without prior mutual deliberation. If peace had not been re-established on the basis of the Four Points by the end of the year, the three Powers promised to 'deliberate without delay upon effectual means for obtaining the object of their alliance'.[2]

The British ministers showed no elation at the signature of the treaty, but in Gavin Henderson's view France welcomed it as the end of the isolation she had endured since 1815. At any rate it marked the end of the Holy Alliance that had operated in Europe for much of that period.[3] In this sense it may have been a significant turning-point, but it was only another step in the unending and tortuous diplomacy that marked both the origins and the whole course of the Crimean War. Now once more the discussion turned to war aims. It was the youngest member of the British cabinet, the duke of Argyll, who first stirred up his colleagues in a long letter addressed to the Foreign Secretary for circulation among the other ministers.[4] He urged that the cabinet should come to a precise understanding on this subject and deprecated the tendency to put the question aside as unnecessary or as too delicate. 'To let things "take their course" in War', he wisely observed, 'is to let

[1] MS. Clar. Dep. C15, fols. 238–47, 19 November 1854.
[2] P.P. 1854–5, LV, E.P. XIII, 1–2 (reprinted in Annual Register, 1854, Appendix to the Chronicle, pp. 536–7).
[3] Henderson, Crimean War diplomacy, pp. 184–9.
[4] MS. Clar. Dep. C14, fols. 706–14, 25 October 1854. The letter is reproduced in full by Argyll in his Autobiography, I, 489–94.

War feed upon, & perpetuate itself.' He professed to believe that the English people would follow wise leadership: 'Public opinion will never be led, so long as it is simply followed', he asserted. It was time, he argued, for the ministers to settle among themselves what they were all willing to accept and this meant going beyond the Four Points, which were too vague. He wanted to know whether it was their intention 'to prosecute the war until Russia was dismembered' or 'to direct the war to the separation of Finland or the re-establishment of Poland', aims that Palmerston had been dreaming about. He continued:

There is one other object of the war which I saw lately proclaimed by an M.P. of some ability & note. It is the resistance of Despotism & the relief of oppressed 'nationalities'. One effect of a lack of definiteness in the language of the Govt. will be that this sort of nonsense will be encouraged. Discussion on the objects of the war, without guidance from something like authority, will be taken up by the different parties in a Popular Assembly each bidding against each other in clap-trap sayings.

'What I dread', he concluded, 'is our going on without some purpose more definitely recognized—afraid of public opinion because we do not try to lead or guide it; shy of each other because we do not know exactly each other's views.'[1] These were wise words, but to gain a consensus on war aims from this cabinet was easier said than done.

Palmerston discussed the subject with Louis Napoleon and Drouyn in Paris and formed the opinion that they 'had no intention or wish for Peace on inadequate conditions or prematurely concluded' and that they looked 'to larger and more decisive operations next year'. Napoleon favoured keeping the Crimea as a lever to be used in negotiation, provided they were not forced to withdraw, which he did not anticipate. He agreed with Palmerston that the conditions under discussion with respect to map changes should not at present be announced, for in the existing state of the war it 'would be like asking for the moon'. In a longer conversation with Drouyn, Palmerston found the foreign minister had very similar views to his own, looking to great territorial changes if the course of events warranted it, and feeling strongly that 'Small Results would not do after our great exertions'. Drouyn argued that if nothing more than the destruction of Sebastopol and the Russian fleet was achieved 'the French nation would say they

[1] According to Henderson (*Crimean War diplomacy*, p. 103) this letter was later circulated among the cabinet and influenced the subsequent development of Allied policy.

had been made the Cats Paw of England, who always wanted the Destruction of the Fleet of other Countries'. 'What of course these remarks pointed out to', Palmerston continued, 'were Georgia and Circassia, the mouths of the Danube, Poland and Finland, matters on which he said his opinion had for two years been the same as those which I told him were mine personally.'[1] Palmerston came back from Paris remarkably confident in the purpose and good faith of the French government, despite their independent dealings with Austria. He told Clarendon that neither the emperor nor Drouyn anticipated the conclusion of peace that winter and that the emperor was looking forward with determination to large-scale operations in the next campaign.[2]

Nevertheless, the Austrians were anxious for an elaboration of the Four Points in order to bind the Western Powers to more precise conditions of peace.[3] Buol had raised the matter even before the treaty of 2 December had been signed, but failed to get a satisfactory response from either Britain or France. Stirred, perhaps, by Argyll's memorandum and by a similar one from Prince Albert,[4] the cabinet approved a despatch on 30 November or 1 December which attempted some elucidation of point 3 with the words: 'It is intended that the maritime preponderance of Russia in the Black Sea shall cease.' This did not seem unreasonable, but it is significant that after the cabinet Aberdeen himself called on Colloredo to warn the Austrians not to take Clarendon's despatch too literally.[5]

Buol expressed his satisfaction with Clarendon's despatch and urged that negotiations with Russia should be begun. Palmerston, in common with Clarendon and Russell, considered the time inopportune for negotiation with Russia: 'we are in Fact in the middle of a Battle upon the issue of which the Conditions of Peace must depend,' he argued; 'and until the Battle is over Each Party must be entitled to assume that victory will be on its side, and we must wait for the Results until we can know how the Two Parties stand.'[6]

[1] MS. Clar. Dep. C15, fols. 238–41, 19 November, and 242–5, 21 November 1854.
[2] Ibid. fols. 259–61, 6 December 1854.
[3] For what follows see Gavin Henderson's very illuminating article, 'The two interpretations of the four points, December 1854', reprinted in Crimean War diplomacy, pp. 98–122.   [4] Argyll, Autobiography, I, 506–7.
[5] Argyll (Autobiography, I, 507) indicates that he obtained a change in wording to ensure that the Christian subjects of the Porte might expect the same protection from the Four Powers collectively as Russia might have promised them alone.
[6] MS. Clar. Dep. C15, fols. 262–4, 10 December 1854 (printed in part in Maxwell, Clarendon, II, 48–9).

The British ministers favoured a stiffer approach on point 3 (respecting the Black Sea), but the French were reluctant to damage the understanding with Austria. The result was, after a good deal of discussion, that the Allied governments agreed to go ahead with an innocuous exchange of notes with Austria regarding the Four Points as a basis of negotiation with Russia and a secret exchange with each other providing for a much more drastic interpretation of point 3, in which they envisaged the destruction of Sebastopol and possibly other Russian fortresses in the Black Sea and the reduction of the Russian fleet on that sea to four ships. With this promise from France in their pockets the British ministers uneasily agreed to the exchange of notes with Austria, which eventually took the form of a protocol signed on 28 December.[1]

The protocol went further than the exchange of notes of 8 August, but not nearly as far as the secret exchange of notes between Britain and France that preceded it. The three governments now agreed:

(1) The exclusive protectorate exercised by Russia over Moldavia, Wallachia and Servia should be replaced by a guarantee of the five Powers and none of the stipulations of former treaties between Russia and Turkey should be revived.

(2) Provision should be made for the free navigation of the Danube.

(3) The Treaty of 1841 should be revised 'to connect the existence of the Ottoman Empire more completely with the European equilibrium, and to put an end to the preponderance of Russia in the Black Sea'; it was indicated that detailed arrangements had to depend on the course of the war.

(4) Russia was to renounce any attempt to revive her former treaties with Turkey.[2]

The Western Allies hoped that even these would be strong enough to deter the Russians from entering peace negotiations prematurely, and when they were presented to Prince Gortchakov, the Russian representative, at an ambassadorial conference in Vienna on 28 December his first reaction tended to confirm their anticipation. Nevertheless, on referral to St Petersburg this version of the Four Points was accepted as a basis of peace negotiations. 'We all think that this Russian acceptance is only a clever dodge to produce dissension between the Western Powers', Clarendon commented acidly.[3] By the time the conference

[1] Henderson, *Crimean War diplomacy*, pp. 105–14.
[2] *P.P. 1854–5*, LV, *E.P.* XIII, 2–3.
[3] Maxwell, *Clarendon*, II, 54.

had opened in Vienna in March 1855, however, the coalition government had fallen and there we must leave the story.[1]

If the coalition had survived it might have come to grief on the shoals of the Vienna peace conference, but, as it was, ministerial differences over wartime foreign policy were not a major factor in its break-up. The differences of emphasis between Aberdeen on the one hand and Russell and Palmerston on the other remained after the outbreak of war, but on the whole they were less divisive than they had been in the preceding twelve months. This was partly because Aberdeen had become fatalistic, his spirit largely broken, and consequently his leadership less effective. Clarendon continued to occupy a middle position and his correspondence with Graham suggests a similarity in their views. Graham, Newcastle and Herbert were all decidedly more warlike than their chief, but preoccupation with war administration left these three with little time for the formulation of foreign policy. Argyll and Granville formed an articulate voice of moderation among the younger members of the cabinet and Wood seems to have held the same middle position. Gladstone was probably closest to Aberdeen in his views, but he did not share his leader's misgivings once the die was cast; with Aberdeen and Argyll, however, he was anxious to restrict the war to its original objectives. While the coalition lasted, the Chancellor of the Exchequer's role in the formulation of war policy was limited: between the problems of war finance and the passage of the Oxford University Act he had his hands full in 1854. (But out of office in 1855-6, as the war dragged on, in his view unnecessarily, he became one of its sharpest critics.) The possibility of rupture within the administration over peace negotiations with Russia never eventuated, since the government fell because of its mismanagement of the war itself. Before turning to this melancholy story, however, there is one other area of diplomatic activity that requires our brief attention.

The Sardinian alliance

The one alliance which actually brought troops into the field against the enemy was the most easily and quickly concluded. This was the agreement with Piedmont which was negotiated just prior to the fall of the coalition. At the end of November Clarendon wrote to Hudson, the

[1] See Henderson, *Crimean War diplomacy*, pp. 114–22. For the sequel see his article, 'The eclipse of Lord John Russell', pp. 33–67.

British minister at Turin, to enquire whether Piedmont might be interested in joining the war. Aberdeen was characteristically unenthusiastic about this development.

There are some expressions in your letter that may appear a little equivocal [he wrote to Clarendon], and rather tend to provoke the Sardinian appetite. It seems rather strange that while you are on the point of signing a treaty of offensive and defensive alliance with Austria, you should engage to protect Piedmont from Austrian attacks. I suppose, however, that you intend, during the war, to protect Lombardy from the much more probable contingency of the renewal of Sardinian invasion.[1]

Clarendon replied that he had no wish for a quarrel with Austria, but that he could not ignore Austria's bad faith in impeding the movements of Omer Pasha in the Principalities.[2] Hudson did not think that there would be any great difficulty in persuading Piedmont to put a contingent in the field, but expected that objections might be raised by Austria and France, who would have 'no wish to see Piedmont take an active part in the war'.[3] On 18 December Clarendon forwarded to Aberdeen an 'important despatch' from Hudson for early consideration of the cabinet.[4] There were apparently some differences of opinion, but on the 23rd Aberdeen told the queen that at a meeting that day the cabinet took a more rational view of the Sardinian proposals. It was decided to make pecuniary conditions easy, but to resist binding commitments calculated to make Austria suspicious.[5] Aberdeen and Queen Victoria were not happy with the despatch that Clarendon prepared to send to Turin and the Prime Minister wrote a rather stiff note to the Foreign Secretary about it. He objected to Clarendon's loose use of the word 'Italy' and was opposed to making any engagements there. 'It is to be hoped that the war will have nothing to do with Italy or its concerns,' he wrote; 'and that the terms of peace will have no relation to its future condition.'[6] The queen demanded changes in the despatch, watering down assurances regarding Britain's interest in the welfare of Italy, and asked to see it again before it was sent.[7] Clarendon was exasperated by the queen's letter and told Aberdeen that the governments

[1] *Ab. Cor. 1854–5*, p. 284, 29 November 1854.
[2] *Ibid.* p. 284, 29 November 1854. This letter presumably follows Aberdeen's.
[3] PRO 30/22/11/F, fols. 1900–3, 8 December 1854.
[4] *Ab. Cor. 1854–5*, pp. 290–1.   [5] R.A. G21, fol. 36.
[6] *Ab. Cor. 1854–5*, pp. 295–6, 24 December 1854.
[7] *Ibid.* p. 297, 24 December 1854.

of the Pope and king of Naples ought no longer to be endured and that the different states of Italy ought not permanently to be occupied by Austrian and French troops. He was sorry to differ with Aberdeen, but he thought that a peace settlement would be a good opportunity to deal with the problem of Italy—just as they had made the settlement of 1814–15 the opportunity of dealing with the slave trade.[1]

At a further cabinet on 27 December it was decided to remove the articles in the proposed treaty relating to Austria and to exclude Piedmont from the peace conference, provisions which Aberdeen mistakenly thought would deter the Sardinians from signing.[2] The queen was quite satisfied by these alterations and considered the revised despatch now to be quite safe. 'Lord Clarendon was rather excited about it last night,' she told Aberdeen, 'which the Queen thought the subject did not call for.'[3] Finally at a cabinet on 16 January 1855 the Sardinian business was settled. Piedmont undertook to contribute 15,000 troops, which were in effect to be paid for by Britain under guise of a loan.[4] The king of Sardinia acceded to the treaty of alliance binding Britain and France and in return the queen and the emperor guaranteed the integrity of his dominions for the duration of the war.[5] The agreements were signed on 26 January, four days before Lord Aberdeen's resignation, and the Sardinian troops arrived in the Crimea in time to participate in the battle of the Tchernaya.[6] Long before this event, however, Lord Aberdeen's administration had collapsed, for its military achievements were less successful than those in the field of diplomacy. It remains, therefore, to examine the events that brought about the demise of the coalition which had hitherto survived so many challenges successfully.

[1] *Ab. Cor. 1854–5*, p. 298, 24 December 1854.
[2] R.A. G21, fol. 45, Aberdeen to queen, 27 December 1854.
[3] *Ab. Cor. 1854–5*, p. 302, 28 December 1854.
[4] R.A. G22, fol. 50, Aberdeen to queen, 16 January 1855.
[5] *Annual Register*, 1855, p. 196.
[6] *Ibid.* Appendix to the Chronicle, pp. 405–6.

17

THE CONDUCT OF THE WAR—
THE INVASION OF THE CRIMEA

The 'Phoney War', April–August 1854—Gallipoli to Varna

This is not the place to attempt any detailed reconstruction of the melancholy story of the Crimean campaign; yet we must consider the salient features of that operation since the fate of the coalition was so dependent on it. For the last six months of the coalition's life its members thought of little else, and public opinion was roused to a great pitch by the remarkable reports from the theatre of war that were being published in *The Times*.[1]

The initial efforts of the British government were, as we have seen,[2] vigorous and effective. Even before the declaration of war the decision had been taken to send a force of some 25,000 men to the East in support of Turkey. Ten regiments had been recalled from the colonies as soon as war was imminent and an advance force of 10,000 men had been sent to Malta at the end of February.[3] A month later these troops proceeded to Gallipoli, where the first French contingents had already arrived and taken the best positions. Here they were joined in due course by the balance of the British force under Lord Raglan, who landed on 2 May.

When the Allied armies were first sent to Turkey the Russians were attacking the Turks across the Danube. The original Allied objective, it will be remembered, as suggested by General Burgoyne, was the defence of Constantinople from a firm base on the Dardanelles, which Graham envisaged as a Torres Vedras. In February Burgoyne had been sent out to Turkey, with the full approval of Louis Napoleon, whom he had visited on the way, in order to advise further on the implementation

---

[1] See W. H. Russell, *The war from the landing in Gallipoli to the death of Lord Raglan* (London, 1855), containing the unrevised original despatches with only minor omissions and alterations.   [2] See above, pp. 251–7.

[3] On 23 February the 28th Regiment and the bulk of the Brigade of Guards departed from Southampton by steamer, arriving at Malta on 5 March, while the 62nd Regiment sailed from Cork in sixteen days. See Russell, *The War*, pp. 1–5, who in his despatches gave full details of ships and regiments in a way that would have shocked the security-minded military of a later day.

THE BLACK SEA

Azov

R. Don

Gheisk

SEA OF
AZOV

R. Kuban

MANGRELIA

ABASIA

Gagri

Redout Kaleh

Trebizond

40°

Berislov

Nikolaev

Kherson

R. Dnieper

Perekop

Taman

Anapa

Kertch

Araba

Kaffa

Simferopol

Eupatoria

CRIMEA

Akmetchet

Tarkan

Sebastopol

Balaclava

B L A C K   S E A

Sinope

200 English miles

150

Scale

100

50

0

35° E

GULF OF PEREKOP

Odessa

R. Dniester

R. Pruth

R. Danube

DOBRUDJA

Silistria

Kustendji
(Constanza)

Baltjik
(Baltjik)

Varna

Shumla

Burgas

B O S P H O R U S

Scutari

Constantinople

SEA OF
MARMORA

30°

448

of these plans. In March he conferred with the Turkish general, Omer Pasha, who seemed quite confident of holding the Russians and who suggested that the Allies might take up positions at Varna, from which they could threaten the Russian flank on the Black Sea. Even at this date Omer spoke of an attack on the Crimea as his favourite project, and made little of its defences.[1]

Writing to Raglan at the end of March, Burgoyne cautiously opened up the possibility of offensive operations such as an attack on the Crimea or a penetration into Georgia, and on 10 April on his return to England he revived this theme, disclaiming the purely defensive views that were attributed to him. Nevertheless, he still emphasised the importance of strong defensive positions in the Dardanelles–Constantinople area as a base for any offensive operations. He was sceptical about the prospects of an expedition to the Crimea, citing the failure of such an operation in Holland in 1799, but he thought the seizure of Anapa near the entrance of the Sea of Azov might be less difficult. He compared the position of the Allies in Turkey with that of the British in the Peninsula, except that the duke of Wellington had the support of the entire population and excellent information regarding the enemy, which in the case of the Russians seemed to be 'totally unattainable'.[2]

At this date even the warlike Russell (writing to Clarendon) was still inclined to stay on the defensive.[3] Towards the end of April, however, in the face of false reports that the Russians had crossed the Balkan, he began to press for increased activity.[4] At a cabinet meeting on the 28th it was proposed to increase the army by 15,000 and the navy by 5,000 men and to embody another 15,000 in the militia to expedite enlistment and to provide sufficient garrisons to relieve a further portion of the regular army for service in the East. An important decision was also taken with respect to the Allied forces already in Turkey, which were now ordered to advance towards the Turkish frontier with a view to the defence of Shumla or operations on the line of the Balkan, but as yet it was left to the Allied commanders to decide exactly how and where their armies would be used.[5] Until their cavalry and artillery arrived there would be

---

[1] Wrottesley, *Burgoyne*, II, 2–27.
[2] *Ibid.* pp. 37–42. Burgoyne attributed his earlier emphasis on defensive positions in part to uncertainty as to French participation.   [3] MS. Clar. Dep. C15, fols. 443–4.
[4] *Ab. Cor. 1854–5*, pp. 110–12, 27 April 1854 (Gooch, *Later correspondence*, II, 161–4).
[5] R.A. G12, fol. 72, Aberdeen to the queen, 28 April 1854; the cabinet decisions contained in this letter corresponded closely to the proposals in Russell's letter to Aberdeen of the previous day.

little opportunity to take the offensive.[1] As soon as all these forces were assembled it was expected that the British commander would have 30,000 men (5,000 more than originally planned) and the French, 50,000; this, Lord Aberdeen told the queen, would 'form a very formidable body for the Russians to encounter'.[2] In the course of the summer, according to Newcastle,[3] a further reserve division was sent out to the East under General Cathcart that brought the total British force up to 34 or 35,000.

At the beginning of June the Allied commanders decided to advance by sea to Varna in support of the Turks, who had valiantly held the Russians on the Danube at Silistria. At the last moment the commander of the French army, Marshal St Arnaud, had attempted to change this plan on the grounds that the Allies were not yet fully prepared to take the field, but eventually on 9 June he gave in to Lord Raglan's insistence.

Actually the Light Brigade had arrived at Varna on 1 June and now it was followed by the First Division, which arrived on the 13th, but with insufficient transport to go forward immediately to the aid of Silistria. Ten days later, on 23 June, the Russians raised the siege and on 7 July the Turks secured a bridgehead across the Danube at Giugevo without any assistance from the Allies other than a few individual Englishmen and the fire of some British gunboats on the river.[4]

Had the Russians succeeded in breaking through the Turkish defences, then the presence of the Allied armies in support might have been invaluable, but the British and French were less prepared to take an early offensive in such a remote theatre of war. The British artillery and cavalry were not all assembled until June and the French siege-train did not arrive until August.[5] Moreover, while the Allied command of large shipping resources of both steam and sail made it possible to bring large numbers of troops and quantities of supplies to the Black Sea, on their arrival the lack of sufficient docking and warehouse facilities led to the loss of much time and efficiency.

[1] MS. Clar. Dep. C15, fols. 491–2, Russell, 16 May 1854; Graham Papers, to Raglan, 8 May 1854.　　　　[2] R.A. G12, fol. 72, 28 April 1854; 8 May 1854.

[3] *P.P. 1854–5*, IX, pt. 2, *Third report from the select committee on the army before Sebastopol*, pp. 188–9.

[4] See Kinglake, *Crimea*, I, 337–49; W. H. Russell, *The War*, pp. 76–85; *P.P. 1854–5*, IX, pt. 2, *Third report*, 165. In his evidence Newcastle admitted that neither army was ready to go to the aid of Silistria before the siege was raised. Most English historians depict St Arnaud as a rather comic-opera sort of general; for a more sympathetic interpretation see B. D. Gooch, *The new Bonapartist generals in the Crimean War*.

[5] MS. Clar. Dep. C15, fols. 491–2, Russell, 16 May 1854.

Commissariat officers, still under the Treasury with all that that implied in red tape, arrived ahead of the troops and made the necessary arrangements for receiving them.[1] Most supplies were sent from England, although some meat, bread and forage were obtained locally. There does not seem to have been any serious shortage of supplies initially although there were some local shortages owing to lack of transport and some complaints about the failure of the commissariat to issue supplies if any of the proper forms were unsigned or missing. The commissariat evidently failed to obtain sufficient animals locally for the movement of stores in the Gallipoli area.[2]

With the failure of the Russians on the Danube the war threatened to become a stalemate. Now that the defence of Constantinople and the Dardanelles was secure, the Allies had to decide whether and how to take the offensive. Opinion in Britain had been moving strongly in favour of an attack on the great Russian naval base of Sebastopol, which was the key to the Black Sea. It is a characteristic of the British people that, although not a military nation, when after the first hesitation they finally commit themselves to war, they refuse to accept half measures. Once the British bulldog sinks in his teeth he is loath to let go.

As we have seen,[3] the British ministers had been discussing the possibility of an attack on Sebastopol several months before their declaration of war, but most of the senior military and naval officers who went out to the Black Sea theatre of war were sceptical of the practicability of the proposal. One exception was Graham's friend Sir Edmund Lyons, second in command of the Black Sea fleet, who wrote to Graham in early April advocating the destruction of Sebastopol.[4] Graham, in

---

[1] According to W. H. Russell (*The War*, pp. 27–8, 61–2) these were insufficient because of the failure to supply any precise information to the commissary officers regarding the number of troops or the anticipated date of their arrival. From the beginning, as Kinglake points out, the Allies operated on the false assumption that stores and transport could be obtained on the open market as needed, despite the scale on which the demands would be made (*Crimea*, IV, 84–5).

[2] *P.P. 1854–5*, I, pt. 2, *Third report*, 113, evidence of duke of Newcastle. According to W. H. Russell the British were much worse off than the French, who arrived a little earlier and were less punctilious in their bargaining with the Turks.

[3] See above, pp. 251–6. According to H. C. F. Bell, Palmerston had demanded such an expedition as early as December 1853 (*Palmerston*, II, 99). In the same month Graham had raised the possibility with Dundas, and Clarendon had instructed Cowley to so inform the French government. See Parker, *Graham*, II, 242; Wellesley, *Paris embassy*, p. 36.

[4] Parker, *Graham*, II, 243. The fleet reconnoitred Sebastopol harbour on 22 March (MS. Clar. Dep. C 14, Graham, 6 April 1854).

reply, expressed his agreement and urged Lyons both to make his views known among his colleagues and to seek all the necessary information for launching such an attack.[1]

As early as 10 April the duke of Newcastle had written to Lord Raglan about the desirability of taking up offensive operations in the event of the Russian advance in Bulgaria coming to a halt, and of these he considered the capture of Sebastopol would be most effective, a theme that he repeated in a letter of 3 May. He instructed Raglan to make careful and secret inquiry regarding the strength of Sebastopol and Russian forces in the Crimea, which he estimated to be only 30,000, an estimate that later was more than doubled.[2] A month later Graham in a private letter to Raglan, while admitting that their information in London was 'most imperfect and unsatisfactory', gave it as his opinion that the capture of Sebastopol and capture of the Russian fleet would be 'the knock-down blows which would win the battle in the shortest time and with the greatest certainty'.[3] When Raglan passed on to him a pessimistic report from Admiral Dundas comparing Sebastopol to Gibraltar and estimating that the Russians had 120,000 men in the Crimea, Newcastle refused to believe the story.[4] The destruction of Sebastopol was now even being urged by some of the more pacific members of the cabinet, such as Wood in a letter to Russell on 9 May[5] and Gladstone in a letter to Palmerston on 22 June.[6]

It is thus clear that the ministry had given much attention to the project of attacking Sebastopol long before *The Times* embarked on a great campaign on 15 June to have such a course undertaken.[7] Indeed as soon as the good news from Silistria arrived Newcastle wrote privately to Raglan to say that the cabinet was unanimously of the opinion that unless the two army commanders felt they were not sufficiently prepared they should now proceed to lay siege to Sebastopol. He then drafted the fateful despatch of 29 June officially ordering Raglan to

[1] Graham Papers, 8 May 1854 (copy).
[2] Martineau, *Newcastle*, pp. 143–4; *P.P. 1854–5*, IX, pt. 2, *Third report*, 116.
[3] Graham Papers, 8 May 1854 (copy); Parker, *Graham*, II, 243.
[4] Martineau, *Newcastle*, pp. 140, 144–5. [5] PRO 30/22/11/D.
[6] P. Guedalla, *The Palmerston papers, Gladstone and Palmerston* (London, 1928), pp. 97–8. A draft of this letter appears in the form of a memorandum in the Gladstone Papers (Add. MS. 44744, fols. 70–1) with no indication that it was sent to Palmerston.
[7] Kinglake in a long passage that reads like an excerpt from a Trollope novel waxed eloquent on the extraordinary influence of *The Times*, with the implication that it was its intervention that stirred the government to action (*Crimea*, I, 357–66; cf. Anthony Trollope, *The warden*, ch. xiv, 'Mount Olympus').

undertake this task and read it to the cabinet that night after a cabinet dinner at Pembroke Lodge which has been dramatically described by Kinglake.[1] Russell later asserted, on reading Kinglake's account of the cabinet's decision, that 'the expedition had occupied the anxious thoughts of the members of the Cabinet for several months and that it had been discussed very carefully and maturely' at a daytime cabinet meeting some days before the dinner meeting at Richmond at which, according to Kinglake, many of the ministers slept while Newcastle read the despatch to Lord Raglan that ordered the invasion.[2]

The terms of the despatch were precise and gave Raglan little leeway. He was told that the difficulties of the siege of Sebastopol were more likely to be increased than diminished by delay, that there was 'no prospect of a safe and honourable peace' until the fortress was reduced, and that 'nothing but insuperable impediment...should be allowed to prevent the early decision to undertake these operations'.[3] The latest intelligence collected by the Foreign Office did not credit the Russians with more than 45,000 men in the Crimea, including naval personnel, and so Raglan was instructed to carry out the operation unless he had information in his possession, unknown to the government at home, which might lead him to consider success improbable. Poor Raglan had no information, because, it is said, his instincts as an English gentleman forbade him to stoop to using the means necessary to get it. (Little could he have imagined the day when a James Bond could be the ideal prototype of a British hero.) More surprising was the failure of the French commander and of the Allied ambassadors in Constantinople to acquire the information in a part of the world where everything was supposed to have its price.[4] The fact is that the senior Allied military and

---

[1] Martineau, *Newcastle*, pp. 145–7.

[2] Kinglake, *Crimea*, I, 368–70; Walpole, *Russell*, II, 226–7. Russell does not deny that some ministers fell asleep and indeed acknowledges that this was a common occurrence at after-dinner meetings, recalling an occasion at Holland House when Lady Holland once walked into a large room in which the cabinet were assembled and found Lord Melbourne asleep on one sofa and Lord Glenelg on another (PRO 30/22/11/D; Walpole omits this anecdote).

[3] Martineau, *Newcastle*, pp. 146–8. Martineau rejects Kinglake's suggestion that the sleepy cabinet failed to examine the restrictive implications of the wording of the despatch by pointing out that its diffuseness suggested that the original had been modified.

[4] Actually in July the Admiralty acquired much more precise intelligence from an agent who had left the Crimea in June and who was able to give circumstantial information regarding roads, harbour, water supply, and the size of the garrison, which he put at 70,000 of whom 40,000 were in Sebastopol (*P.P. 1854–5*, IX, pt. 3, *Fourth report*, 281,

naval officers with the exception of Sir Edmund Lyons had hitherto failed to take the project seriously because they had no heart in it and much preferred to plan a further campaign in Bulgaria.

Raglan's most trusted divisional commander, Sir George Brown, gave it as his opinion that the Great Duke would not have accepted responsibility for such an operation without more information. Nevertheless, Raglan concluded that he had no alternative but to accept the Secretary of State's orders, and he promptly replied to that effect.[1] In acknowledging Raglan's answer Newcastle recognised that it came from a sense of duty rather than conviction. 'God grant that success may reward you and justify us!', he wrote,[2] but it was a prayer that remained unanswered.

Even though the decision had been taken in London and Paris and accepted at Varna there was still some fear among the British ministers that the French would change their minds in view of the negotiations now under way with Austria. In mid July the matter came again before the British cabinet, which stood firm, agreeing with the absent Palmerston, who sent his 'vote' to the duke of Newcastle by letter for pressing on with the invasion 'the moment the two armies are in a Condition to go thither'.[3] 'I think we ought to stick to our Plan & be steady to our Purpose & that is to go to the Crimea', he wrote to Clarendon a week later. 'If we are steady France will stand by us. If we follow the Austrian will-o'-the-wisp we shall be lost in the Quagmire.' Clarendon fully agreed.[4]

The Allied commanders had met on 18 July to consider the new directions received from Paris and London, but such was Lord Raglan's ascendancy among them that the discussion did not turn on the question of whether to accept the orders without question, but rather on the steps to be taken to implement them. Preparations proceeded forthwith, but when news arrived at the end of July of Russian withdrawals in the Principalities the French commander urged that, by eliminating the likelihood of Austrian intervention, this would justify them in abandoning the plans for invasion. Raglan, however, refused to be deflected. A more serious threat to the enterprise came with a severe outbreak of cholera that ravaged the armies and navies of both Allies, slowing down

evidence of Sir James Graham). According to Lord Stanmore and to Sidney Herbert the government acquired 'detailed and accurate' information through a correspondent of Lord Palmerston's (Stanmore, *Herbert*, I, 271–2), but it is not clear whether this was the same source to which Graham referred.

[1] Martineau, *Newcastle*, p. 149.   [2] *Ibid.* p. 150.
[3] *Ibid.* pp. 147–8 n.   [4] MS. Clar. Dep. C15, fol. 134, 24 July 1854.

the preparations and delaying the possible date of attack.[1] Nevertheless, Raglan pressed on, assembling the necessary transports to carry the invasion forces and reconnoitring the coast of the Crimea in the vicinity of Sebastopol. In all this he had the constant support of Sir Edmund Lyons, whose untiring activity was a big factor in successfully completing the very exacting naval preparations.

While decisions were made in London (and in Paris), in fact everything turned on what was done on the shores of the Black Sea, and for two months the British ministers were on tenterhooks, uncertain whether their plans would be executed as they intended,[2] and constantly complaining of Raglan's failure to keep them informed.[3] They knew of the lack of enthusiasm for the operation among the Allied commanders in the theatre, especially the French, whom they never fully trusted, and soon news began to arrive of the ravages of cholera in the Allied armies and navies. Their ire was especially aroused by a foolish and unauthorised operation undertaken by St Arnaud on the Bulgarian front from which three divisions returned ridden with sickness and disease. 'St Arnaud ought to be hung for that expedition to the Dobrucha wh was undertaken without Raglan's knowledge & for the purpose of getting a little separate glory,' Clarendon commented petulantly, '—and it has ended in separate disgrace,' he added, perhaps with a trace of satisfaction.[4]

From the beginning there was a remarkable lack of confidence on the part of the British ministers in their French allies and especially in their strange commander-in-chief in the field. 'What sensible man would have imagined', Palmerston wrote to Clarendon in late August, 'that a man who had passed his Early Life as an actor could all of a sudden become a great General?'[5]

A few weeks later he wrote again: 'It is provoking to find the French

[1] The British Army also lost large quantities of biscuit and boots in a disastrous fire at Varna in August.

[2] See for instance a petulant letter from Palmerston in MS. Clar. Dep. C15, fols. 165–7, 23 August 1854, bewailing what he considered to be the time wasted in getting the armies to the Crimea earlier; also letters from Clarendon, 26, 27, 29 August and n.d. in PRO 30/22/11/D, fols. 1322–47.

[3] E.g. Ab. Cor. 1854–5, pp. 209–10, Newcastle to Aberdeen, 7 September 1854: 'Raglan's letters are as singularly meagre as usual.'

[4] PRO 30/22/11/D, fols. 1326–8, 22 August 1854.

[5] MS. Clar. Dep. C15, fols. 168–9, 25 August 1854. This was unfair since after a dissipated youth St Arnaud had settled down to an army career in 1831, much of which was spent in active service in Algeria. See Gooch, New Bonapartist generals, pp. 20–6.

such dilatory and slack allies: but on the other hand this experience of their way of doing things ought to make us feel more confident that by timely Preparation and due Exertion we may always be able to keep them at Bay as Enemies'.[1] (Palmerston could never forget his early ministerial experiences in the wars with the first Napoleon.) And in September, after receiving official reports of the numbers embarked, Clarendon likewise wrote to Russell: 'What do you think of the French force being inferior to ours after all the boasting of the 70,000 actually there & the 30,000 on the way & St Arnaud writing of himself to the Empr as *the* Cmdr in Chief in virtue of the superior numbers of the French Army? Napoleon I wd not have employed such a Charlatan.'[2]

Nevertheless, it may be noted that in order to cement good relations with France and her ruler, Prince Albert, accompanied by the duke of Newcastle, undertook a visit to Napoleon at Boulogne in early September. In view of the British royal family's earlier attitude to the French emperor and the sceptism of Newcastle and his colleagues about the alliance, the visit was surprisingly successful. It meant much to Louis Napoleon to receive this recognition and with tears in his eyes he told Newcastle 'how impressed he was at the sight of French troops receiving an English Prince at *Boulogne* with "God Save the Queen"'.[3] The British War Secretary pronounced the Boulogne camp a 'complete success', although he was not much impressed by the appearance of the first troops visited, thinking that they looked very young; but at St Omer he reported that the 8,000 men inspected, both infantry and cavalry, were '*very* fine troops'.[4] The prince carried on long conversations with the emperor about many aspects of government in their two countries and was impressed by Napoleon's frankness and candour. Regarding the war outlook the prince recorded:

The E[mperor] was almost the only Person amongst the French at Boulogne who had any hope of success of the expedition agst Sebastopol, and the astonishment was great that our whole party of English Officers were so sanguine about it.—The E. strongly condemned St Arnaud's march into the Dobrudja, which had been positively forbidden.[5]

[1] MS. Clar. Dep. 15, fol. 193, 15 September 1854.
[2] PRO 30/22/11/E, fols. 1421–5, 18 September 1854.
[3] *Ab. Cor. 1854–5*, pp. 205–6, Newcastle, 5 September 1854.
[4] *Ibid.* p. 207, 6 September 1854; PRO 30/22/11/E, fols. 1366–9, Newcastle to Russell, 9 September 1854.
[5] R.A. G16, fol. 150, 1–37, 'Memorandum on my visit to Boulogne', dictated by Prince Albert to General Grey on 12 and 13 September 1854.

There was talk of the emperor making a return visit, a proposal applauded by Clarendon, who wrote to Aberdeen: 'It is not a matter of Court civility but of State policy to keep the Emperor in good humour; for he is France at this moment and embodies the whole *amour propre* of the country, upon which we depend for bringing the war to a successful termination'.[1]

Early victories in the Crimea, September–November 1854

So much eventually went wrong in the Crimea that the achievements tend to be overlooked. In a sense the powers of the Western Allies were too great and allowed them to over-extend themselves. The Russians were never in any danger of gambling an army on the Isle of Wight or the Cherbourg peninsula, but France and Britain together had the sea power to take such risks. Graham described this achievement some time later to the Sebastopol committee:

In the course of a year we have moved somewhere about 60,000 British soldiers to a distance 3,000 miles from this country; we have moved 6,000 horses to that distance; we have moved somewhere about 25,000 or 30,000 French troops from Marseilles to the Crimea, and simultaneously with this very difficulty of supplying the means of transport to the Black Sea, we moved 12,000 French to the Baltic; in the course of last year we moved, principally by steam, somewhere about 150,000 men; and the large portion of them to a point 3,000 miles distant from this country; simultaneously with that we have fed, not only the navy, but the army, and a portion of our allies.[2]

While the Admiralty was responsible for finding the transport to send men and supplies to the East, it was the responsibility of Lord Raglan as the commander in the East and particularly, under him, of Admiral Sir Edmund Lyons to secure the shipping for the transport of the army across the Black Sea. As a result of great exertions the ships were all assembled and a plan of embarkation was worked out by the third week in August. By the 23rd Graham had heard from Lyons that the means of transport were unparalleled, and that the whole army, cavalry, guns and all, could be transported at once, but he added the ominous words '*if the expedition is undertaken*'.[3]

[1] *Ab. Cor. 1854–5*, p. 209, 6 September 1854.
[2] *P.P. 1854–5*, IX, pt. 3, *Fourth report*, 268.
[3] PRO 30/22/11/D, fols. 1330–1, Clarendon to Russell, 23 August 1854 (Clarendon's emphasis). Cf. Graham Papers, to Clarendon, 22 August 1854.

It was cholera rather than lack of transport that caused the agonising delays. Even so, embarkation began on 24 August in systematic fashion, though from the viewpoint of any one individual on the beaches of Varna all may have seemed confusion. Even the critical W. H. Russell, writing in *The Times* for all to read (including the Czar and his commanders), was loud in his praise of the arrangements. After giving a detailed account of the embarkation, regiment by regiment, ship by ship, he continued:

The arrangements for the conveyance of the troops to their destination are of the largest and most perfect character; and when all the transports have united, they will display to the gaze of the enemy an armada of no less than 600 vessels, covered and protected on every side by a fleet with a battery of 3000 pieces of artillery and manned by the bravest seamen in the world.[1]

The British embarked some 27,000 troops, including 1,000 cavalry, 2,700 artillery, and 400 sappers, the French 28,000, mostly infantry, and the Turks 7,000 infantry and some artillery. The British flotilla consisted of 16 men-of-war, 82 transports and 6 tugs purchased for the purpose in Constantinople. The 55 sailing ships among the transports were towed by the tugs and other steamers. The French, with only 52 transports (all but 3 of them sail), were forced to leave their cavalry behind and to load most of their infantry on warships, many of them sail of the line without steamers to tow them. Although embarking the Light Brigade, sixty pieces of artillery, large quantities of ammunition and a very limited number of horses and carts, the British were forced to leave behind them temporarily the Heavy Brigade of cavalry, their siege-train, and a large number of pack-horses.[2]

According to one account, at the last moment, although much needed horses had been left behind, out of compassion the women who had followed the army to Varna and who would have been left there destitute were taken on board the already overloaded ships.[3] Questioned about their presence at the time of the enquiry, the duke of Newcastle gave this curious answer:

[1] W. H. Russell, *The War*, pp. 154–5. The number of vessels is evidently exaggerated.
[2] See Kinglake, *Crimea*, I, 396–9; Martineau, *Newcastle*, p. 161; Sir E. Hamley, *The War in the Crimea* (London, 1890), p. 30; S. Eardley-Wilmot, *Life of Vice-Admiral Edmund Lord Lyons* (London, 1898), pp. 194–200; D. Bonner-Smith and A. C. Dewar (eds.), *Russian War 1854, Baltic and Black Sea official correspondence* (London, 1943), pp. 219–22. There was a separate covering force under Admiral Dundas consisting of 17, or according to Hamley 27, warships.
[3] Cecil Woodham-Smith, *The reason why* (London, 1953), p. 167.

The military authorities, having been accustomed to [allow] a certain number of women to go out with the army, believed that the soldiers would be dissatisfied if they had not their assistance for washing and other purposes for which women generally go with the army.

He believed that fewer went than normally, but admitted that it was unfortunate and said the practice had been abandoned.[1]

The embarkation of such a large and heterogeneous force over open beaches was a gigantic task, but by 4 September it was completed. Even after the Allied fleets had put to sea, however, the French, who had always been sceptical about the wisdom of the expedition, attempted to change its destination.[2] On hearing news of this incident from Raglan, Newcastle wrote in hot indignation to Aberdeen: 'Whilst the armies were on the sea, an attempt was made by our *gallant* Allies to turn tail,— they literally *funked*, and wanted by shabby pretexts to put the whole affair off to next year. Luckily, Raglan and all our officers stood firm, and they are now in for it.' Newcastle also reported that the state of alarm was increasing in Paris, where all the military men were said to anticipate failure. 'We have many red-coated, but white-livered croakers here too', he added bitterly. The strain of the burden of responsibility he carried was beginning to show.[3]

Newcastle's outburst against the French was unfair because there were doubters in his own camp. No less a person than Sir John Burgoyne had written a memorandum on 28 July severely criticising the hazardous nature of the operation.[4] The cabinet appears to have been shaken by this communication and on 11 August Newcastle asked Burgoyne if he would join Raglan as a special adviser. The old general, seven years senior to Raglan, left the next day and arrived in time to sail with the expedition, but too late to introduce any change in the plans.[5] On 29 August shortly after his arrival he prepared a gloomy memorandum in which he declared: 'An attack on Sebastopol at the present time must be considered a most desperate undertaking.' He went on to explain in detail the difficulties of the proposed plan of landing as he saw them and

---

[1] *P.P. 1854–5*, IX, pt. 2, *Fourth report*, 190. Two officers' wives managed to sail with the expeditionary force and allusions in Mrs Duberly's diary indicate that some wives of other ranks did so as well. See E. E. P. Tisdall, *Mrs Duberly's campaigns* (London, 1963).
[2] See Eardley-Wilmot, *Lyons*, pp. 203–5, Lyons to Graham, 13 September 1854.
[3] *Ab. Cor. 1854–5*, p. 221, 28 September 1854. The correspondence of the various British ministers throughout August and early September reveals a high state of tension and frustration as they waited for positive word that the expedition was under way.
[4] Wrottesley, *Burgoyne*, II, 58–60.   [5] *Ibid.* pp. 60–8.

to advocate a landing north of Eupatoria, as less likely to be opposed. He even suggested the possibility of striking inland to seize the strategically important town of Simferopol and at this early date pointed out

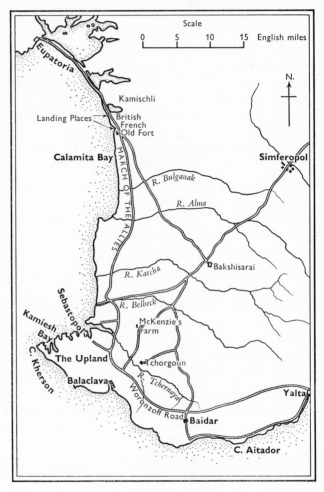

SOUTH-WEST CRIMEA

the advantage of obtaining the use of the harbour of Balaclava.[1] In a letter written home to his family on the same day he said that he was glad he had no responsibility for the operation, 'for I must confess', he wrote, 'I do not understand on what sound principle it is undertaken...

[1] Wrottesley, *Burgoyne*, II, 69–73; cf. an earlier private memorandum written on shipboard which is even more pessimistic (*ibid.* pp. 64–6).

It appears to me to be the most desperate enterprise ever attempted.'[1] St Arnaud frankly told him that they only undertook the expedition because they could not resist the pressure from home.[2]

Raglan met the French objections by himself undertaking a second reconnaissance of the coast in the vicinity of Sebastopol in the swift steamer *Caradoc*, accompanied by senior French and British officers

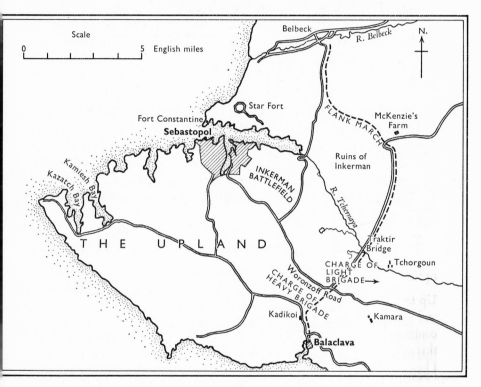

THE UPLAND

(including Burgoyne) and by Admiral Lyons's flagship *Agamemnon*. On a beautiful Sunday morning, 1 September 1854, they sailed closely past the great harbour and along the coast to the north. Raglan agreed that the landing-place originally selected at the mouth of the Katcha, eight miles north of Sebastopol, was unsatisfactory and instead selected a stretch of open beach some twenty miles further to the north on what was ominously called Calamita Bay. Burgoyne, relieved to see no Russian troops north of the Alma, supported this change. St Arnaud,

[1] *Ibid.* pp. 73–4. [2] *Ibid.* p. 77.

who was very ill at the time (he was dying of cancer), signified his willingness to abide by Raglan's decision.[1]

Meanwhile the three fleets were slowly assembling at a prearranged rendezvous, whence they proceeded to take up their positions off the landing beaches. The disembarkation finally began, unopposed, on Thursday 14 September. Considering the complexity of the plan and the necessity of a last-minute change ordered by Admiral Lyons to avoid collision between the English and the French, who began landing further north than was originally intended, the whole operation was carried out successfully. The shortage of transport precluded the landing of tents, with the result that most of the British troops were drenched by a violent rainstorm their first night on shore. Nevertheless, despite all the difficulties encountered, the Allied armies were ready to begin their march south on 19 September. General Airey, the new Quartermaster General, who had learnt to rough it in the Canadian bush, had had some success in collecting some 350 wagons and teams, 67 camels and 253 pack horses, as well as a quantity of livestock and food, which helped to eke out the limited transport and stores which had been landed.[2]

The news of the landing was welcomed with delight by the queen and her ministers at home. Newcastle wrote to Russell with premature optimism:

Up to the present time all the arrangements have been good and successful and whatever may be the results of this great Expedition (which is under the control of higher powers than that of Government or *Press*) I am confident that neither the Country nor the Ministry will have any reason to be ashamed. I have no fear however of a speedy as well as a successful result.

He said that he was already turning over in his mind the preparations for the next campaign, but he confessed that the difficulty was the '*men*'.

[1] See Kinglake, *Crimea*, I, 404–6; Wrottesley, *Burgoyne*, II, 81–3; 'but it is a desperate enterprise', Burgoyne wrote in a private letter, 'forced I believe on Lord Raglan and the French general by taunts from home'.

[2] See Kinglake, *Crimea*, I, chs. XXXIX and XL. Hamley and Hibbert give similar figures but Sir Charles Trevelyan told the Roebuck committee that there were only 193 wagons acquired from the Tartars. He indicated that 1203 pack animals for ammunition and 70 carts with mules were landed with the British troops. Another 266 pack animals and 216 Maltese or Spanish mules with carts were ferried from Varna to Balaclava within two weeks of the landing. The balance of several thousand pack animals were moved overland from Varna to Constantinople, where they were kept as a reserve, supposedly only thirty hours' sailing time from Balaclava (*P.P. 1854–5*, IX, pt. 2, *Third report*, 38–40).

He had to admit that they were 'still very far short of the number already voted by Parliament', but he still hoped to have 10,000 for new regiments providing the need for reinforcements was not too great.[1] Even Sir James Graham acknowledged that he was beginning 'to think that the Horizon brightens on every side'.[2]

So sure were the Government at home of early success that the ministers were already beginning to discuss among themselves and with the French government what should be done with Sebastopol when it fell. Louis Napoleon suggested that the Allies should winter in the Crimea, but destroy the fortifications of the great naval base, and Aberdeen, Russell, Graham, Clarendon, Newcastle, Herbert and Granville were all inclined to agree with this.[3] Only Lansdowne and Palmerston dissented, the former preferring to keep it as a bargaining-counter, the latter because he insisted the Crimea should not be returned to Russia.[4] Aberdeen took a very different view to this, writing to Clarendon: 'With Sebastopol entirely razed, and the fleet captured, I would not give sixpence for the possession of the Crimea in any political view.'[5]

The Allied march on Sebastopol was begun on 19 September under trying conditions. The sequel is well known. The Russians under Prince Menschikoff, soldier as well as diplomat, held the line of the Alma with 33,000 infantry, 3,400 cavalry and 120 guns. On the following day, the 20th, the battle was joined. The poorly coordinated Allied armies had some advantage in numbers, but the Russians enjoyed a commanding position on the high ground to the south of the river and heavier artillery. Rarely can an important battle in modern warfare have been fought with less plan. The French had one of sorts in which part of their army was to make a flanking attack on the seaward side of the Russian army. St Arnaud wanted Raglan to undertake a circuitous attack on the

---

[1] PRO 30/22/11/E, fols. 1451–4, 21 September 1854.

[2] Graham Papers, to Aberdeen, 30 September 1854.

[3] See *Ab. Cor. 1854–5*, pp. 224–5, Graham, 29 September 1854; MS. Clar. Dep. C14, fols. 82–3, Aberdeen, 15 September 1854.

[4] MS. Clar. Dep. C14, fols. 679–82, Lansdowne, 17 September 1854; PRO 30/22/11/E, fols. 1507–10, Clarendon, 1 October 1854. In an earlier letter to Clarendon (MS. Clar. Dep. C15, fols. 182–5, 7 September 1854) Palmerston proposed turning the Crimea over to Turkey. 'An adverse Critic might say catch and kill your Bear before you determine what you will do with his Skin', he added, 'but I think our Bear is as good as taken' (fol. 185).

[5] *Ab. Cor. 1854–5*, pp. 230–1, 3 October 1854. He was content to leave the decision in the hands of the commanders.

other Russian flank, but Raglan refused to make any commitment until he saw the ground. The two commanders made a joint reconnaissance on the morning of the 20th, but Raglan still refused to reveal his hand. He had assured the French commander that he could 'rely upon the vigorous cooperation of the British Army',[1] but now that he saw the ground he refused to contemplate the attack on the Russian inland (right) flank that St Arnaud had envisaged. Eventually, however, about two hours after the battle had begun, but before the French movements on his right had been completed, in response to a further French appeal for support he committed his troops.

Having given his orders, Lord Raglan, accompanied by a small staff, proceeded to separate himself from the army he commanded by advancing fearlessly to an unoccupied knoll, which he perceived well in the rear of the Russian front positions and only a short distance from Menschikoff's own headquarters. It was an extraordinary action for a commanding general, but it did have the effect of causing consternation in the Russian ranks when eventually they saw the English staff officers ensconced in such a position, for they inevitably assumed that the whole line had been breached in this area. Lord Raglan may well have accepted the Tolstoyan view of battle that once the fighting begins no further rational control by the commanders is possible. At any rate he was in a perfect position to view the progress of the fighting, although more awkwardly placed for issuing orders and certainly in considerable danger.[2]

Despite the extravagant claims of the French *communiqué* after the battle, the brunt of the fighting was borne by the British troops, who fought with extraordinary valour and tenacity, considering what they had been through in the preceding month and the rigours of the hot and thirsty march from the beaches on the preceding day. Their discipline and their spirit, however, won the day and by 4.30 in the afternoon the Russians had fled the field. Menschikoff was no more successful in war than in diplomacy, but, as Sir Edward Hamley has observed, 'the battle, as fought, showed a singular absence of skill on all sides'.[3]

[1] Kinglake, *Crimea*, I, 458–9.
[2] The location proved of some advantage for directing artillery fire on the Russian positions.
[3] *War in the Crimea*, pp. 63–4. Hamley gives the British casualties as 2,002, of which 362 were fatal. The French losses were much less and the Turks' nil since they and some of the French were not engaged. The Russians admitted 5,709 casualties (*ibid.* p. 62).

The first news of the Alma victory arrived in England from Stratford via Belgrade on 30 September. Relaying it to Aberdeen, canny Sir James Graham added a political postscript: 'Do not lose sight of your great opportunity; take the tide at its rise, and let us have a new Parliament.'[1] At the same time a false rumour, received from Bucharest, that Sebastopol itself had fallen was widely believed,[2] but by 5 October it was exploded as news arrived of the Allied armies' march around Sebastopol to Balaclava.

From that day to this, opinion has been divided as to whether the Allied armies might have rushed Sebastopol and captured it immediately after the demoralisation of the Russian army on the Alma. Raglan was inclined to such a course, but here old Burgoyne made a successful intervention. He presented a memorandum to Raglan advocating a flank march to enable the Allied armies to take up positions to the south of Sebastopol from which they could undertake a properly conducted siege making use of the little port of Balaclava. Raglan, most taciturn of commanders, merely told him to show it to St Arnaud. The latter discussed the idea with his generals, most of whom were opposed, but the engineer General Bizot supported it and St Arnaud agreed. It was the last important decision that the French commander made, for within a week the poor man had died from cancer which he had been valiantly fighting from the day he was appointed to command.[3]

One significant consequence of this decision was that the Allies abandoned the possibility of blocking the communication lines of the Russian garrison of Sebastopol to the north and of commanding the Crimean peninsula with all that that meant in terms of living off the country, at least with respect to fuel and forage. Instead they condemned themselves, should the initial assault fail, to being hemmed in on a small stretch of barren ground offering nothing to the support of its occupiers.[4]

Nevertheless, once the fateful decision was taken, it was quickly executed. On 25 September the flank march was begun and within a few days the Allied armies had taken up the positions in which they were to be pinned for the next twelve months. The ministers at home, once they had swallowed their initial disappointment that the immediate

---

[1] *Ab. Cor. 1854–5*, pp. 225–6, 30 September 1854.
[2] *Ibid.*
[3] See Wrottesley, *Burgoyne*, II, 93–4; Gooch, *New Bonapartist generals*, pp. 129–31.
[4] See Kinglake, *Crimea*, IV, 82–4, who notes that Commissary General Filder adverted to this danger in a letter to the Treasury on 22 September.

capture of Sebastopol had not been effected, praised the brilliant conception of Raglan's manoeuvre, little anticipating the dreadful stalemate of a siege that was to ensue.[1] The Russians, however, had already shown their determination to resist by sinking seven ships across the entrance of the harbour at Sebastopol to prevent Allied ships from entering it.[2]

Although the British had been on the left in the approach march from the time of landing, they now chose to hold the open right flank since they still had a superiority in cavalry over the French and since they were attracted by the apparent superiority of the harbour of Balaclava, small but landlocked. Unfortunately it was deficient in docking facilities and badly situated for maintaining effective communications with the upland above, where the army took up its positions. The French occupied the tip of the Chersonese peninsula to the west and developed the more open bay of Kamiesh as their port, which in the end proved much more satisfactory than Balaclava.[3] In a despatch covering these developments Raglan admitted that the ground occupied by the British turned out to be very unsatisfactory, broken by deep ravines, rocky and without shelter; the health of the army he reported to be 'still bad but improving'. In passing on this news to Russell, Newcastle observed: 'I think that the general result of the despatch is that there is much cause for anxiety, but I think none (humanly speaking) for apprehension of an unfavourable issue.'[4]

A mixed naval and military garrison was left in Eupatoria, the little port to the north of the original landing-place, but the Allied investment of Sebastopol from the south left the road to the north open and Russian reinforcements from Odessa began to arrive by it in large numbers. The Allied navies attempted to prevent the Russians from crossing the straits into the Crimea but without success, owing to the shallowness of the water in the vicinity of Perekop and the existence of an unknown causeway thirty miles to the east.[5]

Meanwhile preparations for the siege of Sebastopol were made slowly and methodically, which gave the Russians, with the genius of Todleben to guide them, time to prepare their own defences. Under pressure from

[1] PRO 30/22/11/E, fols. 1523–4, 5 October 1854, from Clarendon, and fols. 1537–40, 7 October from Newcastle.
[2] Bonner-Smith and Dewar, *The Russian War, 1854*, pp. 320–1.
[3] Eardley-Wilmot, *Lyons*, pp. 224–7; Gooch, *New Bonapartist generals*, pp. 135–6.
[4] PRO 30/22/11/E, fols. 1598–1601, 23 October 1854.
[5] Eardley-Wilmot, *Lyons*, pp. 232–3; Bonner-Smith and Dewar, *The Russian war, 1854*, pp. 401–5.

Raglan, Dundas reluctantly agreed to naval participation in the initial bombardment which began on 17 October. Although Lyons daringly brought some of the British ships very close inshore, the damage done to the Russian fortifications was limited and the cost high—over 300 casualties and much damage to rigging and superstructures.[1] It demonstrated, as Graham commented to Lyons, that an attack by ships on granite forts at 500 yards was useless.[2]

The bombardment on the landward side was hardly more successful. Early in the day a French powder magazine was exploded by a lucky Russian shot and the French artillery was silenced. The British guns kept up their fire and wrought considerable damage on the Russian defences in the course of the day; as a result of prodigious efforts under cover of darkness, however, these were largely rectified during the night and the disabled Russian guns replaced by naval pieces brought up from the harbour. The pattern of the siege that was to last so many weary months had been set.[3]

At home the fickle public soon felt cheated of victory, and as the situation at the front deteriorated the fortunes of the coalition waned. It is true that these surprising Allied armies, for all their lack of effective leadership, won two more costly victories, Balaclava on 25 October, marked by the gallant but futile charge of the Light Brigade, and Inkerman on 5 November, the bloodiest and most desperate battle of the war. Balaclava was in a sense a drawn battle; the losses were approximately six hundred on each side; the Russians failed to dislodge the Allies and withdrew, but they now held three important hills on the British flank that had previously been Allied outposts, and thus denied to the British the use of the better of the two roads which connected Balaclava to the upland above. Inkerman was a costly defeat for the Russians, who lost 12,000 men, the majority of them killed; Allied losses, the majority British, were 3,286, of whom 740 were killed. The significance of Balaclava was that it demonstrated that the besiegers were themselves besieged, that they controlled no more than a few acres

[1] Eardley-Wilmot, *Lyons*, pp. 242–59.
[2] Graham Papers, from Lyons, 18 October, and to Lyons, 9 November 1854.
[3] A great deal has been written on the Crimean campaign by participants, by contemporary observers, and by more recent historians and popular writers. See the annotated bibliography in Gooch's *New Bonapartist generals*, pp. 270–83, and his article, 'The Crimean War in selected documents and secondary works since 1940', in *Victorian Studies*, I (1958), 271–9; Christopher Hibbert, *The destruction of Lord Raglan* (London, 1961), pp. 349–56.

on one corner of the Crimea.[1] On the other hand Inkerman proved that the Russians were incapable of dislodging the Allied limpet that had attached itself to the outworks of Sebastopol, and in the long run, despite the horrors of the Crimean winter of 1854–5, it was the Allies with their command of the sea who had the better line of communication; this in the end made the fall of Sebastopol inevitable, providing the besiegers remained resolute in their purpose.[2] The immediate situation after Inkerman, however, was one of stalemate, and for the first time it was generally recognised by the Allies that they would probably have to spend the winter in their precarious position.[3] They neither had the strength to take Sebastopol then nor to move.

As soon as he realised this new situation, that is to say late in November, the duke of Newcastle directed that an increased supply of provisions and of fuel should be forwarded from England to keep the depots in Constantinople up to the mark. He also issued orders for the procurement of lumber and other supplies in Constantinople, Vienna and Trieste for the building of huts, in addition to those already arranged in England. Not trusting Constantinople for supplies of lumber, Newcastle also appealed to Graham for assistance in getting them from other sources. On the same day, 17 November, the First Lord replied proposing to send some sailing ships that had just arrived from Canada with lumber direct to Constantinople without breaking bulk. He pointed out that it was much better to use sailing ships immediately available rather than to wait for steamers. Eventually the lumber arrived from England, Malta and Trieste, but with everything else it was long held up in the bottleneck of Balaclava harbour.[4]

For the time being the confidence of the cabinet in the commander-in-chief remained high. Lord Raglan was one of themselves, as Master

---

[1] Throughout the winter the Russians held a line from the coast less than two miles east of Balaclava snaking north to the ruins of Inkerman and thence south-west around Sebastopol, with a salient on the Woronzoff Road less than three miles north of Balaclava.

[2] See Hamley, *War in the Crimea*, chs. VI and VII, or for a very detailed account Kinglake, *Crimea*, vols. II and III.

[3] See *P.P. 1854–5*, IX, pt. 2, *Fourth report*, evidence of duke of Newcastle, p. 120, who said that no conscious decision was made to winter there; it simply grew out of the circumstances.

Writing home immediately after Inkerman, Burgoyne was convinced that any further attempts to take Sebastopol for the present were 'hopeless' (Wrottesley, *Burgoyne*, II, 117–18).

[4] *P.P. 1854–5*, IX, pt. 2, evidence of duke of Newcastle, pp. 121, 128–9; Graham Papers, 18 November 1854.

General of the Ordnance a member of their own administration, a close disciple of the Great Duke and the most respected British military officer of his day. It is true that they complained that his communications were somewhat terse, sometimes non-existent, but all who knew him believed that his presence inspired confidence in both armies. Indeed on receiving the news of Inkerman the queen on the advice of her Prime Minister made Raglan a Field Marshal, a promotion which Graham assured him was hailed unanimously with approbation.[1]

There was more concern with respect to the naval commanders in both theatres of war. Not only were the ministers disappointed with the failure of Napier in the Baltic, but they were also coming to the conclusion that Dundas was an unsatisfactory commander in the Black Sea. The system of seniority had brought him to the top and he happened to be in command in the Mediterranean when the crisis began in 1853. He had commanded in the Baltic as long ago as 1807 and was now 70 years old, but he too was well connected, and had been a member of parliament for many years between the wars. Not knowing how to get rid of him, Graham had hit upon the device of sending Sir Edmund Lyons out as his second-in-command, and fortunately Dundas had accepted Lyons's role; nevertheless he retained the final responsibility and made the final decisions. Increasingly the authorities at home, prompted by stories trickling in from the Crimea,[2] became convinced that Dundas was too cautious and too disinclined to take chances. In particular they blamed him for the failure to prevent the withdrawal of the Russian garrison from Anapa and the blocking of the mouth of the harbour of Sebastopol, as well as for not maintaining a more effective blockade of Russian ports on the Black Sea.

Indeed, Newcastle, temporarily abandoned by most of his colleagues, who had joined in the usual autumn exodus from London, and evidently oppressed by his solitude in the capital, became excited by reports that Dundas was reluctant to bombard the fortifications of Sebastopol and addressed a strange letter to Raglan advising him to call

---

[1] R.A. G19, fols. 65 and 71, 17 and 18 November 1854; Graham Papers, to Raglan, 22 November 1854. Characteristically Raglan was uncomfortable about the promotion because he did not feel that his role in the battle of Inkerman justified it (Hibbert, *Raglan*, p. 270). Kinglake sought to refute the ministerial complaints by pointing to two folio volumes of Raglan's letters to Newcastle, but the fact remains that he did not tell them all they wanted to know (see *Crimea*, IV, 164–5 and 229–30, n. 3).

[2] Layard, who accompanied the invasion fleet, was a constant detractor of Dundas in his correspondence with Russell; see PRO 30/22/11/E, fols. 1395–1402, 16 September 1854; fols. 1648–9, 8 November 1854.

on Lyons to disobey any orders of Dundas that might imperil the well-being of the army.[1] He also wrote to Graham proposing that someone (he was ready to go himself) should go to the Crimea with authority to supersede Dundas if the situation required it.[2] Although Graham had little faith in Dundas, he was not prepared to go that far. It went against the gentleman's code to which he subscribed so to undermine the reputation of another gentleman without more substantial evidence than he had to warrant his taking such decisive action. 'The Crown may appoint whom it pleases,' he wrote to Aberdeen, 'but practically it cannot exercise the power of recall except for reasons which will stand the test of publicity and be free from discussion.' Moreover, he placed full reliance on the presence of Sir Edmund Lyons to exercise a 'salutary influence and control over the conduct of Admiral Dundas'.[3] In this view the conciliatory Aberdeen thoroughly concurred, pointing out that the French admiral was no better. 'It would surely be intolerable to sacrifice an Englishman without very sound ground', he added, 'in order to exalt the reputation of a French Admiral!'[4] It was agreed, however, that Dundas should relinquish his command at the end of the year, which was the normal time for his replacement, and that Lyons should be his successor.

Nevertheless, Graham carried on a singular private correspondence with Lyons behind Dundas's back, telling him the nature of the instructions that had been given to the senior admiral with a view to ensuring their implementation. 'I rely on you', Graham wrote, 'for the infusion of some fire and energy into their [the Allied fleets'] movements. Were it not for your presence with the Fleet I should be in despair.'[5] In replying to this letter Lyons informed Graham that it had been opened by Dundas, to which Graham made the following characteristic response:

I am bound to believe that this was done by mistake; and I cannot bring myself to harbour the suspicion that he read any part of a confidential com-

---

[1] Martineau, *Newcastle*, pp. 166-7.　　　　[2] *Ibid.* pp. 165-6.

[3] *Ab. Cor. 1854-5*, pp. 242-5, 7 October 1854 (printed with omissions in Parker, *Graham*, II, 250-2).

[4] *Ibid.* pp. 246-8, to Graham, 8 October 1854, and p. 253, to Newcastle, 15 October 1854. In thanking Aberdeen for his reply Graham commented: 'It will strengthen my hands; and it will prove to the duke of Newcastle the necessity of proceeding with caution and forbearance in the treatment of Naval and Military Commanders, even when they are less fortunate than ours have been in the Black Sea' (*ibid.* pp. 248-9, 8 October 1854).

[5] Graham Papers, 25 October 1854 (copy).

munication which obviously from the very commencement was addressed to you. There are some things so impossible among Gentlemen that proof is necessary to ensure belief, and this is one.[1]

The situation was an embarrassing one but no more than that since, as Graham observed, by the time his reply reached Lyons Dundas would be handing over the command. One may feel some sympathy for the old admiral, who must have been aware of the general lack of confidence in him. He did, after all, entrust Lyons with a great deal of authority in the invasion and he was right about the ineffectiveness of naval bombardment against such strong shore fortifications as those at Sebastopol, as the costly but ineffective action of 17 October showed.[2]

The collapse of high hopes

Until mid November the siege of Sebastopol appeared to be a not unreasonable operation of war; the hardships borne by the troops, although harsh, were no worse than in any previous war and in some respects were less. They suffered from dysentery and overwork, but they were not ill fed.[3] Britain was a wealthier country than she had been during the Napoleonic Wars and this was reflected in the more lavish scale on which the preparations for the Crimean War were made. The ration scale was more generous;[4] extra supplies of warm clothing were ordered;[5] medical comforts for the sick and wounded were increased;[6] medical establishments were doubled;[7] in November for the

[1] Graham Papers, 4 December 1854 (copy). Graham proceeded to defend his own actions *vis-à-vis* Dundas, saying: 'but with the exception of one or two casual expressions I do not think any letters to you inconsistent with the respect and confidence in the commander in chief'. And he concluded: 'I have also endeavoured to do no wrong to Admiral Dundas. It has been my wish to act fairly between you, and the public good has been my sole object and come what may this is my consolation and sure defence.'

[2] For the official correspondence between Dundas and the Admiralty, which is not very revealing, see Bonner-Smith and Dewar, *Russian war, 1854*, pp. 235–417.

[3] *P.P. 1854–5*, IX, pt. 3, *Fifth report from the select committee on the army before Sebastopol*, p. 3, 18 June 1855.

[4] Ibid., *Fourth report*, evidence of S. Herbert, p. 192; *Hansard*, CXXXVI, 140, S. Herbert, 12 December 1854; Stanmore, *Herbert*, I, 276–7. According to Raglan most of the improvements were initiated by him in the field (PRO/WO/1/371, 1288 Military, despatch no. 164, 30 January 1855).

[5] *P.P. 1854–5*, IX, pt. 2, *Third report*, evidence of duke of Newcastle, pp. 120–1; Stanmore, *Herbert*, I, 278–9.

[6] *P.P. 1854–5*, IX, pt. 2, *Third report*, evidence of duke of Newcastle, p. 139; *Hansard*, CXXXVI, 58–9, 141–3.

[7] *Hansard*, CXXXVI, 141.

first time in British military history female nurses were sent out to the theatre of war to tend the wounded;[1] and on the personal insistence of the Secretary for War the soldiers were allowed to grow beards and throw away the hated stock.[2] So it was planned, but for a combination of reasons the well-meant plans often failed to materialise. Some generals were laws to themselves and continued to insist on the stock.[3] Precious medical supplies needed in the base hospital, which had been moved to Scutari (opposite Constantinople), were left in Varna and apparently never recovered.[4] Other shipments for Scutari went on to Balaclava without being off-loaded *en route* as was intended;[5] iron bedsteads were sent out with the frames on one ship and the legs on another.[6] The shipping was so congested in the little harbour of Balaclava, which lacked the wharves and warehouses necessary for speedy and orderly unloading and which was in constant danger of attack and recapture by the Russians, that many ships were forced to anchor in the dangerous waters outside the harbour and some even returned to England with valuable cargoes still in their holds.[7] Fresh vegetables, especially procured in Constantinople, turned bad on shipboard and had to be jettisoned;[8] green coffee sent in that state to preserve it better became useless for lack of fuel to roast it.[9] Whole shipments of boots proved to be too small,[10] and entrenching tools were pronounced to be of inferior quality.[11] When the government in England first heard of the shortage of medical supplies at Scutari they found it hard to believe, but wasted no time in empowering the ambassador in Constantinople to authorise extraordinary expenditures; there is no evidence, however, that he availed himself of the power.[12]

An ambulance corps was authorised at an early date—a new departure in British military history—but unfortunately pensioners, not physically fit for the work, were enlisted as stretcher-bearers, because the military

[1] See Stanmore, *Herbert*, I, ch. x; Cecil Woodham-Smith, *Florence Nightingale* (London, 1950).
[2] Martineau, *Newcastle*, p. 189, quoting a letter to Lord Raglan, 28 April 1854.
[3] Russell, *The War*, p. 97; Hibbert, *Raglan*, p. 35.
[4] *P.P. 1854–5*, IX, pt. 3, *Fourth report*, evidence of S. Herbert, p. 165.
[5] *Ibid.*, *Fifth report from the select committee*, pp. 10–11.
[6] Stanmore, *Herbert*, I, 303, quoting Herbert to Newcastle, 8 January 1854.
[7] *P.P. 1854–5*, IX, pt. 3, *Fifth report from the select committee*, pp. 11–12.
[8] *Ibid.* p. 16, and pt. 2, *Third report*, evidence of Sir C. Trevelyan, p. 65.
[9] Martineau, *Newcastle*, p. 190.   [10] Stanmore, *Herbert*, I, 296.
[11] *P.P. 1854–5*, IX, pt. 3, *Fifth report from the select committee*, pp. 9–10.
[12] *Ibid.*, evidence of S. Herbert, *Fourth report*, pp. 161–98; Woodham-Smith, *Florence Nightingale*, pp. 159–61.

authorities were unwilling to spare fighting troops.[1] At an early date, Dr Smith, the Director General of the Medical Department, had recommended the provision of hospital ships to evacuate the wounded, but the recommendation had been neglected or overlooked. When this omission came to the attention of the ministers in October, Graham, at the urging of Newcastle, wrote to Admiral Dundas instructing him to fit out two large steamers for the purpose. Dundas failed to do so, anticipating the early fall of Sebastopol. As a result of all this thousands of sick and wounded were evacuated to Scutari in very cramped quarters and under frightful conditions.[2] The wretched condition of the hospitals at Scutari became a notorious scandal when news of it reached the public, although the situation there improved after the arrival of Florence Nightingale and her nurses, the one bright spot in an otherwise dismal story.[3]

All the frustrations and setbacks that marked the first two months of the Crimean campaign were as nothing, however, compared to the calamity that occurred on 14 November in the form of a dreadful storm, which turned the Allied camps into a shambles and wrecked many of their ships loaded with precious supplies of food, forage, winter clothing and ammunition. General Estcourt, the Adjutant General, succinctly described the sad plight of the army, already grim and now desperate, in a letter to Sidney Herbert in which he wrote:

Our position is extremely critical...The guards of the trenches, the working parties, the various armed and unarmed duties...are so severe on the men that they are worn out. Their clothes are worn out, and as you know they have no houses to get shelter in, nor fuel to cook their meals. A storm occurred on Tuesday which brought all our exposure to a crisis; wind which blew down every tent and marquee, not excepting the field hospitals full of sick. Rain and sleet fell and froze upon every one...All day that lasted. Towards night they got their tents pitched again, but very few fires could be lighted. Either no food or uncooked food was all that could be had.

[1] *P.P. 1854–5*, IX, pt. 2, *Third report*, evidence of duke of Newcastle, pp. 167–8. *The Times* (23 January 1855) published a story about a ship being commandeered from Balaclava harbour in a special emergency to take a representative of Lord Raglan's to Constantinople. Half-way across the Black Sea the officer divulged the purpose of his mission to the captain of the ship—the purchase of badly needed footwear for the army. The captain informed him that the ship was loaded with a cargo of boots, which he was waiting to discharge when he was ordered back to sea !

[2] *Ibid.* p. 151, and pt. 3, *Fourth report*, evidence of Sir J. Graham, pp. 270–1; *Fifth report*, pp. 11 and 18; cf. Bonner-Smith and Dewar, *The Russian War 1854*, pp. 416–17.

[3] *P.P. 1854–5*, IX, pt. 3, *Fifth report*, pp. 19–23; see also Woodham-Smith, *Florence Nightingale*, pp. 130–205.

Later in the letter he listed the Army's needs:

We want men—50,000 between us and the French. We want warm clothing.
We want heavy mortars and fresh siege-guns, ours being nearly worn out.
We want more ammunition for small arms as well as great guns. We want
fuel, houses, and we want forage—hay, that is.[1]

Most of these items went down with the twenty-odd ships that
foundered in the storm. Such was the chaos that followed it that when
many of the remaining items arrived they remained unavailable for
months for lack of local transport.

Raglan immediately requisitioned replacements.[2] Likewise, as soon as
he received word of the loss, Newcastle ordered the immediate
replenishment of the lost cargoes and Ordnance agents were sent to the
manufacturing districts with fresh orders. Vessels were secured at short
notice and new supplies of warm clothing had reached the Crimea
before the end of January.[3]

Up until this time the mules and other animals brought by Commissary General Filder from Varna to Balaclava had sufficed to do the job.
When, however, on 8 November he was told that the Army must be
prepared to spend the winter there, he ordered more mules to be sent
from Constantinople, but, inexcusably, they did not arrive until mid
December. On the day before the storm Filder represented to Raglan
the necessity of doing something about the six or seven miles of
unmetalled road between Balaclava and the camp, but Burgoyne, the
chief engineering officer with the expedition, said that nothing could be
done since they did not have the manpower to rebuild it, a task that he
estimated would have taken a thousand men two or three months.[4]
Filder also warned Raglan on this occasion about the unsatisfactory state
of the harbour, which was of course greatly accentuated by the storm of

---

[1] Stanmore, *Herbert*, I, 280–1. Most authorities refer to the hurricane, but the naval
accounts speak of it as a gale or storm.

[2] Kinglake, *Crimea*, IV, 126–7.

[3] *P.P. 1854–5*, IX, pt. 2, *Third report*, evidence of duke of Newcastle, pp. 125–6; *The Times*,
29 January 1855, quoting Raglan's despatch of 13 January.

[4] Martineau, *Newcastle*, pp. 178–9; [P. B. Maxwell,] *Whom shall we hang? The Sebastopol
inquiry* (London, 1855), pp. 139–48; *P.P. 1854–5*, IX, pt. 2, *Third report*, 321–44, evidence
of General Burgoyne, who brushed off many questions on the subject by saying that
before November they did not anticipate any problem with the road since they did not
expect to be there the winter; by that time he maintained there was nothing could be
done about it. His private correspondence in October 1854 reveals that he was by no
means so confident of success then as he intimated to the Roebuck committee. See
Wrottesley, *Burgoyne*, II, 98–118; cf. Kinglake, *Crimea*, IV, 96.

the following day. The heavy rains that followed the storm turned the road into a quagmire impassable to wheeled vehicles. Everything had to be brought up on the backs of the mules and other animals and they could only carry a third of the weight they had drawn in carts. The new burden, combined with the growing lack of forage and the inclement weather, proved too much and resulted in a high rate of mortality among them. Expensive cavalry and artillery horses were put to work as beasts of burden and suffered a similar fate.[1] Although these seven miles of road were the lifeline of the British army, half-hearted efforts to repair it with the help of Turkish labour failed. The result was that the privations of the wretched soldiers in the trenches before Sebastopol were greatly increased and prolonged. Some troops even had to walk the weary fourteen miles for daily rations, in which there were many deficiencies, especially in December.[2] Lumber arrived for much needed hutments, but lack of transport greatly delayed their erection.[3]

General Estcourt wrote to Herbert on 8 December about the serious difficulties involving transport, urging the government to consider how to remedy this chronic failing in the army. He pointed out that the French had an organised transport corps with an adequate supply of mules and their own officers and their own tradesmen all under their Intendant-General, who was a military man (which the British Commissary General was not).

We have a very excellent man as Commissary-General [Estcourt continued charitably], who has a zealous number of officers under him; but there they stop; there is no organized transport. They depend upon the resources of the country. These fail. They are *nil*...The evil is not simply in the failure of the means at the disposal of the Commissary General, but in the disorganization to the Army which the very evident scramble occasions. Every one sees the want of system. Every feeling of regularity is broken down.

Therefore I am convinced that a commissariat without a transport service attached to it of an organized and military character cannot perform its duty in the field, or render the Army efficient for great enterprises. Our provisions are excellent but our transport is rotten. Forage has been denied our *bat*

---

[1] *P.P. 1854–5*, IX, pt. 3, *Fifth report*, 14. General Burgoyne in his evidence was inclined to lay much of the blame on the failure of those responsible to look after their animals properly. 'I consider it', he told the committee, 'a national defect on the part of the British that they do not take care of their horses as other troops do; they do it according to regulations, according to orders but they have not the feeling in themselves to take care of animals' (*ibid.* pt. 2, *Third report*, evidence of General Burgoyne, pp. 321–44).

[2] [Maxwell,] *Whom shall we hang?*, pp. 147–60.

[3] *P.P. 1854–5*, IX, pt. 2, *Third report*, evidence of duke of Newcastle, p. 129.

horses ever since we came into the Crimea...Our cavalry and artillery are at this moment ineffective. The cavalry could not charge and the artillery could not drag the guns into position. A *prodigious* number of both have died. Why? Not only exposure, rain, and cold, but want of hay and straw.[1]

On 18 December he returned to the same theme, bewailing the breakdown of the ambulances because the horses were too weak for lack of forage to do anything. 'All the fault of old Filder', he burst out, less charitably than before, 'because he has not organized transport either of wagons or mules. We shall never do without a great change in that department.'[2]

General Burgoyne expressed very similar views to those of Estcourt. In a letter to England on 5 December he gave the following graphic description of the situation:

Our paramount difficulty now is for means of transport; we are on a ridge of heights from 600 to 800 feet above the sea, and from five to eight miles from our port [Balaclava], the whole way through deep mud and clay, without any made road; the weather, torrents of rain, almost unceasing for weeks, with high cold winds, the animals all exposed in the open air, imperfectly foraged, and the whole in the greatest confusion; animals and drivers, on which our very existence depends, ill-managed, ill-used, and driven rapidly to inefficiency.[3]

He too spoke of the much better organisation of the French transport. 'While our means of transport at this present time is nearly annihilated,' he wrote in another letter, 'we can see theirs working about like bees.'[4] In his evidence before the Roebuck committee he gave it as his opinion that the commissariat was imperfectly organised, that it was overworked, and should be broken up.[5]

While all these criticisms are clearly well founded it should be said in Filder's defence that he was poorly briefed. For instance on 23 October he wrote to Trevelyan to say that while at the moment they were well

[1] Stanmore, *Herbert*, II, 287–8.   [2] *Ibid.* p. 289.

[3] Wrottesley, *Burgoyne*, II, 143.

[4] *Ibid.* p. 154. On another occasion, speaking of the superior organisation of the French army generally, he commented on how much more comfortable and gay the French soldiers were than the poor British, who though very brave no longer smiled. Yet at the same time he insisted that the British officers were superior to the French. While frequently commenting on the better organisation of the French, he also made it clear that they too had their deficiencies in the matter of shelter, of warm clothing and of forage (*ibid.* pp. 169–72, 194, 232–3).

[5] *P.P. 1854–5*, IX, pt. 2, *Third report*, 321–44.

off he was uncertain about the future. 'Lord Raglan will not, in the present state of affairs, give me any definite orders,' he wrote, 'and I can make no preparations. I require always to look three months ahead.'[1]

On 26 December, prodded perhaps by enquiries from London, Raglan asked Filder through the Quartermaster General what preparations he had made to receive the great flow of stores now arriving. Filder replied that the size of the commissariat staff was inadequate owing to overwork and illness and the confined space in Balaclava, but promised to do his best. He complained about the great delay in the sending of horses from Constantinople and pointed out that the conveyance of huts and other special equipment was something far beyond their normal duties. Since there was insufficient ground and not enough pack animals available there were bound to be delays.[2] In November Filder had recommended the recruitment of drivers in Ireland and this was done with little delay.[3] More animals began to arrive in mid December and early January, but the wastage remained excessive. This arose in part from the desertion of Turkish drivers and the pilfering of commissariat horses by the rest of the army.[4]

Once the government was apprised of the situation it made several important if belated decisions on Newcastle's recommendation. The first of these was the establishment of a Land Transport Corps under military control. A Colonel M'Murdo was placed in command and drivers specially recruited in Ireland to replace the unreliable Turkish drivers.[5] Another innovation now authorised was the construction of a railway from Balaclava to the camp; this was entrusted to a private firm

---

[1] *Ibid.*, evidence of Sir C. Trevelyan, p. 49. It may further be said in Filder's defence that he had 1,000,000 lb. of hay on hand but that 800,000 lb. of it was afloat and lost on 14 November (*ibid.* p. 46). Three weeks earlier he had suggested to Trevelyan that additional quantities of hay and biscuit should be shipped from England—he had great difficulty in finding hay in the Black Sea area—and this was done (*ibid.* pp. 40–1), but an earlier suggestion made on 13 September had been ignored (Stanmore, *Herbert*, I, 293–4), because when it was received the Treasury thought the campaign was over (Kinglake, *Crimea*, IV, 101–4).

[2] *P.P. 1854–5*, IX, pt. 2, *Third report*, evidence of Sir C. Trevelyan, pp. 58–60.

[3] *Ibid.* p. 54.

[4] *Ibid.* pp. 60–3.

[5] Stanmore, *Herbert*, I, 292; *P.P. 1854–5*, IX, pt. 2, evidence of duke of Newcastle, p. 167; of Sir John Burgoyne, p. 54. Newcastle informed Raglan on 20 January 1855 that, lacking direct information from him, he had gone ahead with the formation of this Corps under royal warrant. It was to consist of a recruiting wing in England and another in the Crimea of some 3,500 all ranks and 8,000 mules, organised to correspond with the divisions of the army. One-quarter of the drivers were to be British (PRO WO/6/70/84, despatch no. 212).

of contractors, Messrs. Peto and Betts. Their engineers arrived in January, the work was begun on 8 February, and the railway was in operation before the end of March.[1] This, however, was rather a case of locking the barn door after the horse had gone. A large force of navvies sent out in October under proper direction and with the necessary equipment might have built a road that would have been in service for the greater part of the winter.[2] Another innovation undertaken by the duke of Newcastle before leaving office was the laying of a submarine cable between Varna and Balaclava to make possible telegraphic communication between London and the Crimea. This was completed early in 1855.[3]

The confusion in Balaclava harbour, bad before the storm, was indescribable in the months that followed it. Everything floated in its putrid pale green water, the bodies of drowned men and animals, the wreckage and the assorted cargoes of sunken ships, the refuse and the filth from the troops on shore. There seemed to be no order, either in the harbour itself or on land, where the roadway was quite insufficient, where unloaded cargoes were piled helter-skelter, and where supply parties from the camp were kept for hours in the perishing cold and wet waiting for what provisions could be obtained. Men contrasted this shambles with the orderly condition of the little French harbour below Cape Chersonese. Responsibilities at Balaclava were divided between a harbour-master, an officer in charge of transports, and the military authorities on shore.[4]

Admiral Dundas, a rather hostile witness, informed the Roebuck committee that for most of the autumn he was never in Balaclava harbour since he left it to Sir Edmund Lyons, who was there most of the time except the third week in October.[5] Dundas said he had received no complaints regarding the state of Balaclava harbour and that he had

---

[1] Martineau, *Newcastle*, pp. 184–5; Wrottesley, *Burgoyne*, II, 197–8; Hibbert, *Raglan*, p. 304.

[2] *P.P. 1854–5*, IX, pt. 2, *Third report*, evidence of Sir John Burgoyne, p. 333, who admitted that it might have been a good thing to send 1,500 navvies in November and that this would have been better and cheaper than a railway.

[3] *Ibid.*, evidence of duke of Newcastle, p. 173. See also *The Times*, 15 January 1855.

[4] *P.P. 1854–5*, IX, pt. 3, *Fourth report*, evidence of Sir James Graham, pp. 256–88, *Fifth report*, pp. 12–13; Hibbert, *Raglan*, pp. 244–6; Wrottesley, *Burgoyne*, II, 186–7. Admiral Boxer, who was ineffective at Constantinople, was eventually transferred to Balaclava, where he was more successful.

[5] *P.P. 1854–5*, IX, pt. 3, 216–17. Lyons left Balaclava to participate in the bombardment of 17 October.

very good officers there, namely, Admiral Lyons, and Captains Christie and Dacre. In particular, Dundas said he had no criticism to make of Captain Christie, who was in charge of the transports with orders to avoid having too many of them cluttering up the harbour at once. He said Christie had 'a very difficult card to play' since the transport service were not under naval laws and they were 'rather a set of wild fellows' and did what they wanted. According to Dundas, Christie had no responsibility for keeping the harbour clean.[1] When the time came for Lyons to succeed Dundas, ironically the first instruction that Graham gave him was to see that order was established in Balaclava and Constantinople 'as to the unloading of Stores, the anchorage of transports in safety and the return of a portion of them to England for the conveyance back to the Black Sea of Reinforcements and provisions'.[2] These instructions were reiterated in a further letter in which Graham added: 'This can only be regulated in concert with Ld Raglan; who ought to appoint an efficient military officer at each port to co-operate with a naval officer nominated by you.'[3]

Another branch of the service, closely connected with the commissariat, which occasioned much criticism and dissatisfaction was the Ordnance. This department was responsible for executing orders for equipment coming from various branches of the army, but not for distribution in the field, which was looked after by the already over-burdened commissariat. According to Newcastle, who was himself highly critical of the Ordnance, it proved very difficult to tell how these orders were executed and there was clearly a lack of understanding between the Admiralty and the Ordnance as to their specific duties in the consignment of stores aboard ship. Some changes were eventually authorised as a result of these various difficulties. After much pressure from the Secretary for War a system of ordnance stores was inaugurated.[4] There was also some difference between Graham and Newcastle as to whether sea transport should be placed under the War Office or the

[1] *Ibid.* pp. 217–20.
[2] Graham Papers, 18 December 1854. Cf. official orders sent to Dundas on the same day, Bonner-Smith and Dewar, *Russian War 1854*, pp. 406–8.
[3] Graham Papers, 1 January 1855. On 27 January Raglan wrote to Graham about the problems in Balaclava harbour. He welcomed the appointment of two naval officers and said that he could not speak too highly of Admiral Lyons. It is something of a puzzle why the supposedly efficient Lyons had not earlier done something about the chaos in Balaclava harbour.
[4] *P.P. 1854–5*, IX, pt. 2, *Third report*, evidence of duke of Newcastle, pp. 125–7, 145 and 187.

Admiralty. Eventually a compromise was effected with the reconstitution of the old Transport Board.[1]

There was also a serious conflict of personalities on the Board of Ordnance that decreased its effectiveness. The Roebuck committee with good reason criticised the government for failing to replace Raglan as Master General of the Ordnance and for leaving the Department without a second senior officer, the surveyor-general, throughout the crucial summer of 1854. Sir Hew Ross, appointed Lieutenant-General in Raglan's absence, lacked sufficient authority and seemed improperly acquainted with the constitution of the Board. The Roebuck committee also criticised the contract system used by the Ordnance Department.[2]

No branch of the army came in for more criticism than the medical service. The Director General, Dr Smith, complained that he was responsible to five different authorities, but Newcastle said that he made it clear to Smith that 'his real and only master' was the Secretary of State for War. The personal relations between these two men were clearly not harmonious. Smith complained that he was not properly briefed about the coming operation, a charge which Newcastle denied. He said that Smith had a tendency to assume that any order given was carried out and hence to ignore complaints, which never came through official channels. Smith complained that his authority to requisition was always in question.[3] On one occasion he admitted that after a lifetime of economising he found great difficulty in believing that expense was no longer the ultimate consideration. As Sidney Herbert told the Roebuck committee, men like Dr Smith, long used to peace-time economies, were incapable of thinking on the large and lavish scale now demanded.[4]

The conditions in the field hospitals and in the little base hospital at Balaclava, wretched from the beginning, became intolerable as a result of the ravages of the storm and the harshness of the ensuing winter, despite the heroic work of the surgeons. These hospitals were all horribly overcrowded because of the prevalence of cholera, dysentery and other disease and the almost complete lack of medical supplies and beds. It was no longer possible to use waggons to transport the wounded

---

[1] *P.P. 1854–5*, IX, pt. 2, *Third Report*, and pt. 3, *Fifth report*, 10.   [2] *Ibid.* pp. 8–9.

[3] *Ibid.* pt. 2, *Third report*, evidence of duke of Newcastle, pp. 148–59; pt. 3, *Fifth report*, pp. 17–18. Newcastle said that he did not think Smith could 'be held responsible for all the evils in the hospital' at Scutari, but he added: 'Still if it is proved that he did not give directions to remedy them, or take the necessary precaution to prevent them, undoubtedly he is most blameable.'

[4] *Ibid.* pt. 3, 194.

and sick (who greatly outnumbered the wounded) down from the Upland to Balaclava, but eventually the French came to the rescue of their allies by lending 300 *cacolets* to assist in the evacuation.[1]

Conditions in the base hospitals in Scutari were, if possible, worse, because of their greater magnitude, and certainly more disgraceful, since they could more easily have been avoided. Again they were due in part to the lack of supplies, of beds, of proper staff and also to improper drainage which produced a very high fever rate. The basic trouble at Scutari however, was bad management. The military commandant until late in December was a mere major, incapable of supervising an establishment of five or six thousand men which should have been a general's command, and unwilling to take the financial responsibility for the emergency expenditures that had to be authorised. The chief medical officer, a man of equally limited ability, was so overwhelmed with paper work that he never had an opportunity of visiting the wards.[2] The mortality rate in all the hospitals was fearfully high. In the four months from November to February inclusive some 9,000 men died in hospital (about nine times the total number killed in battle from September to November). By the end of February some 13,600 men were sick in hospital, but in the following month the incidence of mortality at Scutari began to fall as a result of long-overdue improvements in the drainage system. By this time the treatment of the patients had been greatly improved thanks to the arrival of Florence Nightingale and her nursing sisters and the munificence of the *Times* fund from which she was able to draw. It was a terrible irony, in view of all the provision that had been made by the government in England, that for months the Scutari hospitals were dependent on medical comforts provided from the fund raised by the paper which had been such a harsh critic of the medical service. Part of the trouble stemmed from the incompetence of the hospital purveyor in Scutari, part from the red tape which tied up the commissary officials, and part from a genuine lack of understanding of the division of responsibilities of the various officials and a failure of any of them to show the initiative needed to cut

[1] Stanmore, *Herbert*, II, 286. The *cacolet* consisted of a pair of chairs strung over the back of a mule on a specially constructed saddle. Estcourt suggested the purchase of these contraptions at Verdon, in the north of France, where they were made (*ibid.* p. 291).

[2] He was superseded for inefficiency, but his eventual successor was a former Principal Medical Officer at Balaclava, who had already been censored there for his 'apathy and lack of interest in the welfare of the sick'. This appointment reflected, as did everything else, on Dr Hall.

through the red tape which bound them. Prime responsibility for the failure of the Medical Services both in the Crimea and at Scutari lay with Dr Hall, the chief medical officer directly responsible to Lord Raglan.[1]

Everything in the Crimea seemed to be part of a vicious circle. The men fell sick in part from overwork, but the high incidence of sickness greatly reduced the number of effective troops and so increased the burden on the survivors. From the beginning one of the hazards of the expedition lay in the limited reserves available. In mid January Estcourt told Herbert that the sick in camp numbered 5,000 and the 'effective strength taking duties' was not much above 13,000.[2] Driblets of reinforcements had been sent out, 1,286 in September, 2,855 in October, 7,037 in November, but many were too young and quickly succumbed.[3] According to one officer writing home in January, one regiment had gone on parade with only one sergeant and seven men, while another regiment only had three effective officers. Many companies, he said, were reduced to seven or eight files.[4]

In contrast, before the end of January the French, thanks to British assistance in the provision of transports, were said to number 70,000. With this extra manpower they gradually gave some assistance to the British and towards the end of January took over responsibility for ground on the right of the British siege-works. The British, however, were always inclined to think that the French failed to assume their proper share, while the French considered the British rather ungrateful for the amount of assistance given. Nevertheless, both commanders were concerned to preserve good relations and the differences did not

[1] See [Maxwell,] *Whom shall we hang?*, chs. 17–21; Hamley, *War in the Crimea*, p. 182; Woodham-Smith, *Florence Nightingale*, chs. VIII and IX; *P.P. 1854–5*, IX, pt. 3, *Fifth report*, pp. 18–22; *Fourth report*, evidence of Sidney Herbert, pp. 165–77; XXXIII, *Report of state of hospitals in Crimea and Scutari*, pp. 3–51. When asked about shortages of port wine Herbert answered: 'You will find complaints in every hospital, even the best London hospitals, that the nurses, and particularly the night nurses, consume a large portion of the stimulant meant for the patients.' This is a reminder that the modern tradition of nursing was only in its infancy.

[2] Stanmore, *Herbert*, I, 291. Estcourt claimed that if they only had lumber to build floors to keep the sick off the ground the suffering would be reduced; but, as we have seen, the materials for huts were slow in arriving for lack of land transport, another part of the vicious circle.

[3] *Hansard*, CXXXVI, 135; 7,561 reinforcements had been sent out before the expedition left Varna for the Crimea, making a total of 18,739 up to the end of November. For Raglan's opinion of the reinforcements see Martineau, *Newcastle*, p. 200.

[4] Wrottesley, *Burgoyne*, II, 195–8, letter of Major J. W. Gordon, R.E., 22 January 1855.

come to a serious crisis. The mutual criticisms were in letters home rather than face to face and on the whole relations between the rank and file of the armies appear to have been good.[1]

The British ministers were appalled by the news that began to reach them in November and December and were especially concerned that for the most part it came from unofficial sources—the correspondent of *The Times* and relatives of officers who received pathetic letters from the front revealing the catastrophic situation. They thought that they had made unprecedented efforts to see that the expeditionary force was well equipped and well supplied and had reason to believe that no such force in British history had ever departed better prepared. Yet now the exact reverse seemed to be the case and they were at a loss to know the reason. They soon began to lose confidence in the commander whom they had appointed, despite the promotion he had been awarded after Inkerman. It was the last vote of confidence that the old man was to receive. The remaining months of his life were overcast by a knowledge of failure and a sense that he had lost the confidence of those at home.

The change may be detected in his correspondence with the duke of Newcastle. Until November Newcastle remained over-sanguine in his view of the situation, but Raglan never gave him cause for this. On 23 October the commander painted a realistic picture of the perilous position in which his army stood and plaintively concluded his letter with the observation that it required, 'and should not be denied, repose'.[2] Throughout December he continued to give brief but gloomy accounts of the state of the army's health and the difficulties under which they laboured.[3] Now a note of disquiet began to enter Newcastle's letters. On 22 December he wrote, not for the first time, to enquire about the cause of 'the complaints which thicken from all quarters of the want of system and organization which prevails in all departments of the camp', and to ask why the French camp was reputed to be in such better condition. He also invited information about the incredible confusion reported in Balaclava harbour and the state of the roads, for which he was being blamed in parliament.[4] Three days later he was enquiring about the alleged shortages of rations of the men in the trenches, saying with some asperity: 'Again, I must repeat, there appears

[1] *Ibid.* pp. 175–6, 200; Hamley, *War in the Crimea*, pp. 176–7; Martineau, *Newcastle*, pp. 234–5; Gooch, *New Bonapartist generals*, pp. 160–2.
[2] Martineau, *Newcastle*, pp. 174–5.
[3] *Ibid.* p. 181. [4] *Ibid.* pp. 229–30.

to be carelessness amongst the higher departments which requires vigorous correction.'[1] On the 29th he began his letter: 'I am really grieved to sing the same song again to-day, but complaints come in so thickly and so strongly that I cannot, if I would, think or write of anything else.' He went on to raise questions about the adequacy of the Quartermaster General and the Adjutant General. 'The truth is,' he wrote, 'General Airey and General Estcourt are much complained of as not being up to their work, and those under them appear to be little capable of supplying their deficiencies.'[2] On 1 January his note became still sharper as he wrote about the growing irritation produced by stories of horses dying of starvation and the deplorable conditions under which the sick and wounded were being evacuated. He foresaw a demand for popular vengeance, 'You and I will come first;' he wrote, 'but those who are most to blame will not escape.' He went on to relate the gossip that was going around that Airey had time to write to fine ladies in London while leaving his duties undone.[3] And finally on 26 January, only a few days before the fall of the government, he wrote in desperation: 'The present condition of the army—wet, cold, and hungry, within seven miles of warm clothing, huts, fuel, and food, must be caused by improvidence of somebody. Who is it?'[4]

One may imagine the growing bitterness with which Lord Raglan received and answered these letters, although in truth some of the questions it seemed beyond his power to answer. With regard to the failure of transport he replied helplessly on 13 January:

I have done all in my power to correct this evil, and so have the officers under me, and I have afforded every support and assistance in my power to Mr Filder; but his establishment is inadequate to his duties, his horse transport dwindles away to nothing, and the Commissariat generally is in a very unsatisfactory state.[5]

In the same letter he admitted that the machinery of the commissariat was undoubtedly defective. 'I do not question either Mr Filder's ability or his zeal', he wrote, 'but his department is not well manned.'

---

[1] Martineau, *Newcastle*, p. 230.   [2] *Ibid.* p. 232.   [3] *Ibid.* pp. 236–7.

[4] *Ibid.* p. 241. Kinglake (*Crimea*, IV, 202–21) is critical of Newcastle for giving too much credence to individual observers, who only saw a small part of the whole picture, and for not showing more confidence in Raglan and his staff. Undoubtedly, when rattled, Newcastle became querulous, but it is hard to see how a responsible minister could avoid pressing a commander who failed to give adequate explanation for all that was going wrong or to propose the proper steps to rectify the situation.

[5] *Ibid.* p. 231.

On 18 January he strongly protested against Newcastle's condemnation of Generals Airey and Estcourt on hearsay evidence and considered that this letter was really an expression of lack of confidence in himself. 'I have been conversant with public business nearly half a century', he wrote, 'and I have never yet known an instance of such condemnation before. I am a witness to their daily labours, their constant toil, and I can with truth say that they merit the tribute of my warmest approbation.' In particular he pronounced General Airey, the one most under fire, as a 'very able man', whom he considered himself fortunate in having. He concluded that he himself no longer enjoyed the confidence of the Secretary for War, but in the Wellingtonian tradition he avowed that his duty to the queen would induce him to persevere, 'apart from all personal considerations'.[1]

Two days later, on receiving the further insinuations about General Airey, he wrote again to say that the only ladies to whom General Airey had written other than his wife were Lady Raglan to assure her of her husband's well-being and a Miss Hardinge to inform her regarding her brother's illness. He continued:

I really cannot understand any gentleman venturing to intrude upon you such an insinuation [nor, by implication, the duke's listening to it].

I cannot say how all these attacks annoy me and add to my anxieties, and these are far from being few.

After looking over copies of his correspondence with Newcastle since the month of October he asserted that he had made clear 'the serious consequences of the state of the roads and of the deficiency of transport'. He also reminded Newcastle that he had referred to a report of Mr Cattley's indicating that the winter climate of the Crimea would require proper shelter. 'You sent me Dr Lee's book, which tended to the belief that the winter here was not rigorous,' Raglan added. 'Mr Cattley's experience shows that he spoke with more *connaissance de cause* than Dr Lee.'[2]

After he left office Sidney Herbert wrote Raglan a long and friendly letter trying to defend Newcastle and to persuade Raglan of the necessity of his keeping the government more fully informed. He pointed out that in reciting stories and accusations brought to his attention

[1] *Ibid.* pp. 233–6.
[2] *Ibid.* p. 239. Cattley, an interpreter and former consul, had warned Raglan about the severity of the Crimean winter in a memorandum which the commander-in-chief had passed on to Newcastle on 23 October. See Kinglake, *Crimea*, IV, 448–50.

Newcastle was not saying that he believed them but asking Raglan for an explanation or contradiction.

One great difficulty, however, which the Cabinet experienced [he went on to say], was the absence of detailed information from yourself. Of the prospects of the siege, its chance of success, and the measures you contemplated for its prosecution, the Cabinet knew nothing direct from yourself, except in the instance of the disagreement between Burgoyne and the French engineers.

I am certain, therefore, that great advantage would result from a more detailed and unreserved communication, either in despatches or private letters, keeping the Government *au fait*, not only of what has happened or is happening, but of your own expectations of what is likely to happen.

He also gently pushed Raglan on another point, writing:

I believe that you have done all that, under the circumstances and the difficulties of the case, could be done, but you know that I have doubted that you were as well served as you ought to be, and I cannot help feeling that you have been too generous to others...But when animals began to die, and forage to be short, and the means of transport to fail, I cannot but think that Mr Filder showed a great want of energy and resource.[1]

Herbert showed more finesse in handling men than Newcastle. His letters to Estcourt, the Adjutant General, as well as the few he wrote to Raglan are more tactful and understanding than those of Newcastle to the commander-in-chief, and Estcourt's letters to Herbert in turn are franker and more informative. Even in the worst days Estcourt was appreciative of what Herbert and others were doing for them. 'You are excellent people, and you do your best, certainly,' he wrote on 8 December in a letter already quoted, 'to make this great and difficult work to *gee*.'[2] Again in a letter of 27 January reporting some improvement at Balaclava as a result of a change of command there, he wrote: 'I have only to say in respect to your office that you have either adopted the suggestions that I have ventured to make, or you have...*anticipated* them. Therefore no stones will be thrown from the Army on your department. In short we centre all our complaints, such as they are, in the want of a military organized transport service.'[3]

[1] Stanmore, *Herbert*, II, 326–30.
[2] *Ibid.* I, 285.
[3] *Ibid.* p. 299. Again on 17 February he wrote: 'If you are out office sleep sound. You have done your duty by the Army. You have *anticipated* most of our wants. The heavy blow to us was the act of Providence. The *Prince* went down at the beginning of the bad weather' (*ibid.* p. 300).

Why, then, had all the vast preparations failed of their purpose? Who was to blame for the disasters that befell this unhappy army? The question has been asked from that day to this, but there is no simple answer. Many complex factors contributed to produce this sorry state of affairs. The mounting of a sea-borne expedition against Sebastopol was probably a legitimate exercise of war, but the ministers were open to criticism for taking such a dangerous gamble in sending a relatively small force with so little provision for reinforcement on such a hazardous operation; yet no military advice seems to have been given them otherwise, with the exception of Burgoyne's warning late in the summer. Clearly, the ministers were over-optimistic that the assault would be completed before winter and neglected to ascertain how inclement the Crimean weather could become. The result was that the provision of winter clothing and housing was made too late, with the consequence that one storm produced disaster.

There is no denying the fact that the Prime Minister's heart was not in the war and that consequently he did not give the overall lead and supervision that are to be found in such great war leaders as the elder Pitt, Lloyd George and Winston Churchill. He was undoubtedly lethargic about undertaking changes in the structure of the military administration and over-solicitous for the feelings and rights of individuals even when the public good might have required changes.[1]

The prime responsibility for the army in the Crimea, of course, fell on the shoulders of the Secretary of State for War. The duke of Newcastle worked under considerable difficulties in the six months after the separation of the War Office from the Colonial Office in that the staff of the new department was inadequate and that for some time it had to make do with provisional accommodation that limited its establishment and delayed its assumption of responsibility for the commissariat.[2] He was critical of the separation of the War Office because it left the Secretary for War with no more power than before and an insufficiency of means. A thorough reorganisation of all the war departments was necessary, but he had been too busy to attempt this and so the anomalies of the minister's relations with the Secretary at War, the Commander-in-Chief, the Ordnance, the Medical Service, *et al.*, continued.[3] Herbert,

---

[1] E.g. in his failure to appoint a new Master General of the Ordnance, in the mistaken belief that a Lieutenant-General in Raglan's absence would do. See his evidence before the Roebuck committee, *P.P. 1854–5*, IX, pt. 3, *Fourth report*, 295–6.

[2] See evidence of Lord Aberdeen, *P.P. 1854–5*, IX, pt. 3, *Fourth report*, 293–7.

[3] *Ibid.* pp. 140–5, 180–1, 193.

on the other hand, strongly endorsed the separation of the two offices when questioned by the Roebuck committee, saying that Newcastle laboured morning, noon and night and that it would have been utterly impossible for him to go on with the Colonial administration. He admitted that there was a lack of communication between the various departments responsible to the Secretary for War, but indicated that in assisting Newcastle he had set up periodic meetings between the heads of these various departments and that before leaving office he had worked out a plan for further reorganisation of these offices.[1]

A more forceful personality than Newcastle would probably have surmounted these difficulties or remedied them more rapidly. Newcastle worked very hard at his job, but he was too inclined to concern himself with detail and he lacked the breadth of vision and the sound judgment of men that his office required. In both these respects Herbert would probably have made a better War minister. Graham was a more efficient and more successful service minister, but he must bear some responsibility for retaining the services of an admiral in whom he lacked confidence—Dundas—who had overall control, despite his disclaimers, of naval operations in the Black Sea, including the ports of Balaclava and Constantinople, which he shared with Lord Raglan. There seems little doubt that the naval officers responsible for arrangements in Balaclava and Constantinople failed to perform their duties in a satisfactory manner.

It is difficult to exonerate Lord Raglan, despite all his fine qualities, which are sometimes too easily forgotten, for failing to keep the government better informed and in failing to make it explicit to his administrative officers, especially the Quartermaster General and the Commissary General, what might be required of them after the investment of Sebastopol was begun. Surely a commander involved in such a precarious operation and dependent on one small and inadequate harbour cannot be excused for failing to say at the beginning that if the operation was to be undertaken at all the facilities of Balaclava had to be improved and its communications with the Upland ensured. If it was the fault of the Commissary General or the Quartermaster General that he had not been apprised of the possible difficulties, why then was he so ready to defend them and to take offence at criticism of their work? Many of the charges against Raglan were false or unfair (for instance, as to his alleged indifference and failure to visit the army), but he was

---

[1] *Fourth report*, 194–8; see ch. xviii for Herbert's proposals.

simply not up to the Herculean task entrusted to him. He was too old and set in his ways, too lacking in imagination and experience. He was not, however, the old fool that some writers have made him out to be.[1]

When the ministers first heard what had gone wrong in the Crimea they tended to blame the Quartermaster General, the Adjutant General and the Commissary General.[2] Probably no man received more blame for what went wrong from critics both in the Crimea and at home than the poor Commissary General.[3] Like most of the generals, Filder was an old man whose experience went back to the Peninsular War, but one who had had a good deal of experience with the British army all over the world since then. He may have done a reasonably efficient job within his terms of reference in the early stages of the campaign, procuring meat, vegetables, transport animals and forage in the Black Sea area by local contracts, but he showed lack of imagination and energy in envisaging the difficulties that might lie ahead and providing for them or in making it sufficiently clear to the Quartermaster General and the Commander-in-Chief what he would need in the way of roads, landing facilities, warehouses and shelter for his animals.

The main fault, however, lay not with individuals but with the system. The British army at that time, as Sidney Herbert said, was only a collection of regiments (and there was little complaint about regimental training and discipline), but most of the field officers had never handled any larger formation. Few of the senior commanders in the army had the training or experience to qualify them to perform their duties effectively, although some worked heroically to master a situation that was beyond them. The system was especially defective in the organisation of the staff, of the ordnance, of the medical services and of the commissariat, which of course up to this time was outside the army proper and only taken over by the War Office at the end of 1854. Hitherto the commissariat had been under the Treasury and in peacetime it was run on Treasury principles of cheese-paring. Its officers were Treasury clerks, not soldiers. They were now burdened with

---

[1] See General Airey's loyal defence of Raglan quoted in Martineau, *Newcastle*, note to pp. 222–3.

[2] See below, pp. 521–7.

[3] Many witnesses before the Roebuck committee who had been in the Crimea were critical of Filder and the commissariat; e.g. General Sir De Lacy Evans, M.P., who commanded the Second Division (*P.P. 1854–5*, IX, pt. 1, *Second report*, 15–58); for a defence of Filder see evidence of Sir C. Trevelyan (*ibid.* pt. 2, *Third report*, 14–108).

extra duties, foreign to them, and they were simply unable to rise to their responsibilities. Having spent a lifetime bound by red tape, they were incapable of cutting it all away overnight. The result was strangulation as men went hungry and animals died for want of filling in forms.[1]

The transfer of the commissariat from the Treasury to the War Office should have undoubtedly taken place earlier. The decision was taken in principle in June but not carried out until 22 December, because Newcastle refused to take direct control of responsibility for it until the War Office moved into new quarters, although he did exercise an overall responsibility. During these crucial five months the Secretary for War had to put up with cramped and inadequate offices in the Prime Minister's house, and so the commissariat remained for that time under Sir Charles Trevelyan in a sort of limbo with no minister taking the close supervision that was necessary.[2] Trevelyan himself, despite his reputation as an able administrator, failed to rise to the occasion and to give the imaginative direction that was required.[3]

It is difficult to say whether the deficiencies in the medical services were due more to the system or to the inadequacies of individuals. Both Newcastle and Herbert were prepared to lay the major blame on the men on the spot. With regard to the shortage of medical stores Herbert said categorically to the Roebuck committee: 'It was not the fault of the system; the system gave a check, but it was gross dereliction of duty on the part of an individual.'[4] In another context he admitted that it was difficult to pin down the blame on an individual and admitted that he knew the public blamed the system, but he responded: 'I do not believe that the difference between one system and another is nearly so great as between one man and another. If you have good men, they will

---

[1] See the evidence of various witnesses before the Roebuck committee, *P.P. 1854–5*, IX, pts. 2, 3 and 4, *Second*, *Third* and *Fourth reports*. Trevelyan warmly defended the commissariat before the committee, claiming that it was better than it had been in the Peninsular War, that it did its job in the Crimea, and that the breakdown was in other branches of the military and naval services, particularly in the Quartermaster-General's branch and in the naval transport branch (*ibid.* pt. 2, *Third report*, 104–7).

[2] See evidence of Lord Aberdeen (*ibid.* pt. 3, *Fourth report*, 292) and the duke of Newcastle (*ibid.* pt. 2, *Third report*, 121). As late as November Gladstone was still querying the wisdom of the transfer, asking whether supply and financial duties could be separated and saying that either the War Department must become the instrument of the Treasury or vice versa (Add. MS. 44744, fols. 82–3, 17 November 1854).

[3] See Jennifer Hart, 'Sir Charles Trevelyan at the Treasury', *E.H.R.* LXXV, 103.

[4] *Ibid.* pt. 3, *Fourth report*, 169.

work a bad system, but the best system will not work with inferior men.'[1]

The men held responsible by the public for what went wrong in the Crimea were bound to be ministers. Clearly the coalition cabinet was to meet its severest test, but even before parliament met it was in the throes of another ministerial crisis, precipitated by a minister who shared the public's lack of confidence in the administration of the war.

[1] *Ibid.* p. 194.

18

THE END OF THE COALITION

Lord John rocks the boat

Lord Aberdeen's heart was never in the war and from the moment it was declared his thought was to confine it to its original objects and to seek an early peace.[1] This, unhappily, was not the leadership that the country wanted and his popularity, never great, continued to diminish. Within the cabinet as well, his direction was lacking as he withdrew further into his shell. Early in September Clarendon observed to Greville that the Prime Minister was out of humour, failed to take interest or to press matters as he should, took hardly any part in cabinet discussions, and failed to reconcile differences among ministers. Clarendon recognised that Aberdeen was a good and honest man, but considered him unfitted for his post, which he did not want, but where he stayed because he knew that the whole machine would fall apart if he left. On the other hand the Foreign Secretary also expressed disgust with Russell's growing discontent and with his disloyalty in allowing his followers to disparage Aberdeen in the way they did.[2]

Aberdeen's friends were naturally concerned at his growing unpopularity and the scurrility of the press attacks on him.[3] On the news of the Alma victory Graham sought to rally him, suggesting that when in Scotland he should make a public speech at Aberdeen. He warned his friend, however, to take no notice of the calumnies that had been circulated against him, referring to the testimony on his behalf by men

[1] Stanmore, *Aberdeen*, p. 258.
[2] *Greville Memoirs*, VII, 59. When Russell wrote disparagingly about Aberdeen's absence from London, Clarendon came quickly to the Prime Minister's defence, pointing out that he was borne down by family worries, that he had not been away since December 1852 and only went to Scotland at this time at the urging of the Court (MS. Clar. C 15, fols. 613–14, Russell, 9 October 1854; Gooch, *Later correspondence*, II, 171–2, 11 October 1854).
[3] *Ab. Cor. 1854–5*, p. 255, Argyll, 13 October 1854, who wrote: 'The personal turn which politics have taken since the break-up of the old Party divisions has led to very disgraceful results; and in no point more disgraceful than in the perpetual and malignant attacks upon you individually, by those who entreated you to join them, when they found that they could hardly do without you.'

such as Hume and Molesworth with whom he had had no previous political connection. Intoxicated by the thought that Sebastopol might already have fallen, Graham proceeded in his most ornate and flowery style to rally the chief:

What we want is a 'Song of Triumph' from the Head of the Government...[he wrote]. Just think of what you have done! Six months have barely elapsed since it [war] was declared and we have closed the White Sea, the Baltic and the Black Sea against even the appearance of the Russian flag. We have sent a larger army to a greater distance in a shorter time than ever before was transported from the shores of England...and the power of England...is exalted higher than ever; and her place among nations is secured. The extravagance of poetry is realized; it is too much for the good citizens of Aberdeen; you have rounded the pillars of Hercules; you have navigated the Aegean; you have passed the Symplegades; you have touched the Chersonese; you have swept the Crimea; and all this has been accomplished in one short summer, while the British fleet at the same time offered battle to the Russians in the harbour of their northern capital, destroyed one of their strongholds in the Baltic, and visited their fastnesses within the Arctic Sea. Here are topics for a song of triumph in which Sovereign and people, Ministers and Parliament, Provosts and Town Councils may cordially join, and in this loud and general acclaim the screeching of slanderers and the hissing of serpents will be drowned and soon forgotten.[1]

The Prime Minister took Graham's advice and made a public appearance on 10 October in Aberdeen, where he was well received. He spoke of his attachment to the Peelite tradition of 'conservative progress' and of his efforts to maintain peace. Nevertheless he promised, now that war had come, to wage it with vigour, and then, although in more moderate language than his friend Graham, he proceeded to dwell on the great achievements that had already been accomplished.[2]

Russell's correspondence with both Clarendon and Graham revealed that he was once again bent on making trouble, meditating, in Newcastle's view, 'the revival of personal projects tending to his own aggrandizement'. In a querulous letter to Graham he complained of 'the

[1] *Ab. Cor. 1854–5*, pp. 235–7, 4 October 1854. He proceeded to extol the achievements of British foreign policy in the past year under Aberdeen's leadership: the 'ancient enmities' of France and Britain obliterated, the evils of war ameliorated by a more civilised treatment of neutral shipping, the good will of Sweden secured, Austria brought into line, Prussia checked, and a reciprocity treaty signed with the United States.

[2] *The Times*, 11 October 1854.

studious withholding of important steps from his cognizance'.[1] 'What can Lord John mean?' poor Aberdeen asked, when he saw the letter. 'I fear mischief,' he added; 'but of the grounds of his complaint I have no conception.' He foresaw a crisis and wondered if Russell acted in combination with Palmerston.[2] Gladstone expressed himself as grievously vexed when he heard this news from Arthur Gordon. 'I must say', he wrote, 'the time has come and more than come to plant the foot firmly, and stand in that direction. We have a little woman to deal with who is of necessity as inevitable as the gates of a certain place: and it is perfectly vain for Lord A. to make concessions to her.'[3] Gladstone's distrust of Lady John was unbounded.

Russell's thinking at this time is reflected in a memorandum, written on 18 October, but apparently not circulated, in which he noted that, like Sir Robert Walpole, he had been leader of the House of Commons so long that he might 'at any time fall before the public lassitude'. Some of his followers differed with him on parliamentary reform; others complained that he failed to get them what they thought their due. 'If this be the evil, the remedy is at hand', he wrote sardonically. 'Lord John Russell has only to retire and take his seat on the back benches.' There were also other difficulties; 'in these days, when religious issues excite so much interest,' he wrote, 'many a vote is determined by the last appointment to a Bishoprick.' Clearly the cabinet would have to come to grips with the situation. 'The mere preparation of measures will not be sufficient,' he concluded; 'some attempt ought to be made to strengthen the general confidence of the House of Commons.'[4]

On 3 November Russell indicated the direction in which his mind was turning when he told Aberdeen that he did not consider that the estimates for the coming year could be framed on the basis of a Secretary at War as well as the Secretary of State for War.[5] Two weeks later he developed this idea in a longer letter, prompted no doubt by his father-in-law, who was warning him of the great 'clamour and indignation gathering against the Government for its neglect of timely

---

[1] *Ab. Cor. 1854–5*, p. 238, Graham to Aberdeen, 3 October 1854; R.A. G17, fol. 89, memorandum of Prince Albert, 7 October 1854; Add. MS. 44319, fols. 75–6, Arthur Gordon to Gladstone, 19 October 1854.

[2] *Ab. Cor. 1854–5*, p. 239, 6 October 1854.

[3] Add. MS. 44319, fols. 77–8, 12 October 1854.

[4] PRO 30/22/11, fols. 1567–75 (partly printed in Walpole, *Russell*, II, 231–2).

[5] *Ab. Cor. 1854–5*, p. 267.

and sufficient exertion in the conduct of the war'.[1] He now proposed not only the abolition of the Secretary at War, but also that the Secretary for War should be in the House of Commons, because of the necessity of having a cabinet minister to satisfy the House on military affairs. Going further than this, he argued that the direction of the war must be constantly and energetically undertaken by the Prime Minister or by a Minister for War 'strong enough to control other departments'. The only minister who met all his requirements, he concluded surprisingly, was his old rival, Lord Palmerston.[2] Russell asked Aberdeen to show his letter to Newcastle, saying that he intended to avoid throwing any blame on the duke. 'Indeed', he wrote, 'I think he deserves very great credit for the exertions he has made. But he has not the authority requisite for so great a sphere.'[3]

Newcastle and Herbert both urged Aberdeen to take any steps he 'thought most conducive to the Public Service', but the Prime Minister did not think Lord John's proposals were either 'advantageous or desirable' and told him so in his considered reply. While recognising the anomaly of the Secretary at War's Office, he thought it objectionable to insist that the Secretary for War must be in the House of Commons. He did not think the House would have any objection to continuing the present arrangement of the Secretary at War moving the estimates, if they were informed that it was a temporary one, for he believed that Herbert was 'deservedly popular and likely to find favour'. He rightly thought that the public would regard the move as the substitution of one man for another, and he did not think that Newcastle's colleagues 'without very strong grounds would wish to place him in such a position'. He pointed out that Palmerston was the same age as he was himself and he could not advise that a man of that age should be asked to perform the work presently being done by two other ministers. Indeed, at the time the War Office was separated from the Colonial Office he understood Russell to express a preference for Newcastle. Aberdeen did not pretend to be a Chatham, which was clearly what Russell wanted, but he pointed to the precedent of the later years of the Napoleonic Wars, when the Prime Minister and the War Minister were in the Lords and the estimates were moved by

---

[1] Walpole, *Russell*, II, 232, quoting Lord Minto, 16 November 1854.
[2] *Ibid.* p. 233, 17 November 1854 (original in Add. MS. 43068, fols. 179–84). For Aberdeen's initial acknowledgment see PRO 30/22/11/F, fols. 1707–8, 18 November 1854.
[3] Add. MS. 43068, fols. 187–8, 18 November 1854.

Palmerston, as Secretary at War, in the Commons.[1] Russell refused to accept Aberdeen's arguments and indicated that he had only agreed to Newcastle's taking the War Office at the time of the division because of the duke's strongly expressed preference for that department and because he (Russell) thought it due to Newcastle 'to presume in favour of his proficiency'. He made it clear, however, that the basic reason for his present proposal was his conviction that 'the Prime Minister must be himself the active and moving spirit of the whole machine, or the Minister of War must have delegated authority to control other departments'. He was ready to abide by the temporary arrangement of a Secretary at War, if only Aberdeen would agree to appoint a Minister of War with 'vigour and authority'.[2] Aberdeen replied at length on 30 November, standing by his previous views and answering some specific charges Russell had brought against Newcastle, regarding the slowness in producing reinforcements. As for Palmerston, Aberdeen argued, he had taken the Home Office in preference to the Admiralty, because the duties were lighter; any change now would be unwarranted and an injustice to a colleague.[3] The arguments on either side were exhausted and in reply Russell merely reverted to his original recommendations, which he now proposed to bring before the cabinet.[4]

Lord John showed the correspondence to Palmerston and was probably taken aback by the latter's strong defence of the office of Secretary at War, which, after all, he had occupied for many years. On the question of his replacing the duke of Newcastle Palmerston was more guarded. He rejected Aberdeen's objections as to his age, but he pointed out that the opportunity for the change was passed; nor was he prepared to blame the present Secretary for what had gone wrong. Without such distinct grounds it would be wrong to break up the government by demanding such a change.[5]

Aberdeen showed the original exchange of letters to Graham, Gladstone and Herbert, who were all highly indignant, and to

[1] Add. MS. 38080, fols. 102–4, 21 November 1854.
[2] Gooch, *Later correspondence*, II, 174–5, 28 November 1854 (original in Add. MS. 43068, fols. 198–206).
[3] PRO 30/22/11/F, fols. 1781–3 (partly printed in Gooch, *Later correspondence*, II, 175–6).
[4] Add. MS. 43068, fols. 221–2, 3 December 1854 (Walpole, *Russell*, II, 235). The whole exchange of correspondence between Aberdeen and Russell is printed in *P.P. 1854–5*, IX, pt. 3, Appendix to *Fourth report*, 355–60, and as an Appendix to *Ab. Cor. 1854–5*, pp. 327–43.
[5] Gooch, *Later correspondence*, II, 176–8, 3 December 1854 (original in PRO 30/22/11/F, fols. 1848–52).

Newcastle, who, according to Prince Albert, 'begged most earnestly to let himself be removed', if this was 'the only mode to keep the Cabinet together'. Nevertheless, according to the same authority, the poor duke was 'deeply mortified by the heartless manner' in which Lord John thus thought to undermine his 'reputation and public position'. When Aberdeen showed the correspondence to the queen she expressed herself as 'horrified' by what she called Lord John's 'wickedness' and 'levity'. In discussing the matter with her and the prince, Aberdeen said it was not yet known whether Palmerston joined Russell, but he rather doubted it; if so the government would be unable to go on, but if not Lord John would probably drop the matter and they would hear no more of it.[1] This proved to be a remarkably accurate forecast of what would happen.

At a cabinet meeting on 4 December Russell said that he had a subject to raise which was 'very important and not very agreeable'. He expressed his opinions about the War Department, but did not indicate his proposals, since, he said, the Prime Minister had refused them. Aberdeen undertook to circulate the correspondence, which was discussed at a cabinet dinner at his house on the 6th. According to Argyll's account of the meeting the Prime Minister observed that Russell's objections really pointed not to a change in the departments, but in the head of the government; 'that if Lord John could get the Cabinet, or any Cabinet, to join him, he (Aberdeen) would not stand for a moment in his way; that he had not wished to keep his present place, but had felt the difficulty in getting out of it, now as much as ever, or more than ever, and he was quite ready to go if he could see his way to any other combination'. Russell made no attempt to criticise Newcastle, but said 'he felt uncomfortable in his position as a leader whom nobody followed'; that he felt the War Minister should be in the Commons and that Palmerston should hold that office. Palmerston, in Argyll's words, 'behaved splendidly' and refused to give Russell any support. He observed that, if ministers were to be turned out for lack of results, then he himself should resign, since all his measures had failed in the last session. Aberdeen gravely observed that Palmerston's failure must have

---

[1] R.A. A 84, fol. 8, 25 November 1854 queen to Aberdeen (copy): R.A. G 20, fol. 17, memorandum of Prince Albert, 24 November 1854; *Letters of Queen Victoria*, III, 67–8, Aberdeen to the queen, 23 November 1854. Graham considered that Aberdeen's removal was Russell's real intention and commented that it was 'not pleasant *to stand upon a mine* when you are about to engage the Enemy in front' (Add. MS. 43191, fols. 270–4, 5 December 1854).

been due to want of vigour and, according to Argyll, the laughter raised by this sally helped to ease the tension. Finding no support from any of his colleagues Lord John told them that he would have to retire after the December adjournment of parliament.[1] The others sought to discourage him and Molesworth argued that it would be unconstitutional for him to defend the government in the December sitting with the intention of resigning. 'This was received with silence,' according to Gladstone, who said that Wood as well as Palmerston pooh-poohed Russell's proposals, but the latter stood by his avowal. 'The meeting ended', according to Gladstone's account, 'with his menace standing before us, and a tacit permission to him to lead and defend the Government at the meeting of Parlt.'[2]

In his report of the meeting to the queen, Aberdeen said that when the constitutional propriety of his staying on through the December sitting of parliament had been questioned Russell had replied that if such was the case he would request Lord Aberdeen to convey his resignation to the queen the following morning. The Prime Minister postponed any decision until he had seen the queen.[3]

According to his wife Lord Clarendon was 'profoundly disgusted with Lord John's selfish and unpatriotic conduct' and sympathetic to the Peelite ministers, Newcastle and Herbert, whose conduct he approved. In a memorandum on Russell's part at the cabinet dinner Clarendon wrote:

John Russell was wrong in his facts, insolent in his assertions and most ill-tempered in his replies. No spoilt child could be more perverse or inaccessible either to kind or firm words, and his look was as if he had plied himself with wine in order to get courage for doing what he felt was wrong, for he several times compared himself to the juryman who complained of the eleven obstinate fellows in the box with him. Everybody was dead against him, though some said nothing...Aberdeen's conduct was a most remarkable contrast and there the matter rests.[4]

One Whig colleague, however, remonstrated with Russell after the meeting. On the following day his candid friend Sir Charles Wood

[1] Argyll, *Autobiography*, I, 508–10.
[2] Add. MS. 44778, fols. 188–90, Gladstone memorandum, 6 December 1854. In a letter to Aberdeen on the following day regarding the inconclusive nature of the meeting Gladstone reiterated Molesworth's point questioning the constitutionality of Russell's proposal to postpone his resignation until after the session (fols. 192–3).
[3] *Letters of Queen Victoria*, III, 72–4, 7 December 1854.
[4] Maxwell, *Clarendon*, II, 53–4. Maxwell misdates the cabinet dinner as 8 December.

addressed to his chief one of his long cajoling epistles, full of unpalatable home truths. He also reminded Russell that six months earlier he had preferred Newcastle to Palmerston in the newly separated War Office and bluntly told him that it was now too late to change. Wood admitted that matters had not been conducted entirely as he might have wished, but he did not think that there was 'much to find fault with'. Indeed he thought it a very remarkable achievement to have put an army of 30,000 men in the field at such short notice, when only two years ago it was said that Britain did not have a movable army of 15,000 or 10,000 men. The home government, he maintained, had sent out an abundance of stores and was not responsible for mismanagement in the field. To change ministers now would be a confession of blunder that 'would be destruction to us all', he argued. 'We must stand together—fight the battle together for the past—work together to make the machine go for the future as it ought to do.' Otherwise they would cut as poor a figure as did Lord Goderich's government in 1827. 'Depend upon it,' he continued, 'the House of C. will support us stoutly...It would be treason & no less to break up the Government at present.'

Admitting that Russell's position as a party leader was a difficult one, he went on to make some interesting observations about the state of party:

Party in the old sense of Pitt & Fox, Whig & Tory, does not exist, & never will again. How soon after the Reform Bill did Lord Grey's apparently irresistible Government break to pieces? Party feeling did not prevent that ...& the formation of the present Government did more in the same direction. But in truth, it is the inevitable result of the change in the construction of the H. of Commons. The old Whig gentry 20 years ago had the traditionary attachment to party. What does such a man as my colleague, a new manufacturer, care for such matters? What do half the new members care for the old Whig party?...I think you must accommodate yourself to the altered political feeling of the H. of C. & the country as to party.

With regard to last session I think you are mistaken. Mostly every question on which we were beaten involved religious feelings more or less. You cannot reason about them, and cannot control men's feelings on such subjects ...[he proceeded to cite examples] These observations apply to the anti-popery matters, and only in a less degree to education and church rates. Our other defeats were on Palmerston's Health bills, where again the feeling of the country is Chadwickean fear...My firm belief therefore is that any leader of the liberal party must be prepared to reconcile himself to conduct on the part of his supporters which never could have occurred in old *party* times.

32-2

Wood reminded Russell of the situation under which the coalition had been formed and of the circumstances that prevented Aberdeen from giving way as intended.

But will what you are now doing render your leading a Government with the Peelites more easy [he continued]? How do you propose to construct a Government if this one is broken up by your going out on such ground? If a Whig Government cannot stand with the Peelites it certainly cannot stand without them. You could not expect Newcastle—Herbert or Graham to serve under you, or Gladstone, when you had broken up the present Government on the alleged conduct of some of them.

He dwelt on the danger of pushing the Peelites back into the arms of the Tories and told Russell that he could not thus 'promote the efficient conduct of the war', but would only put himself in 'a most awkward position'. Therefore, he exhorted Russell for the country's sake and his own to continue the fight together and thus they could defy the Russians in the Crimea and the opposition at home.[1]

On 8 December Russell attended the next cabinet, which met to consider the queen's speech. When he proposed an alteration in the draft to add a clause about strengthening the institutions of the country, Palmerston asked whether that meant Reform. On Russell's replying, 'It might, or it might not,' Palmerston hotly protested any such introduction of the Reform question, direct or indirect, to which Russell was heard to mutter: 'Then I shall bring forward the Reform Bill at once.' In Prince Albert's view Palmerston put on this little act to make it clear to the cabinet that there was no chance of cooperation between him and Russell.[2]

On the following day Aberdeen went down to Windsor, while the cabinet were still working on the throne speech. He told the queen that the whole cabinet were indignant with Russell, nobody more so than Lord Lansdowne, and that Graham and Gladstone were urging him to accept Russell's resignation. Nevertheless, he hesitated to make Russell a martyr; indeed he was certain that the government could not go on without Lord John. The latter had made his position very clear in conversation with Palmerston when he said: 'When the Cabinet was

---

[1] PRO 30/22/11/F, fols. 1886–95, 7 December 1854. For Russell's reply of 9 December, thanking Wood for his interest but defending his own position, see Add. MS. 49531, fols. 86–8.

[2] *Letters of Queen Victoria*, III, 75–6 (from a memorandum by Prince Albert of 9 December 1854).

formed, I always understood that Lord Aberdeen would soon give me up my old place; it has now lasted more than two years, and he seemed to get enamoured with office, and I could not meet the House of Commons in the position I was in last Session.' Palmerston sarcastically asked him what he would say to the country after he had succeeded in bringing the government down. Would he say: 'Here I am. I have triumphed and have displaced in the midst of most hazardous operations, all the ablest men the Country has produced; but I shall take their place with Mr Vernon Smith, Lord Seymour, Lord Minto, and others.' The royal couple and Lord Aberdeen agreed with heavy hearts that when Lord John went, although the time of his resignation was still uncertain, Lord Palmerston must take his place as leader in the House of Commons. Aberdeen found this distasteful not only because of the long mutual opposition between himself and Palmerston, but also from the fact 'that Lord Palmerston loved war for war's sake, and he peace for peace' sake'. He consoled himself, however, with the thought that in this respect Palmerston was no worse than Russell, while, on the other hand, 'he gave greater weight to the consideration of what was practicable'.[1]

On the 9th Aberdeen sent to the queen the cabinet's draft of the speech from the throne with a note to say that there was no further reference in the cabinet to Russell's resignation. 'Towards the end of the Cabinet', he added, 'a very unpleasant discussion took place, raised by Ld J. Russell on the subject of the dismissal of Mr Kennedy...in which he reflected very severely on Mr Gladstone.'[2]

The Peelite members of the cabinet were naturally outraged by Russell's conduct, none more than the duke of Argyll, but unlike Graham and Gladstone, he advised against letting Russell go. 'Under no ordinary circumstances ought it to be tolerated', he wrote to Graham, 'that any member of a government should treat his colleagues as Ld John has lately dealt with one after another *all around*.' Yet he was 'disposed to pass over these displays of temper and personal ambition with the contempt which they deserve', noting that Russell was 'not supported by any one member of his own former party'.[3]

[1] *Ibid.* pp. 74–7.   [2] R.A. A 84, fol. 21, 9 December 1854.
[3] Graham Papers, Sunday [10] December 1854. Argyll also alluded to difficulties regarding the Kennedy case and the proposed appointment of Hayward, in which he suspected that Russell was aiming 'to raise *Whig* against *Peelite*'. 'But I am sure', he concluded, 'that the more we put Ld John in the wrong, by overlooking his caprices and his temper, the better we shall fulfill our duty to the country and to ourselves.'

This is borne out by the letters which one of his Whig colleagues addressed to Russell on the subject. 'I do not agree with you in thinking that Palmerston would be a better Secretary of War than Newcastle', Granville wrote to him on 23 December. 'The best man connected with the Department appears to be Sidney Herbert. He is by far the best judge of men, is practical, unegotistical, and without official nonsense.' He added the interesting observation that Lord Hardinge was not fit to be commander-in-chief at such a crisis, but that he had the merit that he could be bullied by Herbert, Newcastle and the prince into making improvements 'which old military men of sterner stuff would resent'.[1] Lord Lansdowne had expressed a similar viewpoint, saying that he did not see how a minister who had recently been entrusted by his colleagues with such arduous duties as the duke of Newcastle had been, could 'be expected so soon after to transfer them to other hands without a slur upon his character and conduct', especially when they had a speaker 'so able and so popular as Sidney Herbert'[2] to answer military questions in the House of Commons.

Sir Charles Wood returned to the fray with another sixteen pages, once again protesting his loyalty to Russell, but warning him that he was on the verge of a decision that would affect 'the interests of the country and the position of the liberal party'. He repudiated Russell's suggestion that he (Wood) was only concerned with their staying on for the sake of office. 'It is I think only justice to those with whom we have been associated to bear testimony to their uniform straightforwardness,' he wrote, but he regretted that Russell had not been on more intimate terms with the men who directed the War Departments. He reiterated his view that he thought the country would be much better off with a liberal government on grounds of departmental administration alone. In particular he stressed the importance of Russell himself administering the education funds. He denied that the government's measures were 'after the manner of the worst Tories', as Russell had insinuated, and pointed out that the Peelites had shown no indisposition to liberal measures; indeed, on many points, he wrote, 'some of them go as far or further than ourselves'. He reminded Russell that the Peelites had been with him on Reform, but that the temper of the House was against it.

[1] Gooch, *Later correspondence*, II, 180, 23 December 1854.
[2] PRO 30/22/11/F, fols. 1910–13, 10 December 1854. This letter is printed by Walpole (*Russell*, II, 236–7) with an omission and only partly reproduced by Gooch, under the wrong date (*Later correspondence*, II, 179–80); neither includes the sentence about Herbert.

THE END OF THE COALITION

'Now when you complain of the measures of the government as not having been liberal enough, can you say that they have not been as liberal as the liberal party in the H. of Commons approved?' he asked. In fact there was no support for organic change in the old Whig party, while a large portion of the Liberal party took an anti-popery line in opposition to Russell's own principles. He concluded with an earnest appeal to Russell to reconsider his position and listen to the advice of his old colleagues [1]

In the end this combined onslaught was once again too much for the little man, and on 15 December he told Lansdowne that he could throw into the fire an earlier letter setting out his demands, but he reiterated the complaint that he did not think Aberdeen treated him with the confidence that alone could 'enable a leader of the House of Commons to carry on business with satisfaction'.[2]

On the same day Russell attended a cabinet meeting and took part in the discussion as if nothing had ever happened. After the meeting Aberdeen alluded to their correspondence. 'Without any embarrassment, or apparent sense of inconsistency', Aberdeen told the queen, 'he at once admitted that he had changed his intention, and attributed it chiefly to a conversation yesterday with Lord Panmure, who, although a great military reformer, had convinced him that the present was not a fitting time for his proposed changes.' This, of course, was self-deception or worse, since the removal of Aberdeen had been Russell's real object. Nevertheless, the Prime Minister told the queen he felt disposed to be satisfied, despite the element of insecurity that remained and the sense of self-degradation in submitting to such action, since the alternative would lead to greater evils. He said that he had yielded nothing, but that he had 'received Lord John's change without resentment or displeasure'.[3] The storm had subsided for the moment, but the danger was not past.

While this melancholy power struggle was going on behind the closed doors of the cabinet, significant decisions respecting the war were being taken (in addition to those already mentioned in the previous chapter) in an important series of some twenty cabinet meetings held between 10 November and the end of December. The major problem

[1] PRO 30/22/11/F, fols. 1914–22, 11 December 1854. Gooch prints some extracts from this letter (*Later correspondence*, II, 179) without indicating a gap of fourteen pages.
[2] Walpole, *Russell*, II, 237.
[3] *Letters of Queen Victoria*, III, 77–8, 16 December 1854.

in the eyes of the cabinet during this period was reinforcements. Raglan dwelt on this need in despatches of 28 October, 3 and 13 November and 18 December,[1] and the ministers strained, if belatedly and not too effectively, to meet his demands.

It had been a remarkable achievement, as Wood reminded Russell, for the country so quickly to have produced from its small regular army scattered around the world an expeditionary force of some five divisions earlier that year. It had been done by withdrawing troops from garrisons abroad and by stripping depots to bring battalions up to strength, but no sufficient provision had been made for an adequate stream of reinforcements in the event of a prolonged and costly war. A total of 33,586 officers and men, including first-line reinforcements, had been sent to the East before the end of August, of whom 26,800 had been landed in the Crimea before the battle of the Alma.[2] Another 4,141 reinforcements had been sent out in September and October and 7,037 in November.[3] 'If Sebastopol be not taken it will not be for want of means', Graham observed complacently to Herbert early in November in a note spelling out the significance of these figures in terms of shipping.[4]

On 12 December Herbert was able to announce that a total of between 54,000 and 55,000 officers and men had been sent to the East or were in depots awaiting transport.[5] It is difficult to reconcile these figures with the small number available for duty in the trenches in January, but it is a familiar phenomenon of military history that the number of troops actually in the field tends to fall far short of the impressive totals produced on paper by government spokesmen, which do not reflect the extraordinary rates of wastage common to all armies, and which fail to indicate the numbers involved in what today is called the tail of an army. The French emperor complained of this very matter in a conversation with Palmerston, when the latter visited Paris in the latter part of November, saying that he could not understand what had happened to upwards of 70,000 troops which he had sent to the Crimea, when General Canrobert's last report only listed 39,000.[6] In the case of Lord

---

[1] Martineau, *Newcastle*, pp. 199–200.
[2] *P.P. 1854-5*, IX, pt. 2, *Third report*, Appendix, 473, 479. According to this return 7,645 all ranks belonging to regiments joined the Army in the Crimea after the Alma; see also evidence of duke of Newcastle, *ibid.* p. 188.
[3] *Hansard*, CXXXVI, 135, S. Herbert, 12 December 1854.
[4] Herbert Papers, Graham, 7 November 1854.   [5] *Hansard*, CXXXVI, 136–7.
[6] MS. Clar. Dep. C15, fols. 256–8, 24 November 1854.

Raglan's army, as we have seen, the loss from sickness was very high. In August the number of men reported sick was 11,236; in October it had risen to 11,988, and in January it was 23,076.[1]

The war, of course, had stimulated some increase in recruiting, especially in the weeks following the news of the Alma. Between 1 February and 6 November 23,613 men had been recruited, which was 14,500 more than normally would have been the case, and of these some 7,000 came from the militia. Eighteen regiments of militia, numbering some 12,000 men, were embodied in May, June and July, but these were intended for garrison service and, significantly, their colonels had requested that they 'might be protected against the indiscipline and debauchery which the presence of active recruiting parties engenders'.[2] Their strength was not considered sufficient to provide recruits for active service in addition to their primary function.

The two men who probably gave the most thoughtful consideration to this problem of reinforcement were the prince consort and Sidney Herbert. On 11 November the prince wrote to Aberdeen to warn him that the government would never be forgiven if Raglan succumbed for lack of support. Observing that they had reached the bottom of the barrel, that recruiting did not keep pace with the losses, and that the recruits were 'mere boys, unfit for foreign service', he suggested a number of steps that might be taken: the completion of the militia by ballot and the issuance of a proclamation inviting militiamen to join the army; the despatch of militia regiments abroad to release regular regiments from garrison duty for service in the Crimea; authorisation for the enlistment of foreigners and the formation of a foreign legion.[3] Some of these steps had already been thought of by the ministers.

A few days earlier, in a lucid memorandum marshalling all the relevant facts, Sidney Herbert had proposed to increase the number of embodied regiments; he also proposed to withdraw restrictions on recruiting parties visiting embodied regiments and to allow them to recruit up to one-quarter of the embodied regiment's strength. Since the militiaman was a more valuable recruit than the man off the street, he also proposed to increase the bounty for militiamen.[4]

These recommendations were adopted without delay and in the next

[1] P.P. 1854–5, IX, pt. 2, Appendix 10 to *Third report*, 470.
[2] *Ibid.* pt. 3, Appendix 11 to *Fourth report*, 335–8, memorandum of S. Herbert, 6 November 1854.
[3] *Ab. Cor. 1854–5*, pp. 272–4.
[4] P.P. 1854–5, IX, pt. 3, Appendix 11 to *Fourth report*, 335–8.

few weeks Herbert, acting in the absence of the Home Secretary, sent out notices to nine fresh regiments to embody; recruiting was also begun in the existing embodied regiments, which were pronounced to be in a high state of discipline. On 23 November in a second memorandum Herbert proposed a much more extensive embodiment, going beyond the barrack space available, even though it meant billeting the men on local publicans. Under the Mutiny Act the publican received no remuneration beyond a halfpenny a day for salt and what the soldier himself might spend ! Herbert now generously proposed to augment this billet payment to a penny halfpenny or twopence a day, to be paid direct to the publican. He recognised that there might be some problem about clothing, since the troops in the Crimea would have priority, but there was no time to be lost. 'A man enlisted now is worth five embodied next year', he concluded. 'Our army is exhausted and we have a new army to create.'[1]

This further embodiment was also approved by the cabinet, and by 27 November the number of embodied regiments was raised to sixty-one, of which six or nine of the original eighteen were destined for garrison duty in the Mediterranean. By this time, however, the news of Inkerman increased Herbert's apprehension and in a third memorandum he now suggested that recruiting from the newly embodied regiments might go beyond the authorised twenty-five per cent of their strength, for the depots of the line regiments were drained and had to be filled. The army in the East, he observed ominously, had been built up by discounting the future. You might recruit and train 20,000 men in a few months but you could not turn boys into men. As always England was slow at the beginning of a war because of her lack of a large peacetime army. 'Clearly the war with Russia will not be the affair of a year', he concluded.[2]

Early in November Louis Napoleon offered some relief to the overall problem of reinforcements by promising 8,000 additional troops if the British would supply the shipping. Newcastle was inclined to dismiss this offer as insincere and Graham pointed out that the French had the necessary ships since their Baltic fleet had just returned to Cherbourg. Clarendon, however, maintained that they were in no position to reject

[1] Ref. in n. 4 on previous p., pp. 339–40, second memorandum, 23 November 1854.
[2] Ibid. pp. 340–1, third memorandum, 27 November 1854. Newcastle, it may be noted, told the Roebuck committee that he thought too much reliance had been put on recruiting from the militia; he said that he had expressed this view to the Horse Guards, but he did not know with what effect (ibid. pt. 2, Third report, 203)

such assistance, and high words passed between him and the duke of Newcastle at the cabinet meeting of 11 November. He insisted that the ships must be found and when Graham said they were not available the Foreign Secretary asked him whether he had gone to the great steam-ship companies. Sir James put his pride in his pocket, followed up this suggestion, and at the meeting of the 13th announced that the ships were available through the assistance of Mr Samuel Cunard.[1]

Some rearrangement of shipping was required to divert the closest steamers to Toulon, where the French troops were to be picked up. Lord Raglan was instructed to send back to Toulon the three large steamers which had arrived in the Black Sea with British reinforcements; a fourth ship was to sail from England to Toulon, and a fifth was scheduled to call there on 2 December. Further steamers were to be secured to pick up the balance of 2,200 men.[2]

This incident caused Argyll to write to Russell that it had given a 'very rude shock' to his confidence in 'Departmental ideas of the Possible'. He suggested sending the garrison of the Ionian Islands im-mediately to the Crimea and calling a special session of parliament to authorise the immediate release of militia regiments for garrison duty then rather than in March, as Newcastle intended. 'Be so good as to keep this letter to yourself', he added, 'as it might seem like preaching want of confidence in colleagues. But this is not the least my intention or my feeling. I believe Graham and Newcastle administer their Departments well and ably, as much so as anyone I know of could do so. But there are innate tendencies in all Departmental administration which require the vigilance of those who look upon the subject from other points of view.'[3] It may be noted that this interesting letter was sent on the same day that

---

[1] Maxwell, *Clarendon*, II, 49–50; R.A. G18, fol. 134, Aberdeen to the queen, 10 November 1854; Herbert Papers, Graham, 7 November 1854, emphasising the availability of the French Baltic fleet. Palmerston, writing from Paris the following week, supported the French request, arguing that it was not unreasonable, that it was no time for making bargains and that it would be wise to take them up on their promises of reinforcements by helping to supply the transport (MS. Clar. C15, fol. 248, 19 November 1854).

[2] Graham Papers, Graham to Palmerston, 14 November 1854, enclosing a memorandum. Graham pointed out that British army requisitions for transport had been postponed to meet the French request. The shipping situation was well reflected in a letter Graham sent to Newcastle on 18 November which listed five ships to carry 3,250 men between 21 and 25 November and a sixth to carry 500 on 2 December, exclusive of the 90th Regiment, which had sailed that morning, and the ships for the 8,000 French reinforce-ments (Graham Papers).

[3] PRO 30/22/11/F, fols. 1682–7, Argyll, 17 November 1854.

GIVING THE OFFICE

Johnny R – ll. 'I say, Abby, my old-un, the Vestminster sessions is fixed
for the 12th. If you ain't prepared with your defence, you'd better cut.'

(reproduced from *Punch*)

Russell wrote his memorandum urging Newcastle's relinquishment of
the War Office.

Argyll's proposal for a December meeting of parliament was also
taken up by Palmerston, writing from Paris, and on 24 November the
cabinet decided to summon a special meeting for the 12th of the following month. Bills were to be introduced seeking authorisation for the
despatch of six or eight regiments of militia to the Mediterranean to

relieve garrison troops for service in the Crimea, and for the recruitment of foreign adult troops and their training in England.[1] Both measures had been proposed by Prince Albert in his memorandum, and the latter proposal had also been made by Lord Raglan.[2]

Other measures for augmenting the army were worked out by an *ad hoc* committee consisting of the prince consort, the two ministers, Newcastle and Herbert, and the commander-in-chief, Lord Hardinge.[3] Their proposals, which were approved by the cabinet on 1 December,[4] provided for the increase of the establishment of each of the forty-four regiments under Lord Raglan's command from twelve to sixteen companies; eight of these companies were to be with the army, four to be kept training in England, and another four doing advanced training in a great new depot to be formed in Malta, which would hold an army of reserve of 16,000 troops. The depots in England would continuously feed reinforcements into the depot at Malta. Provision was also made for an addition of 880 officers, some to be drawn from the militia on the condition of their bringing 200 men each with them. The quota of the militia volunteers for the army was to be raised from a quarter to a third of their establishments. Finally, a third battalion was to be added to the Rifle Brigade, which, according to the prince, was 'the most popular Corps in the service' and was always 'called upon in an emergency'. It was estimated that 20,000 men would be required to implement these plans, of which 10,000 would come from the militia. Thus everything still turned on increasing the rate of enlistment and eventually this led to an increase in the bounty.

It will be observed that everything that was done was essentially an extension of peacetime regular recruiting; there was no attempt to appeal to the public for volunteers for the duration of the war, as was to be the case in the twentieth century. The public image of the soldier, his low pay and wretched living conditions on the one hand and public parsimony on the other made the concept of a citizen army an unlikely one in the mid-Victorian era. The average Englishman wanted to see

[1] PRO 30/12/ 11 F, fols. 1726–9, Palmerston to Russell, 22 November 1854; R.A. A84, fol. 7, Aberdeen to queen, 24 November 1954.
[2] Stanmore, *Herbert*, I, 238.
[3] *P.P. 1854–5*, IX, pt. 2, *Third report*, evidence of duke of Newcastle, 122; *ibid.* pt. 3, *Fourth report*, evidence of S. Herbert, 191; R.A. G20, fol. 47, memorandum of Prince Albert, 30 November 1854.
[4] R.A. A84, fol. 11, Aberdeen to queen, 1 December 1854; at the same meeting it was resolved to contract with a Mr Peto to build a railway from Balaclava to the camp.

the war fought vigorously, but it did not occur to him that he personally need be involved, beyond perhaps some minor increase in taxation. Moreover, the immediate need was for at least partially trained men, and these were naturally to be sought in the militia, or in foreign recruits. There was no easy or rapid solution to this ever-present problem of manpower, but, before some of the decisions could be implemented, the whole case had to be laid before an anxious parliament, hastily summoned to meet almost on the eve of the first wartime Christmas in forty years.

The December meeting of parliament and the 'Times' change of front

The queen opened the special sitting of the new session on 12 December with a speech from the throne that was both brief and vague. After alluding to the victories of the British and French troops in the Crimea and the need for reinforcements, she was made to say, enigmatically, that, although she expected the prosecution of the war would engage parliament's chief attention, she trusted that 'other Matters of great Interest and Importance' would not be neglected; and she concluded with the pious hope that under God's providence they might bring the war to a successful termination.[1]

In the debate that ensued Lord Derby, as Aberdeen told the queen, despite professions of moderation, indulged in strong censure and criticism, which The Times characterised as 'misrepresentation and captiousness'.[2] While praising the brave deeds of the army in eloquent language he delivered a slashing attack on the government for not doing enough and for its slowness and lack of foresight in what it had done.[3] According to Greville, Newcastle was quite unequal to meeting Derby in debate and his response sounded dull and futile, although in actual fact his case was not a bad one.[4] The Times more charitably pronounced his statement to be 'ingenuous, candid to the verge of discretion, and conclusive on many of the points urged against his administration'.[5] His speech was full of statistics respecting the number of troops and reinforcements that had been sent to the East and the great quantities of equipment that were supplied to them. He admitted that defects had

[1] Hansard, CXXXVI, 1–3.
[2] R.A. G20, fol. 112, 12 December 1854; The Times, 13 December 1854.
[3] Hansard, CXXXVI, 10–36.
[4] Greville Memoirs, VII, 84.　　　[5] The Times, 13 December 1854.

developed in the medical services, but he blamed this not on the medical department itself but 'on that ill-judged economy which prevented an efficient medical department being kept up in time of peace'.[1] All the statistics he could quote to show what had been done could not blot out, however, the stories that were daily appearing about the fearsome suffering of the sick and wounded soldiers. The government was also severely criticised by Lord Ellenborough, who, according to Aberdeen, was answered vigorously by the duke of Argyll.[2]

In the House of Commons the initial opposition attack by Sir John Pakington[3] was answered by Sidney Herbert,[4] who undertook a straightforward narrative of the events of the war in what Greville described as an excellent speech. Presenting statistics with respect to the size of the original force under Lord Raglan's command and the number of reinforcements subsequently sent out, he reminded his hearers why it was that England could never put large reinforcements into the field quickly in the early stages of a war:

It has been the fault of every Parliament; we have always had the same stereotyped system of economy in military affairs...I am as much to blame as anyone...but whenever I have brought forward, as I have done, what are called Peace Estimates, I have constantly been met with Motions for large reductions. I say, therefore, that it has been the fault of all parties, all Administrations, and every Parliament...I have seen Administrations formed of various parties—I have seen them taking different courses on almost every conceivable subject, but on one they have all agreed, and that has been the one to which I have alluded—one of improvident economy.[5]

Herbert was followed by Layard, freshly returned from the Crimea, who as usual was full of criticism of everyone who failed to take his advice. Once again he sought to create division in the coalition by imploring Lord John Russell through the position he held 'as the head of the great Liberal party' to use his influence 'to prevail upon his colleagues to adopt, ere it be too late, a policy' that would 'be more consistent with the honour, the true interests, and the immortal traditions of this mighty empire'.[6]

Disraeli, in a typical jeering harangue, noted the failure of any member of the government to answer Layard and ridiculed Herbert's attempts

[1] *Hansard*, CXXXVI, 36–74.
[2] R.A. G20, fol. 112, Aberdeen to queen, 15 December 1854.
[3] *Hansard*, CXXXVI, 105–23.
[4] *Ibid.* 129–60.   [5] *Ibid.* 136.   [6] *Ibid.* 160–95.

with elaborate statistics to answer charges that had not been made. He attacked the overall planning of the war, or the lack of it, rather than the difficulties arising in the commissariat after forty years of peace.[1] Russell replied briefly, coldly contrasting the patriotism of Pakington's speech with the complete lack of it that he found in Disraeli's, but he made no effort to repudiate Layard's insinuations regarding conflicting opinions in the coalition cabinet.[2] Before the debate was concluded the House was entertained by a brief intervention from Colonel Sibthorp, who, apparently with reference to the Austrian treaty, gratuitously declared that he 'had no very great admiration for foreigners', and that 'he was sure that it would take ninety-nine foreigners to make one thorough good Englishman'.[3]

On 15 December both Houses unanimously agreed to formal motions of thanks to the armed forces in the Crimea and their various commanders.[4] In the Commons Layard inevitably felt constrained to supplement Lord John's eulogy of the two services by relating various stories of valorous deeds drawn from his own experience at the scene of battle, but the occasion was marred by another member denouncing him for derogatory remarks that he was alleged to have made about Admiral Dundas. With some embarrassment Layard had to admit that he had made such criticisms and to promise that he would raise charges on a later occasion.[5] Obviously votes of thanks are somewhat cheapened when in the same breath it is admitted that some of those now thanked may later be impugned. Further embarrassment was occasioned by the discovery that the names of the two senior officers in the Crimean army most open to criticism, those of the Adjutant General and the Quartermaster General, had been inadvertently left off the list. Three days later the duke of Newcastle had sheepishly to admit what in a later day might have been called a Freudian lapse of memory and to request the addition of the names of Generals Estcourt and Airey to the list.[6]

The Foreign Enlistment Bill was first introduced in the House of Lords, where the second reading was debated and passed on 14 December, and the third reading after further debate was approved without a division on the 18th.[7] The purpose of the bill was to allow the government to recruit troops from abroad and to train up to 15,000 in England for despatch to the Crimea. It was criticised severely by Ellenborough,

---

[1] *Hansard*, CXXXVI, 197–215.   [2] *Ibid.* 215–23.   [3] *Ibid.* 230.
[4] *Ibid.* 313–37, 378–414.   [5] *Ibid.* 406–8.   [6] *Ibid.* 423–4.
[7] *Ibid.* 253–91, 344–72, 415–21, 429–61.

Derby and several other peers as being unconstitutional, impolitic and degrading. Ellenborough spoke against the bill at every stage and on one occasion broadened his attack to comment on the lack of aptitude of the ministers for conducting war.[1] Newcastle, Aberdeen, Argyll, Granville and Lansdowne, speaking for the government, emphasised the historical precedents. Granville effectively quoted a speech of Wellington's in support of Derby's Militia Bill of 1852 in which he had dwelt upon the important role played by foreign troops under British command in previous wars, and Newcastle made it clear that the bill did not allow the use of such troops in the United Kingdom. The motion to go into committee was contested and sustained by a vote of 55 to 43.[2] To meet some of the opposition objections the government agreed to reduce the number from 15,000 to 10,000.

The bill was debated through its various stages for four solid days in the House of Commons from 19 to 22 December inclusive.[3] It was defended by Russell, Herbert, Palmerston and others, who again emphasised the historical precedents and its supplementary nature. England had produced, and was capable of producing, large forces on her own, but it was desirable to speed up this process by obtaining additional trained soldiers from Europe. The recruits they were looking for, according to Herbert, were those who had been released from military service in Germany at the age of 26. Every year such men were passing through England on their way to settle in Canada or the United States. When asked whether the British taxpayers would be responsible for the support of their families, Herbert said that they would seek unmarried recruits, but that, where a desirable man might happen to be married, his family could proceed to the colonies.[4] (In this way, presumably, the colonial taxpayer was to be given a chance to participate in the war effort.) When one of the critics argued that the government could not attach great importance to the scheme when they were prepared to limit the number to 10,000, Palmerston quickly pointed out that the limitation was only on the number of such troops to be allowed in the United Kingdom at one time.[5] The government needed no authority to employ foreign troops abroad beyond the vote of the estimates for their support. Sir B. Lytton, Lord Stanley and Disraeli led the opposition from the other side of the House, Disraeli quoting

---

[1] *Ibid.* 349–50.   [2] *Ibid.* 372.
[3] *Ibid.* 507–618, 629–82, 746–87, 794–895.
[4] *Ibid.* 558–9, 769.   [5] *Ibid.* 586.

THE CONDUCT OF THE WAR

various letters from the duke of Wellington to show his low opinion of mercenary troops,[1] but there were also opponents on the Liberal benches. Milner Gibson said that he would have preferred to abstain, but that in conscience he had to vote against the bill. His opposition was on the ground of principle; either the foreigners were to be enlisted over the objection of their own governments or their governments were being asked to connive in an unneutral act.[2] Bright took the opportunity to renew his condemnation of the war and of 'the incapable and guilty administration' which conducted it.[3] Cobden argued that it was positively immoral to ask anyone to fight who had no patriotic interest in the war. 'It is wholesale assassination to employ them,' he avowed. He said it was ridiculous to suppose that any German who had booked his passage from the Rhine to Cincinnati or Buffalo, most probably with his family, was going to break the journey in England to go to Sebastopol.[4] Colonel Sibthorp, expressing his opposition in his own inimitable way—brief, but pungent—is reported to have said: 'The measure was an underhanded measure—a low, dirty, mean, paltry, cowardly measure—a measure unworthy of an English Government.' He reiterated his lack of confidence in the ministers with the exception of the Home Secretary. 'With that exception, the Lord have mercy on such a set!' he piously concluded.[5]

The main interest in the debate lies in the two divisions where, despite strong opposition from the Conservative leaders, Disraeli, Stanley, Pakington, Bulwer Lytton et al., and rebels from their own benches, the government were sustained by comparatively safe majorities; the second reading was passed by 241 to 202[6] and the third reading by 173 to 135.[7] On the second reading the bill was supported by the 30 Peelites who voted and by some 14 independent Conservatives, but it was opposed by 2 independent Irish and 21 Liberals, including Cobden, Bright, and Milner Gibson, most of whom were from midland or northern boroughs.[8]

---

[1] *Hansard*, CXXXVI, 596–9. [2] *Ibid.* 548–52. [3] *Ibid.* 883–93.
[4] *Ibid.* 667–8. [5] *Ibid.* 617. [6] *Ibid.* 618 and Appendix.
[7] *Ibid.* 893–5.
[8] See Appendixes A and B below. The Liberal opponents were: Alcock (Surrey), Bagshawe (Harwich), Baines (Leeds), Baring, Sir F. T. (Portsmouth), Bright (Manchester), Chambers (Greenwich), Cobbett (Oldham), Cobden (Yorkshire—the only county member), Fitzwilliam (Malton), Gardner (Leicester), Geach (Coventry), Milner Gibson (Manchester), Greenall (Warrington), Hadfield (Sheffield), Miall (Rochdale), Muntz (Birmingham), Murrough (Bridport), Ottway (Stafford), Phillimore, J. G. (Leominster), Shelley (Westminster), Smith, J. B. (Stockport).

The Militia Bill had an easier passage. As already indicated, its purpose was to allow the government to send embodied militia regiments abroad, particularly to Gibraltar, Malta and the Ionian Islands, to release the regular army garrisons there for service in the Crimea. While no specific limit was fixed in the bill it was understood that fewer than 15,000 men were required and probably not more than a dozen regiments. One important amendment, however, was accepted by the government, limiting the number allowed to go abroad from any one regiment to three-quarters of its establishment.[1] Derby and Disraeli criticised the principle of the bill in both Houses, but neither was prepared to make an issue of it, and so the bill passed after short debate without any divisions. Disraeli objected that it was unnecessary, a confession of weakness, and calculated to make service in the militia unpopular,[2] while Derby offered the more serious objection that it would prevent the Mediterranean garrisons from being the permanent source of reinforcement that they should be for the Crimea. He appeared to envisage a permanent stream of reinforcements passing to the Crimea through the existing Mediterranean garrisons rather than filling them with troops that could be used nowhere else.[3] In response Lord Granville agreed that this would be very desirable in theory, but in fact they had to make do with what they had.[4]

In introducing the bill in the House of Lords, Newcastle indicated the steps that had been already taken to embody the militia and to encourage enlistment from the militia to the regular army in the Crimea, but he pointed out that these steps alone would not suffice to produce the total number of something like 60,000 that would be required to keep Lord Raglan's army up to strength. For this purpose a large recruiting from the general public was still necessary and therefore the bounty had been increased, the age limit raised from twenty-five to thirty, and the physical requirement with regard to height reduced from five feet six to five feet four inches.[5] In response to a question in the Commons Sidney Herbert made it clear that more regiments had already indicated a wish to volunteer *en masse* than were required.[6]

There were many questions and some objections from members connected with the militia. Colonel Sibthorp was constantly on his feet and among other points demanded that full colonels should be allowed to keep their rank. When Palmerston answered that this would be

[1] *Ibid.* 464–9. [2] *Ibid.* 306–7. [3] *Ibid.* 697–8.
[4] *Ibid.* 710–11. [5] *Ibid.* 685–94. [6] *Ibid.* 473.

impossible the worthy Colonel asked what position then he would be in. With the wisdom of Solomon the Home Secretary replied:

The gallant officer is one of those persons of rank, position, fortune, and social connection in this country whom—with great deference I may be allowed to say—I should wish to see employed in exercising their beneficial influence at home, rather than in command of regiments of militia abroad. And though I should have the greatest confidence in a regiment going into action commanded by the gallant officer, nevertheless he must be conscious that his influence in his own circle at home might be attended with greater advantage to the nation.[1]

The gallant officer was not to be taken in, however, and in his usual devastating way responded: 'In reply to the facetious observations of the noble Lord, all I have to say is, that the sooner he and his colleagues vacate the Treasury bench, give up their salaries, and repair to the seat of war, the better it will be for the country.'[2] Even the Home Secretary had lost the redoubtable Sibthorp's favour.

Parliament adjourned for a month on 23 December with the work of the pre-Christmas sitting completed. The coalition had survived yet another test, but there was no promise that the political weather would improve, let alone the fortunes of their army in the Crimea. Indeed even before the adjournment there was one straw in the wind that boded ill. *The Times* suddenly changed its tune. Up until the middle of December its attitude with respect to the progress of the war had been on the whole optimistic, its tone one of moderate detachment, sometimes even complacency. For instance on 7 November it had said:

Upon the whole we think there is every reason for satisfaction and confidence. We do not appear to have suffered any material repulse... The army has answered, the fleet has exceeded, the expectations formed of its powers; the siege of Sebastopol has been sustained with extraordinary vigour.

It recognised that there was some disappointment that the Allies had 'not carried the strongest fortress in the Russian empire without a struggle',[3] but it pointed out that siege warfare was inevitably slow and uncertain and that there was no real ground for disappointment.[4] By 24 November the note of complacency had disappeared as it was admitted that the first concern now was how to protect the besieging armies. Stress was laid on the need for reinforcements. On several

---

[1] *Hansard,* CXXXVI, 479.   [2] *Ibid.* 480.
[3] *The Times,* 8 November 1854.   [4] *Ibid.* 9 and 18 November 1854.

REMANDED

J – y R – s – ll. 'Well, old boy, what luck?'
A – d – n. 'Weel, I'm just remanded till next sessions.'

(reproduced from *Punch*)

occasions it was asserted that the basic problem was supply[1] and as late as 8 December it was suggested that in this respect the difficulties of the Russians were as great. About the same time boasts were still being made as to the superiority of British over Russian equipment.[2]

When parliament met on 12 December *The Times* called for forbearance in debate. Earlier complaints about the government's lack of

[1] *Ibid.* 16 November and 8 December 1854. [2] *Ibid.* 6 December 1854.

vigour were no longer valid, it maintained, 'for never was war prosecuted so vigorously and resolutely as this at this moment'. On 13 December it indicated that it did not intend to join in an indiscriminate attack on the government for mistakes of the past, although it thought that Sidney Herbert went too far when he seemed to argue that the war had been conducted with 'infallible wisdom'. *The Times* was taken aback, however, by the Foreign Enlistment Bill, which it greeted as completely unexpected and unnecessary, and it contrasted the considerable opposition to this bill with the general support of the Militia Bill.[1]

Then on 19 December the whole attitude of the 'Thunderer' changed dramatically with a leader strongly criticising British army organisation in the Crimea and comparing it unfavourably with the French. In view of all that had been done, it argued, one would expect that the soldiers were enjoying the best of everything, whereas the reverse was the case. 'Our duty is to ascertain, if we can, where the fault of all this waste of life, of time, and of resources lies, in order, if possible, to apply a remedy', it concluded. 'The truth is that organisation and system seem to be completely foreign to the military and official mind.' The theme was resumed on the following day and on the 23rd the note became more strident, as it contrasted the preparations for Christmas festivity in England with the sad lot of the army in the Crimea:

There is no use disguising the matter. We are not speaking from our own correspondence only. We are not saying what we think alone. We say on the evidence of every letter that has been received in this country, and we echo the opinion of almost every experienced soldier or well informed gentleman, when we say that the noblest army England ever sent from these shores has been sacrificed to the grossest mismanagement. Incompetence, lethargy, aristocratic hauteur, official indifference, favour, routine, perverseness and stupidity reign, revel and riot in the camp before Sebastopol, in the harbour of Balaklava, in the hospitals of Scutari, and how much nearer home we do not venture to say.

On the day after Christmas it asserted that it did not expect the early fall of Sebastopol and that if and when the generals asked for more reinforcements a disappointed public would demand, not only reinforcements, but new leadership. It openly criticised the army commander for ignoring the facts of the situation, saying:

We knew that whatever could be done would be done. Yet we have foreseen nothing; and possessing the most ingenious, as well as the richest people in

[1] *The Times*, 15, 18, 19, 20 and 21 December 1854.

the world, we have really shown no more skill or artifice in the siege of Sebastopol than our ancestors would have done 2,000 years ago. All this time we are surpassed by everybody, and only boast a sorry superiority over the Turks, whom, accordingly, we abuse very freely. The French surpass us in their roads, in their port, in their huts, in their food and clothing, in their hospitals, in everything and are beginning to look on our helplessness much as we look on that of our barbarous allies. The Russians surpass all three— French, British and Turks—in everything except in mere physical strength and courage. *There* we come off the best. Yet how disgraceful that England so wealthy, so mechanical and with such infinity of resources, should after all depend upon the rawest material of war—the British soldier—and should be reduced to throw him away by wholesale in order to make up for our want of military science, not to say common sense! That has been the case hitherto though we cannot think that it will last much longer.

These were strong and strange words from a paper that ten days earlier had said that never was war prosecuted so vigorously. What had made it change its mind? A clue to the answer may be found in a further leader printed on the 30th, the last issue of 1854, in which it defended its publication of letters from officers and soldiers in the Crimea. Two months ago, it said, it would have felt constrained not to publish such complaints and criticisms. 'Now the whole Army rushes into print.' Officers and their families care no more for the Horse Guards and chances of promotion, but urge *The Times* to publish their letters and tell the whole truth. Thus the paper now felt that its duty was to publish this evidence and not to cling to 'old hopes or idle conventionalities', when confronted by 'the stern realities of the case' as related in its columns; 'hundreds of letters', it said, 'tell, in uniform language, the almost total disorganization of our army in the Crimea and its awful jeopardy, not from the Russians, but from an enemy nearer home—its own utter mismanagement'.

'It can no longer be doubted, or even denied', this leader continued, 'that the expedition to the Crimea is in a state of entire disorganization.' Recalling all the harrowing details of what had gone wrong in the British camp, it contrasted this with the orderly state of affairs behind the French lines. 'Wherever the British come across the French', it observed bitterly, 'it is to find the same mortifying contrast.' When it was asked what was to be done, some would take the view that it was better that the expedition should fail 'than that one iota of the official system of patronage, of seniority, and of all that semblance of order, that has kept up the illusion of military strength through a profound peace of forty years should be rudely swept away or reformed'. It was better in the view of such people, that the commander-in-chief and his staff should return with honour over the bones of fifty thousand British dead 'than that the equanimity of office and the good humour of society should be disturbed by a single recall, or a new appointment over the heads of those now in command'. *The Times* protested strongly against this view, and said, if the country was to be saved, it must be 'by throwing overboard without a day's delay, all scruples of personal friendship, of official punctilio, of aristocratic feeling and courtly subservience'. This devastating attack concluded with the ominous warning that it was 'a crime in a War Minister, to permit an officer to remain for a single day in the nominal discharge of duties the neglect of which has brought a great and victorious army to the verge of ruin'.[1]

Language such as this marked the sharp rift that lay not far below the surface of Victorian society, between the educated upper middle classes and the old landed aristocracy that still paradoxically played a dominant role in the government of the country a century after the dawn of the Industrial Revolution. Of course many accommodations and adjustments had been made by the upper classes to preserve the balance of power in English society, but at such times of crisis bare nerves were apt to show. In any event it was clear that when parliament reassembled in the new year the coalition would be hard pressed to survive.

Roebuck's motion, Russell's resignation, and the fall of the coalition

While *The Times* delivered its daily broadsides the ministers were not inactive. Herbert's correspondence, while it substantiates many of the evils complained of by *The Times*, disproves charges of apathy and indifference on his part. This is well illustrated in a long letter he wrote to Newcastle on 8 January 1855 in which he urged various steps to set their house in order. 'We have a storm brewing against the working of the military departments,' he wrote, 'and if we intend to outlive it we must make vigorous use of the fortnight between this and the meeting of Parliament.' He favoured Lord Grey's idea of governing the army by a board and suggested that the point would be largely met if they put

---

[1] Kinglake (*Crimea*, IV, 172–202) makes some interesting and pertinent remarks about the role of *The Times*, but he is surely off the mark in suggesting that its sudden attack on Raglan had ministerial inspiration (pp. 214–15).

their meetings with heads of departments on a regular basis, and kept and circulated minutes. He also urged Newcastle to make more use of the cabinet and take more care to keep Lord John fully informed. He went on to discuss practical details that required action, warning that they had 'a terrible arrear to make up in this fortnight'. [1]

The reinvigoration of the army in the Crimea was a still more formidable problem. Herbert and his colleagues continued desperately to rack their brains to determine what could be done to solve the enigma confronting them there of an army disintegrating despite all the steps that had been and were being taken at home to supply it with all its needs. As we have seen, there was growing dissatisfaction with Raglan and his staff, but uncertainty as to how to inject new life into the army command.[2] Nevertheless, the fact was that they could think of no obvious substitutes for the senior appointments.

Surprised at Raglan's unexpected failure in administration, Granville complained of the old-fashioned notions which led him to surround himself with useless young relatives as staff officers and to ask for retired and decrepit generals from England, ignoring the talent of younger but experienced officers already with him in the field.[3] It was Granville's opinion that Raglan should be urged to promote by merit—a Peelite heresy not unacceptable to this younger Whig. The Radical Molesworth said that good nature in refusing to dismiss 'incompetent Heads' at such a time would be a public crime. Argyll told Russell that he agreed with this, but also with Herbert's view that the government at home could 'hardly determine with accuracy or justice' where the 'incompetence' lay. He thought it best to inform Raglan of the government's impression of the Quartermaster General's Department and urge on him the necessity of exercising a 'very *vigorous* judgement'.[4]

---

[1] Stanmore, *Herbert*, I, 303–6. For evidence that this committee or board was already in active operation see PRO 30/22/12/A, fols. 30–3, for a report of the meeting at the War Department, 3 January 1855, attended by Newcastle, Herbert, Hardinge and the Lieutenant-General of the Ordnance, at which arrangements were made for the establishment of the depot at Malta, which was to handle 50,000 men. Directions were given for the despatch of extra beds and bedding, boots and shoes, medical stores, artillery, horses, fuel and panniers.

[2] E.g. PRO 30/22/12/A, *ibid.* fols. 20–3, Lansdowne to Russell, 2 January 1855, who wrote: 'Many people are disposed to think what I should be very loath to admit, that our huge army list and red book does not now contain an amount of capacity equal to carrying on a great war.'

[3] PRO 30/22/11/F, fols. 1941–4, 23 December 1854.

[4] *Ibid.* fols. 1808–9, n.d.

Clarendon and Palmerston were even more outspoken. The former wrote to Russell in early January:

More than enough of everything required for the Army has been sent by the Govt yet the army has been in a state of miserable and disgraceful destitution ...Not only has the administn been defective but the orders of the Govt appear in several instances to have been disregarded...Somebody must be to blame for so much negligence and it wd seem to rest on the Adjutant Genl and the Qr Master Genl. Ld Raglan shd be empowered to remove them... and if he does not do so he shd give his reasons for approving of their conduct.[1]

Palmerston expressed his views even more forcefully to Newcastle:

It is quite clear that in many essential points Raglan is unequal to the task which has fallen to his lot, but it is impossible to remove him...But there are two incompetent men under him holding stations which are the keystones of the organization of the army, and there cannot be the same difficulty in dealing with them. Airey and Estcourt, but especially the former, ought to be removed and better and more active men should be put in their places.[2]

To this Newcastle answered:

I have never concealed my opinion that Airey and Estcourt are not fit for the responsible offices they hold, and I am quite prepared to recommend their removal if better can be found. What, however, can I do? I should not be justified in removing Airey, whom Hardinge recommended as the *best* man for Quarter-Master-General, and whom Raglan appointed as *second best* man, and whose unfitness neither have yet admitted, without having some substitute of marked fitness to send in his place.[3]

Meanwhile the Russell volcano continued to simmer, but for the moment there were no further eruptions. Late in December Lord John prepared a comprehensive memorandum setting out all aspects of the military problems facing them and discussing possible remedies.[4] He minced no words, but his approach was a constructive one. Two days later, however, on 1 January 1855 he was again tempted to bolt and began to write a letter of resignation in which he complained that his advice regarding a more vigorous prosecution of the war had not been taken merely for fear of casting an imputation on the duke of Newcastle. His view was that the effective prosecution of the war was more impor-

[1] PRO 30/22/12/A, fols. 18–19, 2 January 1855, a note in Clarendon's hand initialed 'C'.
[2] Martineau, *Newcastle*, pp. 224–5.
[3] *Ibid.* pp. 225–6.   [4] Walpole, *Russell*, II, 238–40.

tant than the feelings of one man and that he, Russell, could not continue to be responsible for the government's business in the Commons under these circumstances.[1]

He broke off the letter, however, without finishing it and the next day he attended a cabinet which discussed the recruiting of the Foreign Legion, the selection of additional officers for Raglan's staff, and the current negotiations at Vienna. After the meeting the Prime Minister noted to the queen the 'comparatively pacified tone and language assumed by Lord John Russell in Cabinet recently'.[2] Russell's quietness at the cabinet of 2 January may have been explained by a note he received that day from Lord Lansdowne warning him against precipitate action.

Whatever happens the great thing you have to take care of for your own sake as respects publick opinion [his old colleague wrote], is that no break-up should appear to originate in personal feeling on your part. It would never be forgiven.

To prevent this any proposal should be founded on a deliberate view of what errors if any have been or are being committed, *where & when* they have been committed, and from whose fault.[3]

With this advice in mind Russell contented himself for the present with sending Aberdeen a sharp letter saying that nothing could 'be less satisfactory than the result of the recent Cabinets', that Aberdeen himself must direct measures for the effective prosecution of the war, and that Newcastle, Herbert or Hardinge should go to Paris to consult with the emperor and his staff.[4] Poor old Aberdeen was taken aback and answered rather pathetically: 'I was a little surprised by your letter yesterday; for I thought that the recent cabinets were rather satisfactory. Certainly many deficiencies were supplied, defects remedied, and assistance offered to Lord Raglan by the appointment of competent officers.' He also thought some progress had been made in the matter of the Foreign Legion. He had no objection, however, to Newcastle, Herbert or Hardinge going to Paris providing their presence there could really be considered advantageous.[5]

It must be admitted that, except for Herbert, no other minister gave evidence of doing as much hard thinking about the Crimean problem as a whole as did Lord John; Newcastle was too overwhelmed with

---

[1] PRO 30/22/12/A, fols. 14–17, unfinished letter to Aberdeen.
[2] R.A. G21, fol. 73, 2 January 1855.
[3] PRO 30/22/11/A, fols. 20–3, 2 January 1855.   [4] Walpole, *Russell*, II, 240.
[5] PRO 30/22/12/A, fols. 44–5, 4 January 1855 (partly reproduced in Walpole, *Russell*, II, 240).

administrative details to attempt any general appreciation of the situation on paper. Russell's memorandum of 30 December enumerated the principal evils as he saw them and suggested remedies; Herbert, with his greater knowledge, went over Russell's paper carefully, correcting the facts where necessary and elaborating the proposals.[1] Russell saw six basic evils: the soldiers were overworked in the trenches; they had no change of dry clothing on coming out of the trenches; transport animals were dying for lack of forage; the soldiers were on short rations for lack of transport; the men were without huts and wood was scarce; the sick were inadequately cared for and not moved in time. To meet the first point he proposed a re-allocation of responsibilities with the French, since there was no longer the original equality in numbers and never could be. Herbert said that Newcastle had already urged this on Raglan, but that the matter should be taken up directly with the French government; 'it must be done or our army will perish from fatigue', he commented. This was done without delay. On the second point Herbert observed that a constant stream of clothing had been sent to the Crimea, but that it was very difficult to tell what had or had not been received. 'I hope by this time complaints on that head will have been removed', he added. Actually, in a despatch of 13 January received in London two weeks later, Raglan reported the issuance of 'vast quantities of warm clothing', saying that every man had received 'a second blanket, a jersey frock, flannel drawers and socks and some kind of winter coat in addition to a great-coat'.[2] On the third point Herbert pronounced the death of horses from want of forage as 'unaccountable', and suspected that it was due to the lack of ability and experience in the commissariat staff, failing to place sufficiently large orders at Constantinople. Here the solution was the establishment of a separate transport corps, which had been undertaken by the duke of Newcastle. As for the shortage of rations Russell asserted and Herbert agreed that in such an emergency assistance should have been sought from the French. With regard to huts Herbert asserted that all the men's huts and about half the officers' had been sent off; that huts for 13,000 had passed Malta and more for 23,000 had been despatched from Trieste. (In despatches of 6 and 13 January Raglan acknowledged the arrival of the huts in quantity and 'tolerable success' in the heavy work of erecting them.[3]) According to

---

[1] Walpole, *Russell*, II, 238–40; PRO 30/22/12/A, fols. 34–41, 3 January 1855 (Herbert's comments on Russell memorandum). [2] *The Times*, 29 January 1855.
[3] *Ibid.* and 27 January 1855.

Herbert the sick had by then been moved from Balaclava to Scutari and an inquiry was being made into the lack of proper care and comfort for them. He himself had been making arrangements for the creation of a separate hospital corps. Russell concluded his memorandum by dwelling on the lack of coordination between the navy and the army in the matter of supplies and the need for Raglan and Lyons to concert efforts to remedy this. He also suggested, and Herbert fully concurred, that Raglan should be accurately informed as to the number of troops he could expect and be asked to indicate what in his opinion could be done by the Allied armies with the resources at their disposal.

Herbert suggested that Russell's memorandum should be made the basis of a public despatch to Raglan with additional points respecting the failure to build a road or to create divisional depots or to use supplies of forage in Balaclava. Raglan should be urged, if the government's suspicions were well founded, to replace his senior officers and to make use of talent on the spot.[1] Grey, Wood and Clarendon all expressed their agreement with Herbert's views,[2] which he further elaborated in a memorandum for the cabinet.

This paper made an excellent analysis of what had been accomplished to date and what had gone wrong. It admitted that the Allies had underestimated the power of the Russians to reinforce their garrison in the Crimea and noted that the Allies were unlikely to be able to increase their force beyond 100,000. Consequently it would be difficult to maintain superiority and even to remain if Sebastopol was taken. On the other hand they had to face the possibility of the failure of the assault and the possible necessity of evacuation under those circumstances. All the alternatives should be placed before the generals, who should have full discretion. 'They must not consider themselves chained to a rock', he wrote. 'So long as they have no instructions, they may so consider themselves, and our Army might, in the worst of all eventualities, be sacrificed in consequence.' He concluded:

I propose, therefore, first that we should come to a clear decision as to what we think should be done. Secondly, that we should endeavour to obtain from the French Government a concurrence in our opinion, whatever that opinion may be; and, thirdly, that when agreed, instructions in accordance with that opinion should be sent to the allied Generals. Fourthly, that we should require

---

[1] PRO 30/22/12/A, fols. 34–41, 3 January, and 46–9, 6 January 1855.
[2] *Ibid.* fols. 50–3, Sir G. Grey, 8 January 1855; fols. 55–6, Sir C. Wood, 8 January 1855; fols. 65–9, Lord Clarendon, 10 January 1855.

Lord Raglan to state to us, in full, his opinion of the position of the Army, the nature of the operations which he contemplates, and his expectations of success or failure. Fifthly, I think he should likewise give his opinion as to the advantages or disadvantages of an armistice, should the negotiations at Vienna be commenced.[1]

A cabinet meeting held on 9 January was mainly taken up with a consideration of the implications of Russia's acceptance of the Four Points and with great difficulties that were developing in recruiting the Foreign Legion;[2] but in a further meeting on the 11th, Newcastle read a despatch to Raglan that was evidently based on the memoranda of Russell and Herbert and the various recommendations of other ministers with respect to the replacing of Airey and Estcourt. Referring to the numerous reports of deficiencies and generally deplorable conditions coming in from all quarters, Newcastle dwelt on the 'want of foresight or of ability' on the part of some of Raglan's officers that had 'led to an amount of suffering and sickness...which ought to have been avoided'. Initially some allowances might have been made; 'but the experience which has by this time been gained', he wrote, 'should have been sufficient to enable those officers to pursue a system of organization under which disorder and loss would have been of comparatively infrequent occurrence'. He said the evidence of 'neglect or inefficiency' was so overwhelming that he had no alternative but to demand that Raglan conduct an enquiry into the whole question of the internal arrangements of the camp, the supply of provisions and stores and the care of the sick. 'If the army grows weak by disease not attendant upon warfare', he wrote, 'and is perilled by want, exposure and distress which the departmental care of your staff should have provided against, the people of England, regarding results and painfully sensitive to the possibility of a disastrous future, will on behalf of the sufferers and of the national honour call upon your Lordship to recommend such changes as may correct the evils they deplore and ward off the dangers they deprecate.' He promised that any additional aid and expenditure that Raglan might need would be 'cheerfully provided'.[3]

[1] Stanmore, *Herbert*, I, 318–25.
[2] R.A. G21, fol. 111, Aberdeen to queen, 9 January 1855.
[3] PRO WO/6/70/84, no. 202, draft despatch, dated 6 January 1855, which was read to the cabinet on 11 January (R.A. G22, fol. 21, Aberdeen to queen, 11 January 1855). Cf. Kinglake, *Crimea*, IV, 216, who was highly critical of the despatch, which with some reason he described as 'beyond measure wordy'.

The despatch had the queen's warm support, although she regretted that her name had not been included when reference was made to the 'People of England'. Somewhat ingenuously she said that it was 'so delicately worded that it ought not to offend', although it could not help from its matter 'being painful to Lord Raglan'.[1] The Commander-in-Chief was in fact greatly offended and replied with much warmth, not knowing that by that time the duke was out of office. Strongly defending the character and reputation of his staff and repudiating the charges made against them, he proceeded to lecture Newcastle on the organisation of the army, to demonstrate that the Quartermaster General was not responsible for the services entrusted to the commissariat. He did recognise the inadequacies of this branch arising from its lack of trained personnel and said that he had been forced to lend it officers and men from the army. Yet through his whole despatch there was a ring of fatalism. Conditions were deplorable, but they were beyond human control. He asserted his constant concern for ensuring the welfare of his troops, but the means within his reach were inadequate. He made the interesting observation that the organisation of the British army was framed for colonial service and that it was 'undoubtedly defective for operation in the field'. 'This has been the case with all former Armies,' he continued; 'and it did not occur to me to suppose that Her Majesty's Government would be willing to form establishments upon a larger scale, which could not at once be got up in the midst of the active operations of a campaign.' He went on to make some comparisons with the French army, where he observed personnel for certain tasks such as ambulance attendants and hospital orderlies were more easily available because of conscription. The *Intendance* (commissariat), the artillery and the engineers' departments in the French army, he said, were better equipped with what they needed to take the field immediately.[2] It was now almost a year since Lord Raglan had been appointed to his command, but it does not appear to have occurred to him that he had been delinquent in having failed to point all this out at an earlier date and to have made specific recommendations as to what was needed.

In the meantime Herbert pursued the question of coordination

[1] R.A. G22, fol. 21, Aberdeen to queen, 11 January 1855; *Letters of Queen Victoria*, III, 86, 12 January 1855.

[2] Martineau, *Newcastle*, pp. 240–4, refers to two despatches, one dated 6 and one 23 January 1855 (PRO WO/1/371/84, 1288 Military, despatch no. 164, 30 January 1855).

between the army and navy in a long letter to Graham in which he wrote:

I have statement on statement as to the inefficiency and insufficiency of the staff employed at Balaclava confirming the account which we have received now nearly three weeks. The Commissariat has neither the numbers nor the kind of men suited to this purely commercial work. What vexes me is that not a step has been taken here towards remedying it. Newcastle has promised me to get from the London Docks some men who have experience in business of this description and send them out. I hope he has taken steps to effect it.

But I am certain we want good naval direction in Balaclava likewise.

But while we complain of the gross mismanagement and confusion at Balaclava we have unfortunately under our own eyes the same scenes at home. The arrangements about packing our ships are a public scandal... Who is to blame I know not—but this I am conscious of that the Govt which cannot prevent or correct or punish such neglect will become contemptible.

He went on to suggest the necessity of a searching inquiry and the establishment on the part of the departments concerned of some system designed to 'prevent these disastrous failures'.[1]

Graham had already written to Raglan regarding the appointment of a very good officer, Captain Spratt, as port captain of Balaclava. He hoped that Lyons's appointment would lead to better cooperation between the navy and the army. 'I have not been well satisfied with the arrangement of the transport either at Balaclava or at Constantinople,' he wrote. 'The change of Commanders will, I trust, improve the system.'[2] This proved to be the case and Lyons wasted no time in replacing the inefficient Captain Christie, whom he found responsible for much of the confusion in the previous November. Shortly afterwards the whole of the transport arrangements were placed under a unified command as Graham desired.[3]

Russell missed the important cabinet meetings of 9 and 11 January because he had gone to Paris for family reasons. Of course he took the opportunity, as had Palmerston the previous month, to talk with the Emperor Louis Napoleon while he was there. Neither Aberdeen nor the queen welcomed this development, but Clarendon hoped that Russell might help to cement relations with France at a time when negotiations in Vienna were entering a dangerous phase.[4] Russell re-

[1] Graham Papers, Herbert, 7 January 1855.
[2] *Ibid.* Graham to Raglan, 8 January 1855 (copy).   [3] Erickson, *Graham*, p. 356.
[4] PRO 30/22/12/A, fols. 57–60, Clarendon to Russell, 8 January 1855; R.A. G21, fol. 111, Aberdeen to queen, 9 January 1855; *Letters of Queen Victoria*, II, 86–7, queen to Aber-

ceived a friendly welcome from the French emperor and they talked frankly about the various problems facing the alliance, such as Napoleon's proposal to make Russian withdrawal from the Crimea a *sine qua non* for any peace negotiations, and Russell's interest in securing troops from Piedmont. 'With respect to the war,' Russell wrote to Clarendon, 'he observed that France, being a military and continental Power, had great resources and reserves for her army; that England in the same way had great maritime reserves and resources; that it was reasonable that each should use the arm which was strongest, instead of which we both tried to use both arms, and the consequence was that France had exhausted her maritime and England her military means, and that at Sebastopol we had two besieging armies instead of one besieging army.' Lord John fully agreed with all this and seized the opportunity to point out the need of some reallocation of duties since the British army was extended beyond its resources.[1]

Russell returned from Paris on 16 January in time to join a five-hour cabinet meeting at which he reported his conversations with Louis Napoleon. The ministers discussed the differences that had developed between Raglan and Canrobert, but most of their attention was given to diplomatic problems, the approval of a despatch to Westmorland indicating their suspicions regarding Russia's sincerity in the Vienna negotiations, and settlement of the agreement with Sardinia.[2]

Another cabinet meeting on 20 January dealt with some important domestic matters, a Church Rates Bill and a provision for a more effective civil service entrance examination.[3] Consideration was also

deen, 13 January 1855. Of Russell's letter the queen wrote: 'It shows the practice of the Queen's different Cabinet Ministers going to Paris, to have personal explanations with the Emperor, besides being hardly a constitutional practice, must lead to much misunderstanding. How is the Emperor to distinguish between the views of the Queen's Government and the private opinion of the different members of the Cabinet, all more or less varying, particularly in a Coalition Government?'

[1] Gooch, *Later correspondence*, II, 180–2. For Clarendon's reply see PRO 30/22/12/A, fols. 73–8, 12 January 1855. He said that he had proposed another despatch to Raglan warning him of the suspected insincerity of the Russian acceptance of the Four Points and emphasising that negotiations could 'only be accelerated by military success'.

[2] R.A. G22, fol. 50, Aberdeen to queen, 16 January 1855.

[3] R.A. E5, fol. 13, Aberdeen to queen, 20 January 1855. With regard to the civil service he wrote: 'A decision was adopted for rendering the examination for the admission into the various Public Offices much more real and effectual, with examiners independent of the different Departments. This avoids the principle of competition altogether, and obviates the objections made to the scheme of last year; while at the same time it will furnish a more efficient class of servants for public service.'

given to a proposal by Sidney Herbert for the establishment of a Board under the Secretary of State for War, consisting of that minister, the Secretary at War, the Commander-in-Chief and the Master General of the Ordnance. This plan, which went some way to meet Lord Grey's earlier criticisms, was approved at a further meeting on the 21st; Aberdeen assured the queen that the powers of the Commander-in-Chief would remain unchanged, that the royal prerogative would be untouched, and that the new Board would only be an extension of meetings that had already been taking place.[1] The queen said she was prepared to sanction this proposal, on the understanding that the Commander-in-Chief still had access to her and she received the minutes of the new Board.[2]

The Times continued its criticisms throughout January and indeed increased their intensity as the date for the reassembly of parliament approached.[3] On 20 January it complained:

Affairs are left in the same incompetent hands...the Cabinet is engaged in endless discussions which lead to no result...A torpor and lethargy seem to have fallen on the spirit of our rulers; they go on mechanically sending out men and stores to the fatal harbour of Balaklava, without seeming to advert to the fact that men and stores under the present circumstances of the British army are only sent, one to perish, the other to be wasted.

The leader charged that scarcely 2,000 active troops in the British army were in good health and that the whole army faced disaster. A second leader on the same day dwelt on the purposelessness of the pre-Christmas meeting of parliament, claiming that the two measures it passed had remained a dead letter. 'Not a militia regiment has been sent abroad, not a foreigner enlisted at home,' it commented derisively.

Two days later it asked rhetorically why there had been so many long cabinet meetings of late. Was it to solve the Crimean problem, to find a new general or perhaps to entrust the British army to General Canrobert? In its wisdom the 'Thunderer' knew better. It informed its readers that the ministers were met to deal with the great Kennedy case, which it proceeded to explain in satirical terms; perhaps half an hour

[1] R.A. E5, fol. 13 and fol. 8, 21 January 1855; Stanmore, *Herbert*, I, 244.
[2] *Letters of Queen Victoria*, III, 89–90.
[3] E.g. *The Times*, 18 January 1855, which complained that everything in the world was at Balaclava but the army had not the energy to grasp it. It admitted that the ministers were not to blame for the faults of the generals, but observed that they seemed to suffer equally from 'this Crimean helplessness'.

was left over at the end of a meeting for the direction of the war. 'The British public at least will learn with disgust how its rulers are trifling with its anxieties and griefs,' it declared with Pecksniffian solemnity.[1] It is true that this 'little piddling pottering war with Johnny', as Gladstone called it, continued to drag on, and that there was talk of referring it to the cabinet for a decision, but in actual fact Lord John declined 'to submit to the decision of the Cabinet on questions regarding his personal honour'. Certainly the matter did not divert the cabinet from dealing with the conduct of the war, although it absorbed an inordinate amount of time and energy of the three ministers concerned.[2]

To all appearances Russell returned from Paris in rather better spirits and threw himself into the work of the cabinet as if he had given up any idea of early departure. On the 22nd he sent Lord Aberdeen a memorandum proposing an extension to Herbert's Army Board scheme for consideration at the next cabinet, and when the House met on the 23rd he gave notice of his intention to introduce an Education Bill at an early date. When, on the same day, Roebuck gave notice of a motion for a committee of inquiry on the conduct of the war, Russell even discussed the advisability of an amendment with the government whip. Walking home with a colleague after the early adjournment of the House that evening, he gave no hint of the step he was about to take.[3]

Arthur Gordon, Aberdeen's youngest son, chose the night of 22 January to write in his private journal an estimate of the state of the cabinet and its members, in which, ironically, he ventured the opinion that things

[1] *Ibid.* 22 January 1855. *The Times* attack reached a crescendo on the following day when it asserted that the result of the military system developed over the previous half century was 'failure, failure, failure', a perpetually descending bathos of non-performance, confusion, delay, perplexity, impotence and whatever ends in nothings'. It continued: 'The deadlock is absolute, final, inevitable, and desperate, from Whitehall to the camp before Sebastopol. The Minister of War, the Commander-in-Chief at home, the Commander-in-Chief in the Crimea, down to the purveyor of stores at Scutari, and the miserable lad dozing hungry, naked and frostbitten in the trench are all equally dummies.' Nevertheless, it insisted that its quarrel was with the system and not the minister.

[2] Herbert Papers, Gladstone to Herbert, 31 December 1854; Stanmore, *Aberdeen*, pp. 279–80. On 27 and 29 December Aberdeen attributed Gladstone's absence from cabinet meetings to the Kennedy affair, but he told the queen that nothing was said about the matter (R.A. G21, fols. 45 and 54). See above, pp. 377–82. Russell did bring the matter up at the end of a cabinet meeting on 9 December; see above, p. 501.

[3] Stanmore, *Herbert*, I, 245; Stanmore, *Aberdeen*, pp. 280–2; Morley, *Gladstone*, I, 521; Martineau, *Newcastle*, p. 252, quoting a letter of Sir C. Wood. Russell's memorandum (*Ab. Cor. 1854–5*, p. 325) suggested that the proposed Army Board should absorb the Board of Ordnance to avoid overlapping and confusion.

were beginning to 'look better'.[1] Despite his youthfulness his remarks are of interest because of his proximity to the Prime Minister and intimate knowledge of cabinet secrets. Although Russell remained the one source of trouble and weakness, it is noted that he appeared to have given up his projected changes at the War Office and to be inclined towards a policy of peace. 'On the other hand,' Gordon added, 'he is worse than ever about little things,' and it was by no means impossible that he might resign over the Kennedy affair, 'if insensible to the ridicule which would attach to such a proceeding'. Lord Palmerston appeared to be satisfied with the existing arrangements, which Gordon thought 'suited his game'. His comments on Gladstone and Graham were singularly sharp and penetrating.

Gladstone, eager and impulsive [he wrote], is really anxious for a rupture with Lord John, be the consequences what they may. He is wrong. As his Lord-ship [Aberdeen] often says, there is no *perspective* in his views. All objects, great and small, are on one plane with him; and consequently the tiniest sometimes assume the largest dimensions.

Sir James Graham, at once rash and timid, is a warm friend and a dangerous adviser. I wish his Lordship did not listen to him so exclusively. Everyday he comes; to him alone is confidence unreservedly given; and he has more than once contributed to results which he little deserved.

Lord Clarendon is rather unfairly charged with 'insincerity and cowardice', yet Gordon acknowledges his loyalty and affection for Aberdeen and his disgust with Russell's actions. The objection to Clarendon was that he was too fond of dodges; of secretly following Aberdeen's policy, while pretending to adopt Palmerston's. According to Gordon, Palmerston, Lansdowne and Newcastle formed the 'fire-eating war party' in the cabinet. Clarendon, Wood, Granville, Grey, Cranworth and Molesworth were as one with the Peelites, contrary to public opinion, and Russell was quite '*alone*'.

Arthur Gordon's journal entry contains one very significant piece of information that he did not choose to divulge when years later he wrote the biographies of his father and Sidney Herbert. Of the Secretary for War he writes:

The Duke of Newcastle—I hardly dare to write what is known, I believe, to none of his colleagues in the Cabinet—means to resign, not admitting the justice of the outcry against him, but avowing that with such unpopularity he

[1] *Ab. Cor. 1854–5*, Appendix, pp. 378–9.

cannot usefully discharge the duties of the office. He is right and in the long run he will gain by it; but I am afraid his Lordship wishes to appoint Herbert in his place. This will be a mistake. It must, under existing circumstances, be Palmerston. Not that Herbert would not fill the office better, but because if a change is made, this is the only one that will give real confidence.[1]

The following evening, the 23rd, Arthur Gordon and his father returned to a quiet family dinner at Argyll House, following the early adjournment of the two Houses. About ten o'clock Gordon went into the library, as was his custom, to clear the inevitable boxes. In the first one he opened he found a letter of resignation from Lord John. He called his father, who only came under protest, mumbling 'Can't it wait?', but when he saw the letter he was much surprised. His first reaction was one of amusement—Lord John had so often announced his resignation—and then one of relief. This time, however, he was determined to make the resignation stick. He would have no repetition of the scenes recently endured.

He sent his son off to fetch Sir James, who appeared in a dressing gown. On hearing the news he hastily threw on a 'great fur coat' and returned with Arthur to Argyll House in a cab. 'I could not help wondering,' Gordon later wrote in his journal, 'as we jogged along slowly, with our feet in the dirty straw, who had been the last and who would be the next fares of the sleepy driver, and what they had talked and would talk about?'[2] Sir James's thoughts were more down to earth as he began to devise schemes for winning Russell back, but he soon found that Aberdeen was determined not to have it so.

When had Lord John Russell come to his decision? Writing years later Lord Stanmore gave it as his opinion that Russell was not attempting to deceive anybody by his actions during the 23rd and that in actual fact he did not make up his mind until he had arrived home that night.[3] Nor did he do so under the influence of Lady John for she told her father that she had begged him not to write to Lord Aberdeen without consulting his friends. She says that he was prevented by his conscience from doing this.[4] More likely he was impressed by the news that many of his old followers would desert him and the government when the Roebuck motion came to the vote. When he thought of this, all his former doubts and dissatisfaction returned and for the last time he made

[1] *Ibid.* [2] *Ibid.* pp. 380–3, 23 January 1855.

[3] Stanmore, *Aberdeen*, p. 282, and *Herbert*, I, 246.

[4] Walpole, *Russell*, II, 242.

up his mind to part from Lord Aberdeen. No man was more capable of self-deception than Lord John and in a retrospective memorandum on the reasons for his resignation he maintained it was simply on the ground that the House of Commons, following precedents of 1757, 1777 and 1810, had the right to demand such an inquiry as Roebuck now did and that he could not oppose it.[1]

In his formal letter of resignation Russell simply said that he did not see how Roebuck's motion could be resisted, but that since it involved censure of a colleague his only course was to tender his own resignation.[2] In a brief covering note he avowed 'his regard' for Aberdeen's 'personal character' and of his sense of the Prime Minister's 'kindness and liberality'.[3] He sent a copy of his letter of resignation to the queen[4] (a most unusual proceeding) and personal letters of explanation to Palmerston and Granville.[5]

The next morning Aberdeen showed Russell's letter to Newcastle, who immediately offered to resign his office to Palmerston, but the effectiveness of the offer was somewhat reduced, since he spoke of it as a 'sacrifice' to 'appease the public'. Aberdeen then called on Palmerston, who was highly critical of Russell's behaviour; he said that he did not think he could administer the War Department half as well as Newcastle, but that if it was necessary to avoid the dissolution of the government he 'was prepared to try it'.[6] To Russell Palmerston wrote in his most candid manner. He told Lord John that he considered his resignation most ill-timed. Everybody had foreseen such a motion as Roebuck's coming and if he were not prepared to meet it Russell should have warned his colleagues earlier to give them the opportunity of deciding how to meet the difficulty.

As it is [he continued] you will have the appearance of having remained in office aiding in carrying on a system of which you disapproved until driven out by Roebuck's announced Notice and the Government will have the appearance of Self Condemnation by flying from a discussion which they dare not face; while as regards the country the action of the executive will be paralyzed for a time in a critical moment of a great war with an impending negotiation, and we shall exhibit to the world a melancholy spectacle of Dis-

---

[1] PRO 30/22/12/A, fols. 2–8 (partly quoted by Walpole, *Russell*, II, 243).
[2] Walpole, *Russell*, II, 241.   [3] *Ab. Cor. 1855–60*, p. 2, 23 January 1855.
[4] *Letters of Queen Victoria*, III, 90–1.
[5] Fitzmaurice, *Granville*, I, 90. The letter to Palmerston is referred to by Palmerston in a letter quoted below.
[6] *Letters of Queen Victoria*, III, 91–3, memorandum of Prince Albert, 25 January 1855.

organization among our political men at Home, similar to that which has prevailed among our military men abroad. My opinion is that if you had simply renewed the Proposal which you made before Christmas such an arrangement might have been made, and there are constitutional & practical grounds on which such a motion as Roebuck's might have been resisted without violence to any opinions which you may entertain as to the past Period.[1]

The Prime Minister read Lord John's letter to the cabinet, which met at two that afternoon. Newcastle renewed his offer to resign and Palmerston reiterated his position. Grey and Wood both declared it would be impossible to resist Roebuck's motion, but Clarendon suggested that Russell might be induced to withdraw his resignation in view of Newcastle's 'generous offer'. Gladstone objected to this proposal and Lord Aberdeen rejected it, saying 'that they might be justified in sacrificing the Duke to the wishes of the Country, but they could not to Lord John, with any degree of honour'.[2]

In view of the attitude of the Whig members of the cabinet it was decided that the whole cabinet would have to resign. It was agreed that they should meet again on the following day and thereupon Aberdeen went straight off to Windsor to lay their resignations before the queen. After he had gone the ministers decided that Russell should be informed and Sir Charles Wood was commissioned to tell him what had been decided. The unpredictable Russell asked whether he should attend the cabinet on the following day, but Wood advised him against such a course![3]

The queen showed more resolution than her ministers. She refused to accept their resignation, or at least persuaded Aberdeen that he should make one more appeal to them.[4] At the same time she sent a very curt note to Lord John expressing 'her surprise and concern at hearing so abruptly of his intention to desert the Government on the motion of Mr Roebuck'.[5] Russell was much upset by the queen's note and immediately replied, protesting that he had 'sacrificed his position and reputation for two years' and that it was his belief that it would not be

---

[1] PRO 30/22/12/A, fols. 108–9, 24 January 1855 (printed in Ashley, *Palmerston*, II, 301–2).
[2] *Letters of Queen Victoria*, III, 91–3, the prince's memorandum; Maxwell, *Clarendon*, II, 55–6; Add. MS. 44745, fols. 22–8, Gladstone memorandum *re* cabinet of 24 January 1855 (dated 9 March 1855), summarised in Morley, *Gladstone*, I, 522.
[3] *Ab. Cor. 1855–60*, p. 3, Wood to Aberdeen, 24 January 1855. It was Gordon's view that Wood went beyond his mission (Add. MS. 44319, fol. 86, Gordon to Gladstone, 24 January 1855).
[4] *Letters of Queen Victoria*, III, 92–3, prince's memorandum of 25 January 1855.
[5] *Ibid.* p. 91, 24 January 1855.

for the benefit of the country to resist the Roebuck motion. 'It is the cause of much pain to him', he concluded, 'that, after sacrificing his position in order to secure your Majesty's service from interruption, he should not have obtained your Majesty's approbation.'[1]

The queen was not impressed. 'If Lord John will consider, however, the moment which he has now chosen to leave her Government, and the abrupt way in which his unexpected intention of agreeing in a vote implying censure of the Government was announced to her,' she replied, 'he cannot be surprised that she could not express her approbation.'[2]

Lord Aberdeen was gentler in his acceptance of Russell's resignation, and, indeed, in thanking him for his kind personal remarks, he assured Lord John that nothing could ever alter his warm regard for him.[3] Aberdeen actually saw Russell on the 25th and found him 'personally civil', but 'very much excited and very angry' at the letter he had just received from the queen.[4]

When the cabinet reconvened on 25 January, Aberdeen announced the queen's reluctance to accept their resignation and her earnest appeal to them to reconsider.

This wish of the Queen produced a remarkable effect [Gladstone recorded]. Grey led the way in retiring from his position of the preceding day; and the government as a body were saved from the very questionable position in which the course then taken by Grey and his friends would have placed them, that of flying from Roebuck's motion. We all seemed to feel (what Argyll had if I remember right expressed on the previous occasion) that we were bound to abide the sentence of the House of Commons.[5]

It was therefore agreed that on the announcement of Russell's resignation Palmerston should request the adjournment of the House of Commons for twenty-four hours and that the government would then abide by the decision of the House on the Roebuck motion.[6]

Grey apparently reserved the right to retire after the motion was dealt with,[7] but according to Clarendon he was 'perfectly beside him-

---

[1] *Letters of Queen Victoria*, III, 93, 25 January 1855.
[2] *Ibid.* p. 94, 25 January 1855.
[3] Walpole, *Russell*, II, 242, 24 January 1855.
[4] *Letters of Queen Victoria*, III, 94–5, memorandum by the queen, 25 January 1855.
[5] Add. MS. 44745, fols. 28–9, Gladstone memorandum, 25 January, dated 9 March 1855.
[6] *Ibid.* fol. 130, 25 January 1855.
[7] *Letters of Queen Victoria*, III, 84–5, memorandum by the queen, 25 January 1855. Aberdeen again saw the queen at Windsor that evening.

self with rage at Ld John'.[1] Russell was expecting Grey, Granville and Wood to resign and was clearly much disappointed when they failed to do so.[2]

At Russell's request Hayter announced his resignation in the Commons that day and, as planned, Palmerston secured the adjournment of the House on the promise that the Roebuck motion would be proceeded with on the following day.[3] In the meantime Gladstone wrote rather mysteriously to the Prime Minister, saying that he was 'extremely concerned' that they had not consulted Lord Hardinge, who was after all their military expert and 'all but a Minister'.[4] Aberdeen said he had no objection, but presumed that Newcastle had been 'in frequent communication' with Hardinge.[5]

The Times denounced Russell's resignation as 'a wide and painful deviation from the rules of political conduct' which were usually accepted. 'He must be something worse than a bad Minister who can choose such a moment of national calamity for personal resentment or party intrigue', was the harsh verdict of this dread tribunal.[6]

On Friday, 26 January, Aberdeen read Lord John Russell's letter of resignation to the House of Lords and announced that it had been accepted by the queen. He recalled that he would never have formed his government in the first place without Russell's participation, but under the existing circumstances he felt it was only proper that the government should remain in office to meet the motion that was even then being made against it in another place.[7] There was no discussion, for he was immediately followed by Lord Berners who, to quote *The Times*, 'inflicted on the House a disquisition on Roman Catholic processions'.

In the Commons that same afternoon all eyes were on Lord John, who rose from the fourth row to explain his resignation. He admitted that

---

[1] Herbert Papers, Clarendon, 25 January 1855. He was writing to tell Herbert that Lansdowne was very anxious that the Roebuck motion should be met on 'constitutional grounds' and that 'no higher tone should be taken about the conduct of the war' than could be fully sustained by the facts.

[2] *Ab. Cor. 1855–60*, p. 4, Thurs. evening (25 January 1855), C. Dawkins to A. Gordon, reporting a conversation with Hayter, who was using very strong language against Russell. Hayter said he found Wood very angry at Lord John, '*swearing* that he would ruin himself and his party too'. Later Russell complained to Grey that none of his old colleagues had tried to get him to withdraw his resignation! (Gooch, *Later correspondence*, II, 182, 9 February 1855).

[3] *Hansard*, CXXXVI, 941–3.

[4] Add. MS. 44089, fols. 90–1, 25 January 1855 (copy).

[5] *Ibid.* fols. 92–3, 26 January 1855.

[6] *The Times*, 26 January 1855.   [7] *Hansard*, CXXXVI, 943–4.

such a motion as Roebuck's was not unexpected, but he had waited to see from what quarter it came and in what terms it was couched. In view of the 'horrible and heartrending' accounts that arrived every week from the Crimea, he found it impossible in conscience to oppose the motion. He went on in some detail to tell of his differences with Aberdeen since last October, quoting extensively from their correspondence, and emphasised how unsuccessful he had been in getting the change either in personnel or in the machinery of administration that he had advocated. He said that he heard his proposed installation of Palmerston in the War Office was now likely and hoped that he had been instrumental in effecting this by his resignation, since Aberdeen, an honourable man, had given no hint of such change when he accepted the resignation. Russell minced no words; yet he presented his case with a certain effective restraint and concluded with words of personal praise for Aberdeen and of regard for the achievements of his government, especially of the Foreign Secretary and the Chancellor of the Exchequer.[1]

Gladstone and Herbert were of the opinion that Russell carried the House with him as he spoke;[2] certainly he was greeted with cheers from the opposition benches, but feelings on his own side were undoubtedly more mixed. 'He made a very elaborate and dexterous statement,' Aberdeen told the queen; 'but which, altho' very plausible, did not produce a great effect.'[3] The Times, while welcoming Russell's conversion to his new-found principles, asked what he had ever done as Prime Minister or more recently as leader of the House of Commons to put them in practice. It suggested that he would have been more convincing if he had resigned last November; now he only gave the appearance of running away from criticism and leaving his colleagues in the lurch. Having assented to the measures of the government, it was unprecedented that he would not defend them. 'Unhappily', the leader continued magisterially, 'such an action is not calculated to raise the character of Parliamentary government, or to confer additional lustre on the statesman who figures most prominently in this transaction.'[4]

[1] *Hansard*, CXXXVI, 960–74.

[2] Add. MS. 44745, fols. 31–2, Gladstone memorandum dated 9 March 1855 (partly quoted in Morley, *Gladstone*, I, 523). Gladstone says he happened to meet Lady John in the ladies' gallery that evening and found her 'shy and embarrassed as well she might'. 'I told her that Lord John's speech was very kind', he noted, 'but that I did not agree in his mode of viewing or putting the facts', which is about as close as a gentleman can go in telling a lady that her husband is a liar.

[3] *Ab. Cor. 1855–60*, p. 7, 27 January 1855.

[4] *The Times*, 27 January 1855.

Palmerston had asked Gladstone to answer Russell, but it was decided that it would be better not to have a Peelite do so and thus the task devolved on Russell's successor himself. From all accounts his effort was 'singularly unsuccessful'. 'And this is to be our leader', Wood groaned, while Palmerston was still on his feet, and when he sat down Gladstone almost asked him whether there was nothing more to be said.[1] Since there was no response from the other side there was no opportunity for another minister to rise, but later in the day, in speaking to the Roebuck motion, Sir George Grey took the opportunity of expressing his astonishment at Russell's action in no uncertain terms; as Aberdeen observed to the queen, his censure must have been a great blow to Lord John.[2]

Several other speakers in the course of this debate took the opportunity to comment on Russell's statement. In particular Gladstone, speaking on Monday, said what he had been unable to say on Friday, and perhaps more, since in the meantime he had been prompted by Aberdeen, communicating through his son, to refute Russell's charge that it was not permissible to advise in December what was to be done in February. Aberdeen pointed out the very great difference between the voluntary and forced relinquishment by the duke of the War Department, which suggests that, had the government survived the motion, the duke would have resigned.[3]

Gladstone began gently, thanking Russell for his kind words, but he proceeded, by a close examination of the course of events, to show that Lord John had dropped his proposals in mid December and that in January he had been working closely with his colleagues in cabinet, giving no indication that he still harboured these views. Although Gladstone spoke with restraint, he confessed to Aberdeen afterwards that he had wanted to compare Russell on his back bench to Achilles in seclusion, but had been dissuaded from doing so by Wood.[4] Disraeli was much harsher in his treatment of the late President of the Council, whose speech he said he had listened to 'with amazement'. 'It seemed

---

[1] Morley, *Gladstone*, I, 523.

[2] *Hansard*, CXXXVI, 1039; *Ab. Cor. 1855–60*, p. 7.

[3] Add. MS. 44319, fols. 88–90, Gordon to Gladstone [26 January 1855]. Arthur Gordon had objected to Gladstone's being asked to indicate this on the grounds that it would make it an 'official declaration', but his father had merely replied, as many fathers have done before and since: 'Don't argue but do as I tell you.'

[4] *Hansard*, CXXXVI, 1179–83; *Ab. Cor. 1855–60*, p. 8, Arthur Gordon's Journal, 30 January 1855.

to me', he said, 'I was listening to a page of *Bubb Doddington*. Such an all-unconscious admission of profligate intrigue is not to be matched in that record which commemorates the doings of another Duke of Newcastle, who was a Minister of England when the House of Commons was led by Sir Thomas Robinson, and when the opposition was actually carried on by the Paymaster of the Forces and the Secretary at War.' He compared Russell's action with Canning's intrigue to get rid of Castlereagh at the time of the Walcheren expedition, and poked fun at the choice of Palmerston, who was to have been the beneficiary of Russell's intrigue, 'to rebuke with Spartan severity, with more than Lacedaemonian rigour, the illustrious conspirator who had sacrificed himself to the disinterestedness of friendship'. He went on to develop his favourite theme—the frailty of the coalition—saying:

The late Lord President is breaking up the Cabinet, because from the first he anticipated injurious consequences in the conduct of the war from the want of experience and energy of the Duke of Newcastle, and yet he never objected to the office of the Minister for War being conferred on the Duke of Newcastle, because it gave him the means of saving the balance of power [in the coalition], and introducing as Secretary for the Colonies a supporter of his side. Thus, in the struggle to preserve the balance of power, the noble Lord was victorious, but he got bolder, and, not satisfied with his success, he invaded the Principalities, and attempted to drive out the Minister for War also.[1]

Russell had not intended to enter the debate, but these remarks about his statement brought him quickly to his feet when Disraeli sat down. He quietly and briefly begged to differ with Gladstone's interpretation of the events of the past two months, but he rebutted at length and with vigour Disraeli's charge of 'profligate intrigue'. It was scarcely the wisest thing to do this by defending the conduct of Canning, but Russell could never resist an historical argument, and he developed another in his own favour, Lord Grey's replacement of Goderich by Stanley to get the Slavery Emancipation Bill through in 1833. Indeed, he protested that he had done a public service by suggesting Newcastle's transfer before the matter was a public question.[2]

Immediately after Russell's initial statement on Friday, Roebuck introduced his motion for a select committee 'to inquire into the condition of our army before Sebastopol, and into the conduct of those

---

[1] *Hansard*, CXXXVI, 1216–18.   [2] *Ibid.* 1219–22.

Departments of the Government whose duty it has been to minister to the wants of the Army', but he was unable to speak for more than a few minutes because of illness.[1] This put Sidney Herbert, whose task it was to reply on behalf of the government, in a difficult position. He had come prepared to defend their administration of the war against many charges that he expected to be raised against it, but that were not actually made. Everyone was familiar with them, but for Herbert to be the first to introduce them into the Commons debate was an obvious anomaly that did his case no good. Nevertheless, he made as strong a defence of the administration as it was possible to do.[2] He began by stressing the serious limitations of the British army after forty years of peace, which led *The Times* somewhat unfairly to charge him with shifting the blame from the authorities at home to the soldiers in the Crimea. He pointed out the obvious similarities between the state of Raglan's army in the Crimea and Wellington's in the early stages of the Peninsular War. He gave facts and figures to show what had been done and refuted some of the false charges that had been circulating about deficiencies. He even seemed to admit the intervention of the Almighty against them when he said: 'But when we talk of commanding the seas, we are apt to be rebuked by Him at whose breath the stormy wind arises, and we are visited by the terrible calamity which befell our transports a short time ago.'[3] He pointed out the difficulties that would face the work of a select committee and the purposelessness of it since the government already knew what was wrong and were taking the necessary steps to rectify the existing faults and deficiencies. In some detail he outlined what had already been done and what was being done.

But all to no avail. It was clear that had a division been taken on Friday evening it would have gone against the government. The minister's only hope, and that a forlorn one, was that reflection over the weekend on the alleged unconstitutional nature of the resolution would restrain the majority.[4]

The first day's debate produced no great philippics. The strongest speech supporting the motion was delivered by Layard, who claimed he

[1] *Ibid.* 979–82.   [2] *Ibid.* 982–1002.   [3] *Ibid.* 989.
[4] *Ab. Cor. 1855–60*, p. 7, Aberdeen to queen, 27 January 1855. Writing to Gladstone on the 27th, Sir John Young said that he thought the adjournment was favourable to the ministry, for he sensed a lessening of the hostility as the debate continued. 'Some will stay away following Lord John's example', he wrote, 'but the decision will really lie with the opposition; if they bring their men up—I mean Lord Derby's friends—and vote in a body they will have a majority' (Add. MS. 44237, fols. 245–6, 27 January 1855).

had not intended to speak but was moved to do so by the speech of the Secretary at War. Layard made the usual points about the shortage of animals, the lack of winter clothing, the inadequacy of the siege artillery, the hopelessness of running a commissariat with Treasury clerks, the failure of the authorities to take the advice of men with local knowledge, and so on, and his remarks were strengthened by his ability to use the evidence of his own eyes. One of his most significant criticisms was of the army's failure to appoint generals with Indian experience. The only divisional commander (General England) who had been in India had returned under something of a cloud; officers of such tried ability as Sir Colin Campbell had been passed over for divisional commands, which had been given to generals of indifferent ability.[1]

Walpole was the only speaker from the opposition front bench on Friday and he made a very curious contribution, confining himself almost entirely to the question of the desirability of the inquiry.[2] He made it very clear that he did not want to regard the motion as 'in the strict sense casting censure upon the Government'. Rather he hoped that it would lead to the blame being put on the proper persons. He did not want a complete change in administration, but rather a reconstruction of the present ministry. For this reason he particularly regretted the retirement of Lord John Russell. Walpole's idea of reconstruction evidently meant the elimination of the Peelites, for he went on:

I cannot conceal from myself that the experiment of what is called a 'Coalition Government' has again failed, as it always has failed in this country—not from want of ability, not from want of principle, not from want of integrity of character in the men who compose the Government; but it has failed because—as no one can have failed to see who has watched the course and the measures of the Government—there was not one mind pervading them; because there was a difference of opinion amongst the Members of it which was sadly detrimental to the public interests.[3]

The only other minister to speak on the first day was Sir George Grey, who made a strong fighting speech, rebutting the arguments of Layard and others, rebuking the official opposition for being content to

---

[1] Hansard, CXXXVI, 1026–38. Kinglake (Crimea, IV, 56–7) dwells on the failure to make use of officers with Indian army experience, saying that their names were kept in a separate book and that no one would think of interchanging them; 'and from this superstition it resulted', he wrote, 'that for the purpose of ministering to an army in Europe, the power which since the peace of 1815 had waged greater wars than any other was condemned to take the field as a novice'.
[2] Ibid. 1049–57.   [3] Ibid. 1055–6.

hide behind a motion made on the government side, and making it very clear that a vote for the motion was one of confidence in the government.[1]

As usual, light relief on a sombre occasion was unwittingly provided by the irrepressible Colonel Sibthorp. 'He regretted that, upon the side of the House on which he had sat for so long a time, there was so much of the *suaviter in modo*, and so little of the *fortiter in re*.' He was particularly displeased with Walpole's moderation. 'He would remind that right Hon. Gentleman that fair words buttered no parsnips. He (Colonel Sibthorp) had never done it, and never would do it. He had never flattered man, woman or child.' He was not distressed at the warning that the motion would paralyse the government, for in his view they always had been paralysed. 'He was rather anxious to hear also when the Queen (God bless her) was to get rid of this inefficient, weak, loose set.'[2]

The debate was resumed on Monday 28 January with a longish speech by Augustus Stafford, a Conservative member, who, like Layard, had himself visited the theatre of war and thus spoke with some authority, especially about the hospital at Scutari where he had done his best to assist the good work of Florence Nightingale.[3] In all in the course of the two days' debate some five Liberals and twelve Conservatives spoke in support of the motion, while eleven supporters of the government, including three Peelites, opposed it. In a few cases, however, the opposition was to the nature of the motion and indicated no confidence in the government. This was the case with Sir Francis Baring, Vernon Smith, and Monckton Milnes, all of whom spoke more warmly of Lord John than of the continuing ministers.[4] Another Liberal, Bernal Osborne, Secretary of the Admiralty, also expressed concern over Russell's resignation, calling it, to the amusement of the House, 'a great European calamity', but he went on to protest his loyalty to the Prime Minister, 'not only as a good Liberal but as an honest and conscientious politician'. Moreover, Osborne expressed radical and unpopular views about military affairs, more in the language of a *Times* leader than of a junior office-holder. Denouncing the system of purchase as the root of all evil in the army, he said:

[1] *Ibid.* 1038–49.   [2] *Ibid.* 1059–60.
[3] *Ibid.* 1121–35; *Ab. Cor. 1855–60*, p. 8; see also Woodham-Smith, *Florence Nightingale*, pp. 170–4. Gladstone described Stafford's speech as 'cheap', but Arthur Gordon thought the narrative part of it 'simple, clear and effective'.
[4] *Hansard*, CXXXVI, 1015–19, 1057–9, 1156–60.

How is it possible, then, that any but a rich man can enter the army? ['Question!'] I think this is speaking to the question—this is going to your system, which I maintain is rotten. I say it is unfair to sacrifice a Minister of War to the faults of your system, which this House has so often sanctioned and confirmed. I know it is not agreeable to hon. Gentlemen to hear these truths; but I think we have arrived at a crisis when these truths ought to be spoken.[1]

Three Conservatives spoke from the opposition front bench on the second and final day of the debate, Henley (very briefly), Bulwer Lytton and Disraeli. Lytton, after a sharp attack on the government for its failure from the beginning to provide properly for its army in the East, turned to the question of coalitions. He did not, as some of his colleagues had done, deny that coalitions were alien to British tradition. 'I find', he said, 'that most of our powerful, even popular Administrations, have been more or less coalitions...But then there is one indispensable element to a coalition, and that is, that its Members should coalesce.' That element he found wanting in the existing cabinet. 'It had been an union of party interests, but not a coalition of party sentiment and feeling.' He twitted Lord John for his defence of the Whigs against the charge of exclusiveness, saying that in plain words his vindication only amounts to this—'that where the Whigs could not get all the power, they reluctantly consented to accept a part'. As to the view that all English wars were begun with blunders, which were in due course converted into triumphs, he reminded them of a case in point.

Once in the last century [he concluded] there was a Duke of Newcastle, who presided over the conduct of a war, and was supported by a league of aristocratic combinations. That war was, indeed, a series of blunders and disasters. In vain attempts were made to patch up that luckless Ministry—in vain some drops of healthful blood were infused into its feeble and decrepit constitution—the people at last became aroused, indignant, irresistible. They applied one remedy; that remedy is now before ourselves. They dismissed their Government and saved their army.[2]

This peroration was one that might have been made by the speaker's parliamentary leader, who was the next to speak from the opposition benches. Disraeli's speech was not one of his greatest; indeed it was relatively restrained and not very long, perhaps because he considered the outcome inevitable and yet did not want to incur the primary

[1] *Hansard*, CXXXVI, 1135–9.   [2] *Ibid.* 1176–8.

responsibility for the overthrow of the government, which it was by no means certain that the opposition could replace. This was undoubtedly in Lord Derby's mind, but when he saw which way the wind was blowing on Monday evening he sent a curious message urging Disraeli to speak, but as late as possible.[1] Consequently he rose after Gladstone, who replied to Lytton, but before Palmerston.

Affecting great magnanimity, Disraeli refused to be party to any attempt to make one member of the cabinet (or one general officer in the Crimea) the scapegoat. That, he suggested, had been done by some of the duke of Newcastle's colleagues. In fact, in his mind, the duke of Newcastle was not the only minister 'entitled to the notice of Parliament'. To his mind the Home Secretary, for all his great reputation, had been unpardonably slow in producing some important Irish and Scottish militia bills in the previous session, with the consequence that England was stripped of militia to garrison Ireland when regiments of the line in Ireland were sent off to the Crimea. Had the duke of Newcastle done this, they would have heard more about it. In fact, Disraeli argued, the duke of Newcastle had done nothing for which his colleagues were not as responsible as himself. Of course Disraeli had no real sympathy for the duke; he was merely seeking in his usual fashion to pit Peelite against Whig.

I have no personal or political relations with the Duke of Newcastle [he gratuitously told his hearers]. I need not remind the House that there are many reasons why that is not a very popular name on this side of the House. The Duke of Newcastle, as a politician, was trained and bred on the Conservative benches; he owed his introduction to, and his success in public life to, this party; and in our opinion he conducted himself to this party, at a particular moment, with an acerbity of feeling and an ambiguity of conduct, which in his present forlorn condition, we can well afford to forget. But, Sir, I protest against the convenient method which now is brought into habit, of placing all these disasters upon either the mal-administration of an individual or the ill-working of a system.[2]

Clearly he was not trying to excuse the government, but to hang them all together.

Gladstone made a much better speech but he admitted afterwards to Aberdeen that he had never experienced so disagreeable a task and that wherever he turned he felt he had no sympathy.[3] Few topics can have

---

[1] Monypenny and Buckle, *Disraeli*, II, 1372.
[2] *Hansard*, CXXXVI, 1209–13.   [3] *Ibid.* 1178–1206; *Ab. Cor. 1855–60*, p. 8.

been less congenial to this remarkable man, and yet in a quiet and patient manner he talked of affairs of war with as much authority as on happier occasions he dilated on the niceties of public finance or the technicalities of university administration. The gist of his argument was simply that the criticisms had often been exaggerated, and that, although much undoubtedly had gone wrong, the critics overlooked all that had been achieved. Dwelling on the great success of the Minié rifle, only introduced on the eve of the war, he asserted:

It is a weapon capable of the most astonishing execution, as was very remarkably demonstrated at the battle of Inkerman, where it effected the greatest slaughter that has been known for many years. That was, as my right hon. Friend the Secretary at War has justly called it, 'the soldiers' battle', but it would not have been fought in the way it was if it had not been for your War Administration, first of all employing that effective weapon, and thereby changing altogether the character of your infantry, and converting them from mere machines, who fired without thinking or looking, into good and effective marksmen, as the hosts of Russia soon found. Since that time [1851], also, your field artillery has been all but created afresh. In 1852 you had no field artillery. You had no guns or gun-carriages at that time fit for service...[1]

He went on to make a vigorous defence of the conduct of the Secretary for War and to indicate in general terms the steps that had been taken to rectify the deficiencies that had become apparent in December. He rejected the concept of a select committee with scorn as a constitutional absurdity. If they wanted to get rid of the government all they had to do was to refuse to pass its measures, but as to the future of the government he clearly had no illusions. His peroration was not unworthy of the part that he had played in the administration, whose history was now fast drawing to a close:

For my part [he concluded], I believe that mode of proceeding to be worse than useless so far as regards the army in the Crimea. Your inquiry will never take place as a real inquiry; or, if it did, it would lead to nothing but confusion and disturbance, increased disaster, shame at home, weakness abroad; it would convey no consolation to those whom you seek to aid, but it would carry malignant joy to the hearts of the enemies of England, and, for my part, I ever shall rejoice, if this Motion is to-night to be carried, that my last words, as a member of the Cabinet of the Earl of Aberdeen, had been words of solemn and earnest protest against a proceeding which has no foundation

[1] *Hansard*, CXXXVI, 1195.

either in the constitution or in the practice of preceding Parliaments, which is useless and mischievous for the purpose which it appears to contemplate, and which in my judgement is full of danger to the power, dignity and usefulness of the Commons of England.[1]

Palmerston wound up the case for the government with a surprisingly short speech, but his position was undoubtedly a difficult one, not dissimilar to that of another heir-apparent defending the war administration of another failing wartime Prime Minister in our own century. He confirmed a point already made by Gladstone as to solidarity of the coalition, saying that in all their discussions they never thought of what party they originally belonged to. 'I warn you against giving encouragement to vulgar clamour against a coalition,' he warned, 'because I will venture to say that in the present state of political parties in this country, you will never be able to form a Government, strong enough to carry on its affairs with the support of Parliament, that is not founded more or less upon the principle of coalition.' He may already have been contemplating the possibility that he soon would be trying to form a ministry on this necessary principle. At any rate, few government leaders in the House of Commons can have concluded a debate in words more clearly looking forward to the likelihood of defeat than did Lord Aberdeen's new House leader on this occasion.

So, I trust [he concluded], whatever may be the fate of the Government, whatever may be the decision of this night's debate, that when the House has settled what Government it will have—when the House shall have given its confidence to any set of men who may be hereafter entrusted with the conduct of public affairs, they will give their support to that Government— that they will enable it to carry out the wishes and determination of the nation.[2]

After a final brief contribution from Roebuck the House divided and the motion was carried by a vote of 305 to 148.[3] In the majority there were 220 Conservatives, two Peelites (H. A. Bruce and J. Walter) and 83 Liberals, including twelve Irish, plus one Liberal and one Conservative teller. The minority consisted of 100 Liberals, 34 Peelites and 14 Conservatives, plus two Liberal tellers. Thus a considerable number of Liberals absented themselves from the vote, including Russell, Cobden, Bright and Milner Gibson. Indeed, apart from two or three

[1] *Ibid.* 1205–6.   [2] *Ibid.* 1222–6.
[3] *Ibid.* 1230–3. See Appendixes A and B below.

prominent Radicals, most of the Liberal dissidents were little-known backbenchers.

The next morning Gladstone called on Lord Aberdeen before the midday cabinet and observed that the enormous majority against them 'not only knocked us down but sent us down with such a whack, that one heard one's head thump as it struck the ground'. After some conversation about the preceding day's debate, they left for the final cabinet meeting. It was snowing heavily, as it had been all morning, and Aberdeen wanted to take Gladstone in his carriage, but he preferred to trudge off through the snow, saying that 'it made him feel rural'.[1]

After the formalities of the meeting were completed the Prime Minister, accompanied by his son, caught the two o'clock train for Windsor. 'The grey towers of the castle were relieved by a background of yet greyer and gloomier sky,' Arthur Gordon recorded, 'and the large damp snow flakes fell, slowly, thickly, and sullenly round us as we walked up from the station. I parted from my father at the gate with a sigh. I watched him cross the court through the snow, and then passing through the Norman gate, and turning into the cloisters, I ran down the hundred steps and crossed the bridge to Eton.'[2] The Aberdeen coalition was at an end.

[1] *Ab. Cor. 1855–60*, pp. 8–9, Arthur Gordon's Journal, 30 January 1855.
[2] *Ibid.* 109.

CONCLUSION

The sequel is beyond the scope of this book, but in broad outline it is well known. Derby and Russell were alike unable to form governments; the former for lack of support from outside his own party, the latter because no Whig, with the dubious exception of Palmerston, would join him; and Lansdowne declined on grounds of health. The queen was forced to fall back on Palmerston, the inevitable, who reformed the coalition, less Aberdeen and Newcastle, although a few weeks later he lost Graham, Gladstone, Herbert and Cardwell, when he failed to oppose the setting up of the Roebuck committee of inquiry. The Palmerstonian Whig–Liberal ministry survived for three years and in due course brought the war to its conclusion.

Two not unrelated questions remain to be considered. First of all, why did Britain, the wealthiest, the freest and technologically the most advanced country in Europe, fail to play a more effective role in the Crimean War? Secondly, why did the Aberdeen coalition collapse so ignominiously after it had survived for two years a wide variety of challenges? *The Times*, in effect, raised the first question when it began its devastating attack on the conduct of the war, asking how such a wealthy and ingenious people as the British could fail so miserably in tackling the practical problems of waging war.

The evidence that we have considered suggests that on the whole the army was more immediately responsible for what went wrong in the Crimea than the government. In the long run, however, the politicians were responsible for the state of the army and the calibre of the officers commanding it. As we have seen, *The Times* condemned the aristocratic 'establishment' of that day, and, although its charges were exaggerated, undoubtedly here is where much of the trouble lay. Britain's economic strength and commercial supremacy were for the most part the achievement of her men of business and her technicians. These men built their commercial empires, but as yet, with some exceptions, they did not aspire to play a leading role in government, provided they were free to do as they chose and were not burdened by heavy taxes. By and large, the government of the country was still in the hands of the ruling class who had run it for centuries. They were an enlightened aristocracy, always ready to tolerate a certain amount of

549

recruitment from below, and they had made a certain accommodation with the times by effecting some reform of parliament and of the central administration; their approach to the responsibilities of government, however, tended to remain casual and amateur. Yet there were elements among them who instinctively saw the necessity of abandoning this outdated attitude and making government a matter for professionals, on both the political and administrative levels. This was pre-eminently the view of the Peelites, first under Peel himself; and later it was exemplified in the careers of Gladstone and Cardwell. (All three were sons of prosperous business men, who as a result of their education and natural abilities had themselves been accepted into the aristocratic establishment.) Peel and his colleagues were always critical of the amateur and cavalier approach of the Whigs to weighty matters of government and particularly to public finance. The great fiscal reforms of the period were the work of Peel and Gladstone, and it was Gladstone and Cardwell who were responsible eventually for the reform of the civil service and the army. There were, however, important elements in the Liberal party that supported and welcomed such reforms and herein lay the justification for the ultimate fusion of the Peelites and the Liberals.

There was indeed an irony in the fact that the chief administrative responsibility for the conduct of the war lay in the hands of Peelite ministers and that they failed, but it is doubtful whether others would initially have been any more successful. The accretion of centuries was not to be swept away overnight. It is true that the Peelites stood for greater efficiency in government, but they were not revolutionaries. Indeed they were conservative reformers, whose approach to reform was pragmatic and utilitarian. They wanted to make the machinery of government work more efficiently, but not to upset the framework of society. The Peelite contribution to army reform was still fifteen years in the future. The Crimean War came upon them too quickly and overwhelmed them.

Nor were all the Peelites equally effective. Aberdeen was intellectually and emotionally sympathetic to Peel's ideals, but he was not himself naturally a man of business. He was quite ready to support parliamentary and civil service reform, but he was at his most conservative when it came to army reform, where he was content to abide by the views of the duke of Wellington and the prejudices of the queen. Newcastle was potentially more liberal, but lacked the imagination needed in the hour of crisis; Gladstone was not interested in the army and Cardwell was not in the cabinet. Had Sidney Herbert been at the War Office he might have effected the more necessary adjustments, but the problem was basically a long-term one and no government coming into office on the eve of a European war could be held fully responsible for inadequacies of the British military system. Unfortunately for the Aberdeen coalition, it was the first British wartime administration to face the glare of modern newspaper publicity resulting from the presence of correspondents in the field with the army. This brings us to our second question concerning the collapse of the coalition.

There are really two questions, the narrower one as to the coalition's responsibility for what had gone wrong with the war, which we have partly answered, and the larger one regarding the viability of the coalition itself. If it had not fallen on this issue, would it not have collapsed on another?

There is no doubt that Aberdeen was not cut out to be a war leader. As we have seen, his heart was not in it and there was foundation to Russell's criticism when he implied that there was a lack of initiative in the Prime Minister. His replacement in the course of the war was politically a natural occurrence, similar to the replacement of Addington in 1804, of Asquith in 1916, and of Neville Chamberlain in 1940. It was probably less necessary than on those other occasions, for the Crimean was not a war of the same magnitude as the others and it was nearer to an end when the change was effected. Indeed it may be argued that the change made little difference, but all the same a political need was met.

The duke of Newcastle was clearly not an ideal Minister for War and his colleagues, other than Russell, were too gentlemanly in their consideration of his personal feelings. A more decisive Prime Minister than Aberdeen, with more insight into the problems of running and winning a war, would have grasped the opportunity offered by the division of the War Office and the Colonial Office in June of 1854. There was no lack of zeal on the poor duke's part; he was the most conscientious of ministers and did not spare himself in any way, but he simply became overwhelmed by detail. He proved to be a poor judge of men and lacking in imagination. He was also too standoffish and over-critical of others, particularly of the French allies. Sidney Herbert, who gave him much unofficial assistance, would probably have been a much better War Minister. He certainly showed more of an eye for the problem as a whole and would not have become as submerged by detail. It is hard to believe that he would not have been a better choice than either Palmerston or Lord Panmure, Newcastle's successor. Whether he would have had the physical stamina to stand up to the strain of the office is a matter of question. Indeed the strain of the same office in peacetime half a dozen years later was to prove too much for him.

Yet when all these criticisms of Aberdeen and Newcastle are admitted, the fact remains that the change in ministers probably did not make any significant difference to the outcome of the war, although it more than likely prolonged it because of Palmerston's reluctance to make peace. It is clear that the major steps towards reform had been taken before the Aberdeen administration went out of office. The deficiencies in huts and clothing had been largely made up, the Balaclava Railway was under construction, the chaos in the harbour was being brought under control by new and more successful officers, a Land Transport Corps was being organised, a reinforcement depot was being set up in Malta, a telegraphic cable was being laid across the Black Sea to the Crimea, improvements had been made in the hospitals at Scutari, the French had been persuaded to accept a larger share of the trenches, more in proportion to their numbers, and on the other hand the British had given them needed assistance in the matter of sea transportation. The War Office and the Colonial Office had been separated. The commissariat had been transferred from the Treasury to the War Office and a new Board was in process of being established to coordinate the various independent departments responsible for the army. By the spring the lot of the army was vastly improved, although there were still to be disappointing and costly setbacks before the final objective was attained. Sebastopol did not fall until September and months before that Lord Raglan was dead. The final victory was mainly the achievement of the French army, now greatly superior in numbers, but it could not have been attained without the earlier victories to which the British had made the greatest contribution in men and valour.

The larger question regarding the viability of the coalition may be rephrased. Was its fall an accident of war, or the failure of the coalition to coalesce? In other words, was the vote on the Roebuck motion merely the occasion of a break-up that was bound to come sooner or later? As we have seen, the first year of the coalition's existence was on the whole a marked success, while the second was largely one of frustration and failure in the field of domestic legislation. Was this owing, it may be asked, to the intrinsic weakness of the government itself or to external forces beyond its control? From the beginning everyone knew that its majority was a precarious one, liable to disappear whenever a sufficient number of the various independent elements in the House of Commons sided with the official opposition on a particular issue. After the collapse of two successive administrations in 1852, the House was not prepared for another change in 1853; moreover, the imagination of the majority was captured by Gladstone's budget of that year. By 1854 the honeymoon was over, but, more important, the politicians had become preoccupied with the war and had cooled to further reform. The growing undependability of the government leader in the Commons was the final straw. When he went the edifice collapsed. Time after time in the entire twenty-five months of its duration Lord John Russell had proved to be an indigestible element in the coalition, but it is equally clear that there were no obvious divisions within the cabinet on party lines. This was the case in all the crises that the government faced and it was most dramatically emphasised in the repudiation of Russell by all his former Whig colleagues at the end. Palmerston and the other Whig ministers were genuinely anxious to keep the Peelites in the government when it was reformed, and had it not been for the snag of the Roebuck committee the union of 1859 might have been anticipated, but that is another story.

Gladstone may not have been ready in 1855 for the step he ultimately took in 1859. In the intervening years he and his friends strongly criticised the Palmerston government on many counts, but they never returned to the Conservative party. Had the Crimean War not delayed Lord Aberdeen's intended retirement, Russell might well have succeeded him as Prime Minister under happier circumstances than those of 1855 and Gladstone have been persuaded to stay. In domestic policy he had more in common with Russell than with Palmerston who, had it not been for the accident of 1855, might have faded out of the picture at a much earlier date than he actually did. These, however, are speculations beyond the role of the historian. The most important consequence of the Aberdeen coalition was that it proved the possibility of the heirs of Peel joining with Whigs and Radicals one day to form a new Liberal party. The final date of the merger was uncertain when the coalition fell, but 1859 was a natural sequel to the experiment of 1852–5.[1] The elimination of the Peelite element from the Conservative party and its eventual absorption into a revitalised Liberal party was a major event in the history of political parties in the nineteenth century. The history of the Aberdeen coalition was an important chapter in that transformation.

[1] This book was completed before the appearance of John Vincent's *The formation of the Liberal party 1857–1868* (London, 1966).

APPENDIXES

In both appendixes the letter C indicates a pro-coalition vote, i.e. against the Derby government in division 1 or with the coalition in the other divisions; the letters AC (anti-coalition) indicate the opposite. Parentheses indicate a different reading of the same bill. In some cases the vote was actually taken on an amendment and the reading itself passed without a division. The choice of divisions has been limited to those for which division lists are published by *Hansard*.

AN ANALYSIS OF THE VOTES OF PEELITE MEMBERS 1852–5[1]

	1	2	3	4	5	6	7	8	9	10	11	12	13	14
A'Court, C. H. (Wilton)	C		C	(AC)	C	C	C		C	C		C	C	C
Baring, F. (Thetford)	C		C	C	C		C							
Baring, H. B. (Marlborough)	C		C	C	C	C	C	C	C	C				
*Bruce, Ld E. (Marlborough)	C		C		C	C	C	C		C	C			C
Bruce, H. A. (Merthyr-Tydvil)	C	C	C	C	C	C			C	C	C	C		C
*Cardwell, E. (Oxford City, 4 Jan. 1853)	C	C	C	C	C	C	C	C	C	C	C	C	C	C
*Charteris, F. (Haddingtonshire)	C	C	C	C	C	C	C	C	C	C	C	C	C	C
*Clinton, Ld R. (Notts.)	C	C			C	C	C		C					C
Denison, E. (Yorks., W.R.)	C		C	C	C	C	C	C	C		C		C	C
*Drumlanrig, Visc. (Dumfriesshire)	C	C	C	C	C	C	C	C	C				C	C
*Fitzroy, H. (Lewes)	C	C	C	C	C	C	C	C			C	C	C	C
*Gladstone, W. E. (Oxford)	C	C	C	AC	C	C	C	C	C	C		C	C	C
Goulburn, H. (Cambridge)	C		C	C	C			C	C	C	AC		C	C
*Graham, Sir J. (Carlisle)	C		C	AC	C	C	C	C	C	C	AC	C		C
Greene, T. (Lancaster, 18 Apr. 1853)	C				C		C	C	C	C		C	C	C
Hanmer, Sir J. (Flint)	C		C	C	C	C	C	C	C	C	C	C	C	C
Harcourt, G. G. (Oxfordshire)	C		C	(C)	C	C	C		C	C			C	C
Heneage, G. F. (Lincoln)	C	C	C	C	C	C		C	C		C		C	
Herbert, H. A. (Kerry)	C	C	C	C	C	C	C	C	C	C	C		C	C
*Herbert, S. (Wilts. N.)	C	C	C	(AC)	C	C	C	C	C	C			C	C
*Hervey, Lord A. (Brighton)	C	C	C	(AC)	C	C	C	C	C	C		C	C	C

Table of votes on coalition/anti-coalition divisions (one-time Conservative members)[1]

Hogg, Sir J. W. (Honiton)	C	C	C	C	C		C	C	C	C			C	C
Jermyn, Earl (Bury St Edmund's)	C	C	C	C	C	C	C		C	C	C		C	C
Johnstone, Sir J. (Scarborough)	C	C	C	C	C		C		C	C			C	C
Legh, G. C. (Ches. N.)	C		C	AC	C	C	C		C	AC	C	C		
Lewis, Sir T. F. (Radnor)	C	(C)	C	(C)	C				C	C	C			
Lockhart, A. E. (Selkirkshire)	C		C	AC	C	C	C		C	AC	C		C	C
*Lowe, R. (Kidderminster)	C		C	C	C	C	C	C	C	C	C	C	C	C
Milnes, R. M. (Pontefract)	C	C	C	C	C	C	C	C	C	C	C	C	C	C
*Monck, Visc. (Portsmouth)	C	C	C	C	C	C	C	C	C	C			(C)	C
Mostyn, E. (Flintshire)	C	C	C	C	C	C	C	C	C	C	C	C	C	C
Mure, Col. W. (Renfrewshire)	C	C	C	C	C	C	C		C	C	C	C	C	C
Norreys, Ld (Abingdon)	C				C									
Palmer, Roundell (Plymouth, 2 June 1853)	C		C	C	C	C	C	C	C	C				
*Peel, F. (Bury)	C		C	AC	C	C	C		C			C		AC
Peel, Sir R. (Tamworth)		(C)		AC	C	C	C			C	C			C
Phillimore, R. J. (Tavistock, 1 Feb. 1853)				C	C	C	C	C	C	C	C	C		C
Sutton, J. H. M. (Newark)	C	C	C	C	C	C	C	C	C	C	C			C
Vernon, G. E. H. (Newark)	C	C	C	C	C	C	C		C	C	C	C		C
Wall, C. B. (Salisbury)	C	C	C	C	C	C	C		C	C	C	(died autumn 1853)		
Walter, J. (Nottingham)	C	C	C	C	C	C	C						(C)	AC
Wickham, H. W. (Bradford)	AC	AC	C	C	C	C	C	C	C			AC	AC	C
Wortley, J. A. S. (Buteshire)	AC	AC	C	C	C	C	C					AC	AC	C
Young, Sir J. (Cavan)	C	C	C	C	C	C	C		C	C	C	C	C	C
Total coalition votes	39	26	41	34	43	40	37	28	37	39	31	21	31	35
Total anti-coalition votes	0	2	0	6	0	0	0	0	0	0	4	2	0	1

[1] I.e. one-time Conservative members who did not support the Disraeli budget and who gave fairly consistent support to the coalition, although in a few cases this proved to be a little shaky. I have included H. A. Bruce, who is sometimes classified as a Liberal, but not Sir R. Fergusson, whom I have accepted as a Whig. Charteris became Lord Elcho in 1854.

* Office-holders, including household appointments.

APPENDIX B

AN ANALYSIS OF THE VOTES OF 36 INDEPENDENT CONSERVATIVES 1852–5

	1	2	3	4	5¹	6	7²	8	9	10	11	12	13	14
*Acland, Sir T. D. (Devon N.)	AC	—	AC	AC	C	C	C	C	C	C	—	—	C	C
Baring, T. (Huntingdon)	—	—	AC	C	AC	—	C	—	C	AC	—	—	AC	C
*Beckett, W. (Ripon)	AC	—	AC	AC	C	—	C	—	C	C	AC	AC	—	AC
*Benbow, J. (Dudley)	AC	—	—	—	C	C	C	—	—	—	—	—	—	—
Bramston, T. W. (Essex, S.)	AC	C	AC	AC	C	C	C	C	C	—	AC	C	C	AC
*Christy, S. (Newcastle-under-Lyme)	AC	—	C	(AC)	C	C	—	—	—	AC	AC	—	AC	AC
*Cocks, T. S. (Reigate)	AC	C	C	AC	C	C	C	AC	C	AC	AC	C	AC	AC
*Colville, C. R. (Derbyshire, S.)	—	—	(C)	AC	AC	C	—	—	AC	C	AC	C	—	AC
Coote, Sir C. (Queen's)	AC	C	C	—	C	C	C	—	—	—	—	—	—	—
*Cubitt, Sir W. (Andover)	AC	—	AC	C	AC	—	—	—	—	C	AC	AC	AC	AC
Dundas, G. (Linlithgowshire)	—	AC	C	AC	C	—	C	—	—	—	AC	—	C	AC
East, Sir J. B. (Winchester)	AC	AC	C	AC	C	C	C	C	—	AC	AC	—	AC	AC
*Egerton, E. C. (Macclesfield)	AC	—	AC	AC	C	C	—	C	—	—	AC	—	AC	—
*Egerton, W. T. (Ches. N.)	AC	—	—	AC	AC	C	—	C	C	C	AC	C	—	C
*Emlyn, Visc. (Pembrokeshire)	—	C	C	AC	C	—	—	AC	AC	AC	AC	AC	AC	AC
Evelyn, W. J. (Surrey, W.)	AC	C	(C)	AC	AC	C	—	—	C	C	—	C	AC	AC
*Fitzgerald, W. R. S. (Horsham)	AC	C	C	—	—	—	—	—	AC	C	AC	—	AC	AC
Gladstone, J. N. (Devizes)	AC	C	C	AC	C	C	—	—	C	C	—	AC	—	C
*Hardinge, C. S. (Downpatrick)	AC	AC	—	—	AC	—	C	C	AC	C	—	AC	C	C
Heathcote, Sir W. (Oxford U., 8 Feb. 1854)	AC	C	C	AC	C	C					AC		C	C
Heneage, G. H. W. (Devizes)	AC	—	C	AC	C	—	—	C	C	C	AC	—	—	C
*Hughes, W. B. (Carnarvon)	AC	AC	AC	AC	C	C	C	AC	C	C	AC	C	C	C
Inglis, Sir R. (Oxford U.)	AC	AC	AC	AC	C	C	C	C	C	C	AC	C	C	C

(Chiltern H, Feb. 1854)

558

★Johnstone, Jas. (Clackmannan)	C	—	AC	AC	C	C	C	C	C	—	—	—	AC	C
MacGregor, Jas. (Sandwich)	AC	AC	AC	AC	C	AC	C	C	C	—	AC	AC	AC	AC
★Owen, Sir J. (Pembroke)	AC	—	C	C	C	—	C	—	C	C	—	—	C	C
★Patten, J. W. (Lancs. N.)	—	—	C	AC	C	—	—	—	C	C	AC	—	C	C
Peel, Col. J. (Huntingdon)	C	—	AC	AC	—	—	C	—	C	—	AC	—	C	C
Philips, J. H. (Haverfordwest)	AC	C	—	AC	C	C	—	C	C	C	AC	—	C	—
Pritchard, J. (Bridgenorth, 23 Mar. 1853)		—	AC	C	C	—	C	—	C	C	—	—	AC	AC
★Sandars, G. (Wakefield)	AC	—	AC	C	C	—	C	—	C	AC	AC	AC	AC	AC
★Smollett, A. (Dumbartonshire)	AC	—	(C)	—	—	C	C	—	C	C	AC	AC	C	—
Stephenson, R. (Whitby)	AC	—	AC	AC	C	—	C	—	—	C	AC	—	C	C
★Stirling, W. (Perthshire)	AC	C	(C)	—	C	AC	C	C	C	C	AC	AC	C	—
Stuart, H. (Bedford)	—	—	C	AC	C	C	C	—	—	C	AC	AC	—	—
★Wyndham, W. (Wilts. S.)	AC	C	C	AC	C	—	C	C	C	C	—	—	—	C
Total coalition votes	2	11	18	4	28	21	27	12	23	20	0	5	12	12

Sir T. D. Acland, Sir John Owen and W. Wyndham might have been included in the Peelite list had they not voted for the Disraeli budget. Jas. Johnstone and J. W. Patten, who did not vote for the Disraeli budget, might also have been included, but their voting pattern does not seem quite strong enough to justify it. The line between the most independent of these Conservatives and the most uncertain of the Peelites is by no means distinct and admittedly somewhat arbitrary.

In addition there were at least twenty-two other Conservatives who voted against their party two or three times on these fourteen divisions. They were: C. B. Adderley, E. Ball, E. S. Cayley, Sir E. Dering★, H. Drummond, J. M. Gaskell, Admiral W. Gordon (Aberdeen's brother), Col. F. V. Harcourt, E. Lascelles, G. Hudson, Col. Lindsay★, J. Masterman★, W. Michell, E. G. D. Pennant, M. Portal, Lord W. Powlett, H. K. Seymer, J. G. Smyth, G. Tomline★, Sir R. Vyvyan, Lord C. Wellesley, L. T. Wigram.

[1] Other Conservatives supporting the Gladstone income tax (col. 5) were: H. Drummond, Adm. W. Gordon, Col. F. V. Harcourt, G. Hudson, Col. Lindsay, J. Masterman, Col. E. Pennant, Ld W. Powlett, J. G. Smyth, Ld C. Wellesley, F. R. West, B. T. Woodd.

[2] Other Conservatives supporting the India Bill (col. 7) were: Sir J. Bailey, T. W. Booker, C. Butt, I. Butt, H. M. Cairns, Sir A. Campbell, E. S. Cayley, Visc. Chelsea, S. Child, J. C. Cobbald, Sir W. Codrington, H. B. Coles, H. L. Corry, D. A. Davies, R. Davison, Sir E. Dering, Sir J. Duckworth, F. Floyer, B. S. Follett, Sir W. P. Gallwey, A. L. Goddard, Sir E. Gooch, Adm. Gordon, W. O. Gore, E. Greaves, R. B. Hale, Col. Harcourt, Sir E. Hayes, J. C. Herries, Lord Hotham, G. Hudson, W. Hume, N. Kendall, E. Lascelles, Sir T. H. Maddock, R. Malins, W. Michell, Sir G. Montgomery, O. Morgan, J. Mowbray, G. J. Noel, Col. North, M. Portal, D. Pugh, P. Rolt, F. Scott, Visc. Seaham, H. K. Seymer, J. G. Smyth, R. Spooner, J. Tollemache, G. H. Vansittart, Sir R. Vyvyan, D. Waddington, Ld C. Wellesley, L. T. Wigram, E. Wodehouse.

★ Names mentioned as possible Peelites in the Gladstone Papers, 1852.

THE ABERDEEN MINISTRY

(as it stood at the meeting of the parliament on 10 February 1853)[1]

IN THE CABINET

First Lord of the Treasury . . .	Right Hon. Earl of Aberdeen
Lord Chancellor	Right Hon. Lord Cranworth
Chancellor of the Exchequer . . .	Right Hon. William Ewart Gladstone
President of the Council . . .	Right Hon. Earl Granville
Privy Seal	His Grace the Duke of Argyll
Home Secretary	Right Hon. Viscount Palmerston
Foreign Secretary	Right Hon. Lord John Russell
Colonial Secretary	His Grace the Duke of Newcastle
First Lord of the Admiralty . . .	Right Hon. James Robert George Graham, bt.
President of the Board of Control . .	Right Hon. Sir Charles Wood, bt.
Secretary at War	Right Hon. Sidney Herbert
First Commissioner of Works and Public Buildings . . . . . }	Right Hon. Sir William Molesworth, bt.
	Most Hon. Marquess of Lansdowne

NOT IN THE CABINET

General Commanding-in-Chief . .	Right Hon. Viscount Hardinge
Master General of the Ordnance . .	Right Hon. Lord Raglan
President of the Board of Trade . .	Right Hon. Edward Cardwell
Paymaster of the Forces, and Vice-President of the Board of Trade . . . }	Right Hon. Lord Stanley of Alderley
Chancellor of the Duchy of Lancaster .	Right Hon. Edward Strutt
Postmaster-General	Right Hon. Viscount Canning
Secretary of the Admiralty . . .	Ralph Bernal Osborne, esq.
Attorney-General	Sir Alexander James Edmund Cockburn, knt.
Solicitor-General	Sir Richard Bethell, knt.
Judge-Advocate General . . .	Right Hon. Charles Pelham Villiers
Chief Poor-Law Commissioner . .	Right Hon. Matthew Talbot Baines

SCOTLAND

Lord Advocate	Right Hon. James Moncrieff
Solicitor-General	Robert Handyside, esq.

[1] From *Annual Register, 1853*, Appendix to the Chronicle.

APPENDIXES

IRELAND

Lord Lieutenant	Right Hon. Earl of St Germans
Lord Chancellor	Right Hon. Maziere Brady
Chief Secretary	Right Hon. Sir John Young, bt.
Attorney-General	Right Hon. Abraham Brewster
Solicitor-General.	William Keogh, esq.

QUEEN'S HOUSEHOLD

Lord Steward	His Grace the Duke of Norfolk
Lord Chamberlain	Most Hon. Marquess of Breadalbane
Master of the Horse	His Grace the Duke of Wellington
Mistress of the Robes	Duchess of Sutherland

THE FOLLOWING CHANGES TOOK PLACE DURING THE YEAR

IN THE CABINET. The Earl of Clarendon, *Foreign Secretary, vice* Lord John Russell, *a Seat in the Cabinet without Office.*

NOT IN THE CABINET. James Crauford, Esq., *Solicitor-General for Scotland, vice* Robert Handyside, Esq., *a Lord of Session.*

THE FOLLOWING CHANGES TOOK PLACE IN THE YEAR 1854[1]

IN THE CABINET. Lord John Russell, *Lord President of the Council, vice* Earl Granville. The Duke of Newcastle, *Secretary of State for War (a new Secretaryship).* Sir George Grey, *Secretary of State for the Colonies, vice* the Duke of Newcastle. Earl Granville, *Chancellor of the Duchy of Lancaster (with a seat in Cabinet), vice* Right Hon. Edward Strutt, *resigned.*

NOT IN THE CABINET. Thomas Mackenzie, Esq., *Solicitor-General for Scotland, vice* James Crawford, Esq., *a Lord of Session.*

[1] *The Annual Register 1854,* Appendix to Chronicle.

THE BUDGETS OF 1853–4 AND 1854–5[1]

(1) 18 April 1853

REVENUE

Head of Revenue	Basis of estimate £	Estimate £	Result £	Remarks
Customs	20,680,000	20,022,000	20,703,048	New duties imposed, net
Excise	14,640,000	14,391,000	15,263,549	gain, £1,344,000
Stamps	6,700,000	7,000,000	6,956,819	Old duties reduced or
Taxes	3,250,000	3,250,000	3,241,701	repealed, net loss
Income tax	5,550,000	5,845,000	6,117,303	£1,656,000
Post office	900,000	900,000	1,104,000	
Crown lands	390,000*	390,000	395,888	
Miscellaneous	320,000	320,000	511,450	
Old stores	460,000	460,000	481,146	
Total	52,890,000	52,578,000	54,774,905	
Surplus	807,000	495,000	3,524,785	
Deficiency	—	—	—	

EXPENDITURE

Head of Service	Estimate £	Result £	Remarks
Debt	27,804,000	27,738,927	The estimate for the Army as here given
Cons. fund charges	2,503,000	2,500,529	includes the vote for the Commissariat;
Army	6,582,000 ⎱ 6,415,000		and the estimate for the Navy includes
Militia	530,000 ⎰		that for the Packet Service, though
Navy	7,035,000	6,942,769	Mr Gladstone stated them separately
Ordnance	3,053,000	2,900,000	
Miscellaneous	4,476,000	4,471,559	
Kafir War	200,000	230,000	
Unclaimed dividends	—	51,336	
Total	52,183,000	—	
Estimated saving on conversion of stock	100,000	—	
Total	52,083,000	51,250,120	

[1] Based on Sir Stafford H. Northcote's, *Twenty years of financial policy*, pp. 387–8.

* The estimate for the Crown Lands was swelled by a sum of £135,000 on account of repayments in respect of Metropolitan Improvements.

(2) 6 March and 8 May 1854

REVENUE

Head of Revenue	Basis of estimate £	Estimate £	Result £	Remarks
Customs	20,175,000	20,875,000	20,496,659	Income tax raised to 14d. in
Excise	14,595,000	17,495,000	16,179,169	the £. Duty on Scotch
Stamps	7,090,000	7,090,000	6,965,514	and Irish spirits raised.
Taxes	3,015,000	3,015,000	3,036,136	Malt duty raised from
Income tax	6,275,000	12,832,000	10,515,369	2s. 8½d. to 4s. per bushel.
Post office	1,200,000	1,200,000	1,299,156	Sugar duties raised
Crown lands	259,000	259,000	272,572	Amount of unfunded debt
Miscellaneous	320,000	320,000	316,904	created this year:
				£
Old Stores	420,000	420,000	414,674	Exchequer bills 1,750,000
Total	53,349,000	63,506,000*	59,496,154	Exchequer bonds 5,375,513
Surplus	—	—	—	
Deficiency	2,840,000	3,543,000*	6,196,808	£7,125,513

EXPENDITURE

Head of Service	Estimate, 6 March £	Estimate, 8 May £	Result £	Remarks
Debt	27,546,000	27,546,000	27,864,533	
Cons. fund charges	2,460,000	2,460,000	1,839,290	
Army and commiss.	7,502,000	7,802,000 ⎱	8,380,882	
Militia	530,000	1,030,000 ⎰		
Navy and packets	8,280,000	12,830,000	14,490,105	
Ordnance	3,846,000	4,486,000	5,450,720	
Miscellaneous	4,775,000	4,775,000	5,867,432	
Extraordinary military services	1,250,000	2,100,000	1,800,000	
Total	56,189,000	63,039,000	65,692,962	

* This sum shows the estimated ultimate produce of the new taxes, but the whole amount expected within the year was £59,496,000, the deficiency of £3,543,000 being provided for by the issue of Exchequer bonds.

A DIPLOMATIC CALENDAR 1853-4

1853

9 Jan.   Seymour conversations.
13 Jan.   Russian military and naval movements in the Black Sea area.
9 Feb.   Russell despatch—satisfies the Czar.
12 Feb.   Leiningen mission—successfully presses Austrian claims with Turkey.
2 Mar.   Menschikoff arrives at Constantinople.
7 Mar.   Rose summons Dundas with the fleet.
16 Mar.   Menschikoff makes his 'drastic demands'.
19 Mar.   French government decides to send a squadron to the Aegean.
20 Mar.   British inner cabinet vetoes Rose's summons of the fleet.
5 Apr.   Stratford arrives at Constantinople.
5 May   Details of Holy Places dispute settled.
  Menschikoff demands special privileges for the Orthodox Churches.
9 May   Stratford encourages the sultan, but refuses naval support.
10 May   Menschikoff presses a secret alliance on the Turks.
13 May   Menschikoff forces resignation of Turkish ministers and appointment of
  Reschid.
17 May   Turkish grand council opposes Russian demands.
18 May   Menschikoff refuses Reschid's proposals.
19 May   Meeting of four ambassadors to the Porte; their offer of good offices declined.
20 May   Menschikoff refuses final offer of Reschid.
22 May   Menschikoff leaves Constantinople.
27 May   Czar orders occupation of the Principalities.
31 May   Russian ultimatum to Turkey regarding the Principalities (received in
  Constantinople, 10 June).
  British cabinet authorises Stratford to summon fleet.
2 June   British fleet ordered to the Aegean.
13 June   British fleet arrives at Besika Bay.
14 June   French fleet joins British at Besika Bay.
16 June   Britain and France ask Austria to summon a conference.
  Turkey turns down Nesselrode ultimatum of 31 May.
17 June   Russian legation closed in Constantinople.
19–21 June   British ministers exchange memoranda on the crisis.
2 July   Russian occupation of the Principalities; Nesselrode circular of explanation.
7 July   Cabinet approves Clarendon's draft convention; also approves an alternate
  French draft.
20 July   'Turkish ultimatum' extracted from the Porte by Stratford.
24 July   Vienna conference of ambassadors opened by Buol.
29 July   Vienna conference rejects 'Turkish ultimatum'—prepares Vienna note based on
  French draft.
1 Aug.   Vienna note despatched to St Petersburg and Constantinople.
2 Aug.   Clarendon informs Stratford of Britain's acceptance of the Vienna note.
5 Aug.   Russia accepts the Vienna note.
12 Aug.   Stratford demands Turkish acceptance of the note.

APPENDIXES

16 Aug. Commons debate on Eastern Question.

20 Aug. Prorogation of parliament.

Turkey rejects Vienna note unless amended.

3 Sept. Ministerial meeting in London to discuss the Turkish modifications; Russell memorandum.

11–12 Sept. Constantinople riots; Allied ambassadors call up small warships.

13 Sept. Russia rejects Turkish modifications.

14 Sept. Four Allied ships approach Constantinople.

15 Sept. British proposal of a Four-Power interpretation of the Vienna note.

17 Sept. Nesselrode's 'violent interpretation' of the Vienna note revealed; France and Britain abandon it.

20 Sept. Buol declares Vienna conference closed.

23 Sept. Aberdeen and Clarendon order Stratford to summon the fleet to Constantinople.

26 Sept.–4 Oct. Turkish grand council meets; decides to declare war.

Russian and Austrian emperors meet at Olmütz; their proposals.

4 Oct. Turkish ultimatum to Russia to quit the Principalities.

Stratford receives fleet orders but delays.

5 Oct. France rejects Olmütz proposals.

7–8 Oct. British cabinet meeting confirms rejection of Olmütz proposals; authorises fleet to enter the Black Sea.

12 Oct. Cabinet considers Clarendon's draft note based on Stratford's proposals.

20 Oct. Ambassadors summon fleets to Constantinople.

22 Oct. Stratford sends his draft note to Vienna.

Allied fleets enter the Dardanelles.

23 Oct. Turks begin hostilities.

24 Oct. Clarendon despatches his draft note to Constantinople.

25 Oct. Buol announces Russian offer to enter peace negotiations.

Buol rejects Stratford note.

30 Oct. Czar writes to Queen Victoria.

Prince consort and ministers exchange memoranda.

5 Nov. Clarendon note arrives in Constantinople; not accepted by the Turks.

16 Nov. Cabinet decides to ask Turks to indicate armistice terms.

20 Nov. Buol asks British and French governments to submit proposals.

24 Nov. Turks reject Austrian note regarding Russian overture.

Arrival of Allied fleets at Constantinople.

29 Nov. Anglo-French proposals (collective note) forwarded to Vienna.

30 Nov. Battle of Sinope.

3 Dec. Collective note approved at Vienna; forwarded to Constantinople.

7 Dec. Clarendon sends unofficial warning to St Petersburg.

14 Dec. Resignation of Palmerston.

15 Dec. Stratford and ambassadors submit project to Turks.

16 Dec. Stratford holds back collective note.

17–20 Dec. Cabinet orders fleet into Black Sea.

22–24 Dec. Cabinet agrees to French demands regarding Russian ships in the Black Sea.

24 Dec. Return of Palmerston accepted.

26 Dec. Stratford decides to send fleet into Black Sea.

31 Dec. Allied fleets leave for Black Sea.

Turks agree to Stratford's project.

1854

3 Jan.	Allied fleets complete entry into Black Sea.
6 Jan.	Warning to Russian admiral delivered at Sebastopol.
11 Jan.	Seymour informs Nesselrode of instructions to Black Sea fleet.
20 Jan.	Stratford proposals reach St Petersburg from Vienna.
28 Jan.	Orloff arrives in Vienna with counter-proposals.
31 Jan.	Louis Napoleon appeals to Nicholas.
2 Feb.	Vienna conference rejects Russian proposals.
4–5 Feb.	Russian ambassadors recalled from Paris and London.
7 Feb.	British and French governments recall their ambassadors from St Petersburg.
8 Feb.	Orloff leaves Vienna.
9 Feb.	Nicholas rejects Louis Napoleon's appeal.
27–28 Feb.	British and French governments despatch a summons to the Russian government with approval of Austrian government.
28 Feb.	First British army detachments sail for the East.
4 Mar.	Prussia gives limited support to Allied summons.
19 Mar.	British and French consuls present summons to Nesselrode, who refuses a reply.
27–28 Mar.	Britain and France declare war on Russia.

BIBLIOGRAPHY

1. Manuscript Sources
2. Printed Sources
3. Biographies, Memoirs, Letters

4. Monographs and other secondary works
5. Articles
6. Works of Reference

1 *Manuscript Sources*

Aberdeen Papers, British Museum, Add. MSS. 43039–43358.

Bright Papers, British Museum, Add. MS. 43383.

Broughton Papers, British Museum, Add. MS. 43757.

Clarendon Papers, Bodleian Library, Oxford.

Cobden Papers, British Museum, Add. MSS. 43649–50.

Crown Copyright Records, PRO WO 6/70/85 and WO 1/371/84.

Gladstone Papers, British Museum, Add. MSS. 44086–44835.

Graham Papers, Netherby Manor, Longtown, Cumberland; microfilmed copies consulted at University Library, Cambridge, and Newberry Library, Chicago.

Halifax Papers, British Museum, Add. MS. 43531.

Herbert Papers, Wilton House Archives, Wilton, Wiltshire.

Newcastle Papers (fifth duke), University of Nottingham Library.

Russell Papers, Public Record Office. PRO 30/22/10, PRO 30/22/11, and PRO 30/22/12 cover the years 1852–5, each with subdivisions A, B, C, etc. Recatalogued and repaginated in 1963 after this research was completed. I have endeavoured to revise all the references.

—— British Museum, Add. MSS. 38080 (miscellaneous correspondence).

Royal Archives, Windsor Castle, Papers of Queen Victoria and Prince Albert (R.A. A23, A84, C28, C42, C47, E3, E5, F11, F35, G6, G7, G10, G12, G13, G14, G17, G18, G19, G20, G21, Y154).

2 *Printed Sources*

Aberdeen Correspondence, privately printed by Lord Stanmore. In the British Museum there are nine volumes, with varying titles or no titles for the period 1846–1862, one of which is dated Colombo, 1885. These comprise a full and accurate selection of all the major correspondence, excluding routine letters re engagements, etc. (*Ab. Cor.*)

The Annual Register, *1852* to *1855* (four volumes).

Hansard's Parliamentary Debates, 3rd series, vols. CXXIII (December 1852) to CXXXVI (January 1855).

Parliamentary Papers, *1852–3*, *1854–5* and *1855* Readex microprint edition of *British Sessional Papers 1801–1900*, ed. by E. L. Erickson (New York, 1942?–1960) (*P.P.*), including:

    Eastern Papers, parts I to XII, *P.P. 1854*, vol. LXXI (*E.P.*)

Five *Reports from the Select Committee on the Army before Sebastopol,
P.P. 1854–5*, vol. IX, parts 1, 2 and 3;
Papers Relating to the Reorganization of the Civil Service, P.P. 1854–5,
vol. XX.
*A collection of public general statutes passed in the sixteenth and seventeenth
years of the reign of Her Majesty Queen Victoria 1852–3*. London, 1853.
The Times, July 1852 to January 1855.

3 *Biographies, Memoirs, Letters*
In alphabetical order of subjects

The life of George fourth earl of Aberdeen, K.G., K.T. By Lady Frances Balfour.
2 vols. London, n.d.
The earl of Aberdeen. By Sir Arthur Gordon (Lord Stanmore). New York,
1893.
George Douglas, eighth duke of Argyll, autobiography and memoirs, edited by the
dowager duchess of Argyll. 2 vols. London, 1906.
The life of John Bright. By George Macaulay Trevelyan. London, 1913.
Life and correspondence of Field Marshal Sir John Burgoyne. By Lt. Col. G.
Wrottesley. 2 vols. London, 1873.
Life of Stratford Canning, Viscount Stratford de Redcliffe. By S. Lane-Poole.
2 vols. London, 1887.
Edward T. Cardwell: Peelite. By A. B. Erickson (Transactions of the Ameri-
can Philosophical Society, new series, vol. 49, part 2). Philadelphia, 1959.
*The life and letters of George William Frederick, fourth earl of Clarendon, K.G.,
G.C.B.* By Sir Herbert Maxwell. 2 vols. London, 1913.
The life and times of Sir Edwin Chadwick. By S. E. Finer. London, 1952.
The life of the marquis of Dalhousie. By Sir William Lee-Warner. 2 vols.
London, 1904.
The private letters of the marquis of Dalhousie. London, 1910.
John Thaddeus Delane. By A. I. Dasent. 2 vols. New York, 1908.
Lord Derby and Victorian conservatism. By Wilbur Devereux Jones. Oxford,
1956.
The life of Benjamin Disraeli, earl of Beaconsfield. By William Flavelle Mony-
penny and George Earle Buckle. Rev. ed., 2 vols. New York, 1929.
Mrs Duberly's campaigns. By E. E. P. Tisdall. London, 1963.
Lord Ellenborough. By A. H. Imlah. Cambridge, Mass. and London, 1939.
The life of William Ewart Gladstone. By John Morley. 3 vols. London and
Toronto, 1903.
Gladstone's speeches: descriptive index and bibliography. By Arthur Tilney
Bassett. London, 1916.
The career of Arthur Hamilton Gordon, first Lord Stanmore 1829–1912. By J. K.
Chapman. Toronto, 1964.

The public career of Sir James Graham. By Arvel B. Erickson. Oxford and Cleveland, 1952.

Life and letters of Sir James Graham, second baronet, of Netherby, P.C., G.C.B., 1792–1861. By Charles Stuart Parker. 2 vols. London, 1907.

The life of Granville George Leveson Gower, second Earl Granville, K.G., 1815–1891. By Lord Edmond Fitzmaurice. 2 vols. London, 1905.

The Greville memoirs, ed. by L. Strachey and R. Fulford. Vols. VI and VII. London, 1938.

Correspondence of Abraham Hayward, ed. by Henry Carlisle. 2 vols. London, 1886.

Sidney Herbert: Lord Herbert of Lea—a memoir. By Lord Stanmore. 2 vols. London, 1906.

Life and letters of Benjamin Jowett. By E. Abbott and L. Campbell. 2 vols. London, 1897.

Life and works of Sir James Kay-Shuttleworth. By Frank Smith. London, 1923.

Life of Vice-Admiral Edmund, Lord Lyons. By Capt. Sydney Eardley-Wilmot. London, 1898.

Life and letters of Lord Macaulay. By G. O. Trevelyan. 2 vols. London, 1908 ed.

Rt. Hon. Sir William Molesworth, bt, M.P. By Mrs Fawcett. London, 1901.

The life of Henry Pelham, fifth duke of Newcastle, 1811–1864. By John Martineau. London, 1908.

Florence Nightingale, 1820–1910. By Cecil Woodham-Smith. London, 1950.

The Palmerston papers: Gladstone and Palmerston, ed. by P. Guedalla. London, 1928.

The triumph of Lord Palmerston: a study of public opinion in England before the Crimean War. By Kingsley Martin. London, rev. ed. 1963.

The Life and correspondence of Henry John Temple, Viscount Palmerston. By Hon. Evelyn Ashley. 2 vols. London, 1879.

Lord Palmerston. By H. C. F. Bell. 2 vols. London, 1936.

The destruction of Lord Raglan: a tragedy of the Crimean War, 1854–5. By Christopher Hibbert. London, Pelican ed., 1963.

Memoirs of the life and correspondence of Henry Reeve. By J. K. Laughton. 2 vols. London, 1898.

The later correspondence of Lord John Russell 1840–1878, ed. by G. P. Gooch. 2 vols. London, 1925.

The life of Lord John Russell. By Spencer Walpole. 2 vols. London, 1891.

Lord Shaftesbury. By J. L. and Barbara Hammond. London, 1936.

Life of Archibald Campbell Tait. By R. T. Davidson and W. Benham. 2 vols. London, 1891.

Letters of Queen Victoria, ed. by A. C. Benson and Viscount Esher. First series, vols. II and III. London, 1907.

4   *Monographs and other secondary works*

(For biographical studies see above, section 3)

Adamson, J. W. *English education, 1789–1902.* Cambridge, 1930.

Anderson, Olive. *A liberal state at war.* London, 1967.

Birchenough, C. *History of elementary education in England and Wales from 1800 to the present.* London, 1914.

Bonner-Smith, D. and Dewar, A. C. (eds.). *Russian War, 1854: Baltic and Black Sea: Official correspondence.* Navy Records Society, vol. 83. London, 1943.

Bourne, H. R. Fox. *English newspapers, chapters in the history of journalism.* 2 vols. London, 1887.

Buxton, Sydney. *Finance and politics: an historical study 1783–1885.* London, 1888.

Clapham, J. H. *An economic history of modern Britain: free trade and steel, 1850–1886.* Cambridge, 1932.

Cohen, Emmeline W. *The growth of the British civil service, 1780–1939.* London, 1941.

Dodwell, H. H. *The Indian empire, 1858–1918.* Vol. VI of *The Cambridge History of India.* Cambridge, 1932.

Dreyer, F. 'The Russell Administration, 1846–1852', unpublished doctoral thesis, St Andrew's University.

Glover, Richard. *Peninsular preparation.* Cambridge, 1963.

✗ Gooch, Brison D. *The new Bonapartist generals in the Crimean War: distrust and decision-making in the Anglo-French alliance.* The Hague, 1959.

Grant, James .*The newspaper press: its origins, progress and present position.* 3 vols. London, 1887.

Halévy, Elie. *A history of the English people in the nineteenth century,* vol. III, *The triumph of reform, 1830–1841,* trans. G. Watkins. London, 1950 ed.

Hamley, Sir E. B. *The war in the Crimea.* London, 1891.

✳ Henderson, Gavin. *Crimean war diplomacy.* Glasgow, 1947.

Henriques, Ursula. *Religious toleration in England, 1787–1833.* London and Toronto, 1961.

✳Humphries, R. A. *The diplomacy of British Honduras, 1638–1901.* London, 1961.

Hutchins, B. L. and Harrison, A. *A history of factory legislation.* Westminster, 1907.

Keith, A. B. *A constitutional history of India, 1600–1935.* London, 1936.

Kinglake, A. W. *The invasion of the Crimea.* 9 vols. 4th ed. New York, 1880.

Maccoby, S. *English Radicalism, 1832–1852.* London, 1935.

Mallet, C. E. *A history of the university of Oxford.* Vol. III. London, 1937.

[Maxwell, Peter Benson.] *Whom shall we hang? The Sebastopol enquiry.* London, 1855.

Moore, R. J. *Sir Charles Wood's Indian policy 1853–66.* Manchester, 1967.

Moses, Robert. *The civil service of Great Britain.* New York, 1914.

Northcote, Sir Stafford H. (1st earl of Iddesleigh). *Twenty years of financial policy.* London, 1862.

Owen, David. *English philanthropy, 1660–1960.* Cambridge, Mass., 1964.

⊬ Puryear, V. J. *England, Russia and the Straits question, 1844–56.* Berkeley, 1931.

—— *International economics and diplomacy in the Near East.* Stanford and London, 1935.

Rees, J. *Short fiscal and financial history of England, 1815–1918.* London, 1921.

Roberts, David. *Victorian origins of the British welfare state.* New Haven, 1960.

Roth, Cecil. *A history of the Jews in England.* Oxford, 1964.

Russell, W. H. *The war from the landing at Gallipoli to the death of Lord Raglan.* London, 1855.

Seymour, Charles. *Electoral Reform in England and Wales: the development and operation of the parliamentary franchise, 1832–1885.* New Haven and Oxford, 1915.

Shehab, F. *Progressive taxation: a study in the development of the progressive principle in the British income tax.* Oxford, 1953.

Simpson, F. A. *Louis Napoleon and the recovery of France, 1848–56.* London, 1923.

⊬Southgate, Donald. *The passing of the Whigs, 1832–1886.* London, 1962.

Stokes, Eric. *The English Utilitarians and India.* London, 1959.

Taylor, A. J. P. *Englishmen and others.* London, 1956.

Temperley, Harold. *England and the Near East—the Crimea.* London, 1936.

Tillyard, A. I. *A history of university reform.* Cambridge, 1913.

Ward, W. R. *Victorian Oxford.* London, 1965.

Wellesley, F. A. (ed.). *The Paris embassy during the second empire.* London, 1929. (Containing extracts from the Cowley Papers.)

⊬Williams, Mary Wilhelmine. *Anglo-American isthmian diplomacy, 1815–1915.* Washington, 1916.

Woodham-Smith, Cecil. *The great hunger.* London, 1963.

—— *The reason why.* London, 1953.

Whyte, J. H. *The Independent Irish party, 1850–1859.* Oxford, 1958.

Young, G. M. and Handcock, W. D. (eds.). *English historical documents, 1833–1874.* London, 1956.

5 Articles

Anderson, Olive. 'Great Britain and the beginnings of the Ottoman public debt, 1854–1856'. *Hist. J.,* VII (1964), 47–63.

Bell, Herbert C. 'Palmerston and parliamentary representation'. *J.M.H.* IV (1932), 186–213.

Clark, G. Kitson. 'Statesmen in disguise', *Hist. J.,* II (1959), 19–39.

Conacher, J. B. 'Peel and the Peelites, 1846–1850'. *E.H.R.*, LXXIII (1958), 431–52.

—— 'Party politics in the age of Palmerston', in Appleman, P., Madden, W. A. and Wolff, M. (eds.), *1859: Entering an age of crisis*. Bloomington, pp. 163–80.

—— (ed.). 'A visit to the Gladstones in 1894' (a memorandum by Lady Aberdeen), *Victorian Studies*, II (1958), 155–60.

—— 'Mr Gladstone seeks a seat', *Canadian Historical Association Report— 1962*, pp. 55–67.

Edinburgh Review, CXVII (1863), 307–52 (review of Kinglake's *Invasion of the Crimea*).

Gladstone, W. E. 'The history of 1852–1860 and Greville's latest journals', *E.H.R.* II (1887), 281–302.

—— 'The declining efficiency of parliament', *Quarterly Review*, XXCI (1856), 521–70 (reviewing *Hansard's parliamentary debates, 1856*).

Gooch, B. D. 'A century of historiography on the origins of the Crimean War', *A.H.R.* LXII (1956), 33–58.

—— 'The Crimean war in selected documents and secondary works since 1940', *Victorian Studies*, I (1957), 271–9.

Hart, Jennifer. 'Sir Charles Trevelyan at the treasury'. *E.H.R.* LXXV (1960), 92–110.

Howard, R. E. 'Brunnow's reports on Aberdeen'. *Camb. Hist. J.* IV (1934), 312–21.

Hughes, E. 'Charles Trevelyan and civil service reform, 1835–1855'. *E.H.R.* LXIV (1949), 53–88, 206–34.

—— 'Civil service reform, 1853–1855'. *History*, XXVII (1942), 51–83; revised and reprinted in *Public Administration*, XXXII (1954).

Martin, B. K. 'The resignation of Lord Palmerston in 1853'. *Camb. Hist. J.*, I (1923), 107–12.

Moore, R. J. 'Abolition of patronage in the Indian civil service and the closing of Haileybury college'. *Hist. J.*, VII (1964), 246–67.

Puryear, V. J. 'New lights on the origins of the Crimean war'. *J.M.H.*, III (1931), 219–34.

Roberts, David. 'Lord Palmerston at the home office'. *The Historian*, XXI (1958–9), 63–81.

Schmidt, B. 'Diplomatic preliminaries of the Crimean war'. *A.H.R.*, XXV (1919), 36–67.

Stuart, C. H. 'The formation of the coalition cabinet of 1852'. *Trans. R. Hist. Soc.*, 5th series, IV (1954), 45–68.

Temperley, Harold. 'Stratford de Redcliffe and the origins of the Crimean War'. *E.H.R.*, XLVIII (1933), 601–21, and XLIX (1934), 265–98.

—— 'The alleged violations of the straits convention by Stratford de

Redcliffe between June and September 1853'. *E.H.R.*, XLIX (1934), 657–72.

⇟Van Alstyne, R. W. 'Great Britain, the United States and Hawaiian independence, 1850–1855'. *Pacific Historical Review*, IV (1835), 15–24.

—— 'Anglo-American relations, 1853–1857'. *A.H.R.*, XLII (1937), 496–7.

—— 'British diplomacy and the Clayton–Bulwer treaty, 1850–1860'. *J.M.H.*, XI (1939), 149–93.

6 Reference Works

Members of parliament: return of two orders of the honourable the house of commons, dated 4 May 1876 and 9 March 1877: part II: ordered by the house of commons to be printed, 1 March 1878.

Dod, C. R. *Electoral facts, 1832–1852* (1853).

—— *Parliamentary companion, 1853.*

MacCalmont, F. H. *Parliamentary poll book.* London, 1879.

INDEX

Aberdeen, 4th earl: correspondence with Russell, 1852, 5; Graham's advice to, 9; attends Woburn conclave, 9; recommended to queen, 9–11; not recommended by Derby, 11; summoned by queen, 12; conversations with Lansdowne, Graham and Russell, 12–13; accepts queen's commission, 14; difficulties with Russell, 15–21; support for Jewish emancipation, 18; other cabinet appointments, 21–4; distribution of lesser offices, 24–32; announces formation of government and its policy, 33; equates terms Liberal and Conservative, 34; criticisms of his statement, 34–5; insistence on Peelite strength, 36; purchase of Argyll House, 37; biographical sketch, 38–9; Gladstone's *Letter to*, 47; views on his new administration, 49; on good will in cabinet, 51; and Russell's resignation of Foreign Office, 51–4; altercation with Derby, 55; and defeat on advertisement duty, 63; supports Gladstone budget, 66; Wood's threat of resignation, 68–9; congratulates Gladstone, 70; defends budget in Lords, 76; on Gladstone's success, 77; favours early India bill, 80–4; opposes Lord Grey on transportation, 99; Clergy Reserves bill, 101; Jewish Disabilities bill, 104–5; appointment of committee on Maynooth, 106–7 and 107 n. 1; Irish crisis of June, 1853, 107–10; and education, 110; fills 105 columns of *Hansard*, 119; effectiveness as leader, 120; relations with queen, 125–8; and Russell's succession, 127–8, 173–4, 190–1; and patronage, 129–34; trusts Russians, 138, 143; earlier connection with Eastern Question, 139–41; and re-appointment of Stratford, 144–5; opposes Palmerston's proposals, 149; appealed to by Brunnow, 150, 153; and calling up of fleet, 152; pessimistic, 153; inability to control situation, 154–5; urges peace policy, 156–7; resists proposals of Palmerston, 157, and of Russell, 158; defends government policy, 160; on Stratford de Redcliffe, 164–5; visits Osborne, 175; remains in London, 174–6; on Turkish demands, 177; at ministerial council, 3 September, 179–80; Dardanelles question, 180–1; pressed by Brunnow, 182; difficulties with Russell, 183–4; on *Morning Chronicle*, 186; authorises movement of fleet to Constantinople, 188–90; reluctant to retire, 190–1; on Olmütz proposals, 192–3; misses Graham, 194; account of cabinet meetings, 195–8; excuses to queen, 200; considers new note, 202–4; objects to a London conference, 205, 210; on the Turks, 207; differences with Clarendon, 212–14; views on Russell's Reform bill, 215, 218, 230; Palmerston's resignation, 219–22; offers Home Office to Russell and George Grey, 223–5; proposes to bring Cardwell into cabinet, 223; return of Palmerston, 227–9; efforts to restrain Russell after Sinope, 234–41; resents French pressure, 234; filled with foreboding, 243; welcomes Stratford's note, 245; and Orloff mission, 247; heavyhearted at ultimatum, but welcomes Austrian support, 249; complains to Clarendon of *Times* leak, 249–50; preparations for war, 257; his remorse, 258–61; Mme Lieven's lament to, 260–1; failure of his policy, 264–7; and press attack on Prince Albert, 261–73; defends his foreign policy, 275, 276, 277, 283; queen's speech, 291; Reform bill, 293–4; opposes its postponement, 296–7; accepts postponement, 300–1; reluctant to abandon bill, 303–6; discusses replacement of Russell, 307–8; supports proposed civil service reforms, 317; asks Baines to remain in office, 349; urges Russell to remain in government, 359;

Civil service reform, taken up by Gladstone, 119; genesis of Northcote-Trevelyan Report, 312–14; content of the Report, 315–16; comments of Jowett, 316–17; of Gladstone's colleagues, 317; Gladstone correspondence with Graham re Report, 317–21; with Russell, 321–3; Report approved by Cabinet and queen, 423–4; bill drawn up, 324; Trevelyan–Delane correspondence re Report, 324–5; criticism of Arbuthnot, 325–6; public reception of Report, 326–7; parliamentary debate, 327–9; opinion of experts invited and published, 329–31; the sequel, 331–2; cabinet decision re examinations, 20 January 1855, 529 and n. 3

Clanricarde, 1st Marquis, claims pressed, 27; grieved at non-appointment, 30 n. 2; omission from cabinet, 35; motion re anti-French speeches, 56; on Eastern Question, 166–7, 168–9, 274–7; on civil service report, 328; questions government on war, 390; attacks Aberdeen, 392, 393; attacks conduct of the war, 418–19; *and also* 413

Clarendon, 4th earl: at Woburn conclave, 9–10; and cabinet negotiations, 15–16, 20, 23–6; weakness as a debater, 24; upbraids Reeves, 25–6; temporary omission from cabinet, 35; biographical sketch, 37, 42; succeeds Russell at Foreign Office, 52–3; and 1853 budget, 66–8, 70; and India bill, 84; 'scene' with Derby, 101; on Irish crisis, June 1853, 110; his effectiveness, 120; on Stratford de Redcliffe, 145; firm with Brunnow, 147; despatch to St Petersburg, 150–2; and disposition of fleet, 151–2; instructions to Stratford, 151, 154; relations with colleagues, 154–5; prepares draft convention, 159; complains of Nesselrode memorandum, 159; under pressure from Palmerston, 155 n. 1, 160–1, 204; sends draft project to Seymour and Stratford, 161; instructs Stratford to press Vienna Note, 163; dissatisfaction with Stratford, 164–5, 177, 189, 210; answers questions on foreign policy, 166–7; on Eastern Question, 168; Aberdeen supports against Palmerston, 173; diplo-

matic negotiations, August–December 1853, 175–214; comments on Aberdeen, 176 and n. 2; quarrel with Russell, 182–3; Aberdeen's opinion of, 184, 214; despatch of fleet to Constantinople, 188; his dejection, 189; opposes Olmütz proposals, 192; proposals to cabinet, 195–6; despatch to Vienna, 8 October, 197; explanation to Lewis, 199–200, 201–2; draft note of 24 October, 202–5; comments on Palmerston memorandum, 207–8; approves Stratford's note, 209–10; preparation of collective note, 211–13; differences with Aberdeen, 212, 214; Palmerston's resignation, 222, 224 n. 4, 228 n. 3; agrees to fleet entry to Black Sea, 236; discussion of naval operations in Black Sea, 237–43; and Stratford's note, 244–5; Orloff mission, 247; Napoleon's appeal to Czar, 248; addresses ultimatum to Russia, 249; on leak to *Times*, 250; on consular arrangements in Russia, 250–1; criticises Kinglake on origins of the war, 261–2; and responsibility for Crimean War, 265–7; publication of blue-books, 274; annoyance at Aberdeen, 276; defence of his policy, 277–8; on declaration of war, 282–3; on convention with France, 283; Reform bill, 301; opposes civil service reform plan, 323; high opinion of his despatches, 366; Paris visit of Duke of Cambridge, 371; answers critics, 391; on Aberdeen speech, 392–3; foresees campaign against Dundas, 393; concurs in Russell's army proposals, 403; defends position of Austria, 413; defends foreign policy, 419; and Greytown affair, 422; proposed Swedish alliance, 423–8; indignant at Austro-French manoeuvres, 433; negotiations with Austria, 436–40; and peace negotiations based on Four Points, 442–4; and Sardinian alliance, 444–6; observations on Aberdeen, 492 n. 2; on Russell's conduct, 498; on incompetence in army command, 522; Gordon's opinion of, 532; and Russell resignation, 534; *and also* 119 n. 1, 193, 221, 263, 347, 368, 463, 536

Clayton–Bulwer treaty, 421

INDEX

Gladstone, W. E. (*cont.*)
debate, 339–40; reprimands Cecil, 340; on admission of Dissenters to Oxford, 342; defends himself, Russell and government, 357; on party system, 367 n. 1; on selection of ecclesiastical appointees, 373; responsible for recommendation of Lawley as colonial governor, 376; on difficulty of procuring suitable colonial governors, 377; informs Aberdeen of necessity of dismissing Kennedy, 378; correspondence with Russell on Kennedy dismissal, 378–9; states views on Kennedy affair, 380, 531; his character, and coalition government, 381; defends stand in Kennedy affair, 381–2; and row with Bank of England, 382; and budgets of 1854, 387; proposes doubled income tax, 388; and debt conversion, 388–9; argues for paying war expenses by taxation, 388–9; and Aberdeen's Russia speech, 392; agrees with Russell's army proposals, 403; on division of authority, 405; explains proposed cabinet changes to Canning, 407–8; comments on Lady John Russell, 408; regrets at inability to defend Aberdeen, 418; on proposed Swedish alliance, 424, 426, 431; on relations with Austria, 430–1; views close to Aberdeen's, 444; advocates firm stand toward Russell, 494; on Russell's threats, 498; urges acceptance of Russell resignation, 500; Russell critical of, 501; Gordon's views of, 532; and Russell resignation, 538 and n. 2, 539; on Roebuck motion, 545–6; discusses defeat with Aberdeen, 548; future relations with Liberal party, 549–53; *and also* 45, 128, 138, 238, 266, 351, 360, 402, 406, 496, 540

Glasgow, 232
Glass, reduction in duties, 65
Glenelg, Lord, 277
Gordon, Arthur, Aberdeen's son and biographer, 38 n. 1, 204 n. 1, 212 and n. 3; warns Gladstone of government crisis, 358–9; wins seat vacated by Lawley, 376; indignant with Russell, 391–2; on his father's feelings, 418; his election, 418 n. 1; views on cabinet ministers, 531–3; and reception of Russell resignation, 533; accompanies father to Windsor, 548; *and also* 406, 535 n. 3

Gordon, Sir Willoughby, urged consolidation of army authorities into one office, 396

Gortchakov, Prince, represents Russia at Vienna conference, 28 December 1854, 443

Goulburn, Henry: confers with Peelite leaders, 13; not in Aberdeen ministry, 28; and University Reform debate, 339

Graham, Sir James: friendly to Russell, 5; suspected by Young, 7; advises Aberdeen, 9; role in ministerial negotiations, 12–24, 29–30; reconciliation with Peelites, 13; considered for peerage, 14; suspects Lady John Russell, 15; declines Home Office and Exchequer, 16; opposes Russell's leading House without office, 18–19; calls coalition cabinet a 'tessellated pavement', 24; attacked by Derby, 34; biographical sketch, 40–1; returned at by-election, 50; speech critical of French government, 56–7; on 1853 budget, 61, 66, 68; and India Bill of 1853, 81–4, 91; on Irish crisis, June 1853, 109–10; and Naval Coast Volunteer bill, 115; views on colleagues, 120, 121, 128–9; visit to Balmoral, 127–8; on Palmerston's fleet proposal, 149; despatch of fleet to Aegean, 151–2; views on policy towards Russia, 156; opposes naval reconnaissance in Black Sea, 158; bitter critic of Stratford, 165, 179; on Cobden–Palmerston clash, 172; Russell's proposed succession to Aberdeen, 173; visits naval establishments, 175; safety of fleet at Besika Bay, 180; on *Morning Chronicle*, newspaper advertising and press leaks, 187; remains at Balmoral, 194; critical of cabinet decisions, 198; reports developments to Herbert, 202–4; and Russell's Reform bill, 216–24, 229–30; on Sinope, 236; Russell's Black Sea proposal, 237–41; war plans, 251–4; naval preparations, 254–6; on policy to neutrals, 254–5; defends government foreign policy, 278–9; Reform Club dinner to Napier, 280–1; Russell Reform bill, 296 n. 1, 297–8, 299, 301, 302, 307, 312; criti-